Privacy-Aware
Knowledge Discovery

Chapman & Hall/CRC
Data Mining and Knowledge Discovery Series

SERIES EDITOR
Vipin Kumar

University of Minnesota
Department of Computer Science and Engineering
Minneapolis, Minnesota, U.S.A

AIMS AND SCOPE

This series aims to capture new developments and applications in data mining and knowledge discovery, while summarizing the computational tools and techniques useful in data analysis. This series encourages the integration of mathematical, statistical, and computational methods and techniques through the publication of a broad range of textbooks, reference works, and handbooks. The inclusion of concrete examples and applications is highly encouraged. The scope of the series includes, but is not limited to, titles in the areas of data mining and knowledge discovery methods and applications, modeling, algorithms, theory and foundations, data and knowledge visualization, data mining systems and tools, and privacy and security issues.

PUBLISHED TITLES

UNDERSTANDING COMPLEX DATASETS:
DATA MINING WITH MATRIX DECOMPOSITIONS
David Skillicorn

COMPUTATIONAL METHODS OF FEATURE
SELECTION
Huan Liu and Hiroshi Motoda

CONSTRAINED CLUSTERING: ADVANCES IN
ALGORITHMS, THEORY, AND APPLICATIONS
Sugato Basu, Ian Davidson, and Kiri L. Wagstaff

KNOWLEDGE DISCOVERY FOR
COUNTERTERRORISM AND LAW ENFORCEMENT
David Skillicorn

MULTIMEDIA DATA MINING: A SYSTEMATIC
INTRODUCTION TO CONCEPTS AND THEORY
Zhongfei Zhang and Ruofei Zhang

NEXT GENERATION OF DATA MINING
Hillol Kargupta, Jiawei Han, Philip S. Yu,
Rajeev Motwani, and Vipin Kumar

DATA MINING FOR DESIGN AND MARKETING
Yukio Ohsawa and Katsutoshi Yada

THE TOP TEN ALGORITHMS IN DATA MINING
Xindong Wu and Vipin Kumar

GEOGRAPHIC DATA MINING AND
KNOWLEDGE DISCOVERY, SECOND EDITION
Harvey J. Miller and Jiawei Han

TEXT MINING: CLASSIFICATION, CLUSTERING,
AND APPLICATIONS
Ashok N. Srivastava and Mehran Sahami

BIOLOGICAL DATA MINING
Jake Y. Chen and Stefano Lonardi

INFORMATION DISCOVERY ON ELECTRONIC
HEALTH RECORDS
Vagelis Hristidis

TEMPORAL DATA MINING
Theophano Mitsa

RELATIONAL DATA CLUSTERING: MODELS,
ALGORITHMS, AND APPLICATIONS
Bo Long, Zhongfei Zhang, and Philip S. Yu

KNOWLEDGE DISCOVERY FROM DATA STREAMS
João Gama

STATISTICAL DATA MINING USING SAS
APPLICATIONS, SECOND EDITION
George Fernandez

INTRODUCTION TO PRIVACY-PRESERVING DATA
PUBLISHING: CONCEPTS AND TECHNIQUES
Benjamin C. M. Fung, Ke Wang, Ada Wai-Chee Fu,
and Philip S. Yu

HANDBOOK OF EDUCATIONAL DATA MINING
Cristóbal Romero, Sebastian Ventura,
Mykola Pechenizkiy, and Ryan S.J.d. Baker

DATA MINING WITH R: LEARNING WITH
CASE STUDIES
Luís Torgo

PRIVACY-AWARE KNOWLEDGE DISCOVERY: NOVEL
APPLICATIONS AND NEW TECHNIQUES
Francesco Bonchi and Elena Ferrari

Chapman & Hall/CRC
Data Mining and Knowledge Discovery Series

Privacy-Aware Knowledge Discovery

Novel Applications and New Techniques

Edited by
Francesco Bonchi
Elena Ferrari

CRC Press
Taylor & Francis Group
Boca Raton London New York

CRC Press is an imprint of the
Taylor & Francis Group, an **informa** business

A CHAPMAN & HALL BOOK

CRC Press
Taylor & Francis Group
6000 Broken Sound Parkway NW, Suite 300
Boca Raton, FL 33487-2742

First issued in paperback 2018

© 2011 by Taylor and Francis Group, LLC
CRC Press is an imprint of Taylor & Francis Group, an Informa business

No claim to original U.S. Government works

ISBN-13: 978-1-4398-0365-3 (hbk)
ISBN-13: 978-1-138-37410-2 (pbk)

Visit the Taylor & Francis Web site at
http://www.taylorandfrancis.com

and the CRC Press Web site at
http://www.crcpress.com

Contents

II   Traces and Streams   109

5   Catch, Clean, and Release: A Survey of Obstacles and Opportunities for Network Trace Sanitization   111

Keren Tan, Jihwang Yeo, Michael E. Locasto, and David Kotz

6   Output Privacy in Stream Mining   143

Ting Wang and Ling Liu

III   Spatio-Temporal and Mobility Data   161

7   Privacy Issues in Spatio-Temporal Data Mining   163
Aris Gkoulalas-Divanis and Vassilios S. Verykios

8   Probabilistic Grid-Based Approaches for Privacy-Preserving Data Mining on Moving Object Trajectories   183
Gyözö Gidófalvi, Xuegang Huang, and Torben Bach Pedersen

V Biomedical Data   281

VI Web Usage Data

14 Issues with Privacy Preservation in Query Log Mining

*Ricardo Baeza-Yates, Rosie Jones, Barbara Poblete, and Myra
Spiliopoulou*

15 Preserving Privacy in Web Recommender Systems

*Ranieri Baraglia, Claudio Lucchese, Salvatore Orlando, Raffaele
Perego, and Fabrizio Silvestri*

VII Social Networks   393

16 The Social Web and Privacy: Practices, Reciprocity and Conflict Detection in Social Networks   395

Seda Gürses and Bettina Berendt

Preface

Awareness that privacy protection in data mining is a crucial issue has driven the attention of many researchers in the last decade, leading to a proliferation of different solutions for enabling the potential benefits of data mining while preserving user privacy, confidentiality and freedom.

As an interesting example of the privacy risks connected with data mining, consider what has happened with the publication in 2006 of the America On-line (AOL) query log. This data, which included 20 million Web queries from 650,000 AOL users, underwent only naive anonymization before being made available to millions of people on the Web. One of the benefits of publishing such a dataset is allowing data mining practitioners and researchers to analyze a precious kind of information that usually is available only inside search engine companies. However, the immediate problem with this massive release was that many of the users who were registered on the log had issued personally identifying (or semi-identifying queries), which combined with other searches, made it possible to map some of them to real people. A few of these people even had their identities published along with their searches, which in many cases represented private information.

This is just one of many examples, critical from the point of view of user privacy, that in the last years have generated awareness of this topic, and have driven the research towards the design of privacy-preserving data mining techniques able to offer privacy guarantees, without giving up the potential benefits of the knowledge discovery activity.

The issues connected to the protection of individual privacy while performing data analysis are therefore rooted in the real-world, and concern academia, industry, government, and society in general. The issues are global; this is also witnessed by the fact that many governments are struggling to set national and international policies on privacy for data mining endeavors. Furthermore, in industry, this interest is made evident by the fact that major corporations are allocating significant resources to study and develop commercial products that address these issues.

At a coarse granularity, we can divide privacy-preserving approaches into two main categories, namely *privacy-aware data mining*, and *privacy-aware data publishing*.

In the first category fall all those solutions devising new ad hoc data mining algorithms for a given set of privacy constraints. Typical examples are the *"distribution reconstruction"* approaches, where privacy preservation is obtained by perturbing the data. The goal is to avoid the identification of the original data, while, at the same time, allowing, by means of some specialized data mining algorithms the reconstruction of the data distribution at an aggregate level, sufficient to perform the mining. Another technique falling in this category is the *"distributed privacy preserving data mining"* approach, aimed at computing, by means of secure multiparty computation protocols, a common data mining model from several distributed datasets, where each party owning a portion of the data does not communicate its dataset to the other parties involved in the computation.

In the second category, namely privacy-aware data publishing, fall all those solutions where privacy-issues are tackled once and for all by the data owner before publishing the data, and after that, any data mining algorithm can be applied by the data analyst, even traditional algorithms and not necessarily privacy preserving ones. The objective of the owner is making it impossible for a malicious adversary to re-identify individuals in the published data, while keeping high quality and usability of the data itself. The most well-known approach in this category is *k-anonymity*.

A common aspect of the two categories is that originally the methods have been mainly developed for simple tabular data, and the devised techniques are not directly applicable in more complex applications, managing different kinds of data and domain-specific background knowledge.

As an example of this, consider k-anonymity. The traditional k-anonymity approach applies to relational tables. The basic assumptions are that the table to be anonymized contains entity-specific information, that each tuple in the table corresponds uniquely to an individual, and that attributes are divided in quasi-identifiers (i.e., those attributes whose values in combination can be linked to external information to re-identify the individual to whom the information refers) and sensitive attributes (publicly unknown attributes that we want to keep confidential). The k-anonymity principle requires that each tuple is indistinguishable from at least other $k-1$ tuples with respect to the quasi-identifiers. Although it has been shown that the k-anonymity model presents some flaws and limitations, and that finding an optimal k-anonymization is NP-hard, the k-anonymity model is still practically relevant and in recent years a large research effort has been devoted to developing algorithms for k-anonymity. However, changing the context from simple relational tables to differently structured kinds of data (e.g., graph-structured social network data, data streams), makes the classical definition of k-anonymity no longer applicable, at least not straightforwardly.

Additionally, beyond the structure and complexity of the data, different applications have different domain-specific background knowledge that can be used to threaten the privacy of the individuals. For instance, in mobility data anonymization there are geographical constraints, such as the road network, that might open inference channels that can be used to reconstruct the original data, thus making useless obfuscation attempts that do not keep it in consideration.

Therefore, the increasing heterogeneity and complexity of these new forms of data and applications call, on the one hand, for new forms of patterns and models, together with new algorithms to discover such patterns and models efficiently, and, on the other hand, require new privacy-preservation models to be defined. In this context, several novel results have recently arisen in the privacy, the database, and the data mining research communities for which a uniform presentation is still missing.

The goal of this research frontier book is therefore to collect and present the ongoing investigations in the field of privacy-preserving data mining techniques for many novel applications' domains that must face the increasing heterogeneity and complexity of new forms of data: medicine, biology, Web, social networks, mobility observation systems, etc. Because of its goal, the book does not cover only some well-established results, on the contrary it presents complex domains where, while the privacy issues are almost clear and well defined, the solutions are still preliminary and in continuous development. From this perspective, this book represents a reference for ongoing research, as well as a relevant collection of open problems in these domains for future investigation.

The book is structured into seven parts, providing in-depth coverage of some of the most novel reference scenarios for privacy-preserving techniques.

Part I is orthogonal to the other parts, as it presents general techniques that can be applied in more than one of the application domains discussed in the rest of the book.

Chapter 1 is an introductory chapter providing an overview of the privacy issues in data mining activity, as well as an overview of the main privacy-preserving data publishing and mining techniques. Then, Monreale et al. also discuss privacy preservation in complex application domains, focusing in particular on mobility data analysis. Finally, the chapter also presents a brief overview about how data privacy has been considered in the legal frameworks of different countries.

In Chapter 2 Terrovitis et al. investigate the preservation of privacy in the publication of sparse *multidimensional data*. Multidimensional data stem from several application areas in the form of set-values, sequences, trajectories, time series, Web logs and even multirelation database schemas. Multiple dimensions pose significant challenges in the sanitation of the data. The most profound challenge is the inherent difficulty of creating equivalence classes with common values in a large number of dimensions. Nevertheless, when data are sparse high-dimensional vectors, it is possible to devise solutions that permit publishing the data and preserving the privacy of the associated individuals, with an acceptable information loss. Terrovitis et al. explain the difficulties in sanitizing multidimensional data and explain how sparcity can be exploited to find efficient anonymizing techniques. The chapter also offers a survey of the best-known techniques and the most important open challenges in this area, including the anonymization of Web log data.

In Chapter 3 Abul presents a general framework for *knowledge hiding* from diverse databases, providing concrete problem definitions for particular knowledge and data formats and applications. The kind of database, sensitive knowledge format, data mining task and data distortion metrics are all relevant to the problem definition and to development of solution techniques. The chapter first provides a comprehensive survey of knowledge hiding in the context of frequent itemset and association rule mining, and then a preview of knowledge-hiding problems in emerging application domains and their associated open research challenges.

In Chapter 4 Saygin and Nergiz present a widely used approach for privacy-preserving data publication and mining, namely *condensation*. In condensation-based methods, instead of the actual data, the aggregate (condensed) data are published. Condensation is done in a way that the statistical properties of the data are preserved so that they can still be used for data mining purposes. The chapter provides an overview of the privacy issues in sequence data and gives a sketch of condensation-based methods for privacy-preserving sequence data publishing with two representative types of sequence data, which are *strings* and *trajectories*.

Part II contains two chapters: the first one about network traces sanitization, and the second one about privacy in data stream mining.

Chapter 5 analyzes privacy risks connected to the sharing of *network traces*. Tan et al. introduce sanitization as an attempt to protect both the privacy of network users and the secrecy of operational network information. In particular, the chapter presents, through a review of the literature, the main methods for sanitizing network traces. Additionally, the chapter illustrates the main dimensions according to which sanitization techniques can be evaluated, and ends with a discussion on some challenging open issues in the field of network traces sanitization.

Chapter 6 by Wang and Liu focuses on the protection of *output privacy in data mining*, with a particular focus on *data streams*. Output privacy refers to avoiding the disclosure of sensitive patterns through mining output. This is an important issue, so far less considered than the problem of preserving the privacy of the input of a mining tool. After a review of the related literature, the chapter focuses on output privacy protection for frequent-pattern mining, up to now the most intensively studied mining task. After formalizing the possible privacy breaches and attack model, the chapter overviews Butterfly, a light-weighted, proactive solution for data stream output privacy.

Part III is about privacy in spatio-temporal data mining and mobility data analysis.

In Chapter 7 Gkoulalas-Divanis and Verykios discuss privacy issues in *spatio-temporal data mining*. The chapter first initiates this topic by introducing the readers to a real-world application, the mining of user mobility data, discussing the benefits as well as the threats that emerge from spatiotemporal data mining, and the reason why traditional approaches to privacy preservation are inappropriate for the handling of this type of data. Then

Gkoulalas-Divanis and Verykios present a taxonomy and a detailed description of a set of novel algorithms that has been recently proposed to guarantee privacy-aware mining of historical spatiotemporal data, focusing on their strengths and weaknesses. Finally, the chapter concludes with a discussion of open problems in this area.

In Chapter 8 Gidófalvi et al. propose a general framework that allows user location data to be anonymized, thus preserving privacy, while still allowing interesting patterns to be discovered. The framework allows users to specify individual desired levels of privacy that the data collection and mining system will then meet. Privacy-preserving methods are proposed for two core data mining tasks, namely finding dense spatio-temporal regions and finding frequent routes.

Location-based applications might require the application of privacy-preserving techniques at transaction time (*online* techniques), or upon the subsequent release of portions of transaction history (*offline* techniques).

In Chapter 9 Bettini et al. provide a brief survey of proposals for both classes of techniques, further classifying them according to their specific goal, reference architecture, and evaluation methods. A technically deeper discussion is devoted to online anonymization when the adversary can recognize traces of requests from the same user, and to online location obfuscation in proximity services, like friend-finder services.

Part IV deals with time series analysis.

In Chapter 10 Papadimitriou et al. consider privacy preservation in time series analysis using the perturbation method that introduces uncertainty to the data. In this method, the actual values of the time series are modified by adding noise. However, if the additional noise does not have the same compressibility properties as the original data, then it can be detected and filtered out, reducing uncertainty and therefore privacy. Thus, by making the perturbation "similar" to the original data, the proposed method can both preserve the structure of the data better and make breaches harder.

In Chapter 11 Fu and Zhu discuss the privacy issues in time series data mining. A segment-based method for preserving privacy in time series data mining is proposed. The experimental results show that the method is effective against privacy attacks and in the meantime maintains classification performance.

Part V is about biomedical data. It contains two chapters: one dealing with genomic data and the other addressing the problem of privacy-aware information sharing of health data.

In Chapter 12 Malin et al. deal with the protection of clinical and genomic data during data mining. This is a very challenging issue due to many factors, some of them going beyond computer science, such as the regulatory context, the familial implications, and the high-dimensionality of the problem. Research in this area is still in its infancy; as such, the main goal of the chapter is to provide the reader with a set of guidelines to tackle the issue of privacy-preserving data mining of clinical and genomic data, rather than to survey and compare the related literature. To better understand the domain, the chapter also surveys the regulatory basis underlying the sharing of such data, it then analyzes the privacy violations that may occur, and discusses how they can be addressed.

In Chapter 13 Trojer et al. present a real-life scenario in the Hong Kong Red Cross Blood Transfusion Service (BTS) to highlight the privacy issues connected to health data sharing. Then, after a review of the state of the art in the field, the chapter presents a privacy-aware information sharing method for two specific data mining tasks, that is, classification and cluster analysis, and discusses its applicability to the Hong Kong BTS.

Part VI is about Web applications. It contains two chapters dealing with query log mining and Web recommender systems, respectively.

Chapter 14 by Baeza-Yates et al. is about query log mining. In particular, they discuss how k-anonymity can be applied in this scenario, and the problems that still remain unresolved. Other anonymization techniques based on noise addition are surveyed as well.

In Chapter 15 Baraglia et al. analyze some of the most relevant proposals of recommender systems to have appeared so far, according to a set of dimensions which include how and to what extend they preserve privacy. From the analysis of the state of the art, it emerges that a system able to cope with all the identified privacy risks still does not exist. As a first step towards the development of a comprehensive privacy-preserving recommender system, the second part of the chapter presents $\pi SUGGEST$ and discusses the privacy guarantees it provides.

Part VII is about social networks and contains three chapters analyzing privacy issues related to the management of social network data under different perspectives.

In Chapter 16 Gürses and Berendt propose a re-investigation of the concept of privacy in the context of social networks arguing that in such a scenario privacy is not only about hiding or controlling information. The chapter focuses on two main privacy threats, that is, those arising from transitive access control and from the disclosure of relational information.

In Chapter 17 Carminati et al. address the problem of how to protect users' personal data from other social network participants and from the social network hosting company. Various threads to privacy are considered, such as those related to the disclosure of relationship information for access control purposes or the inference of private information from public information available in user profiles. Moreover, the chapter shows how access control mechanisms can be used to protect user profile privacy.

A complementary aspect of social network privacy is addressed in Chapter 18, where Hay et al. focus on the problem of privacy-preserving analysis of network data, which is one of the most important requirements needed to facilitate sharing of such data. In particular, the chapter illustrates, through a review of the literature, two main methods towards a privacy-preserving analysis of network data. According to the first, the owner modifies the data so that user privacy is not violated before their release, whereas in the second method it is the query result that is modified by the owner in a privacy-preserving way before its release to the requesting user. Additionally, the chapter provides an analysis of the main privacy attacks on network data.

A heterogeneous audience can benefit from this book. First, the book can be a valuable resource for researchers, both in academia and industry, working on security, privacy, and data mining, to be updated with cutting edge issues in the field. This book is also ideal for researchers from other computer-science disciplines, as well as for researchers working in other fields (e.g., statistics, marketing, law) who wish to get acquainted with this new and challenging area and integrate it with their own fields. Second, the book could be used as a reference book for senior undergraduate or graduate courses in information security and data mining, which have a special focus on privacy and/or data mining.

The editors would like to thank all the people who made possible the successful completion of this project. First of all, we would like to thank the publishing team at Chapman & Hall. In particular, we would like to thank Randi Cohen, who constantly supported us throughout the whole process. We also want to express our gratitude to the authors of the chapters, for their insights and excellent contributions to this book. Most of them also served as referees for chapters written by other authors. We wish to thank all of them, as well as all the other reviewers, for their constructive and comprehensive reviews.

MATLAB® is registered trademark of The MathWorks, Inc. For product information, please contact:

The MathWorks, Inc.
3 Apple Hill Drive
Natick, MA 01760-2098 USA
Tel: 508 647 7000
Fax: 508-647-7000
E-mail: info@mathworks.com
Web: www.mathworks.com

Dr. Francesco Bonchi
Yahoo! Research
Prof. Elena Ferrari
University of Insubria, Italy

About the Editors

Francesco Bonchi is a senior research scientist at Yahoo! Research
Barcelona, Spain, where he is part of the Barcelona Social
Mining Group. He received his PhD in computer science from
the University of Pisa, in 2003. His research interests have
spanned different areas of data mining over the years, including data mining query languages and systems, data mining
applications in various domains, and privacy-preserving data
mining. His recent research interests include mining query-
logs, social networks, and social media. Dr. Bonchi has served
as program co-chair of the fourth International Workshop on
Knowledge Discovery in Inductive Databases (KDID 2005),
the first IEEE International Workshop on Privacy Aspects of Data Mining
(PADM 2006), the first and the second ACM SIGKDD International Workshop on Privacy, Security, and Trust in KDD (PinKDD 2007 and 2008), and
the 21st European Conference on Machine Learning and the 14th European
Conference on Principles and Practice of Knowledge Discovery in Databases
(ECML-PKDD 2010).

Elena Ferrari is a full professor of computer science at the University
of Insubria, Italy, where she heads the Database & Web Security Group. She received a PhD in computer science from the
University of Milan in 1998. Her research activities are related to various aspects of data and application security and
privacy. She received the IEEE Computer Society's presti-
gious 2009 Technical Achievement Award for "outstanding
and innovative contributions to secure data management."
She has served as program co-chair of the 4th ACM Symposium on Access Control Models and Technologies (SAC-
MAT'04), co-chair of the third IFIP WG 11.11 International Conference on
Trust Management, the first and second ACM SIGKDD International Workshop on Privacy, Security, and Trust in KDD, the first COMPSAC'02 Workshop on Web Security and the Semantic Web. Prof. Ferrari is on the editorial
board of the *IEEE Transactions on Knowledge and Data Engineering*, the
Transactions on Data Privacy, and the *International Journal of Information
Technology*. She is a member of ACM and a senior member of IEEE.

Contributors

Osman Abul
TOBB University of Economics and
    Technology
Ankara, Turkey

Ricardo Baeza-Yates
Yahoo! Labs
Barcelona, Spain

Ranieri Baraglia
ISTI-CNR
Pisa, Italy

Bettina Berendt
Katholieke Universiteit Leuven
Leuven, Belgium

Claudio Bettini
University of Milan
Milan, Italy

Barbara Carminati
University of Insubria
Varese, Italy

Christopher Cassa
Harvard-MIT Division of Health
    Sciences and Technology
Boston, Massachusetts, USA

Elena Ferrari
University of Insubria
Insubria, Italy

Dario Freni
University of Milan
Milan, Italy

Yongjian Fu
Cleveland State University
Cleveland, Ohio, USA

Benjamin C. M. Fung
Concordia University
Montreal, Quebec, Canada

Gyözö Gidófalvi
Uppsala University
Uppsala, Sweden

Aris Gkoulalas-Divanis
Vanderbilt University
Nashville, Tennessee, USA

Seda Gürses
Katholieke Universiteit Leuven
Leuven, Belgium

Michael Hay
University of Massachusetts
Amherst, Massachusetts, USA

Xuegang Huang
Aalborg University
Aalborg, Denmark

Patrick C. K. Hung
University of Ontario
Oshawa, Ontario, Canada

Sushil Jajodia
George Mason University
Fairfax, Virginia, USA

David Jensen
University of Massachusetts
Amherst, Massachusetts, USA

Rosie Jones
Yahoo! Labs
Boston, Massachusetts, USA

Panos Kalnis
KAUST
Thuwal, Saudi Arabia

Murat Kantarcioglu
University of Texas at Dallas
Dallas, Texas, USA

George Kollios
Boston University
Boston, Massachusetts, USA

David Kotz
Dartmouth College
Hanover, New Hampshire, USA

Cheuk-Kwong Lee
Hong Kong Red Cross Blood
    Transfusion Service
Hong Kong, China

Feifei Li
Florida State University
Tallahassee, Florida, USA

Ling Liu
Georgia Institute of Technology
Atlanta, Georgia, USA

Michael E. Locasto
University of Calgary
Calgary, Canada

Claudio Lucchese
ISTI-CNR
Pisa, Italy

Bradley Malin
Vanderbilt University
Nashville, Tennessee, USA

Nikos Mamoulis
The University of Hong Kong
Hong Kong, China

Sergio Mascetti
University of Milan
Milan, Italy

Gerome Miklau
University of Massachusetts
Amherst, Massachusetts, USA

Anna Monreale
University of Pisa
Pisa, Italy

Lalita Narupiyakul
University of Ontario
Oshawa, Ontario, Canada

Mehmet Ercan Nergiz
Sabanci University
Istanbul, Turkey

Salvatore Orlando
Ca'Foscari University of Venice
Venice, Italy

Spiros Papadimitriou
IBM T.J. Watson Research Center
Hawthorne, New York, USA

Torben Bach Pedersen
Aalborg University
Aalborg, Denmark

Dino Pedreschi
University of Pisa
Pisa, Italy

Ruggero G. Pensa
University of Torino
Torino, Italy

Raffaele Perego
ISTI-CNR
Pisa, Italy

Barbara Poblete
Yahoo! Labs
Santiago, Chile

Yucel Saygin
Sabanci University
Istanbul, Turkey

Fabrizio Silvestri
ISTI-CNR
Pisa, Italy

Myra Spiliopoulou
University of Magdeburg
Magdeburg, Germany

Keren Tan
Dartmouth College
Hanover, New Hampshire, USA

Manolis Terrovitis
IMIS "Athena" Research Center
Athens, Greece

Bhavani Thuraisingham
University of Texas at Dallas
Dallas, Texas, USA

Thomas Trojer
University of Innsbruck
Innsbruck, Austria

Vassilios S. Verykios
University of Thessaly
Volos, Greece

Ting Wang
Georgia Institute of Technology
Atlanta, Georgia, USA

X. Sean Wang
University of Vermont
Burlington, Vermont, USA

Jihwang Yeo
Dartmouth College
Hanover, New Hampshire, USA

Philip S. Yu
University of Illinois at Chicago
Chicago, Illinois, USA

Ye Zhu
Cleveland State University
Cleveland, Ohio, USA

Part I

General Techniques

Chapter 1

Anonymity Technologies for Privacy-Preserving Data Publishing and Mining

Anna Monreale

Computer Science Dept., University of Pisa, Italy

Dino Pedreschi

Computer Science Dept., University of Pisa, Italy

Ruggero G. Pensa

Computer Science Dept., University of Torino, Italy

1.1 Introduction

Data mining is gaining momentum in society, due to the ever increasing availability of large amounts of data, easily gathered by a variety of collection technologies and stored via computer systems. Data mining is the key step in the process of Knowledge Discovery in Databases, the so-called KDD process. The knowledge discovered in data by means of sophisticated data mining techniques is leading to a new generation of personalized intelligent services. The dark side of this story is that the very same collection technologies gather personal, often sensitive, data, so that the opportunities of discovering knowledge increase hand in hand with the risks of privacy violation. When personal, possibly sensitive data are published and/or analyzed, one important question to take into account is whether this may violate the right of individuals whose data is referred to — the *data subjects* — to have full control of their personal data. Some examples of data collection containing personal sensitive information include:

- Retail market basket data: the analysis of purchase transaction data can reveal customer preferences, not only strategic and competitive information for a company;

- Social networking data: may disclose personal data, such as phone numbers and e-mail address, but more importantly may reveal relationships among people;

- E-Mails: the contents of e-mails can reveal secrets and interests of a person, besides the identity of the correspondents;

- Phone calls: the list of user's phone calls may reveal the contacts of each user;

- Mobility and location data: a collection of space-time tracks left by a mobile device may reveal the movements of a user, and the place visited.

Clearly, each of the above forms of data may potentially reveal many facets of the private life of the data subjects: but the danger is brought to a limit if the various forms of data can be linked together, painting a precise portrait even of a supposedly unknown person, whose name, or other indirect identifier, has been removed from the data. Quoting Robert O'Harrow Jr. in *No Place to Hide* (Free Press, 2005): "Most of privacy violations are not caused by the revelation of big personal secrets, but by the disclosure of many small facts in a row. Like killer bees, one is just a nuisance, but a swarm can be lethal."

Protecting private information is an important problem in our society: despite the commonsense belief that it is impossible to protect privacy in the digital era, the lack of trustable privacy safeguards in many current services and devices is at the basis of a diffusion that is often more limited than expected; also, people feel reluctant to provide true personal data, if not absolutely necessary. In several countries, many laws have been enacted, that regulate the right to the protection of personal data. In general, these laws regulate the type of information that may be collected and how this information may be stored and used. Privacy is not limited to the individuals: companies and public organizations, such as hospitals, have the necessity to protect strategic information that provides competitive assets, or the privacy of their patients. The term *corporate privacy* is used in these cases, to make a distinction from *individual privacy*.

Many recent research works have focused on privacy-preserving data mining and data publishing in order to provide some forms of data protection, and possibly to adhere to the existing legislation. Usually, these works propose techniques that allow to publish data and/or to extract knowledge while trying to protect the privacy of users and customers (or respondents) represented in the data. Some of these approaches aim at individual privacy, while others aim at corporate privacy. Unfortunately, some realistic examples show that transforming the data in such a way to guarantee anonymity is a very hard task in the general case. Indeed, in some cases supposedly anonymous datasets can leave open unforeseen doors to a malicious attacker, that can link the personal data of an individual and the identity of the individual itself (the so-called linking attack). Therefore, many issues remain open and require further investigation. Despite an increasing interest in privacy, there exists a lack of technology in privacy-preserving data publishing and mining. This problem is reflected in the lack of communication and collaboration between the law researchers and professionals that study the definitions of the privacy regulations and the scientists that try to develop technical privacy-preserving solutions. The existing regulations pose challenges to the development of the technical solutions for the privacy issue, but we agree with [7] that this problem can only be achieved through an alliance of technology, legal regulations and social norms.

1.1.1 Privacy vs. Utility

In general, the data anonymity problem requires finding an optimal trade-off between privacy and utility. From one side, we would like to transform the data in order to avoid the re-identification of individuals whose data is referred to. Thus, we would like to publish safely the data for analysis and/or mining tasks without risks (or with negligible risk) for each data subject. From the other side, we would like to minimize the loss of information that reduces the effectiveness of the underlying data when it is given as input to data mining methods or algorithms. Therefore, the goal is to maintain the maximum utility of the data. In order to measure the information loss introduced by the anonymization process it is necessary to define measures of utility; analogously, we need to quantify the risks of privacy violation.

1.1.2 Attacks and Countermeasures

The techniques for privacy preservation strongly depend on the nature of the data that we want to protect. For example, many proposed methods are suitable for continuous variables but not for categorical variables (or the other way around), while other techniques employed to anonymize sequential data such as clinical data or tabular data are not appropriate for moving object datasets. Clearly, different forms of data have different properties that must be considered during the anonymization process. We believe that it is necessary to adopt a *purpose-oriented* anonymity framework, based on the definition of: (i) specific hypotheses on the form and the nature of the data, and (ii) specific hypotheses on the attack model for privacy violation. First, a valid framework for privacy protection has to define the background knowledge of the adversary, that strongly depends on the context and on the kind of data. Second, an attack model, based on the background knowledge of the attacker, has to be formalized. Third, a specific countermeasure associated to that attack model has to be defined in terms of the properties of the data to be protected. The definition of a suitable attack model is very important in this context. Different assumptions on the background knowledge of an attacker entail different defense strategies. Indeed, it is clear that when the assumption on the background knowledge changes, the anonymity approach to be adopted also changes significantly. Consider, for example, that an attacker gains access to a spatio-temporal dataset and that he/she knows some spatio-temporal points belonging to some trajectory of an individual. Two cases are possible: (a) the attacker knows the exact points or (b) the attacker knows these points with a given uncertainty threshold. The attacker can try to re-identify the respondent by using his/her knowledge and by observing the protected database. Specifically, he/she should generate all the possible candidate trajectories by using the background knowledge as constraints. Clearly, the defense strategy that it is necessary to use in the case (b) might be unsuitable for the case (a), because the assumption (b) is weaker than the assumption (a). This does not mean that assumption (b) is not valid, as it can be adequate for particular situations where (a) is unrealistically strong.

1.1.3   Privacy-Preserving Data Mining and Statistical Disclosure Control

The problem of protecting privacy when disclosing information is not trivial and this makes the problem scientifically attractive. It has been studied extensively in two different communities: in data mining, under the general umbrella of *privacy-preserving data mining*, and in statistics, under the general umbrella of *statistical disclosure control*. Often, the different communities have investigated lines of work which are quite similar, sometimes with little awareness of this strong tie. In this chapter, we will provide a survey of the main anonymity techniques proposed by the two different communities, analyzing them from the two perspectives. The Figure 1.1 shows a taxonomy tree that describes our classification of the privacy-preserving techniques.

1.1.4   Anonymity in Data Protection Laws

We also provide a brief discussion on how the concept of anonymous data is defined in the most influential privacy regulations enacted internationally. The baseline of this discussion is that no satisfactorily precise definition of data anonymity is up to date available: given that, it is unrealistic to define anonymity as the theoretical impossibility to re-identify the data subject(s) by looking at their data, the legal definitions adopt concepts like reasonableness, or disproportion of efforts — agreeable yet vague concepts, weakly actionable to the purpose of assessing the degree of anonymity protection supported by a given technology or organizational procedure. This observation brings evidence that more work is needed to make anonymity definitions operational in the juridical practice: in this precise sense, there's a strong need for quantifi-

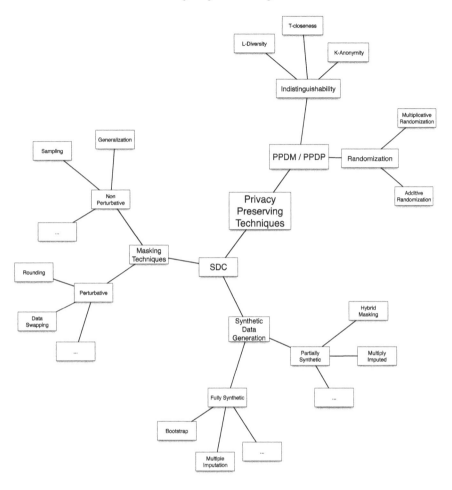

FIGURE 1.1: Taxonomy of privacy-preserving techniques

able notions of privacy and anonymity that can help privacy laws and privacy technologies to have a stronger impact on people's life.

1.1.5 Anonymity in Complex Data

Also, a discussion about anonymity in complex data domain is provided, in order to underline that the techniques proposed for tabular data are not always suitable for data of more complex nature, where specific semantics may offer to the attackers more means to link the data with external knowledge. Specifically, we focus our attention on spatio-temporal data and a brief overview on the recent approaches for the anonymity of this particular form of data is provided, while other chapters in this book have a similar aim toward other forms of data, including query logs, (social) networking data, etc.

1.1.6 Plan of the Chapter

The chapter is organized as follows. Section 1.2 provides an overview on the main privacy-preserving data publishing and mining techniques proposed by the data mining community. Section 1.3 presents the main techniques for anonymity of microdata proposed by the statistical disclosure control community. An overview on how privacy has been considered in the legal frameworks of different countries is presented in Section 1.4. Section 1.5 discusses the privacy issues in complex domains, focusing the attention on the context of spatio-temporal data and describes some approaches proposed for anonymity of this type of data. Finally, Section 1.6 concludes.

1.2 Anonymity for Data Publishing and Mining

We have discussed how the importance of privacy-preserving data publishing and mining is growing. In this section, we provide an overview of the anonymity techniques proposed in the literature.

1.2.1 Anonymity by Randomization

Randomization methods are used to modify data with the aim of preserving the privacy of sensitive information. They were traditionally used for statistical disclosure control [2] and later have been extended to privacy-preserving data mining problems [8]. Randomization is a technique for privacy-preserving data mining using a noise quantity in order to perturb the data. The algorithms belonging to this group of techniques first of all modify the data by using randomization techniques. Then, from the perturbed data it is still possible to extract patterns and models.

In literature, there exist two types of random perturbation techniques:

- additive random perturbation

- multiplicative random perturbation.

1.2.1.1 Additive Random Perturbation

In this section, we will discuss the method of *additive random perturbation* and its applications in the data mining problem. This method can be described as follows. Denote by $X = \{x_1 \ldots x_m\}$ the original dataset. The new distorted dataset, denoted by $Z = \{z_1 \ldots z_m\}$, is obtained drawing independently from the probability distribution a noise quantity n_i and adding it to each record

$x_i \in X$. The set of noise components is denoted by $N = \{n_1, \ldots, n_m\}$. The original record values cannot be easily guessed from the distorted data as the variance of the noise is assumed large enough. Instead, the distribution of the dataset can be easily recovered. Indeed, if X is the random variable representing the data distribution for the original dataset, N is the random variable denoting the noise distribution, and Z is the random variable describing the perturbed dataset, we have:

$$Z = X + N$$
$$X = Z - N$$

Notice that, both m instantiations of the probability distribution Z and the distribution N are known. In particular, the distribution N is known publicly. Therefore, by using one of the methods discussed in [8, 6], we can compute a good approximation of the distribution Z, by using a large enough number of values of m. Then, by subtracting N from the approximated distribution of Z, we can compute N approximation of X. At the end of this process individual records are not available, while we obtain a distribution only along individual dimensions describing the behavior of the original dataset X.

The additive perturbation method has been extended to several data mining problems. But, it is evident that traditional data mining algorithms are not adequate as based on statistics extracted from individual records or multivariate distributions. Therefore, new data mining approaches have to be devised to work with aggregate distributions of the data in order to obtain mining results. This can sometimes be a challenge. In the works presented in [8, 70, 71] authors propose new techniques based on the randomization approach in order to perturb data, and then we build classification models over randomized data. In particular, the work in [8] is based on the fact that the probability distribution is sufficient in order to construct data mining models as classifiers. Authors show that the data distribution can be reconstructed with an iterative algorithm. Later, in [6] Agrawal and Aggarwal show that the choice of the reconstruction algorithm affects the accuracy of the original probability distribution. Furthermore, they propose a method that converges to the maximum likelihood estimate of the data distribution. Authors in [70, 71] introduce methods to build a Naive Bayesian classifier over perturbed data. Randomization approaches are also applied to solve the privacy-preserving association rules mining problem as in [57, 28]. In particular, the paper [57] presents a scheme attempting to maximize the privacy to the user and to maintain a high accuracy in the results obtained with the association rule mining. While in [28], authors present a framework for mining association rules from randomized data. They propose a class of randomization operators more effective than uniform distribution and a data mining approach to recover itemset supports from distorted data.

1.2.1.2　Multiplicative Random Perturbation

For privacy-preserving data mining, *multiplicative random perturbation* techniques can also be used. There exist two types of multiplicative noise. The first one applies a logarithmic transformation to the data, and generates a random noise that follows a multivariate normal distribution with mean equal to zero and constant variance. Then, this noise is added to each element of the transformed data. Finally, the antilog of the noise-added data is taken. The second approach generates random noise by truncated normal distribution with mean equal to 1 and small variance, and then multiplies this noise by the original data. This method preserves the inter-record distances approximately. Therefore, in this case it is possible to reconstruct both aggregate distributions and some record-specific information as distance. This means that the multiplicative random perturbation method is suitable for many data mining applications. For example, in the work presented in [18] authors showed that this technique can be applied to the problem of classification. Moreover, the technique is suitable for the problem of privacy-preserving clustering [53, 54]. The work in [53] introduces a family of geometric data transformation methods (GDTMs) that distort confidential numerical attributes in order to meet privacy protection in clustering analysis. Oliveira et al. in [54] address the problem of guaranteeing privacy requirements while preserving valid clustering results. To achieve this dual goal, the authors introduce a novel spatial data transformation method called Rotation-Based Transformation (RBT) and for distributed privacy-preserving data mining as shown in [45]. The main techniques of multiplicative perturbation are based on the work presented in [37].

1.2.1.3　Strengths and Weakness of Randomization

The main advantage of the randomization method is that it can be implemented at data-collection time, because it is very simple and does not require knowledge of the distribution of other records in the data for the data transformation. This means that the anonymization process does not need a trusted server containing all the original records.

The problem of the randomization is that it does not consider the local density of the records and thus, all records are handled equally. Outlier records can be compared to records in denser regions in the data and thus, this can make an attack easier. Another weakness of the randomization framework is that it does not provide guarantees in case of re-identification attack done by using public information. Specifically, if an attacker has no background knowledge of the data, then the privacy can be difficult to compromise. Instead, in [3], authors showed that the randomization method is unable to effectively guarantee privacy in high-dimensional cases. Moreover, they provide an analysis revealing that the use of public information makes this method vulnerable. In [38] Kargupta et al. challenged the effectiveness of randomization methods, showing that the original data matrix can be obtained from the randomized data matrix using a random matrix-based spectral filtering technique.

1.2.2 Anonymity by Indistinguishability

As said in the previous section, the randomization method has some weakness. The main problem is that it is not safe in case of attacks with prior knowledge. When the process of data transformation for privacy-preserving is not to be performed at data-collection time, it is better to apply methods that reduce the probability of record identification by public information. In literature three techniques have been proposed: *k-anonymity*, *l-diversity* and *t-closeness*. These techniques differ from the randomization methods as they are not data-independent.

1.2.2.1 *k*-Anonymity

One approach to privacy-preserving data publishing is *suppression* of some of the data values, while releasing the remaining data values exactly. However, suppressing just the identifying attributes is not enough to protect privacy, because other kinds of attributes, that are available in public such as age, zip-code and sex can be used in order to accurately identify the records. These kinds of attributes are known as *quasi-identifiers* [63]. In [62] it has been observed that for 87% of the population in the United States, the combination of Zip Code, Gender and Date of Birth corresponded to a unique person. This is called *record linkage*. In this work, authors proposed *k*-**anonymity** in order to avoid the record linkage. This approach became popular in privacy-preserving data publishing. The goal of *k*-anonymity is to guarantee that every individual object is hidden in a crowd of size k. A dataset satisfies the property of *k*-anonymity if each released record has at least $(k-1)$ other records also visible in the release whose values are indistinct over the quasi-identifiers. In *k*-anonymity techniques, methods such as *generalization* and *suppression* are usually employed to reduce the granularity of representation of quasi-identifiers. The method of *generalization* generalizes the attribute values to a range in order to reduce the granularity of representation. For instance, the city could be generalized to the region. Instead, the method of *suppression*, removes the value of an attribute. It is evident that these methods guarantee privacy but also reduce the accuracy of applications on the transformed data.

The work proposed in [59] is based on the construction of tables that satisfy the *k*-anonymity property by using domain generalization hierarchies of the quasi-identifiers. The main problem of the *k*-anonymity is to find the minimum level of generalization that allows us to guarantee high privacy and a good data precision. Indeed, in [50], Meyerson and Williams showed that the problem of optimal *k*-anonymization is NP-hard. Fortunately, many efforts have been done in this field and many heuristic approaches have been designed as those in [43, 12]. LeFevre et al. in [43] propose a framework to implement a model of *k*-anonymization, named full-domain generalization. They introduce a set of algorithms, called *Incognito* that allows us to compute a *k*-minimal generalization. This method generates all possible full-domain generalizations of a given table and thus, uses a bottom-up breadth-first search of the domain generalization hierarchy. In particular, it begins by checking if the single quasi-identifiers attributes satisfy the k-anonymity property and removing all the generalizations that do not satisfy it. In general, for each iteration i the *Incognito* algorithm performs these operations for the subset of quasi-identifiers of size i. Another algorithm, called k-*Optimize* is presented in [12] by Bayardo and Agrawal. This approach determines an optimal k-anonymization of a given dataset. This means that it perturbs the dataset as little as is necessary in order to obtain a dataset satisfying the k-anonymity property. In particular, the authors try to solve the problem to find the power-set of a special alphabet of domain values. They propose a top-down search strategy, i.e., a search beginning from the most general to the more specific generalization. In order to reduce the search space k-*Optimize* uses pruning strategies. Another interesting work has been proposed in [65], where a bottom-up generalization approach for k-anonymity is presented. Instead, in [33] the authors introduced a method of top-down specialization for providing an anonymous dataset. Both these algorithms provide masked data that are still useful for building classification models.

The problem of k-anonymization can be seen as a search over a space of possible multi-dimensional solutions. Therefore, some work used heuristic search techniques such as genetic algorithms and simulated annealing [36, 67]. Unfortunately, by applying these approaches the quality of the anonymized data is not guaranteed and often they require high computational times.

Aggarwal et al. proposed an approach based on clustering to implement the k-anonymity [4]. The same basic idea is used in [24], where the authors described how to use micro-aggregation for obtaining k-anonymity. Moreover, it has been studied how some approximation algorithms guarantee the quality of the solution of this problem [50, 5]. In particular, in [5] the authors provide an $O(k)$-approximation algorithm for k-anonymity that uses a graph representation. By using a notion of approximation, authors try to minimize the cost of anonymization, due to the number of entries generalized and the degree of anonymization.

In literature, there also exist applications of the k-anonymity framework that preserve privacy while publishing valid mining models. For example, in [9, 10, 11] the authors focused on the notion of individual privacy protection in frequent itemset mining and shift the concept of k-anonymity from source data to the extracted patterns.

Finally, another application of the k-anonymity notion is proposed in [56], where the authors addressed the problem of anonymizing sequence dataset trying to preserve sequential frequent pattern mining results. They reformulated the anonymization problem as the problem of hiding all the sequences occurring less than k times in the original sequence dataset.

Based on the definition of k-anonymity, new notions such as l-diversity [46] and t-closeness [44] have been proposed to provide improved privacy.

1.2.2.2 *l*-Diversity

In literature, there exist many techniques based on the k-anonymity notion. It is due to the fact that k-anonymity is a simple way to reduce the probability of record identification by public information. Unfortunately, the k-anonymity framework in some cases can be vulnerable; in particular, it is not safe against homogeneity attacks and background knowledge attacks, that allow to infer the values of sensitive attributes. Suppose that we have a k-anonymous dataset containing a group of k entries with the same value for the sensitive attributes. In this case, although the data are k-anonymous, the values of the sensitive attributes can be easily inferred (Homogeneity Attack). Another problem happens when an attacker knows information useful to associate some quasi-identifiers with some sensitive attributes. In this case the attacker can reduce the number of possible values of the sensitive attributes (Background Knowledge Attack). In order to eliminate this weakness of the k-anonymity the technique of l-diversity was proposed [46]. The main aim is to maintain the diversity of sensitive attributes. In particular, the main idea of this method is that every group of individuals that can be isolated by an attacker should contain at least l *well-represented* values for a sensitive attribute. A number of different instantiations for the l-diversity definition are discussed in [46, 68].

1.2.2.3 *t*-Closeness

l-diversity is insufficient to prevent an attack when the overall distribution is skewed. The attacker can know the global distribution of the attributes and use it to infer the value of sensitive attributes. In this case, the t-**closeness** method introduced in [44] is safe against this kind of attack. This technique requires that the distribution of a sensitive attribute in any equivalence class is close to the distribution of the attribute in the overall table. The distance between the two distributions should be no more than a threshold t [44].

1.3   Statistical Disclosure Control

The aim of Statistical Disclosure Control (SDC) is to protect statistical data. In particular, it seeks to modify the data in such a way that they can be published and mined without compromising the privacy of individuals or entities occurring in the database. In other words, SDC seeks to provide safe techniques against linking attacks. Moreover, after the data protection, data analyses have to be possible and the results obtained should be the same or similar to the ones that would be obtained analyzing the data before the protection.

The youngest sub-discipline of SDC is the microdata protection. It aims at protecting static individual data, also called *microdata*. In this section, we provide a survey of SDC methods for microdata, the most common data used for data mining.

A microdata set X can be viewed as a table or a file with n records. Each record related to a respondent contains m values associated to m attributes. The attributes can be classified in the following categories: *Identifiers, Quasi-identifiers, Confidential attributes* and *Non-confidential attributes*.

As stated above, the purpose of SDC is to prevent confidential information from being linked to specific respondents, thus we will assume all the identifiers have been removed from the original microdata sets to be protected.

In the literature, several microdata disclosure protection methods have been proposed. Microdata protection methods can classified as follows: *masking techniques* and *synthetic data generation techniques*.

Masking techniques, usually, generate a modified version of the original microdata set, which is still suitable for statistical analysis although the respondents' privacy is guaranteed and can be divided in two sub-categories [66]: Non-perturbative and Perturbative. Synthetic data generation techniques, instead, produce new data that replace the original data and preserve their key statistical properties. The released synthetic data are not referred to any respondent. Hence, the release of this data cannot lead to re-identification. The techniques can be of two kinds: *fully synthetic techniques* and *partially synthetic techniques*.

1.3.1   Non-Perturbative Masking Techniques

Non-perturbative techniques do not modify the original dataset; rather, these methods produce a protected dataset by using suppressions or reductions of details in the original dataset. Some of these methods are suitable only for categorical data while others are suitable for both continuous and categorical data.

Non-perturbative methods include: *Sampling, Generalization, Global Recoding* and *Local Suppression*.

1.3.1.1   Sampling

Sampling methods allow us to publish a sample of the original microdata [66]. Thus, the protected microdata contains only the data about a part of the whole population. In this way, the probability of not finding the data about a specific respondent in the protected microdata may be not null; this reduces the risk of re-identification of a respondent. These methods are not suitable for continuous data.

1.3.1.2 Generalization

Generalization provides protected microdata by replacing the values of a given attribute by using more general values [59]. This technique first of all defines a *generalization hierarchy*. The most general value of this hierarchy is at the root of it while the most specific values are represented by the leaves. The generalization method, thus, replaces the values represented by the leaf nodes with one of their predecessor nodes. A particular case of generalization is the global recoding technique. Clearly, it is possible to generate different generalizations of a microdata set.

1.3.1.3 Global Recoding

The Global Recoding method reduces the details in the microdata by substituting the value of some attributes with other values [25, 26]. For a continuous attribute, the method divides in disjoint intervals the domain of that attribute. Then it associates a label to each interval and finally, replaces the real attribute value with the label associated with the corresponding interval. For a categorical attribute, the method combines several categories in order to form new and less specific categories and then the new value is computed. Two particular global recoding techniques are the *Top-coding* and the *Bottom-coding*. The first one [25, 26] is a method based on the definition of *top-code*, that is an upper limit. The idea is that values above a certain threshold are replaced with the top-code. Similarly, the second one [25, 26] is based on a notion of *lower limit*, named *bottom-code*, that is used to replace any value lower than this limit. *Top-coding* and *Bottom-coding* can be applied to both continuous attributes and to categorical attributes that can be linearly ordered.

1.3.1.4 Local Suppression

The Local Suppression method [59] suppresses the value of some individual or sensitive attributes, by replacing them with a missing value. In this way the possibility of analysis is limited. DeWaal et al. in [22] discussed the combinations of local suppression and global recoding techniques.

1.3.2 Perturbative Masking Techniques

Perturbative techniques alter the microdata set before publication for preserving statistical confidentiality. The statistics computed on the dataset protected by perturbation do not differ significantly from the ones computed on the original microdata set. In general, a perturbative approach modifies the microdata set by introducing new combinations of values and making unique combinations of values in the original microdata set. In the following, we describe the main approaches belonging to this group of techniques.

1.3.2.1   Random Noise

These methods perturb microdata set by adding random noise following a given distribution [55]. In general, the *additive noise*, given X_j the j-th column of the original microdata, replaces each x_{ij} $(i = 1 \ldots n)$ with $x_{ij} + e_{ij}$, where e_j is an error vector. Two kinds of additive noise exist in the literature: *uncorrelated* and *correlated*. In the former, e_{ij} is a vector of normally distributed errors drawn from a random variable with mean equal to zero and with a variance that is proportional to those of the original attributes. This does not preserve variances and correlation coefficients, but preserves mean and covariance. In the latter, the co-variance matrix of the errors is proportional to the co-variance matrix of the original data; therefore, this technique also preserves correlation coefficients. Additive noise is often combined with *linear* or *non linear* transformations [41, 61]. This means that before publishing the microdata, linearly /non linearly transformation has to be applied on the data after the process of noise addition. Notice that additive noise is usually not suitable to protect categorical data. As stated in Section 1.2.1 the Randomization techniques introduced by the data mining community come from the methods traditionally used in statistical disclose control described now.

1.3.2.2   Data Swapping

In order to perturb the data another technique can be used, i.e., so-called *Data Swapping*. This technique does not change the aggregate statistical information of the original data, although the confidentiality of individual sensitive information is preserved. The basic idea is to switch a subset of attributes between selected pairs of records in the original database [29]. In this way, the data confidentiality is not compromised and the lower order frequency counts or marginals are preserved. Therefore, certain kinds of aggregate computations can be performed without compromising the privacy of the data.

1.3.2.3   Rank Swapping

Rank Swapping [25] is seen as a variation of the swapping method. It is possible to apply this technique to both continuous and categorical attributes, which can be sorted by using an order relationship. The idea is to rank the values of an attribute according to their ascending order. Then, each value is swapped with another value, guaranteeing that the swapped records are within a specified rank-distance of one another.

1.3.2.4   Resampling

The Resampling technique [25, 23] replaces the values of a sensitive continuous attribute with the average value computed over a given number of samples of the original population in the microdata set. Specifically, if we consider h independent samples $S_1, \ldots S_h$ of the values of T_i (an original attribute). This method sorts the samples considering the order of original values. Then, it computes the set $\bar{t}_1, \ldots, \bar{t}_n$ where each $\bar{t}_j$ is the average of the j-th ranked values in $S_1, \ldots S_h$ and n is the number of records. Finally, the masked attribute is generated replacing each original value of the attribute with the correspondent average value.

1.3.2.5 Rounding

Rounding replaces original values of attributes with rounded values. In order to replace the value of an attribute, the technique defines a *rounding set*, that for example contains the multiples of a given base value. Then, it selects rounded values in this set. Usually, this method is suitable for continuous data. In case of multivariate original datasets, univariate rounding is usually performed, i.e., the rounding is applied on one attribute at a time. However, in [66, 20] authors show that it is possible to perform multivariate rounding.

1.3.2.6 PRAM

PRAM (Post RAndomized Method) [42, 26] allows one to perturb categorical value for one or more attributes by using a probabilistic mechanism, namely a Markov matrix. Each row of this matrix contains the possible values of each attribute. It is important to notice that the choice of the Markov matrix affects the risk of disclosure and information loss.

1.3.2.7 MASSC

MASSC (Micro-Agglomeration, Substitution, Sub-sampling and Calibration) [60] is a perturbative technique that consists of four steps:

- *Micro-agglomeration*: Records in the original microdata set are partitioned into different groups. Each group contains records with a similar risk of disclosure. Moreover, each group is formed using the quasi-identifiers in the records. Intuitively, records with rare combinations of values for quasi-identifiers are considered to be at a higher risk and thus, they should be in the same group.

- *Substitution*: An optimal probabilistic strategy is used to perturb the data.

- *Sub-sampling*: Some attributes or whole records are suppressed by using an optimal probabilistic subsampling strategy.

- *Optimal calibration*: In order to preserve a specific statistical property, the sampling weights, used in the previous step, are calibrated.

This technique is not suitable for datasets containing continuous attributes.

1.3.2.8 Micro-Aggregation

The Micro-Aggregation technique, described in [25], groups individual record into aggregates of dimension k. Next, given a group, its average value is computed and then it is published instead of individual values. In this kind of method an important notion is the *maximal similarity function*, which is used in order to form the groups. Finding an optimal grouping solution is a difficult problem [52], so some heuristic algorithms have been proposed to maximize similarity. There are different variations of micro-aggregation approaches. For example, some of them use different grouping strategies for the perturbation of different attributes. Other methods, instead, use the same grouping.

Another strategy consists in substituting the original value of all tuples (or part of them) in a group with the mean. Micro-aggregation is proposed for protecting both continuous attributes and categorical data.

1.3.3 Fully Synthetic Techniques

Fully synthetic techniques generate a set of data that is completely new. This means that the released data are referred to any respondent. Hence, no respondent can be re-identified. Different techniques exist that can be applied only on categorical or continuous data, or on both of them. Some methods belonging to this category are: *Cholesky decomposition* [49], *Bootstrap* [30], *Multiple imputation* [58], *Latin Hypercube Sampling* [31].

1.3.3.1 Cholesky Decomposition

This technique is based on the Cholesky matrix decomposition method and consists of five steps [49]:

1. Represent the original microdata set X as a matrix with N rows (tuples) and M columns (attributes)

2. Compute the co-variance matrix C over X

3. Generate a random matrix of $N \times M$ elements, named R, such that its co-variance matrix is the identity matrix I

4. Compute the Cholesky decomposition D of C, such that $C = D^t \times D$

5. Generate the synthetic data X' by matrix product $R \times D$.

Notice that X' and X have the same co-variance matrix. Indeed, this approach preserves variance, co-variance and mean of the original microdata set. This method is suitable for continuous attributes.

1.3.3.2 Bootstrap

This technique generates synthetic data by using Bootstrap methods [30]. In particular, it computes the p-variate cumulative distribution function F

of the original dataset X with p attributes. Then, it alters the function F in order to transform it into another similar function F'. Finally, this last function is sampled to generate a synthetic dataset X'.

Notice that this method is particularly suitable for continuous data.

1.3.3.3 Multiple Imputation

The multiple imputation technique [58] considers a dataset X of N tuples corresponding to a sample of N respondents belonging to a larger population of M individuals. Moreover, it divides the attributes into: background attributes (A), non-confidential attributes (B) and confidential attributes (C). The first ones are available for the whole population, while the second ones and the last ones are only known for the N individuals.

This method is performed in three steps:

a. Construct a multiply imputed population of M individuals starting from X. In this population there are N tuples of X and k matrices (B, C) for the $M - N$ remaining individuals. Notice that k is the number of multiple imputations.

b. Predict a set of couples (B, C) starting from the attributes A using a prediction model. In this way, the whole population has a value for each kind of attribute, some values will be imputed while others will be original.

c. Draw a sample X' of N records from the multiply imputed population. This is can be repeated k times in order to produce k replicates of (B, C) values. At the end, k multiply imputed synthetic datasets are obtained and in order to assure that no original data are contained in synthetic datasets, when the sample is drawn the N original tuples are excluded.

Multiple imputation method works on both categorical and continuous data.

1.3.3.4 Latin Hypercube Sampling

Latin Hypercube Sampling [31] is a technique that provides both the univariate and the multivariate structure of the original dataset. Usually, univariate structures are the mean and covariance of an attribute, while a multivariate structure is the rank correlation structure of the data. The main problem of this technique is that it is time-intensive and its complexity depends on the number of statistics to preserve on synthetic data and on the values to be reproduced.

The Latin Hypercube Sampling method can be used on both categorical and continuous data.

1.3.4   Partially Synthetic Techniques

Partially synthetic techniques produce a dataset, where the original data and synthetic data are mixed. In literature, several techniques belonging to this category have been proposed and in the following we describe the main ones.

1.3.4.1   Hybrid Masking

The Hybrid Masking method [21] is based on the idea of combining original and synthetic data in order to mask the data. Usually, this technique generates synthetic records. Using a distance function, each original record is matched with synthetic record. The masked data are obtained by combining the paired records. For the combination the values in these records can be added or multiplied.

1.3.4.2   Information Preserving Statistical Obfuscation

This technique, proposed in [17], explicitly preserves certain information contained in the data. The data are assumed to be composed of two kind of information for each respondent: *public data* and *specific survey data*. Before releasing the data, this approach alters the public data by a perturbation operation, while it discloses the specific survey data without alteration. Usually, both sets of data are released for a subset of respondents. The new set of data maintains a certain set of statistics over the original public data.

1.3.4.3   Multiply Imputed Partially Synthetic Data

This technique alters confidential attributes by using the multiple imputation method to simulate them, while releasing the others attributes without alteration [32]. The basic idea is that only the confidential attributes should be protected. This method can be applied to both categorical and continuous data.

1.3.4.4   Blank and Impute

The Blank and Impute technique [55] is suitable for both categorical and continuous data. First of all, it selects some records randomly and then deletes the original values of a set of attributes in these records. The deleted values are replaced by a sort of imputation method.

1.4 Anonymity in Privacy Regulations

In recent years, privacy has been one of the most discussed jurisdictional issues in many countries. Citizens are increasingly concerned about what companies and institutions do with their data, and ask for clear positions and policies from both the governments and the data owners. Despite this increasing need, there is not a unified view on privacy laws across countries. In some of them (e.g., Spain, Portugal) the right to privacy has been established as a constitutional principle; in other countries (e.g., USA) there exist multiple law articles that deal with special cases. In this section we will present an overview on how privacy has been considered in the jurisdiction of Canada, United States and European Union.

1.4.1 Privacy Laws in Canada

Canada's first response at the government level to the call for protection of personal information — or data protection, as it is frequently called in Europe — was to introduce data protection provisions into the Canadian Human Rights Act. Subsequently, the Canadian Charter of Rights and Freedoms outlined that everyone has "the right to life, liberty and security of the person" and "the right to be free from unreasonable search or seizure," but never mentioned directly the concept of privacy. However, in 1982, Parliament enacted purpose-specific legislation — the federal Privacy Act. This act puts limits and obligations on over 150 federal government departments and agencies, on the collection, use and disclosure of personal information. It also gives Canadians the right to find out what personal information the federal government has about them by making a formal request under the Privacy Act. The Office of the Privacy Commissioner of Canada has the authority to investigate complaints. The Act came into force the following year.

The governments of all provinces and territories in Canada, except for Newfoundland and Labrador, also have legislation governing the collection, use and disclosure of personal information. The legislation varies from province to province, but the general right to access and correct personal information exists in all, and each has a commissioner or ombudsman who is authorized to handle complaints.

Canada also promulgates an important act concerning more specifically the private sector. The 2000 Personal Information Protection and Electronic Documents Act, or PIPED Act, regulates, in provinces without a similar legislation, how private sector organizations collect, use and disclose personal information in the course of business activities. This Act has been implemented in three stages: in 2001 the federally regulated private sector, for example banks and international air carriers, is covered; in 2002 it covered personal health information collected, used or disclosed by federally regulated organizations;

from 2004 it covers information collected in the course of any commercial activity in any province or territory in Canada, including provincially regulated organizations. At the beginning of 2004, the only province exempted from the federal PIPED Act was Quebec. Quebec businesses are not covered by the PIPED Act, but must comply with the Quebec private sector privacy law.

The PIPED Act establishes ten principles that organizations must follow when collecting, using and disclosing personal information in the course of commercial activity. Among them: identifying purpose, consent, limiting collection, limiting use, disclosure and retention. Substantially it supports and promotes e-commerce by "protecting personal information that is collected, used or disclosed in certain circumstances, by providing for the use of electronic means to communicate or record information or transactions." It states that an organization "may collect, use or disclose personal information only for purposes that a reasonable person would consider are appropriate in the circumstance," but does not apply to data "rendered anonymous" and does not mention any example of "reasonable" method of identification.

In 2004, the Canadian Institutes of Health Research (CIHR) proposed a clarification of PIPEDA that offers an interpretation of "reasonableness" as a reasonably foreseeable method of identification or linking of data with a specific individual. However, it also refers to anonymized data as information permanently stripped of all identifiers, such that the data has no reasonable potential for any organization to make an identification. Finally, it states that reasonable foreseeability should be assessed with regard to the circumstances prevailing at the time of the proposed collection, use, or disclosure.

1.4.2 Privacy Laws in the United States

In the United States, the right to privacy is the right to be let alone, in the absence of some "reasonable" public interest in a person's activities, like those of celebrities or participants in newsworthy events. Invasion of the right to privacy can be the basis for a lawsuit for damages against the person or entity violating the right. The right to privacy is not mentioned in the Constitution, but the Supreme Court has interpreted several of the amendments as creating this right. One of the amendments is the Fourth Amendment, which stops the police and other government agents from searching us or our property without "probable cause" to believe that we have committed a crime. Other amendments protect our freedom to make certain decisions about our bodies and our private lives without interference from the government. Rights derived from the Fourth Amendment are limited by the legal requirement of a "reasonable expectation of privacy." The due process clause of the 14th amendment generally only protects privacy of family, marriage, motherhood, procreation, and child rearing. The Constitution, however, only protects against state actors. Invasions of privacy by individuals can only be remedied under previous court decisions.

Invasion of privacy is a commonly used cause of action in legal pleadings.

In the United States, the development of the doctrine regarding this tort was largely spurred by an 1890 Harvard Law Review article written by Samuel D. Warren and Louis D. Brandeis on The Right of Privacy. Modern tort law includes four categories of invasion of privacy, i.e., intrusion of solitude, public disclosure of private facts, false light, and appropriation. In particular, public disclosure of private facts arises where one person reveals information which is not of public concern, and the release of which would offend a reasonable person. Disclosure of private facts includes publishing or widespread dissemination of little-known, private facts that are non-newsworthy, not part of public records, public proceedings, not of public interest, and would be offensive to a reasonable person if made public. Although partial regulations exist, there is no all-encompassing law regulating the acquisition, storage, or use of personal data in the US. In general terms, in the US, whoever can be troubled to key in the data is deemed to own the right to store and use it, even if the data were collected without permission. Moreover, in the United States today there are separate privacy laws for medical information, financial information, library records, video rental records, GPS tracking, and numerous other classes of data.

In the US, the use of GPS trackers by police requires a search warrant in some circumstances, but use by a private citizen does not, as the Fourth Amendment does not limit the actions of private citizens. Other laws, like the common law invasion of privacy tort as well as state criminal wiretapping statutes (for example, the wiretapping statute of the Commonwealth of Massachusetts, which is extremely restrictive) potentially cover the use of GPS tracking devices by private citizens without consent of the individual being so tracked.

1.4.3   Privacy Laws in the European Union

Unlike in the United States, the right to data privacy is heavily regulated and rigidly enforced in Europe. Article 8 of the European Convention on Human Rights (ECHR) provides a right to respect for one's "private and family life, his home and his correspondence," subject to certain restrictions. The European Court of Human Rights has given this article a very broad interpretation in its jurisprudence. According to the Court's case law, the collection of information by officials of the state about an individual without his consent always falls within the scope of Article 8. Thus, gathering information for the official census, recording fingerprints and photographs in a police register, collecting medical data or details of personal expenditures and implementing a system of personal identification has been judged to raise data privacy issues.

The government is not the only entity which may pose a threat to data privacy. The Convention for the Protection of Individuals with regard to Automatic Processing of Personal Data was concluded within the Council of Europe in 1981. This convention obliges the signatories to enact legislation concerning the automatic processing of personal data, which many duly did.

As all the member states of the European Union are also signatories of the European Convention on Human Rights and the Convention for the Protection of Individuals with regard to Automatic Processing of Personal Data, the European Commission was concerned that diverging data protection legislation would emerge and impede the free flow of data within the EU zone. Therefore the European Commission decided to harmonize data protection regulation and proposed the Directive (95/46/CE) on the protection of personal data, which was voted in the 1995 by the European Parliament, and which member states had to transpose into law by the end of 1998.

Personal data covers both facts and opinions about the individual. It also includes information regarding the intentions of the data controller towards the individual, although in some limited circumstances exemptions will apply. With processing, the definition is far wider than before. For example, it incorporates the concepts of "obtaining," "holding" and "disclosing." Also, mobility data has been considered within this jurisdictional framework by the Directive 2006/24/CE of the European Commission.

All EU member states adopted legislation pursuant to this directives or adapted their existing laws. Each country also has its own supervisory authority to monitor the level of protection. In particular, a critical principle of the EU Directive, which has also been proposed in national jurisdictions, is the 26th considerandum, which states:

> Whereas the principles of protection must apply to any information concerning an identified or identifiable person; whereas, to determine whether a person is identifiable, account should be taken of all the means likely reasonably to be used either by the controller or by any other person to identify the said person; whereas the principles of protection shall not apply to data rendered anonymous in such a way that the data subject is no longer identifiable;...

This principle raises important discussions on how to measure the "reasonableness" of identifying means. Clearly, many parameters are likely to be involved in the definition of *reasonable*, such as, computational resources to be employed in term of time and money, number of possible linked sources to be considered for re-identification, and so on. A considerable effort should be then undertaken by both computer scientists and law experts in order to provide a clear and usable framework to guide privacy policy definitions, and to support the decisions of judges and lawyers.

1.5   Anonymity in Complex Data

We have seen how many research efforts have focused on privacy-preserving data mining and data publishing. Most research, however, addresses the anonymity problems in the context of general tabular data, while relatively little work has addressed more complex forms of data in specific domains, although this kind of data is growing rapidly: examples include social networking data, spatio-temporal data, query log data, and more. The analysis of these data is very interesting as they are semantically rich: such richness makes such data also very difficult to anonymize, because the extra semantics may offer unexpected means to the attacker to link data to background knowledge. Traditional techniques used for tabular datasets cannot be directly applied, so typically the standard approaches must be adjusted appropriately. A survey of techniques for anonymity of query log data is presented in [19]. In this work the author seeks to assess some anonymity techniques against three criteria: a) how well the technique protects privacy, b) how well the technique preserves the utility of the query logs, and c) how well the technique might be implemented as a user control. In [72] Zhou et al. propose a brief systematic review of the existing anonymity techniques for privacy preserving publishing of social network data. Another interesting work is presented in [47], where Malin introduces a computational method for the anonymization of a collection of person-specific DNA database sequences. The analysis of person-specific DNA sequences is important but poses serious challenges to the protection of the identities to which such sequences correspond.

In this section we focus our discussion on spatio-temporal data showing that in recent years some reasonable results have been obtained by solutions that consider the particular nature of these data. The increasing availability of spatio-temporal data is due to the diffusion of mobile devices (e.g., mobile phones, RFID devices and GPS devices) and of new applications, where the discovery of consumable, concise, and applicable knowledge is the key step. Clearly, in these applications privacy is a concern, since a pattern can reveal the behavior of a group of few individuals, compromising their privacy. Spatio-temporal datasets present a new challenge for the privacy-preserving data mining community because of their spatial and temporal characteristics.

Standard approaches developed for tabular data do not work for spatio-temporal datasets. For example, randomization techniques, discussed above, which modify a dataset to guarantee respondents' privacy while preserving data utility for analyses, are not applicable on spatio-temporal data, due to their particular nature. Therefore, alternative solutions have been suggested: some of them belong to the category of *confusion-based algorithms* others belong to the category of approaches of *k-anonymity for location position collection*. All these techniques try to guarantee location privacy for trajectories.

The approaches in [35, 39, 40, 27] belong to the first category and provide confusion/obfuscation algorithms to prevent an attacker from tracking a complete user trajectory. The main idea is to modify true trajectories or generate fake trajectories in order to confuse the attacker. In [13, 14, 34, 16] authors presented techniques belonging to the second category. The main aim of these techniques is to preserve the anonymity of a user obscuring his route. They use the notion of k-anonymity adapted for the spatio-temporal context.

k-anonymity is the most popular method for the anonymization of spatio-temporal data. It is often used both in the works on privacy issues in location-based services (LBSs) [15, 48] and in the works of anonymity of trajectories [1, 51, 69]. In the work presented in [1], the authors study the problem of privacy-preserving publishing of moving object databases. They propose the notion of (k, δ)-anonymity for moving object databases, where δ represents the possible location imprecision. In particular, this is a novel concept of k-anonymity based on co-localization that exploits the inherent uncertainty of the moving objects whereabouts. In this work authors also propose an approach, called *Never Walk Alone*, for obtaining a (k, δ)-anonymous moving object database. The method is based on trajectory clustering and spatial translation. In [51] Nergiz et al. address privacy issues regarding the identification of individuals in static trajectory datasets. They provide privacy protection by: (1) first enforcing k-anonymity, meaning every released information refers to at least k users/trajectories, (2) then reconstructing randomly a representation of the original dataset from the anonymization. Another approach based on the concept of k-anonymity is proposed in [56], where Pensa et al. present a framework for k-anonymization of sequences of regions/locations. The authors also propose an approach that is an instance of the proposed framework and that allows to publish protected datasets while preserving the data utility for sequential pattern mining tasks. This approach, called *BF-P2kA*, consists of three steps. During the first step, the sequences in the input dataset D are used to build a prefix tree, representing the dataset. The second step, given a minimum support threshold k, anonymizes the prefix tree. This means that sequences, whose support is less than k, are pruned from the prefix tree. Then, part of these infrequent sequences is re-appended in the prefix tree, by using the notion of longest common sub-sequence. The third and last step is to post-process the anonymized prefix tree, as obtained in the previous step, to generate the anonymized dataset of sequences D'. Yarovoy et al. in [69] study problem of k-anonymization of moving object databases for the purpose of their publication. They observe the fact that different objects in this context may have different quasi-identifiers and so, anonymization groups associated with different objects may not be disjoint. Therefore, a novel notion of k-anonymity based on spatial generalization is provided. In this work, authors propose two approaches that generate anonymity groups satisfying the novel notion of k-anonymity. These approaches are called *Extreme Union* and *Symmetric Anonymization*.

Finally, we also mention the very recent work [64], where Terrovitis and Mamoulis suggest a suppression-based algorithm that, given the head of a trajectory, reduces the probability of disclosing its tail. This work is based on the assumption that different attackers know different and disjoint portions of the trajectories and the data publisher knows the attacker's knowledge. So, the proposed solution is to suppress all the dangerous observations in the database.

1.6 Conclusion

In this chapter, we presented an overview of the main techniques for ensuring anonymity in data publishing and mining. In particular, we described the approaches proposed both by the data mining community and by the statistical disclosure control community. Often, the work done by these communities is very similar. Moreover, we presented an overview on how anonymity has been considered in the privacy jurisdiction of different countries. Finally, we concluded with a discussion about the anonymity issues in complex data, focusing our attention on spatio-temporal data. Usually, the anonymity techniques proposed for tabular data are not suitable for complex data, such as social networking data, spatio-temporal data, query log data and web log data; therefore new approaches have to be developed. We presented very recent works tackling the problem of anonymity in the particular context of spatio-temporal data.

What have we learned by this critical perspective? The main lesson is that if we strive to a general concept of anonymity in personal data, we are doomed to obtain rather weak definitions, both in the legal and in the data analysis fields. Talking in general of tabular data describing personal information leads to slippery concepts such "reasonableness," "disproportionate effort" referred to re-identification; from the analytical side, a clear trade-off for balancing analytical utility and risk of re-identification is missing. Researchers in data mining and statistic disclosure control seem to have learned this lesson, and the most recent results are focusing on specific, yet interesting, forms of data: the assumption of a particular data semantics helps in defining convincing background knowledge assumptions for adversarial attacks, and, in turn, precise countermeasures and formal protection models. This is a crucial step in identifying formal measures of privacy risk, that may in turn affect regulations, and provide quantifiable counterparts of the adjective "reasonable." We tried to provide one instance of this "purpose-oriented anonymity," with reference to mobility data: other examples can be found in the other chapters of this book.

Anonymity in data publishing and mining is a young, exciting research arena, with plenty of open issues, some of which, if solved, can have a great impact on society, and change the way information technology is perceived today.

Acknowledgments

Ruggero G. Pensa is co-funded by Regione Piemonte. Dino Pedreschi acknowledges support by Google, under the Google Research Award program.

References

[1] O. Abul, F. Bonchi, and M. Nanni. Never walk alone: Uncertainty for anonymity in moving objects databases. In *ICDE*, pages 376–385, 2008.

[2] N. R. Adam and J. C. Wortmann. Security-control methods for statistical databases: A comparative study. *ACM Computing Surveys*, 21(4):515–556, 1989.

[3] C. C. Aggarwal. On randomization, public information and the curse of dimensionality. In *ICDE*, pages 136–145, 2007.

[4] G. Aggarwal, T. Feder, K. Kenthapadi, S. Khuller, R. Panigrahy, D. Thomas, and A. Zhu. Achieving anonymity via clustering. In *PODS*, pages 153–162. ACM, 2006.

[5] G. Aggarwal, T. Feder, K. Kenthapadi, R. Motwani, R. Panigrahy, D. Thomas, and A. Zhu. Anonymizing tables. In *ICDT*, volume 3363 of *LNCS*, pages 246–258, 2005.

[6] D. Agrawal and C.C. Aggarwal. On the design and quantification of privacy preserving data mining algorithms. In *PODS*. ACM, 2001.

[7] R. Agrawal. Privacy and data mining. In *ECML/PKDD*, 2004.

[8] R. Agrawal and R. Srikant. Privacy-preserving data mining. In *SIGMOD*, pages 439–450. ACM, 2000.

[9] M. Atzori, F. Bonchi, F. Giannotti, and D. Pedreschi. Blocking anonymity threats raised by frequent itemset mining. In *ICDM*, pages 561–564. IEEE Computer Society, 2005.

[10] M. Atzori, F. Bonchi, F. Giannotti, and D. Pedreschi. k-anonymous patterns. In *PKDD*, pages 10–21, 2005.

[11] M. Atzori, F. Bonchi, F. Giannotti, and D. Pedreschi. Anonymity preserving pattern discovery. *VLDB Journal*, 17(4):703–727, 2008.

[12] R. J. Bayardo and R. Agrawal. Data privacy through optimal k-anonymization. In *ICDE 2005*, pages 217–228, 2005.

[13] A. R. Beresford and F. Stajano. Location privacy in pervasive computing. *IEEE Pervasive Computing*, 2(1):46–55, 2003.

[14] A. R. Beresford and F. Stajano. Mix zones: user privacy in location-aware services. In *PerCom Workshops*, pages 127–131. IEEE Computer Society, 2004.

[15] S. Mascetti and C. Bettini. Preserving k-anonymity in spatio-temporal datasets and location-based services. First Italian workshop on PRIvacy and SEcurity (PRISE), Rome, June 2006.

[16] C. Bettini, X. S. Wang, and S. Jajodia. Protecting privacy against location-based personal identification. In *VLDB Workshop SDM 2005*, volume 3674 of *LNCS*, pages 185–199. Springer, 2005.

[17] J. Burridge, L. Franconi, S. Polettini, and J. Stander. A methodological framework for statistical disclosure limitation of business microdata. *Technical Report 1.1-D4*, CASC Project, 2002.

[18] K. Chen and L. Liu. Privacy preserving data classification with rotation perturbation. In *ICDM*, pages 589–592. IEEE Computer Society, 2005.

[19] A. Cooper. A survey of query log privacy-enhancing techniques from a policy perspective. *ACM Trans. Web*, 2(4):1–27, 2008.

[20] L. H. Cox and J. J. Kim. Effects of rounding on the quality and confidentiality of statistical data. In *Privacy in Statistical Databases*, volume 4302 of *LNCS*, pages 48–56, 2006.

[21] R. A. Dandekar, J. Domingo-Ferrer, and F. Sebé. Lhs-based hybrid microdata vs rank swapping and microaggregation for numeric microdata protection. In *Inference Control in Statistical Databases*, pages 153–162. Springer-Verlag, 2002.

[22] A. G. DeWaal and L. C. R. J. Willenborg. Global recodings and local suppressions in microdata sets. In *Proceedings of Statistics Canada Symposium'95*, page 121132, 1995.

[23] J. Domingo-Ferrer and J. M. Mateo-Sanz. On resampling for statistical confidentiality in contingency tables. In *Computers & Mathematics with Applications*, pages 13–32, 1999.

[24] J. Domingo-Ferrer and J. M. Mateo-Sanz. Practical data-oriented microaggregation for statistical disclosure control. *IEEE TKDE*, 14(1):189–201, 2002.

[25] J. Domingo-Ferrer and V. Torra. *A Quantitative Comparison of Disclosure Control Methods for Microdata*, pages 111–133. Elsevier, 2001.

[26] J. Domingo-Ferrer and V. Torra. Distance-based and probabilistic record linkage for re-identification of records with categorical variables. *Butlletí de l'ACIA*, 28:243–250, 2002.

[27] M. Duckham and L. Kulik. A formal model of obfuscation and negotiation for location privacy. In *Pervasive*, pages 152–170, 2005.

[28] A. V. Evfimievski, R. Srikant, R. Agrawal, and J. Gehrke. Privacy preserving mining of association rules. In *SIGKDD*, pages 217–228. ACM, 2002.

[29] S. E. Fienberg and J. McIntyre. Data swapping: Variations on a theme by dalenius and reiss. In *Privacy in Statistical Databases*, volume 3050 of *LNCS*, pages 14–29. Springer, 2004.

[30] S. E. Fienberg. A radical proposal for the provision of micro-data samples and the preservation of confidentiality. *Technical Report 611*, Carnegie Mellon University Department of Statistics, 1994.

[31] A. Florian. An efficient sampling scheme: Updated latin hypercube sampling. *J. Probabilistic Engineering Mechanics*, 7(2):123–130, 1992.

[32] L. Franconi and J. Stander. A model based method for disclosure limitation of business microdata. *Journal of the Royal Statistical Society D-Statistician*, 51:1–11, 2002.

[33] B. C. M. Fung, K. Wang, and P. S. Yu. Top-down specialization for information and privacy preservation. In *ICDE*, pages 205–216, 2005.

[34] M. Gruteser and X. Liu. Protecting privacy in continuous location-tracking applications. *IEEE Security & Privacy*, 2(2):28–34, 2004.

[35] B. Hoh and M. Gruteser. Protecting location privacy through path confusion. In *SECURECOMM '05*, pages 194–205. IEEE Computer Society, 2005.

[36] V. S. Iyengar. Transforming data to satisfy privacy constraints. In *KDD*, pages 279–288. ACM, 2002.

[37] W. Johnson and J. Lindenstrauss. Extensions of Lipshitz mapping into Hilbert space. *Contemporary Math.*, 26:189–206, 1984.

[38] H. Kargupta, S. Datta, Q. Wang, and K. Sivakumar. On the privacy preserving properties of random data perturbation techniques. In *ICDM '03*, page 99. IEEE Computer Society, 2003.

[39] H. Kido, Y. Yanagisawa, and T. Satoh. An anonymous communication technique using dummies for location-based services. In *International Conference on Pervasive Services*, pages 88–97. IEEE Computer Society, 2005.

[40] H. Kido, Y.Yanagisawa, and T. Satoh. Protection of location privacy using dummies for location-based services. In *ICDE Workshops*, page 1248, 2005.

[41] J. J. Kim. A method for limiting disclosure in microdata based on random noise and transformation. In *Survey Research Method Section, American Statistical Association*, pages 370–374, 1986.

[42] P. Kooiman, L. Willenborg, and J. Gouweleeuw. Pram: A method for disclosure limitation of microdata. Research paper no. 9705, 1997.

[43] K. LeFevre, D. J. DeWitt, and R. Ramakrishnan. Incognito: Efficient full-domain k-anonymity. In *SIGMOD*, pages 49–60. ACM, 2005.

[44] N. Li, T. Li, and S. Venkatasubramanian. t-closeness: Privacy beyond k-anonymity and l-diversity. In *ICDE*, pages 106–115. IEEE, 2007.

[45] K. Liu, H. Kargupta, and J. Ryan. Random projection-based multiplicative data perturbation for privacy preserving distributed data mining. *IEEE TKDE*, 18(1):92–106, 2006.

[46] A. Machanavajjhala, J. Gehrke, D. Kifer, and M. Venkitasubramaniam. l-diversity: Privacy beyond k-anonymity. In *ICDE*, page 24. IEEE Computer Society, 2006.

[47] B. Malin. Protecting DNA sequence anonymity with generalization lattices. *Methods of Information in Medicine*, 44(5):687–692, 2005.

[48] S. Mascetti, C. Bettini, X. S. Wang, and S. Jajodia. k-anonymity in databases with timestamped data. In *TIME*, pages 177–186, 2006.

[49] J. M. Mateo-Sanz, A. Martinez-Balleste, and J. Domingo-Ferrer. Fast generation of accurate synthetic microdata. In *Privacy in Statistical Databases, vol.3050 of LNCS*, pages 298–306. Springer, 2004.

[50] A. Meyerson and R. Williams. On the complexity of optimal k-anonymity. In *PODS '04*, pages 223–228. ACM, 2004.

[51] M. E. Nergiz, M. Atzori, and Y. Saygin. Perturbation-driven anonymization of trajectories. Technical Report 2007-TR-017, ISTI-CNR, Pisa, Italy, 2007. 10 pages.

[52] A. Oganian and J. Domingo-Ferrer. On the complexity of optimal microaggregation for statistical disclosure control. *Statistical Journal of the United Nations Economic Comission for Europe*, 18:345–354, 2001.

[53] S. R. M. Oliveira and O. R. Zaiane. Privacy preserving clustering by data transformation. In *SBBD*, pages 304–318, 2003.

[54] S. R. M. Oliveira and O. R. Zaiane. Data perturbation by rotation for privacypreserving clustering. *Technical Report* TR04-17, Department of Computing Science, University of Alberta, Edmonton, Canada, 2004.

[55] Federal Committee on Statistical Methodology. Statistical policy working paper 22, may 1994. Report on Statistical Disclosure Limitation Methodology.

[56] R. G. Pensa, A. Monreale, F. Pinelli, and D. Pedreschi. Pattern-preserving k-anonymization of sequences and its application to mobility data mining. In *PiLBA*, 2008.

[57] S. Rizvi and J. R. Haritsa. Maintaining data privacy in association rule mining. In *VLDB*, pages 682–693, 2002.

[58] D. B. Rubin. Discussion of statistical disclosure limitation. *Journal of Official Statistics*, (9(2)):461–468, 1993.

[59] P. Samarati. Protecting respondents' identities in microdata release. *IEEE TKDE*, 13(6):1010–1027, 2001.

[60] A. C. Singh, F. Yu, and G. H. Dunteman. Massc: A new data mask for limiting statistical information loss and disclosure. In *The Joint UNECE/EUROSTAT Work Session on Statistical Data Confidentiality*, pages 373–394, 2003.

[61] G. R. Sullivan. *The use of added error to avoid disclosure in microdata releases*. PhD thesis, Ames, IA, USA, 1989. Supervisor-Fuller, Wayne A.

[62] L. Sweeney. Uniqueness of simple demographics in the U.S. population. Technical report, Laboratory for International Data Privacy, Carnegie Mellon University, Pittsburgh, PA, 2000.

[63] L. Sweeney. k-anonymity: A model for protecting privacy. *International Journal of Uncertainty, Fuzziness, and Knowledge-Based Systems*, 2002.

[64] M. Terrovitis and N. Mamoulis. Privacy preservation in the publication of trajectories. In *MDM*, pages 65–72, 2008.

[65] K. Wang, P. S. Yu, and S. Chakraborty. Bottom-up generalization: A data mining solution to privacy protection. In *ICDM*, pages 249–256. IEEE Computer Society, 2004.

[66] L. Willenborg and T. DeWaal. *Elements of Statistical Disclosure Control*. Springer-Verlag, 2001.

[67] W. E. Winkler. Using simulated annealing for k-anonymity. Technical Report 7, US Census Bureau.

[68] X. Xiao and Y. Tao. Anatomy: Simple and effective privacy preservation. In *VLDB*, pages 139–150. ACM, 2006.

[69] R. Yarovoy, F. Bonchi, L. V. S. Lakshmanan, and W. H. Wang. Anonymizing moving objects: how to hide a mob in a crowd? In *EDBT*, pages 72–83, 2009.

[70] J. Z. Zhan, S. Matwin, and L. Chang. Privacy-preserving collaborative association rule mining. In *DBSec*, pages 153–165, 2005.

[71] P. Zhang, Y. Tong, S. Tang, and D. Yang. Privacy preserving Naive Bayes classification. In *ADMA*, volume 3584 of *LNCS*, pages 744–752. Springer, 2005.

[72] B. Zhou, J. Pei, and W. Luk. A brief survey on anonymization techniques for privacy preserving publishing of social network data. *SIGKDD Explor. Newsl.*, 10(2):12–22, 2008.

Chapter 2

Privacy Preservation in the Publication of Sparse Multidimensional Data

Manolis Terrovitis

IMIS, Research Center "Athena," Greece

Nikos Mamoulis

Dept. of Computer Science, The University of Hong Kong, PR of China

Panos Kalnis

Div. of Mathematical and Computer Sciences and Engineering, The King Abdullah University of Science and Technology, Saudi Arabia

2.1 Introduction

Nowadays, most human activities leave some trace in a digital registry. Whether one buys something in a supermarket or gets admitted in the hospital, an entry to her credit card history or to her medical record will be made. Data collected this way can be used to improve the quality of services, e.g., companies can adjust faster to the needs of the consumers, or even contribute to science advancement; doctors can study the medical histories of thousands or even millions of patients. On the other hand, such data collections pose a significant threat to the privacy of the individuals that are associated with them. Even if some information that directly identifies a person (e.g., the name or the social security number) is removed from a database record, the individual that is associated to the record can be identified by linking the remaining information (e.g., age, zip code of residence) to external knowledge (e.g., a public voters table).

In most privacy protection settings, we assume that a part of the disseminated information is publicly known and can be used as a link between the

id	Age	Region	Disease		id	Age	Region	Disease
1	25	Thessaloniki	flu		1	[20-40]	Northern Greece	flu
2	34	Drama	cancer		2	[20-40]	Northern Greece	cancer
3	35	Athens	pleuritis		3	[20-40]	Central Greece	pleuritis
4	22	Athens	AIDS		4	[20-40]	Central Greece	AIDS
5	39	Thessaloniki	cancer		5	[20-40]	Northern Greece	cancer
6	20	Megara	gastritis		6	[20-40]	Central Greece	gastritis

(a) original   (b) anonymized

FIGURE 2.1: Example database

anonymized database and the external knowledge possessed by the attacker. The attributes that comprise this linking information are usually termed the *quasi identifier*. For example, in the database of Fig. 2.1.a, where medical information about patients is revealed, "age" and "region" form the quasi identifier, since an attacker might have this knowledge about individuals from another source. Using this transformation she could identify the associated person to each record. For example, if there is a unique person in a demographics database who is age 22 and resides in Athens, then an observer of the database of Fig. 2.1.a can infer that he/she is infected by AIDS. With k-anonymity [23] the initial database is transformed in such a way that any tuple is indistinguishable from another $k − 1$ tuples, based on the quasi identifier. Each group of tuples with identical quasi identifier is an *equivalence class*. A simple transformation that would prohibit linkage to an external knowledge source would be to generalize the values of the quasi identifiers in order to achieve equivalence classes of cardinality at least k. For instance, the transformed table of Figure 2.1.b satisfies 3-anonymity, since each entry is indistinguishable from at least 2 more entries based on their quasi identifier. Anonymization algorithms have to balance two conflicting aims: a) the provision of the required privacy guarantee and b) to keep as much as possible of the original information. This is translated in an effort to perform the minimum amount of transformations for achieving the desired privacy guarantee. In most cases the transformations create equivalence classes where all quasi identifiers are identical. To achieve this they employ a variety of techniques like generalization, suppression and perturbation. l-diversity [17] imposes an even stricter requirement to k-anonymity; the publicly known information cannot be linked with any sensitive value on the anonymized table with probability higher than $1/l$. For example, the transformation shown in Figure 2.1.b may not be acceptable, since the probability (2/3) of a tuple in the "Northern Greece" equivalence class to be associated to cancer may be considered too high.

If the domain of the quasi identifiers is small compared to the size of the database, then it is likely that many different entries will share the same quasi identifiers and few transformations will be needed. Imagine for example that in the database of Figure 1.a we only have 100 different values for age (1–100 years old) and 10 distinct regions. There are 1000 different quasi identifiers based on these attribute domains. If the database contained millions of entries and we wanted to achieve k-anonymity for a very small k, it is quite likely that no transformations would be required. On the other hand, if the database contained more attributes that could be used as quasi identifiers, e.g., nationality, gender, weight, height etc, then the anonymizer's job would be harder; the domain of a quasi identifier grows exponentially to the number of its attributes and it would be a lot easier for the adversary to uniquely identify a person in the original database.

Anonymization techniques can be seen as efforts to bring together data points scattered in the quasi-identifier space. Collections of such points are replaced by a single point or by a multi-dimensional region that encloses them. Most utility metrics that measure the quality of the data are affected by the scattering of the data which are grouped together. Thus, quality is disproportional to the volume of the multi-dimensional region that encloses an equivalence group; the more clustered the original data are, the less information loss is introduced when they are placed in the same equivalence class. As the number of attributes in the quasi identifiers grows, it becomes harder to detect clusters of high quality, and the information loss is very high. This effect, known as the curse of dimensionality, appears also in other areas of data management, for example in indexing. For example, it has been shown that as dimensionality of the data increases there is always a point where the privacy cannot be protected by any other means but for completely suppressing all the data [4] (or generalizing to one point).

While publishing very high dimensional data with a privacy guarantee seems impossible in its general case, in many real-world cases it becomes feasible, due to the fact that data in these applications are *sparse*, i.e., they have non-trivial values only in a small subset of their dimensions. Examples of such data are numerous; market basket data are sparse multidimensional binary vectors with each different product being a distinct dimension, whose domain takes two values 1 (bought) and 0 (not bought). The same holds for medical histories, each different disease is a distinct dimension with a domain of two values indicating if the specified disease appears in the medical history or not. Basically, any type of data where we can have an arbitrary number of different entries for the same person must be treated as a multidimensional single entry, since the combination of these individual entries can be used to identify the associated person.

This chapter provides a survey of the anonymization techniques that appear in the research literature for sparse multidimensional data. In Section 2.2 we provide a detailed overview of the some generic anonymization techniques that do not specialize in a single type of data processing or in data from a specific application area. We focus mostly on three methods: the multirelational k-anonymity, an adjustment of l-diversity to the sparse multidimensional space and the k^m-anonymity. In Section 2.3 we examine the privacy problems and the anonymization solutions for web log data. Finally, in Section 2.4 we conclude the chapter.

2.2   Generic Methods

In sparse multidimensional data only a small percentage of the data space dimensions (attributes) has non-trivial values. The majority of the dimensions has a zero or undefined value, depending on the application semantics. A common example of sparse data are transactional data, like the ones depicted in Figure 2.2. The data represent retail sales; in the first column we store the *id* of the user who did a transaction and in the rest of the columns the *ids* of the products that were bought in the transaction. We can model the data in three different ways. In Figure 2.2.a the transactions are modeled in the most intuitive way: as set values. Each tuple has two attributes; the customer *id* and a set-valued attribute with all the *IDs* of the products. In Figure 2.2.b we model the transactions as fixed-length binary vectors, with as many attributes as the total number of products that appear in the database. Each attribute that models a product can take two values: 1, if the customer bought the product, and 0, if the customer did not buy it. Storing data in this way has significant storage requirements since we explicitly model not only positive knowledge (i.e., the fact that someone bought a product) but also negative. This model helps in understanding the difficulty of grouping the data due to the extremely high dimensionality. Finally, Figure 2.2.c converts the set-valued representation to a compact, strictly relational model, where each tuple has two attributes: the customer *id* (which is no longer a key) and one of the products she bought. For each transaction we need as many tuples as the number of products she bought.

All data representations in Figure 2.2 are equally expressive, and anonymization can adopt any of them, depending on how helpful they are in presenting the anonymization algorithm. In any case, the adversary will use the attributes that describe the products as quasi identifiers and will try to re-identify the the person that bought them. If the publisher adopts *k*-anonymity as a privacy guarantee and wants to present a 2-anonymous version of the database, he must create equivalence classes of size at least 2 that have the same quasi identifier. Such anonymized versions of the data that are depicted in Figures 2.2.a and 2.2.b are presented in Figures 2.3.a and 2.3.b respectively. In this example, the publisher has created equivalence classes with the same quasi identifier by suppressing several products. Note that an algorithm for simple relational *k*-anonymity would work on the data if they are modeled as in 2.2.b. Such algorithms, like Incognito [16], have an exponential

User ID	item
1	a
1	b
1	c
2	b
2	c
2	d
3	a
3	b
4	d
4	e
5	b
5	f

User ID	items
1	a,b,c
2	b,c,d
3	a, b
4	d, e
5	b, f

User ID	a	b	c	d	e	f
1	1	1	1	0	0	0
2	0	1	1	1	0	0
3	1	1	0	0	0	0
4	0	0	0	1	0	1
5	0	1	0	0	0	1

(a) set-values   (b) bitmap   (c) relational

FIGURE 2.2: Three different representations of the same dataset

complexity to the number of dimensions, so although they might do the job, they would never manage to sanitize high dimensional data in a reasonable amount of time.

The case is a bit more complicated for the data as depicted in Figure 2.2.c. If we simply run an anonymization algorithm that is used for simple relational tables in literature we could get a database like the one depicted in Figure 2.3.d, which is problematic. It may be that each quasi identifier appears at least 2 times, but still the database is not anonymous. An adversary who knows a person who bought the products c and d can identify her as the customer with $id = 2$ and discover that she also bought the product a. A correct anonymization would be the one depicted in Figure 2.3.c. The problem with algorithms that were designed for single relational tables, is that they also assume that all tuples are independent; there are no tuples that refer to the same person or at least no such information is revealed in the publication. An important point here is that a collection of data which has an arbitrary amount of entries for the same person or entity, has to be treated, for privacy preservation purposes, as a collection of single independent multidimensional entries for each person. In the context of the example of Figure 2.2, we should assume that we have a single entry for each person with dimensionality equal to the number of products that appear in the database.

The anonymization methods for the simple relational tables, can exhaustively explore all combinations of generalizations or suppressions in all dimensions of the data, hence they can provide an optimal solution. In the case of sparse multidimensional data the solution space is huge, and most anonymization algorithms focus on heuristics that find a local optimum. They borrow ideas from the data mining research and they try to cluster similar data together and then transform each cluster to an equivalence class. In the rest of the section we detail further three such techniques: multirelational

User ID	items
1	a,~~b~~,~~e~~
3	a,b
2	~~b~~,~~c~~,~~d~~
5	b,~~f~~
4	~~d~~,~~e~~

User ID	a	b	c	d	e	f
1	1	1	~~1~~	0	0	0
3	1	1	0	0	0	0
2	0	1	~~1~~	~~1~~	0	0
5	0	1	0	0	0	~~1~~
4	0	0	0	~~1~~	0	~~1~~

(a) set values   (b) bitmap

User ID	item
1	a
3	a
1	b
2	b
3	b
5	b
1	e
2	e
2	~~d~~
4	~~d~~
4	e
5	f

User ID	item
1	a
3	a
1	b
2	b
3	b
5	b
1	c
2	c
2	d
4	d
4	e
5	f

(c) relational - correct   (d) relational - wrong

FIGURE 2.3: Anonymized versions of the data of Figure 2.2

k-anonymity, l-diversity for sparse multidimensional data and k^m-anonymity.

2.2.1 Multirelational k-Anonymity

Multirelational k-anonymity was proposed in [21, 20] and extends the notion of k-anonymity to multiple relations. The idea is that information associated to a specific person is spread in many different relational tables, which have several functional dependencies. For example in Figure 2.4 we see a database that contains data about the medical treatment of patients. In Table T_p we store the disease of a patient, in table T_d the doctors that treated her and in T_m the medicine that each doctor prescribed for each patient. The *pid* acts as a foreign key from T_d to T_p and *sid* acts as a foreign key from T_m to T_d. A naive way to anonymize this database would be to create a bitmap table as we did in Figure 2.2.b and use some anonymization algorithm for simple relational tables. Again, the high dimensionality would make this approach impractical.

To tackle the dimensionality problem the authors of [21] propose the MiR-aCle algorithm (for MultiRelAtional CLustEring), which is a clustering-based anonymity algorithm. Before explaining the algorithm further we need some basic assumptions and definitions. The method assumes that in the database schema there is a special type of table termed *person specific table.*

DEFINITION 2.1 Person specific table *(PT)* *A table is called person specific if and only if it has a primary key that corresponds to a real person*

SID	patient	doctor
1	1	Kalnis
2	1	Mamoulis
3	1	Terrovitis
4	2	Who
5	2	Mamoulis
6	2	House
7	3	Terrovitis
8	3	House
9	3	Mamoulis
10	4	Terrovitis
11	4	House

SID	medicine
1	antibiotic 1
2	vitamin C
2	painkiller 2
3	eye surgery
4	antibiotic 1
5	painkiller 2
6	ear surgery
7	dental fillings
8	antibiotic 3
9	vitamin C
10	dental denture

patient	disease
1	cancer
2	flu
3	ulcer
4	gastritis

FIGURE 2.4: Original database for a hospital

SID	patient	doctor
1	1	*Pathologist*
2	1	Mamoulis
3	1	*Surgeon*
4	2	*Pathologist*
5	2	Mamoulis
6	2	*Surgeon*
7	3	Terrovitis
8	3	House
*	*	*
10	4	Terrovitis
11	4	House

SID	medicine
1	antibiotic 1
2	vitamin C
2	painkiller 2
3	*surgery*
4	antibiotic 1
5	*surgery*
6	ear surgery
7	*dental operation*
*	*
10	*dental operation*

patient	disease
1	cancer
2	flu
3	cancer
4	gastritis

FIGURE 2.5: The anonymized database of Figure 2.4

Table T_p is a person specific table in the context of the Figure 2.4. We assume that in each relational schema we have one person-specific table *PT* and all the remaining tables are functionally depended (directly or indirectly) on the *PT*. The multirelational *k*-anonymity for a database having the aforementioned schema is defined as follows:

DEFINITION 2.2 Multirelational *k*-anonymous database *A database D is k-anonymous if and only if the following properties hold:*

1. *any query involving selection, projection and join on the database tables returns either zero or at least k (not necessarily distinct) tuples.*

2. *any query involving selection, projection and join that includes the primary key vip of PT returns at least k distinct values for vip.*

3. *the join of all tables of D_{pub} contains all and only generalized versions of the tuples that appear in D.*

Regarding the third property, a tuple *g* is a generalization of tuple *t* if every attribute of *g* has the same or a generalized version of the value of the respective attribute in *t*. The anonymization procedure guarantees certain properties and in doing so it has some limitations. These properties and assumptions are:

- **Schema Preservation**. The anonymized database is structurally equivalent to the original database. The tables have the same attributes and the *PT* table has the same primary key.

- **Dependency Preservation**. The anonymized database preserves the original functional dependencies.

- **Snowflake Schema**. We assume that the original database has a snowflake schema:

  1. No connection keys between tables are quasi-identifiers. If that does not hold, it is possible to transform the database to a form which satisfies this property.

  2. Every table except *PT* contains only one foreign key.

  3. All tables are directly or indirectly functionally dependent on *PT*. This means they either have a foreign key to *PT* or to a table that is dependent on *PT*.

Given a database with a snowflake schema the MiRaCle algorithm can produce a new database D_{pub} which is *k*-anonymous. The MiRaCle algorithm can use as a base any existing clustering based anonymity algorithm [6, 10, 19]. The snowflake schema allows abstracting the data of the database as a forest of trees, each of which has as root a single entry *e* of the *PT* table, i.e., a single person. A tree represents the nested relation that is associated with a single entry *e*. Each node of the tree represents a quasi identifier (i.e., a relation tuple) and each edge represents a functional dependency, i.e., a foreign key. Example trees from the database of Figure 2.4 are depicted in the leftmost part of Figure 2.6. Each path of a tree (excluding the root) corresponds to a combination of quasi-identifier values (at different tables linked by foreign key relationships), therefore each path should appear in at least k different trees (which correspond to different vip identifiers of PT), in order to satisfy k-anonymity. The MiRaCle algorithm considers the database as a collection of such trees and performs the following basic operations:

1. It clusters the data in the quasi identifier space. The clusters should be large enough to guarantee the k-anonymity, i.e., they must have at least k members.

2. It creates one representative for each cluster which is a generalization of all its members.

3. It replaces all the values of the quasi identifiers of all clusters' members, with the respective generalized values of each cluster's representative.

There are two key points in the algorithm: a) the creation of the representative and b) the definition of the distance between two trees. The representative is created by making the necessary generalizations to the underlying data, so that the result is anonymous i.e., the entities cannot be distinguished based on their quasi identifiers. The basic operation is the *anonymization* of two trees. This anonymization takes as input two distinct trees and results to two trees with common (possibly generalized) quasi identifiers. The anonymization happens top down. First, the root elements are generalized to the lowest common generalized value (the root includes the quasi identifiers that exist in the PT table — there are no such quasi identifiers in our example), then the children are coupled based on their distance and the same anonymization procedure is called for all pairs. An example of this process is graphically depicted in Figure 2.6. The distance between two trees is defined as the generalization cost for making them anonymous. The detailed algorithm and the exact distance definition can be found in [21]. Figure 2.5 shows the anonymized database of Figure 2.4.

2.2.1.1   Summary

Multirelational k-anonymity extends the traditional k anonymity to a multirelational setting. Even with its restrictive assumptions, the extension is significant, since the model covers many real world databases and more can be transformed to abide with the snowflake schema requirements. The MiRaCle algorithm manages to anonymize the database a lot faster than a traditional k-anonymity algorithm would on the bitmap representation of the data. The only problem is that the strict extension of the k-anonymity to the multidimensional space of the multirelational schema requires extensive transforma-

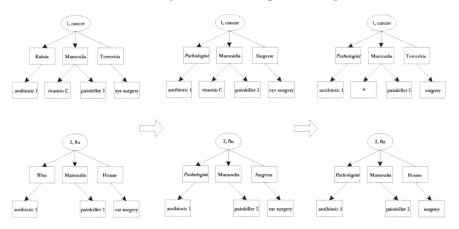

FIGURE 2.6: The anonymization procedure for two trees from the database of Figure 2.4

tions on the original data. The transformations incur an information loss that might be unacceptable in certain cases.

2.2.2 l-Diversity for Sparse Multidimensional Data

In Section 2.2.1 we saw a method for transforming a special form of multidimensional data, i.e., a relational database with a snowflake schema, to a k-anonymous database. k-anonymity guarantees that any tuple will be indistinguishable w.r.t. the quasi identifiers. However, if there is a sensitive value that is linked to the majority of individuals in an equivalence class then it will be associated to an individual with high probability, regardless of the anonymity guarantee. For example, if all patients of the first data cluster in the database of Figure 2.3 had the same disease, e.g., cancer, k-anonymity would not be able to hide this fact. To avoid such privacy breaches l-diversity requires that each equivalence class in the anonymized dataset has diverse sensitive values with the most frequent not appearing in more that $1/l$ records of the equivalence class.

An l-diversification method for sparse high dimensional data without any structural constraints has been proposed in [11]. The most convenient data representation for explaining the anonymization procedure is that of the bitmap, e.g., in the form of the dataset of Figure 2.7.a. It assumes two types of binary attributes; sensitive ones (e.g., *viagra* and *antibiotics*) which are unknown to the attacker, and the rest, which are potentially known to the attacker and act as quasi identifiers. The anonymization method is based on perturbation. It groups transactions into equivalence classes, which are l-diverse and then it publishes the quasi identifiers and the sensitive values of each group (with their frequencies) disassociated, as in Figure 2.7.c.

User ID	chocolate	ice cream	beer	oranges	viagra	antibiotic
Nikos	1	0	1	0	0	1
Manolis	1	0	1	0	0	0
Panos	0	1	0	1	1	0
Maria	0	1	1	0	0	0
Eleni	1	0	1	1	0	0

(a) Original dataset

User ID	chocolate	ice cream	beer	oranges	viagra	antibiotic
Nikos	1	1	0	0	0	1
Manolis	1	1	0	0	0	0
Eleni	1	1	1	0	0	0
Maria	0	1	0	1	0	0
Panos	0	0	1	1	1	0

(b) Band matrix of the dataset

User ID	chocolate	ice cream	beer	oranges	sensitive items
Nikos	1	1	0	0	
Manolis	1	1	0	0	antibiotic, 33%
Eleni	1	1	1	0	
Maria	0	1	0	1	viagra, 50%
Panos	0	0	1	1	

(c) Published dataset

FIGURE 2.7: An example transaction log dataset and its l-diverse anonymization

The published data provide the l-diversity guarantee which is expressed as follows:

DEFINITION 2.3 *A transaction set D is l-diverse if the probability of associating any transaction $t \in D$ with a particular sensitive item does not exceed $1/l$.*

Unlike perturbation based methods for simple relational data [26], which create the equivalence classes without taking into account the quasi identifiers, the anonymization method of [11], creates groups that have similar QIs. This way, useful correlations between QIs and sensitive items are preserved. These correlations can be captured by the $KL\_Divergence$ metric [14]. This metric compares the original distribution of a sensitive value in all the equivalence classes of the original data (i.e., all groups with identical QI values), to the distribution of the same value in the equivalence classes of the published data.

The *KL_Divergence* is given by the following equation:

$$KL\_Divergence = \sum_{\forall C} Act_C^s \log \frac{Act_C^s}{Est_C^s} \qquad (2.1)$$

Where C stands for an equivalence class and s for a sensitive value. Act_C^s is given by the formula:

$$Act_C^s = \frac{occurences\ of\ s\ in\ C}{occurences\ of\ s\ in\ D}$$

Act_C^s is the ratio of the occurrences of a sensitive value s in the equivalence class C in the original data. Est_C^s expresses the same ratio for the published data. The *KL_Divergence* builds on these ratios to give an overall measure for the correlations that are preserved in the anonymized data. The algorithm presented in this section aims at preserving the correlations between QIs and sensitive values and uses *KL_Divergence* to measure the quality of its results.

The algorithm for *l*-diversity is a clustering algorithm, but it uses a heuristic to sort the data in such a way that clusters are created from transactions that appear closely placed in the sorted dataset. The algorithm first organizes the data into a *band matrix* by performing permutations of rows and columns in the original table. A band matrix has the general form shown in Figure 2.8, where all elements of the matrix are 0, except for the main diagonal d_0, a number of U upper diagonals $(d_1, \ldots, d_U)$ and a number of lower diagonals $(d_{-1}, \ldots, d_{-L})$. The objective in the transformation of the original bitmap matrix to a band matrix is to minimize $U + L$. The problem has been shown to be NP-hard, so a heuristic is used; the *Reverse Cuthill-McKee* (RCM) algorithm [9]. The RCM algorithm works only for symmetric matrices, which is not the case for most datasets, where the number of transactions $|D|$ is usually considerably greater than the number of dimensions. This can be easily tackled by padding the original matrix with 0 columns (fake items that do not appear in the database).

Once the data is transformed according to RCM, the next step is to create anonymized groups of transactions. To fulfill the privacy requirement, each sensitive transaction (i.e., transactions that contain sensitive items) needs to be grouped with non-sensitive transactions or sensitive ones with different sensitive items. The grouping is achieved with the *Correlation-aware Anonymization of High-Dimensional Data* (CAHD) heuristic. CAHD is a greedy heuristic that capitalizes on the data correlation, and groups together transactions that are close-by in the band matrix representation.

Consider the example in Figure 2.9 where non-sensitive transactions are shown light-shaded, and sensitive ones dark-shaded. CAHD scans the transaction set D in row order, finds the first sensitive transaction in the sequence, and attempts to form an equivalence class for it. For each transaction t_0 CAHD will examine the $a \times l$ transactions that precede it and the $a \times l$ transactions that follow it, in order to create the anonymization equivalence

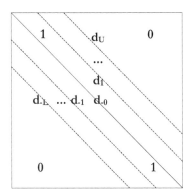

FIGURE 2.8: The abstract form of a band matrix. The shaded part stands for 1s and the empty part for 0s

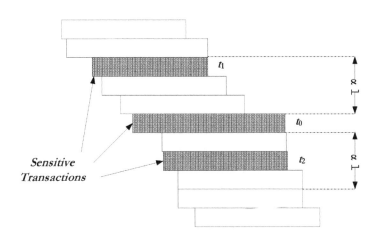

FIGURE 2.9: The CAHD heuristic.

class. $a \in \mathbb{N}$ is a system parameter which restricts the range of the search. The algorithm adopts a *one-occurrence-per-group* policy that allows only one occurrence of each sensitive item in each equivalence class. Therefore, any transactions that contain a common sensitive item with t_0 or with some other transaction that has already been considered as a candidate for the equivalence class, are skipped. Out of the $2 \times a \times l$ transactions the $l - 1$ of them that have the largest number of QI items in common with t_0 are chosen to form the equivalence class. All selected transactions are then removed from D and the process continues with the next sensitive transaction in the order.

2.2.2.1 Summary

The anonymization algorithm presented in this section extends the *l*-diversity guarantee to the sparse multidimensional setting, where each transaction can have different QIs and multiple sensitive values. The algorithm combines advantages of both generalization and perturbation methods; it avoids the great information loss that generalization on highly dimensional data would incur, and unlike random perturbation, it creates equivalence classes where the correlation between the QIs and the sensitive values is preserved to a certain degree. One drawback of the anonymization technique is its memory requirements; the creation of the band matrix requires keeping in memory a matrix of $|D| \times |D|$ size.

2.2.3 k^m Anonymity

In Sections 2.2.1 and 2.2.2 we outlined two strict extensions of *l*-diversity and *k*-anonymity to a sparse multidimensional setting. Both these approaches tried to preserve the original definitions of *k*-anonymity and *l*-diversity, as they appear in the simpler relational anonymization problems. Still, the assumptions of these definitions may not fit in all cases of sparse multidimensional data. The k^m anonymity approach we present in this section revisits some of them:

- *There are two different types of data: sensitive attributes and quasi identifiers.* Since each tuple can have numerous dimensions, whose number might reach several thousands, it is not always clear which dimensions describe sensitive and which non-sensitive data. Moreover, the definition of sensitive might be very subjective and hence all should be treated as sensitive values. On the other hand, merely the existence of multiple sensitive values means that the knowledge of some of them can lead an adversary to the others. When we have a single sensitive value per record then there is little to hide from an adversary that somehow has acquired this information. In the presence of multiple sensitive values, the privacy preserving transformation must make some provision for the possibility that these sensitive values will act as quasi identifiers. For example, if a doctor has treated a patient in the past and knows some of the sensitive details of her medical history, should she be able to discover all other entries in the patient's medical record? Based on this ambiguity of what is a quasi identifier and what is not, the k^m anonymity treats all items as quasi identifiers and as sensitive values at the same time; it assumes that the attacker might know any of them but on the other hand it will prohibit her or him from identifying less than k records that contain them.

- *The attacker knows all quasi identifiers.* In the case of few dimensions that are densely populated the most natural assumption is to assume adversaries that know all quasi identifiers that appear in a record. In a sparse multidimensional setting where thousands of different dimensions might act as quasi identifiers, this is not always the most reasonable assumption. While it makes sense not to set a boundary between quasi identifiers and sensitive values, it also makes little sense assume that the number of quasi identifiers an attacker might know is fixed. On the other hand, in a context where there are no quasi identifiers and sensitive values, there is little privacy gain in protecting a few values in a record where the adversary already knows the majority of entries. Therefore, there should be an upper bound to the number of known items to the attacker (per transaction) in order for the anonymization to be practical.

- *Negative knowledge is equal to positive knowledge.* In classic k-anonymity and l-diversity, negative knowledge, i.e., nulls or zeroes in some fields, is equally important to positive knowledge. For example, in the classic setting, an adversary who tries to discover information in a transaction log, might know that a customer bought products a and b but not c, so she or he is able to distinguish between the following records: $\{a, b, c\}$ and $\{a, b\}$. This is not the common case for sparse multidimensional data. In the presence of potentially thousands of dimensions with zero or null values (depending on the semantics) it is not very easy for an adversary to know positively that a substantial number of them are empty. This is also the case from the application point of view. It is a lot easier for an adversary to discover that a supermarket customer bought some products, than to know for certain that he did not buy some others. The same holds for medical records; it is easier to know that someone had a certain disease than to be certain that he never had it. Assuming that the adversary cannot use any negative knowledge to identify a certain record greatly reduces the difficulty of the problem without increasing significantly the threat to privacy.

Assume that we have a database of sparse multidimensional data, in the form of set-values as in Figure 2.2.a. The definition of k^m-anonymity follows:

DEFINITION 2.4   *Given a database D no attacker that has background knowledge of up to m items of a record $t \in D$ can use these items to identify less than k tuples from D.*

In other words, any subset query of size m or less, issued by the attacker, should return either nothing or more than k answers. Note, that the adversary can have only *positive* knowledge; he is aware of only the existence of a value in a record, not of its absence.

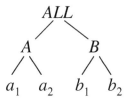

FIGURE 2.10: A generalization hierarchy

id	contents
t_1	$\{a_1, b_1, b_2\}$
t_2	$\{a_2, b_1\}$
t_3	$\{a_2, b_1, b_2\}$
t_4	$\{a_1, a_2, b_2\}$

(a) original database (D)

id	contents
t'_1	$\{A, b_1, b_2\}$
t'_2	$\{A, b_1\}$
t'_3	$\{A, b_1, b_2\}$
t'_4	$\{A, b_2\}$

(b) transformed database (D')

FIGURE 2.11: Transformation using $\{a_1, a_2\} \to A$

The anonymization procedure proposed in [24] is based on generalization. Unlike the approach of multirelational k-anonymity, where the algorithm follows a *local recoding* approach (i.e., the same quasi identifier values can be differently generalized in each cluster), the k^m-anonymization algorithm follows a *global recoding* approach. This means that every appearance of the same value is generalized to the same generalization level throughout D. The generalization of each value happens according to a generalization hierarchy like the one depicted in Figure 2.10. In this hierarchy, a_1 and a_2 can be a generalized to A and A and B can be generalized to ALL, which is the root of the hierarchy and stands for the ultimate generalization of all items in D. It should be noted that if one value needs to be generalized, then all its siblings in the hierarchy tree, must be generalized too. The anonymization algorithm tries to find a "cut" in the generalization hierarchy that guarantees k^m anonymity and the the same time minimizes the information loss (see Figure 2.12). The "cut" is simply the level of generalization that must be applied to each value of D. The information loss, used as quality criterion in [24], is an extension of the *Normalized Certainty Penalty* (NCP) [27]. Let $\mathcal{I}$ be the domain of D and let p be an item in $\mathcal{I}$. Then:

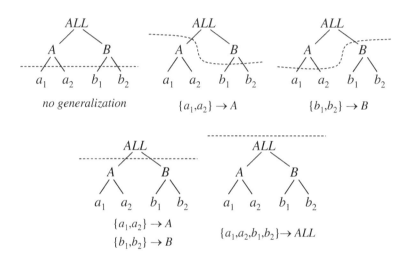

FIGURE 2.12: Possible "cuts" for the generalization hierarchy

$$NCP(p) = \begin{cases} 0, & |u_p| = 1 \\ |u_p|/|\mathcal{I}|, & otherwise \end{cases}$$

where u_p is the node of the item generalization hierarchy where p is generalized. $|u_p|$ and $|\mathcal{I}|$ are the number of leaves under u_p and in the entire hierarchy, respectively. Intuitively, the NCP tries to capture the degree of generalization of each item, by considering the ratio of the total items in the domain that are indistinguishable from it. For example, in the hierarchy of Figure 2.10, if a_1 is generalized to A in a transaction t, the information loss $NCP(a_1)$ is $2/4$. The NCP for the whole database weights the information loss of each generalized item using the ratio of the item appearances that are affected to the total items in the database. If the total number of occurrences of item p in the database is C_p, then the information loss in the whole database due to the generalization can be expressed by:

$$NCP(D) = \frac{\sum_{p \in \mathcal{I}} C_p \cdot NPC(p)}{\sum_{p \in \mathcal{I}} C_p}$$

The most effective algorithm for transforming a database to a k^m anonymous one is an *a priori* based algorithm. The *a priori* algorithm is inspired
by its namesake data mining algorithm, and it is based in the *a priori* principle: if the database is k^i-anonymous it should certainly be k^{i-1}-anonymous.
The algorithm exploits this property of k^m-anonymization and transforms the
original database to a k^m-anonymous one, in m passes over D. At the first
pass it generalizes every itemset of size 1 (1-itemset) that has support less
than k, in step 2 it generalizes all 2-itemsets with support less than k and so
on. An itemset i_g is a generalization of an itemset i if $\forall o \in i \Rightarrow g(o) \in i_g$ and
i_g does not contain any other item. A generalization $g(o)$ of item o is the item
o itself or any other item that appears as its ancestor in the hierarchy tree.
The basic idea of the anonymization procedure is to count the support of all
itemsets of size m and to perform the necessary item generalization so that
all the resulting itemsets should appear with support over k. For example,
a 2^2-anonymization of the table in Figure 2.11.a appears in Figure 2.11.b.
In this procedure there are two challenging issues: a) how to keep track of
the support of all the m-sized itemsets and b) how to choose the generalization that introduces the smallest information loss. In order to keep track of
the support of each m-itemset the algorithm keeps a memory resident trie
termed *count tree*, like the one depicted in Figure 2.13. The trie is a compact
representation of all m-itemsets and all their possible generalizations. The
number of m-itemsets that appear in D is $\binom{|\mathcal{I}^*|}{m}^*$, which even for relatively
small m can be huge. The *a priori* principle offers a way to reduce memory
requirements. In the i-th step the algorithm performs the required item generalizations $\{o_1, \ldots, o_n\} \rightarrow \{o_1, \ldots, o_n\}$ for making the database k^i-anonymous.
In the $i+1$-th step the combinations that contain previously generalized items
$\{o_1, \ldots, o_n\}$ are ignored and only the combinations that contain the generalized items $\{g(o_1), \ldots, g(o_n)\}$ will are into account. Since many different items
get generalized to a single item, the number of combinations of generalized
items will be significantly smaller. Finally, in the m-th step the database will
be k^m-anonymous. At each step the generalizations are selected using two
criteria: a) whether the generalization at question creates a generalized itemset with support of at least k and b) the lowest information loss. By keeping
track of the support of all generalized itemsets in the count tree, it is easy to
verify whether a generalization is adequate to produce a generalized itemset
with support at least k. The information loss can be easily calculated from
the statistics of the dataset. The final result of the algorithm is a cut of the

---

$^*\mathcal{I}^*$ is the set of all items that appear in D and all their possible generalizations

generalization hierarchy that guarantees that the database is k^m-anonymous. For more details see [24].

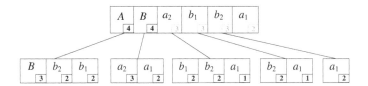

FIGURE 2.13: The count tree for the database of Figure 2.11

2.2.3.1 Summary

The k^m-anonymization model makes significantly different assumptions about the data compared to the multirelational k-anonymity and the l-diversity algorithms presented in Sections 2.2.1 and 2.2.2. It provides a weaker form of privacy protection, in the sense that it does not cover adversaries who know all quasi identifiers, and it does not take into account negative knowledge and l-diversity. At the same time it is suitable for data where the distinction between sensitive and non-sensitive values is not clear, it protects from adversaries who already know some sensitive values and introduces a lower information loss. Depending on the privacy and utility requirements it offers an alternative option to the data publisher.

2.2.4 Other Methods

An interesting anonymization proposal for sparse multidimensional data is that of (h, k, p)-cohesion [28, 29]. The (h, k, p)-cohesion guarantee extends l-diversity to sparse multidimensional spaces in a conditional way, similar to the way k^m-anonymity extends k-anonymity. It assumes that items are classified as sensitive and non-sensitive with the latter acting as quasi identifiers. A (h, k, p)-coherent database is defined as follows:

DEFINITION 2.5 *A database D_{pub} is (h, k, p)-coherent if no attacker who knows up to p items from a record can identify less than k-tuples and the most common sensitive item in the query result does not appear with probability over h.*

The (h, k, p)-cohesion guarantees both k-anonymity and l-diversity (with the h parameter acting like l in the l-diversity of Section 2.2.2). The algorithm from [28, 29] for transforming a database D to a (h, k, p)-coherent database D_{pub} is based on item suppression. The suppression happens globally; if an item is suppressed then all its occurrences are suppressed. The information loss is calculated based on the items that get suppressed and the weight that is associated with each of them. An important property of the coherent databases is that they retain the original support of all the itemsets that appear in the published database.

In [5] the authors propose to preserve the privacy when publishing text or sparse multidimensional data by using sketches. Every record $t = \{o_i, \ldots, o_n\}$ is approximated with a sketch $t_s = \{s_1, \ldots, s_m\}$. By varying the number of sketch components m, the publisher can handle the trade-off between utility (reconstruction error) and privacy level.

Finally, in [25] the authors provide an anonymization technique that uses suppression in order to guarantee l-diversity in sequences. Unlike the approach of [29] they suppress only some occurrences of each item. The sequences in the context of [25] are trajectories, i.e., sequences of points, but the algorithm can easily be adjusted to other settings.

2.3 Privacy Preservation in Web Logs

The privacy preservation in the publication of web logs has lately attracted a significant amount of interest. Research interest has been motivated after the dissemination of AOL query logs [1] and the Netflix Prize dataset [2] and the real privacy breach problems that followed [8, 7, 18]. Research has been focused on these two data publications, since they are both characteristic cases of a large amount of important web data; web search query logs and user profiles. Web query logs carry information of paramount importance to several application areas. Website owners can use them to better understand what users want, manufacturers can faster discover what consumers are asking for, market experts can discover new trends in consumer behavior and polling companies and news agencies can monitor the current issues of major interest. Being information-rich data, the query logs can also reveal very private aspects of the user's life, from health issues to the state of household income (even numbers qualifying as credit card numbers were revealed in the AOL data [3]). Anonymizing such data poses some unique challenges for two main reasons:

- The data are extremely high dimensional (10M terms for 650k users for the AOL data) and extremely sparse; 90% of the terms that appear in the logs of AOL are unique. Removing the unique terms will result to a log 54% smaller that the original, and by removing the terms that appear 3 times of fewer (97% of the total terms) the resulting log will be only 31% of the original [3].

- The semantics of the data are unclear. It is far from trivial to understand what the user is searching for, just by looking at the query term. This makes practically impossible the use of generalization as an anonymization method.

There are several papers that study attack models against the privacy of the users [12, 13, 15]. The authors demonstrate that by taking advantage of user behavior (e.g., most users query their own name [13]) or by using simple techniques for guessing a user's name from her user-ID [12], the real names of the users can be easily revealed. In [15] the authors further demonstrate that anonymizing the data by using a token-based hashing scheme is not safe. Even if the publisher replaces certain query terms with a hash value, an attacker with statistical background knowledge can breach the privacy of the persons who posed the queries.

In [3] the authors offer a solution for anonymizing query logs that uses two different techniques. First, they propose a secret sharing scheme that masks a rare query until it has appeared t times. The motivation for this is that the publisher might want to perform incremental publications of a web search log, and a query that is rare at first, might prove to be frequent after some point. The second anonymization technique that appears in [3], breaks the user's query sessions into smaller sessions, where the queries are thematically related. This way, it not only reduces the information available for each user, but it also creates users that have their queries relatively close in the data space.

In a very different approach, the authors of [22] try to protect the website privacy in query logs. This form of privacy focuses on protecting confidential information related to websites, like visits to internal documents, query terms that lead to internal pages and keywords that position the website in the Web. In this context the adversary can be a competitor website that has access to its own query logs (which are complete and related), in addition to the information it can find from the anonymized query log and from public search engines. By mapping one's own log to the anonymized query log, it can possibly infer with higher probability the anonymized references to the competitor websites. The proposed anonymization procedure relies on removing the queries that share many common results with other queries.

2.4   Conclusion

In this chapter we presented a survey of the latest developments in the privacy preserving publication of sparse multidimensional data. We saw that recording an arbitrary amount of information for a single person is equivalent, in the most common case, to a single sparse multidimensional record. Such recordings might be transaction logs, profiles, medical histories, even tuples from multiple relations that are linked via some functional dependency. No matter how the information about a person is modeled, if it is possible for the attacker to infer that it is associated with a single individual, every part of it might act as a quasi identifier. In Section 2.2 we detailed two methods that extended the k-anonymity and the l-diversity models to the multidimensional setting and presented the k^m-anonymity, which offers a new privacy guarantee based on assumptions specific to a sparse multidimensional domain. We concluded our survey with a brief presentation of other similar methods in Section 2.2.4 and a discussion about privacy preservation in the publishing of web logs in Section 2.3.

The privacy preservation techniques we presented offer some basic solutions, but they are far from covering every data type and utility need in sparse multidimensional data. The inherent problems of dimensionality, which prevent the publisher from easily identifying closely related data, and the possibility that many quasi identifiers might exist in a single record, pose some very hard challenges in efficiently anonymizing such data. The case of web query logs, where research has merely identified some attack models and very few solutions have been proposed is a characteristic example. Still, since data from numerous real world applications are essentially sparse multidimensional data, we believe that the research interest will further increase in the future.

References

[1] AOL research Web site, no longer on-line. http://research.aol.com.

[2] Netflix prize faq. http://www.netflixprize.com/faq, download on February 16, 2009.

[3] E. Adar. User 4xxxxx9: Anonymizing query logs. In *Workshop on Query Log Analysis at the 16th World Wide Web Conference*, 2007.

[4] Charu C. Aggarwal. On k-anonymity and the curse of dimensionality. In *VLDB '05: Proceedings of the 31st international conference on Very large data bases*, pages 901–909. VLDB Endowment, 2005.

[5] Charu C. Aggarwal and Philip S. Yu. On privacy-preservation of text and sparse binary data with sketches. In *SDM*. SIAM, 2007.

[6] Gagan Aggarwal, Tomás Feder, Krishnaram Kenthapadi, Samir Khuller, Rina Panigrahy, Dilys Thomas, and An Zhu. Achieving anonymity via clustering. In *PODS '06: Proceedings of the Twenty-Fifth ACM*

SIGMOD-SIGACT-SIGART Symposium on Principles of Database Systems, pages 153–162, New York, NY, USA, 2006. ACM.

[7] M. Arrington. AOL proudly releases massive amounts of private data. http://www.techcrunch.com/2006/08/06/aol-proudly-releases-massive-amounts-of-user-search-data/, 2006.

[8] M. Barbaro and T. Zeller. A face is exposed for AOL searcher no. 4417749. New York Times, 2006.

[9] E. Cuthill and J. McKee. Reducing the bandwidth of sparse symmetric matrices. In *Proceedings of the ACM 24th National Conference*, pages 157–172, New York, NY, USA, 1969. ACM.

[10] Josep Domingo-Ferrer and Vicenc Torra. Ordinal, continuous and heterogeneous k-anonymity through microaggregation. *Data Mining and Knowledge Discovery*, 11:195–212(18), September 2005.

[11] Gabriel Ghinita, Yufei Tao, and Panos Kalnis. On the Anonymization of Sparse High-Dimensional Data. In *Proc. of ICDE*, 2008.

[12] Rosie Jones, Ravi Kumar, Bo Pang, and Andrew Tomkins. "I know what you did last summer": query logs and user privacy. In *CIKM '07: Proceedings of the Sixteenth ACM Conference on Conference on Information and Knowledge Management*, pages 909–914, New York, NY, USA, 2007. ACM.

[13] Rosie Jones, Ravi Kumar, Bo Pang, and Andrew Tomkins. Vanity fair: privacy in querylog bundles. In *CIKM '08: Proceeding of the 17th ACM Conference on Information and Knowledge Management*, pages 853–862, New York, NY, USA, 2008. ACM.

[14] Daniel Kifer and Johannes Gehrke. Injecting utility into anonymized datasets. In *SIGMOD '06: Proceedings of the 2006 ACM SIGMOD International Conference on Management of Data*, pages 217–228, New York, NY, USA, 2006. ACM.

[15] Ravi Kumar, Jasmine Novak, Bo Pang, and Andrew Tomkins. On anonymizing query logs via token-based hashing. In *WWW '07: Proceedings of the 16th International Conference on World Wide Web*, pages 629–638, New York, NY, USA, 2007. ACM.

[16] Kristen LeFevre, David J. DeWitt, and Raghu Ramakrishnan. Incognito: Efficient Full-domain k-Anonymity. In *Proc. of ACM SIGMOD*, pages 49–60, 2005.

[17] Ashwin Machanavajjhala, Johannes Gehrke, Daniel Kifer, and Muthuramakrishnan Venkitasubramaniam. l-Diversity: Privacy Beyond k-Anonymity. In *Proc. of ICDE*, 2006.

[18] A. Narayanan and V. Shmatikov. Robust de-anonymization of large sparse datasets. In *In SP '08: IEEE Symposium on Security and Privacy*, pages 111–125, 2008.

[19] M. Ercan Nergiz and Chris Clifton. Thoughts on k-anonymization. *Data and Knowledge Engineering*, 63(3):622–645, 2007.

[20] M. E. Nergiz, C. Clifton, and A.E. Nergiz. Multirelational k-anonymity. In *Proc. of ICDE*, pages 1417 – 1421, 2007.

[21] M. E. Nergiz, C. Clifton, and A.E. Nergiz. Multirelational k-anonymity. *IEEE Transactions on Knowledge and Data Engineering (TKDE)*, to appear.

[22] Barbara Poblete, Myra Spiliopoulou, and Ricardo Baeza-Yates. Website privacy preservation for query log publishing. In *In PinKDD'07: Workshop on Privacy, Security and Trust in Data Mining at the ACM SIGKDD*, pages 80–96, 2007.

[23] Latanya Sweeney. k-Anonymity: A Model for Protecting Privacy. *International Journal of Uncertainty, Fuzziness and Knowledge-Based Systems*, 10(5):557–570, 2002.

[24] M. Terrovitis, N. Mamoulis, and P. Kalnis. Privacy-preserving Anonymization of Set-valued Data. *Proceedings of the VLDB endowment (PVLDB)*, 1(1), 2008.

[25] Manolis Terrovitis and Nikos Mamoulis. Privacy Preservation in the Publication of Trajectories. In *Proc. of Int. Conf. on Mobile Data Management (MDM)*, 2008.

[26] Xiaokui Xiao and Yufei Tao. Anatomy: simple and effective privacy preservation. In *VLDB '06: Proceedings of the 32nd International Conference on Very Large Data Bases*, pages 139–150. VLDB Endowment, 2006.

[27] J. Xu, W. Wang, J. Pei, X. Wang, B. Shi, and A. Fu. Utility-Based Anonymization Using Local Recoding. In *Proc. of SIGKDD*, pages 785–790, 2006.

[28] Yabo Xu, Ke Wang, Ada Wai-Chee Fu, and Jian Pei. Publishing sensitive transactions for itemset utility. In *ICDM '08: Proceedings of the 8th IEEE International Conference on Data Mining*, 2008.

[29] Yabo Xu, Ke Wang, Ada Wai-Chee Fu, and Philip S. Yu. Anonymizing transaction databases for publication. In *KDD '08: Proceedings of the 14th ACM SIGKDD International Conference on Knowledge discovery and Data Mining*, pages 767–775, New York, NY, USA, 2008. ACM.

Chapter 3

Knowledge Hiding in Emerging Application Domains

Osman Abul

TOBB University of Economics and Technology, Ankara, Turkey

3.1 Introduction

Without any doubt data is among the most valuable assets of many profit or non-profit organizations including government agencies, corporations and non-governmental institutions. Apart from daily operational use, this is simply because data is the source of precise information and knowledge that organizations need to stay in business, i.e., their success heavily depends on better data utilization. Fast-pacing technological advancements provide organizations with easy collection of massive volumes of data, the utilization of which is organization-dependent, e.g., ranging from simple querying to complex analysis like data mining. However, the process is not straightforward as data management *per se* has long been known as a tough issue as it encompasses several non-trivial aspects, e.g., indexing, integrity, consistency and security. Fortunately, database management systems provide tools to simplify the processes to some extent by means of automation. The security aspect can simply be cast as enforcing a set of data protection policies to limit unauthorized accesses to individual data elements and their aggregations. In a broader sense, the security measures extend to the disclosure limitation of knowledge, patterns/rules derivable from the data. Clearly, security measures are indispensable requirements whenever sensitivity issues do exist. Sensitive data, information or knowledge when disclosed, either intentionally or accidentally, can potentially lead to privacy, anonymity or secrecy violations. This is a serious issue as the violations may cause countless troubles, e.g., unauthorized disclosure of sensitive personal data is a crime in many countries.

In the typical database publishing scenario, an organization maintains a database, and releases it as a whole or in part to third parties, mainly for *do-it-yourself* kind of queries and analysis. We distinguish two basic models of database release: *physical* and *logical*. In the physical release model, interested parties can obtain the released database as a whole. In the logical release model, third parties can not get their own copy but are allowed to query against the shared database with restrictions based on their privileges. In the former, since the to-be-released database may contain sensitive raw data (e.g., salary of general manager), the data publisher simply erases or mixes such entries before the release. The challenge here is to maintain data integrity and statistics. We call this operation *data-level sanitization*. In the latter, third parties are not allowed to query sensitive data directly but only some aggregate information (e.g., average salary of managers) over the sensitive/nonsensitive data. Unfortunately, even simple inferences are shown to be enough to extract sensitive information even though it can not be queried directly. To see, consider that the salary of individual managers is sensitive, but their average salary, is allowed to be queried. In case there is only one manager, then anybody can easily learn the sensitive information through issuing the aggregate query. This is known as the *inference problem* and studied in the context of statistical databases; see [18] for a survey. In this setting, selectively denying to answer some queries can be seen as sanitization since it preserves the disclosure. We call this operation *information-level sanitization*.

The main objective with *data-level sanitization* and *information-level sanitization* is the protection of privacy of individuals. However, privacy protection of individuals is not the only sensitivity issue. Consider for instance that the database is not necessarily about individuals but its content implies valuable patterns which must be kept inaccessible to third parties. In this case, we speak about the "privacy of patterns" and *knowledge-level sanitization*.

The positive side of data mining has long been known. However, it is now a serious threat to database security as data mining techniques allow extraction of almost every derivable knowledge including the sensitive data. Privacy-aware data mining, i.e., the study of data mining side effects on privacy, has rapidly become a hot research area [16, 8, 49, 12] since its introduction in 1991 by O'Leary [35]. Since then, many completely different problem formulations with differing objectives and techniques have been introduced and studied in established data mining domains. *Knowledge hiding* is one of such formulation approaches aimed at hiding some knowledge tagged sensitive from shared databases. Other approaches include data obfuscation/perturbation, secure multi-party computation, secure knowledge sharing and k-anonymity [12].

Many different approaches for knowledge hiding have emerged over the years, mainly in the context of frequent itemset and association rule mining.

But emerging real-world applications' data demands (and associated knowledge demands) are versatile with a wide-spectrum: from unstructured (e.g., text) databases to structured (e.g., graph) databases. This in turn calls for advanced data analysis and respective sensitive knowledge hiding formulations.

In this chapter, we introduce the generic knowledge hiding problem which is to be used as a template in the development of concrete knowledge hiding tasks. We consider there are at least three dimensions for data mining activities depending on (i) the kind of dataset, e.g., relational, structured and text (ii) the kind of data mining task, e.g., associations, clustering and classification (iii) the kind of knowledge format, e.g., itemsets, rules, patterns and clusters. Since knowledge is the focal point in knowledge hiding, we select it to be the main dimension to organize the content. To this end, we first present the generic knowledge hiding problem and obtain specializations for certain knowledge formats and discuss respective sanitization approaches. Then, we present the frequent itemset hiding problem, the classical knowledge hiding domain, and related association rule hiding problem. After that, we continue with the (relatively new) problem of sequential knowledge hiding. Following this, we visit other emerging domains for which the knowledge hiding task is not addressed at all or is immature. For those knowledge hiding domains, we present our view of problem, definitions and possible approaches. Finally, we provide conclusions along with challenging future research directions.

3.2   Knowledge Hiding

Knowledge hiding refers to the activity of concealing patterns that hold in a database that is going to be published, and that are considered as sensitive by the data owner. When the database is published as it is, privacy of the sensitive patterns may be put at risk due to data mining threats. Knowledge hiding is usually obtained by a sanitization process over the database in such a way that the sensitive knowledge can no longer be inferred, while the database utility is preserved as much as possible.

We classify the knowledge in a corporate knowledge-base of an organization along two dimensions: *sensitivity* and *derivability*. The two dimensions define four categories as shown in Figure 3.1. The sensitive knowledge is simply the knowledge that must be kept private to the organization and the derivable knowledge is the knowledge that can be obtained by application of data mining techniques on organization owned data. Since sensitivity is a subjective matter, the sensitive knowledge needs to be stated explicitly, or should be extracted automatically through organizational security policy exploitation.

DEFINITION 3.1 (Ability to derive)   *Data mining algorithm A,* *when run with parameter set Θ, is said to have ability to derive knowledge K from database $\mathcal{D}$ iff K appears, either directly (i.e., by visual inspection) or indirectly (i.e., by reasoning), in its output. The ability to derive (entailment) relation is denoted as $(A, \mathcal{D}, \Theta) \vdash K$. K is said to be derivable at Θ from $\mathcal{D}$, denoted $(\mathcal{D}, \Theta) \vdash K$, if there exists any mining algorithm A such that $(A, \mathcal{D}, \Theta) \vdash K$. Moreover, given $\mathcal{D}$ and Θ the set of derivable knowledge is denoted as $KSet_{(\mathcal{D},\Theta)}$; i.e., any knowledge K with the property $(\mathcal{D}, \Theta) \vdash K$ is in $KSet_{(\mathcal{D},\Theta)}$. Note that the parameter set Θ is always implicit in any mining algorithm as there is no parameterless learning/mining [31].*

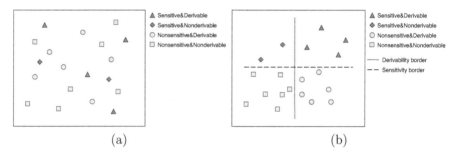

(a)   (b)

FIGURE 3.1: Corporate knowledge-base: (a) four categories (b) same information organized into four quadrants along the sensitivity and derivability border

Figure 3.1(b) reveals that anybody having access to the organizational data can derive the knowledge in the first and fourth quadrants by using appropriate data mining tools. Since the knowledge in the first quadrant is sensitive as well, the indirect disclosure of it (through database sharing) must be limited. There are basically two strategies to provide the limitation; 1) no publish, i.e., do not share data with third parties or do not make it public, 2) publish after transform, i.e., share a variant of the database which limits the sensitive knowledge disclosure. The first approach is the easiest and the most secure way of the limitation but it is too restrictive, i.e., prevents discovery of some useful (but not necessarily sensitive) knowledge from the data by third parties. Clearly the second approach, provided that disclosure of no sensitive knowledge is risked, is preferred for better utilization of the data. Taking the second strategy, we formalize the knowledge hiding problem below.

Problem 1 (The Generic Knowledge Hiding) *Let $\mathcal{K}^s = \{K_1, \dots, K_n\}$ be the set of sensitive knowledge that must be hidden from $\mathcal{D}$ at Θ. The Knowledge Hiding problem requires to transform $\mathcal{D}$ into a database $\mathcal{D}'$ such that:*

1. $KSet_{(\mathcal{D}',\Theta)} \cap \mathcal{K}^s = \emptyset$

2. the difference between $\mathcal{D}$ and $\mathcal{D}'$ is minimized.

The problem requires to sanitize the input database $\mathcal{D}$ in such a way that a set of sensitive patterns $\mathcal{K}^s$ is hidden, while most of the information in $\mathcal{D}$ is maintained. The resulting database, $\mathcal{D}'$, is the released one. The first requirement asks all sensitive knowledge to be *hidden* in $\mathcal{D}'$, i.e., none of it is derivable. The second requirement asks to minimize the sanitization effects on data quality, i.e., any analysis on $\mathcal{D}'$ gives almost the same results as it is done on $\mathcal{D}$. The requirement, in other words, is keeping $\mathcal{D}'$ as similar as possible to $\mathcal{D}$.

The purpose with the second requirement of Problem 1 is to maintain data quality for any kind of data analysis, e.g., data statistics, data mining and simple querying. In other words, the intended receiver of released data is data centric applications. In some other domains, however, data is intensionally made available for data mining purposes, i.e., the intended receiver of released data is knowledge centric applications. For this reason, we define another variant of the knowledge hiding problem below.

Problem 2 (The Generic Knowledge Hiding) *Let $\mathcal{K}^s = \{K_1, \ldots, K_n\}$ be the set of sensitive knowledge that must be hidden from $\mathcal{D}$. The Knowledge Hiding problem requires to transform $\mathcal{D}$ into a database $\mathcal{D}'$ such that:*

1. *there is no hiding failure, i.e., $KSet_{(\mathcal{D}',\Theta)} \bigcap \mathcal{K}^s = \emptyset$;*

2. *the number of misses, $|KSet_{(\mathcal{D},\Theta)} \setminus KSet_{(\mathcal{D}',\Theta)}|$, is minimized;*

3. *the number of fakes, $|KSet_{(\mathcal{D}',\Theta)} \setminus KSet_{(\mathcal{D},\Theta)}|$, is minimized.*

The first requirement in the problem definition 2 requires that no sensitive knowledge is disclosed through $\mathcal{D}'$. To increase the utility of $\mathcal{D}'$ w.r.t. knowledge conveyed, the second requirement calls for the solutions where knowledge in original database $\mathcal{D}$ is preserved as much as possible. The third requirement is to ensure that only valid mining models are obtained through $\mathcal{D}'$. This is an important issue in (life)-critical domains where fake knowledge can lead to unrecoverable damages. The concepts of *hiding failure*, *misses* and *fakes* are graphically shown in Figure 3.2. Note that in Figure 3.2(d) the first requirement is softened to obtain partial hiding solutions, solutions sacrificing the privacy of some sensitive knowledge. This mechanism, indeed, provides the data publisher more flexibility and a knob to balance the utility vs. privacy tradeoff. In that case, the first requirement becomes $|KSet_{(\mathcal{D}',\Theta)} \bigcap \mathcal{K}^s|$ minimized. When the privacy requirements are too tough to meet, even the best no hiding failure solutions may end up with totally useless data. In this case, partial hiding solutions may be resorted to at the cost of some privacy loss.

The problems 1 and 2 are very general definitions, which is why they are attributed generic, which (i) do not make the form of knowledge, the kind of database, and applicable data mining techniques concrete, and (ii) do not say *how* the sanitization is actually performed. The second is more related to

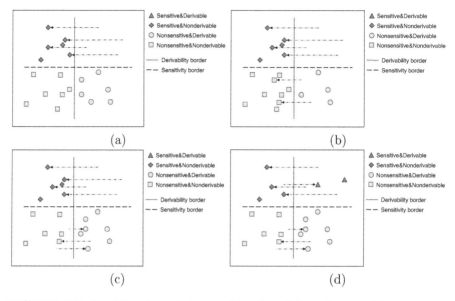

FIGURE 3.2: Sensitive knowledge sanitization: (a) perfect sanitization: no hiding failure, no misses and no fakes (b) non-perfect sanitization: no hiding failure, no fakes but misses (c) non-perfect sanitization: no hiding failure but misses and fakes (d) non-perfect sanitization: hiding failure, misses and fakes

algorithmic solution approaches to the concrete problems posed in the first. In what follows, we provide our view of concrete knowledge hiding problems for certain domains and solution approaches from the literature. We first survey the classical knowledge hiding domain: frequent itemset and association rule hiding from transactional databases. Then we shift our focus to the emerging knowledge hiding domains, the domains for which the literature has already addressed the data mining tasks but not the respective knowledge hiding problems. In this work, we show that the generic problem definitions can serve as a template for a wide range of concrete knowledge hiding problem formulations.

3.3   Itemset Hiding

An *item* is a symbol or an event corresponding to a real-world entity and an *itemset* is a finite set of such items. For instance, bread, blue, pain, egg, milk, and rain are all items and $\{blue, rain, egg\}$ make an itemset over them. However, sensible itemsets usually are those drawing items from the same domain. For instance, the itemset $\{blue, rain, egg\}$ may lack a consistent interpretation but the itemset $\{bread, egg\}$ does, as the latter has clear a interpretation in the sense of a shopping basket content. The notion of *frequent itemset* is the study of rate of co-appearance of items in transaction databases, e.g., market-basket databases where each shopping basket (containing a number of items, hence an itemset, purchased together) is modeled as a transaction. Given a frequent itemset, an itemset appearing in a sizeable portion of transactions, one can reason that there is a strong correlation among items (in the itemset). Therefore, such an itemset is a pattern (a piece of knowledge) that can be used for numerous purposes. For instance, in the market-basket case a frequent itemset is a pattern showing the consumer behaviors that can be used to offer new deals. Clearly, such a pattern has a commercial value and may be considered sensitive.

DEFINITION 3.2 (Frequent Itemset Mining) *Let* $\mathcal{I} = \{i_1, i_2, \ldots, i_n\}$ *be a set of items, and itemset X be any non-empty subset of $\mathcal{I}$. X is called k-itemset if its cardinality is k, i.e., $|X| = k$. The transaction database, $\mathcal{D}$, is an unordered collection of transactions T; each of which is an itemset over $\mathcal{I}$, i.e., $T \in 2^{\mathcal{I}} - \emptyset$. The support set of an itemset X in $\mathcal{D}$, denoted $S_{\mathcal{D}}(X)$, is the set of transactions in $\mathcal{D}$ that contains X, i.e., $S_{\mathcal{D}}(X) = \{T : X \subseteq T \text{ and } T \in \mathcal{D}\}$. The cardinality of $S_{\mathcal{D}}(X)$ is called the support, denoted $sup_{\mathcal{D}}(X)$, of X in $\mathcal{D}$, i.e., $sup_{\mathcal{D}}(X) = |S_{\mathcal{D}}(X)|$. For a user-defined minimum support threshold σ (a non-negative integer), the frequent itemset mining problem is to find all itemsets X having support of at least σ in $\mathcal{D}$. The resulting itemsets are called frequent (a.k.a. large) itemsets and formally denoted as $F_{(\mathcal{D}, \sigma)} = \{X : X \subseteq \mathcal{I}, X \neq \emptyset, sup_{\mathcal{D}}(X) \geq \sigma\}$.*

Since the introduction [5, 6] of the frequent itemset mining problem, the research community has mainly concentrated on developing fast algorithms to support counting of exponentially growing itemsets space. To this end, one of the most useful properties is the anti-monotonic **a priori** property: *if an itemset is not frequent none of its superset can be frequent*, or equivalently *if an itemset is frequent then all of its subsets are frequent too*. As a result, support counting of large portions of itemsets can be avoided to gain efficiency. After the Apriori algorithm [5] which is exploiting Apriori property, several other algorithms have been developed using different approaches, techniques and advanced data structures [39, 23, 4].

Most of the time, an objective criterion of being frequent is not enough to understand the usefulness, and some additional subjective criteria are often needed. Recognizing this fact, constrained frequent itemset mining is proposed to mine only those itemsets that are in the focus of user interests [34]. In another view, the user is given the opportunity to control the data mining output. One of the most important side effects of the constraints is the efficiency obtained through pushing the constraints deep inside the mining process.

DEFINITION 3.3 (Constrained Frequent Itemset Mining)   *Given the set of items $\mathcal{I}$, a constraint C is a mapping from itemset space to boolean space, i.e., $C : 2^{\mathcal{I}} \rightarrow \{true, false\}$. Given a set of constraints $\mathcal{C}$, transaction database D and minimum support threshold σ, constrained frequent itemset mining requires finding the set of itemsets, denoted $CF_{(\mathcal{D},\sigma,\mathcal{C})}$, that are frequent and satisfying all the constraints. Formally, $CF_{(\mathcal{D},\sigma,\mathcal{C})} = \{X : X \in F_{(\mathcal{D},\sigma)} \text{ and } \forall C \in \mathcal{C},\ C(X) = true\}$.*

Depending on the constraint types, there are variants of the constrained frequent itemset mining problem in the context of transaction databases. Most of the constraints are defined over the attributes (e.g., category, price and weight in market-basket transactions) of itemsets. Most common constraints defined over numeric attributes are minimum, maximum, average and variance. In a nutshell, constrained frequent itemset mining generalizes the frequent itemset mining where being frequent is a particular kind of constraint. Constraints are usually classified into a number of categories for efficient processing. Many useful constraints are (or can be relaxed to) either monotone or anti-monotone. Anti-monotone constraints allow us faster production of frequent itemsets as they can be easily pushed deep inside the level-wise bottom-up mining process. Other classes of constraints that possess certain nice properties are *succinct* and *convertible* constraints [11]. Efficient mining with mixed categories of constraints is still a challenging problem; for details see [11].

Regardless of constrained or unconstrained frequent itemset mining, with relatively small σ and large/dense databases, the output grows very large and easily becomes unmanageable. To reduce the size of the output, materialization of some trivial/redundant/implied itemsets can be avoided. Closed and/or maximal itemsets help in that direction [14].

Whatever the problem specification of frequent itemset mining, the knowledge (the output patterns) is in the form of itemsets. Considering what is common, sensitivity of some of the itemsets, we define the frequent itemset hiding problem next to protect itemset privacy against all forms (e.g., unconstrained, constrained and maximal) of frequent itemset mining problem formulations.

3.3.1   Frequent Itemset Hiding

Frequent itemset hiding is a specialization of generic knowledge hiding problem (Problem 2) as defined next.

Problem 3 (Frequent Itemset Hiding) *Let $\mathcal{K}^s = \{X_1, X_2, \ldots, X_n\}$ with $X_i \in 2^{\mathcal{I}} - \emptyset, \forall i \in \{1, \ldots, n\}$, be the set of sensitive itemsets that must be hidden from $\mathcal{D}$. Given a disclosure threshold ψ, the Frequent Itemset Hiding Problem requires to transform $\mathcal{D}$ into a database $\mathcal{D}'$ such that:*

1. $\forall X_i \in \mathcal{K}^s : sup_{\mathcal{D}'}(X_i) < \psi;$

2. $\sum_{X \in (2^{\mathcal{I}} - \emptyset) \setminus \mathcal{K}^s} |sup_{\mathcal{D}}(X) - sup_{\mathcal{D}'}(X)|$ *is minimized.*

The first requirement asks for lowering the support of sensitive itemsets below ψ level. This ensures that no frequent itemset mining algorithm can derive the itemsets in $\mathcal{K}^s$ at minimum support $\sigma = \psi$, hence they are hidden. The second requirement is the minimization objective which calls for solutions destroying supports of nonsensitive itemsets as little as possible. To ease the second requirement, the first requirement can be recast as allowing some hiding failure. This is in fact due to the tradeoff between hiding failure and misses as introduced in Problem 2.

We note that perfect solutions (no hiding failure, no misses and no fakes) are almost impossible but only non-perfect solutions are possible (see Figure 3.2). To this end, we dichotomize solution proposals based on whether they guarantee no hiding failure or not.

3.3.1.1 *No Hiding Failure* Methods

The work by Atallah et al. [9] proved that the frequent itemset hiding problem (their problem is a simpler form of Problem 3) is NP-Hard. Their operation to solve the problem is to remove (suppress) items from transactions. They also proposed heuristics to solve the problem by selectively reducing the support of sensitive itemsets. The algorithm iterates over the set of sensitive frequent itemsets until none of them is frequent. Let's suppose that a k-itemset $X \in \mathcal{K}^s$ is selected to be hidden. A level-wise traversal, starting from X and ending at a singleton included in X, is carried out on the itemset lattice as described next. Over all $k - 1$ subsets of X, the respective supports are reviewed and the subset with the maximum support is chosen as the new point for the traversal. This process is iterated until $k = 1$, at which time a singleton itemset is found. An occurrence of this singleton itemset is suppressed in one of the supporting transactions of X. The criteria for this decision is minimal effect on the number of 2-itemsets of the transaction, which is somewhat equal to distorting remaining large-itemsets that this transaction is providing support to. Since the support of X is reduced one-at-a-time fashion, the whole operation is repeated until X's support reaches below the disclosure threshold. The heuristic hides all sensitive itemsets, i.e., no hiding failure, and also targets minimal distortion of non-sensitive itemset supports. Since the sole operation is suppression, the algorithm does not introduce fake patterns.

A linear time (w.r.t. $|\mathcal{D}|$) sanitization algorithm employing sliding window approach is presented in [36]. The algorithm is intended to hide the knowledge of association rules but it is actually hiding frequent itemsets. For each batch of window size K, the algorithm consists of five steps: (1) identifying sensitive and nonsensitive transactions in the batch, (2) selecting victim item, (3) building the sensitive transaction list for every sensitive itemset and computing the number of sensitive transactions to be sanitized, (4) sorting the sensitive transactions by size, (5) sanitizing the transaction by removing victim item. Two main characteristics of the algorithm are being scalable to large databases and allowing different sensitivity thresholds, i.e., rather than a common threshold, for each sensitive itemset. The algorithm is hiding failure and fake pattern free.

A border-based approach is presented in [45]. The idea is to preserve the shape of positive border (of frequent itemsets) during sanitization as much as possible. The algorithm first computes the minimal set of sensitive itemsets, as sensitive itemsets may have containment relationships, from the user-specified sensitive itemsets and hides each of them one-by-one after ordering based on cardinality (descending) and support (ascending). Next, the elements of positive border intersecting with every single item in the sensitive itemset at hand is determined and a weight factor is computed for each candidate (a pair of a single item and a transaction supporting it). The minimum weight candidate is selected for suppression and the candidate selection is repeated until the sensitive itemset gets support less than the disclosure threshold. The weight measures the degree to which the candidate will distort the nonsensitive frequent itemsets. However, the algorithm is not scalable to large and dense databases, especially when the size of positive border grows large. The algorithm is hiding failure and fake pattern free.

Gkoulalas-Divanis and Verykios [20] present another border-based approach. Their method minimizes a distance metric defined between $\mathcal{D}$ and $\mathcal{D}'$, and also satisfies constraints generated from the given frequent itemset hiding problem specification. These together are combined to obtain an instance of constraint-satisfaction problem which is solved by integer programming techniques after reducing the problem size to manageable limits. An extension of the work is given in [21] where they add artificial transactions (called database extension) to the original database and formulate the knowledge hiding problem as a constraint-satisfaction problem to be solved by integer programming techniques. The database extension can cause fake patterns but may greatly lower misses. In other words, it provides a tradeoff between misses and fakes. Both methods have a nice property that whenever a solution with no misses and no hiding failure is possible, they are guaranteed to find it.

3.3.1.2 *Hiding Failure* Methods

We recognize that *no hiding failure* methods can be stopped earlier in order to prevent further data utility drop by means of intentionally allowing some level of hiding failure. The stopping criteria can be formalized based on a notion of data quality reduction, or alternatively on a notion of tradeoff between sensitivity/utility. However, no method presented in the previous section has explicitly considered this option. In case the data utility is not satisfactory with no hiding failure methods, another option could be to remove some (relatively less) sensitive itemsets from the initial sensitive itemset list and employ a no hiding failure solution method afterwards. These two options in fact define frameworks that utilize no hiding failure solutions to obtain hiding failure solutions.

Lee et al. [28] proposed a sanitization matrix based approach which is not hiding failure free. The sanitization matrix has dimensions $|\mathcal{I}| \times |\mathcal{I}|$ where the entries are restricted to be $\{-1, 0, 1\}$. Before the transformation, the database $\mathcal{D}$ is converted into the matrix representation where the matrix has size $|\mathcal{D}| \times |\mathcal{I}|$, and the entries are either 0 (non-existence of the item in the transaction) or 1 (otherwise). The matrix representation of $\mathcal{D}'$ is then obtained by multiplying the $\mathcal{D}$ matrix with the sanitization matrix. To give 0 or 1 entries, the multiplication results are truncated to zero or one. Clearly, if the sanitization matrix is the identity matrix, then $\mathcal{D}'$ is equal to $\mathcal{D}$. The challenge is to selectively turn some non-diagonal elements of the sanitization matrix into -1 so that support of sensitive itemsets reduce while the support of others are affected as little as possible. Authors present three greedy algorithms to do so. The main heuristic selects the entry (j, k), to be replaced with -1, such that itemset $\{i_j, i_k\}$ exists in some sensitive itemsets but does not exist in any nonsensitive itemsets.

3.3.1.3 Metrics

Following distortion metrics are studied in the context of itemset hiding to assess the quality of the sanitization process.

- Item level support distortion [36]: It is the relative support difference between $\mathcal{D}$ and $\mathcal{D}'$ at item level, i.e., $\frac{\sum_{i_j \in \mathcal{I}} sup_{\mathcal{D}}(i_j) - sup_{\mathcal{D}'}(i_j)}{\sum_{i_j \in \mathcal{I}} sup_{\mathcal{D}}(i_j)}$.

- Frequent pattern distortion [3]: It is the ratio of frequent patterns hidden, i.e.,
$$\frac{|\mathcal{F}_{(\mathcal{D},\sigma)}| - |\mathcal{F}_{(\mathcal{D}',\sigma)}|}{|\mathcal{F}_{(\mathcal{D},\sigma)}|}$$

- Nonsensitive frequent pattern distortion [28]: It is the ratio of number of hidden frequent nonsensitive itemsets to the number of all nonsensitive frequent itemsets, i.e., $\frac{\mathcal{F}_{(\mathcal{D},\sigma)} \setminus \mathcal{F}_{(\mathcal{D}',\sigma)} - \mathcal{K}^s}{\mathcal{F}_{(\mathcal{D},\sigma)} - \mathcal{K}^s}$. In effect, it measures the degree of the misses' cost.

- Frequent pattern support distortion [3]: It is the mean value for relative support differences of all frequent itemsets in $\mathcal{D}'$ w.r.t. $\mathcal{D}$, i.e.,
$$\frac{1}{|\mathcal{F}_{(\mathcal{D}',\sigma)}|} \sum_{S \in \mathcal{F}_{(\mathcal{D}',\sigma)}} \frac{sup_{\mathcal{D}}(S) - sup_{\mathcal{D}'}(S)}{sup_{\mathcal{D}}(S)}$$

Besides the distortion metrics, another line of metrics is proposed to assess the difficulty of the sanitization problem at hand. Difficulty metrics are given below.

- The number of sensitive itemsets, i.e., $|\mathcal{K}^s|$, [45]: Clearly, the larger it is the more difficult the problem is.

- Average support difference (from the threshold) [45]: It measures the mean distance of sensitive itemset supports from the threshold, i.e., $\sum_{X \in \mathcal{K}^s} \frac{sup_{\mathcal{D}}(X) - \sigma}{|\mathcal{K}^s|}$. The larger it is the more difficult the problem is.

- Average length of sensitive itemsets [45]: It is simply the $\sum_{X \in \mathcal{K}^s} \frac{|X|}{|\mathcal{K}^s|}$. Intuitively, the smaller it is the more difficult the problem is.

- Overlap rate [28]: It measures the ratio of common items in sensitive and nonsensitive frequent itemsets. Formally, it is computed as $\frac{|\{X:X \in \mathcal{K}^s\} \cap \{X:X \in KSet_{(\mathcal{D},\Theta)} - \mathcal{K}^s\}|}{|\{X:X \in \mathcal{K}^s\} \cup \{X:X \in KSet_{(\mathcal{D},\Theta)} - \mathcal{K}^s\}|}$. Clearly, the smaller it is, the easier the problem is.

3.4 Association Rule Hiding

Associations are typically expressed with association rules over the itemsets. Association rule mining, formally defined next, is finding all significant association rules derivable from a given dataset.

DEFINITION 3.4 (Association Rule Mining) *Let* $\mathcal{I} = \{i_1, i_2, \ldots, i_n\}$ *be a set of items, and itemsets* X *and* Y *be any non-empty subsets of* $\mathcal{I}$*. An association rule is an implication of the form* $X \Rightarrow Y$ *where* $X \cap Y = \emptyset$*.* X *is called the left-hand side (*lhs*) or antecedent and* Y *is called right-hand side (*rhs*) or consequent. The rule* $X \Rightarrow Y$ *is said to hold in transaction database* $\mathcal{D}$ *with support* s *and confidence* c *if (i)* $sup_{\mathcal{D}}(X \cup Y) \geq s$ *and (ii)* $\frac{sup_{\mathcal{D}}(X \cup Y)}{sup_{\mathcal{D}}(X)} \geq c$*. Given the minimum support threshold* σ *and the minimum confidence threshold* $minconf$*, the association rule mining problem is to find all significant association rules holding in the database with at least* σ *support and* $minconf$ *confidence.*

For any rule $X \Rightarrow Y$, $X \cup Y$ must be frequent. This is the main reason that association rule mining typically employs frequent itemset mining first and then generates rules and computes their confidences next. The second step is much faster to solve compared to the first step [5]. This is why these two problems are usually treated in the same context in the literature. But, we consider these two separately, since the output knowledge formats differ.

3.4.1 Association Rule Hiding

Association rule hiding is a specialization of the generic knowledge hiding problem (Problem 2) as defined next.

Problem 4 (Association Rule Hiding)

Let $\mathcal{K}^s = \{X_1 \Rightarrow Y_1, X_2 \Rightarrow Y_2, \ldots, X_n \Rightarrow Y_n\}$ be the set of sensitive associa-tion rules that must be hidden from $\mathcal{D}$. Given the pair of disclosure threshold parameters (ψ_1, ψ_2), the Association Rule Hiding problem requires to trans-form $\mathcal{D}$ into a database $\mathcal{D}'$ such that:

1. *the support of every rule in $\mathcal{D}$ is less than ψ_1, i.e., $\forall X_i \Rightarrow Y_i \in \mathcal{K}^s$: $sup_{\mathcal{D}'}(X_i \bigcup Y_i) < \psi_1$; or*
   the confidence of every rule is less than ψ_2, i.e., $\forall X_i \Rightarrow Y_i \in \mathcal{K}^s$: $\frac{sup_{\mathcal{D}'}(X_i \bigcup Y_i)}{sup_{\mathcal{D}'}(X_i)} < \psi_2$;

2. *$\sum_{X \in (2^{\mathcal{I}} - \emptyset) \setminus \mathcal{S}} |sup_{\mathcal{D}}(X) - sup_{\mathcal{D}'}(X)|$ is minimized, where $\mathcal{S} = \{X \bigcup Y : X \Rightarrow Y \in \mathcal{K}^s\}$.*

Note that the first of the conditions relates to sensitive knowledge disclosure prevention while the second relates to the utility (data/knowledge quality) reduction minimization.

The canonical approach to association rule hiding is to reduce support and/or confidence of sensitive rules. To this end, one can easily use any method developed for frequent itemset hiding to reduce the support after transform-ing $\mathcal{K}^s = \{X_1 \Rightarrow Y_1, X_2 \Rightarrow Y_2, \ldots, X_n \Rightarrow Y_n\}$ into $\mathcal{K}^s = \{X_1 \bigcup Y_1, X_2 \bigcup Y_2, \ldots, X_n \bigcup Y_n\}$. However, association rule hiding of-fers more flexibility compared to itemset hiding as confidence reduction is the other possibility.

A support/confidence framework is introduced in [17] where the authors present three strategies: (i) increasing the support of rule antecedent, (ii) de-creasing the support of rule consequent, and (iii) decreasing rule support. Clearly, the first two strategies are to reduce the rule confidence while the last one is to reduce the rule support. One of the important limitations of the strategies is the assumption of the disjointness of the sensitive rules, i.e., sensitive rules do not share items. An extension of [17] is presented in [50]. Another support/confidence framework is presented in [41]. The authors intro-duce unknowns (symbol ?) in binary data matrix representation. The notion, replacing some zeros and ones with unknowns, brings ranges for true values of support and confidence of rules. The objective is then to reduce the support and/or confidence of all rules below the disclosure parameters. The authors give three algorithms for sanitization. Since both zeros and ones can be turned to unknowns, the reconstruction of the source database and recovery of hidden patterns are shown to be impossible. Wu et al. [52] introduce a limited side effect rule hiding problem, which we call inverse association rule hiding, where the roles of the objective and the constraint in Problem 2 are reversed. That is, the misses and fakes are avoided altogether at the expense of disclosure of some sensitive rules.

3.4.2 Variations of Association Rule Mining

Several variations of association rule mining have been investigated in the literature. Generalized association rules are studied in [43]. Generalized association rule mining involves a hierarchy (*isa* relationships) of predefined item generalization and finds all high support and high confidence association rules over the generalized itemsets. The work by Srikant and Agrawal [44] extends the standard association rule mining problem to relational tables where both categorical and quantitative attributes present.

There are several other variations of the association rule mining but they can be considered as special cases of constrained association rule mining. Constraints are typically defined through some identified interestingness measure [37, 34]. For instance, strong negative association [40] is a particular kind of constraint. Negative association rules have the same form as regular association rules but the significance measure differs. By definition, negative association rules are those rules where (i) both the antecedent and the consequent are frequent itemsets, and (ii) the interestingness measure, deviation of expected support from the actual support, exceeds a minimum threshold. Causal association rules, another variant, are studied in [42]. Correlation mining is studied in [13] and [29].

Unfortunately, no knowledge hiding problem is explicitly addressed for any of those variations. But respective knowledge hiding problem instances can be obtained following the template similar to the formulation in Problem 4, i.e., first specifying knowledge hiding constraints and then data/knowledge utility maximization criteria.

3.5 Sequential Pattern Hiding

In an itemset the order of items is immaterial, however in many domains (e.g., web clicks and spatio-temporal traces of moving objects) the order is crucial. When the event ordering matters in data space, it typically matters in knowledge space too. Sequential pattern mining aims at finding significant patterns by also taking the event ordering into account.

Let $\mathcal{D}$ be a database of sequences, where each $T \in \mathcal{D}$ is a finite sequence of a set of symbols (itemset) from an alphabet Σ: $T = \langle t_1, \ldots, t_{T_n} \rangle$ where $t_i \subseteq \Sigma, \forall i \in \{1, \ldots, T_n\}$. We denote the set of all sequences as $\{2^\Sigma - \emptyset\}^*$. A sequence $U \in \Sigma^*$ is a subsequence of a sequence $V \in \Sigma^*$, denoted $U \sqsubseteq V$, if U can be obtained by deleting some symbols from V, i.e, $U = \langle u_1, \ldots, u_m \rangle$ is subsequence of $V = \langle v_1, \ldots, v_n \rangle$ if there are m indices $i_1 < \ldots < i_m$ such that $u_1 \subseteq v_{i_1}, \ldots, u_m \subseteq v_{i_m}$. Similar to sequence databases, a *sequential pattern* is defined as a sequences of itemsets.

The support of a sequence S is the number of sequences in $\mathcal{D}$ that are supersequences of S: $sup_{\mathcal{D}}(S) = |\{T \in \mathcal{D} \mid S \sqsubseteq T\}|$. The classical problem of mining frequent sequential patterns [7] requires, given a database $\mathcal{D}$ and a minimum support threshold σ, to compute all patterns that have a support not less than σ: $\mathcal{F}(\mathcal{D}, \sigma) = \{S \in \{2^{\Sigma} - \emptyset\}^* \mid sup_{\mathcal{D}}(S) \geq \sigma\}$.

The sequential pattern hiding problem is defined as follows to protect sensitive patterns from discovery by sequential pattern mining algorithms, e.g., [7].

Problem 5 (Sequential Pattern Hiding) *Let* $\mathcal{K}^s = \{S_1, S_2, \ldots, S_n\}$ *with* $S_i \in \{2^{\Sigma} - \emptyset\}^*, \forall i \in \{1, \ldots, n\}$, *be the set of sensitive sequential patterns that must be hidden from* $\mathcal{D}$. *Given a disclosure threshold* ψ, *the Sequential Pattern Hiding problem requires to transform* $\mathcal{D}$ *into a database* $\mathcal{D}'$ *such that:*

1. $\forall S_i \in \mathcal{K}^s, sup_{\mathcal{D}'}(S_i) < \psi$;

2. $\sum_{S \in \{2^{\Sigma} - \emptyset\}^* \setminus \mathcal{K}^s} |sup_{\mathcal{D}}(S) - sup_{\mathcal{D}'}(S)|$ *is minimized.*

In what follows we overview the two important classes of the sequential pattern hiding problem: one-dimensional (simple) sequences and two-dimensional (spatio-temporal) sequences.

3.5.1 Simple Sequences

A simple sequence is a sequence where each event in the sequence is a singleton, i.e., contains exactly one item. The simple sequence hiding problem is introduced in Abul et al. [3] as defined next, where the problem is also shown to be NP-Hard, and a polynomial sanitization algorithm is developed for effective sanitization.

Problem 6 (Simple Sequence Hiding) *Let* $\mathcal{K}^s = \{S_1, S_2, \ldots, S_n\}$ *with* $S_i \in \Sigma^*, \forall i \in \{1, \ldots, n\}$, *be the set of sensitive simple sequence patterns that must be hidden from* $\mathcal{D}$. *Given a disclosure threshold* ψ, *the Simple Sequence Hiding Problem requires to transform* $\mathcal{D}$ *into a database* $\mathcal{D}'$ *such that:*

1. $\forall S_i \in \mathcal{K}^s, sup_{\mathcal{D}'}(S_i) < \psi$;

2. $\sum_{S \in \Sigma^* \setminus \mathcal{K}^s} |sup_{\mathcal{D}}(S) - sup_{\mathcal{D}'}(S)|$ *is minimized.*

Note from the definition that both the transactions and the sensitive patterns are in the form of simple sequences.

The sanitization is accomplished by replacing some items in the selected transactions by a special symbol Δ not in Σ. As an example, consider $T = \langle a, a, b, e, c, b, a, e \rangle \in \mathcal{D}$ be a simple sequence (transaction) and $S = \langle a, b, c \rangle$ be a sensitive pattern. Since $S \sqsubseteq T$, T supports S and contributes by 1 to $sup_{\mathcal{D}}(S)$. To reduce the support, we can replace the first b in T to give $T' = \langle a, a, \Delta, e, c, b, a, e \rangle \in \mathcal{D}'$ so that T' fails to give support to S. Notice that there are many ways to introduce Δ symbols to reduce the support. In the example, for instance, $T' = \langle \Delta, \Delta, b, e, \Delta, b, a, e \rangle \in \mathcal{D}'$ reduces support too, but apparently it is less effective as it overly distorts data.

For effective sanitization, the polynomial sanitization algorithm exploits two heuristics (i) *local*, and (ii) *global*. Both of the heuristics are based on the notion of matchings; a matching (match) between a sensitive itemset $S = \langle u_1, \ldots, u_m \rangle$ and a transaction $T = \langle v_1, \ldots, v_n \rangle$ is defined as an assignment to $i_1 < \ldots < i_m$ such that $u_1 = v_{i_1}, \ldots, u_m = v_{i_m}$. The local heuristic works as follows. Given a sequence to be sanitized, the algorithm suppresses the event which is involved in the most matches with the sensitive sequences. This way, the number of different matches of the candidate sequence to sensitive sequences are reduced as much as possible in a single suppression operation. The global heuristic exploits the fact that if the total number of matchings is small, the sanitization can be performed with little data distortion. More precisely, the heuristic selects top $(1 - \psi) * |\mathcal{D}|$ transactions to undergo sanitization after sorting all transactions of $\mathcal{D}$ in increasing order of total number of matches. The overall algorithm only suppresses some events in selected sequences and hence does not introduce fake patterns, and it is hiding failure free.

The same work also extends sequence hiding for constraints of *maximum gap*, *minimum gap* and *maximum window*, which are the typical constraints of sequential pattern mining tasks. When the constraints are specified, the sanitization can be achieved with smaller data distortion compared to the no constraints case. In the above example for instance, with maximum window of three, no sanitization is necessary as there is no matching of S that can fit in the maximum window of three within T. This is why handling constraints in knowledge hiding problems are important. The work also discusses an extension to hide general sequences defined according to Problem 5.

3.5.2   Spatio-Temporal Sequences

Abul et al. [2] studied hiding spatio-temporal patterns from moving object databases. Moving object databases contain a bag of spatio-temporal movements where each movement is a sequence of spatio-temporal points.

In the mentioned work, the only hiding operator is *coarsening* which is defined as removing a spatio-temporal point in a given trajectory. The coarsening operator is shown to be safe with respect to fake pattern generation. The problem is formally defined as next, where two points are considered the same provided that they have exactly the same spatial location but their temporal dimensions may differ at most τ time units. Since it is almost impossible to have two points equal in spatial coordinates, the notion of background network (graph) is assumed where spatial points coincide with graph vertices.

Problem 7 (Pattern Hiding by Coarsening) *Given a trajectory T, a set of sensitive trajectory patterns $\mathcal{K}^s = \{P_1, \ldots, P_n\}$ and time tolerance τ. The*

Pattern Hiding by Coarsening problem requires to transform T into another trajectory T' using coarsening operations only, and such that:

1. $\forall P_i \in \mathcal{K}^s . T' \not\sqsupseteq_\tau P_i$;

2. *the number of coarsening operations is minimized.*

where $T \sqsupseteq_\tau P$, meaning that T supports P (with time tolerance τ), is spatio-temporal support relation. Note that, for simplicity the definition is restricted only to involve sanitization of a single trajectory. Clearly, in practice it is always generalized to a database of trajectories after introducing a minimum support as it is done with simple sequences.

In the same study, the Spatio-Temporal pattern hiding problem is shown to be NP-Hard, and a sanitization algorithm, which exploits similar heuristics as the ones explained in Section 3.5.1, is developed. The attack model is shown to be very different from simple sequences as an adversary knowing the map of the location can reconstruct the hidden points due to lack of alternatives. This is noted in the same work and a k-secure path constraint is further enforced. The constraint ensures for each removed point that there are at least k alternative paths between the flanking left-out points so that the removed points can not be reconstructed. Increasing values of k provides better security but results in more data distortion.

3.6 Classification Rule Hiding

A classification rule is an implication from a feature (attribute-value) space to a value in the domain of the class attribute. Classification rules typically follow the schema of relational tables, and are constructed from the table by employment of a rule mining algorithm such as C4.5 [38]. Given a relational table, rule learning algorithms output a set of rules that hold in the table. In the literature various forms of classification rules are studied [31]; in what follows we focus our attention on conjunctive rules with categorical attributes.

DEFINITION 3.5 (Classification Rule Mining) *Consider a relational table (database) $\mathcal{D}$ with the schema $\mathcal{D}(A_1, A_2, \ldots, A_m, C)$ where $A_i s$ are predictive attributes for the class attribute C. A classification rule R is of the form $\wedge (A_i, a_i)^k \Rightarrow C$, where each $A_i \in \{A_1, A_2, \ldots, A_m\}$ and a_i is a value from the domain of A_i, and $1 \leq k \leq m$. The rule R is said to hold in the database $\mathcal{D}$ with confidence c if its classification accuracy is c or above. The classification rule mining problem is then to find classification rules (and their respective confidences) having a high (i.e., at least c) accuracy.*

Considering that some of the rules are sensitive, the source database must be sanitized before sharing so that the rules can not be derived. The classification rule hiding problem tackles the issue.

Problem 8 (Classification Rule Hiding) *Let $\mathcal{K}^s = \{R_1, R_2, \ldots, R_n\}$ be the set of sensitive classification rules that must be hidden from $\mathcal{D}$. Given the confidence threshold c, the Classification Rule Hiding problem requires to transform $\mathcal{D}$ into a database $\mathcal{D}'$ such that:*

1. *the confidence of every rule in $\mathcal{K}^s$ is less than c,*

2. *the confidence of nonsensitive rules are changed as little as possible.*

The canonical solution to Problem 8 requires to modify the database such that no classification model covering the sensitive rules at the specified confidence can be built.

Compared to the frequent itemset and association rule hiding, there is limited work for the classification rule hiding problem in the literature. Johnsten and Raghavan [26] present a classification rule hiding methodology for a specific kind of classification algorithm so-called decision-region based. Their sanitization operator is suppression, updating selected table entries with NULL values. Only the predictive attributes of unprotected objects are suppressed. Protected objects are those that are supposed to contain NULL values for the class attribute in the released database. Security policies are formulated around the class-accuracy set concept. Each member of the class-accuracy set is a pair of class-confidence values defined separately for each and every protected object. There are four security policies defined over the class-accuracy set, namely *maximum threshold*, *maximum range*, *protected threshold*, and *protected rank*. For maximum threshold policy, for instance, the set is said to be satisfied if the maximum accuracy is less than a user defined threshold. When the set is unsatisfied, some predictive attributes of unprotected objects are suppressed until the satisfaction is ensured.

A reconstruction-based approach is taken in Natwichai et al. [33]. Instead of suppressing some values, first of all a set of valid classification rules is generated from the database and presented to the data publisher for a sensitivity check. A decision tree is constructed from the nonsensitive rules and a database conforming to the tree is reconstructed for publishing. The reconstructed database clearly holds the nonsensitive rules but the not sensitive ones, hence it can be safely published. The key challenge in the approach is how to construct the decision tree. To this end, authors present an information-gain driven heuristic to guide the construction.

A template-based privacy preservation is presented in [51], where the problem formulation is different from Problem 8 in a few respects. First, the schema of the database is $\mathcal{D}(M_1, M_2, \ldots, M_m, \Pi_1, \Pi_2, \ldots, \Pi_p, C)$, where M_is are nonsensitive (masking) attributes and Π_js are sensitive attributes, and C is the usual class attribute. Second, the form of sensitive knowledge is defined through inference templates. An inference template is of the form $< IC \rightarrow \pi, h >$, where inference channel IC contains some attributes from masking attributes and π is a value vector from Π_js and h is the confidence threshold. Given a set of templates, selected values from masking attributes are generalized until the template is satisfied, i.e., the true confidence of the template falls below h. Authors show that the generalization is monotonic, i.e., every generalization comes closer to the satisfaction. The key challenge is how to select attributes and values for generalization. To this end, an information gain directed heuristic is provided as well. Authors' formulation is mostly concerned with the individual privacy rather than the rule privacy.

3.7 Other Knowledge-Hiding Domains

Data mining is such a hot and lively research area that new data mining problems and their variants are emerging constantly from diverse application domains. Although numerous data mining problems and variants are already established for many domains, the respective knowledge hiding problems are either not addressed at all or only recently introduced but not studied in depth. Cluster mining, outlier mining, text mining, link mining and XML mining are among the best examples. In this section, we briefly cover not all but some important data mining domains and highlight the respective knowledge hiding problems.

3.7.1 Cluster Hiding

Clustering is the process of grouping similar objects together. The task usually involves partitioning the data objects in a number of groups or segments, called clusters. Clustering is an old field of data mining and extensively studied in the literature [25]. One of the main uses of clustering is to summarize (or abstract) the data objects and hence reduce the database size. Depending on the nature of the database and the clustering algorithm applied, there are several ways of representing clusters, including dendrograms, means and counts, sample points, spatial areas, and probability distributions. Clearly, some clusters may be sensitive (e.g., the cluster of loyal customers) while some others are not. Note that, the sensitivity here is not related to the privacy of individuals but the privacy of the group knowledge they form.

Unfortunately, cluster hiding has not been studied in the literature yet. However, once the structure of the sensitive clusters has been identified, the concrete knowledge hiding problem can be defined following the generic approach presented in Problem 1. For example, taking the methodology in [26], the database can be clustered and presented to the data publisher for sensitivity tagging of clusters. In the second round, the underlying objects can be modified to distort the sensitive clusters.

3.7.2   Outlier Hiding

In many domains and datasets, there are usually a few items (either data or knowledge) that are radically different from the rest. These rare and exceptional items are referred to outliers (a.k.a. anomalies). There are basically two uses of outliers in the data mining process (i) outlier removal (ii) outlier mining [22]. The former is usually addressed when the outliers are treated as noise, e.g., erroneous data entry, and data mining algorithms are sensitive to the noise, whereas in the latter, the detection of outliers is of particular interest to obtain precious knowledge, e.g., abnormal city traffic. In case some of the outliers are deemed sensitive and can be surfaced by outlier mining algorithms, such outliers must be hidden before the data release.

By definition outlier patterns/rules have limited coverage in the dataset. This suggests that the respective sanitization can be done relatively easily with very limited side effects. Unfortunately, outlier hiding has not been studied in the literature.

3.7.3   Text Hiding

Text mining refers to the activity of deriving knowledge from unstructured (text) data [24]. Due to unstructured data, the pre-processing part (from free text to term vector) of text mining is extensive, requiring techniques from information retrieval, natural language processing and information extraction. Once a term vector is obtained, each document can be treated as a structured data object where attributes are the (weighted) terms. Over this representation, text classification, clustering and association mining tasks can be formulated depending on the analysis purpose. So, a piece of knowledge (including the sensitive ones) can be reduced to either classification rules, clusters or associations. Sanitization can be achieved by suppressing identified terms from some documents or simply by suppressing a subset of the document set. However, care must be taken, as the original data can be pre-processed in various ways to surface the sensitive knowledge from the supposedly sanitized database.

To the best of our knowledge, no knowledge hiding work has been done in the text mining context. We believe that text data will be one of the challenging domains for knowledge hiding in the near future. On the other hand, data-level sanitization has been addressed to hide sensitive data from text documents. One of the first works in this line is the *Scrub* system [46]. The Scrub system is designed to remove personally-identifying information in medical records of free text. For instance it can detect (possibly sensitive) patient names, phone numbers, addresses, diagnoses and any other personal information in physician notes. After detecting such words, it scrubs them before sharing the records. Unfortunately, simple detection techniques are not adequate for de-identification as there are so called quasi-identifiers like the one in the context "He developed Hodgkins while acting as the U.S. Ambassador to England ..." [46]. Hence, this kind of personally-identifying information should also be detected using a reasoning mechanism. The work by Velupillai et al. [48] presents recent standards and software, and an application for the de-identification task from medical records.

In many domains, full de-identification (removing every personally-identifying information) is too strict, as anonymization in a group may suffice. In principle, given a free text, anonymization can be done manually by a domain expert. Clearly, this approach is too costly, hence full or semi automatic anonymization methods are demanded. Medlock [30] proposes an NLP-based textual anonymization method where features are identified using a syntax tree, and presented to a human annotator for sensitivity classification. Anonymization is then carried out by replacing sensitive features with more general categories, e.g., a particular noun phrase with "NP."

Chakaravarthy et al. [15] present a document sanitization approach which models a (free text) document as a term vector. In their model, the document refers to a set of entities. The sensitive knowledge is to prevent the adversaries from learning which entities the document refers to. Separate from the document, there is a list of protected entities for which an adversary is assumed to know the term vectors but not whether the document refers to a particular entity. The document sanitization task is then to make a given term vector (of a protected entity) anonymous w.r.t. the published document. To formalize the notion, authors define K-safety privacy protection, requiring there to be at least $K-1$ other individuals (in the released document) matching the term vector of every protected entity. Their technique requires to delete some terms in the document to meet the K-safety. Note that, the notion of K-safety is very similar to k-anonymity privacy protection [47] (no individual is identifiable within less than k individuals) studied in relational databases.

3.7.4 Link Hiding

In the classical data mining, objects are treated as independent entities and only their attributes are included in the mining process, leaving the possible relations among them ignored. However, many datasets collected today, e.g., social networks and scientific data, also contain different kinds of inter-object relationships. Link mining is the study of objects, their attributes and relationships in the mining process [19]. Thus it also includes web mining and hypertext mining as special cases.

The natural data representation for link mining is the graph where nodes correspond to objects with attributes and edges to inter-object relations. Both objects and relations can be heterogeneous, for instance authors and articles as objects, and co-authorship and same-venues as relations. Getoor and Diehl [19] present common link mining tasks as follows.

- Object ranking: The objective is to order the objects, e.g., ranking pages in a keyword-based web search, based on some criteria.

- Object classification: This is the usual classification task enriched with the inter-object relation information.

- Object clustering: This is the usual clustering task enriched with the inter-object relation information.

- Object identification: Object identification is the task of finding different references to the same object.

- Link prediction: Link prediction is predicting the existence of relations, e.g., friendship, between objects.

- Subgraph discovery: Given a set of graphs, subgraph discovery is finding subgraphs that occur in a significant number of the graphs. The task is sometimes called frequent subgraph pattern mining and there are several algorithms proposed for the task, e.g., Span [53].

- Graph classification: Graph classification is the classification task used where the objects are graphs.

The privacy problem has been addressed for graph data especially for the social networking databases, but they are mostly concerned with individual privacy and anonymity [32] rather than the pattern/rule privacy. Backstrom et al. [10] studied social network anonymization, where each node in the graph corresponds to an individual, and edges between nodes correspond to inter-action. Their attack model is understanding whether there is an interaction between targeted pairs of nodes from anonymized (in the sense pseudo names are assigned to nodes, and made intact otherwise) social networking graph data. Hence, an attacker must locate the targeted pairs within the anonymized network and simply check the existence of edges. It has been shown that, with relatively small effort, adversaries can succeed whatever the topology and the size of the released network data.

To the best of our knowledge, no knowledge hiding work has been done in the link mining context. Due to the complexity of data, the knowledge hiding problem here is probably much more complex and challenging than for the transactional databases.

3.7.5   XML Hiding

XML is a language used to define tree-structured documents containing data and meta-meta (tags defining the meaning of data) together. Most structured and semi-structured data can be formatted as XML documents to be shared for numerous applications, including database publishing, business-to-business transactions, remote procedure calls and so on. XML mining is the study of mining XML formatted documents to generate knowledge. XML mining is a broad area, since most databases can be modeled as XML documents and various mining models (e.g., association rules, clustering and classification) can be adapted to deal with XML data.

Johnsten et al. [27] presented a methodology for knowledge hiding from XML documents. Their methodology has five steps: (1) identify sensitive knowledge, (2) identify target data mining model, (3) formulate security policies, (4) apply a sanitization algorithm, and (5) generate a report for the process. In particular, they study the association rule hiding from an XML document, which is essentially a set of transactions encoded as XML, and formulate security policies using Bacchus' probability logic. Their sanitization approach is to remove tagged items until the security policies are satisfied.

3.8 Meta-Knowledge Hiding

The implicit assumption in the knowledge hiding scenario is that the form of sensitive knowledge exactly matches the form of knowledge that appears in the mining results. However, this is not true in all real-world problems, because sensitive knowledge can be defined in meta-knowledge level. Meta-knowledge hiding was recently introduced in Abul [1]. In that work, a concrete meta-knowledge hiding problem, so called co-occurring sensitive frequent itemsets, is studied.

Co-occurring frequent (*co-frequent* for short) itemsets is a group of itemsets that appear all together in the mining results. In other words, the itemset group is sensitive if every itemset within it appears in the mining results, and nonsensitive if any of the itemset is missed. This kind of sensitivity definition can be found in many domains. Consider the example from the shopping domain: where there are two deals (itemsets): D1={*popcorn, peanut*} and D2={*bread, butter*}. Here the sensitive knowledge is that both deals have received customer interest. So, to hide this meta-knowledge, suppressing either of D1 or D2 suffices but hiding both is superfluous. The co-frequent itemsets and the respective hiding problem are formally defined next.

DEFINITION 3.6 (Co-Frequent Itemsets) *Let C be any non-empty subset of $F_{(\mathcal{D}, \sigma)}$, i.e., $C \in 2^{F_{(\mathcal{D}, \sigma)}} - \emptyset$, then the set of itemsets in C are called co-frequent itemsets. In other words, any non-empty subset of frequent itemsets is a co-frequent itemset.*

In a special case, when $C = \{X_1, X_2\}$ (i.e., $|C| = 2$), then X_1 and X_2 are called pairs of co-frequent itemsets. The definition can be easily extended to triples, quadruples and so on. Additionally, the definition also applies in the trivial case of $C = \{X_1\}$, i.e., $|C| = 1$. Note that unlike associations which require itemsets to appear in the same set of transactions, co-frequent itemsets allow itemsets to occur in different sets of transactions as long as they are all frequent.

Problem 9 (Co-Frequent Itemset Hiding) *Let $\mathcal{K}^s = \{C_1, C_2, \ldots, C_n\}$ be the set of sensitive co-frequent itemset sets that must be hidden from $F_{(\mathcal{D}, \sigma)}$. Co-Frequent Itemset Hiding Problems require to transform $\mathcal{D}$ into a database $\mathcal{D}'$ such that:*

1. $\forall C_i \in \mathcal{K}^s : C_i \nsubseteq F_{(\mathcal{D}', \sigma)}$;

2. $\sum_{X \in (2^{\mathcal{I}} - \emptyset)} |sup_{\mathcal{D}}(X) - sup_{\mathcal{D}'}(X)|$ is minimized.

The same work shows NP-Hardness of the problem and its connection, namely one-to-many reduction, to the standard frequent itemset hiding problem. A solution framework implementing the reduction, with a hitting set based heuristics, has been given too.

3.9 Conclusion

Knowledge hiding has roots from data and information hiding where sensitive individual data and related aggregations are protected in open databases against querying tools. Data and information hiding have been a great challenge for inferences from statistical databases since the '70s, at which time data mining was in its infancy. Before data mining was mature, there was limited risk of disclosing sensitive knowledge through data publishing. However, with the sophisticated and wide range of data mining tools available today, data mining has become a real threat to sensitive knowledge protection. Nowadays limiting the disclosure of sensitive knowledge is an essential requirement in provision of data publishing. So, protecting sensitive knowledge is not just an option for many situations, but a must.

To date sensitive knowledge hiding is extensively studied in the context of frequent itemsets and association rules from transactional databases. But it is only recently that some other knowledge formats and databases have gotten (limited) interest. Yet, the problem has not been addressed at all for many emerging and/or established domains of data mining. Recognizing that sensitive knowledge can be found everywhere in many contexts of data publishing, this work is aimed at drawing attentions to the problem, especially in emerging domains of data mining. We conjecture that emerging knowledge hiding domains of classification rule hiding, cluster hiding, outlier hiding, text hiding, link hiding, specially formatted databases (like XML) and meta-knowledge hiding will receive more interest from the research community in the near future.

References

[1] O. Abul. Hiding co-occurring frequent itemsets. In *2nd International Workshop on Privacy and Anonymity in the Information Society (PAIS'09), in conjunction with ICDT/EDBT'09*, 2009.

[2] O. Abul, M. Atzori, F. Bonchi, and F. Giannotti. Hiding sensitive trajectory patterns. In *6th International Workshop on Privacy Aspects of Data Mining (PADM'07), in conjunction with ICDM'07*, 2007.

[3] O. Abul, M. Atzori, F. Bonchi, and F. Giannotti. Hiding sequences. In *Third ICDE International Workshop on Privacy Data Management (PDM'07), in conjunction with ICDE'07*, 2007.

[4] R. C. Agarwal, C. C. Aggarwal, and V. V. Prasad. A tree projection algorithm for generation of frequent itemsets. *Journal of Parallel and Distributed Computing*, 61:350–371, 2000.

[5] R. Agrawal, T. Imielinski, and A. Swami. Mining association rules between sets of items in large databases. In *Proceedings of the 1993 ACM SIGMOD International Conference on Management of Data (SIGMOD'93)*, pages 207–216, 1993.

[6] R. Agrawal and R. Srikant. Fast algorithms for mining association rules in large databases. In *Proceedings of the 20th International Conference on Very Large Databases (VLDB'94)*, pages 487–499, 1994.

[7] R. Agrawal and R. Srikant. Mining sequential patterns. In *Eleventh International Conference on Data Engineering (ICDE'95)*, pages 3–14, Taipei, Taiwan, 1995.

[8] R. Agrawal and R. Srikant. Privacy-preserving data mining. In *Proceedings of the 2000 ACM SIGMOD International Conference on Management of Data (SIGMOD'00)*, pages 439–450, 2000.

[9] M. Atallah, E. Bertino, A. K. Elmagarmid, M. Ibrahim, and V. S. Verykios. Disclosure limitation of sensitive rules. In *Proceedings of the 1999 IEEE Knowledge and Data Engineering Exchange Workshop (KDEX'99)*, pages 45–52, 1999.

[10] L. Backstrom, C. Dwork, and J. Kleinberg. Wherefore art thou r3579x?: anonymized social networks, hidden patterns, and structural steganography. In *Proceedings of the 16th International Conference on World Wide Web (WWW'07)*, pages 181–190, 2007.

[11] F. Bonchi and C. Lucchese. Extending the state-of-the-art of constraint-based pattern discovery. *Data and Knowledge Engineering (DKE)*, 60(2):377–399, 2007.

[12] F. Bonchi, Y. Saygin, V. S. Verykios, M. Atzori, A. Gkoulalas-Divanis, S. V. Kaya, and E. Savas. Privacy in spatiotemporal data mining. In Fosca Giannotti and Dino Pedreschi, editors, *Mobility, Data Mining and Privacy*, pages 297–333. Springer, 2008.

[13] S. Brin, R. Motwani, and C. Silverstein. Beyond market basket: Generalizing association rules to correlations. In *Proceedings of the 1997 ACM SIGMOD International Conference on Management of Data (SIGMOD'97)*, 1997.

[14] D. Burdick, M. Calimlim, and J. Gehrke. MAFIA: A maximal frequent itemset algorithm for transactional databases. In *Proceedings of the 17th IEEE International Conference on Data Engineering (ICDE'01)*, pages 443–452, 2001.

[15] V. T. Chakaravarthy, H. Gupta, P. Roy, and M. K. Mohania. Efficient techniques for document sanitization. In *Proceeding of the 17th ACM Conference on Information and Knowledge Management (CIKM'08)*, pages 843–852, 2008.

[16] C. Clifton and D. Marks. Security and privacy implications of data mining. In *Proceedings of the 1996 ACM SIGMOD International Conference on Management of Data (SIGMOD'96)*, pages 15–19, February 1996.

[17] E. Dasseni, V. S. Verykios, A. K. Elmagarmid, and E. Bertino. Hiding association rules by using confidence and support. In *Proceedings of the 4th International Workshop on Information Hiding*, pages 369–383, 2001.

[18] C. Farkas and S. Jajodia. The inference problem: A survey. *ACM SIGKDD Exploration Newsletter*, 4(2):6–11, 2002.

[19] L. Getoor and C. P. Diehl. Link mining: A survey. *SIGKDD Explor. Newsl.*, 7(2):3–12, 2005.

[20] A. Gkoulalas-Divanis and V. S. Verykios. An integer programming approach for frequent itemset hiding. In *Proceedings of the 2006 ACM Conference on Information and Knowledge Management (CIKM'06)*, 2006.

[21] A. Gkoulalas-Divanis and V. S. Verykios. Exact knowledge hiding through database extension. *IEEE Transactions on Knowledge and Data Engineering*, 21(5):699–713, 2009.

[22] J. Han and M. Kamber. *Data Mining: Concepts and Techniques.* Morgan Kaufmann, 2005.

[23] J. Han, J. Pei, Y. Yin, and R. Mao. Mining frequent patterns without candidate generation: A frequent-pattern tree approach. *Data Mining and Knowledge Discovery*, 8(1):53–87, 2004.

[24] A. Hotho, A. Nurnberger, and G. Paa. A brief survey of text mining. *LDV Forum - GLDV Journal for Computational Linguistics and Language Technology*, 20(1):19–62, 2005.

[25] A. K. Jain, M. N. Murty, and P. J. Flynn. Data clustering: a review. *ACM Comput. Surv.*, 31(3):264–323, 1999.

[26] T. Johnsten and V. V. Raghavan. A methodology for hiding knowledge in databases. In *Proceedings of the 2002 IEEE International Conference on Privacy, Security and Data Mining (CRPITS'02)*, pages 9–17, 2002.

[27] T. Johnsten, R. B. Sweeney, and V. V. Raghavan. A methodology for hiding knowledge in XML document collections. In *27th Annual International Computer Software and Applications Conference (COMPSAC'03)*, 2003.

[28] G. Lee, C.-Y. Chang, and A. L. P. Chen. Hiding sensitive patterns in association rules mining. In *28th Annual International Computer Software and Applications Conference (COMPSAC'04)*, pages 424–429, 2004.

[29] Y. K. Lee, W. Y. Kim, Y. D. Cai, and J. Han. Comine: Efficient mining of correlated patterns. In *Proceedings of the Third IEEE International Conference on Data Mining (ICDM'03)*, pages 581–584, 2003.

[30] B. Medlock. An introduction to NLP-based textual anonymisation. In *The International Conference on Language Resources and Evaluation (LREC'06)*, 2006.

[31] T. M. Mitchell. *Machine Learning.* McGraw-Hill Higher Education, 1997.

[32] A. Narayanan and V. Shmatikov. De-anonymizing social networks. *IEEE Security & Privacy*, (in press), 2009.

[33] J. Natwichai, X. Li, and M. Orlowska. A reconstruction-based algorithm for classification rules hiding. In *Proceedings of the 17th Australasian Database Conference (ADC'06)*, pages 49–58, 2006.

[34] R. T. Ng, L. V. S. Lakshmanan, A. Pang, and J. Han. Exploratory mining and pruning optimizations of constrained associations rules. *SIGMOD Rec.*, 27(2):13–24, 1998.

[35] D. E. O'Leary. Knowledge discovery as a threat to database security. In Gregory Piatetsky-Shapiro and William J. Frawley, editors, *Knowledge Discovery in Databases*, pages 507–516. AAAI/MIT Press, 1991.

[36] S. R. M. Oliveira and O. R. Zaïane. Protecting sensitive knowledge by data sanitization. In *Proceedings of the Third IEEE International Conference on Data Mining (ICDM'03)*, pages 211–218, 2003.

[37] E. Omiecinski. Alternative interest measures for mining associations. *IEEE TKDE*, 15(1):57–69, 2003.

[38] J. Ross Quinlan. *C4.5: Programs for Machine Learning*. Morgan Kaufmann, 1993.

[39] A. Savasere, E. Omiecinski, and S. Navathe. An efficient algorithm for mining association rules in large databases. In *Proceedings of 21st International Conference on Very Large Data Bases (VLDB'95)*, pages 432–444, 1995.

[40] A. Savasere, E. Omiecinski, and S. B. Navathe. Mining for strong negative associations in a large database of customer transactions. In *Proceedings of the 14th IEEE International Conference on Data Engineering (ICDE'98)*, 1998.

[41] Y. Saygin, V. S. Verykios, and C. Clifton. Using unknowns to prevent discovery of association rules. *ACM SIGMOD Record*, 30(4):45–54, 2001.

[42] C. Silverstein, S. Brin, R. Motwani, and J. Ullman. Scalable techniques for mining causal structures. In *Data Mining and Knowledge Discovery*, pages 594–605, 1998.

[43] R. Srikant and R. Agrawal. Mining generalized association rules. In *Proceedings of the 21st International Conference on Very Large Databases (VLDB'95)*, 1995.

[44] R. Srikant and R. Agrawal. Mining quantitative association rules in large relational tables. In *Proceedings of the 1996 ACM SIGMOD International Conference on Management of Data (SIGMOD'96)*, 1996.

[45] X. Sun and P. S. Yu. A border-based approach for hiding sensitive frequent itemsets. In *Proceedings of the Fifth IEEE International Conference on Data Mining (ICDM'05)*, pages 426–433, 2005.

[46] L. Sweeney. Replacing personally-identifying information in medical records, the scrub system. In *AMIA*, pages 333–337, 1996.

[47] L. Sweeney. k-anonymity: a model for protecting privacy. *International Journal on Uncertainty Fuzziness and Knowledge-Based Systems*, 10(5), 2002.

[48] S. Velupillai, H. Dalianis, M. Hassel, and G. H. Nilsson. Developing a standard for de-identifying electronic patient records written in swedish:

Precision, recall and f-measure in a manual and computerized annotation trial. *International Journal of Medical Informatics*, in press, May 2009.

[49] V. S. Verykios, E. Bertino, I. N. Fovino, L. P. Provenza, Y. Saygin, and Y. Theodoridis. State-of-the-art in privacy preserving data mining. *ACM SIGMOD Record*, 33(1):50–57, 2004.

[50] V. S. Verykios, A. K. Elmagarmid, E. Bertino, Y. Saygin, and E. Dasseni. Association rule hiding. *IEEE TKDE*, 16(4):434–447, 2004.

[51] K. Wang, B. C. M. Fung, and P. S. Yu. Template-based privacy preservation in classification problems. In *Proceedings of the Fifth IEEE International Conference on Data Mining (ICDM'05)*, pages 466–473, 2005.

[52] Y-H. Wu, C-M. Chiang, and A. L. P. Chen. Hiding sensitive association rules with limited side effects. *IEEE TKDE*, 19(1):29–42, 2007.

[53] X. Yan and J. Han. gSpan: Graph-based substructure pattern mining. In *Proceedings of the Second IEEE International Conference on Data Mining (ICDM'02)*, pages 721–724, 2002.

Chapter 4

Condensation-Based Methods in Emerging Application Domains

Yucel Saygin

Faculty of Engineering and Natural Sciences, Sabanci University, Istanbul, Turkey

Mehmet Ercan Nergiz

Faculty of Engineering and Natural Sciences, Sabanci University, Istanbul, Turkey

4.1   Introduction

Sequence data can be defined as ordered data units which may be extended with other dimensions such as space and time for specific applications. Many forms of new and emerging data types are actually in the form of sequences. For example, DNA or protein sequences from bio-informatics, click streams from the Web, and spatio-temporal trajectories of moving objects from GPS or GSM applications are few of such popular data types. Masses of collected sequence data, naturally attracted data mining researchers to develop algorithms for extracting patterns or descriptive models from sequences. In fact, one of the early data mining papers considers customer purchase sequences as the target data source [4] to discover frequently appearing sequences of customer purchases. Another seminal data mining paper is on mining frequent episodes from event sequences which proposed methods for discovering event sequences in the form of sequential or concurrent events. [17].

The sequence data type is versatile enough to provide data models for many applications. For example DNA is a sequence of amino acids, and time series is an ordered sequence of temporally annotated values. When we include location as well as time information, then we obtain spatio-temporal traces of moving objects in the form of trajectories. Knowledge hidden in masses of raw sequence data could be harvested with data mining technology obtaining frequently occurring subsequences, or patterns within sequence data, clusters of sequences, or predictive models. For example, in the case of trajectory data which is a sequence of time-stamped locations of an individual or an object in general, we may find the frequently followed paths, in the form of subsequences, or we can obtain places periodically visited by the same person. These frequent subsequences show the movement habits of individuals. Using sequence clustering techniques, we can obtain the collective movement behavior of people at different periods of time. Such descriptive models could be used for traffic management and city planning. With classification algorithms, we can learn the activities of people with respect to their movement behavior, movement speeds, etc. In the light of these applications, one can easily see that sequence data contains valuable information to be harvested with data mining technology.

Besides being an invaluable source of information, sequence data about individuals are also extremely sensitive from a privacy perspective. DNA data contain a lot of information about how prone we are to certain types of disease, which we may not want to share with health insurance companies. A typical example is the Huntington's disease which is a neurological degenerative disease that affects people after their 30's and shows itself by degeneration in cognition and movement. There are genetic predictive tests for persons who have an affected parent or relative. The test can predict in almost all cases whether the subjects will develop the disease at some stage in their life. Our trajectories also contain very sensitive information since they show the places we visit, our habits and so on. An interesting work by Malin and Sweeney shows that location data and genomic data may in fact be used together to identify genetic information of individuals [16]. Their re-identification method is based on the fact that people visit multiple hospitals in sequence, which collect both sensitive data such as our DNA, and non-sensitive data which can be linked with further analysis.

Privacy issues need to be considered when performing data mining tasks on sensitive data which includes sequence data as well. From a general perspective, privacy may be compromised when the released data contain private information. Privacy may also be compromised even when only the data mining models are released [10]. For example, there may be patterns which could be linked to individuals. This issue has been investigated in the context of association rules in [26, 6] where rules with very high confidence could be used to infer sensitive values. Therefore, privacy can be handled at the data preprocessing level or model construction level depending on how the data mining is going to be performed and by whom.

When the datasets are going to be released, proper de-identification techniques need to be applied to prevent the private data to be linked with personal identifiers [24, 25]. One effective way of de-identification is anonymization in which data values (e.g., nation: USA, age: 12) are replaced with more general values (e.g., nation: America, age: [10-20]) to create a certain degree of indistinguishability between sets of tuples. Research on this area proposed several privacy metrics to address various types of applications. Among these metrics, k-anonymity [24, 25] ensures each individual in the dataset is indistinguishable with at least $k-1$ other individuals, however does not fully protect against the identification of sensitive attributes. ℓ-Diversity [14], t-closeness [13], (α,k)-anonymity [29], and discernibility [22] enforce diversity in the sensitive attributes of indistinguishable groups thus bound the probability that an individual in the dataset possesses a sensitive attribute. Another metric, δ-presence [19], protects the existence or non-existence of individuals in a released dataset when the information on the presence of individuals is considered sensitive (e.g., releasing a diabetes dataset).

Although the early anonymization algorithms did not consider data mining as the main utility of the released data, later on this has changed and data mining aware anonymization techniques have been developed [31, 7, 12]. A recently proposed method for privacy preserving data mining is based on condensation of the data which was partially inspired by the notion of k-anonymity. The main idea of condensation is to release the "condensed drops rather than the vapor itself" [2]. In database terms, condensation-based approach partitions the multidimensional data into groups with well-defined statistical properties which are essential for data mining. This ensures privacy at the data preprocessing step of knowledge discovery process. For example, suppose a dataset contains a vector of values `<10,11,13,20>`. An anonymization would make these values indistinguishable by replacing them with their generalizations; `<[10-20],[10-20],[10-20],[10-20]>` where `a-b` denotes the range of values from `a` to `b`. Note that such a process destroys the statistics (e.g., mean, variance, $\cdots$) in the original data. A condensation-based approach would return four values drawn from a random variable X with domain 10-20. We pick the distribution of X such that we preserve enough statistics from the data. An example distribution might be a normal with mean and variance of the original values. Such a condensation of the vector might look like `<11,12,13,17>`.

In this chapter, we will first define the general notion of sequences which can be extended with other dimensions such as time and space for different applications. Then we will briefly discuss the state of the art data mining algorithms on sequence data; after that we will look at the privacy issues arising from the emerging applications. We will then discuss how the currently proposed condensation-based methods for privacy preserving data mining apply for sequence data, and provide future directions for research.

4.2   Sequence Data Types

In this section, we are going to formalize the sequence data and provide an overview of possible sequence data types together with some motivating applications. Our focus will be two types of sequences. The first one is the ordered data units without time-stamp information. This can be considered as a more general form of sequence. Amino Acid sequences which are the basic building blocks of proteins, performing most of the functions within our body, are an example of these types of sequences. The second type of sequence data we are going to consider is time-stamped locations, also called spatio-temporal data, which is becoming more and more popular with emerging applications such as location based services though GPS equipped devices. GSM network also provides location information with triangulation and signal strength based techniques precise enough for location-based services which means that location-based services will be even cheaper and more popular in near future. Location measurements in the form of movement traces of moving objects collected over a period of time can further be preprocessed to obtain trajectories of people, which is another emerging data type.

One of the initial sequence mining work aims to find frequent sequences of customer purchases where the database consists of a set of records of the form: (CID, date, time, SetOfItems) where CID is the customer identifier, date and time are the date and time of the purchase of a set of items. The sequences of sets of items purchased by the same customer identified are by the CID and ordered by date and time for a sequence for a CID. The whole database of purchase records can be transformed into a set of sequences this way. The problem now, is to find frequently occurring sequential patterns with respect to a threshold value. A sequential pattern is of the form: $(is_1, is_2, is_3, ..., is_k)$ where each of is_i is a set of items. A DNA sequence, on the other hand, is represented as: $L_1, L_2, L_3....L_k$ where each of L_i is from the set of letters A, C, G, T.

A trajectory is a sequence of locations visited by an individual or a moving object together with the times of visit. The actual movement behavior is continuous. However, the trajectories collected and stored are a spatio-temporal approximation of the actual movement behavior. We define a trajectory database in an object-oriented way as in [20]. A trajectory dataset T is a set of private entities or trajectories (e.g., $T = \{tr_1, \cdots, tr_n\}$, $|T| = n$). Each private entity tr_i is an ordered set of spatio-temporal 3D volumes (e.g., points) composed of time (e.g., t) and location (x and y) dimensions (e.g., $tr_i = \{p_1, \cdots, p_{m_i}\}$ where $p_k = < t_k, x_k, y_k >$, $|tr_i| = m_i$). We assume that the t_i, x_i and y_i components are ranges of values defined as $t_i : [t_i^1 - t_i^2]$, $x_i : [x_i^1 - x_i^2]$ and $y_i : [y_i^1 - y_i^2]$ where $[a - b]$ denotes all numbers q such that $a \leq q \leq b$. Each tr_i is ordered by their subtime component t_i^1. tr_is refer to the individuals. Each triplet has its own range and specifies a 3D volume. An individual with a trajectory tr_i resides in a geographic rectangle specified by $[x_i^1 - x_i^2]$ and $[y_i^1 - y_i^2]$ at some time in $[t_i^1 - t_i^2]$. According to this definition, generalization of a trajectory is also a trajectory. We use the following notation for components to express their length; $|x_i| = |x_i^1 - x_i^2|$, $|y_i| = |y_i^1 - y_i^2|$, $|t_i| = |t_i^1 - t_i^2|$.

4.3 An Overview of Mining and Privacy-Preserving Publishing of Sequence Data

The initial work by Agrawal and Srikant considered sequences of customer transactions and developed algorithms to find frequent sequences of sets of items purchased belonging to the same customer [4]. The database mined was sequences of customer transactions. The algorithm proposed was based on the Apriori property for early pruning of infrequent sequences. The work on frequent episode mining proposed by Mannila et al. [17], assume an event sequence and define the notion of parallel and serial episodes. They then propose a sliding window algorithm to extract frequent episodes from the event sequence.

The notion of sequences was enriched by adding the time component to define temporal sequences. The time dimension in temporal sequences, enabled the analysis of periodic and partial periodic patterns from event sequences by Han et al. in [9]. The work by Han et al., assumes that the events with a time reference occur with certain periodicity and they propose index-based algorithms for mining partial periodic patterns from time series data.

The basic notions of temporal sequences were applied to many domains such as mining of web logs, and DNA sequences[18], [27]. Spatio-temporal data mining has also been investigated in the past by the data mining researchers [23]. A recent EU funded project, GeoPKDD (Geographic Privacy-aware Knowledge Discovery and Delivery),* considers time referenced location data of individuals in the form of trajectories. The GeoPKDD project considers the collection, representation, analysis, and visualization of trajectory datasets while paying special attention to privacy at every step. Trajectories of individuals are further analyzed to obtain frequent patterns of visited places [8] and they are enriched with semantic information via stops and moves.

Privacy preserving data publishing research considers data mining as one of the target applications for the released data. One of the seminal papers in privacy preserving data mining considers classification as the data mining objective [5]. Authors propose an algorithm based on random perturbation, mixing additive or multiplicative noise with the data so that actual values in the dataset are not learned, yet the data mining results gathered from the per-

---

*http://www.geopkdd.eu/

turbed data will not deviate significantly from the results gathered from the original data. The work on condensation-based approach for string anonymization for privacy preserving data publishing also considers the classification problem of strings [3]. The anonymization work on trajectories considers clustering as the main data mining objective and shows that the anonymized data produces clusters almost as good as the original data [20].

4.4 Condensation-Based Methods

In the context of this chapter we look at two specific methods and applications based on condensation. The first one is the condensation-based method for string data, and the second one is a condensation-based method for trajectory data.

Since condensation-based methods were not proposed as a generic metric for anonymization but for privacy preserving data analysis, we are going to name condensation-based methods for both anonymization, and call it a generic method for privacy preserving data mining.

One of the initial papers on privacy preserving data mining exploits the fact that some data mining methods can be used without seeing the actual data but just the statistical properties [5]. Condensation-based methods for privacy preserving data mining exploit the same assumption. In fact one of the early algorithms for efficient clustering of large data can be considered to lay the foundation of condensation-based methods. The work by Zhang et al., [34] did not consider privacy but considered memory constraints. The basic idea was to use the notion of a clustering feature (CF) to summarize a group of data points. CF for a cluster C containing N points with dimensionality d, is a triple (N, LS, SS), where N is the number of data points in C, LS is the linear sum of the data points in C, and SS is the square sum of the data points in C. The authors prove the additivity property of clustering features where the CF of a cluster C, which is the union of C_1 and C_2, is the sum of the clustering features of C_1, and C_2. This means that CF vectors for clusters can be built incrementally by scanning the database once. The summary information stored in CFs can also be used to calculate the properties of clusters, such as the centroid, the radius, and the diameter of a cluster. These properties describe the quality of clusters and can be used to calculate distances among clusters.

Most condensation-based techniques proposed so far have the same skeleton:

- Use a clustering method to group similar individuals. Each group satisfies a constraint enforced by the privacy metric. Similarity is captured by a predefined distance metric. Most algorithms differ in their definition of distance.

• From each group, construct representatives with similar statistics. Which statistics are preserved depends on the algorithm.

4.4.1   Privacy Metrics and Attack Models

The privacy metrics for condensation-based methods are based on anonymization and the notion of k-anonymity. The data quality metrics are based on the utility of data for data mining and querying.

It has been shown that just removing unique identifiers (e.g., social security number (SSN) from a dataset is not enough for de-identification. Quasi-identifier attributes (e.g., age, sex, address,$\cdots$) can still be used to map individuals to private information. k-Anonymity is defined in [25, 24], as a privacy standard to protect against identification of individuals in such person specific datasets. A dataset is k-anonymous if each record over quasi-identifiers appears at least k times. k-Anonymity property ensures that a given set of quasi identifiers can at best be mapped to a group of at least k entities in the dataset. The most common technique being used to anonymize a given dataset is value generalizations and suppressions. In multidimensional space, the counterpart of these operations is replacing a set of points with the minimum bounding box that covers the points. It should be noted that k-anonymization via generalizations and suppressions preserves the truth of the data, explaining the data at a higher granularity.

For condensation-based methods for privacy preserving data mining, the notion of k-indistinguishability was used as the privacy standard. A record is said to be k-indistinguishable, when the datasets contain at least $k-1$ other records from which the data record cannot be distinguished, which is the same idea used for defining the notion of k-anonymity.

Authors in [3] propose k-indistinguishability as the privacy metric for their condensation-based approach for string data. Their attack model assumes that partial or complete information about the individual fragments of the strings is available. The purpose of anonymization is to make sure that it is no longer possible to use the string fragments in order to make inferences about the identities of the original strings. This assumption was motivated by the work of Malin and Sweeney [15] which shows that genotype data can be identified through clinical phenotype data. For example, genetic diseases can be identified as specific patterns in the DNA sequence of an individual. In light of this, k-indistinguishability of strings ensures that k strings within a group are indistinguishable from each other as in the case of a k-anonymous database.

The notion of k-anonymity was also used for trajectories, but the algorithms to achieve k-anonymity of trajectory data is quite different from tabular data, since the data consists of sequences of points which are dependent on each other, therefore they need to be considered as a whole.

For trajectory datasets, although no uniquely identifying information is released, the trajectories could still be linked to individuals by using time-referenced location information as a quasi identifier. The following adversarial behavior is assumed for anonymization of trajectories:

1. The adversary may already know some portion of the trajectory of an individual in the dataset and may be interested in the rest. (e.g., adversary knows that a particular person lives in a particular house. He also knows that she leaves the house and comes back home at specified times. He is interested in finding the locations she visited.)

2. The adversary may already know the whole trajectory of an individual but be interested in some sensitive information about the individual. This is a concern if some sensitive information is also released, as part of the database, for some of the spatio-temporal triplets or for some individuals. Sensitive information, for example, could be the requests done by the individual to location based services.

4.4.2   Comparison of Condensation-Based and Other Privacy Approaches

Given the adversary model explained in Section 4.4.1, three techniques have been proposed to de-identify data.

1. Perturbation-based techniques apply multiplicative or additive noise on each numerical data value. While information about each individual is distorted, noise wears off in aggregate analysis (i.e., the vector of values $<12, 14, 42, 48>$ from the attribute domain age can be perturbed as $<12 + X_1, 14 + X_2, 42 + X_3, 48 + X_4>$ where each $X_i \in [0..1]$ has a uniform distribution).

2. Generalization-based techniques (or anonymization techniques) apply generalizations on data cells to form groups of similar tuples and introduce indistinguishability within each group. Most privacy metrics from this domain are designed to capture a desired level of indistinguishability. Generalizations can be carried out over user supplied domain generalization hierarchies, by assuming some total order over each attribute [11] or through set operations [21], (i.e., assuming the 2-anonymity metric, the same vector can be generalized as $<[10-20], [10-20], [40-50], [40-50]>$). For sequence data, two points belonging to two sequences can be generalized by replacing them with the minimum bounding covering the two points.

3. Condensation-based techniques sample data values from the area covered by each group but tries to preserve as much statistics as possible, (i.e., assuming the 2-indistinguishability metric [2], the same vector can be condensed in a most trivial way as $<X_1 \in [10-20], X_2 \in [10-20], X_3 \in [40-50], X_4 \in [40-50]>$ where each X_i has a uniform distribution.).

The advantages of condensation-based over perturbation-based techniques are as follows:

- Perturbation is applied over each attribute independently. The technique ignores the joint distribution of attributes, thus correlation between attributes is not captured. Whereas, the original work on condensation-based privacy preservation preserves second order statistics.

- There is no notion of distinguishability of individuals in a perturbed dataset. Privacy metric is defined over the parameters of the noise and may not translate well in a real world applications. However, condensation creates groupings, and privacy metrics are expressed in terms indistinguishability within groupings.

The advantages of condensation over anonymization are as follows:

- Condensation-based method works with pseudo-data while anonymization produces a generalized version of the original data records.

- One of the biggest challenges in anonymization (of tabular or sequence data) is the difficulty in extracting information contained in the output. Most data mining and statistical applications work on atomic data values while anonymization maps the data to a heterogeneous domain. Condensation, however, does not change the domain of the output dataset. (In fact, one solution offered to overcome this challenge in anonymization literature is to reconstruct another dataset from the anonymization by random sampling [21]. This is basically a condensation technique.)

- For sequence data, use of minimum bounding boxes in anonymization discloses uncontrolled information about the exact locations of the points. (E.g., in the case of two trajectories, two non-adjacent corners give out the exact locations.) This problem is weakened in a condensation-based approach since released data does not contain real points.

- A disadvantage of k-anonymity for tabular data is that k-anonymization requires domain generalization hierarchies or at least a total order assumption to capture the semantics of the data. While condensation could also benefit from hierarchies, the underlying methodology guarantees that (in large enough data) the distribution of the data is preserved in the output data. Thus, condensation does not suffer from the lack of hierarchies or total orders as much as an anonymization does.

4.4.3   Condensation-Based Methods for Tabular Data

Condensation-based methods for privacy preserving data mining were proposed by Charu Aggrawal and Philip S. Yu in [2] for numerical data. They further extended their work for privacy preserving mining of sequence data [3]. Condensation-based methods for privacy preserving data mining in general could be considered in the context of privacy preserving data publishing.

Condensation-based techniques ensure that the data is condensed and only pseudo data showing similar statistics with the original data is released, which is enough for data mining applications. Their work on sequence condensation needs to be looked at from a data mining perspective. In condensation-based methods, they do not require new algorithms for privacy preserving data mining, rather, they map the original dataset into an anonymized version. These anonymized data are generated in such a way as to match the characteristics of the original data. The clusters are generated in a way to preserve k-distinguishability.

This approach uses a methodology which condenses the data into multiple groups of predefined size. For each group, certain statistics are maintained. Each group has a size of at least k, which is referred to as the indistinguishability level of that privacy-preserving approach. The greater the indistinguishability level, the greater the amount of privacy. At the same time, a greater amount of information is lost because of the condensation of a larger number of records into a single statistical group entity.

In the case of tabular data, the whole database is partitioned into groups of records. Let's say a group contains the records $(X_1, X_2, ... X_k)$ where each of X_i represents a d dimensional record in the group. The information maintained for each group is the following [2]:

- The sum of corresponding values for each attribute j (first order sum)

- For each pair of attributes (i, j), the dot product of the corresponding attribute values is maintained (second order sum).

- Total number of records k within the group

The summary information given above is enough to calculate the mean of an attribute and the covariance between pairs of attributes within the group.

Given a database, creation of the groups is a simple task. A random data point is picked, and the nearest $k - 1$ data points to it are selected to form the initial group, and these k points are removed from the database. The remaining groups are formed iteratively using the same approach. The above mentioned first and second order sums are maintained for each group. The groups constructed are used to create an anonymized dataset. For dynamic datasets, as new data arrives, it is assigned to the nearest group and a group is divided into two after its size exceeds $2k$ as in the case of a $B+$ tree with order k. This is very similar to the BIRCH clustering technique [34] which maintains a hierarchy of cluster statistics in the form of a tree which is dynamically constructed.

Proposed approaches for condensation-based privacy preserving data mining was tested and it was shown that the classifier accuracy for kNN classification is within acceptable limits, and therefore the techniques could be considered as successful for privacy preserving classification.

4.4.4 Condensation-Based Methods for Strings

Condensation-based method for strings have similar characteristics to condensation-based methods for tabular data in that they are both based on the concept of k-indistinguishability, and summary statistics of groups of strings. The summary statistics which contains first and second order information about the distribution of the symbols in the strings are further used to generate pseudo-strings. The aggregate behavior of the new set of strings preserves the following key characteristics of the original dataset:

- composition,

- the order of the intra-string distances,

- the accuracy of data mining algorithms.

Let us assume that we have a database D containing N strings $S_1, S_2, ...S_N$ from which we would like to create an condensed database D^* that satisfies k-indistinguishability. The algorithm followed by [3] is as follows:

- The algorithm first creates r segments such that each segment has at least k strings and strings in each segment have similar length.

- Each string in a given segment is converted to a template of equal size. This is done through a normalization phase such that each position i of the template is expressed in terms of weights over the space of symbols.

- Templates in each segment then are grouped into clusters such that each cluster contains k templates and the distances between the templates within the same group are minimized. The distance of two templates is the sum of distances of weights over all index positions.

- From each cluster, the first and the second order statistics are calculated. The first order statistics for index position i and symbol q is given by the average weight of q at index i in all templates. The second order statistics for index position i and symbols p and q is the average correlation of two symbols between the ith and $i + 1$th position.

- The algorithm creates k pseudo-strings from each cluster by using the statistics. The first symbol is generated from the first order statistics, subsequent symbols are generated from the second order statistics.

Note that the use of second order statistics captures only the correlations between the symbols that are next to each other. However, it is also possible to modify the algorithm to extract higher order statistics. Note also that the condensation of k strings is created from the combined statistics of templates in a given cluster. Thus, the set of pseudo-strings are indistinguishable and it is no longer possible to use the attack scenario where the information about portions or fragments of the strings are used to identify the entire string.

4.4.5 Condensation-Based Methods for Sequential Patterns

In case of sequential patterns, the privacy threat appears when the frequency of patterns is less than a certain value k, where the sequences may be linked with individuals and reveal their movement habits. A solution is to k-anonymize the sequence database where each sequence appears with at least $k-1$ other sequences. The resulting set of sequences should preserve the sequential pattern mining and clustering results as the utility metric. The original sequence database is transformed in such way that the (sub)sequences with support less than k in the original dataset are removed in the anonymized dataset. Given an attack scenario where an adversary knows part of the sequence belonging to a person, and that s/he also knows that this person is present in the database, s/he has a probability of $1/k$ of reconstructing the entire sequence. The anonymization algorithm, called *SS-P2kA* (Sequence Segmentation Pattern-Preserving k-Anonymization) uses a prefix tree in order to model the original sequence dataset as a compact way of representation. Sequences are further segmented to create groups of similar sequences as the basis for anonymization. The segmentation is performed on infrequent sequences which may cause privacy violation, and they are segmented into their frequent sub-sequences.

4.4.6 Condensation-Based Methods for Trajectory Data

Trajectory data is a special case of sequences, containing location measurements collected over time. These are processed to extract trajectories and could be enriched with semantic information such as speed, activity, point of interest etc. Anonymization of trajectories could be considered as a way of privacy preserving publishing of trajectories. The common approach followed by two representatives of this area of research [1, 20] involves clustering of similar trajectories to come up with groups to anonymize. Then random points are released as representative points, so the last step is randomization, which mimics condensed trajectories.

For the condensation-based methods for trajectory datasets, we are going to consider two approaches which have similarities and differences in terms of the methods they are using. The first one uses the inherent imprecision of the GPS measurements of trajectories together with clustering for anonymization and the algorithm is called Never Walk Alone (NWA) [1]. The second one is a anonymization-based approach which uses string alignment together with clustering for trajectory anonymization and we name it the Trajectory Grouping and Alignment (TGA) approach [20].

4.4.6.1   Never Walk Alone

NWA defines an uncertain trajectory as a cylindrical volume with radius δ. Two trajectories t_1 and t_2 are co-localized if the euclidean distance between the corresponding points (with respect to time) in these two trajectories is less than δ. Given the parameters k, and δ, and a trajectory dataset, we would like to obtain D' with minimum distortion where D' satisfies (k, δ)-anonymity, which means that for a given trajectory t in D', there should be at least $k-1$ other trajectories co-localized with t with distance threshold δ. In the light of these definitions, the NWA algorithm anonymizes a given set of trajectories in three steps:

- Pre-processing: The distance metric used in NWA assumes that the input trajectories have the same length and span the same time interval. To enforce this requirement, the algorithm first partitions the database such that the trajectories in each partition start and stop at the same time. However, this creates many small partitions when applied to raw data. To prevent this, the algorithm generalizes the time domain according to a user supplied parameter and increases the number of trajectories per partition.

- Clustering: The algorithm clusters each partition into groups of size k. The algorithm also tries to minimize the size of each cluster.

- Space Translation: Trajectories in each cluster are shifted in space such that the trajectories become a (k, δ)-anonymity set.

4.4.6.2   Trajectory Grouping and Alignment Approach

The basic idea of condensation based on Trajectory Grouping and Alignment (TGA) is to protect the privacy of individuals against an adversary by using:

- k-Anonymity: anonymize the dataset so that every trajectory is indistinguishable from $k-1$ other trajectories.

- Reconstruction: release atomic trajectories sampled randomly from the area covered by anonymized trajectories.

k-Anonymity limits the adversary's ability to link any information to an individual, while reconstruction further prevents leakage due to anonymization. Since reconstruction is just sampling from anonymized data, expectation on the amount of privacy-utility depends only on the anonymization. As an anonymization is required to satisfy the privacy constraints, it also needs to maximize the utilization. An anonymization with a reconstruction that better explains the data is considered to be highly utilized. The underlying algorithm can be summarized as follows:

- The algorithm first clusters the trajectory database such that each group contains at least k trajectories.

- The trajectories in each group are anonymized with respect to each other. Points of anonymized trajectories become 3D volumes.

- The algorithm reconstructs each trajectory by sampling from the 3D volumes.

The anonymization needs to consider the quality of the data and the generalization-based approach uses the log-cost metric given in Equation 4.1 to measure the quality of the anonymized data. The log-cost of a given generalized trajectory tr^* is a measure proportional to the number of distinct atomic trajectories that are contained in tr^*. As the number of trajectories that can be inferred by the generalization increases, the log-cost of the generalization increases and so does the ambiguity on the whereabouts of the original trajectory. The log-cost metric can capture space and time sensitivity by assigning different weights to these dimensions.

$$LCM(tr^*) = \sum_{p_i \in tr^*} w_s(\log |x_i| + \log |y_i|) + w_t \log |t_i| \qquad (4.1)$$

In TGA, two points are anonymized by replacing them with the minimum bounding box containing the points. Two trajectories t_1 and t_2 are anonymized by matching each point on t_1 with some point in t_2 such that the log-cost of the resulting anonymization is minimized.

In the clustering phase, the distance metric between two trajectories is defined as the log-cost of their anonymization. The distance metric being used does not assume the trajectories have the same number of points.

4.4.7   Comparison of the Methods

The attack model for the condensation-based approach for string data is the same as in [16]. Parts of the strings, as in the case of DNA fragments, could be used together to infer identities. In case of sequence anonymization, the fact that the frequency of sequences is lower than k was proposed as a privacy violation. In case of trajectories, the frequently followed paths and locations were assumed to be quasi-identifiers.

When we compare the condensation-based anonymization of trajectories, we see that NWA protects privacy by shifting trajectory points in space that are already close to each other in time. Clusters of k trajectories are forced to be close to each other so that they fall in the same area of uncertainty given by a user parameter representing the GPS precision. NWA makes use of heuristics to minimize the total distance between the original trajectories and the translated trajectories. TGA adapts the original k-anonymity definition to trajectory databases. The algorithm relies on the generalization of points both in space and time and enforces that at least k trajectories fall in the same generalized volume. TGA optimizes against a utility metric that correlates with the total volume of the generalized regions. The utility metric can be set to be sensitive to space or time, meaning it can also capture similarities between the trajectories that are close in space but far away in time. TGA makes use of clustering techniques to group similar trajectories. Similarities are captured by a distance metric that is based on point alignment thus clustering technique can also work on non-euclidean spaces such as string databases. As the output, TGA releases random trajectories sampled from the generalized volumes.

4.5   Conclusions and Open Research Problems

In this chapter, we provided some characteristics of sequence data with representative data types, such as DNA sequences and spatio-temporal trajectories. Privacy metrics and attack models were given on these datasets and condensation-based methods were explained for privacy preserving data publishing. Data anonymization in general, which is rooted in late 90s, can be considered as the basis of condensation-based methods. However, the main motivation of condensation-based methods is data mining, therefore their target is different. A comparison with condensation-based methods and anonymization techniques is needed in terms of their privacy guarantees and their utility with respect to data mining algorithms.

Although various anonymization algorithms were proposed for different applications and different data types, a general framework is yet to be proposed for complex data types involving sequences. A benchmark is needed to assess the utility of the proposed methods. For example the condensation-based method was tested against kNN classification, and for trajectories, data utility is measured with respect to the clusters produced from the anonymized data.

We see the first steps to apply k-anonymization/condensation techniques to spatio-temporal databases; however, the research in this area is still far from the current state of the art in anonymization technology. As also mentioned in Section 4.1, more recent works on anonymization showed weaknesses of k-anonymity and changed/improved its definition to other privacy models (e.g., ℓ-diversity, t-closeness, (α,k)-anonymity, and discernibility [22], δ-presence, $\cdots$) that better fit into real world applications. Surely, new techniques that provide better privacy guarantees need to be designed for spatio-temporal databases.

In addition to modeling new privacy metrics, recent developments in privacy technology also showed that instead of generalizing/perturbing quasi identifiers, an anatomization approach that permutes only sensitive information gives the same privacy guarantees while ensuring a higher level of utility [30, 33]. However, current techniques in spatio-temporal databases do not even distinguish sensitive from non-sensitive (e.g., the part of the trajectory of a person showing him/her going to a hospital should surely be de-identified. However, there is not much point to de-identify the fact that the same person leaves his/her home). Having such a distinction between sensitive/non-sensitive points and applying different levels of protection to each class surely has potential to create more utilized databases.

One recent observation in anonymization-based privacy protection technology is that adversaries that know the underlying anonymization technique can discover more than the anonymization and the privacy metric allow [28, 32]. The condensation-based techniques are also prone to such attacks (e.g., points are more likely to be in the center of a rectangle for spatio-temporal anonymizations), but it is an open question as to what extent this is a privacy threat. New countermeasures need to be taken to provide resistant condensations in case of such strong adversaries.

Finally, harmonization of the technology, law, and regulations is an important issue for privacy preserving data analysis and publishing in general. For example, what should be the value of "k" in case of anonymization or condensation? When regulations enforce a privacy parameter such as a very high value of parameter "k" in case of k-anonymity, this may require a lot of generalization or data perturbation, resulting in a dataset which has no value for data mining.

Acknowledgments

This work was partially funded by the Information Society Technologies program of the European Commission, Future and Emerging Technologies under IST-014915 GeoPKDD project, and The Scientific and Technological Research Council of Turkey (TUBITAK) National Young Researchers Career Development Programme under grant number 106E116.

References

[1] Osman Abul, Francesco Bonchi, and Mirco Nanni. Never walk alone: Uncertainty for anonymity in moving objects databases. In *Proceedings*

of the 24st IEEE International Conference on Data Engineering (ICDE 2008).

[2] Charu C. Aggarwal and Philip S. Yu. A condensation approach to privacy preserving data mining. In *Proceedings of the 9th International Conference on Extending Database Technology (EDBT 2004)*, pages 183–199.

[3] Charu C. Aggarwal and Philip S. Yu. A framework for condensation-based anonymization of string data. *Data Min. Knowl. Discov.*, 16(3):251–275, 2008.

[4] Rakesh Agrawal and Ramakrishnan Srikant. Mining sequential patterns. In *Proceedings of the 11th IEEE International Conference on Data Engineering (ICDE'95)*.

[5] Rakesh Agrawal and Ramakrishnan Srikant. Privacy-preserving data mining. *SIGMOD Rec.*, 29(2):439–450, 2000.

[6] Maurizio Atzori, Francesco Bonchi, Fosca Giannotti, and Dino Pedreschi. Anonymity preserving pattern discovery. *VLDB J.*, 17(4):703–727, 2008.

[7] Benjamin C. M. Fung, Ke Wang, and Philip S. Yu. Top-down specialization for information and privacy preservation. In *ICDE'05: Proceedings of the 21st International Conference on Data Engineering*, pages 205–216, Washington, DC, USA, 2005. IEEE Computer Society.

[8] Fosca Giannotti, Mirco Nanni, Fabio Pinelli, and Dino Pedreschi. Trajectory pattern mining. In *Proceedings of the 13th ACM SIGKDD International Conference on Knowledge Discovery and Data Mining (KDD 2007)*, pages 330–339.

[9] Jiawei Han, Guozhu Dong, and Yiwen Yin. Efficient mining of partial periodic patterns in time series database. In *Proceedings of the 15th IEEE International Conference on Data Engineering (ICDE'99)*.

[10] Murat Kantarcıoğlu, Jiashun Jin, and Chris Clifton. When do data mining results violate privacy? In *Proceedings of the 2004 ACM SIGKDD International Conference on Knowledge Discovery and Data Mining*, pages 599–604, Seattle, WA, August 22-25 2004.

[11] Kristen LeFevre, David J. DeWitt, and Raghu Ramakrishnan. Mondrian multidimensional k-anonymity. In *ICDE'06: Proceedings of the 22nd International Conference on Data Engineering*, pages 25–35, Atlanta, GA, April 3-7 2006.

[12] Kristen LeFevre, David J. DeWitt, and Raghu Ramakrishnan. Workload-aware anonymization. In *KDD '06: Proceedings of the 12th ACM SIGKDD International Conference on Knowledge Discovery and Data Mining*, pages 277–286, New York, NY, USA, 2006. ACM.

[13] Ninghui Li and Tiancheng Li. t-closeness: Privacy beyond k-anonymity and l-diversity. In *ICDE'07: Proceedings of the 23nd International Conference on Data Engineering*, Istanbul, Turkey, April 16-20 2007.

[14] Ashwin Machanavajjhala, Johannes Gehrke, Daniel Kifer, and Muthuramakrishnan Venkitasubramaniam. ℓ-diversity: Privacy beyond k-anonymity. In *ICDE'06: Proceedings of the 22nd IEEE International Conference on Data Engineering*, Atlanta Georgia, April 2006.

[15] Bradley Malin and Latanya Sweeney. Inferring genotype from clinical phenotype through a knowledge based algorithm. In *Pacific Symposium on Biocomputing*, pages 41–52, 2002.

[16] Bradley Malin and Latanya Sweeney. How (not) to protect genomic data privacy in a distributed network: using trail re-identification to evaluate and design anonymity protection systems. *Journal of Biomedical Informatics*, 37(3):179–192, 2004.

[17] Heikki Mannila, Hannu Toivonen, and A. Inkeri Verkamo. Discovery of frequent episodes in event sequences. *Data Min. Knowl. Discov.*, 1(3):259–289, 1997.

[18] Bamshad Mobasher, Olfa Nasraoui, Bing Liu, and Brij M. Masand, editors. *Advances in Web Mining and Web Usage Analysis, 6th International Workshop on Knowledge Discovery on the Web, WebKDD 2004, Seattle, WA, USA, August 22-25, 2004, Revised Selected Papers*, volume 3932 of *Lecture Notes in Computer Science*. Springer, 2006.

[19] Mehmet Ercan Nergiz, Maurizio Atzori, and Chris Clifton. Hiding the presence of individuals in shared databases. In *SIGMOD'07: Proceedings of the 2007 ACM SIGMOD International Conference on Management of Data*, Beijing, China, June 11-14 2007.

[20] Mehmet Ercan Nergiz, Maurizio Atzori, Yucel Saygin, and Baris Guc. Towards trajectory anonymization: a generalization-based approach. *Transactions on Data Privacy*, 2(1):1010–1027, 2009.

[21] Mehmet Ercan Nergiz and Chris Clifton. Thoughts on k-anonymization. *Data and Knowledge Engineering*, 63(3):622–645, December 2007.

[22] Aleksander Øhrn and Lucila Ohno-Machado. Using boolean reasoning to anonymize databases. *Artificial Intelligence in Medicine*, 15(3):235–254, March 1999.

[23] John F. Roddick and Kathleen Hornsby, editors. *Temporal, Spatial, and Spatio-Temporal Data Mining, First International Workshop TSDM 2000 Lyon, France, September 12, 2000, Revised Papers*, volume 2007 of *Lecture Notes in Computer Science*. Springer, 2001.

[24] Pierangela Samarati. Protecting respondents' identities in microdata release. *IEEE Trans. Knowl. Data Eng.*, 13(6):1010–1027, 2001.

[25] Latanya Sweeney. k-anonymity: A model for protecting privacy. *International Journal of Uncertainty, Fuzziness and Knowledge-Based Systems*, 10(5):557–570, 2002.

[26] Vassilios S. Verykios, Ahmed K. Elmagarmid, Elisa Bertino, Yücel Saygin, and Elena Dasseni. Association rule hiding. *IEEE Trans. Knowl. Data Eng.*, 16(4):434–447, 2004.

[27] Jason Tsong-Li Wang, Mohammed Javeed Zaki, Hannu Toivonen, and Dennis Shasha, editors. *Data Mining in Bioinformatics*. Springer, 2005.

[28] Raymond Chi-Wing Wong, Ada Wai-Chee Fu, Ke Wang, and Jian Pei. Minimality attack in privacy preserving data publishing. In *VLDB'07: Proceedings of the 33rd International Conference on Very Large Data Bases*, pages 543–554. VLDB Endowment, 2007.

[29] Raymond Chi-Wing Wong, Jiuyong Li, Ada Wai-Chee Fu, and Ke Wang. (α, k)-anonymity: An enhanced k-anonymity model for privacy preserving data publishing. In *KDD'06: Proceedings of the 12th ACM SIGKDD International Conference on Knowledge Discovery and Data Mining*, pages 754–759, New York, NY, USA, 2006. ACM.

[30] Xiaokui Xiao and Yufei Tao. Anatomy: Simple and effective privacy preservation. In *VLDB'06: Proceedings of 32nd International Conference on Very Large Data Bases*, Seoul, Korea, September 12-15 2006.

[31] Jian Xu, Wei Wang, Jian Pei, Xiaoyuan Wang, Baile Shi, and Ada Wai-Chee Fu. Utility-based anonymization using local recoding. In *KDD '06: Proceedings of the 12th ACM SIGKDD International Conference on Knowledge Discovery and Data Mining*, pages 785–790, New York, NY, USA, 2006. ACM.

[32] Lei Zhang, Sushil Jajodia, and Alexander Brodsky. Information disclosure under realistic assumptions: privacy versus optimality. In *CCS '07: Proceedings of the 14th ACM Conference on Computer and Communications Security*, pages 573–583, New York, NY, USA, 2007. ACM.

[33] Qing Zhang, N. Koudas, D. Srivastava, and Ting Yu. Aggregate query answering on anonymized tables. *Data Engineering, 2007. ICDE 2007. IEEE 23rd International Conference on*, pages 116–125, April 2007.

[34] Tian Zhang, Raghu Ramakrishnan, and Miron Livny. Birch: An efficient data clustering method for very large databases. In *Proceedings of the 1996 ACM SIGMOD International Conference on Management of Data (SIGMOD'96)*.

Part II

Traces and Streams

Chapter 5

Catch, Clean, and Release: A Survey of Obstacles and Opportunities for Network Trace Sanitization

Keren Tan, Jihwang Yeo

Institute for Security, Technology Studies, and Society, Dartmouth College, Hanover, New Hampshire

Michael E. Locasto

University of Calgary, Calgary, Canada

David Kotz

Institute for Security Technology Studies, Dartmouth College, Hanover, New Hampshire

5.1 Introduction

The sharing of network trace data provides important benefits to both network researchers and administrators. Sharing traces helps scientists and network engineers compare and reproduce results and the behavior of network tools. The practice of sharing such information, however, faces a number of obstacles. Network traces contain significant amounts of sensitive information about the network structure and its users. Thus, researchers wishing to share traces must "sanitize" them to protect this information. We distinguish the terms "anonymization" and "sanitization": "anonymization" attempts to protect the privacy of network users, and "sanitization" attempts to protect the privacy of network users *and* the secrecy of operational network information. In contrast, freely sharing full-capture traces happens rarely and usually re-

111

quires either close, pre-established personal relationships between researchers or extensive legal agreements (as in the PREDICT repository [51]). Furthermore, most real-world traces contain a large volume of information with features along many different dimensions, making the problem of identifying and masking sensitive data non-trivial.

It remains difficult to precisely specify a policy regarding the type and structure of information that should be sanitized, let alone provide a reliable method that ensures the conclusive suppression of such information in the shared trace. Thus, two main categories of concerns arise: (1) legal and ethical obstacles to capturing information derived from human interaction for research purposes and (2) operational difficulties arising from a lack of effective tools and techniques for suppressing sensitive information. In this chapter, we survey a selection of both seminal and recent papers to summarize the reasons for these concerns, identify the work that has been done to help address or overcome them, and frame what we have come to view as the next major problem in this space: the invention of metrics describing the *quality* of a particular sanitization or anonymization technique on a given dataset.

We find that network researchers face a dilemma: although they can hypothesize about network data properties and prototype sanitization tools, they find it difficult to obtain real network traces to test these hypotheses and tools and verify whether they are correct, or to operate with any utility on real-world networks, respectively. Fortunately, network research is far from stagnant because researchers have put a significant amount of effort into (or find creative ways of) obtaining access to large, meaningful traffic traces from real production networks.

5.1.1   Challenges for Trace Collection and Sharing

The daunting challenge of creating and maintaining a network monitoring infrastructure involves obtaining legal and administrative approval, reaching out to the campus or corporate community, implementing extensive security and control measures, maintaining internal records and documentation, and (sometimes) undergoing external security audits (see Section 5.6). This investment of time and effort can restrict the ability to capture meaningful amounts of network data to larger or well-funded organizations. In such an environment, *sharing becomes an essential feature of networking research.* Yet, the legal, ethical, and privacy issues of capturing and sharing production network traces threatens to chill such sharing and to eliminate this form of applied research.*

---

*Some point out that simulation provides an alternative to using real traffic data. For certain types of research (e.g., anomaly-based intrusion detection), simulation is unlikely to prove useful, as the details of a real data sample are important, not just those properties derived from aggregate statistics).

Many of the relevant laws are unclear about the legality of capturing and releasing network traces [58]. Even if such laws were amended to include specific exceptions for research use of network traces, as some advocate [11], individual privacy would still need protection and organizations would still wish to protect operational details. For example, network administrators may wish to share data for operational, not research purposes, but privacy concerns remain. Moreover, the network operator may wish to protect other information of proprietary or operational significance, such as the structure of the network, the identity of important servers, or how the network itself responds to particular types of threats.

We recognize the inherent trade-off between **privacy** and **usefulness**. Sanitization methods intentionally degrade the quality of a network trace to protect against trace users who actively seek to extract sensitive information from the trace, and inevitably reduce the type and content of features useful for non-malicious research. It is difficult to simultaneously achieve privacy and usefulness. A relationship exists between the amount of information shared and the level of risk an organization or individual assumes in sharing that information. *Methods of sanitization or anonymization seek to bound the level of risk as information sharing increases, but they can also bound the utility of the resulting data.*

5.1.2 Real-World Network Trace Sharing Efforts

Although they may seem abstract, privacy concerns are far from theoretical, and recent incidents involving real datasets have increased such concerns. The release of and subsequent de-anonymization attacks against the AOL dataset [29], the release of the Enron email archive [25], and the de-anonymization attack on the Netflix competition dataset [45] show how easily simple methods of content anonymization can be broken and highlight the risk posed by data once considered "private" or confidential.

Yet, the utility of sharing traces is so compelling that several efforts exist to share varying amounts and types of network trace data, including CAIDA, CRAWDAD, and PREDICT.

CAIDA (Cooperative Association for Internet Data Analysis) [12] collects several different types of network data (including topology, security, traffic characteristics, routing, real time monitors, and performance related data) at geographically and topologically diverse locations. CAIDA makes this data available to the research community while preserving the data donors' privacy. Currently its data repository has more than 230,000 data files. DatCat [21] is a CAIDA project providing the Internet Measurement Data Catalog (IMDC), a searchable registry of information about network measurement datasets. It aims to provide a searchable index of available network datasets and to enhance the documentation of the dataset via a public annotation system.

CRAWDAD (Community Resource for Archiving Wireless Data At Dartmouth) [19] provides a collection of trace data from wireless-network and mobile-computing researchers around the world. As of July 2010, CRAW-DAD.org has over 2337 users from 73 countries. It now makes 60 datasets and 23 tool sets available through the archive, with several more in the pipeline. Over 200 papers have been published with or about CRAWDAD datasets. In addition, a Dartmouth-wide wireless monitoring infrastructure has contributed to the CRAWDAD repository since 2001.

PREDICT (Protected Repository for the Defense of Infrastructure Against Cyber Threats) [51] is sponsored by the Department of Homeland Security (DHS) Science and Technology (S&T) directorate. The datasets in this repository, which include security-relevant network traces and host logs, are only available to qualified cyber defense researchers and only in the United States.

The DSHIELD [24] repository of firewall logs is one of the earliest examples of sharing intrusion alert information. Newer sharing efforts like Open-Packet.org tend to have a more limited number of datasets.

5.1.3   Terminology

Since this chapter assumes a focus on network traces, rather than other types of data collections (notably databases), our terminology reflects this bias by referring to packets, headers, and other network-related terms. Within the world of network traces, however, many specific types exist (such as SNMP logs, IP packet dumps, or Netflow traces), each with their own organization, data types, and information peculiarities. The content of a network trace includes not only the information from a network protocol (such as IP and MAC addresses, or port numbers), but also other metadata such as timestamps, session duration, or a wireless device's geographical coordinates. Such diversity of network traces makes it difficult or impossible to construct a universal algorithm for uniformly sanitizing all types of network traces. Moreover, due to a lack of understanding of (or documentation about) what information a trace might contain, trace sanitization can be much more challenging than it might initially appear.

We assume a general model for a network *trace* that holds a series of *records*. Each record contains a tuple of several *fields*. Each component represents a specific *feature*, such as source and destination MAC address, source and destination IP address, and time stamp.

Sanitization techniques can be applied independently to specific fields or sets of fields, and can include intra-record methods (hiding correlations between fields of a single record), inter-record methods (hiding correlations between multiple records in a trace), and inter-trace methods (hiding correlations between traces captured from different devices or at different times). Section 5.2 gives a detailed review of the sanitization techniques, especially IP-address anonymization techniques, and introduces several state-of-art network trace sanitization tools.

De-sanitization techniques extract sensitive information from the sanitized network traces. These techniques can be classified into two categories: direct de-sanitization attacks and indirect de-sanitization attacks. While a direct de-sanitization attack exploits the flaws and limitations of some sanitization techniques, an indirect attack often leverages implicit information from the sanitized trace or auxiliary information from other sources. As an interesting example of the indirect attack, a CRAWDAD user suggested that the characteristic scanning behavior of a well-known Internet worm could be used to reverse the anonymization of IP addresses in some traces. Section 5.3 introduces current de-sanitization techniques and demonstrates several sucessful de-sanitization practices.

5.1.4 Database Sanitization and Privacy-Preserving Data Mining

A large body of research has been also conducted from the database and data mining community on sanitization metrics (and techniques) and privacy-preserving data mining [1].

Anonymity is widely used as a key measure of privacy in sanitized databases [49]. One specific anonymity metric is "k-anonymity" [55], which in the database setting is defined such that a system provides k-anonymity protection if each record in the database cannot be distinguished from at least $k-1$ other records, with respect to every set of quasi-identifiable non-sensitive attributes. Machanavajjhala et al. demonstrate some severe problems with k-anonymity, however, especially when the attacker uses background knowledge, and propose "l-diversity" as a more powerful privacy definition than k-anonymity [43]. Li et al. show some limitations of l-diversity, in that it is neither necessary nor sufficient to prevent attribute disclosure, and propose a privacy notion called "t-closeness" that protects against attribute disclosure [40].

Although from these metrics we may gain some insights for network trace sanitization, they have made some assumptions that are specific to the database setting. For example, each of these metrics assumes that the set of "sensitive" attributes are known *a priori*, which is difficult to assume for network traces [16, 17]. Moreover, the metrics are purely *static* and *syntactic* in that they only consider the distribution of attribute values in the sanitized database and do not aim to capture the *dynamic* change of the adversary's *semantic* knowledge [9].

Instead, Shannon's entropy is often used as a simple indicator of anonymity and a measure of the adversary's knowledge gain in a network trace. Many information-theoretic metrics have been proposed [22, 56, 14, 16], including the degree of anonymity [22, 16] and the measure of the adversary's knowledge gain [16].

Producing sanitized data that have "good" utility for various data mining tasks is an important research goal in privacy-preserving data mining [9]. There are two approaches for measuring utility: a workload-independent measure, i.e., a utility measure that can be used for any data mining tasks, and a workload-dependent measure. Although workload-independent measures of utility are ideal for broader uses of published datasets, they inevitably use "workload-independent" or "syntactic" properties, such as the amount of generalization and suppression [13], average size of quasi-identifier equivalence class [43], or preservation of marginals [33]. Such "syntactic" measures, however, are of little use for some specific data mining tasks such as classification algorithms and therefore several workload-dependent utility measures such as accuracy of data-mining algorithms have also been studied [9, 31, 39, 60].

We believe that both workload-independent (syntactic) and workload-dependent (semantic) approaches are applicable to *usefulness* metrics for network trace sanitization. For specific applications like network security analysis, some approaches define and exploit a workload-dependent usefulness metric [64, for example]. However, there is limited research on workload-independent metrics for the usefulness of a trace for network analysis. We discuss more details about the usefulness metric for network sanitization in Section 5.4 and 5.5.

5.1.5 Chapter Organization

As network and security researchers, we have faced many obstacles, challenges, and problems in our efforts to share network trace information with others, be it wireless frames or intrusion alerts. Our experience building and maintaining CRAWDAD has shown us the promise of trace sharing. Similarly, our experience building the 200-sniffer Dartmouth Internet Security Testbed (DIST [23]) informs our opinion about the cost to create such systems and their utility as a shared infrastructure for a wider community. Our experience led us to want a deeper understanding of the issues involved in safely sharing network traces.

We organize this chapter to reflect the structure of our own foray into this topic: a progression we hope will ease the reader's journey. We start by identifying other overviews of sanitization techniques and selecting those we believe provide a novel perspective. In particular, the work of Ohm et al. highlights the legal issues surrounding network monitoring for research [58]. That paper serves as a wake-up call for the wider networking community, because collecting and sharing network data has several subtle pitfalls that tend to get overlooked simply because computer scientists are rarely trained as social-science researchers or legal experts.

Gattani et al. define a comprehensive reference model that can capture anonymization problems [28]. They introduce the notion of *universal information*, which is the complete truth regarding the users and the network where the trace was recorded. They show that the raw trace is only a subset of the universal information and as such cannot contain the universal information in its entirety. They propose a new entity set consisting of *collector, auditor, analyst*, and *adversary*, where the *auditor* was missing in the traditional entity set. They define the auditor to be an entity internal to the organization, who works with the collector to guarantee the privacy, accuracy and usability of a sanitized trace. As the only entity that can access the universal information, the auditor emulates the role of an adversary, as demonstrated by Coull [16]. Their reference model is reasonable, and they demonstrate its utility by applying it to Coull's work; the comprehensiveness of the model has not been verified with enough examples, however. Therefore, we do not use their model in describing and comparing a variety of problems and methods in this chapter.

Kelly et al. survey the state of the art in metrics for precisely quantifying the information leakage from anonymized network data [32]. They offer a comprehensive summary of existing anonymity metrics and compare them in terms of *applicability* (whether a metric is useful for data privacy or communication privacy), *complexity* (whether the method requires substantial computation), and *practicality* (reflecting the trade-off between practicality and mathematical rigor). In this paper, we not only address the issues and problems of anonymity metrics but also on research of *usefulness metrics* that quantify how useful the sanitized trace is for the researchers to analyze the trace.

Porras et al. propose nine risks and challenges [50]. They group these challenges into three categories: network sensors that generate data, repositories that collect data and make them available for analysis, and the network infrastructure which delivers the data from the sensors to the repository. Similarly, Bishop et al. pay special attention to the interactions between the multiple actors (collector, analyst, and adversary) involved in a sanitization problem [5, 20]. Coull et al. suggest that the research on anonymizing census microdata may also provide several useful insights on how to effectively anonymize network traces [17].

These surveys serve as a starting point to explore various themes in the field. We organize our own report into three main sections bracketed by this Introduction and an argument about three critical open problems for trace sanitization (Section 5.5). The main sections consider, in turn, sanitization techniques (Section 5.2), methods of attacking these techniques (Section 5.3), and current proposals for evaluating the strength of sanitization and sanitization effects on datasets (Section 5.4). We seek to highlight the coevolution between ways to perform sanitization [18, 59, 65, 61, 26, 48, 30, 66, 52, 62, 8, 46, 35, 44, 6, 41, 42], de-sanitization techniques [36, 8, 48, 18, 16], and methods of measuring [16, 64] the success of both such efforts.

Finally, we close with a consideration of various "gaps" in the space of sanitization and sanitization techniques. We posit that the largest such gap is the difference between the type of information sanitization tools operate on (and thus report on) and the type of information meaningful to a human operator to help them assess the quality of a particular sanitization pass over a specific dataset. Although several researchers [5, 50] note that network data sanitization requires methods that simultaneously protect sensitive or private information and preserve information useful for analysis, there has been only limited development of usable quantitative metrics for measuring privacy protection for network data (e.g., the degree of anonymity [16]).

5.2   Sanitization

To share network traces while preserving privacy, the trace publishers draft sanitization policies according to their specific privacy concerns. These policies explicitly or implicitly determine which sanitization methods to apply and how.

In this section, we review current research on sanitization, with a focus on techniques and tools. Here, "techniques" refer to specific methods or algorithms that solve a specific sanitization problem. Because different fields in the network trace possess different characteristics, they require different sanitization techniques; other techniques are needed to sanitize some inferable and implicit information, such as network topology. A sanitization "tool," on the other hand, provides a systematic solution for a range of applications. A sanitization tool usually implements a set of sanitization techniques and provides a convenient interface to its user.

5.2.1   Sanitization Techniques

General techniques to sanitize specific network trace fields can be classified into a few categories [18, 59]: destruction, fixed transformation, variable transformation, and typed transformation. *Destruction* removes part of, or all, the information from a field, for example, complete removal of the TCP payload, or the removal of the least significant bits of the IP address. *Fixed transformation* uses a single pseudonym value to substitute all values appearing in a field, e.g., to replace the field with zero. Intrinsically this is same as destruction. *Variable transformation* provides more flexibility by using different pseudonym values according to the context of the field. One example is to substitute an original IP address with different pseudonym values according to the type of upper-layer protocols, such as HTTP or SMTP. *Typed transformation*, also called permutation in the most general sense, is a one-to-one mapping between a pseudonym value and a distinct value of the original field. "Prefix-preserving" address anonymization, a common technique, belongs to this category.

Among all the fields in the network trace, the IP address has received most research attention. There are several types of IP-address anonymization techniques based on different design considerations [65, 59]. IP-address partial destruction removes the rightmost IP-address bits, which identify an individual host on a subnet. Prefix-preserving anonymization (pseudonymization) is a special case of permutation that preserves the hierarchical nature of IP addresses and is often preferred to random permutations. There are two general classes of prefix-preserving IP address anonymization techniques: the strict bitwise-preserving approach [44, 61, 26], and Pang's "divide-and-conquer" approach [48].

In the strict bitwise-preserving approach, two anonymized IP addresses will have a common n-bit prefix if and only if the un-anonymized IP addresses have a common n-bit prefix. Minshall implemented one approach to such prefix-preserving anonymization in TCPdpriv with the "A50" option [44]. Xu and Fan showed that such prefix-preserving anonymization functions all follow a canonical form. They proposed a cryptography-based, prefix-preserving anonymization technique, which is implemented in Crypto-PAn, without the need for a prefix table [61, 26]. A geometric interpretation of this prefix-preserving anonymization technique can be described as follows [30]. The collection of all possible IP addresses can be represented by a complete binary tree (see Figure 5.1). For IPv4 addresses the height of the tree is 32, and for IPv6 it is 128. Each leaf node of the tree represents a distinct IP address, and each non-leaf node corresponds to a bit position, indicated by the height of the node, and a bit value, indicated by the branch direction from its parent node. The set of distinct addresses present in the unanonymized trace can be represented by a subtree of this complete binary tree. This subtree is called the *original address tree*. A prefix-preserving anonymization function can be viewed as specifying a binary variable for each non-leaf node of the *original address tree*. This variable determines whether the anonymization function "flips" this bit or not. Applying this anonymization function to the *original address tree* results in an *anonymized address tree*. Based on Xu and Fan's work, Harvan [30] extended this algorithm to preserve SNMP's lexicographical-ordering property. Zhang and Li [66] observed that a trace is often used by different research groups at the same time. Since each group has a distinct trustworthy level, one network trace needs to be anonymized separately to fulfill each group's requirement. Thus, if there are n research groups, there will be n copies of anonymized trace from one original trace. They proposed a scheme that only generates one copy of an anonymized trace, but the users with different knowledge (secret keys) may recover different traces from this single copy. Ramaswamy [52] presented an online prefix-preserving anonymization algorithm — top-hash subtree-replicated anonymization — with low processing requirements and small space complexity.

Unlike the above bitwise-preserving approaches, Pang's approach [48] remaps the IP addresses differently based on the type of addresses, either *external addresses* or *internal addresses*. All *external addresses* — the IP addresses that do not belong to the trace publishing organization — are remapped using the IP address anonymization algorithm in Crypto-PAn. All *internal addresses* — the IP addresses that belong to the trace publishing organization — are divided into the subnet portion and host portion. These two portions are remapped independently and preserve only whether two addresses belong to the same subnet. This means that all hosts in a given subnet

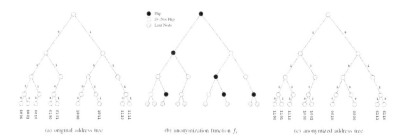

FIGURE 5.1: Geometric interpretation of prefix-preserving anonymization function: (a) represents nine addresses from a 4-bit address space as a binary tree; (b) shows a randomly chosen anonymization function, that is, a set of nodes in the tree are flipped to generate anonymized addresses; (c) shows the anonymized 4-bit addresses produced by applying the anonymization function from (b).

in the original trace will also appear in the same subnet in the anonymized trace. Note that this mapping does not preserve the relationship between subnets. For example, two 24-bit subnet numbers that share a 20-bit prefix in the original trace will not necessarily also have a 20-bit common prefix in the anonymized trace. Pang suggested that this anonymization approach can also be applied to the MAC address.

However, several researchers have criticized current prefix-preserving techniques. Ylonen demonstrates that the prefix-preserving anonymization in TCPdpriv with the "A50" option is not necessarily good enough to keep a well-informed adversary from determining where the data were collected [62]. In Crypto-PAn's prefix-preserving anonymization, any given bit of the anonymized address is dependent on all previous bits of the unanonymized addresses; Coull et al. argue that this kind of dependence causes a single de-anonymization to affect all anonymized addresses that share a common prefix with the true unanonymized addresses [18]. Moreover, Brekne et al. present a set of attacks employing active packet injection and frequency analysis to systematically compromise individual IP addresses protected by the anonymization techniques implemented in TCPdpriv and Crypto-PAn [8, 46]. They propose transaction-specific anonymization schemes that use stream ciphers to encrypt each bit of an IP address and do not preserve the one-to-one mapping between the original and the anonymized IP addresses at all. By individually performing pseudo-random permutation on the subnet and host portions of internal IP addresses, Pang's approach reduces linkability among anonymized addresses more than Crypto-PAn's approach and is more robust against Coull's attack [18]. However, Coull shows that some sensitive information, such as network topology and network servers, can still be inferred from traces anonymized by Pang's approach [18].

5.2.2   Sanitization Tools

Many network trace sanitization techniques have been proposed; some of these techniques are also implemented as software tools. As mentioned above, Crypto-PAn implements the cryptography-based prefix-preserving anonymization technique proposed by Fan and Xu [61, 26]. It uses the Rijndael cipher (AES algorithm) as its underlying pseudorandom function and has the following properties: a one-to-one mapping from unanonymized to anonymized IP addresses, a prefix-preserving mapping, and consistent address mapping across traces. TCPurify [6] is a packet-capture program with sanitization capabilities. After recognizing the Ethernet or IP header, it removes all data payload before storing the packet (except for certain protocols), and does a reversible randomization on IP addresses without preserving network prefix information. TCPdpriv [44] also anonymizes packet traces, with several options to process IP address and TCP/UDP port numbers. TCPdpriv provides prefix-preserving anonymization of IP addresses using a prefix table on a per-trace basis, and thus may not provide a consistent mapping: a particular address will likely be anonymized to different pseudonym addresses in different traces. CANINE (Converter and ANonymizer for Investigating Netflow Events) provides multiple format conversion utilities and integrates several sanitization methods, such as IP anonymization and time stamp sanitization, on NetFlow logs [41, 42]. AnonTool, an open-source implementation of a set of anonymization APIs, aims to build an anonymization assembly line, up to the application level, by expressing the anonymization policy as several sets of sequential function calls [35].

Compared to the sanitization tools above, tcpmkpub [48] and FLAIM [59] provide a more comprehensive and flexible solution. Both of them implement a generic framework for sanitizing network traces. These two frameworks have several common characteristics: (1) User-defined sanitization policies are described by a set of explicit rules using a dedicated language. Figure 5.2 gives an example of PCAP header sanitization rule used in tcpmkpub. The XML-based language used by FLAIM is called the *Module Schema Language*. A snippet of this language is shown in Figure 5.3. (2) The framework follows a modular design and is extensible. Many sanitization primitives and common algorithms, such as truncation and prefix preserving, are implemented and integrated into the framework. Users can also develop their new sanitization techniques as modules and plug these new modules into the framework. (3) tcpmkpub supports sanitization for multiple layers: link layer, network layer and transport layer. FLAIM supports sanitization for several types of logs. For each type of log, FLAIM implements a parser module respectively.

It is important to mention that all available sanitization tools can only do a "one-way job." That is, they can only sanitize a network trace, but they can not provide the user any feedback about the quality of sanitization, such as how much privacy information has been removed or kept in the trace. The goal of sanitization is to pursue a balance between protecting privacy and preserv-

```
- <policy>
  - <field name="IPV4_DST_IP">
    - <BinaryPrefixPreserving>
        <passphrase>abracadabra</passphrase>
      </BinaryPrefixPreserving>
    </field>
  - <field name="IPV4_SRC_IP">
    - <BinaryBlackMarker>
        <numMarks>8</numMarks>
        <replacement>0</replacement>
      </BinaryBlackMarker>
    </field>
  - <field name="TS_SEC">
    - <RandomTimeShift>
        <lowerTimeShiftLimit>60</lowerTimeShiftLimit>
        <upperTimeShiftLimit>600</upperTimeShiftLimit>
        <secondaryField>NONE</secondaryField>
      </RandomTimeShift>
    </field>
```

FIGURE 5.2: PCAP header sanitization rules used in FLAIM.

```
FIELD          (TCP_srcport, 2,     KEEP)
FIELD          (TCP_dstport, 2,     KEEP)
FIELD          (TCP_seq,     4,     KEEP)
FIELD          (TCP_ack,     4.     KEEP)
FIELD          (TCP_off.     1.     KEEP)
FIELD          (TCP_flags,   1,     KEEP)
FIELD          (TCP_window,2,       KEEP)
PUTOFF_FIELD        (TCP_chksum,       2,      ZERO)
FIELD          (TCP_urgptr,  2,     KEEP)
FIELD          (TCP_options, VARLEN, anonymize_tcp_options)
PICKUP_FIELD(TCP_chksum,         0,     recompute_tcp_checksum)
FIELD          (TCP_data.    RESTLEN, SKIP)
```

FIGURE 5.3: TCP sanitization rules used in tcpmkpub.

ing trace's utility. Since no perfect sanitization techniques exist, choosing and tuning these techniques affects the final sanitization result greatly. As noted by many researchers [48, 59, 16, 61], exploring the relationship between the strength and utility of sanitization is an important task for future research.

5.3 De-Sanitization

In security research, we often perform a *worst-case* analysis that assumes an adversary has almost unlimited resources and knowledge to launch an attack on the examined target. Due to the intrinsic complexity of network trace sanitization, we must admit that there are few, if any, available network-trace sanitization schemes that can provide a *water-tight* guarantee under the *worst-case* analysis. That we hold this opinion is not to degrade the value of sanitization research presented in Section 5.2 but rather to emphasize that current de-sanitization research has been remarkably creative and successful.

According to the attack strategies employed by an adversary, we classify current de-sanitization research into two categories: *direct attacks* that exploit the limitations of an anonymization algorithm [8, 46, 18], and *indirect attacks* that use implicit information contained in the trace [18, 27, 2, 47, 38], auxiliary information obtained from other sources [38, 18, 47], and new techniques from other research fields, such as machine learning and pattern recognition [15, 7, 47, 2], to uncover sensitive information from the anonymized network trace.

One example of a direct attack exploits a flaw in Crypto-PAn [61]. As mentioned in Section 5.2, Crypto-PAn implements a strict bitwise-prefix-preserving anonymization algorithm, and any given bit of the address anonymized by Crypto-PAn depends on all previous bits of the anonymized addresses. This dependence enables a de-anonymization on one address to affect all anonymized addresses that share a common prefix with the true address [18]. For instance, if an anonymized address $a = a_1 a_2 \ldots a_{n-1} a_n$ is deanonymized to reveal its true address $t = t_1 t_2 \ldots t_{n-1} t_n$, then the adversary also learns that the anonymized address of another true address $t^* = t_1 t_2 \ldots t_{n-1} t_n^*$. should be $a^* = a_1 a_2 \ldots a_{n-1} a_n^*$. Because t and t^* have a common prefix of $n - 1$ bits, their anonymized addresses a and a^* must also have the same $(n-1)$-bit prefix. Based on this idea, Brekne et al. proposed an attack against Crypto-PAn that uses packet injection and frequency analysis to compromise individual addresses in multilinear time [8, 46]. Pang's "divide-and-conquer" approach is regarded as an improvement over Crypto-PAn by processing the subnet and host portions of internal IP address respectively, and thus it decreases the linkability among anonymized addresses [48].

From a trace publisher's view, an indirect attack is probably more dangerous and much harder to defend than a direct attack. Although Pang's *tcpmkpub* [48] is regarded as one of the most state-of-art and comprehensive sanitization solutions, Coull's work [18] shows that this solution is far from enough to provide a "water-proof" protection for a lot of sensitive information. For instance, a "dominant state analysis" characterizes the behavior of each host and then classifies these hosts into logical groups, such as a possible server or an ordinary client, based on their behavior profiles. The subnet clustering algorithm takes advantage of the prefix-preserving anonymization to extract information about the underlying network topology. By associating the above information extracted from the anonymized trace with other auxiliary information, such as DNS records, SMTP traffic, ARP traffic and publicly available website information, their experiment shows that they can not only completely deanonymize some public hosts but also depict detailed traffic properties at some observation points.

Moreover, recent research has extended such indirect de-sanitization attacks to the wireless-network domain. Many researchers have shown that an IEEE 802.11 wireless device's chipset, the firmware or the driver can be identified by either passive fingerprinting [27, 2] (in which the adversary simply observes network traffic) or active fingerprinting [7] (in which the adversary sends out probes and observes the responses). Whether passive or active, these techniques work by building a database of the unique variations in protocol behaviors, as seen across different vendors or implementations, and later discerning the make and model of an unknown Wi-Fi network interface by observing this behavior in network traffic. Knowledge of the brand used by a Wi-Fi user may, when combined with other external information, allow an adversary to de-anonymize that user's traffic within a trace. Using auxiliarly location information, Kumar's work shows the possibility to categorize Wi-Fi users based on their gender [38]. As a further step, Pang et al. demonstrate that by using so-called "implicit identifiers," such as network destinations, SSID probes, broadcast packet size and IEEE 802.11 MAC protocol fields, an adversary can accurately pin down user identities in some circumstances [47].

The above de-sanitization research shows that there is no one sanitization technique that can handle all situations. Any flaw in an anonymization algorithm can lead to disastrous privacy leakage. Beyond the robustness of the anonymization algorithm applied, a desirable outcome depends on the properties of the original unanonymized trace, such as the type and volume of implicit information contained in the trace. To maximally defend against an indirect attack, the trace publisher should have a comprehensive view of the anonymization problem. This means that when sanitizing a trace, the trace publisher should not only focus on the trace itself but also take all auxiliary information into consideration. As shown above, the combination of auxiliary information plays a vital role in a de-sanitization. We regard the progress in network trace de-sanitization as a valuable and indispensable complement to anonymization research.

5.4   Evaluation of Sanitization

Methods to evaluate the efficacy of sanitization methods seem somewhat underdeveloped compared to the wide variety of actual suppression techniques and attacks. Most evaluation papers naturally focus on both quantitative and qualitative measures [16, 64, 10], but some consider the aspects of traces that can be exploited in the sanitization process. For example, the remote and local port features reveal more distinguishing information than the time stamp feature, and therefore re-examining the anonymization policy on these features may improve the efficacy of sanitization [16]. Settling on a particular metric of sanitization effectiveness is difficult, in part due to the variety of features in network traces. It is not immediately clear, for example, how one might meaningfully compare the sanitization of IP addresses with the anonymization of user browsing profiles.

There seem to be two broad types of metric. First, *sanitization metrics* measure how well the sanitization method has fulfilled predefined requirements. In view of the definition of sanitization, the predefined requirements may be those for privacy or secrecy. Second, *usefulness metrics* measure how well the sanitized traces remain useful to the researchers for the purpose of trace analysis.

Table 5.1 summarizes some representative evaluation papers with regard to evaluation metrics, evaluated sanitization methods, and evaluation methods.

Coull et al. [16] evaluate two well-known anonymization methods, CryptoPAn [61] and Pang [48], in terms of the privacy requirement. For the evaluation, they de-anonymize the sanitized data on a few selected fields to quantify the anonymity of the data. They defined the anonymity of each object (e.g., each host) with respect to a feature (e.g., port number) by calculating the entropy of the "similarity" distribution. For an object A, the similarity distribution consists of the probability $P_F(A, i)$ over N objects. This probability expresses how similar the object A is to an unanonymized object i with respect to the feature F. If the anonymity of the object A (in this case, the entropy of the object A) is close to its minimum value (zero), then there probably exists an unanonymized object that is similar to A with respect to the feature F. Otherwise, if the anonymity of the object A is close to its maximum value, $logN$, then the object is not more similar to any one unanonymized object than any other unanonymized object.

Yurcik et al. compare a variety of sanitization methods in terms of how they trade-off anonymity and usefulness [64]. They use the SCRUB-tcpdump network packet anonymization tool [63] to perform various anonymization methods on all fields of the data. The anonymization methods include replacing values with a predefined constant (*black marker*), mapping values to any valid permutation (*pure randomization*), hashing values with a small key (*keyed randomization*), and classifying values into groups (*grouping*). They ex-

Table 5.1: Representative evaluation papers

Paper	Metric	Methods Evaluated	Evaluation Method
Coull [16]	the anonymity of each object (e.g., network host) defined by calculating the entropy from the probability distribution on the object identity	CryptoPAn [61], Pang [48]	simulate adversary's behaviors and compare anonymization techniques by examining the impact on the anonymity of the data.
Yurcik [64]	tradeoff between privacy protection vs. research usefulness (security analysis capability)	black marker, pure randomization, keyed randomization, bilateral classification, and grouping	calculate the difference of intrusion-detection-system alarms before and after the anonymization.
Burkhart [10]	tradeoff between privacy protection (host identification) vs. research usefulness (anomaly detection capability)	IP address truncation	privacy risk is evaluated using a metric based on conditional entropy and usefulness is evaluated using ROC (Receiver Operating Characteristic) curve, i.e., true positive rate of anomaly detection.

amine, as the usefulness metric, the difference in the number of alarms from the Snort IDS, an intrusion-detection system [54], before and after a trace is anonymized.

They showed that some fields (Transport Protocol Number and Total Packet Length) have a zero-sum tradeoff, meaning that "the more network data is anonymized for privacy-protection, the less value the network data may be for security analysis" [64]. However, most of the other fields have a more complex tradeoff (not zero sum), suggesting that both privacy and usefulness can be achieved in certain cases.

More recently, Burkhart et al. investigated the tradeoff between data utility for anomaly detection and the risk of host identification for IP address truncation [10]. They evaluated the risk of de-anonymizing individual IP addresses using a metric based on conditional entropy [4, 37]. For measuring data utility, they compared the detection rates of the DoS and Scan attacks based on IP-based detection metrics (e.g., unique address counts and Shannon entropy) computed on the original traces with those based on IP-based detection metrics computed on anonymized traces. According to their results, truncation effectively prevents host identification but degrades the utility of data for anomaly detection.

They found that the degree of utility degradation depends on the detection metrics used for anomaly detection (e.g., unique address counts vs. entropy) [10]. For example, the entropy detection metrics are more resistant to truncation than unique address counts because the entropy detection metrics better represent the distribution of flows per IP address than the unique address counts metrics, even when the IP addresses are truncated. They also noticed that the detection quality of anomalies degrades much faster in internal addresses than in external addresses. Specifically, the usefulness of internal address counts is lost even for truncation of only 4 bits while the usefulness of external address entropy is virtually unchanged even for truncation of 20 bits.

Research on methods to evaluate the efficacy of sanitization methods is obviously in its infancy, and many research questions remain. Among them, two issues draw our attention more than others: first, only a few evaluation metrics, either sanitization metrics or usefulness metrics, have been suggested that can precisely quantify the efficacy of network data sanitization. Second, even when a metric can give a precise measure of the sanitization efficacy, there may exist a large gap between the semantics of the metric and the semantics understood by users of the sanitization tool, or of the network trace. We discuss these two issues more deeply in Sections 5.5.2 and 5.5.3.

5.5   Challenges and Open Problems

Sanitizing network traces is about managing risk [48]. The amount of risk depends on both the trace publisher's policies and assumptions about the attacker's knowledge and capability. The trace publisher drafts sanitization policies according to his/her specific privacy or secrecy concerns, and these sanitization policies are mapped to a set of sanitization techniques and their configuration. Generally the trace publisher has a "benign wish" when sanitizing traces, that is, to preserve the trace's usefulness as much as possible. However, there is a tradeoff between privacy and usefulness during sanitization. In choosing a sanitization approach, the trace publisher balances privacy and usefulness, informally evaluating the risk that an adversary will be motivated and capable of exposing sensitive information by leveraging benign information the publisher chooses to leave in the trace. Therefore, a top-level challenge for trace-sanitization research is to help trace publishers deal with the tradeoff between anonymity and usability.

In this section, we discuss several challenges to achieve this goal. The challenges include how to quantify private or sensitive information, what metrics to use for evaluating the sanitization result, and how to interpret the sanitization result.

5.5.1   Quantifying Sensitive Information

To protect personal or proprietary interests, the trace publisher would like to know how much private or proprietary information is contained in the trace. This may be difficult, however, for two reasons.

First, the boundary between sensitive and insensitive fields is obscure and changing over time. Some fields of a packet are obviously "sensitive," while others are not. It is well known that a port number is useful to identify a specific service, a MAC address is enough to identify a unique NIC, and an IP address may be useful to identify a specific host. For some other fields, the degree of sensitivity is not clear at first glance, but they actually may contain private information. For example, recent research shows that an attacker can fingerprint a physical host by using only the clock drift in TCP timestamps [34]. The length of an HTTP/TCP connection can identify the web server (if a well-known public server), and the order of IP addresses contained in SYN packets can be used to partly reconstruct the anonymized IP addresses [36]. The point here is that with the development of new techniques, fields that seem to be safe today may become sensitive in the future.

Second, in addition to the explicit values described in each field of a packet or an entry in a log, there is information "implicitly" contained in the network traces. For example, such information includes the traffic pattern of a host, the topology of the traced network, and the mutual relationships between hosts.

Previous sanitization research mainly focused on anonymizing explicit values, and neglected this implicit information. As a result, some de-sanitization techniques, such as dominant state analysis and subnet clustering [18], can dig out valuable information.

We think a great amount of information exists intrinsically in the traces or is intentionally preserved by the specific sanitization technique, such as the network topology discovered by subnet clustering but preserved by Pang's prefix-preserving method [48]. Although trace publishers who intentionally preserve such useful information may be willing to take the risk of de-sanitization, others may not realize that they are preserving such information, or that new methods can extract more than they expect. Nevertheless, we regard this kind of de-sanitization research to be important, if only to inspire new sanitization methods and to help determine the privacy bounds of those methods.

5.5.2 Metrics for Evaluating Sanitization Results

Trace publishers sanitize their traces to achieve both their "sanitization" goals (to protect both personal and operational information) and "usefulness" goals (to protect research value); after sanitization, presumably, they would like to know whether their goals are actually achieved. To evaluate whether their goals are achieved, we need metrics for measuring the degree of sanitization and usefulness of the sanitized traces. It would be even better if these metrics could also be used to help control the tradeoff between the degree of sanitization and usefulness.

Although several generic "anonymity" metrics have been suggested [55, 22, 56, 14], and some were specifically suggested for network traces [16], we have yet to find any generic metric for the "usefulness" of a trace for network analysis. For specific applications like security analysis, some approaches define and exploit a usefulness metric [64, for example].

Different research interests have different understandings of and requirements for the usefulness of network traces. For example, network-security research for wired networks pays most attention to the TCP/IP layers and above, and does not often address the link layer. In the wireless-network security world, however, the focus is largely on the link layer [3]. Even for the same feature in a network trace, such as timestamp, Quality-of-Service research may require micro-second resolution [53], while other research, such as Delay Tolerant Networks, may be satisfied with minute-level resolution. Because of diverse research interests, it is infeasible to generalize the notion of "usefulness" by including the semantics of all possible usages. We think that there is another avenue for future research on the usefulness metric: we need a range of possible metrics that each apply to one or more trace features, then we need a framework that allows one to compose these per-feature metrics to provide an overall metric for the trace's usefulness.

5.5.3   Interpreting Sanitization Results

Although some evaluation papers report comparison results [16, for example], such as which sanitization method is most effective for a given trace and what kind of trace is most effectively sanitized when the same sanitization method is applied, there needs to be more research on how to develop an explicit evaluation stage that informs the trace publisher about the quality of the sanitization result in terms of various sanitization metrics, and on methods to effectively communicate the results to the trace publisher.

Indeed, trace publishers may find it difficult to interpret a sanitization result in terms of sanitization metrics. Generally, publishers are most interested in how to use sanitization methods or tools and how well the methods or tools achieve the publishers' initial goals, that is, for anonymity and usefulness. Therefore, they may prefer an intuitive interpretation of the sanitization result rather than rigorous metrics expressed in complicated mathematics. For example, although entropy has been used often in anonymity research [22, 56, 14], it may be difficult for trace publishers to intuitively interpret an entropy-based metric.

Thus, it remains an open problem to present the evaluation results as high-level feedback about the quality and limits of the sanitization. The feedback may report how well each of the user-specified sanitization goals is achieved, and if any goal fails, to identify a reason and to recommend a method that may resolve the conflict resulting from the tradeoff between anonymity and usability.

5.6   Case Study: Dartmouth Internet Security Testbed

In Section 5.1.1 we noted the that it is often tremendously difficult to obtain permission to collect network traces on a production network, not to mention the logistical and technical challenges of establishing a robust and effective trace-capture system. In this section, we offer as a case study our experiences in deploying the Dartmouth Internet Security Testbed (DIST) [23]. We hope this case study offers practical lessons for others who may wish to collect network traces within their own enterprise.

Several years ago, in January 2006, we sought to build a large testbed for conducting network-security research at Dartmouth College. The testbed would contain both wired- and wireless-network components, and would cover a substantial fraction of the campus production network. The wireless-network infrastructure would be used initially for trace capture, but the hardware would also be useful for other wireless-network experiments including controlled studies of Wi-Fi network attacks. The wired-network infrastructure would only be used for capture and real-time analysis of traffic on the campus backbone network. Although research was the primary purpose of and motivation for the infrastructure, the Dartmouth network-operations group was enthusiastically interested in leveraging the infrastructure and the researchers' results for operational monitoring of the network.

The wireless-network infrastructure consists of about 210 Wi-Fi access points, of the same brand and model Dartmouth uses to provide its production Wi-Fi network on campus. We had developed a scalable network-monitoring and intrusion-detection software base in our MAP project [57], in which we reflash the Aruba AP70 access points with OpenWRT Linux and run our own software for sniffing on the Wi-Fi network interface. This software uses pcap to capture Wi-Fi frames and packs multiple frames into a custom format for transmission to our central server for real-time analysis and (optionally) storage.

The wired-network infrastructure includes a one-way feed of the campus network traffic, from a span port on one of the backbone routers, into a server located in the central computing facility. The research goal was to install and evaluate various network intrusion-detection systems, including several developed by Dartmouth researchers under previous projects, to evaluate their real-time performance on huge traffic flows.

Needless to say, the installation and operation of such an infrastructure requires careful planning and communication with the relevant campus departments. Although we had been collecting Wi-Fi network traces since 2001, the new wireless-network infrastructure was going to capture an order of magnitude more data, and the new wired-network infrastructure was going to capture data that had never been captured for research purposes at Dartmouth. Furthermore, the physical installation of over 200 Wi-Fi access points in about 10 large buildings around campus meant drilling holes into walls, leading to potential concerns about aesthetics.

The first step was to obtain permission from the Network Services group within Peter Kiewit Computing Services (PKCS), the central campus IT office. This step was easy, because we had developed the concept in collaboration with Network Services. We are fortunate to have a group of talented professionals who are also enthusiastic collaborators with researchers. We have repeatedly heard from colleagues, however, that this hurdle is very difficult in their organizations.

The next step was to obtain formal permission from Dartmouth's Committee for Protection of Human Subjects (CPHS). CPHS services as the Institutional Review Board (IRB) for Dartmouth; all universities with federal research funding are required to operate an IRB so that research involving human subjects can be evaluated to ensure that risks are acceptable and subjects provide informed consent where appropriate. Our Wi-Fi network tracing effort was approved by CPHS several years prior, and our proposed effort was a subset of what we had done earlier, so a simple renewal was sufficient. Our wired-network effort was new, however, so we submitted a new project application to CPHS.

Meanwhile, we set out to obtain permission from the department heads located in the buildings where we hoped to place Wi-Fi sniffers. These buildings included the main library complex, the school of engineering, the school of business, a gymnasium, a student center, several dormitories, and several academic buildings. In some cases, we chose sites where renovation was underway and our sniffers (and their wiring) could be easily installed in the construction process, requiring less cost and no inconvenience to the building residents. In all cases, we met personally with the lead staff in each department, describing what we planned to do. We walked through their building, sometimes repeatedly, discussing in detail the placement of sniffers and their wiring. Each building required several months of planning to obtain permission, choose sites, confirm the sites with department staff, obtain quotes from electricians, install the wiring, and install the sniffers.

During this process, Sicker et al. published a paper on the legal issues involved in network trace capture [58]. The paper provides a thoughtful review of the many issues involved, and yet concludes that the legal status of network trace-collection for research purposes is not entirely clear. We consulted with the university counsel in depth, and with outside consultants, concluding that such trace collection could proceed as long as the research activity was closely coupled with network-operations activity. We had involved PKCS Network Services from the start, but we adjusted our research program to more directly meet their needs; our trace-capture facility can now support both operational and research goals simultaneously.

Furthermore, because of the scale of this effort, and the sensitive issues related to the privacy of network users, we met with several leadership groups on campus to explain our plans, answer their questions, obtain their feedback, and ultimately seek official approval from the College to proceed with trace collection. In particular, we met with the high-level faculty committee responsible for sponsored research and the provost-level council that includes all campus deans. In both cases we obtained valuable feedback that helped us to clarify our operating parameters. We developed an increasingly crisp understanding of the privacy risks and our mechanisms for mitigating those risks.

Ultimately, we decided to conduct a careful, objective study of our trace-collection infrastructure and our privacy-protection mechanisms. The College hired an outside expert, a researcher with several years of network-tracing experience in academic settings, to visit campus, interview the research teams, and to study our trace-collection infrastructure in detail. This visit served as a tremendous help to us, providing a critical eye to help us recognize where our plans could be improved or become more specific. In the end, based on the expert's advice and internal deliberations, the College leadership decided that the risks posed by the wired-network infrastructure (given the type of data needed by the researchers) were not easily mitigated, and the wired-network capture will not proceed. For the Wi-Fi infrastructure, we decided to add additional layers of security — to ensure that the infrastructure itself can not be compromised by attackers — and additional layers of encryption and in-line anonymization to protect the privacy of network users. If, in the future, we make non-trivial changes to our data-collection infrastructure we will again ask the expert to evaluate our plans.

An important part of the process is communication and public notice, especially since informed consent is not feasible in an open wireless network covering numerous buildings and a shifting population. Every one of our sniffers is labeled with the URL of our website describing the project. We are posting notices at the entries to each building, informing visitors of the data-collection effort and directing them to the website for further information. At the request of the library, we are posting notices on every table in public areas of the library. Finally, we issued a press release describing our research and the scope of the data collection.

At this writing, our Wi-Fi sniffing infrastructure is ready to begin operation. We include several layers of security on the sniffers, including extremely limited services, narrow firewall openings, no crypto keys in persistent storage, and frequent defensive port-scans. We discard all but the MAC layer from each frame, then encrypt each packet of captured frames before sending them to the server; at the server they are decrypted and immediately anonymized before being used for inline analysis or storage for offline analysis. The anonymization map is generated anew for each experiment, using a random seed that is discarded after use. As a result, very little sensitive information is captured and the most sensitive components (MAC addresses and SSIDs) are thoroughly anonymized.

The result is, we expect, a highly secure, privacy sensitive, scalable capture system for Wi-Fi networks, larger and more secure than any other ever assembled. We intend to use the infrastructure to collect operationally useful data for Network Services, and to serve our own ongoing research in trace anonymization techniques.

5.7 Summary and Conclusion

It can be technically and logistically challenging to collect large amounts of real network data. Sharing such data with the larger research community becomes an imperative for advancing scientific progress. Similarly, network operators and engineers look for ways to reliably share network traces to help analyze network problems. Unfortunately, legal, ethical, and privacy concerns complicate these sharing efforts.

In this chapter, we survey methods for sanitizing traces, methods for de-sanitizing traces, and methods for evaluating sanitization algorithms and tools. We discuss much of the research that describe methods to (or demonstrate the failure of methods to) protect the privacy of network users and the confidentiality of certain network properties.

Although this body of work contains numerous examples of methods for sanitizing a particular feature or set of fields (that is, identifying such information and blanking it out or transforming it in some way to suppress it), these methods are often bypassable by de-sanitization techniques that consider inter-feature or inter-record relationships or external information.

We hypothesize that, because researchers and network operators who want to share trace data have access to only a few tools for quantitatively assessing the *quality* of a particular sanitization technique or resulting dataset, it is difficult for much substantial progress to be made on anticipating and defeating de-sanitization attacks. In essence, the risks of certain classes of sanitization methods are not well understood because metrics for evaluating the efficacy of classes of de-sanitization attacks are in their infancy.

Efforts to improve our ability to measure the efficacy of sanitization are of paramount concern. As we note above, metrics, be they simple measures of a particular feature or complicated mathematical models, face an underlying problem: there is a large gap between their semantics and the semantics understood by users of the sanitization tool, or of the network trace. The key problem is that the semantics of sanitization success remains unclear and unintuitive for trace producers and (legitimate) trace consumers. Any such metric must simultaneously convey (1) how well sensitive information has been suppressed (that is, the level of effort for an attacker to recover this information) and (2) the potential loss for legitimate research or operational uses. Metrics that have these semantics can then be used with confidence in decisions about which traces, portions thereof, or derivative statistics can or should be shared with various consumers.

Acknowledgments

This chapter results from a research program in the Institute for Security, Technology, and Society (ISTS), supported by the U.S. Department of Homeland Security under Grant Award Number 2006-CS-001-000001, by the CRAWDAD archive at Dartmouth College (funded by Award 0454062 from the National Science Foundation), and by the NetSANI project at Dartmouth College (funded by Award CNS-0831409 from the National Science Foundation). The views and conclusions contained in this document are those of the authors and should not be interpreted as necessarily representing the official policies, either expressed or implied, of the U.S. Department of Homeland Security or the National Science Foundation.

References

[1] Charu C. Aggarwal and Philip S. Yu. *Privacy-Preserving Data Mining: Models and Algorithms.* Springer-Verlag, 2008.

[2] Kevin Bauer, Damon Mccoy, Ben Greenstein, Dirk Grunwald, and Douglas Sicker. Using wireless physical layer information to construct implicit identifiers. In *Proceedings of HotPETS 2008*, July 2008.

[3] John Bellardo and Stefan Savage. 802.11 denial-of-service attacks: Real vulnerabilities and practical solutions. In *Proceedings of the USENIX Security Symposium*, pages 15–28. USENIX, August 2003.

[4] Michele Bezzi. An entropy based method for measuring anonymity. In *Security and Privacy in Communications Networks and the Workshops, 2007. SecureComm 2007. Third International Conference on*, pages 28–32, Sept. 2007.

[5] Matt Bishop, Rick Crawford, Bhume Bhumiratana, Lisa Clark, and Karl Levitt. Some problems in sanitizing network data. In *Proceedings of the IEEE International Workshops on Enabling Technologies: Infrastructure for Collaborative Enterprises (WETICE)*, pages 307–312. IEEE Press, 2006.

[6] Ethan Blanton. TCPurify: A "sanitary" sniffer, 2000. http://masaka.cs.ohiou.edu/~eblanton/tcpurify/.

[7] Sergey Bratus, Cory Cornelius, David Kotz, and Daniel Peebles. Active behavioral fingerprinting of wireless devices. In *Proceedings of the ACM Conference on Wireless Network Security (WiSec)*, pages 56–61. ACM Press, New York, NY, USA, 2008.

[8] Tønnes Brekne, André Årnes, and Arne Øslebø. Anonymization of IP traffic monitoring data: Attacks on two prefix-preserving anonymization schemes and some proposed remedies. In *Proceedings of the International Symposium on Privacy Enhancing Technologies (PET)*, volume 3856 of *Lecture Notes in Computer Science*, pages 179–196. Springer-Verlag New York, Inc., NY, USA, 2005.

[9] Justin Brickell and Vitaly Shmatikov. The cost of privacy: destruction of data-mining utility in anonymized data publishing. In *Proceedings of the 14th ACM SIGKDD International Conference on Knowledge Discovery and Data Mining (KDD '08)*, pages 70–78. ACM, August 2008.

[10] Martin Burkhart, Daniela Brauckhoff, Martin May, and Elisa Boschi. The risk-utility tradeoff for IP address truncation. In *Proceedings of the 1st ACM Workshop on Network Data Anonymization (NDA '08)*, pages 23–30. ACM, October 2008.

[11] Aaron J. Burstein. Toward a culture of cybersecurity research. *Technical Report* 1113014, UC Berkeley Public Law Research Paper, 2008.

[12] Cooperative Association for Internet Data Analysis (CAIDA), 2008. http://www.caida.org/.

[13] V. Ciriani, S. De Capitani di Vimercati, S. Foresti, and P. Samarati. k-Anonymity. In T. Yu and S. Jajodia, editors, *Secure Data Management in Decentralized Systems*. Springer-Verlag, 2007.

[14] Sebastian Clauß. A framework for quantification of linkability within a privacy-enhancing identity management system. In Güter Müller, editor, *Proceedings of Emerging Trends in Information and Communication Security*, volume 3995 of *Lecture Notes in Computer Science*, pages 191–205. Springer-Verlag New York, Inc., NY, USA, 2006.

[15] S. E. Coull, M. P. Collins, C. V. Wright, F. Monrose, and M. K. Reiter. On web browsing privacy in anonymized netflows. In *Proceedings of the USENIX Security Symposium*, pages 1–14. USENIX, 2007.

[16] Scott Coull, Charles Wright, Fabian Monrose, Angelos Keromytis, and Michael Reiter. Taming the Devil: Techniques for evaluating anonymized network data. In *Proceedings of the Annual Symposium on Network and Distributed System Security (NDSS)*. IEEE Press, February 2008.

[17] Scott E. Coull, Fabian Monrose, Michael K. Reiter, and Michael D. Bailey. The Challenges of Effectively Anonymizing Network Data. In *Proceedings of the Cybersecurity Applications & Technology Conference For Homeland Security (CATCH '09)*, pages 230–236, March 2009.

[18] Scott E. Coull, Charles V. Wright, Fabian Monrose, Michael P. Collins, and Michael K. Reiter. Playing Devil's advocate: Inferring sensitive information from anonymized network traces. In *Proceedings of the Annual Symposium on Network and Distributed System Security (NDSS)*. IEEE Press, February 2007.

[19] Community Resource for Archiving Wireless Data At Dartmouth (CRAWDAD), 2007. http://www.crawdad.org/.

[20] R. Crawford, M. Bishop, B. Bhumiratana, L. Clark, and K. Levitt. Sanitization models and their limitations. In *Proceedings of the Workshop on New Security Paradigms (NSPW)*, pages 41–56. ACM Press, New York, NY, USA, 2007.

[21] Internet measurement data catalog (DatCat), 2008. http://www.datcat.org.

[22] Claudia Díaz, Stefaan Seys, Joris Claessens, and Bart Preneel. Towards measuring anonymity. In *Proceedings of the International Symposium on Privacy Enhancing Technologies (PET)*, volume 2482 of *Lecture Notes in Computer Science*, pages 54–68. Springer-Verlag New York, Inc., NY, USA, 2002.

[23] Dartmouth Internet Security Testbed, 2010. `http://www.cs.dartmouth.edu/~dist/`.

[24] DHSIELD, 2008. `http://www.dshield.org/`.

[25] The Enron email dataset, 2008. `http://www.cs.cmu.edu/~enron/`.

[26] Jinliang Fan, Jun Xu, Mostafa H. Ammar, and Sue B. Moon. Prefix-preserving IP address anonymization: measurement-based security evaluation and a new cryptography-based scheme. *Computer Networks*, 46(2):253–272, 2004.

[27] Jason Franklin, Damon McCoy, Parisa Tabriz, Vicentiu Neagoe, Jamie Van Randwyk, and Douglas Sicker. Passive data link layer 802.11 wireless device driver fingerprinting. In *Proceedings of the USENIX Security Symposium*. USENIX, 2006.

[28] Shantanu Gattani and Thomas E. Daniels. Reference models for network data anonymization. In *Proceedings of the ACM Workshop on Network Data Anonymization (NDA)*, pages 41–48. ACM Press, New York, NY, USA, 2008.

[29] Saul Hansell. AOL removes search data on group of web users, 8 August 2006. `http://www.nytimes.com/2006/08/08/business/media/08aol.html`.

[30] M. Harvan and J. Schonwalder. Prefix- and lexicographical-order-preserving IP address anonymization. In *Proceedings of the IEEE/IFIP Network Operations and Management Symposium (NOMS)*, pages 519–526, 2006.

[31] Vijay S. Iyengar. Transforming data to satisfy privacy constraints. In *KDD '02: Proceedings of the eighth ACM SIGKDD International Conference on Knowledge Discovery and Data Mining*, pages 279–288, New York, NY, USA, 2002. ACM.

[32] Douglas J. Kelly, Richard A. Raines, Michael R. Grimaila, Rusty O. Baldwin, and Barry E. Mullins. A survey of state-of-the-art in anonymity metrics. In *Proceedings of the ACM Workshop on Network Data Anonymization (NDA)*, pages 31–40. ACM Press, New York, NY, USA, 2008.

[33] Daniel Kifer and Johannes Gehrke. Injecting utility into anonymized datasets. In *SIGMOD '06: Proceedings of the 2006 ACM SIGMOD In-*

ternational Conference on Management of Data, pages 217–228, New York, NY, USA, 2006. ACM.

[34] Tadayoshi Kohno, Andre Broido, and K. C. Claffy. Remote physical device fingerprinting. *Proceedings of the IEEE Symposium on Security and Privacy (S&P)*, 2005.

[35] D. Koukis, S. Antonatos, D. Antoniades, E. P. Markatos, and P. Trimintzios. A generic anonymization framework for network traffic. In *Proceedings of the IEEE International Conference on Communications (ICC)*, volume 5, Istanbul, Turkey, June 2006. IEEE Press.

[36] D. Koukis, Spyros Antonatos, and Kostas G. Anagnostakis. On the privacy risks of publishing anonymized IP network traces. In *Proceedings of the International Conference on Communications and Multimedia Security (CMS)*, volume 4237 of *Lecture Notes in Computer Science*, pages 22–32. Springer-Verlag New York, Inc., NY, USA, 2006.

[37] A. Kounine and M. Bezzi. Accessing disclosure risk in anonymized datasets. In *FloCon 2008*, January 2008.

[38] Udayan Kumar, Nikhil Yadav, and Ahmed Helmy. Gender-based feature analysis in campus-wide wlans. *SIGMOBILE Mob. Comput. Commun. Rev.*, 12(1):40–42, 2008.

[39] Kristen Lefevre, David Dewitt, and Raghu Ramakrishnan. Workload-aware anonymization. In *KDD*, 2006.

[40] Ninghui Li, Tiancheng Li, and Suresh Venkatasubramanian. t-closeness: Privacy beyond k-anonymity and ℓ-diversity. In *Proc. of ICDE*, pages 106–115, 2007.

[41] Y. Li, Adam Slagell, K. Luo, and W. Yurcik. CANINE: A combined conversion and anonymization tool for processing netflows for security. In *Proceedings of the International Conference on Telecommunication Systems, Modeling and Analysis*, November 2005.

[42] K. Luo, Y. Li, Adam Slagell, and W. Yurcik. CANINE: A netflow converter/anonymizer tool for format interoperability and secure sharing. In *Proceedings of FLOCON Network Flow Analysis Workshop*, September 2005.

[43] Ashwin Machanavajjhala, Johannes Gehrke, Daniel Kifer, and Muthuramakrishnan Venkitasubramaniam. ℓ-diversity: Privacy beyond k-anonymity. In *Proc. of ICDE*, pages 24–85, 2006.

[44] Greg Minshall. TCPdPriv: Program for eliminating confidential information from traces, 2005. http://ita.ee.lbl.gov/html/contrib/tcpdpriv.html.

[45] Arvind Narayanan and Vitaly Shmatikov. Robust de-anonymization of large sparse datasets. In *Proceedings of the IEEE Symposium on Security and Privacy (S&P)*, pages 111–125. IEEE Press, 2008.

[46] Lasse Overlier, Tonnes Brekne, and Andre Arnes. Non-expanding transaction specific pseudonymization for IP traffic monitoring. In Yvo Desmedt, Huaxiong Wang, Yi Mu, and Yongqing Li, editors, *Proceedings of Cryptology and Network Security (CANS)*, volume 3810 of *Lecture Notes in Computer Science*, pages 261–273. Springer-Verlag New York, Inc., NY, USA, 2005.

[47] Jeffrey Pang, Ben Greenstein, Ramakrishna Gummadi, Srinivasan Seshan, and David Wetherall. 802.11 user fingerprinting. In *Proceedings of the ACM International Conference on Mobile Computing and Networking (MobiCom)*, pages 99–110. ACM Press, New York, NY, USA, 2007.

[48] Ruoming Pang, Mark Allman, Vern Paxson, and Jason Lee. The devil and packet trace anonymization. *ACM SIGCOMM Computer Communication Review*, 36(1):29–38, 2006.

[49] Andreas Pfitzmann and Marit Hansen. Anonymity, unobservability, and pseudonymity: A consolidated proposal for terminology, February 2008. http://dud.inf.tu-dresden.de/Anon_Terminology.shtml.

[50] Phillip Porras and Vitaly Shmatikov. Large-scale collection and sanitization of network security data: risks and challenges. In *Proceedings of the Workshop on New Security Paradigms (NSPW)*, pages 57–64. ACM Press, New York, NY, USA, 2007.

[51] Protected Repository for the Defense of Infrastructure against Cyber Threats (PREDICT), 2008. http://www.predict.org.

[52] Ramaswamy Ramaswamy and Tilman Wolf. High-speed prefix-preserving IP address anonymization for passive measurement systems. *ACM/IEEE Transactions on Networking (TON)*, 15(1):26–39, January 2007.

[53] Maxim Raya, Jean-Pierre Hubaux, and Imad Aad. DOMINO: Detecting MAC layer greedy behavior in IEEE 802.11 hotspots. *IEEE Transactions on Mobile Computing*, 5(12):1691–1705, 2006.

[54] Martin Roesch. Snort: A free, open source network intrusion detection and prevention system, 1998. http://www.snort.org/.

[55] P. Samarati and L. Sweeney. Protecting privacy when disclosing information: k-anonymity and its enforcement through generalization and suppression. *Technical Report* SRI-CSL-98-04, Computer Science Laboratory, SRI International, 1998.

[56] Andrei Serjantov and George Danezis. Towards an information theoretic metric for anonymity. In *Proceedings of the International Symposium on Privacy Enhancing Technologies (PET)*, volume 2482 of *Lecture Notes in Computer Science*, pages 41–53. Springer-Verlag New York, Inc., NY, USA, 2002.

[57] Yong Sheng, Guanling Chen, Hongda Yin, Keren Tan, Udayan Deshpande, Bennet Vance, David Kotz, Andrew Campbell, Chris McDonald, Tristan Henderson, and Joshua Wright. MAP: A scalable monitoring system for dependable 802.11 wireless networks. *IEEE Wireless Communications*, 15(5):10–18, October 2008.

[58] Douglas C. Sicker, Paul Ohm, and Dirk Grunwald. Legal issues surrounding monitoring during network research. In *Proceedings of the Internet Measurement Conference (IMC)*, pages 141–148. ACM Press, New York, NY, USA, 2007.

[59] Adam Slagell, Kiran Lakkaraju, and Katherine Luo. FLAIM: A multi-level anonymization framework for computer and network logs. In *Proceedings of the USENIX Large Installation System Administration Conference (LISA)*, December 2006.

[60] Ke Wang, Benjamin C. M. Fung, and Philip S. Yu. Template-based privacy preservation in classification problems. In *ICDM '05: Proceedings of the Fifth IEEE International Conference on Data Mining*, pages 466–473, Washington, DC, USA, 2005. IEEE Computer Society.

[61] Jun Xu, Jinliang Fan, M. H. Ammar, and S. B. Moon. Prefix-preserving IP address anonymization: measurement-based security evaluation and a new cryptography-based scheme. In *Proceedings of the IEEE International Conference on Network Protocols (ICNP)*, pages 280–289, November 2002.

[62] Tatu Ylonen. Thoughts on how to mount an attack on tcpdpriv's "-a50" option, 2009. http://ita.ee.lbl.gov/html/contrib/attack50/attack50.html.

[63] William Yurcik, Clay Woolam, Greg Hellings, Latifur Khan, and Bhavani Thuraisingham. SCRUB-tcpdump: A multi-level packet anonymizer demonstrating privacy/analysis tradeoffs. In *Proceedings of the IEEE International Workshop on the Value of Security through Collaboration (SECOVAL)*, pages 49–56. IEEE Press, September 2007.

[64] William Yurcik, Clay Woolam, Greg Hellings, Latifur Khan, and Bhavani M. Thuraisingham. Toward trusted sharing of network packet traces using anonymization: Single-field privacy/analysis tradeoffs. *Technical Report* 0710.3979v2, arXiv, 2007.

[65] Jianqing Zhang, Nikita Borisov, and William Yurcik. Outsourcing security analysis with anonymized logs. In *Proceedings of the International*

Workshop on the Value of Security through Collaboration (SECOVAL). IEEE Press, 2006.

[66] Qianli Zhang and Xing Li. An IP address anonymization scheme with multiple access levels. In Ilyoung Chong and Kenji Kawahara, editors, *Proceedings of Information Networking: Advances in Data Communications and Wireless Networks (ICOIN)*, volume 3961 of *Lecture Notes in Computer Science*, pages 793–802. Springer-Verlag New York, Inc., NY, USA, 2006.

Chapter 6

Output Privacy in Stream Mining

Ting Wang

Distributed Data Intensive Systems Lab, College of Computing, Georgia Institute of Technology, Atlanta, Georgia

Ling Liu

Distributed Data Intensive Systems Lab, College of Computing, Georgia Institute of Technology, Atlanta, Georgia

6.1 Introduction

Privacy preservation is widely recognized as an important requirement in large-scale data integration and data mining systems that involve private personal information, e.g., medical data or census data. Individuals were usually unwilling to contribute their information if they knew that the privacy of the data could be compromised. A plethora of work has been done on preserving *input privacy* for static data [4, 8, 17, 26, 29], which assume an untrusted mining-service provider and enforces privacy restrictions and regulations by modifying the raw data before performing the mining task, wherein the goal is to achieve a desired balance between privacy and utility.

In a strict sense, however, privacy preservation not only refers to preventing unauthorized access to raw data that could lead to leakage of sensitive information, but also includes eliminating unwanted disclosure of sensitive patterns through mining output; that is, the published mining output should not be informative enough to infer properties possessed only by a few individuals, which we refer to as *output privacy*. The existence of output-privacy risk is explained by the fact that existing input-privacy-preserving techniques are designed to make the patterns constructed over sanitized data as close as, if not identical to, that built over raw data, in order to guarantee the output

143

utility. This *no-outcome-change* property is considered as a pillar of privacy-preserving data mining [6]. As long as the significant statistical information of raw data is preserved, the risk of disclosing private information exists; also, one can conclude that the preservation of input and output privacy is not necessarily equivalent.

For instance, consider a nursing-care database that records the observed symptoms of the patients in a hospital. By mining such a database, one can discover valuable information about syndromes characterizing particular diseases. The released mining output, however, can also be leveraged to uncover combinations of symptoms that are so special that only rare people match them. This qualifies as severe threats to individuals' privacy. Assume that Alice knows that Bob has certain symptoms a, b, but not c ($\bar{c}$). By analyzing the mining output, she finds that only one person in the hospital matching the specific combination of $\{a, b, \bar{c}\}$, and only one having all $\{a, b, \bar{c}, d\}$. She can then conclude that the one must be Bob, who also has the symptom d. Furthermore, by studying another medical database, she might learn that the combination of $\{a, b, \bar{c}, d\}$ is linked to a rare disease with high chance. This clearly qualifies as a privacy-intruding conclusion.

The example above exposes an output-privacy breach in a single-time mining output release; this issue is even more severe in stream mining, wherein the mining results need to be published in a continuous and in-time manner: not only a single-time release might contain privacy breaches, but also multiple releases could potentially be exploited in combination, given the overlap of the corresponding input data.

This chapter presents a survey of a variety of countermeasures against mining-output inference in literatures, with the aim of pinpointing individual research efforts on the grand map of output-privacy protection, and identifying open issues and technical challenges worthy of further investigation.

The first part of this chapter presents an overview of privacy preservation techniques in data mining. Specifically, we attempt to answer the following three questions. First, what is the current state of the research on privacy protection in data mining, especially stream mining? Second, what is the difference between input and output privacy protection? Third, is it sufficient to apply the input-privacy-preserving models and techniques developed to date for protecting output privacy?

The second part is devoted to a brief survey of the research on output privacy by taking a close examination at a variety of countermeasures against adversarial inference over mining output. In particular, we discuss two categories of approaches, namely, *reactive* and *proactive* approaches, and analyze their strengths and weaknesses.

In the final part of this chapter, we conduct a concrete case study of a light-weighted countermeasure in the context of frequent-pattern mining over data streams, a well known data mining problem. We exemplify this case to illustrate the general principles of designing output-privacy solutions for data mining, especially stream mining. We conclude this chapter with discussing

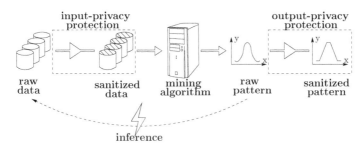

FIGURE 6.1: Overall framework of privacy-preserving data mining. © IEEE 2008 [35].

open issues and technical challenges that demand further work.

6.2 Grand Map of Privacy-Preserving Data Mining

Recently, the data management and mining community has witnessed a gradual shift to the *database-as-service* paradigm [19]: an increasing number of data mining and management tasks are outsourced to third-party service providers. While offering reliable storage and powerful computation capabilities, such services also open the door for compromising individuals' private sensitive information, e.g., disease history, salary, and credit information. Understandably, it is unacceptable to directly present the raw data to the mining-service provider; rather, the input data should be *sanitized* before the mining task is performed. As illustrated in the first three steps of Figure 6.1, this process is referred to as *input-privacy* protection.

6.2.1 Input Privacy

Intensive research efforts have been directed to addressing input-privacy concerns. The work of [2, 4] paved the way for the rapidly expanding field of privacy-preserving data mining; they established the main theme of privacy-preserving data mining as to provide sufficient privacy guarantee while minimizing information loss of mining output. Under this framework, a variety of techniques have been developed.

The work [2, 4, 17] applied data perturbation, specifically random noise addition, to association-rule mining, with the objective of maintaining sufficiently accurate estimation of frequent patterns while preventing disclosure of specific records. In the context of privacy-preserving data classification, the work in [8] identified the important geometric properties with respect to classification models, and presented a random rotation perturbation scheme that preserves data privacy while maintaining the perfect data utility for classification.

For centralized data publication, group-based anonymization approaches have been considered. The existing work can be roughly classified into two categories: the first one aims at devising anonymization models and principles as the criteria to measure the quality of privacy protection, e.g., k-anonymity [29], l-diversity [26], and $(\epsilon, \delta)^k$-dissimilarity [36]; the second category of work explores the possibility of fulfilling the proposed anonymization principles, meanwhile preserving data utility to the maximum extent [23, 27]. Cryptographic tools have also been used to construct privacy-preserving data mining protocols, e.g., secure multi-party computation [25, 32]. Nevertheless, all these techniques focus on protecting input privacy for static data.

Quite recently, the work [24] addressed the problem of preserving input privacy for streaming data, by on-line analysis of correlation structures of multivariate streams. The work [6] distinguished the scenario of data custodian, wherein the data collector is entrusted, and proposed a perturbation scheme that guarantees no change in mining output. In [20, 22], it is shown that a hacker could potentially employ spectral analysis to separate artificially added random noises from real values in multi-attributed data.

6.2.2   Output Privacy

It might seem at the first glance that there would be no privacy violation if the input raw data is effectively sanitized before being sent to the service provider, i.e., sufficient input-privacy protection. Unintuitively, from the released mining output (statistically significant patterns), it is still possible to infer patterns that match only few individuals appearing in the database (vulnerable patterns). This phenomenon is explained by the fact that in order to maintain mining-output utility, input-privacy-preserving techniques are designed to make the mining output constructed over sanitized data as close as, if not identical to that built over raw data; therefore, as long as the statistically significant information of original data is preserved in the sanitized data, the risk of exposing individuals' private information exists.

As a concrete example, let us consider frequent-pattern mining over data streams. An itemset is a subset of a finite set of items. A database consists of a set of records, each corresponding to a non-empty itemset. The support of an itemset I with respect to a database is defined as the number of records in the database, which contain I as a subset. Frequent-pattern mining [3] aims at finding all itemsets with support exceeding a user defined threshold, called the *minimum support*. With the setting of data stream, a sliding-window model is usually applied [9, 30]: the set of records within a most recent sliding window is considered as a dataset, and one attempts to discover all frequent patterns appearing in this window.

Figure 6.2 illustrates a snapshot of a data stream, wherein $a \sim h$ and

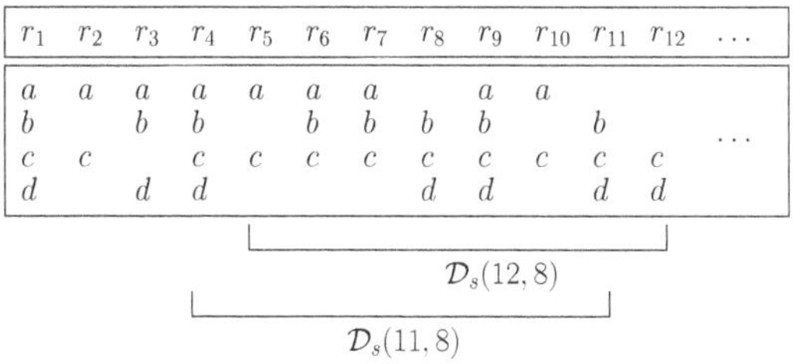

r_1	r_2	r_3	r_4	r_5	r_6	r_7	r_8	r_9	r_{10}	r_{11}	r_{12}	...
a	a	a	a	a	a	a		a	a			
b		b	b		b	b	b	b		b		...
c	c		c	c	c	c	c	c	c	c	c	
d		d	d				d	d		d	d	

$$\mathcal{D}_s(12,8)$$

$$\mathcal{D}_s(11,8)$$

FIGURE 6.2: A snapshot of a data stream, where $\mathcal{D}_s(n, m)$ denotes a sliding window of size m and with the most recent record as n. © IEEE 2008 [35].

$r_1 \sim r_{12}$ represent the set of items and records, respectively. Assuming the minimum support as 3, within the window $r_5 \sim r_{12}$ ($\mathcal{D}_s(12,8)$), the set of itemsets $\{c, bc, ac, abc\}$ are all frequent, since their support values exceed 3. The release of these patterns, however, is not safe, since given their support, one is able to infer the support of the pattern $a\bar{b}c$ (where $\bar{x}$ represents the negation of an item x) to be 1. This indicates that a unique record (r_{12}) in the database exhibits the pattern $a\bar{b}c$, which is clearly a privacy violation against the individual corresponding to this very record.

Though the example above only exposes a privacy breach in the output of frequent-pattern mining, such a breach essentially exists for all data mining tasks, as long as the statistically significant information is preserved in the mining output. It is also noted that this privacy issue is even more severe in stream mining: the mining results need to be published in a continuous manner; not only might a single release contain privacy breaches, but also multiple releases could potentially be exploited in combination, given the overlap of the corresponding input data. Taking the sliding window model as an example, in addition to the leakage in the output of each single window (*intra-window* breach), the output of multiple overlapping windows could be combined to infer sensitive information (*inter-window* breach), even if each window itself contains no privacy breach per se.

A question therefore naturally arises: is it sufficient to apply input-privacy-preserving mechanisms to address output-privacy concerns? Unfortunately, most input-privacy-preserving models and techniques developed to date fail to satisfy the requirement of countering inference attacks over mining output: many of these proposals develop data perturbation techniques to sanitize the raw data while keeping the constructed patterns possibly close to that built over the raw data. The existing methods differ from one to another in terms of concrete mechanisms used to maximize the input-privacy guarantee and at the same time minimize output-utility loss due to data perturbation. Nevertheless, the adversarial attack over input data (raw records) is significantly different from that over mining output (patterns or models), which makes the existing studies on the attack resilience of input-privacy-preserving techniques inapplicable for the inference attack over mining output.

Therefore, one can conclude that in addition to the input-privacy-preserving mechanism, it is necessary to introduce another layer of protection, *output-privacy* protection, into the privacy-preserving data mining framework, shown as the last step of Figure 6.1.

6.3   From Statistical Databases to Data Mining

From the mid 70s through early 80s, the research on statistical databases has produced extensive publications on disclosure control in the context of statistical query processing, and documented a variety of adversarial inference techniques over published aggregation-query results, and correspondingly, a wealth of defense mechanisms. It is noted that the essence of output-privacy protection in data mining is similar to that of disclosure control in statistical databases: both concern providing statistical information without compromising sensitive information regarding individuals.

Nevertheless, they also exhibit significant differences which render the techniques and models developed in one domain not directly applicable for the other. First, query processing in statistical databases typically involves only simple statistical quantities, e.g., min, max, and avg; while mining output (model or pattern) usually demonstrates much more complicated structures, leading to more delicate requirements for output utility. Second, compared with statistical databases, output-privacy protection in data mining usually faces stricter requirements regarding processing time and space; this is especially true for the case of stream mining, wherein it is required to release output in an in-time manner when processing a high-rate incoming data stream. Thus, computational intensive analysis adopted by statistical databases is usually not an option for protecting output privacy.

This section presents a brief survey of a plethora of inference-control mechanisms, with the aim of analyzing their strengths, weaknesses, and underlying assumptions. In general, existing solutions can be roughly classified into two categories: the *reactive* approaches, which attempt to analyze the statistical output to detect all potential breaches and then eliminate them, i.e., the *detecting-then-removing* paradigm; the *proactive* approaches, which require no explicit detection of breaches, and aim at immunizing the output from malicious inference by injecting an appropriate amount of uncertainty while preserving its utility. We summarize the literatures on these two categories of approaches in Section 6.3.1 and 6.3.2, respectively.

6.3.1 Reactive Approaches

The most straightforward solution to preserving output privacy is to detect and eliminate all potential privacy breaches, i.e., the *detecting-then-removing* strategy, which stemmed from disclosure control in statistical databases. The concrete mechanisms, according to their applied scenarios, can be categorized as either *query restriction* or *data perturbation*. The query restriction family includes controlling the size of query results [18], restricting the overlap between successive queries [15], suppressing the cells of small size [12], and auditing queries to check privacy compromises [11]; the data perturbation family includes sampling microdata [14], swapping data entries between different cells [13], and adding noises to the microdata [31] or the query results [14]. As shown in [1], however, the proposed techniques can hardly meet the requirements of providing high-precision statistics, meanwhile preventing exact or partial disclosure of personal information.

In the data mining community, the detecting-then-removing paradigm has also been applied to address privacy breaches in a variety of mining tasks. In the context of stream mining, the solutions typically follow a two-staged scheme: in the first stage, one detects all intra-window breaches and eliminates them using the techniques developed for static data, e.g., adding fake records, or suppressing vulnerable transactions [5]; in the second stage, by referring to the released output in previous windows, one further blocks the inter-window inference. One line of research efforts attempts to propose general frameworks for detecting potential privacy breaches. For example, the work [21] proposes an empirical testing scheme to evaluate if a learned classifier violates privacy constraints. Another line of works focus on proposing algorithms to address detected breaches for specific mining tasks. For instance, it is shown in [5] that association rules could be exploited to infer information about individual records; while the work [34] proposes a scheme to block inference of sensitive patterns satisfying user-specified templates by suppressing certain raw records (transactions).

Unfortunately, most reactive approaches suffer from two major drawbacks. First, the detection of breaches typically requires complicated computation over entire dataset and bookkeeping of voluminous history output. Such complex results are usually negative in tone [10] for online stream mining applications, which feature limited processing time and space. Second, even at such high costs, the operations of removing the detected breaches by modifying raw data usually twist the output, e.g., suppression and addition [5], and result in significant decrease of output utility.

6.3.2 Proactive Approaches

In contrast to the detecting-then-removing paradigm, the proactive approaches neither rely on uncovering which part of mining output could be leveraged for succeeding the output-inference attack, nor depend on detecting all vulnerable patterns existing in the data. More concretely, analogous to sanitizing raw input data to seal sensitive-information leakage, the proactive approaches adopt the concept of "sanitized pattern" [35] and intelligently modify output patterns produced by data mining processes, with the objective of significantly reducing the risk of malicious inference, while maximally preserving the utility of output patterns. This scenario is shown as the last step in Figure 6.1.

The validity of proactive approaches is based on the next two key observations. First, in a number of mining applications, users do not expect exact patterns or models; rather, they care more about the semantic relationships among these patterns, e.g., the ranking of frequent patterns in terms of support. It is thus tolerable to sacrifice trivial precision of each pattern, given that such output utility is guaranteed. Second, the inference attacks over mining output, either intra-window or inter-window, usually involve multiple patterns. If one introduces trivial uncertainty into each pattern, the accumulated uncertainty in the inferred patterns could be considerable, spiritually similar to the *butterfly effect*. The more complicated the inference, i.e., harder to detect, the more uncertain the inferred result.

Based on these two observations, light-weighted output-privacy preservation solutions can be constructed using primitives such as random perturbation. The intuition is that by sacrificing trivial precision of each published pattern, it significantly heightens the uncertainty of sensitive patterns, thus blocking both intra-window and inter-window inference. Requiring neither to explicitly detect intra-window or inter-window breaches, nor to refer to any previous output, such solutions can be readily incorporated into the stream mining process, without affecting the processing efficiency. A typical proactive countermeasure follows a two-staged paradigm: in the first phase, one focuses on countering malicious inference by amplifying the uncertainty of sensitive patterns through carefully controlled random perturbation; in the second phase, with the hard privacy guarantee, one maximally preserves pattern-specific output utility by further refining the output patterns.

Compared with the wealth of reactive techniques developed to date, the attention given to the proactive approaches is still fairly limited. In a representative work [35] of this category, Wang and Liu proposed a proactive approach in the context of frequent-pattern mining over data streams. The next section presents a case study of the techniques and models of [35], with the aim of summarizing the general principles of designing proactive output-privacy solutions and identifying open issues and technical challenges.

6.4 Case Study: Frequent-Pattern Mining over Streams

We start with introducing the privacy breach existing in the output of frequent-pattern mining over streams and the associated attack model that exploits such breaches; we then proceed to presenting the detailed design of BUTTERFLY, a light-weighted, proactive solution; we conclude this case with a set of general principles of designing output-privacy protection solutions.

6.4.1 Concepts and Models

Output privacy, in general, refers to the requirement that the output (pattern or model) of a mining process does not disclose sensitive information regarding any few participating individuals. In the context of frequent-pattern mining, examples of such sensitive information are usually in the form of patterns with low support. Recall the example of nursing-care records in Section 6.1. The disclosure of such patterns through mining-output inference could lead to uncovering sensitive information regarding victim individuals.

This privacy concern is captured by the notion of *vulnerable pattern*. Intuitively, vulnerable patterns are those matching only few records with respect to the given database. The vulnerability of a pattern is quantitatively measured by a threshold, called the *vulnerable support*. Specifically, given a database $\mathcal{D}$, let $\mathcal{P}$ denote the set of patterns appearing in $\mathcal{D}$. Based on the minimum and vulnerable support, $\mathcal{P}$ can be classified into three disjoint classes: *frequent* patterns $\mathcal{P}_f$, those with support above the minimum support, *hard vulnerable* patterns $\mathcal{P}_{hv}$, those with support below the vulnerable support, and *soft vulnerable* patterns $\mathcal{P}_{sv}$, those with support lying between the vulnerable and minimum support.

The frequent patterns expose the significant statistics of the underlying data, and are often the candidate in the mining process. The hard vulnerable patterns represent the properties possessed by only few individuals; it is thus unacceptable that they are disclosed or inferred from the mining output. The soft vulnerable patterns neither demonstrate statistical significance, nor violate the privacy of individual records; therefore, they are not contained in mining output, but it is usually tolerable that they are learned from the mining output.

In the context of frequent-pattern mining over data streams, the problem of protecting output privacy can be stated as: *for each sliding window, prevent the disclosure or inference of any hard vulnerable patterns with respect to this window from the mining output.*

Although the output of frequent-pattern mining contains only frequent patterns (the minimum support is much greater than the vulnerable support), an adversary might still be able to infer hard vulnerable patterns from the released frequent patterns and their associated support. A more detailed dis-

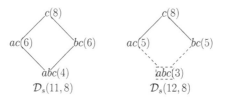

FIGURE 6.3: Intra-window and inter-window breaches, where the two lattices correspond to the sliding window $\mathcal{D}_s(11, 8)$ and $\mathcal{D}_s(12, 8)$ in FIGURE 6.2. © IEEE 2008 [35].

cussion is given in the following.

6.4.2   Breaches and Attacks

Next, we expose an adversary model that exploits the well known *inclusion-exclusion* principle. We will use the following notations: given two itemsets I and J, let $I \oplus J$ denote their union, $J \ominus I$ represent the set difference of J and I, and $\mathcal{T}(P)$ be the support of a pattern (itemset) P.

6.4.2.1   Lattice Structure

As a special case of multi-attribute aggregation, computing the support of an itemset I is to generalize over all the attributes of $J \ominus I$ $(I \subset J)$; one can thus apply the standard work of multi-attribute aggregation, a lattice structure [28]. We use the notation $\mathcal{X}_I^J = \{X | I \subseteq X \subseteq J\}$ to represent both the set of itemsets and their corresponding lattice structure. An example of a lattice $\mathcal{X}_c^{abc}$ is shown in Figure 6.3.

6.4.2.2   Deriving Pattern Support

Consider the two itemsets I and J, if the support values of all the nodes of $\mathcal{X}_I^J$ are available, one is able to derive the support of the pattern of the form $I \oplus (\overline{J \ominus I})$, according to the inclusion-exclusion principle. For example, in Figure 6.3, assume that the support of $\mathcal{X}_c^{abc}$ is given with respect to the sliding window of $r_5 \sim r_{12}$ $(\mathcal{D}_s(12, 8))$. One can derive $\mathcal{T}(\overline{ab}c)$ as follows: $\mathcal{T}(\overline{ab}c) = \mathcal{T}(c) - \mathcal{T}(ab) - \mathcal{T}(ac) + \mathcal{T}(abc) = 1$.

6.4.2.3   Estimating Itemset Support

Since the support of any pattern is non-negative, according to the inclusion-exclusion principle, if the support of $\mathcal{X}_I^J \ominus \{J\}$ is available, one is able to estimate the lower and upper bounds for $\mathcal{T}(J)$. For example, in Figure 6.3, given the support of c, ac, and bc with respect to $\mathcal{D}_s(12, 8)$, one can establish the bound for $\mathcal{T}(abc)$ as $[2, 5]$. When the lower and upper bounds meet, one can exactly determine the actual support. This technique is used in [7] to mine non-derivable frequent itemsets. In our context, an adversary leverages this technique to exploit the privacy breaches existing in the mining output.

Based on these two primitives, an adversary is able to carry out inference over the output of frequent-pattern mining, with both intra-window and inter-window attacks.

6.4.2.4 Intra-Window Inference

For a stream mining process without output-privacy protection, the released frequent itemsets in one specific window might contain intra-window breaches, which could be leveraged by an adversary through the technique of deriving pattern support.

More formally, if J is a frequent itemset, then according to the Apriori rule [3], all $X \subseteq J$ are frequent, which are supposed to be reported with their support; thus, the information is available to compute the support of any pattern of the form $I \oplus (\overline{J \ominus I})$ for $I \subset J$. This also implies that the number of possible breaches to be checked is potentially exponential in terms of the number of items.

Even if the information of J is unavailable, i.e., the lattice of $\mathcal{X}_I^J$ is incomplete to infer $I \oplus (\overline{J \ominus I})$, one could possibly apply the technique of estimating itemset support first to complete some missing "mosaics," then derive vulnerable patterns. Moreover, the itemsets under estimation themselves could be vulnerable.

6.4.2.5 Inter-Window Inference

Meanwhile, in a stream mining process, the output of previous windows could also be leveraged to infer the vulnerable patterns within the current window, and vice versa, even though no vulnerable patterns could be inferred from the output of each window per se.

Consider the two windows $\mathcal{D}_s(11, 8)$ and $\mathcal{D}_s(12, 8)$ shown in FIGURE 6.3. Assume the minimum and vulnerable support as 4 and 1, respectively. In $\mathcal{D}_s(11, 8)$, no vulnerable pattern exists; while in $\mathcal{D}_s(12, 8)$, abc is inaccessible (shown in a dashed box). From the available information of $\mathcal{D}_s(12, 8)$, the best guess about abc is $[2, 5]$. Clearly, this bound is not tight enough to estimate that the pattern $\overline{abc}$ is vulnerable. Hence, both windows are currently immune to intra-window inference.

Nevertheless, if one is able to derive that $\mathcal{T}(abc)$ decreases by 1 from $\mathcal{D}_s(11, 8)$ and $\mathcal{D}_s(12, 8)$, based on the information released in $\mathcal{D}_s(11, 8)$ (i.e., $\mathcal{T}(abc) = 4$), the exact support value of abc in $\mathcal{D}_s(12, 8)$ could be inferred, and the vulnerable pattern $\overline{abc}$ is uncovered. Sketchily, the main idea of inter-window inference is to first estimate the transition of the support of certain itemsets from previous windows to the current one, using the technique of estimating itemset support, and then to uncover vulnerable patterns, using the technique of deriving pattern support.

6.4.3   Butterfly: A Proactive Solution

Here, we present BUTTERFLY, a light-weighted, proactive solution for output privacy in frequent-pattern mining over streams. As discussed in Section 6.3.2, a proactive approach trades trivial precision degradation of each frequent itemset to significantly amplify the uncertainty of vulnerable patterns, while guaranteeing that the semantic relationships among frequent itemsets are preserved. BUTTERFLY achieves this objective in two phases: first, it amplifies the uncertainty of vulnerable patterns by injecting proper amount of randomness into each frequent itemset; second, it maximally preserves the output utility, under the hard privacy guarantees.

6.4.3.1   First Phase

In the first phase, one employs perturbation to inject uncertainty into the mining output. Note that the perturbation over mining output is significantly different from that over input data. In input perturbation, the data utility is defined on the overall statistical characteristics of input data. The perturbed data is fed as input into the following mining process. There tends to be no utility constraints for individual data values. In output perturbation, however, the sanitized output is directly presented to end users, and the data utility is defined over each individual value. Specifically, there are two types of utility constraints for the perturbed output. First, each reported value should enjoy sufficient precision; that is, it should not deviate from actual value too far. Second, the semantic relationships among the values should be preserved to the maximum extent.

More concretely, on the support of each frequent itemset, a value randomly drawn from certain statistical distribution is added; thus, from the adversary's perspective, the original value is now a statistical distribution characterized by the parameters of *bias* β and *variance* σ^2.

Intuitively, the perturbation distorts the exact support of frequent itemsets; it can be shown that the precision degradation of a specific frequent itemset is proportional to $(\beta^2 + \sigma^2)$. Meanwhile, the privacy is achieved by the accumulated estimation uncertainty at vulnerable patterns; it can be proved that the privacy protection for a specific vulnerable pattern is proportional to σ^2 (a detailed discussion in [35]).

The relationships between frequent itemsets and vulnerable patterns offer three key implications, which guarantee the effectiveness of this approach against both intra-window and inter-window inference attacks. First, the uncertainty of involved frequent itemsets are accumulated in the infered vulnerable patterns. Moreover, the more complicated the inference, i.e., hard to be detected, the higher the uncertainty. Second, the exact support values of vulnerable patterns are usually small (only few records match vulnerable patterns), adding trivial uncertainty makes it hard to tell the existence of such patterns in the database, i.e., if the support is zero or less than the vulnerable support. Finally, the inter-window inference follows a two-staged strategy: first

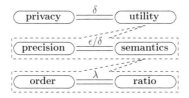

FIGURE 6.4: Multi-level trade-offs in output privacy protection.

deduce the transition of frequent itemsets between contingent windows, then infer the vulnerable patterns. The uncertainty associated with both stages further lowers the adversary's chance.

Meanwhile, there is a natural trade-off between the output utility and the privacy protection. In the BUTTERFLY framework, this trade-off is flexibly adjustable by setting the variance σ^2 and bias β. Specifically, the variance controls the overall balance between privacy and utility, while the bias gives a finer control over the balance between precision and other utility metrics, as will be discussed in the next phase. Typically, a lower variance produces higher-precision output, but also reduces the uncertainty of vulnerable patterns. This trade-off is illustrated as the first layer of Figure 6.4.

6.4.3.2 Second Phase

The first step treats each frequent itemset uniformly (the same bias setting for all the frequent itemsets) without taking account of their semantic relationships. Though easy to implement and effective against inference attacks, this simple scheme might easily violate the semantic constraints that are directly related to the specific applications of the mining output, thus reducing the output utility. In this phase, we intend to further refine the basic scheme by taking semantic constraints into the map, and preserving them to the maximum extent.

Specifically, in the context of frequent-pattern mining, one is particularly interested in two types of semantic relationships, namely, *absolute order* and *relative frequency*. By absolute order, we refer to the ranking of frequent itemsets according to their support. In a number of applications, users pay special attentions to the ordering of itemsets, rather than their actual support values, e.g., querying the top-ten-popular purchase patterns. By relative frequency, we mean the ratio of two support values. In certain applications, users care more about this relative quantity, instead of the absolute values, e.g., computing the confidence of association rules.

Recall that the balance between privacy guarantee and overall output utility (including both absolute precision and semantic relationships) is controlled by the setting of variance. The trade-off between absolute precision and semantic relationships in the mining output is adjusted by the setting of bias, shown as the second layer of Figure 6.4. Intuitively, by intelligently adjusting the bias, one minimizes the probability that the absolute order or the relative frequency of a pair of frequent itemsets is distorted.

Unfortunately, it can be proved that finding the optimal bias setting is NP-hard, while [35] provides polynomial solutions for finding near-optimal settings with respect to absolute order and relative frequency preservations, based on dynamic programming and Markov's inequality.

Finally, while the bias settings for optimizing order and ratio preservations achieve the maximum utility at their ends, in some applications wherein both semantic relationships are important, it is desired to balance the two factors to achieve the overall optimal quality. A simple solution could be to set the bias with a weighted linear combination of the settings suggested by the order and ratio preserving schemes, shown as the third layer of Figure 6.4.

6.4.4 Lessons Learned

Through the detailed case study above, we can obtain a set of general principles regarding designing efficient output-privacy solutions in data mining, especially stream mining.

First, the mining output typically involves more complicated structures, e.g., classification tree, frequent patterns, and regression functions, than the simple statistics, e.g., min, max, and avg, as concerned by statistical databases, which makes detecting output-privacy breaches much more difficult. Hence, proactive solutions are generally preferable to reactive ones, which is especially true for cases with strict processing-time and -space constraints.

Second, in designing a proactive solution, it is imperative to carefully control the amount of uncertainty injected into the mining output. A proper setting should satisfy that it offers sufficient protection for the vulnerable patterns targeted by the adversary, and it distorts the precision of each published pattern to the minimum possible extent. Determining the optimal setting of injected uncertainty, however, requires fully analyzing the attack model and the implicit structures of the mining output.

Last but not least, the rich semantic relationships are the valuable information requested by end users; they are therefore also the output utility we aim to preserve in protecting output privacy. Due to their complicated structures, e.g., the relative frequency and absolute order coexist, the preservation of semantic relationships usually boils down to complicated optimization problems, e.g., quadratic programming [33], and efficient near-optimal solutions are often a must.

6.5 Roadmap for Future Research

In contrast to the wealth of techniques and tools available for preserving the privacy of input data, the study of protecting output privacy is still fairly limited, and a great number of issues and challenges remain open, which are worth much further investigation. Here, we identify several important directions for future research.

While this chapter mostly focuses on output-privacy protection, in general, it is beneficial to consider the preservation of input and output privacy in a uniform framework, because of their interleaved nature. For example, both care about maximizing the utility of mining output, and preventing inference against underlying individual data contributors. We envision that a unified input- and output-privacy-preserving mechanism could lead to better output utility and consistent privacy guarantee.

This chapter presents a detailed study of output-privacy protection for frequent-pattern mining, arguably the most intensively studied mining task. A recent paper [37] looked at the problem of preventing malicious inference over the output of association-rule mining. To our best knowledge, there is no systematic study yet on the threats for mining tasks other than the two. As we have pointed out, while one can conceive general principles for designing output-privacy solutions, the detailed mechanisms need to be implemented and deployed according to the specific characteristics of targeted applications and adversarial attack models.

Random value distortion is investigated as the main technique of preserving output privacy in most literature, and extensive studies have been conducted on its implicit characteristics [3, 4, 35]. It is haunted by a number of drawbacks; for instance, it unavoidably introduces errors into the mining output. For some applications, other privacy enhancing techniques might lead to better performance. For example, the rotation transformation technique [8] perfectly preserves the geometric properties of the input data, crucial to learning classification models. Hence, it would be beneficial to explore such alternative primitives to construct superior output-privacy solutions.

6.6 Conclusion

In this chapter, we presented an overview of the state-of-the-art in output-privacy protection for data mining, especially stream mining. We discussed a variety of models and techniques designed to counter inference attacks over mining output, and analyzed their strengths and weaknesses. We also summarized a set of general principles regarding designing efficient output-privacy solutions, through a detailed case study of a light-weighted, proactive countermeasure, BUTTERFLY, in the context of frequent-pattern mining over data streams. Finally, we identified several research directions that are worth further investigation.

Acknowledgments

This work is partially funded by grants from NSF CISE CyberTrust program and NDF NetSE program, an IBM Faculty award, and IBM SUR grant.

References

[1] N. Adam and J. Wortman. Security-control methods for statistical databases. *ACM Computing Surveys*, 21(4), 1989.

[2] D. Agrawal and C. Aggarwal. On the design and quantification of privacy preserving data mining algorithms. In *Proc. of PODS*, 2001.

[3] R. Agrawal and R. Srikant. Fast algorithms for mining association rules. In *Proc. of VLDB*, 1994.

[4] R. Agrawal and R. Srikant. Privacy preserving data mining. In *Proc. of SIGMOD*, 2000.

[5] M. Atzori, F. Bonchi, F. Giannotti and D. Pedreschi. Anonymity preserving pattern discovery. *The VLDB Journal*, 16(4), 2006.

[6] S. Bu, L. Lakshmanan, R. Ng and G. Ramesh. Preservation of pattern and input-output Privacy. In *Proc. of ICDE*, 2007.

[7] T. Calders and B. Goethals. Mining all non-derivable frequent itemsets. In *Proc. of PKDD*, 2002.

[8] K. Chen and L. Liu. Privacy preserving data classification with rotation perturbation. In *Proc. of ICDM*, 2005.

[9] Y. Chi, H. Wang, P. Yu and R. Muntz. Moment: Maintaining closed frequent itemsets over a stream sliding window. In *Proc. of ICDM*, 2004.

[10] F. Chin and G. Ozsoyoglu. Statistical database design. *ACM Transactions on Database Systems*, 6(1), 1981.

[11] F. Chin and G. Ozsoyoglu. Auditing and inference control in statistical databases. *IEEE Transactions on Software Engineering*, SE-8(6), 1982.

[12] L. Cox. Suppression methodology and statistical disclosure control. *Journal of American Statistics Association*, 75(370), 1980.

[13] T. Dalenius and S. Reiss. Data swapping: a technique for disclosure control. *Journal of Statistical Planning and Inference*, 6, 1982.

[14] D. Denning. Secure statistical databases with random sample queries. *ACM Transactions on Database Systems*, 5(3), 1980.

[15] D. Dobkin, A. Jones and R. Lipton. Secure databases: protection against user inferences. *ACM Transactions on Database Systems*, 4(1), 1979.

[16] G. Duncan, S. Fienberg, R. Krishnan, R. Padman and S. Roehrig. Disclosure limitation methods and information loss for tabular data. *Confidentiality, Disclosure, and Data Access: Theory and Practical Applications for Statistical Agencies*, pp 135-166, Elsevier, 2001.

[17] A. Evfimevski, R. Srikant, R. Agarwal and J. Gehrke. Privacy preserving mining of association rules. In *Proc. of SIGKDD*, 2002.

[18] I. Fellegi. On the question of statistical confidentiality. *Journal of American Statistics Association*, 67(337), 1972.

[19] H. Hacigümüş, B. Iyer, C. Li and S. Mehrotra. Executing SQL over encrypted data in the database-service-provider model. In *Proc. of SIGMOD*, 2002.

[20] Z. Huang, W. Du and B. Chen. Deriving private information from randomized data. In *Proc. of SIGMOD*, 2005.

[21] M. Kantarcioglu, J. Jin and C. Clifton. When do data mining results violate privacy?. In *Proc. of KDD*, 2004.

[22] H. Kargupta, S. Datta, Q. Wang and K. Sivakumar. On the privacy preserving properties of random data perturbation techniques. In *Proc. of ICDM*, 2003.

[23] K. LeFevre, D. DeWitt and R. Ramakrishnan. Mondrian multidimensional k-anonymity. In *Proc. of ICDE*, 2006.

[24] F. Li, J. Sun, S. Papadimitriou, G. Mihaila and I. Stanoi. Hiding in the crowd: privacy preservation on evolving streams through correlation tracking. In *Proc. of ICDE*, 2007.

[25] Y. Lindell and B. Pinkas. Privacy preserving data mining. In *Proc. of CRYPTO*, 2000.

[26] A. Machanavajjhala, J. Gehrke, D. Kifer and M. Venkitasubramaniam. L-diversity: privacy beyond k-anonymity. In *Proc. of ICDE*, 2006.

[27] H. Park and K. Shim. Approximate algorithm for k-anonymity. In *Proc. of SIGMOD*, 2007.

[28] W. Scott. *Group Theory*, Prentice Hall, 1964.

[29] L. Sweeney. K-anonymity: a model for protecting privacy. *Int. J. Uncertain. Fuzziness Knowl.-Based Syst.*, 10(5), 2002.

[30] W. Teng, M. Chen and P. Yu. A regression-based temporal pattern mining scheme for data streams. In *Proc. of VLDB*, 2003.

[31] J. Traub, Y. Yemini and H. Woznaikowski. The statistical security of a statistical database. *ACM Transactions on Database Systems*, 9(4), 1984.

[32] J. Vaidya and C. Clifton. Privacy preserving association rule mining in vertically partitioned Data. In *Proc. of SIGKDD*, 2002.

[33] S. Vavasis. Quadratic programming is in NP. *Information Processing Letter*, 36(2), 1990.

[34] K. Wang, B. Fung and P. Yu. Handicapping attackers confidence: an alternative to k-anonymization. *Knowl. and Info. Syst.*, 11(3), 2007.

[35] T. Wang and L. Liu. Butterfly: protecting output privacy in stream mining. In *Proc. of ICDE*, 2008.

[36] T. Wang, S. Meng, B. Bamba, L. Liu and C. Pu. A general proximity privacy principle. In *Proc. of ICDE*, 2009.

[37] Z. Zhu, G. Wang and W. Du. Deriving private information from association rule mining results. In *Proc. of ICDE*, 2009.

Part III

Spatio-Temporal and Mobility Data

Chapter 7

Privacy Issues in Spatio-Temporal Data Mining

Aris Gkoulalas-Divanis

Department of Biomedical Informatics (DBMI), Vanderbilt University, 2525 West End Ave, Suite 800, Nashville, Tennessee

Vassilios S. Verykios

Department of Computer & Communication Engineering, University of Thessaly, Volos, Greece.

7.1 Introduction

The remarkable progress that is evidenced nowadays in the areas of telecommunications and indoor/outdoor location tracking technologies, such as GPS, GSM and UMTS, has made possible the tracking of mobile devices (and subsequently their human companions) at an accuracy that spans from a few hundred meters to only a few meters. As ubiquitous computing pervades our society, the available wireless network infrastructures can be used to sense and record the movement of people, animals, and vehicles, thus generating large volumes of geo–spatial, mobility data. From this perspective, we have nowadays the means of collecting, storing and processing mobility data of an unprecedented quantity, quality and timeliness.

A mobility dataset is composed of a series of spatio-temporal observations (3D points), which capture the changes in the physical location of a set of moving entities throughout a certain amount of time, usually discretized in a set of time instants. People, as well as animals, are entities that move purposely in order to accomplish certain goals. For example, as well stated in [4], "the movements of people may greatly depend on their occupation, age, health condition, marital status, and other properties." In all cases, the movement traces that are left behind by the mobile devices of the users are an excellent source of information which can aid traffic engineers, city managers and environmentalists toward decision making in a wide spectrum of contexts, such as urban planning, traffic engineering, forecasting of traffic–related phenomena, fleet management, wildlife rescuing, and locating environmental pollution. As an effect, the analysis of the user movement traces by means of appropriate patterns and models extracted through the application of modern data mining technologies, can potentially lead to a source of knowledge of extreme usefulness. The existing large volumes of mobility data, as exemplified by trajectory data collected during the course of various mobile applications (primarily attributed to the usually high update rates that are used for their collection), makes the manual analysis of this data impossible.

Mobility data is a unique and complex data type due to its spatio-temporal nature. As an effect, traditional data mining approaches are in most cases inappropriate to handle this type of data as they fail to account for both its spatial and its temporal characteristics. Spatio-temporal data mining [19, 24, 18] is emerging as a very challenging area of research, targeting the in-depth analysis of large spatio-temporal datasets, such as datasets of user mobility. However, we should realize that spatio-temporal data mining can become a double-edged sword. As it becomes evident, in the wrong hands this type of emergent knowledge may lead the way to an abuse scenario, where highly sensitive personal information or sensitive aggregate knowledge patterns are revealed to unauthorized, potentially malevolent, entities. In the case of mobility data, some examples of misuse include user tailing, surveillance, and user profiling. Generally speaking, the personal mobility data, as sensed through the available telecommunication infrastructures, represents an extremely sensitive source of information; its potential disclosure to untrusted parties may severely jeopardize the privacy of the individuals to whom this data refers [6] or lead to the identification of knowledge patterns that depict trends of the data which are considered as sensitive. Dobson and Fisher [9] describe the severity of the unauthorized disclosure of personal mobility data or emergent knowledge patterns mined from this data, as "a new form of slavery characterized by location control." To effectively address the privacy concerns regarding the mining of mobility (and, generally, of spatio-temporal) data, a novel set of specially, crafted privacy preserving data mining methodologies has been recently proposed. The aim of these methodologies is to enable the privacy-aware sharing of mobility data in a way that either (i) protects the sensitive data itself prior to the course of data mining or (ii) protects the sensitive knowledge patterns that would otherwise be revealed from the data, if the data were mined by the existing data mining technology.

The rest of this chapter is organized as follows. In Section 7.2 we elaborate on the research challenges that pertain to the mining of spatio-temporal data as well as the privacy-aware mining of mobility data. Section 7.3 presents a taxonomy of the state-of-the-art algorithms for the offering of privacy in the course of spatio-temporal data mining, along with their strengths and weaknesses. Following that, Section 7.4 provides a roadmap along with potential future trends in this area of research. Finally, Section 7.5 summarizes and concludes this work.

7.2 Research Challenges

To motivate the research challenges in the privacy-aware mining of spatio-temporal data, we consider the real-world application of mining datasets of user mobility. Mobility data raises a series of important research challenges with respect to its mining, primarily due to the fact that it is referenced both in space and time. The existing techniques for the mining of mobility (and generally of spatio-temporal) data can be classified along the following principal dimensions: (i) the type of extracted knowledge patterns, (ii) the population in reference (i.e., the coverage of the patterns), and (iii) the data dimension that is in focus. With respect to (i), methodologies have been proposed that extract different types of patterns; clustering, association rule mining, classification rule mining, sequential pattern mining, and trend discovery are some among the data mining tasks that have been investigated in the context of spatio-temporal data. Some of the algorithmic approaches that have been proposed for the mining of spatio-temporal data extend existing techniques for knowledge discovery in classical relational or transactional data to take into consideration the spatio-temporal annotations in the course of mining. With respect to (ii), *local* methodologies have been proposed for the mining of patterns that characterize only a portion of the population that is recorded in the dataset (e.g., a subset of individuals or a limited spatial/temporal or spatio-temporal region), as well as *global* patterns that summarize the trends in the complete data space.

We consider the third dimension of the proposed classification to be the most prevalent. Due to the complexity of spatio-temporal data mining, few approaches exist that handle both the space and the time dimension of the data equally well. Indeed, most of the proposed approaches focus only on one dimension of the data, by either suppressing or devaluing the information that is offered by the other dimension. Specifically, in spatial data mining approaches [25] focus is given on the spatial characteristics of the dataset, while any temporal characteristics of the data are suppressed. Similarly, temporal data mining approaches [17] give emphasis on the temporal dimension of the data, while the spatial dimension is suppressed. Within the domain of temporal data mining, sequential pattern mining [29] has received particular attention and has influenced most of the approaches that have been proposed so far for the privacy-aware mining of spatio-temporal datasets. The sequential pattern mining framework (in the context of spatio-temporal data) requires that the spatial dimension of the data is simplified to a number of items denoting specific places of interest, while the temporal dimension simply provides the ordering of these items in user transactions (trajectories). The goal of these methodologies is to discover ordered sequences of items (i.e., sequential patterns) that occur in a significant portion of the data.

The existing challenges in the mining of spatio-temporal data have highly influenced the methodologies that have been proposed so far for the privacy-aware mining of mobility data. As it becomes apparent, simple de-identification, i.e., removal of just the obvious identifiers from the user trajectories (e.g., the user ID, the user name, etc) is insufficient to protect the privacy of the users once the dataset is publicly released (shared). This is due to the spatio-temporal nature of the data which enables data recipients to use publicly available information, such as the white pages, along with geocoded information, in order to search for certain public places based on the spatio-temporal coordinates in the released data. For example, an adversary may use publicly available data sources (such as a map together with a phone directory) to locate the houses of a set of users and collocate this information along with the released user trajectories. Since users typically start their day by leaving their house to go to work, this information can easily expose the identities of the owners of at least some of the publicized trajectories. This is due to the fact that location information, especially when released together with detailed time information, may become a "quasi-identifier" that can be used to link specific individuals to de-identified released data. On the other hand, the knowledge patterns that can be mined from historical datasets of user mobility may also infringe user privacy by enabling intrusive inferences regarding the habits or the sexual preferences of a portion of the population, or even providing the means for unsolicited advertisement and user profiling. As it becomes evident, both the protection of the sensitive mobility data prior to the course of data mining, as well as the hiding of sensitive knowledge patterns that can be found through the mining of historical datasets of user mobility, are very challenging problems that postulate extensive research.

7.3   A Taxonomy of the Privacy Methodologies

In the last few years, a set of privacy preserving methodologies have been proposed for the protection of sensitive data and/or sensitive knowledge related to user mobility. Existing methodologies can be partitioned into two broad categories [12]: (i) those that protect the sensitive data related to user mobility prior to the course of data mining, and (ii) those that hide sensitive knowledge patterns that summarize user mobility, identified as a result of the application of data mining. The first category of methodologies collects data perturbation and obfuscation approaches that distort the original dataset to facilitate privacy-aware publication of mobility data (see Section 7.3.1), as well as distributed privacy-aware approaches for secure multiparty computation (see Section 7.3.2). On the other hand, the second category of methodologies treats the mobility data as sequential data and applies sequential pattern hiding techniques to prevent the disclosure of the sensitive patterns in the course of sequential pattern mining (see Section 7.3.3). After the application of these approaches, only the nonsensitive patterns, summarizing users' movement behavior, survive the mining process, while the sensitive ones are suppressed in the data mining result. In the sections that follow, we investigate the methodologies that have been proposed along each of these lines of research.

7.3.1 Data Perturbation and Obfuscation

Data perturbation and obfuscation approaches aim at sanitizing a spatio-temporal dataset depicting user mobility, in such a way that an adversary can no longer match the recorded movement of each user to a particular individual (thus reveal the identity of the user based on his/her recorded movement in the released dataset). In what follows, we consider that user mobility is captured as a set of trajectories that depict the locations and times in the course of each user's history of movement. We assume that these location–time recordings occur at a reasonably high rate that allows the tracking of user movement in the original dataset. For example, an adversary could use these recordings to track the user down to his/her house or place of work, even if the user trajectory was not accompanied by an explicit identifier, such as the user ID, the social security number or the name of the user. Moreover, we assume the existence of a trusted entity, such as the data owner, who has complete knowledge of the data, as well as the possible threats related to its publication.

Hoh and Gruteser [14] present a data perturbation algorithm that is based on the idea of path crossing. The proposed approach identifies when two non-intersecting trajectories that belong to different users are reasonably close to each other and generates a fake crossing of these two trajectories in the released dataset. The goal of this approach is to prevent an adversary from successfully tracking a complete user trajectory and thus identifying the corresponding user. Provided that many crossings of trajectories exist in the released dataset, the probability that an adversary succeeds in following the same individual prior to and after a crossing, sufficiently deteriorates. As the authors demonstrate, path confusion can be formalized as a constrained non-linear optimization problem which, when given the trajectories of two users within a bounded area where a crossing has to occur, estimates the perturbed locations for each user such that their trajectories meet within a pre–specified time period. At each generated fake user location toward the meeting of the two trajectories, the algorithm takes special care to keep the enforced perturbation of the exact user location within reasonable bounds. In order to achieve

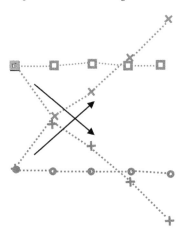

FIGURE 7.1: An example of path crossing between two users who in reality move in parallel (the black arrows indicate the perturbed paths and their artificial crossing).

this, each perturbed (fake) location has to reside within a given perturbation radius (indicating the maximum allowable perturbation) from the original user location. Figure 7.1 presents an example of path perturbation for two users who in reality move in parallel. As is expected, a larger radius increases the degree of privacy that is offered to the users but also deteriorates the utility of the released dataset. Equivalently, a smaller radius offers less privacy to the users but achieves a better utility of the publicized data. Through experiments the authors prove that the proposed algorithm limits the duration in which an adversary can successfully track the same individual in the sanitized dataset. This approach is the first to apply data perturbation to camouflage sequences of spatio-temporal points, thus offering spatio-temporal privacy to released datasets of user mobility. However, due to its way of operation it fails to offer privacy in low density areas where the probability of the paths of two users to be close in proximity is small.

Hoh, et al. [15] improve [14] by introducing a new empirical measure to quantify the privacy that is offered in a dataset of publicized spatio-temporal observations referring to user trajectories. The proposed measure calculates the time that a user can be successfully tracked (by an adversary) based on the knowledge of his/her user trajectory. To achieve that, it calculates the time that elapsed between two consecutive occasions where the adversary could not determine (at least with sufficient certainty) the next spatio-temporal observation in the trajectory of the user. By using this measure, the authors propose a path perturbation strategy that relies on data coarsening to exclude a limited amount of spatio-temporal observations from a user trajectory. The applied coarsening strategy ensures that the corresponding user cannot be tracked (at least with sufficient certainty) by an adversary, for a time that exceeds a pre–specified time threshold (a.k.a. the maximum time to confusion). To achieve this goal, the perturbation algorithm discloses a location–time recording of a user trajectory (as it appears in the original dataset) to the released data, only if the time that has elapsed since the last point of confusion is below the pre–specified time threshold. An extension of this algorithm, that offers increased privacy guarantees about what can be learned by an adversary, is also examined. The proposed methodology is proven to provide strict privacy guarantees for people who move in low density regions.

Terrovitis and Mamoulis [27] consider datasets that depict user mobility in the form of sequences of places that each user has visited in the course of his/her movement. For each user, the authors assume the existence of a transaction in the dataset that contains the list of places that this user has visited (e.g., based on his/her card transactions), set out in the order of visit. No other information of spatial or temporal nature (e.g., the exact time of each visit) is assumed to be known. Based on this type of data, the authors propose a suppression technique that removes some of the places that were visited by specific users to protect their identity from adversaries who hold partial information on the user trajectories. Specifically, an adversary is considered to be any individual who has knowledge of certain places that were visited (as well as the sequence in which they were visited) by some of the users, for whom he/she knows their identity. To exemplify, consider a bank which has many branches in a city. Each branch of the bank has some ATM machines that people can use to perform regular money transactions. Whenever a person uses the ATM of the bank, his or her transaction is recorded. Now assume that the bank manager possesses an anonymized version of the original dataset of user mobility, where he/she identifies that some of the users that appear in the dataset have visited certain branches of this bank. By using this information it is possible that the manager can learn the identity of some of the users who are recorded in the dataset and then identify the other places that these users have visited in the course of their movement. To protect the privacy of the users when publicizing their movement data, the proposed methodology assumes that the data holder has knowledge of the sets of places (i.e., the projection of the dataset) that are known to each individual adversary. In our example, the data holder knows the branches of the bank that the bank manager controls. By using this information, the data holder can compute the probability by which the corresponding adversary can infer the identity of a user in the publicized dataset, based on the projection of the data that the adversary holds.

The proposed suppression strategy operates in an iterative fashion to minimize the probability of a given adversary to associate (based on his/her data projection) a place that appears in the publicized data to the identity of a person whose movement is recorded in the dataset. Figure 7.2 presents an example of the proposed algorithm where the original dataset T (see Figure 7.2(a)) is transformed into its sanitized counterpart T' (see Figure 7.2(c)), which can

id	trajectory
t_1	$b_1 \rightarrow a_1 \rightarrow b_2$
t_2	$b_1 \rightarrow a_1 \rightarrow b_2 \rightarrow a_3$
t_3	$b_1 \rightarrow a_2 \rightarrow b_2$
t_4	$b_1 \rightarrow b_2 \rightarrow a_2$
t_5	$b_1 \rightarrow b_3 \rightarrow a_1$
t_6	$b_3 \rightarrow a_1$
t_7	$b_3 \rightarrow a_2$
t_8	$b_3 \rightarrow a_2 \rightarrow a_3$

(a) *exact data (T)*

id	trajectory
t_1^B	$b_1 \rightarrow b_2$
t_2^B	$b_1 \rightarrow b_2$
t_3^B	$b_1 \rightarrow b_2$
t_4^B	$b_1 \rightarrow b_2$
t_5^B	$b_1 \rightarrow b_3$
t_6^B	b_3
t_7^B	b_3
t_8^B	b_3

(b) *B's knowledge (T_B)*

id	trajectory
t'_1	$b_1 \rightarrow a_1 \rightarrow b_2$
t'_2	$b_1 \rightarrow a_1 \rightarrow b_2$
t'_3	$b_1 \rightarrow a_2 \rightarrow b_2$
t'_4	$b_1 \rightarrow b_2 \rightarrow a_2$
t'_5	$b_3 \rightarrow a_1$
t'_6	$b_3 \rightarrow a_1$
t'_7	$b_3 \rightarrow a_2$
t'_8	$b_3 \rightarrow a_2$

(c) *transformed database (T')*

(d) *the map of locations*

FIGURE 7.2: An example of data suppression to generate a safe projection T' of data T, with respect to the partial knowledge T_B of an adversary B.

be safely released to adversary B. As is shown in Figure 7.2(b), B's knowledge consists of all the places b_i from which he/she can retrieve information that can lead him/her to the identity of specific users. When selecting which locations to suppress from the original dataset, the proposed algorithm tries to minimize the side-effects that are introduced to the dataset. For example, location a_3 (suppressed from transactions t_2 and t_8) and location b_1 (suppressed from sequence t_5) lie close to their neighboring points (i.e., $\{b_2, a_2\}$, and $\{b_3\}$ respectively) in the original sequences (as demonstrated in Figure 7.2(d)). On the positive side, this is the first work to offer privacy by considering many adversaries, each holding a projection of the original data, who want to use their projection to infer sensitive locations with high certainty. However, as the experimental evaluation indicates, the proposed methodology is expected to perform well only when the size of the original data is large and the knowledge of each adversary (i.e., his/her projection) is limited. Furthermore, the reduction of the original spatio-temporal observations per user to plain sequences of places of interest (without any temporal annotation) leads to substantial information loss.

Nergiz, et al. [20] also rely on the sequential nature of mobility data and propose a coarsening strategy to generate a dataset that consists only of $\mathcal{K}$–anonymous sequences and thus can be safely released. The principle of $\mathcal{K}$–anonymity (originally proposed by Samarati and Sweeney [23, 26] in the context of relational data and recently adapted to different types of data) requires that each released data record must be indistinguishable from at least $\mathcal{K}$–1 other records with respect to a certain set of identifying variables. In the case of spatio-temporal data the identifying variables are space and time. The proposed algorithm aims at generating a dataset from the original data such that every trajectory (sequence) in the released dataset becomes indistinguishable from at least $\mathcal{K}$–1 other trajectories (sequences). Furthermore, to enhance the privacy guarantees that are offered by the privacy methodology in the released dataset, the authors perform a sampling of the anonymized trajectories to generate representatives of users' movements and then publish the representatives instead of the real anonymized user trajectories.

The proposed anonymization process operates in two phases. First, the trajectories are consolidated into groups of $\mathcal{K}$ based on a similarity measure that quantifies the cost-optimal anonymization. The similarity measure that is used is inspired from the research on string alignment [13]. The employed strategy iteratively selects the most similar trajectory to the (representative of the) already co-clustered ones, uses it to compute the new representative (trajectory) of the cluster and then identifies the trajectory from the dataset that lies closest to the representative. The same process continues until $\mathcal{K}$ trajectories are grouped together. Then, the co-clustered trajectories are removed from the dataset and the same operation reiterates among the remaining trajectories. In the second phase, the trajectories in each cluster are anonymized. The anonymization process operates as follows: It computes a matching between the points of each pair of co-clustered trajectories. The matched points in a pair of trajectories are replaced by their Minimum Bounding Rectangle (MBR) enclosure, while the unmatched ones are suppressed. The resulting coarsened trajectory is then used instead of its origins to participate in the following matches. As a result of this phase, every cluster of trajectories is simplified to one representative (coarsened) trajectory. Figure 7.3 shows how the anonymization is accomplished in the case of three trajectories tr_1, tr_2, and tr_3. First, the trajectories are aligned and then pairwise anonymized. The last sketch of Figure 7.3 demonstrates the employed point matching.

After the trajectory anonymization process, each representative trajectory is a $\mathcal{K}$–anonymization of the co–clustered trajectories from which it was constructed. The last step in the proposed approach regards the release of a representative sample coming from the anonymized trajectories (sequences) to the end user. The employed reconstruction process probabilistically generates a set of sample trajectories from the anonymized data by uniformly selecting points from the MBR of each representative trajectory and using these

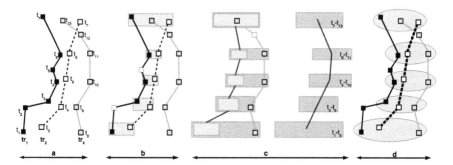

FIGURE 7.3: An example of the two–phase trajectory anonymization process proposed in [20], presented in a series of steps.

points to reconstruct the original trajectories. As the authors demonstrate, by applying this strategy the reconstructed data does well in explaining the original data while preserving the privacy of the individuals whose movement is recorded in the data.

Abul, et al. [1] propose a $\mathcal{K}$–anonymity strategy that relies on the inherent uncertainty with respect to the whereabouts of user trajectories in historical datasets of user mobility [28]. As the authors mention, due to the inherent imprecision of sampling and positioning systems, trajectories of moving objects can no longer be considered as 3D polylines, consisting of (x, y, t) elements. Instead, the authors represent the uncertainty of a trajectory by using a cylindrical volume that consists of a series of disks, defined for the different time intervals of user movement (see Figure 7.4). The sampling time is assumed to be the same for all trajectories and within each time interval the corresponding user is assumed to move linearly and at a constant speed. The proposed anonymity algorithm identifies trajectories that are close to each other in time and enforces space translation to put them also close to each other in space. We should note that due to space translation, some of the trajectory points of a user trajectory are moved from their original location to another location. The algorithm operates as follows: First, it generates clusters of at least $\mathcal{K}$ members (trajectories) by employing a clustering technique that constraints the radius of the identified clusters. Then, it applies space translation in order to transform each cluster to a $\mathcal{K}$–anonymity region by relocating the trajectories that participate in this cluster to a cylinder of a certain diameter δ. An example of a 2–anonymity region (cylinder) of diameter δ is presented in Figure 7.5. The enforced clustering technique proceeds as follows. First, the farthest trajectory from the dataset center is selected. Second, a sequence of pivot trajectories are chosen, such that each one is the farthest trajectory from the previously selected pivots. Third, the $K–1$ trajectories that are nearest to each selected pivot are captured as a cluster. Given a threshold of maximum allowable radius for a cluster, the algorithm ensures that the co–clustered

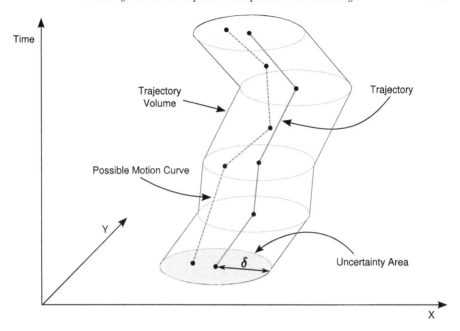

FIGURE 7.4: Modeling the uncertainty regarding the whereabouts of a user trajectory.

objects do not produce a cluster that violates this threshold. Finally, each remaining (unclustered) trajectory is included to the cluster of its nearest pivot, provided that it does not violate the maximum radius threshold. In any case, if a trajectory is selected to be added to a cluster and this leads to the violation of the maximum radius threshold, the trajectory is simply trashed.

On the positive side, the employed representation of uncertainty with respect to the whereabouts of user trajectories by means of a cylinder rather than a grid, serves much better the model of trajectory anonymity and introduces less distortion to the trajectory data. On the negative side, the quality of the employed clustering approach depends heavily on the maximum radius threshold that is used. When this threshold is small, the methodology leads to more coherent clusters but may potentially also lead to a large amount of trajectories being trashed. On the other hand, when the threshold is large it leads to few trajectories being trashed but the quality of the produced anonymity sets deteriorates.

7.3.2 Privacy-Aware Knowledge Sharing

The previous category of approaches aims at generating a privacy-aware counterpart of the original dataset, which can be safely shared with untrusted third parties as it contains only nonsensitive data. Secure Multiparty Com-

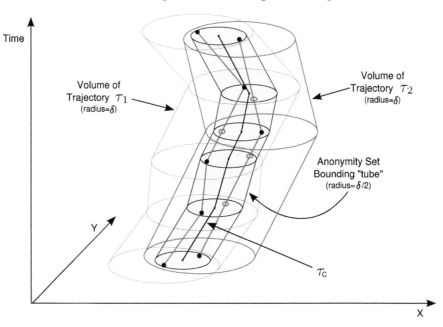

FIGURE 7.5: An example of a 2–anonymity set of diameter δ.

putation (SMC) provides an alternative family of approaches that can safely protect the sensitive data that appears in a dataset. The SMC approaches consider a set of collaborators who wish to collectively mine their data but are unwilling to disclose their own datasets to each other. As it turns out, this distributed privacy preserving data mining problem can be reduced to the secure computation of a function based on distributed inputs and it is thus solved by using cryptographic approaches. Pinkas [22] elaborates on this close relation that exists between privacy-aware data mining and cryptography. In SMC, each party contributes to the computation of the secure function by providing its private input. A secure cryptographic protocol that is executed among the collaborating parties ensures that the private input that is contributed by each party is not disclosed to the others. Most of the applied cryptographic protocols for multiparty computation result in some primitive operations that have to be securely performed: secure sum, secure set union, and secure scalar product. Clifton, et al. [8] elaborate on these operations.

SMC has been studied in the context of user mobility (and more generally on spatio-temporal) data. Inan and Saygin [16] were the first to propose a privacy-aware methodology for the clustering of a set of spatio-temporal datasets, owned by different parties. To perform clustering, a similarity measure is necessary to quantify the proximity between two objects (e.g., the user trajectories), such that in the computed clustering solution the co–clustered objects are more similar to one another than to objects belonging in different clusters. As part of this work, the authors propose a secure protocol that can be employed to enable the pairwise secure computation of trajectory similarity among all the trajectories of the different parties, thus building a global matrix of trajectory similarity. By using this matrix, a trusted third party can perform the clustering on behalf of the users and communicate the computed clustering results back to the collaborating parties. The proposed privacy preserving protocol supports all the necessary basic operations for the computation of trajectory similarity based on widely adopted trajectory comparison functions: (i) Euclidean distance, (ii) longest common subsequence, (iii) dynamic time warping, and (iv) edit distance. The protocol makes the following assumptions: (i) it assumes the semi–honest model in which all the parties follow the protocol but may also store any information that they receive from other parties in order to infer private data, (ii) the parties do not mutually share any other kind of information, and (iii) the mobility data that is to be clustered follows a horizontal partitioning (i.e., each party contributes a set of trajectories to participate in the clustering process).

The proposed methodology operates as follows: (i) every involved party, including the trusted party, generates pairwise keys which are used to disguise the exchanged messages, (ii) each party locally computes the trajectory similarity matrix (based on the commonly accepted trajectory comparison function) for its own trajectories and securely transmits it to the trusted party, (iii) for every pair of trajectories that belong to the datasets of different parties, the two parties execute the protocol to compute the similarity of their trajectories, build a similarity matrix based on their trajectories, and subsequently transmit it to the trusted party, and (iv) the trusted party uses the computed matrix of trajectory similarity based on the trajectories of all the collaborating parties, in order to perform trajectory clustering. An interesting observation is that by using this technique, the trusted party is free to choose any clustering algorithm, depending on the requirements of the data holders, in order to perform the clustering of the trajectories.

7.3.3 Sequential Pattern Hiding

The extraction of frequent patterns from mobility data has primarily focused on the sequential nature of the datasets by extracting frequent subsequences of user mobility (e.g., Cao, et al. [7], Giannotti, et al. [10]). Giannotti, et al. [11] proposed the integration of spatial and temporal information in the extracted mobility patterns by temporally annotating the sequences with transition times from one element (place of interest) to another. The resulting patterns (called $\mathcal{T}$–patterns) depict the frequent movement behavior of the objects whose trajectories are recorded in the dataset. An example of a $\mathcal{T}$–pattern is Home $\xrightarrow{15min}$ Park $\xrightarrow{30min}$ Work. In a similar manner, the approaches that have been proposed for the hiding of mobility patterns apply knowledge hiding in the form of sequential pattern hiding, where a set of sequences in the original data are considered to be sensitive. Such sequences, similar to the notion of LBQIDs originally proposed in [5], capture the behavior of a limited amount of individuals, whose movement is recorded in the dataset, and thus can easily lead to their identification. In what follows, we present some approaches that aim at hiding sensitive sequences.

Abul, et al. [3] model the problem of trajectory hiding to that of sequential pattern hiding. The authors consider that pertinent to every sensitive sequence is a disclosure threshold that defines the maximum number of sequences in the sanitized database that are allowed to support the sensitive sequence. The sequence sanitization operation is based on the use of unknowns to mask selected elements in the sequences of the original dataset. As the authors prove, the problem of sanitizing a sequence from the original dataset, while introducing the least amount of unknowns, is NP–hard and thus one needs to resort to heuristics to identify an efficient solution. The proposed heuristic operates as follows: For each sensitive sequence, the algorithm searches all the sequences of the original database to identify those in which the sensitive sequence is a subsequence (a sequence S1 is a subsequence of another sequence S2 if it can be obtained by deleting some elements from S2). For every such sequence of the original dataset, the algorithm examines in how many different ways this sequence becomes a subsequence of the sensitive one. Each "different way" (also called a matching) is counted based on the position of each element in the sequence that participates in the generation of the sensitive sequence. As an effect, for each element of the sequence coming from the original dataset, the algorithm maintains a counter depicting the number of matchings in which it is involved. To sanitize the sequence, the algorithm iteratively identifies the element of the sequence which has the highest counter (i.e., it is involved in most matchings) and replaces it by an unknown, until the sensitive sequence is no longer a subsequence of the sanitized one. As a result of this operation, the sensitive sequence becomes unsupported by the sanitized sequence. In order to enforce the requested disclosure threshold the algorithm applies this sanitization operation in the following manner: For each sensitive sequence, all the sequences of the original dataset are sorted in ascending order based on the number of different matchings that they have with the sensitive sequence. Then, the algorithm sanitizes the sequences in this order, until the required disclosure threshold is met in the privacy-aware version of the dataset. The authors have developed extensions of this approach for the handling of time constraints, such as min/max gap and max window.

A similar approach to [3], which operates by removing (instead of masking) elements from temporally annotated sequences [10] representing user mobility in an underlying network of user movement, is presented in the work of Abul, et al. [2]. The employed network topology confines the movement of the users to a set of allowable routes. Each edge of the network is assumed to be a directed straight line which is annotated to denote the minimum time that is required for its traversal (i.e., the traversal of the corresponding road part). Given the underlying network, a trajectory pattern can be represented as a time labeled sequence $u_0 \xrightarrow{a_1} u_1 \xrightarrow{a_2} \ldots \xrightarrow{a_m} u_m$, where u_i denotes a vertex of the network and a_j is the minimum time that is required for the transition from one vertex to the next one. A user trajectory supports a trajectory pattern if it is a time-consistent (based on the annotations) subsequence of the pattern. The proposed hiding approach identifies all the user trajectories that support a sensitive trajectory pattern and sanitizes some of them through coarsening, such that the pattern becomes insignificant. The employed sanitization strategy ensures that the sequences that participate in the sanitized dataset remain consistent to the underlying network. It operates in exactly the same manner as [3] to select which spatio-temporal points will be removed from which trajectories, and to perform the necessary sanitization. The authors propose an extension of this strategy which protects the publicized data from inference attacks regarding the lack of alternative paths. In this type of attack, a malevolent user can infer some of the suppressed points in a sanitized user trajectory if there is only one path between two consecutive vertices in the user trajectory, which is time-consistent to the network. The solution that is proposed requires the suppression of spatio-temporal points in the original user trajectories such that between two released points there exist at least k alternative time-consistent paths that the user may have followed in the meanwhile. Thus, the user is adequately protected.

Pensa, et al. [21] propose a sequential pattern hiding methodology that aims at removing all the infrequent subsequences from a dataset of user mobility. The proposed algorithm operates in four steps: (i) a prefix tree is generated based on the sequences of the original dataset, (ii) the infrequent subsequences are pruned away from the tree, thus the prefix tree is anonymized, (iii) part of the removed frequent subsequences (lost as a side-effect of the brute-force pruning operation) are re-appended to the prefix tree, and (iv) the sequences of the prefix tree are used to generate the sanitized dataset, which can be safely released. In the first step, the prefix tree is constructed by inserting each sequence of the original dataset as a path of the tree (each element of the sequence is a node and two nodes are joined together by an edge). For the insertion, the algorithm locates the longest prefix path in the tree that is common to the sequence and then the sequence is accordingly inserted. Following the insertion operation, the support of each node in the common prefix path is updated based on the support that the sequence has in the original dataset. After all the sequences are inserted to the prefix tree, the tree is pruned based on the user-specified support threshold. The applied pruning operation aims at the removal of all the infrequent subtrees from the tree; however, it also loses some of the frequent sequences. The support of each path (sequence) in the pruned tree is accordingly updated. Following that, a portion of the lost frequent subsequences are re-appended to the pruned tree. This is achieved through the increment of the support of certain nodes in the tree based on the support of the corresponding subsequences. The final step of the proposed methodology regards the generation of the sanitized dataset based on the sequences that are currently represented in the prefix tree. To generate the sanitized counterpart of the original dataset, the proposed algorithm visits the sequences (paths) of the prefix tree and for each visited path it appends the corresponding sequence (based on its support) to the sanitized dataset. Although very interesting, the proposed methodology suffers from the following shortcomings: (i) it assumes that all the infrequent subsequences of a dataset are sensitive which is a rather strong assumption; as an effect it may cause significant distortion to the original dataset, as well as lose some frequent patterns of the original data due to side-effects, (ii) it does not operate well on sparse datasets where there exist many infrequent subsequences, and (iii) the anonymization strategy makes an implicit assumption regarding the frequent part of the sequences (i.e., where the frequent items appear in each sequence), as the pruning of the prefix tree is conducted on its lower part.

7.4   Roadmap and Future Trends

Data mining is a rapidly evolving field counting numerous conferences, journals and books that are dedicated to this area of research. As new forms of data come into existence, as well as new application areas and challenges arise, it becomes evident that innovative privacy preserving data mining methodologies will also have to be proposed to keep pace with this progress. Spatio-temporal data mining is one of the most recent and prominent directions of privacy preserving data mining. As spatio-temporal and geo-referenced datasets grow, a novel class of applications is expected to appear that will be based on the extraction of behavioral patterns of user mobility. Clearly, in these applications privacy is a major concern and thus novel privacy preserving methodologies will have to be proposed to protect those patterns that are sensitive with respect to the privacy of individuals.

As it became apparent from section 7.3, few approaches have been proposed so far that achieve to address some of the special requirements of spatio-temporal datasets. A basic drawback of the existing methodologies is that they fail to treat space and time equally well. Instead, most of the approaches that have been proposed put their effort on the adequate treatment of either the spatial or the temporal dimension of the data, but not both. As a result, user mobility data is often transformed into sequential data, where the spatial component is reduced to a set of places of interest (events) and the time component (apart from providing the total ordering of these events in the sequence) is disregarded. Thus, we feel that there is plenty of room for research in this interesting and challenging area.

As presented earlier, privacy preserving data mining in the context of spatio-temporal data has been investigated towards three broad research directions: (i) data perturbation approaches, (ii) distributed secure multiparty computation approaches, and (iii) knowledge hiding approaches. Based on the number of published works per direction, it becomes evident that most of the research effort has been placed toward the development of data perturbation methodologies, while few approaches have been devised to support the other two directions. We believe that in the upcoming years, data mining researchers will put more effort in devising novel algorithms for the hiding of user mobility patterns, especially due to the urging need of these methodologies in various application contexts. The hiding of sensitive spatio-temporal patterns referring to user mobility imposes far greater challenges than traditional knowledge hiding, since specially crafted algorithms are necessary to identify all the important correlations that exist within the datasets. Furthermore, the mining of sensitive knowledge, depicted in the form of associations in mobility datasets, may allow for the use of different measures of pattern interestingness than the currently employed metrics. As an effect, new knowledge hiding techniques may have to be investigated that will successfully conceal this novel type of sensitive knowledge.

7.5   Summary and Conclusions

In this chapter we provided an overview to the area of privacy in spatio-temporal data mining, highlighted its research challenges, as well as presented a taxonomy of the state-of-the-art privacy methodologies that have been proposed to tackle this problem. Although still in its infancy, privacy preserving spatio-temporal data mining has attracted a lot of research attention and already counts a number of methodologies both with respect to sensitive data protection and to sensitive knowledge hiding. However, as we discussed in the provided roadmap, there is still a lot of work to be done, especially with respect to methodologies that hide spatio-temporal knowledge. We feel that in the upcoming years this research area will display important findings and attract even more researchers from similar disciplines.

Acknowledgments

The authors would like to thank the anonymous reviewers for their thoughtful comments and suggestions that led to the improvement of the quality of this work.

References

[1] O. Abul, F. Bonchi, and M. Nanni. Never walk alone: Uncertainty for anonymity in moving objects databases. In *Proceedings of the 24th IEEE International Conference on Data Engineering (ICDE)*, pages 376–385, 2008.

[2] O. Abul, M. Atzori, F. Bonchi, and F. Giannotti. Hiding sensitive trajectory patterns. In *Proceedings of the 7th IEEE International Conference on Data Mining Workshops (ICDMW)*, pages 693–698, 2007.

[3] O. Abul, M. Atzori, F. Bonchi, and F. Giannotti. Hiding sequences. In *Proceedings of the 23rd International Conference on Data Engineering Workshops (ICDEW)*, pages 147–156, 2007.

[4] N. Andrienko, G. Andrienko, N. Pelekis, and S. Spaccapietra. *Basic Concepts of Movement Data*, chapter 1, pages 15–38. Mobility, Data Mining and Privacy: Geographic Knowledge Discovery. Springer Berlin Heidelberg, 2008.

[5] C. Bettini, X. S. Wang, and S. Jajodia. Protecting privacy against location–based personal identification. In *Proceedings of the Second VLDB Workshop on Secure Data Management (SDM)*, pages 185–199, 2005.

[6] F. Bonchi, Y. Saygin, V. S. Verykios, M. Atzori, A. Gkoulalas-Divanis, S. V. Kaya, and E. Savas. *Privacy in Spatiotemporal Data Mining*, chapter 11, pages 297–333. Mobility, Data Mining and Privacy: Geographic Knowledge Discovery. Springer Berlin Heidelberg, 2008.

[7] H. Cao, N. Mamoulis, and D. W. Cheung. Discovery of collocation episodes in spatiotemporal data. In *Proceedings of the 6th International Conference on Data Mining (ICDM)*, pages 823–827, 2006.

[8] C. Clifton, M. Kantarcioglou, X. Lin, and M. Zhu. Tools for privacy preserving distributed data mining. *SIGKDD Explorations*, 4(2):28–34, 2002.

[9] J. E. Dobson and P. F. Fisher. Geoslavery. *IEEE Technology and Society Magazine*, 22(1):47–52, 2003.

[10] F. Giannotti, M. Nanni, and D. Pedreschi. Efficient mining of temporally annotated sequences. In *Proceedings of the 6th SIAM International Conference on Data Mining (SDM)*, pages 346–357, 2006.

[11] F. Giannotti, M. Nanni, F. Pinelli, and D. Pedreschi. Trajectory pattern mining. In *Proceedings of the 13th ACM SIGKDD International Conference on Knowledge Discovery and Data Mining (KDD)*, pages 330–339, 2007.

[12] A. Gkoulalas-Divanis and V. S. Verykios. *Privacy Preserving Data Mining: How far can we go?*, pages 1–21. Handbook of Research on Data Mining in Public and Private Sectors: Organizational and Governmental Applications. IGI Global, 2009. Accepted — Currently in press.

[13] D. Gusfield. Efficient methods for multiple sequence alignment with guaranteed error bounds. *Bulletin of Mathematical Biology*, 55(1):141–154, 1993.

[14] B. Hoh and M. Gruteser. Protecting location privacy through path confusion. In *Proceedings of the 1st International Conference on Security and Privacy for Emerging Areas in Communications Networks (SECURECOMM)*, pages 194–205, 2005.

[15] B. Hoh, M. Gruteser, H. Xiong, and A. Alrabady. Preserving privacy in GPS traces via uncertainty–aware path cloaking. In *Proceedings of the 14th ACM Conference on Computer and Communications Security (CCS)*, pages 161–171, 2007.

[16] A. Inan and Y. Saygin. Privacy preserving spatiotemporal clustering on horizontally partitioned data. In *Proceedings of the 8th International Conference on Data Warehousing and Knowledge Discovery Engineering (DAWAK)*, pages 459–468, 2006.

[17] S. Laxman and P. S. Sastry. A survey of temporal data mining. *Sadhana*, 31(2):173–198, 2006.

[18] N. Mamoulis, H. Cao, G. Kollios, M. Hadjieleftheriou, Y. Tao, and D. W. Cheung. Mining, indexing, and querying historical spatiotemporal data. In *Proceedings of the 10th ACM SIGKDD International Conference on Knowledge Discovery and Data Mining (KDD)*, pages 236–245, 2004.

[19] M. Nanni, B. Kuijpers, C. Körner, M. May, and D. Pedreschi. Spatiotemporal data mining. In *Mobility, Data Mining and Privacy*, pages 267–296. Springer Berlin Heidelberg, 2008.

[20] M. E. Nergiz, M. Atzori, and Y. Saygin. Towards trajectory anonymization: A generalization–based approach. In *Proceedings of the ACM GIS Workshop on Security and Privacy in GIS and LBS*, pages 1–10, 2008.

[21] R. G. Pensa, A. Monreale, F. Pinelli, and D. Pedreschi. Pattern–preserving $\mathcal{K}$–anonymization of sequences and its application to mobility data mining. In *Proceedings of the International Workshop on Privacy in Location Based Applications*, pages 1–17, 2008.

[22] B. Pinkas. Cryptographic techniques for privacy preserving data mining. *SIGKDD Explorations*, 4(2):12–19, 2002.

[23] P. Samarati. Protecting respondents' identities in microdata release. *IEEE Transactions on Knowledge and Data Engineering*, 13(6):1010–1027, 2001.

[24] S. Shekhar, R. R. Vatsavai, and M. Celik. Spatial and spatiotemporal data mining: Recent advances. In *Next Generation of Data Mining*, pages 549–584. Chapman & Hall/CRC, 2008.

[25] S. Shekhar, P. Zhang, Y. Huang, and R. R. Vatsavai. *Trends in Spatial Data Mining*, chapter 3, pages 357–380. Data Mining: Next Generation Challenges and Future Directions. AAAI/MIT Press, 2004.

[26] L. Sweeney. $\mathcal{K}$–anonymity: A model for protecting privacy. *International Journal on Uncertainty, Fuzziness and Knowledge Based Systems*, 10(5):557–570, 2002.

[27] M. Terrovitis and N. Mamoulis. Privacy preservation in the publication of trajectories. In *Proceedings of the The 9th International Conference on Mobile Data Management (MDM)*, pages 65–72, 2008.

[28] G. Trajcevski, O. Wolfson, K. Hinrichs, and S. Chamberlain. Managing uncertainty in moving objects databases. *ACM Transactions on Database Systems*, 29(3):463–507, 2004.

[29] Q. Zhao and S. S. Bhowmick. Sequential pattern mining: A survey. *Technical Report*, Center for Advanced Information Systems, School of Computer Engineering, Nanyang Technological University, Singapore, 2003.

Chapter 8

Probabilistic Grid-Based Approaches for Privacy-Preserving Data Mining on Moving Object Trajectories

Gyözö Gidófalvi

Dept. of Information Technology, Uppsala University, Uppsala, Sweden

Xuegang Huang

Dept. of Computer Science, Aalborg University, Aalborg, Denmark

Torben Bach Pedersen

Dept. of Computer Science, Aalborg University, Aalborg, Denmark

8.1 Introduction

The efficient management of moving object databases has gained much interest in recent years due to the development of mobile communication and positioning technologies. A typical way of representing moving objects is to use the trajectories. Much work has focused on the topics of indexing, query processing and data mining of moving object trajectories, but little attention has been paid to the preservation of privacy in this setting. In many applications such as intelligent transport systems (ITS) and fleet management, floating car data (FCD), i.c., tracked vehicle locations, are collected, and used for mining traffic patterns. For instance, mining vehicle trajectories in urban transportation networks over time can easily identify dense areas (roads, junctions, etc.), and use this for predicting traffic congestion. By data mining the periodic movement patterns (objects follow similar routes at similar times) for individual drivers, personalized, context–aware services can be delivered. However, exposing location/trajectory data of moving objects to application servers can cause threats to the *location privacy* of individual users. For example, a service provider with access to trajectory data can study a user's personal and potentially sensitive habits. The naïve approach of keeping the user's identity a secret by hiding / encoding the user's ID does not work: Frequent user locations, such as the home and office addresses can be found by first self–correlating the user's trajectory, and then cross–referencing the frequent locations with publicly available spatial data sources, e.g., *The Yellow Pages*, thereby revealing the user's identity.

In recent years, the study of privacy–preserving data mining has appeared due to the advances in data collection and dissemination technologies which force existing data mining algorithms to be reconsidered from the point of view of privacy protection. Various privacy concepts and measures, such as *k–anonymity* and *l–diversity*, and related privacy–preservation techniques, such as perturbation, condensation, generalization and data hiding with conceptual reconstruction have been proposed in the general setting. However, research that investigates the extension or applicability of these privacy concepts and measures to the spatio-temporal domain, in particular the privacy–preserving data mining of moving object trajectories has been limited. Hence this chapter is focused on addressing the unique challenge of obtaining detailed, accurate patterns from anonymized location and trajectory data.

To this extent, after a thorough status report on research works related to the issue of privacy–preserving data mining on moving object trajectories, first, the chapter proposes a novel *anonymization framework* for the preservation of location privacy on moving object trajectories. In this framework, users specify their requirements of location privacy, based on the notions of *anonymization rectangles* and *location probabilities*, intuitively saying how precisely they want to be located in given areas. Second, the chapter shows a *common problem* with existing methods that are based on the notion of *k–anonymity*. This problem allows an adversary to infer a frequently occurring location of a user, e.g., the home address, by correlating several observations. Third, the chapter presents an effective *grid–based framework* for data collection and mining over the anonymized trajectory data. The framework is based on the notions of *anonymization grids* and *anonymization partitionings* which allow effective management of both the user–specified location privacy requirements and the anonymized trajectory data. Along with the framework, three *policies* for constructing *anonymization rectangles*, called *common regular partitioning*, *individual regular partitioning*, and *individual irregular partitioning* are presented. All three policies avoid the aforementioned privacy problem of existing methods. Fourth, the chapter presents a client–server architecture for an efficient implementation of the system. A distinguishing feature of the architecture is that anonymization is performed solely on the client, thus removing the need for trusted middleware. Fifth, the chapter presents techniques for solving two basic trajectory data mining operations within the proposed anonymization framework, namely *finding dense spatio-temporal areas* and *finding frequent routes*. The techniques are based on probabilistic counting.

Finally, extensive experiments with prototype implementations show the effectiveness of the approach, by comparing the presented solutions to their non–privacy–preserving equivalents. The experiments show that the framework still allows most patterns to be found, even when privacy is preserved.

The rest of this chapter is organized as follows. Section 8.2 reviews related work. Section 8.3 discusses anonymization models of trajectory data. Section 8.4 presents the grid–based anonymization framework, while Section 8.5 presents an empirical evaluation. Finally, Section 8.6 concludes and points out future directions for research.

8.2   Related Work

Privacy protection in databases has been a core area in the database research community and many related topics have appeared in the literature, such as access control, inference control and statistical databases. The increasing availability, the sensitive nature and unique characteristics of location data about moving objects quickly made location privacy an increasingly important and interesting research subtopic. Finally, the potential value of the knowledge that can be extracted from such location data has made spatio-temporal data mining a hot area of research. The following sections review related work in these areas.

8.2.1   General Privacy Concepts

The problem of anonymizing person–specific datasets (e.g., hospital records) has led to the introduction of a number of general privacy concepts and measures. As it is demonstrated in [28], the simple removal of unique identifiers (e.g., SSN, name) does not suffice, as a set of *quasi–identifiers* (e.g., ZIP code, date of birth, sex) together with some external public data sources (e.g., voting registers) can be used to link an individual uniquely or with very high probability to a single record in the dataset, which contains one more more *sensitive attributes* (e.g., disease). To protect against such exposure, *k–anonymity* requires the values of the quasi–identifiers to be suppressed or generalized such that for each quasi-identifier value there are at least k records in the dataset with the same value. As pointed out in [23], while k such records are indistinguishable from each other w.r.t. the quasi–identifier, i.e., form an *equivalence class*, the privacy of the individual is threatened if the values for the sensitive attribute(s) in the equivalence class are not sufficiently diverse. Hence, *l–diversity* requires the sensitive attribute(s) to take on at least l different values in each equivalence class.

8.2.2   Location Privacy

The rapid developments in mobile computing, communication, and localization technologies fuel the emergence and adoption of LBSes. Since the locations of the LBS users can be used as quasi–identifiers to access sensitive information about the individual [6, 16], in recent years location privacy quickly became a public concern and hot research topic. Most of the research in this area focuses on either one of the following two tasks: 1) the *online* provision of privacy–preserving LBS, or 2) the *offline* privacy–preserving publication of the collected location sequences, i.e., trajectories of moving objects. However, most recently, methods have been proposed to facilitate the combined tasks of providing *trajectory anonymity* for LBS.

Privacy–Preserving LBS: To eliminate location privacy concerns, several papers have proposed privacy–preserving LBS solutions, which try to effectively deliver the LBS to the user without exposing the exact user location to the LBS provider [6, 9, 13, 16, 12, 20, 25, 33]. These solutions provide privacy either by spatio-temporal generalization or by mixing exact user locations with dummy locations. Spatio-temporal generalization can be based on a minimum area requirement and/or a k–*anonymity* requirement, whereby the locations of k users are aggregated, i.e., substituted by a "cloaking" rectangle that includes all k locations, so that the location of an individual user is not distinguishable [12, 20]. Dummy locations can either be real locations of other users or synthetic locations that exhibit some spatial characteristics [33]. When dummy locations are those of other users, they can either be acquired from a trusted middleware, often termed an *anonymizer*, that is aware of the exact locations of all the users at all times [6, 12, 20, 25], or they can be acquired from neighboring users communicating in a P2P network [9, 13]. In both cases, however, users must *trust* a component of the system, either a server or each other to determine the set of k user locations. In a *special* setting, one in which user locations *cannot* be used as quasi–identifiers, but can be "secret" or "embarrassing," a solution that does not require trusted components, but allows the lossless k–*anonymous* collection of exact trajectories has been proposed [17]. However, a solution for the same task in an environment that contains only untrusted components is unknown and likely to be computationally prohibitive in the *general* setting, one in which user locations *can* be used as quasi–identifiers.

Privacy–Preserving Publications of Trajectories: k-*anonymity* based privacy–preserving LBS solutions are developed with the aim of protecting the sensitive location–based queries (LB–query) of users. As such, they generalize the location of a single LB-query of a user in such a way that the source of the LB–query, i.e., the user, is indistinguishable from $k-1$ other potential sources (users). In a sense, the privacy that is provided is for a single LB–query at a particular time and location. This point–wise k–*anonymity* guarantee fails to protect the privacy of users that issue *sequences* of LB–queries, when a *subset* of the generalized LB–queries at frequently visited private locations (e.g., home, work, . . .) are used as a quasi–identifier to link a particular user to a generalized trajectory, which may contain not general enough cloaking rectangles and reveal sensitive locations. To aid the useful analysis of trajectory datasets while protecting against the above described privacy threat, in recent years a number of methods have been proposed for the task of privacy–preserving publication of trajectories [1, 2, 3, 26, 30]. Based on the nature of the problem, all these methods assume that a trusted entity has collected the trajectories and aims to sanitize it before releasing it to un-trusted third parties for further analysis. The methods are either based 1) on data perturbation and or obfuscation [3, 26, 30], or 2) on sequential pattern hiding techniques [1, 2, 27]. All methods apply a general mining technique, clustering [3, 26, 30] or frequent pattern mining [1, 2, 27], to either group and spatio-temporally generalize k nearby trajectories to ensure privacy [3, 26], or to identify and obfuscate a subsequence of the locations in the trajectories that can be used as quasi–identifiers or are sensitive [1, 2, 27, 30].

Trajectory Anonymity for LBS: Privacy–preserving LBS solutions offer methods to point-wise anonymize LB–queries in an online fashion. Methods for privacy–preserving publication of trajectories provide methods to anonymize entire trajectories in an offline fashion. However, since LBS provi- ders have the ability, and most likely the intention, to store and analyze sequences of service requests, i.e., trajectories, most recently methods have been proposed to provide trajectory anonymity for LBS [18, 19]. Essentially, these proposals combine two methods, one from each of the previously discussed research areas. As in the previous proposals, both of these methods are based on a trusted middleware that receives and stores all the LB–queries of the users, extracts patterns from the stored data, and depending on the current user locations and the extracted patterns anonymizes the current user locations such that, if possible, the anonymity of trajectories, or at least, the point–wise anonymity of locations is guaranteed.

8.2.3 Spatio-Temporal Data Mining

Spatio-temporal data mining is an ongoing topic in the database community. Approaches have appeared for finding dense areas of moving objects [21, 22, 29] and extracting spatio-temporal rules and patterns [14, 31]. The present proposal is focused on discovering areas with potential traffic jams and roads that are frequently used by drivers. Two very related papers [21, 22] study the querying of spatio-temporal regions with a high concentration of moving objects. The first paper [21] divides the data space into a uniform grid so that the density query is simplified to reporting cells that satisfy the density conditions. This solution provides fast answers, but can lead to *answer loss* (as termed in the second paper [22]), such as regions that cover boundaries of several cells with a high density of objects (but each individual cell does not contain enough objects to be dense). The second paper [22] provides a new definition of density query that eliminates answer loss and proposes a two-phase filter–and–refinement algorithm for computing the density queries. A method to provide approximate answers to *distinct* spatio-temporal aggregation is proposed in [29], where aggregation is grid–based, and the distinct criterion is time– and space–effectively solved by combining a spatio-temporal index (aRB–tree) and sketches. Finding frequently traveled routes taken by moving objects has many applications in telematics, ITS and LBS. This has been recognized recently in [15], where frequent route mining is mapped to frequent itemset mining, after trajectories are transformed to a set of spatio-temporal grid cells. The proposed solution takes a similar approach to finding frequent routes, but focuses on the privacy preserving aspect of the data mining.

A lot of recent research work has focused on techniques for privacy–preserving data mining [5]. This topic has appeared due to the advances in data collection and dissemination technologies which force existing data mining algorithms to be reconsidered from the point of view of privacy preservation. Various papers have recently addressed privacy-preserving data mining. Important techniques include perturbation, condensation, and data hiding with conceptual reconstruction. Paper [32] presents a good review of these techniques. The techniques proposed in this chapter follow the spirit of a common strategy used for privacy–preserving data mining, namely *generalization*.

It is evident from the presented related work review that k–*anonymity* based anonymization of locations and trajectories has several problems. First, the so far proposed solutions for the *general* setting require trusted components for finding the locations/trajectories of the other $k-1$ users. Second, the notion of location privacy that is guaranteed by k–*anonymity* may not be satisfactory in the case where a large number of moving objects stay in a small area where users do not want to be observed (such as a red light district). This problem can be eliminated by requiring cloaking rectangles to have a minimum area [25]. Third, the cloaking rectangles calculated for the same user for the same location at different times depend on locations of the other $k-1$ users, and hence may vary in extent and location. This, in a sense *non-deterministic* or *probabilistic* nature of cloaking rectangles sacrifices location privacy, as demonstrated later. Fourth, traditional mining methods cannot be easily and effectively adapted to the anonymized location or trajectory.

Hence, in comparison to the so-far proposed methods, this chapter does not consider k–*anonymity* and does *not* assume the existence of trusted components for providing the k–*anonymous* "cloaking" rectangles. Instead, it focuses on novel ways to conceal the actual moving object trajectories while still allowing the data mining algorithms on the LBS server to extract detailed, accurate traffic patterns and rules from the anonymized trajectory data. Note that the proposed anonymization framework does *not even aim* to provide *k–anonymity*. The reason is that for some applications, e.g., traffic services in remote areas, even a rather small k will cause the reported rectangles to become extremely large, and thus worthless for the purpose of mining. Instead, the proposed framework performs a *spatial anonymization* that meets the user's requirements for location privacy. The framework proposed in this chapter is largely based on a prior publication of the authors [16]. However, the chapter significantly extends the framework to include an additional basic trajectory data mining operation, namely *finding frequent routes*. Furthermore, the chapter also significantly extends the discussion on the previously proposed *multi–grid extension* of the framework. This extension provides several fruitful research directions.

8.3   Spatio-Temporal Anonymization

In the context of moving object trajectories, generalization refers to mapping elements of a trajectory (time stamped locations) to a set of coarser space–time regions. The following sections formally define this mapping using rectangular regions, give an intuitive definition of location privacy in terms of the mapped regions, and discuss ways to avoid two potential pitfalls that can lead to privacy breaches.

8.3.1   Definition of Location Privacy

For the simplicity of the discussion, it is assumed that the time domain $\mathbb{T}$ is totally ordered and the non–negative numbers are used as the time domain. The trajectory of a moving object in 2–dimensional (2D) space can be described by a sequence of tuples $S = \langle (loc_1, t_1), \ldots, (loc_n, t_n) \rangle$ where $loc_i \in \mathbb{R}^2$ ($i = 1, \ldots, n$) describe locations, and $t_1 < t_2 < \ldots < t_n \in \mathbb{T}$ are irregularly spaced but temporally ordered time instances, i.e., gaps are allowed.

The trajectory is anonymized by reducing the spatio-temporal resolution of the 2D space. One basic method is to enclose the trajectory in one or more space–time rectangles, denoted as an *anonymization rectangles*. A formal definition is as follows:

DEFINITION 8.1   Given an area size `areasize` $\in \mathbb{R}^2$ and a probability threshold `maxLocProb` $\in [0..1]$, an **anonymization rectangle** satisfying (`areasize`, `maxLocProb`) for a moving object o is a three–tuple (R, t_s, t_e), where $t_s < t_e \in \mathbb{T}$ are two time instances, and R is a 2D rectangle such that the maximum probability can be *inferred* about o being in any subregion A of size *areasize* in R during the period $[t_s, t_e]$ is at most `maxLocProb`.

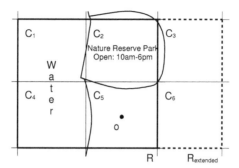

FIGURE 8.1: Location Privacy.

DEFINITION 8.2   Given an area size `areasize` $\in \mathbb{R}^2$, the maximum probability that can be *inferred* about the whereabouts of object o inside R is called the **location probability** of R and is denoted as $R.LocProb$.

Privacy preservation in spatio-temporal datasets is challenging because spatio-temporal datasets are so rich in correlations, allowing many "privacy attack" strategies that are difficult to counteract and sometimes even to anticipate. The proposed method is believed to protect against the most obvious threats, namely, 1) detection of frequent private/personal/individual locations due to self–correlations in historical spatio-temporal (trajectory) datasets, 2) detection of the current position due to physical mobility constraints on objects (maximum speed, road network, spatio-temporal restrictions in general).

In the definitions, *inferred* is emphasized, because the straightforward, uniform spatio-temporal probability distribution for the location of an object o does not hold for any rectangle $R \in \mathbb{R}^+$. By relating external spatial and/or temporal data sources, which put limitations on the possible locations of o, more specific distributions can be derived that sacrifice the privacy of o. This is illustrated in Figure 8.1, where anonymization rectangle R of o is composed of 4 unit–area cells (c_1, c_2, c_4, c_5). Not combining any external data sources, $R.LocProb = 1/4$. Knowing that cells c_1 and c_4 are covered by water, $R.LocProb = 1/2$. Finally, knowing about the location and opening hours of the Nature Resort Park in cell c_2 and the current time (8am), $R.LocProb = 1$. Clearly, relating more and more spatio-temporal, external data sources to R raises the location probability of it, and guarantees less privacy for o. One natural way to guarantee a location probability of at most `maxLocProb`, is to spatially, or temporally, extend R to $R_{extended}$, such that $R_{extended}.LocProb \leq$ `maxLocProb`. Section 8.4.2 describes how such an extension can be done practice to protect location privacy.

If the currently known spatio-temporal probability distribution for the location of an object o is denoted as PD_o, then any kind of "extra" external spatio-temporal information can be modeled as a function $F(PD_o)$ that returns a

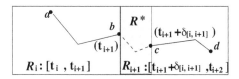

FIGURE 8.2: Time Delay Factor.

new spatio-temporal probability distribution PD'_o. If the location probability of o at certain locations is then over the threshold `maxLocProb` with the new distribution, there is a problem that needs to be handled somehow, most often by enlarging the area partitions.

Intuitively, the whole trajectory of a moving object can be enclosed in a single rectangle so that the anonymity of the trajectory is preserved. However, as the trajectories are often very long, the rectangles can be very big, so that it becomes impossible for the data mining algorithms to return any useful results. The proposed method provides an **anonymized format** of the trajectory by cutting a long trajectory into pieces and enclosing each piece in an anonymization rectangle. This format can give opportunities for doing data mining without sacrificing location privacy.

8.3.2 Practical "Cut–Enclose" Implementation

The "cut–enclose" procedure splits the whole trajectory of a moving object o into a set of polylines which correspond to a set of time periods $\{[t_1, t_2], [t_2, t_3], [t_3, t_4], \ldots, [t_{k-1}, t_k]\}$, such that at any time instance $t_i \in \{t_2, t_3, \ldots, t_{k-1}\}$, object o's trajectory crosses an edge between two neighboring anonymization rectangles. As illustrated in Figure 8.2, o's trajectory crosses the edge between R_i and R_{i+1} at location b at time instance t_i. Since around this instance t_i, o is more likely to be close to the edge between R_i and R_{i+1}, the probability value $R_{i+1}.LocProb$ will temporarily be higher, which might sacrifice the location privacy of o. More specifically, from the time spent in the previous anonymization rectangles, their sizes, and relative locations to each other, a malicious server can easily maintain a linear movement model of o. Using this movement model, when o sends the anonymization rectangle R_{i+1}, the malicious server can *deduce* a *possible location range* R^* of o, such that $R^*.LocProb > $ `maxLocProb`.

To avoid this situation and preserve the location privacy of o, a **time delay factor** $\delta_{[i,i+1]}$ for delaying the sending of the anonymous rectangle R_{i+1} after leaving R_i is introduced. The factor $\delta_{[i,i+1]}$ can be calculated as follows. Object o can maintain the same linear movement model about its own movement as the malicious server can. Hence, at any time instance $t^* > t_i$, having entered R_{i+1}, o can calculate R^* and $R^*.LocProb$. As time progresses, the size of R^* is monotonically increasing and $R^*.LocProb$ is monotonically decreasing. Hence,

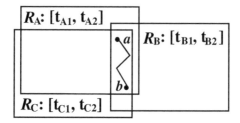

FIGURE 8.3: Overlapping Area.

at some time point $t^s > t_i$, when the associated $R^*.LocProb \leq$ `maxLocProb` it is *safe* for o to send R_{i+1} to the server. The time delay factor is then $\delta_{[i,i+1]} = t^s - t_i$.

Most moving objects are confined to road networks. In the presence of road networks, more sophisticated movement models are possible. Actual values for the time delay factor have been investigated for a number of network–based movement models on real-world datasets in [10], but this work has a different aim, namely to aid tracking.

8.3.3　Problems with Existing Methods

To construct an anonymization rectangle for a given piece of trajectory, one naïve method is to randomly choose a location in the vicinity of the trajectory and use this location as the center to build the anonymization rectangle based on a predefined size. Another method, in order to provide *location k–anonymity* [20, 12, 25], is to build the anonymization rectangle that encloses this piece with trajectory pieces of $k - 1$ other moving objects.

However, these two methods can lead to an undesired *loss of location privacy*. Sensitive locations that need to be kept private, or trajectory pieces that lead to these, are often revisited by the objects many times, at a similar time of day. For example, objects (users), in the evening hours return to their *home* using the same path (trajectory piece). If on different occasions the anonymization rectangles for this trajectory piece are constructed in a *nondeterministic* way, either randomly or based on time–varying user locations, the location of the trajectory piece can be narrowed down to the *intersection* of these anonymization rectangles. This leads to an undesirable loss of privacy. In the example of Figure 8.3, object o returns to its *home* b using the same trajectory piece $[a, b]$ on three different occasions at the same time of the day. On the three occasions, three anonymization rectangles R_A, R_B, and R_C are constructed, such that they all contain the trajectory piece $[a, b]$. Based on the multiple visits, the location of $[a, b]$ can be narrowed down to the small overlapping area of the anonymization rectangles.

The next section presents a grid-based anonymization framework and several methods for constructing anonymization rectangles in a *deterministic* way on this grid, thereby avoiding the privacy loss described above. The grid-based anonymization framework also allows for an efficient implementation of the "cut–enclose" procedure described in Section 8.3.2.

8.4 Grid-Based Anonymization Framework

A basic method to anonymize location is to reduce the spatial resolution. Thus, instead of randomly constructing the anonymization rectangles or building the rectangles based on trajectories of other moving objects, the anonymization rectangles for all moving objects are built based on a single, predefined 2D grid. The following sections discuss the proposed grid-based framework in detail.

8.4.1 Grid-Based Anonymization

Denote the whole 2D Euclidean space by $\mathbb{R}^2$. Then, the definitions of an *anonymization grid* and *anonymization partitioning* are as follows.

DEFINITION 8.3   An **anonymization grid** (briefly, a grid) G is a uniform grid of $\mathbb{R}^2$ with a predefined origin $O \in \mathbb{R}^2$ as the starting point and a side length l. An **anonymization partitioning** (briefly, a partitioning) is a set of pairwise disjoint sets of grid cells covering all of G.

As illustrated in Figure 8.4(a), given a starting point $O \in \mathbb{R}^2$, the anonymization grid (briefly, the grid) G uniformly divides the whole space into square–shaped **grid cells**, each of which has side length l. Each grid cell has an ID value, such as $c_1, c_2, \ldots$ in Figure 8.4(a). A *partition* of a partitioning that is defined on the grid is a set of grid cells.

Next, several policies for constructing **anonymization partitionings** based on the anonymization grid are developed. All of the partitionings are constructed *deterministically*, thereby avoiding the privacy loss due to overlapping partitions.

Common Regular Partitioning (CRP): The simplest policy is to define a single, regular partitioning that is used by all the objects. A partitioning is called **regular** if all the partitions are rectangles with side lengths $i_x \times l$ and $i_y \times l$, where i_x and i_y are integers.

Such a regular partitioning can be seen as a coarser grid on the 2D space. As illustrated in Figure 8.4(a), given the grid (the grid of thin lines), the partitioning (the grid of thick lines) is defined by an origin O and $i_x = 3, i_y = 3$. In the example the grid cells c_1, c_2, c_3 belong to the partition p_1. With the

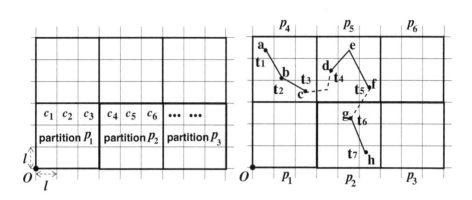

(a) Anonymization Grid and Partitioning.

(b) Anonymized Trajectory.

FIGURE 8.4: Grid-Based Anonymization of Trajectories.

grid and partitioning, a moving object trajectory can be transformed to a set of non-overlapping anonymization rectangles to preserve anonymity. For instance, given the trajectory $\langle (a, t_1), (b, t_2), \ldots, (h, t_7) \rangle$ in Figure 8.4(b), a grid on the 2D space is built and the partitioning on the grid is made. The partitions are denoted as $p_1, \ldots, p_6$ in the figure and they are non-overlapping rectangles. As described in Section 8.3.2, given the time delay factor δ, the whole trajectory is cut into several pieces with $t_4 - t_3 = \delta$ and $t_6 - t_5 = \delta$. Then, the whole trajectory is transformed into a list of anonymization rectangles $\langle (p_4, t_1, t_3), (p_5, t_4, t_5), (p_2, t_6, t_7) \rangle$.

The above described partitioning guarantees the same minimal level of privacy for all users in any region of the space. This policy for partitioning is termed the Common Regular Partitioning (CRP) policy.

Fundamental spatio-temporal data mining tasks, like finding dense spatio-temporal regions, are based on simple counts or identities of the users that are present in a given spatio-temporal region. Since according to the CRP policy all users report the same set of grid cells for the same location, the spatio-temporal granularity of any pattern found is *lower bounded* by the size of a partition. In the example in Figure 8.4(b), the size of the common partition is 9 grid cells, hence the smallest dense ST-region that can be found will be 9 grid cells.

Individual Regular Partitioning (IRP): Not all objects require the same level of location privacy. This requirement of individual objects can easily be accommodated in the anonymization grid-based framework. Objects requiring higher levels of privacy construct and use a regular partitioning with larger partitions, while objects requiring lower levels of privacy define and use a regular partitioning with smaller partitions. This policy for partitioning is termed the Individual Regular Partitioning (IRP) policy.

Besides being more flexible in terms of the objects' privacy requirements, the IRP policy allows the discovery of patterns of spatio-temporal granularity that is equal to the size of a single grid cell (if enough data is present).

Individual Irregular Partitioning (IIP): Objects may have different location privacy requirements in different regions of space. For example, most objects (users) desire a higher level of location privacy when being at *home* or the *work place* than when being in transition or when being in other general areas of the city. This requirement of individual objects can again be easily accommodated in the proposed grid-based anonymization framework. Objects can be allowed to individually define privacy levels for regions in space that reflect their needs. The definition of these regions can be either manual, or can be aided by discovering frequent (presumably sensitive) locations of individual objects. Since the selection or discovery of these sensitive locations can be accomplished on the client side, it can be kept private. This policy for partitioning is termed the Individual Irregular Partitioning (IIP) policy.

The IIP policy also allows the discovery of patterns of spatio-temporal granularity that is equal to the size of a single grid cell. The additional ability to define spatially varying privacy levels not only adds more privacy control, but it is also expected to allow the discovery of more patterns with finer spatio-temporal granularity. This is due to the fact that most objects are expected to require higher levels of location privacy in relatively small subregions. The more detailed patterns are expected to be more useful for ITS applications.

With the proposed grid-based framework, the knowledge one can infer about the whereabouts of a user does not depend on the number of samples collected. The certainty of the inference only depends on the amount of external spatio-temporal information available for the anonymous rectangle.

8.4.2   System Architecture

The grid-based anonymization framework is implemented based on a client/ server architecture. As illustrated in Figure 8.5, the server side has three components, the *anonymity component* which defines one or more grids and communicates them to the client, the *storage component* which collects the anonymization rectangles sent from the clients and stores the data on disk, and the *data mining component* which discovers certain patterns and rules either directly from the incoming data stream or from the historical data retrieved from the storage component.

The clients are responsible for accepting an anonymization grid and developing a partitioning based on the grid. In practice, the partitioning will be made in one of two ways: a) the user selects among a small number of pre–computed partitionings to find one that meets their privacy requirements, or b) the partitioning is computed by a dedicated program on the client, based

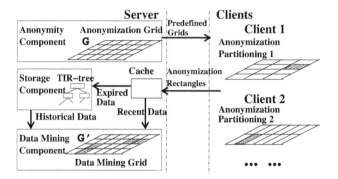

FIGURE 8.5: System Architecture.

on user input about privacy requirements. Both a) and b) take available background knowledge into account. The framework can also handle the presence of road networks. If road networks are dense compared to the partition size, the framework can be used without modification. If not, the partitions have to be enlarged so that each partition contains enough road to get a location probability that is comparable to those of the other partitions.

These client- and grid-specific partitionings are stored on the clients and only anonymization rectangles (in the form of sets of grid cells), which are computed *at the clients*, are transmitted to the server. It is assumed that the client has a fair amount of storage and CPU power, but not more than what can be found in most currently available smart phones or PDAs.

Saving a partitioning at the client side does not take much space. For a regular partitioning, where partitions form a regular grid, it is enough to store the starting point and the side length of the partitioning. Finding the partition that corresponds to a location is a matter of simple arithmetic. For a non-regular partitioning, where partitions do not form a regular grid, i.e., are of different size and/or shape, partitions can be kept in an R–tree. Finding the partition that corresponds to a location can be done by issuing a stabbing query on the R–tree for the location. The communication cost between the clients and the server is very low since the grids can be described with the starting point and side length l of the grid, and the anonymization rectangles only involve a few data fields (i.e., coordinates of the client's current partition and the time instances).

The clients always send their current anonymization rectangle, i.e., their current partition, to the server. When the anonymized data is transmitted to the server, it is stored in two places. To be able to perform data mining on historical data, the data is first stored in a time-interval R-tree (TIR–tree in Figure 8.5) on disk. The TIR-tree is a 1-dimensional R-tree that indexes the data on the time intervals. To be able to perform online data mining on the current data, the data is also stored in a *cache*, with a FIFO replacement policy as follows. According to the size of the cache, when a new anonymization rectangle of a moving object arrives, either the previous anonymization rectangle of this moving object (if in the cache) or the oldest data in the cache is deleted.

The system architecture in Figure 8.5 supports data mining on both historical trajectories and recent data. Each anonymization grid in the anonymity component corresponds to an in-memory instance of the same grid in the data mining component. For instance, the anonymization grid G in Figure 8.5 corresponds to the data mining grid G′ (it is assumed that the data mining component has enough memory to store G′). Based on this architecture, in the following, algorithms for discovering *dense spatio-temporal areas* and *frequent routes* on the anonymized trajectory data are presented.

8.4.3 Finding Dense Spatio-Temporal Areas

Discovering dense areas is one of the most common topics for spatial and spatio-temporal data mining. Existing research work has explored density clustering [11], spatio-temporal dense area discovery [31] and density queries [22]. For dense area discovery on the anonymized trajectory data, the most basic operation is to find those grid cells that contain a large amount of moving objects during specified time intervals. In the anonymized format, objects are present in a grid cell with some *probability* only. Hence, a **time interval probabilistically dense spatio-temporal area query**, or *dense ST–area query* for short, is proposed.

Specifically, suppose a moving object o corresponds to a partition P on a given anonymization grid G, a partition cell $p \in P$ contains o's trajectory during time interval $[t_s, t_e]$, and p includes grid cells $c_1, c_2, \ldots, c_k$. p is used as the anonymization rectangle for o's trajectory and each grid cell $c_i \in p$ has the location probability $c_i^o.LocProb = 1/k$ for o at any time instance during $[t_s, t_e]$. Let O^{c_i} be the set of moving objects whose anonymization rectangles include the grid cell c_i in at least one time instance during the time interval $[t_s, t_e]$. Then $c_i.count = |O^{c_i}|$ and $c_i.prob = \sum_{o \in O^{c_i}} c_i^o.LocProb/|O^{c_i}|$. Intuitively, $c_i.count$ is the *maximum* number of objects that *can* be inside c_i during $[t_s, t_e]$, while $c_i.prob$ is the *average* location probability of the objects that can be inside c_i during $[t_s, t_e]$. Consequently, $c_i.prob \times c_i.count$ is the *expected* number of objects inside c_i during $[t_s, t_e]$. Furthermore, the *pattern certainty* $c_i.cert = \prod_{o \in O^{c_i}} c_i^o.LocProb$ is defined as the probability of *actually* having $c_i.count$ number of moving objects inside of c_i during $[t_s, t_e]$.

A grid cell c_i is said to be **probabilistically dense** during $[t_s, t_e]$ if $c_i.count \geq$ min_count and $c_i.prob \geq$ min_prob, for some given threshold values min_count and min_prob. Thus, the **dense ST–area query** is formulated as follows:

DEFINITION 8.4   A dense ST-area query $Q = ([t_s, t_e], \text{min\_count},$

min_prob) retrieves all the grid cells whose corresponding *count* and *prob*
values during $[t_s, t_e]$ are greater than or equal to min_count and min_prob,
respectively.

To process a *dense ST–area query*, the first step is to compute the *count* and
prob values for each grid cell c_i for the specified time interval $[t_s, t_e]$. Based on
the system architecture in Figure 8.5, a range query over the TIR–tree needs
to be issued to find all the anonymization rectangles whose time periods have
intersections with $[t_s, t_e]$. Results of the range query are used to fill in the
count and *prob* values for each cell c_i of the data mining grid G'. Then the set
of dense ST–grid cells is:

$$D = \{c_i : c_i.count \geq \mathtt{min\_count} \wedge c_i.prob \geq \mathtt{min\_prob}\}$$

During the query time interval $[t_s, t_e]$ a moving object can leave and later
reenter a given grid cell c_i. To avoid counting such an object multiple times
for c_i, a hash array of object IDs is maintained and values for $c_i.count$ and
$c_i.prob$ are only updated when an object ID is encountered for c_i for the first
time. If only approximate counts are considered, these can be more effectively
obtained using the methods from [29].

As it will be seen in Section 8.5, the cutoff criteria for dense areas presented
above is in some cases not strict enough, thus generating too many dense areas
(false positives). To remedy this, the alternative *steepest slope* cutoff criteria is
introduced, which is calculated by first sorting the expected counts for dense
areas passing the first criteria in descending order, finding the deltas between
any two consecutive values, and making the cutoff where the (negative) delta
is the smallest, i.e., where the "slope" is steepest.

The *dense ST–area query* can be seen as an atomic operation over the
anonymized trajectory data. Advanced and complex data mining functions
can be made by assembling this operation with other basic query types.

8.4.4   Frequent Route Mining

Finding frequently traveled routes taken by moving objects has many applications in telematics, ITS and LBS. One such application, an intelligent
rideshare application, was recently proposed in [15]. To aid such applications,
the task of retrieving frequent routes of moving objects can be seen as another
slightly more complicated, but equally important atomic operation over the
anonymized trajectory data. Hence, conforming the proposed anonymization
framework in the following, the **time interval** *probabilistically* **frequent
route query**, or *frequent route query* for short, is introduced.

The present proposal adopts an approach from [15] to answer a *frequent
route query* in the anonymization grid based framework. Namely, in the
present proposal trajectories are represented as a set of spatio-temporal grid
cells, and the task of finding sharable long patterns in trajectories is posed as

finding maximal frequent itemsets, i.e., frequent sets of spatio-temporal grid cells, a common task in data mining. The following paragraphs describe this mapping between problem instances formally.

Similarly to Section 8.4.3, it is assumed that for any historical time interval $[t_s, t_e]$ the locations of moving objects can be retrieved from the server side storage component in form of anonymization rectangles, which are stored as a set of grid cells, with corresponding location probabilities. To construct a spatio-temporal grid cell representation of trajectories, trajectories are split inside the query time interval into m sub-trajectories of duration $d = (t_e - t_s)/m$, by issuing m d–long time interval queries to the server side storage component at time instances $t_s, t_s + d, t_s + 2d, \ldots, t_e - 2d, t_e - d$. For each query result, the returned grid cell IDs are combined with the starting time of the query to form spatio-temporal grid cells. As a result of this transformation, a trajectory that falls inside the query time interval is represented as a set of spatio-temporal grid cell IDs, each of which is associated with a location probability. After this transformation, the traditional frequent itemset framework in [4] is modified by mapping the problem of finding frequent routes to the problem of finding maximal frequent itemsets as follows.

Conforming to the naming convention used in the traditional frequent itemset mining framework, a spatio-temporal grid cell ID is equivalently referred to as an *item*. Then, a *transformed trajectory* t inside the query time interval, equivalently referred to as a *transaction* is a two–tuple (X, P), where X is an *itemset* and P are the corresponding probabilities of the items in X. For a given transaction $t = (X, P)$, the probability of an item $i \in X$ is denoted as *i.prob*. Given a user-defined threshold `min_prob`, a transaction $t = (X, P)$ *probabilistically satisfies* an itemset Y if $Y \subseteq X$ and $\forall i \in Y \cap X$, *i.prob* $\geq$ `min_prob`. Given a set of transactions, the *probabilistic support* of an item i, denoted as *i.count* is the number of transactions that probabilistically satisfy the itemset $Y = \{i\}$. Similarly, the probabilistic support of an itemset Y, denoted as *Y.count* is the number of transactions that probabilistically satisfy all items $i \in Y$. Given a user-defined threshold `min_count`, an item i is *probabilistically frequent* if *i.count* $\geq$ `min_count`. Similarly, an itemset Y is probabilistically frequent if *Y.count* $\geq$ `min_count`. An itemset Y is a *maximal probabilistically frequent itemset* if there does not exists a probabilistically frequent itemset X such that $Y \subset X$.

Using this modified frequent itemset framework, referred to as the *probabilistically frequent itemset framework*, a **frequent route** is defined to be a maximal probabilistically frequent itemset. Consequently, the **frequent route query** is formulated as follows:

DEFINITION 8.5   A **frequent route query** $Q = ([t_s, t_e], \texttt{min\_count}, \texttt{min\_prob})$ retrieves all the maximal probabilistically frequent itemsets during $[t_s, t_e]$.

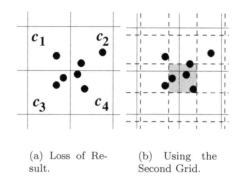

(a) Loss of Result. (b) Using the Second Grid.

FIGURE 8.6: *Multi–Grid Extension* to Overcome Answer Loss.

It is important to note that frequent routes returned by the query are not necessarily continuous in space or time. For example, a large set of objects may share the beginning and end of a route, but may make different detours in the middle of their trajectories. Such discontinuous, frequent routes can still be of great interest to telematics and ITS.

To answer a *frequent route query*, a prominent maximal itemset mining algorithm, MAFIA [8], is adopted to the probabilistic frequent itemset framework as follows. A transaction t can probabilistically satisfy an itemset $Y = \{i_k\}$ iff $i_k \in t$ and $i_k.prob \geq$ min_prob. Hence, before the mining, items having a location probability less than min_prob are deleted from transactions. This preprocessing guarantees that all maximal frequent items mined in the traditional framework, will be maximal probabilistically frequent itemsets. Such a preprocessing of transformed transactions is a straightforward, linear time operation, which not only allows a simple, but also an efficient mapping between the two frameworks and tasks. Since items that have location probabilities less than min_prob cannot appear in a maximal probabilistically frequent itemset, eliminating them from the transactions before mining reduces the search lattice and ultimately computation cost.

8.4.5   Multi-Grid Extension

The above methods are simple to implement but cannot discover all patterns (dense ST-areas or frequent routes) at the grid cell level. For example, as it is illustrated in Figure 8.6(a), while grid cells c_1, c_2, c_3, c_4 have several moving objects (dots in the figure), for a threshold min_count $= 4$, none of the four cells are reported as dense, since the *count* value of each is less than 4, even though the dark area in Figure 8.6(b) has the size of a grid cell and is dense.

A *multi-grid extension* of the anonymization framework can avoid such answer loss along with providing several other benefits. In the *multi–grid extended* anonymization framework the server provides several anonymization grids with different uniformly distributed starting points and distributes these grids to the moving objects so that there are equal amount of objects that build their partitioning based on each of the anonymization grids. The power of the *multi-grid extension* lies in the ability to allow for the propagation of probabilistic counts of a grid cell c defined on a grid G to cells c' (defined on another grid G') that overlap with c. How this propagation is performed and how it can avoid answer loss and provide additional benefits, while preserving location privacy is discussed next.

Given a uniform base grid G with side length l and predefined origin $O \in \mathbb{R}^2$, the *multi-grid extended* anonymization framework defines $n^2 - 1$ additional uniform grids $G_{(i,j)}$ with side length l and respective origins $(O_x + i * l/n, O_y + j * l/n)$, where $i, j \in \{0, 1, \ldots, n-1\}$. Note that $G_{(0,0)}$ is the base grid. The totality of the defined grids essentially forms a high resolution uniform regular grid G^* over $\mathbb{R}^2$ and effectively subdivides any given grid cell into a number of grid subcells. To efficiently utilize the power of the high resolution grid G^*, in the *multi-grid extended* anonymization framework, probabilistic counts of a grid cell c defined on a grid G are accumulated in the grid cells of G^* that are contained in c. To propagate probabilistic counts across grid boundaries, the *multi-grid extended* anonymization framework sums the accumulated probabilistic counts in the grid cells of G^*, and updates the probabilistic counts in the grid cells of the coarser grids by summarizing the sum of the accumulated probabilistic counts in the grid cells of G^*.

It is easy to see that regardless of which grid each of the objects in the dense ST-area (gray cell in Figure 8.6(b)) uses to construct anonymization partitions, accurate probabilistic counts can be summarized for the dark grid cell by applying meaningful summary statistics, e.g., max, average, sum, etc., to the sums of the accumulated probabilistic counts in the grid cells of G^* that are contained in the dark grid cell. Thus, the *multi–grid extended* anonymization framework can avoid answer loss.

A perhaps even more powerful feature of the *multi–grid extension* is that by mapping the probabilistic counts to a higher resolution grid, the extended framework allows the construction of spatio-temporal data mining algorithms that can discover higher resolution patterns. Essentially, the sum of the accumulated probabilistic counts in the grid cells of G^* is a high resolution *probabilistic spatio-temporal probability distribution* (*pstpd*) of objects.

It is important to note that while the *multi-grid extended* anonymization framework allows the derivation of a non-uniform *pstpd* of objects at a (virtually) arbitrarily high resolution, the anonymization framework still preserves location privacy. Specifically, while for any given grid cell c that is reported by a specific object o, the high resolution (non-uniform) *pstpd* of objects, c^*, is known, object o can be in any subregion of c with equal probability. The above is true, because the presence of o in any subregion of c, results in o reporting the grid cell c, which in turn results in the derivation of the *same* c^*. This guarantees that the location privacy of the object o is preserved.

Finally, as the *multi-grid extension* is based on projecting probabilistic counts between high and low resolution uniform regular grids, its implementation can be efficiently supported by grid–based indexes. Due to the abundance of research possibilities that the *multi–grid extension* represents, its implementation and evaluation is left for future research.

8.5   Evaluation

To evaluate the effectiveness of the proposed grid-based anonymization framework, a large set of experiments using realistically simulated trajectories were conducted to determine the accuracy of the proposed probabilistic data mining algorithms under different conditions and parameter settings.

In recent research [24] it has been shown that the degree of spatio-temporal generalization that common privacy-preserving solutions perform to guarantee location or trajectory *k–anonymity* heavily depends on the characteristics of the input trajectory dataset. It is argued and is shown that random moving object simulators in general, and in particular the commonly used network-based moving object simulator [7] (which is also used in the present evaluation), only partially capture the characteristics of real-world trajectory datasets. This fact however, does not invalidate the results of the present evaluation as the proposed anonymization framework is not based on the principle of *k–anonymity* and the degree of generalization is independent of the characteristics of the data and is solely controlled by user-defined anonymity parameters.

The following three sections describe a) the simulated trajectory datasets, the experimental setup and the evaluation criteria, b) the results of the experiments involving the *dense ST–area queries*, and c) the results of the experiments involving *frequent route queries*, respectively.

8.5.1   Experimental Setup and Evaluation Criteria

To evaluate the *dense ST-area query* and *frequent route query* algorithms, Brinkhoff's network-based generator of moving objects [7] is used to generate trajectories on the Oldenburg network. 600 to 3000 trajectories are generated for the time period from 0 to 100 and sampled at every time unit. To capture the real-world time span between two consecutive time instances, for all the trajectories, the average distance between every two subsequent reported locations is calculated. The average distance is $234.96m$, which is about 14 seconds travel time for a $60km/hour$ moving object. Thus, the actual time span between two consecutive time instances is about 14 seconds. The default time span for all the queries is 50 time instances, i.e., 11.6 minutes.

To implement the grid-based anonymization framework, the anonymization grid is generated based on the minimum bounding rectangle (MBR) of the Oldenburg network. A randomly chosen anonymization partitioning based on the grid is assigned to each generated trajectory. The default grid is a 40×40 partitioning on the MBR of the Oldenburg network. Based on the Oldenburg network data, the size of each grid cell is $589m \times 672.9m$. In the experiments, the grid partitioning is also tuned from 20×20 to 50×50 to observe the performance. The three policies are applied on the trajectories with the anonymization grid. To implement the CRP policy, two fixed partitionings are made, where each user has 2×2 or 4×4 grid cells. In the IRP policy, every user partition contains at most 4×4 grid cells. In the IIP policy, each moving object is set to use the anonymization partition (each partition contains at most 4×4 grid cells) that covers the start location of the moving object. After the object is out of this partition, it uses the lowest level of privacy so that each partition equals to a grid cell.

The experiments focus on evaluating the accuracy of the probabilistic data mining algorithms, i.e., the amount of false positives and false negatives. A false negative is the error of not finding a pattern that does exist in the data. A false positive is the error of finding a "pattern" that does not exist in the data. To compare the algorithms, the algorithms are also applied on an ideal case, where the partitioning of every user equals the anonymization grid, and the results of this case are used as the evaluation target. Suppose the actual amount of dense grid cells is D, the number of false positives P and false negatives N are collected for every algorithm and the ratio between these values and D are reported, called the *false positive rate* (FPR) and *false negative rate* (FNR), respectively. The choice of these measures over the precision and recall measures used in information retrieval is because of conceptual simplicity. In the present case different kinds of errors are related to the same reference set (D), whereas in information retrieval the same set of correctly retrieved patterns are related to the set of all true patterns (recall) and to the set of retrieved patterns (precision). Hence, more accurate results are characterized by lower error rates rather than by higher recall and precision. However, it holds that Recall=1-FNR and Precision=(1-FNR)/(1-FNR+FPR).

8.5.2 Dense ST–Area Queries

In the experiments involving the *dense ST–area queries*, the *count* and *prob* values are tuned to observe the amount of false positives and false negatives. Experiments have also been conducted to test the effect of grid size, time span and amount of trajectories on the accuracy. As seen in Figure 8.7(a) to Figure 8.7(e), there are very few false negatives and the amount of false positives grows in certain cases. In particular, based on Figure 8.7(a), with the growth of *count* values, more false positives appear. With the experiment on the *prob* value (Figure 8.7(b)), it is possible to reach an optimal situation by tuning this *prob* value for each policy. For instance, the IRP policy has fewer false positives when *prob*= 0.1 and so has IIP when *prob*= 0.3. An observation from Figure 8.7(c) is that the amount of false positives grows with the grid size. The explanation for this is as follows. As the grid becomes denser, there are fewer really dense grid cells, but the amount of dense cells found through the three policies does not decrease very much, so the reported ratio value becomes larger. Figure 8.7(d) and Figure 8.7(e) show that the increase of the time span and the amount of trajectories reduces the amount of false positives for all the policies.

To test how the steepest slope cutoff criteria influences the algorithms, the *count* and *prob* values are tuned to observe the amount of false positives and false negatives on the different policies. As illustrated in Figure 8.7(f) and Figure 8.7(g), the cutoff criteria decreases the amount of false positives but, compared to the same settings in Figure 8.7(a) and Figure 8.7(b), brings more false negatives. Thus, considering all the parameters for the three policies, the following are the **recommendation** settings for the *dense ST-area query*:

The IIP is the most effective policy for doing dense ST–area query *with privacy protection. The second and third best choice is the CRP policy with* 2×2 *partitioning and the IRP policy, respectively. For all the policies, certain optimal situation on the amount of false positives and false negatives can be reached by tuning the prob value. To increase the time span and amount of trajectories will improve the performance of all approaches.*

Based on the **recommendation**, an experiment is conducted to compare the different policies with their optimal settings. In this experiment, the amount of trajectories is increased to 1000 and optimal *prob* values are used for each policy. Figure 8.7(h) presents the results. The CRP policy with each partition containing 2×2 cells and the IIP policy shows the most promising performance. These two policies guarantee a precision level that makes them useful for most applications.

8.5.3 Frequent Route Queries

In the simulated moving object datasets, objects move between a source and a destination location, obeying the limitations of the road network and traffic conditions. However, there is little regularity in the selection choice for the source and destination locations. Hence, one can expect to find longer frequent routes, only if there are a large number of objects on the road network at the same time. Thus in the experiments involving the *frequent route queries*, to find sufficiently large number of patterns as a basis for the evaluation of the accuracy of the algorithm, the largest dataset (3000 objects) and the largest query time span (120 seconds) were used.

For a *frequent route query*, a pattern is a maximal set of spatio-temporal grid cells. Since two patterns are very unlikely to be exactly the same, to be able to evaluate false positive and false negative errors, an *approximate* matching criteria between two patterns is defined as follows: A pattern p_1 is *f–contained* in a pattern p_2, if at least f fraction of the items that are in p_1 are also in p_2.

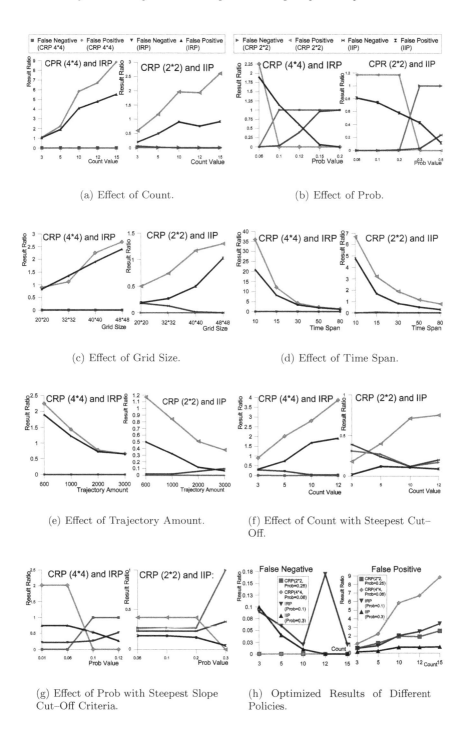

FIGURE 8.7: Experiments on Dense ST–area Queries.

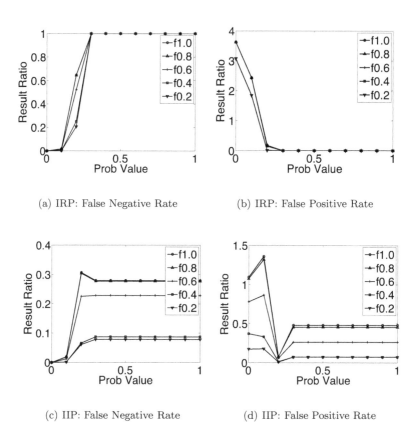

(a) IRP: False Negative Rate   (b) IRP: False Positive Rate

(c) IIP: False Negative Rate   (d) IIP: False Positive Rate

FIGURE 8.8: Experiments on Frequent Route Queries.

The *frequent route query* experiments for fixed min_count = 5, evaluate
the accuracy of the three anonymization policies for various *prob* values and
f-containment. The results of the experiments for the IRP and IIP policies are
shown in Figure 8.8. Results for the CRP (2 x 2) policy have been excluded
from the figure, because the varied parameters had little to no effect on the
results. For all *f-containments* for min_prob ≥ 0.3 the false positive rate was
0, while the false negative rate was 1. For min_prob < 3, the opposite was true.
The reason for this behavior is that in the CRP policy with 2×2 partitioning
all grid cells have a location probability of 0.25. The false positive rate of
0 for min_prob ≥ 0.3 is due to the fact that under this setting no patterns
(out of which none are false) are found in the anonymized data. A similar
behavior is observable for the IRP policy, except the false positive rate, for
sufficiently low min_prob values, is between 3 and 3.5. This is due to the fact
the average partition size for the IRP policy is 9 cells, which gives rise to
a lot more patterns. As expected, the best performance is obtained by the

IIP policy, where for `min_prob` = 0.3 the false negative rate is 0.37 and the false positive rate is 0.47. *The experiments show that for low* `min_prob` *values the IRP policy, but even more so, the IIP policy provides accurate and useful frequent route mining results.*

8.6 Conclusions and Future Work

Motivated by the possible loss of location privacy for LBS users, this chapter proposed a general grid–based framework that allowed user location data to be anonymized. Thus, privacy is preserved, but interesting patterns could still be discovered. The framework allowed users to specify individual desired levels of privacy and developed three policies for implementing that. Privacy-preserving methods were proposed for a core data mining task, namely *finding dense spatio-temporal regions*. An extensive set of experiments evaluated the methods and showed that the framework still allowed most patterns to be found, even when privacy was preserved.

Future work will be along three paths. First, the *multi-grid extension* will be further investigated as it offers a direction for getting more detailed and accurate data mining results without violating the privacy. Second, in addition to the CRP, IRP and IIP policies, it is possible to develop more policies for creating anonymization rectangles suitable for different real world situations. Third, since the grid–based anonymization framework is a simple and general framework for privacy–preserving data mining on moving object trajectories, it is planned to be extended to support more kinds of spatio-temporal data mining algorithms, e.g., spatio-temporal (density–based) clustering.

References

[1] O. Abul, M. Atzori, F. Bonchi, and F. Giannotti. Hiding Sequences. In *Proc. of the 23rd International Conference on Data Engineering Workshops, ICDEW*, pp. 147–156, 2007.

[2] O. Abul, M. Atzori, F. Bonchi, and F. Giannotti. Hiding Sensitive Trajectory Patterns. In *Proc. of the 7th IEEE International Conference on Data Mining Workshops, ICDMW*, pp. 693–698, 2007.

[3] O. Abul, F. Bonchi, and M. Nanni. Never Walk Alone: Uncertainty for

Anonymity in Moving Objects Databases. In *Proc. of the 24th IEEE International Conference on Data Engineering, ICDE*, pp. 376–385, 2008.

[4] R. Agrawal, T. Imilienski, and A. Swami. Mining Association Rules between Sets of Items in Large Databases. In *Proc. of the International Conference on Management of Data, SIGMOD*, pp. 207–216, SIGMOD Record 22(2), 1993.

[5] R. Agrawal and R. Srikant. Privacy–Preserving Data Mining. In *Proc. of the International Conference on Management of Data, SIGMOD*, pp. 439–450, SIGMOD Record 29(2), 2000.

[6] C. Bettini, X. S. Wang, and S. Jajodia. Protecting Privacy Against Location–Based Personal Identification. In *Proc. of the VLDB Workshop on Secure Data Management, SDM*, pp. 185–199, Springer, 2005.

[7] T. Brinkhoff. A Framework for Generating Network–Based Moving Objects. *Geoinformatica*, 6(2):153–180, Springer, 2002.

[8] D. Burdick, M. Calimlim, and J. Gehrke. MAFIA: A Maximal Frequent Itemset Algorithm for Transactional Databases. In *Proc. of the 17th International Conference on Data Engineering, ICDE*, pp. 443-452, IEEE Computer Society, 2001.

[9] C. -Y. Chow, M. F. Mokbel, and X. Liu. A Peer–to–Peer Spatial Cloaking Algorithm for Anonymous Location–Based Services. In *Proc. of the 14th ACM International Symposium on Geographic Information Systems, ACM–GIS*, pp. 171–178, ACM, 2006.

[10] A. Civilis, C. S. Jensen, and S. Pakalnis. Techniques for Efficient Road–Network–Based Tracking of Moving Objects. *IEEE Transactions on Knowledge and Data Engineering, TKDE*, 17(5):698–712, IEEE Educational Activities Department, 2005.

[11] M. Ester, H. P. Kriegel, J. Sander, and X. Xu. A Density–Based Algorithm for Discovering Clusters in Large Spatial Databases with Noise. In *Proc. of the 2nd International Conference on Knowledge Discovery and Data Mining, KDD*, pp. 226–231, AAAI Press, 1996.

[12] B. Gedik and L. Liu. Location Privacy in Mobile Systems: A Personalized Anonymization Model. In *Proc. of the 25th International Conference on Distributed Computing Systems , ICDCS*, pp. 620–629, IEEE Computer Society, 2005.

[13] G. Ghinita, P. Kalnis, S. Skiadopoulos. PRIVE: Anonymous Location Based Queries in Distributed Mobile Systems. In *Proc. of the 16th International Conference on World Wide Web, WWW*, pp. 371–380, ACM, 2007.

[14] G. Gidófalvi and T. B. Pedersen. Spatio-Temporal Rule Mining: Issues and Techniques. In *Proc. of the 7th International Conference on Data*

Warehousing and Knowledge Discovery, DaWaK, volume 3589 of Lecture Notes in Computer Science, pp. 275–284, Springer, 2005.

[15] G. Gidófalvi and T. B. Pedersen. Mining Long, Sharable Patterns in Trajectories of Moving Objects. In *Proc. of the 3rd Workshop on Spatio-Temporal Database Management, STDBM*, volume 174 of Online Proceedings of CEUR–WS, pp. 49–58, CEUR–WS, 2006.

[16] G. Gidófalvi, X. Huang, and T. B. Pedersen. Privacy–Preserving Data Mining on Moving Object Trajectories. In *Proc. of the 2008 International Conference on Mobile Data Management, MDM*, pp. 60–68, IEEE Computer Society, 2007.

[17] G. Gidófalvi, X. Huang, and T. B. Pedersen. Privacy–Preserving Trajectory Collection. In *Proc. of the 16th ACM SIISPATIAL International Conference on Advances in Geographic Information Systems, ACM–GIS*, pp. 387–390, ACM, 2008.

[18] A. Gkoulalas-Divanis and V. S. Verykios. A Free Terrain Model for Trajectory K–Anonymity. In *Proc. of the of the 19th International Conference on Database and Expert Systems Applications, DEXA*, pp. 49–56, 2008.

[19] A. Gkoulalas-Divanis, V. S. Verykios, and M. F. Mokbel. Identifying Unsafe Routes for Network–Based Trajectory Privacy. In *Proc. of the SIAM International Conference on Data Mining, SDM*, pp. 942–953, 2009.

[20] M. Gruteser and D. Grunwald. Anonymous Usage of Location–Based Services Through Spatial and Temporal Cloaking. In *Proc. of the 1st International Conference on Mobile Systems, Applications and Services, MobiSys*, pp. 31–42, ACM, 2003.

[21] M. Hadjieleftheriou, G. Kollios, D. Gunopulos, and V. J. Tsotras. On–Line Discovery of Dense Areas in Spatio-Temporal Databases. In *Proc. of the 8th International Symposium on Spatial and Temporal Databases, SSTD*, volume 2750 of Lecture Notes in Computer Science, pp. 306–324, Springer, 2003.

[22] C. S. Jensen, D. Lin, B. C. Ooi, and R. Zhang. Effective Density Queries on Continuously Moving Objects. In *Proc. of the 22nd International Conference on Data Engineering, ICDE*, pp. 71–81, IEEE Computer Society, 2006.

[23] A. Machanavajjhala, J. Gehrke, D. Kifer, and M. Venkitasubramaniam. *l*–Diversity: Privacy Beyond *k*–Anonymity. In *Proc. of the 22nd International Conference on Data Engineering, ICDE*, p. 26, IEEE Computer Society, 2006.

[24] S. Mascetti, D. Freni, C. Bettini, X. S. Wang, and S. Jajodia. On the Impact of User Movement Simulations in the Evaluation of LBS Privacy–Preserving Techniques. In *Proc. of the International Workshop on Privacy in Location Based Applications, PiLBA*, p. 1, 2008.

[25] M. F. Mokbel, C.-Y. Chow, and W. G. Aref. The New Casper: Query Processing for Location Services without Compromising Privacy. In *Proc. of the 32nd International Conference on Very Large Data Bases, VLDB*, pp. 763–774, ACM, 2006.

[26] M. E. Nergiz, M. Atzori, and Y. Saygin. Towards Trajectory Anonymization: A Generalization–Based Approach. In *Proc. of the ACM GIS Workshop on Security and Privacy in GIS and LBS, SPRINGL*, pp. 1–10, 2008.

[27] R. G. Pensa, A. Monreale, F. Pinelli, and D. Pedreschi. Pattern–Preserving k–Anonymization of Sequences and its Application to Mobility Data Mining. In *Proc. of the International Workshop on Privacy in Location Based Applications, PiLBA*, p. 1, 2008.

[28] L. Sweeney. K–Anonymity: A Model for Protecting Privacy. *International Journal of Uncertainty, Fuzziness and Knowledge–Based Systems, IJUFKS*, 10(5):557–570, World Scientific Publishing, 2002.

[29] Y. Tao, G. Kollios, J. Considine, F. Li, and D. Papadias. Spatio-Temporal Aggregation Using Sketches. In *Proc. of the 19th International Conference on Data Engineering, ICDE*, pp. 214–226, IEEE Computer Society, 2004.

[30] Manolis Terrovitis and Nikos Mamoulis. Privacy Preservation in the Publication of Trajectories. In *Proc. of the The 9th International Conference on Mobile Data Management, MDM*, pp. 65–72, 2008.

[31] I. Tsoukatos and D. Gunopulos. Efficient Mining of Spatiotemporal Patterns. In *Proc. of the 7th International Symposium on Advances in Spatial and Temporal Databases, SSTD*, pp. 425–442, Springer, 2001.

[32] V. S. Verykios, E. Bertino, I. N. Fovino, L. P. Provenza, Y. Saygin, and Y. Theodoridis. State–of–the–art in Privacy Preserving Data Mining. *SIGMOD Record*, 33(1):50–57, ACM, 2004.

[33] T.-H. You, W.-C. Peng, and W.-C. Lee. Protecting Moving Trajectories with Dummies. In *Proc. of the 2007 International Conference on Mobile Data Management, MDM*, pp. 278–282, IEEE, 2007.

Chapter 9

Privacy and Anonymity in Location Data Management

Claudio Bettini

DICo, Università degli Studi di Milano, Milan, Italy

Sergio Mascetti

DICo, Università degli Studi di Milano, Milan, Italy

Dario Freni

DICo, Università degli Studi di Milano, Milan, Italy

X. Sean Wang

CS, University of Vermont

Sushil Jajodia

CSIS, George Mason University

9.1 Illustration of the Problem

A growing number of applications and services include among their parameters a spatial and temporal characterization of some of the objects that they store and process. These applications are enabled by technologies, like GPS, WiFi positioning, or cellular network based methods, that can provide real-time data about the position of moving objects.

Some applications do not permanently store location data that is just received, processed, and deleted. This is sometimes enforced as a privacy preserving policy in the provisioning of location based services (LBS). However, in most cases, location data are permanently stored as any other data, to provide a better service (e.g., to understanding direction and speed of objects, or even trajectories) as well as for historical records and accounting purposes. The huge amount of spatio-temporal data collected by these applications is currently stored in many different ways, since a standard has not emerged yet; Moving-object databases and spatial extensions of standard database management systems are the main options. A very active research area is investigating the efficient storage, processing, and retrieval of trajectory data.

Most of this data is acquired in the form of transactions. Examples are periodic location updates from GPS-monitored vehicles, spatial nearest-neighbor requests, ATM transactions with location and timestamp, georeferenced emergency calls. Privacy issues arise both in the acquisition of this data, and in the subsequent release from the repositories where the data is stored. If we consider that an adversary may be able to obtain one or more transactions at the time they are acquired, a defense technique must be applied at each transaction, as proposed in the case of requests to LBS. The situation is analogous to having a stream of data in which each element coming from the stream must be transformed in order to prevent privacy threats. We call these techniques *online* privacy preserving techniques. Depending on the adversary model, the transformation function should take into account different knowledge, including, for example, how the previous elements of the stream have been transformed. On the contrary, *offline* techniques operate a transformation on a whole dataset of transactions acquired in a given time window. Many of the trajectory privacy preserving techniques proposed in data mining are offline techniques, considering the one-shot release of the whole dataset. A less investigated privacy problem is the sequential release of subsets of the transactions dataset covering different and possibly overlapping time windows. In this case, offline techniques have to take into account the possible correlations among published data. Note that the extreme case in which a release occurs for each time window containing a single time instant degenerates to the problem requiring online defense techniques.

This chapter provides a brief survey of proposals for both classes of techniques, further classifying them accordingly to their specific goal, reference architecture, and evaluation methods. A technically deeper discussion is devoted to online anonymization when the adversary can recognize traces of requests from the same user, and to online location obfuscation in proximity services, like friend-finder services.

A detailed survey of offline techniques has been proposed by Bonchi et al. [9], while another survey covering some online and offline techniques has been written by Ghinita [15]. An independent line of research has investigated context-based access control systems and privacy policy based approaches with specific reference to location and trajectory data. Two surveys of results from these approaches have been written recently by Verykios et al. [40], and by Ardagna et al. [2].

9.1.1 Typical Application Scenarios and Intuitive Threats

There is a privacy threat whenever an adversary is able to associate the identity of a user to information that the user considers private. In the case of LBS, this *sensitive association* can be possibly derived from location-based requests issued to service providers. More precisely, the identity and the private information of a single user can be derived from requests issued by a group of users as well as from available background knowledge. Figure 9.1 shows a graphical representation of this general privacy threat in LBS.

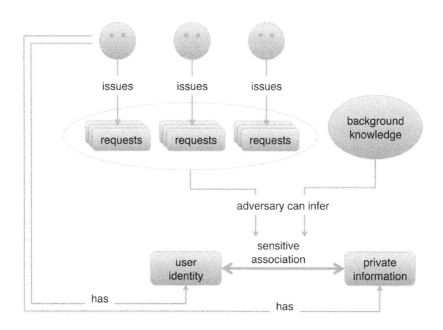

FIGURE 9.1: General privacy threat in LBS

More generally, an adversary can obtain a *sensitive association* by looking at one or more *transaction records* containing location data that can be acquired at transaction time, or after they have been stored in a repository, like e.g., a moving-object database. The user identity, if not explicitly given, can be possibly inferred by joining so called quasi-identifier data in the record with the adversary's background knowledge. For example, the workplace of an individual can act as a quasi-identifier if external knowledge is available to restrict the set of individuals that can possibly be in that location. To complete the sensitive association, the adversary associates the user identity with private information found in the transaction itself or derived from transaction data. Location data can play the role of quasi-identifier in certain transactions, and of private information in others. This holds for other transaction data as well. In the following we will often use the term "request" as a specific kind of transaction since our reference application is LBS, but our arguments hold for general transactions including location data, like for example, vehicle tracking and fleet monitoring.

Examples of intuitive threats follow:

- Alice issues an LBS request for a georeferenced dating service. Since Alice does not want to reveal that she uses this service, she drops any explicit identifier (like her name) from the service request. The adversary obtains the request and matches the location from where the request was issued (possibly a given office or shop) with external information this adversary acquired about who is at that location at that time, obtaining the sensitive association between Alice and a request for a dating service.

- Alice asks for a taxi through an LBS so that her location is automatically sent to the taxi company. If an adversary obtains the request and is able to re-identify Alice (possibly by the phone number) he can obtain the sensitive association between Alice and the specific place where she was when she called the taxi, while this may be private information to Alice.

- Alice is using a friend finder service to see which of her contacts are in proximity. She periodically issues multiple service requests, containing her updated position, using her nickname as pseudo-identifier (PID). These requests are stored in a database on the service provider. An adversary is able to obtain part of this database. He is interested in recognizing who was in a specific sensitive place appearing in a record, but he only finds a PID that does not lead to an individual based on the information in the record itself. However, by considering all the records with the same PID he obtains a trajectory pattern that reveals the home address and the workplace of the person associated with that PID. Using public knowledge, the adversary can then associate that PID with a restricted group of individuals, making Alice a likely candidate for the sensitive association he is trying to obtain.

9.1.2 The Need for Specialized Defense Techniques

In the last years, database researchers have extensively investigated privacy issues in the release of database views, both for data mining purposes and for micro data release. Hence, a natural question is why the same techniques cannot be applied to the problem illustrated above. The answer is that some of the techniques and concepts can be indeed applied. However, considering both LBS requests and moving-object databases, the main conceptual difference is that records have a spatio-temporal attribute value, and it is well known that both space and time have a very specific semantics that calls for specialized data management methods. The extension of the k-anonymity concept [37] to time stamped databases has been first investigated by Mascetti et al. [32]. A concept analogous to k-anonymity has been first proposed for LBS by Gruteser [20], and the counterpart of l-diversity and t-closeness, to name some of the proposed variants, have been studied as well [6].

A possible mapping between LBS requests, or more generally location data acquisition, and databases, is to consider all the requests/acquisitions received in a given time granule as the tuples of a table, with each tuple having a respondent and a location as the value of a spatial attribute. Considering the flowing of time, this mapping leads to a sequence of tables each one time stamped with a given time granule. Hence, the privacy problem in location data management is to release versions of these tables so that no sensitive associations can be derived. This task, on one side requires techniques specialized for the semantics of spatio-temporal data, and on the other side requires anonymization techniques for sequential data publication that are not yet fully understood by the database community.

9.2 State of the Art

In this section, we provide a brief survey of the location data privacy literature. This is not meant to be a thorough survey, but a pointer to the literature for various aspects of privacy protection for this kind of data.

Like in any system aimed at providing protection, it is important to have clear assumptions about the context in which privacy protection is to be applied. While some papers in the literature give explicit assumptions, others only provide implicit ones. Once assumptions have been identified, different techniques may apply. Based on this observation, we organize our brief survey in two subsections, namely assumptions and techniques. We will end this section with a classification of the main approaches proposed in the literature.

9.2.1 Assumptions

A *privacy attack* (or, for short, an *attack*) is a specific method used by an adversary to obtain the sensitive association.

In order to specify an attack, we first characterize the *adversary model* by defining which is the private information the adversary aims to obtain, which are the circumstances under which the adversary can acquire transaction data and which are the *background knowledge* and the *inferencing abilities* available to the adversary. More specifically, we identify six aspects that mainly characterize the adversary model:

1. which part of transaction data is private information
2. which part of transaction data is quasi-identifier,
3. ability of the adversary to recognize transactions from the same user,
4. ability of the adversary to distinguish transactions from different users,
5. knowledge of the defense technique, and
6. online versus offline acquisition of location data.

Private information   The target private information is the type of information that the adversary would like to associate with a specific individual, like, for example, her political orientation, or, more specifically, her location. In LBS privacy, we are mostly concerned with two types of private information, namely service request and location. For the former, the concern is the association of a user with the (entire) LBS request, while for the latter, the concern is the association of a user with the location from where the LBS request is issued. As observed in Section 9.1, simply deleting the identifying information from service requests is not sufficient to address these concerns. An adversary may be able to use information other than that contained in the request to re-associate the request or the location back to the user. Note that encrypting LBS requests with a general purpose encryption function does not solve the problem, because in this case the service provider needs to decipher the content in order to satisfy the request itself, and he is not a trusted entity.

Quasi-identifiers   Either part of the sensitive association can be discovered by joining information in a request with external information. When we discover the identity of the issuer (or even restrict the set of candidate issuers) we call the part of the request used in the join *quasi-identifier*. For example, when the location data in the request can be joined with publicly available presence data for the same location to identify an individual, we say that location data acts as quasi-identifier. In some cases location is considered as quasi-identifier even when the real quasi-identifier is a pattern, or a sequence of locations, like a trajectory. Similarly to privacy preserving database publication, the recognition of the information that can act as quasi-identifier in a service request is essential to identify the possible attacks (as well as to design appropriate defenses).

Transactions from the same user: Snapshot versus historical attacks
Most of the approaches presented so far in the literature [20, 34, 24, 7] have proposed techniques to ensure a user's privacy in the case in which the adversary can acquire a single request issued by that user. More specifically, these approaches implicitly or explicitly assume that the adversary is not able to *link* a set of requests i.e., to understand that the requests have been issued by the same (anonymous) user.

When this assumption is made, we say that the corresponding threats are limited to the *snapshot case*. Intuitively, it is like the adversary can only obtain a snapshot of the messages being exchanged for the service at a given instant, while not having access to the complete history of messages.

In contrast with the snapshot case, in the *historical case* it is assumed that the adversary is able to *link* a set of requests. Researchers [5, 22] have considered such a possibility. Several techniques exist to *link* different requests to the same user, with the most trivial ones being the observation of the same identity or pseudo-id in the requests, and others being based on spatiotemporal correlations. We call *request trace* a set of requests that the adversary can correctly associate to a single user. More dangerous threats can be identified in contexts characterized by the historical case as explained in [8].

Transactions from different users: Single versus multiple-issuer attacks When the adversary model limits the requests that can be obtained to those being issued by a single (anonymous) user, we say that all the attacks are *single-issuer attacks*. When the adversary model admits the possibility that multiple requests from multiple users are acquired, and the adversary is able to understand if two requests are issued by different users, we have a new important category of attacks, called *multiple-issuer attacks*. Note that this is an orthogonal classification with respect to snapshot and historical. Consequently, it is possible to identify four classes of attacks: snapshot single-issuer, snapshot multiple-issuer, historical single-issuer and, finally, historical multiple-issuer. For example, if we consider the case in which the adversary has access to the communication channel between one user and the SP, then the adversary can apply attacks in the historical and single-issuer category since it can obtain requests issued in different time instants by a single user. As another example, if the adversary obtains a part of the database of a service provider containing the requests issued by all the users in a single time instant (or in a short period of time), then the adversary can apply attacks in the snapshot and multiple-issuer category.

In the area of privacy in databases, the multiple-issuer attack is known as *homogeneity attack* [27]. In Example 9.1 we show that, if the adversary is able to reason with requests issued by different users, then the user's privacy can be violated even if k-anonymity is guaranteed.

Example 9.1

Let r_1 and r_2 be two requests issued by users u_1 and u_2, respectively, with the same service specific parameters p that each of them considers as private information. In order to enforce anonymity of the two users, r_1 and r_2 are independently generalized into r_1' and r_2', respectively; suppose that the generalization leads to $\{u_1, u_2\}$ as the set of possible issuers of both r_1' and r_2', making each request 2-anonymous. However, if the adversary knows that the issuer of r_1' is different from the issuer of r_2', then, even if he is not able to associate each request with its issuer, he can infer that both u_1 and u_2 issued a request with private parameters p, hence violating their privacy. ⬜

Knowledge of the defense technique In security it is usually assumed that the adversary knows the algorithms used for protecting information. We have shown that the first proposals for LBS privacy protection ignored this aspect leading to solutions subject to so called *inversion* attacks [29]. Considering spatial cloaking as a defense technique, the intuition is that if the adversary knows how a given location is generalized to an area and the area returned by the generalization is different for each point in the space, the adversary, looking at the generalized location can consider each candidate point and check if it could be generalized to the area he is observing. This process can effectively reduce the set of candidate locations. Hence, depending on the assumption in the adversary model about the knowledge of the defense algorithm and of its parameters we distinguish *def-aware* attacks from *def-unaware* attacks.

Online versus offline acquisition of location data Location data can be acquired online, at transaction time, or offline as a stored dataset, with single or multiple releases. This assumption affects when and where the defense is to take place. If we are considering LBS, and the user wants to maintain privacy when each request is delivered to the service provider, an *online* defense technique should be applied, namely protecting each request at the time it is issued. One implication of this assumption is that the privacy protection mechanism does not have information about any future requests (but may have the knowledge of the past requests). A different scenario occurs when location data have been collected by a trusted party and portions of the data are acquired, possibly for data analysis, by an untrusted party. This is the typical scenario considered by privacy preserving location data mining. In this case, a *offline* defense can be applied, considering a static large number of location data tuples possibly representing moving-object trajectories. As mentioned in Section 9.1, it is important to clarify in the adversary model specification if multiple releases of datasets may occur, and if the same data can be present in different release (possibly protected in different ways).

9.2.2 Techniques

Defense techniques can be categorized referring to the attacks' classification reported above, depending on which specific attacks they have been designed for. However, there are other important characteristics to distinguish defense approaches:

1. Anonymization,
2. PI-Obfuscation,
3. Encryption,
4. Centralized or decentralized, and
5. Theoretical or experimental evaluation.

Anonymity based defenses   The different defense techniques can be classified as *anonymity-based* if they aim at protecting the association between an individual and her private information by avoiding the re-identification of the individual. This is achieved by transforming the parts of the transaction acting as quasi-identifiers.

PI-Obfuscation based defenses   *PI-Obfuscation-based* techniques aim to protect the same association by transforming the private information contained in the transaction, often assuming that the identity of the individual can be obtained. The techniques proposed in the literature to obfuscate location information implicitly or explicitly assume that user identity is known to the adversary or could be discovered. Therefore, these techniques protect users' privacy by preventing the release of the user's precise location that is the target private information. Since PI-obfuscation based defenses do not aim at protecting users' anonymity, they ignore which part of the request is a quasi-identifier.

Encryption based defenses   *Encryption-based* techniques use methods that can potentially protect both the identity of the issuer and the private information in the request. The most interesting defenses in this class are based on private information retrieval (PIR) techniques. The general objective of a PIR protocol is to allow a user to issue a query to a database without the database learning the query.

Centralized or decentralized defenses   Centralized defenses assume the existence of of one or more trusted entities that collaborate to preserve the privacy of the users. In the case of LBSs, these entities act as proxies for service requests and responses between the users and the service providers. Decentralized defenses, on the contrary do not assume the existence of any trusted entity. Among the benefits of centralized defenses are a) the ability of the trusted entity to use information about a group of users (e.g., their location) in order to more effectively preserve their privacy, and b) the availability of more computational and communication resources than the users' devices. The main drawbacks are considered the overheads in updating the information about the users, and the need for the users to actually trust these entities.

Theoretical or empirical evaluations   An important property of a defense proposal is the set of methods used for the validation of the specific proposed technique. In some cases, formal results, based on some assumptions, have been provided so that a certain level of privacy is guaranteed in all scenarios in which the assumptions hold. In other cases, only an experimental evaluation, usually on synthetic data is provided. This approach may be critical, for example in location-based services, when the actual service deployment environment does not match the one used in the evaluation.

9.2.3   Literature Summary

Each privacy protection technique appeared in the literature may be characterized by the assumptions it makes, and by the particular choices regarding the six aspects illustrated above. In the following we briefly illustrate for each defense category, the main features of the proposed approaches.

Online defenses based on PI-obfuscation   The idea of protecting location privacy by obfuscating location information was first proposed by Gruteser et al. [21]. The technique is aimed at avoiding the association of a user with a *sensitive area* she is crossing or approaching, by appropriately suspending user requests to ensure that the location of the user may be confused among at least other k areas. The proposed technique is a centralized solution, and correctness is evaluated experimentally. The impact is not clear if the adversary is aware of the defense technique.

Table 9.1 summarizes the main properties of the techniques based on PI-obfuscation. Note that these techniques do not address the problem of how the user's identity is obtained and hence in these contributions it is not specified which information act as quasi-identifier.

Techniques proposed by Kido et al. [26] and Yiu et al. [42] have the same assumptions and techniques. Both use fake information to provide protection to the actual user location. Kido et al. [26] uses a set of fake requests along with the actual request, while Yiu et al. [42] uses a single fake location to obtain k-NN (Nearest Neighbor) points of interests to the actual location. Both methods are decentralized solutions, and are effective even if the adversary is aware of the defense mechanism. The evaluation methods are different. The former was evaluated empirically, while the latter was evaluated both theoretically and empirically.

Finally, we also mention in this class of techniques the interactive protocol between the client and the SP proposed by Duckham et al. [13] to compute 1-NN queries when the user's location is generalized. The paper does not tackle the problem of how to compute the generalized location information provided by the client, and hence it does not consider the problem of the adversary knowing the generalization function.

Online encryption-based defenses   The first encryption-based technique proposed in the literature protects users' privacy in the LBSs that compute range queries among static resources [25]. On the contrary, Ghinita et al. propose a solution for the private computation of 1-NN queries [16]. Both techniques are proved to solve the privacy problem under the most conservative assumptions as they do not reveal any information about the requests

Paper	Assumptions						Techniques	
	Private Information	Quasi Identifier	Snapshot or Historical	Single or Multiple issuers	Knowledge of defense		Centralized or Decentralized	Theoretical or Empirical Eval
IEEESP-04 [21]	Location	Not spec.	S	S	No		C	E
Pervasive-05 [13]	Location	Not spec.	S	S	No		D	-
SWOD-05 [26]	Location	Not spec.	S	S	Yes		D	E
ICDE-08a [42]	Location	Not spec.	S	S	Yes		D	T/E

Table 9.1: Summary of techniques based on PI-obfuscation

to the adversary. The solutions do not need any centralized entity, and their correctness is shown theoretically. While these promising solutions provide strong privacy guarantees, currently they seem to involve high computational and communication overheads that pose concerns about their applicability.

Two encryption-based defenses have also been proposed to guarantee privacy protection in friend finder applications [43, 30]. These techniques use data encryption to obfuscate the location information disclosed when using a friend finder application. The solution proposed in [43] is designed for a decentralized architecture while the other ([30]), in order to reduce the computational and communication costs, requires a centralized architecture and includes an optional generalization step run by the centralized trusted entity. These techniques are described in more details in Section 9.3.2.

Table 9.2 shows the main properties of this class of defenses.

Paper	Assumptions						Techniques	
	Private Information	Quasi Identifier	Snapshot or Historical	Single or Multiple issuers	Knowledge of defense		Centralized or Decentralized	Theoretical or Empirical Eval
PALMS-08 [25]	Service, Location	Location	H	M	Yes		D	T
SIGMOD-08 [16]	Service, Location	Location	H	M	Yes		D	T/E
PET-07 [43]	Location	Location	S	S	Yes		D	T
MDM-09a [30]	Location	Location	S	S	Yes		C	T/E

Table 9.2: Summary of online techniques based on encryption

Offline Anonymity-based defenses for single release   Three articles deal with the single-release situation in a multiple-issuers and historical scenario (see Table 9.3). That is, there is a database of locational data, and we are interested in releasing the data to the public. Abul et al. in [1] study a database of locations of moving objects, each moving object being a privacy entity (e.g., mobile user) and each location represented by a circle of certain radius (instead of a precise point). In order to avoid any adversary from figuring out the exact trajectory of a particular moving object, the radii of the location data are appropriately extended and the center possibly moved so that each object will have $k-1$ other objects "walking with it" in the sense that all k objects are not revealing their precise locations, but are only known to walk within a given radius of a precise (virtual) trajectory in the space-time. Nergiz et al. in [35] address a similar problem and propose a technique to guarantee user's k anonymity by making each user's trace indistinguishable from the traces of other $k-1$ users. This is obtained through the suppression and the generalization of the locations that compose the traces. In the two papers it is not assumed that the adversary knows the generalization function.

Terrovitis et al. address a different problem [39]. They consider trajectories as sequences of addresses that users pass through, and adversaries are assumed to have some trajectory projections (sub-trajectories of some users), each one associated to a user's identity. Adversaries can join their projections to the sequences in the database, and hence track the rest of the (whole) trajectories of the same users, resulting in a privacy breach if the database is not altered in some way. In the proposed solution, data suppression is used to break the adversaries' ability to associate a particular sub-trajectory to a whole one with enough certainty.

Paper	Private Information	Quasi Identifier	Snapshot or Historical	Single or Multiple issuers	Knowledge of defense	Centralized or Decentralized	Theoretical or Empirical Eval
	Assumptions					Techniques	
ICDE-08b [1]	Location	Location	H	M	No	C	T/E
TDP-09 [35]	Location	Location	H	M	No	C	T/E
MDM-08 [39]	Service and some locations	Some locations	H	M	Yes	C	T/E

Table 9.3: Summary of offline techniques

Online anonymity-based defenses Table 9.4 summarizes the main characteristics of the online defenses based on anonymity. A first group of articles proposes techniques to contrast snapshot, single-issuer attacks with the adversary unaware of the defense technique. All the methods are based on enlarging, or generalizing, the area in the user request in order for the area to contain at least k-users. The techniques in this first group do not guarantee anonymity if the adversary is aware of the defense technique (*def-aware* attacks).

Paper	Assumptions					Techniques	
	Private Information	Quasi Identifier	Snapshot or Historical	Single or Multiple issuers	Knowledge of defense	Centralized or Decentralized	Theoretical or Empirical Eval
MobiSys-03 [20]	Service	Location	S	S	No	C	E
VLDB-06 [34]	Service, Location	Location or not spec.	S	S	No	C	E
WWW-08 [3]	Service, Location	Location or not spec.	S	S	No	C	E
SSTD-07a [17]	Service	Location	S	S	No	D	T/E
ACMGIS-06 [11]	Service	Location	S	S	No	D	E
WWW-07 [18]	Service	Location	S	S	Yes	D	T/E
TKDE-07 [24]	Service	Location	S	S	Yes	C	T/E
TMC-08 [14]	Service	Location	S	S	Yes	C	T/E
JLBS-08 [29]	Service	Location	S	S	Yes	C	T/E
SDM-05 [8]	Service	Location Patterns	H	S	Yes	C	T
SSTD-07b [10]	Service	Location	H	S	Yes	C	E
ACMGIS-07 [41]	Service	Location	H	S	No	C	E
MDM-09b [31]	Service	Location	H	S	Yes	C	T/E
IEEEPC-03 [4]	Location	Location	H	S	No	C	E
CCS-07 [23]	Location	Location	H	S	Yes	C	E
PerCom-07 [6]	Service	Location	S	M	Yes	C	-
TIME-09 [36]	Service	Location	H	M	Yes	C	E

Table 9.4: Summary of online techniques based on anonymity

The first generalization algorithm that appeared in the literature applying the concept of k-anonymity to LBS, was named *IntervalCloaking* [20]. The idea of the algorithm is to iteratively divide the total region to find the smallest area with at least k-users. In this case, location is considered as a quasi-identifier while the implicit private information is the use of the service. Indeed, when location acts as quasi-identifier it cannot act in the same request as private information at least not at the same spatial granularity. To cover cases in which identity can be inferred and location acts as private information, extensions to the above work have been proposed [34, 3]. The proposed techniques include a second parameter used to control the amount of location information disclosed. According to our classification, these approaches aim to provide both anonymity and PI-obfuscation. All of the above proposals are evaluated experimentally, and use a centralized defense with a trusted entity in charge of finding the cloaking area. In the following we call this entity Location-aware Trusted Server (LTS).

Other two articles in this group loosen the LTS assumption by adopting a decentralized strategy [11, 17]. Chow et al. [11] proposed a decentralized solution called *CloakP2P* in which it is assumed that users can communicate with each other using an ad-hoc network to form a group of k users. The generalized request is issued to the server through a user randomly chosen in the group. In another approach, Ghinita et al. [17] modify the centralized algorithm (the *Hilbert Cloak* algorithm mentioned below, [18]) to work in a distributed environment. The algorithm is formally validated.

A second group of papers is aimed to provide privacy protection against *def-aware* attacks. Ghinita et al. propose a distributed algorithm is based on a distributed B^+-tree on the Hilbert space-filling curve over the protection space [18]. The technique is formally validated, but is subject to scalability problems as the number of users increases. (The same authors propose a method to increase the efficiency over this one, but then the solution is not safe against *def-aware* attacks [17].) The last three papers in this group propose centralized defenses against *def-aware* attacks. Kalnis et al. [24] propose the *Hilbert Cloak* algorithm that provides anonymity. A different algorithm, called *CliqueCloak* is proposed by Gedik et al. [14]. The main difference with respect to the *IntervalCloaking* algorithm is that *CliqueCloak* computes the generalization among the users that actually issue a request and not among the users that are potential issuers. Mascetti et al. present three generalization algorithms that are proved to guarantee anonymity in this category [29]. The aim is to provide anonymity while minimizing the size of the generalized area. The algorithm that results to have the better performance with respect to this metric is called *Grid*. The correctness of the algorithms in the three above papers is formally proved, and their performances are also experimentally evaluated.

The third group of papers departs from the above two groups in assuming historical attacks. The use of spatio-temporal generalization functions to defend from historical attacks has been first proposed in [8], by considering specific patterns of locations as quasi-identifiers, and generalizing the current request's location in order to preserve historical k-anonymity. The proposed centralized algorithm assumes the adversary is aware of the defense technique. A similar strategy, considering single locations as quasi-identifiers, and progressively applying spatial generalizations is proposed by Chow et al. [10] and

Xu et al. [41]. The technique proposed in the former paper aims at providing protection against a *def-aware* attacks, while both techniques proposed in the latter seem to assume *def-unaware* attacks. The techniques proposed in the two papers are evaluated through experiments. The work in [31] is part of this group and will be more extensively presented in Section 9.3.1.

A different approach consists in altering or suppressing the requests in order to prevent requests linking and consequently to enhance anonymity. The solution proposed by Beresford et al. [4] consists in changing a user's pseudo-identifier when the user enters in a mix zone. Intuitively, a mix zone is a spatial area such that, if an individual crosses it, then it will not be possible to link her future requests (outside the area) with previous ones (before entering the area). A different solution proposed by Hoh et al. [23] aims to prevent request linking while maintaining high spatial accuracy by suppressing the requests that could be linked with the previous ones.

Finally, the last group includes papers considering the ability of the adversary to understand that two or more requests are issued by different users, resulting in what we call *multiple-issuer* attacks. To our knowledge, the first paper considering this attack was proposed by Bettini et al. [6] and is restricted to the snapshot case. The defense is based on properly generalizing location as a quasi-identifier in such a way that at least l requests with different private values have been issued from each group of undistinguishable users (the anonymity set). This approach captures a concept similar to l-diversity in database publication [27]. An extension to the historical case using a combination of anonymity and PI-obfuscation techniques is proposed by Riboni et al. [36].

9.3 Emerging Techniques for Online Privacy Preservation in Location Data Management

In this section we focus on two different categories of online defenses presenting new promising techniques against privacy attacks. The first category aims at preserving the anonymity of issuers of LBS requests, and concerns defenses against historical attacks. The second aims at preserving location privacy in the deployment of social network applications involving alerts on the proximity of individuals.

9.3.1 Historical Anonymization

Most related work on anonymity in LBS implicitly or explicitly assumes as a worst case that the adversary has *complete location knowledge*, i.e., in order to be safe in the occasional situation in which the adversary knows which individuals are in a location at a given time, it is assumed he always may acquire from external sources the identities of users in a given location. Similarly, the papers that consider the historical case conservatively assume that the adversary can link all the requests issued by the same user. Clearly, in many scenarios, and for certain types of adversaries, these assumptions are too conservative. A natural question arises: is it possible to provide privacy protection under these very conservative assumptions without excessively degrading the quality of service?

To answer this question, Mascetti et al. [31] apply the notion of *historical k-anonymity* previously defined by Bettini et al. ([8]) to evaluate in a realistic scenario if requests can be maintained historically k-anonymous under these conservative assumptions. The intuition is that a request r is historically k-anonymous if there are at least k users that can be the potential issuer of each request r' in the same request trace as r. The authors consider spatial generalization as the defense technique maintaining the issuer's location within the generalized region and propose to use the perimeter of the region to measure the degradation of the quality of service. The parameter P_{max} is introduced to represent the maximum tolerable degradation of the quality of service; The idea is that if the generalized region of a request has a perimeter larger than P_{max}, then the SP is not able to provide the service with a sufficiently high quality and hence the request is considered useless. In the same paper the authors describe the *OptimalLength* algorithm that computes the generalization of a set of requests from a single issuer. The algorithm guarantees to produce generalized regions with perimeter not larger than P_{max} and to maximize the number of consecutive historically k-anonymous requests. Note that the *OptimalLength* algorithm is not applicable in practice, since it is an offline algorithm and it also has a very high complexity. Instead, the purpose of the *OptimalLength* is to compute an upper bound to the length of consecutive requests that can be generalized by any spatial generalization algorithm. The experimental results (described in detail in [31]) give evidence that it is not possible to generalize more than few consecutive requests in a request trace, and hence that under these excessively conservative assumption it is not possible to provide protection while guaranteeing a minimum quality of service. This actually contradicts some of the positive results that have appeared in the literature (e.g., [10, 41]).

The above negative result supports the need for an adversary's model that is sufficiently conservative to guarantee protection against a broad range of attacks but that, at the same time, is not overly conservative, since this makes privacy preservation unachievable, at least through spatial generalization.

A first attempt to design a model with these characteristics was presented in a work by Bettini et al. ([8]) in which spatio-temporal patterns, as opposed to single locations, are considered quasi-identifiers. For example, a user can consider the trajectory from her home to her job as a quasi-identifier pattern if it is repeated more than 3 times in a week. Another attempt with a different approach is proposed in a work by Terrovitis et al. ([39]). This paper, which considers the problem in the offline case, assumes that there are only some locations where users can be identified by an adversary.

A similar approach is used by Mascetti et al. for the online problem [31]. In their work it is assumed that the total area where the service is provided is partitioned into a visible region A_v and a hidden region A_h. Intuitively, when a user is in A_v, it is assumed that the adversary knows the exact location where she is, while, when she is in A_h, it is assumed that the adversary only knows she's in A_h without any more information. In addition, the paper also relaxes the assumption about the adversary's ability to link requests. Indeed, the paper considers the case in which each user has one or more pseudo-identifier (PID), and one is included in each of her requests.* While a single PID would be the standard, each user can obtain a new PID when this is necessary to preserve her privacy, at the cost of a degradation of the quality of service (in terms of service personalization and overhead). Under this assumption, a request is linked with all the requests issued with the same PID, which is a subset of all the requests issued by the same user.

In the same paper, the authors propose the *ProvidentHider* algorithm to provide protection under these relaxed assumptions. The algorithm has three main characteristics. First, it tries to use a PID that had already been used in previous requests by the same user. A new PID is only used if none of the PIDs used in previous requests can be used to guarantee the required level of anonymity without generating a region with perimeter larger than P_{max}. Second, the algorithm does not generalize any request that is issued from a hidden location, and computes the generalization of the requests issued from a visible location only considering the locations of the other visible users. The rationale is that if a user u is in a hidden location, then the adversary cannot tell her apart from other hidden users (at the time), and generalization does not usually help to significantly increase the number of users that are indistinguishable with u. As a consequence of this property and since it is also assumed that the adversary knows the generalization function, he also knows that no user in a hidden location can be the issuer of a request with a generalized location. Hence, the users in the hidden location do not contribute to increase the anonymity of a request, even if their location is in the generalized region. The last characteristic is that the algorithm always computes generalized regions that, while having a perimeter smaller than P_{max}, are larger than those that would be strictly necessary to generalize the request. The idea is that when a request r is issued, the algorithm tries to generalize its location so that there are as many users as possible that are indistinguishable with the issuer u. The purpose is to maximize the probabilities that when a new request is issued by the same user, it is possible to generalize it so that at least k of these users are potential issuers. If this generalization can be found, it is

---

*This is not an unrealistic assumption, since there are LBSs that take advantage of the usage of PID, for example for service personalization. In this sense PIDs are similar to cookies in Internet services.

possible to re-use the same pseudo-ID used in the generalization of r, hence avoiding to degrade the QoS.

While experiments show that *ProvidentHider* can be effectively used in real applications, this contribution should be considered a preliminary result. The main problem with this approach is that it guarantees privacy protection only under the assumption that when a user is in A_h, the adversary does not actually know where the user is located (except for the fact that the user is in A_h). Consequently, an error in the definition of A_h can lead to a privacy violation. A possible solution can be based on a probabilistic approach in which, instead of using only a boolean value (visible or hidden) to model a user's "visibility," it is possible to specify the probability that the adversary can observe the user in a given location at a given time. This solution presents some technical issues, including the re-definition in probabilistic terms of the notion of anonymity. However, this approach presents some major advantages. For example, assume that it is possible to evaluate that an adversary can identify a user in a given location with probability 0.01. With the "boolean" approach, in order to be safe, it is necessary to assume that location as visible, and hence the privacy protection guarantees anonymity also in case the adversary identifies each user in that location. This is safe, but clearly excessively conservative. On the contrary, with the probabilistic approach it is possible to provide a defense that guarantees a probabilistic notion of anonymity versus an adversary that actually has 0.01 probability to identify the user in that location. Clearly, the probabilistic notion of anonymity is weaker than the deterministic one used so far in the literature; However, it is likely that an algorithm that guarantees probabilistic anonymity can also provide a much better QoS. This trade-off in our opinion deserves a deep investigation.

9.3.2   Location Obfuscation in Friend Finder Services

Friend finder services are becoming a very popular category of LBS. Using a friend finder service, a subscriber obtains location information about other participants, called *buddies*. Depending on the service, buddies can either be pre-determined (i.e.: a contact list of already-known users), or dynamically retrieved (e.g.: users which meet certain search criteria). Most of the current applications show the position of close-by friends participating in the service. However, many users may be concerned about revealing their exact location to the other buddies or even to the SP, and this could prevent them from using this kind of service.

In order to classify the service provided by typical friend finder applications, we considered a special class of services called *proximity based services*, whose primary goal is to inform users about which buddies (or, more generally, entities) are in a given range of proximity, without revealing their exact location. In order to achieve this purpose, the user issues a *proximity query*. Technically, a proximity query is a spatial range query on the database of users' locations, using a fixed proximity threshold as range. Eventually, the user can choose to communicate her exact location only to selected buddies. It should be noted that the friend finder service is only one of the possible instances of proximity based services.

Some of the general purpose solutions for LBS privacy, like those presented in Section 9.2, can possibly be adapted to provide privacy protection for this service. However, some techniques have been specifically designed for this kind of application with the aim of enhancing the quality and the efficiency of the service [43, 12, 30]. In the following we summarize the proposed techniques. To evaluate the quality of a technique, we identify three criteria called *privacy*, *service precision* and *system costs*. The measure of the privacy achieved using a certain technique can be expressed as the size of the area of uncertainty in which a potential adversary cannot locate a user participating in the service. Although some techniques can guarantee a minimum privacy requirement, the size of the uncertainty region should be as large as possible, because it is desirable to achieve more privacy than strictly required. The service precision measures the impact of a privacy preserving technique on the quality of service. For example, it may occur that the result of a proximity query include users whose distance from the issuer is above the requested threshold. The precision for this class of services is defined as the percentage of times the correct answer is given to the issuer about the proximity condition of the buddies. Finally, the system costs consist in the measure of communication and computational costs: as this service can be mainly oriented to mobile devices, the costs should be as low as possible.

In the service considered by Cox et al., a user determines if a buddy is in proximity if she can receive a broadcasted radio signal emitted by the buddy's device [12]. The proposed privacy solution aims to encrypt the identity information included in broadcast packets so that only selected users are able to decrypt this information. In practice, the proposed solution ensures that only a user's buddies can determine the proximity of that user. While this solution can be practical in certain cases, it has two main drawbacks. First, the solution to the proximity problem does not make it possible to specify a distance threshold different from the one imposed by the physical limits of the radio technology. Second, the solution to the privacy problem, does not allow a user to specify the minimum uncertainty region with respect to her buddies. For example, if the area in which the radio signal can be received is smaller than the uncertainty region of a user, a privacy violation occurs.

Zhong et al. [43] propose three privacy-preserving techniques consisting in a secure computation protocol based on public-key cryptography. All the protocols are based on a buddy-to-buddy communication, in which a user (the issuer), queries each of her buddies to check whether they are in proximity or not. This decentralized architecture, by avoiding interactions with an SP, avoids any privacy concern when the SP is not trusted. On the other side, communication costs are likely to be much higher than in a centralized architecture, especially when each proximity query involves a large number of buddies. The first protocol, called *Louis*, involves a third semi-trusted party (which participates to the secure computation without learning any location information) and is divided in two phases. In the first phase, consisting of four communication steps, the issuer needs to know whether her distance from the buddy is above or below a certain threshold. The second optional phase, consisting in two additional communication steps, is meant to run only for buddies which are in proximity, and lets the users exchange their exact location. Skipping the second phase of the protocol, however, does not ensure that the location of a user can not be discovered. In fact, if an adversary knows the location information of some buddies, as well as the answer of the first phase of the protocol run with an attacked user, he may be able to triangulate the position of the user. In the second protocol, called *Lester*, one of the participating users learns the exact distance from the other after only two communication steps. However, thanks to a property of the cryptosystem used in this protocol, the amount of work needed by an issuer to discover the distance can be controlled by the other user. The intuition is that, as the computation time needed to calculate the exact distance grows linearly with the distance, and exponentially with a parameter chosen by the queried user, it should be possible to calculate the exact distance in reasonable time only when users are nearby. The last protocol, called *Pierre*, divides the plane on a grid of cells, where the edge of a cell is equal to the proximity threshold previously determined by the users. After two communication steps, the issuer needs to know whether the contacted buddy is located in her same cell or in one of the adjacent cells. With this protocol is it not possible to narrow down the exact location of the user inside a cell. The approximation given by the cells, however, has an impact on the service precision, as the distance between two users in adjacent cells may be bigger than the proximity threshold.

We have been working on the same problem, and we proposed three protocols which can always guarantee certain user-specified minimum privacy requirements ([30]). As already observed, location privacy can be expressed as the size of the area of uncertainty that a potential adversary has about the user's position. Applied to a real-world map, this can be represented by a geographic area in which it is not possible to exclude any of the points as a possible position of the user. Therefore, the entire space can be partitioned in several areas of uncertainty. Formally, this can be modeled by using the notion of *spatial granularity*. A spatial granularity is defined as a subdivision of the spatial domain in non-overlapping regions, called *granules*. In order to specify a user's location privacy requirements, spatial granularities can be used, considering each granule being a minimum uncertainty region. A user can desire different privacy preferences with respect to the SP or with respect to the buddies. Two spatial granularities are considered in the protocols, called G_A^{SP} and G_A^{U}, to define the minimum location privacy required with respect to the SP and any other buddy, respectively. The first protocol is totally centralized and is called *SP-Filtering*. By using this protocol, two subscribers A and B send their obfuscated locations (i.e., spatial granules containing their real locations), according to their privacy requirement

G_{SP}, to the SP. Given the obfuscated locations, the SP computes the minimum and maximum possible distance. If the minimum distance is above the distance threshold δ_A, the SP communicates to A the message "B is not in proximity." If the maximum distance is below the distance threshold, then A is informed that "B is in proximity." In the other cases, the SP cannot state precisely whether B is in proximity or not, and it sends A the message "B is possibly in proximity." This centralized approach significantly reduces the communication costs if compared to the distributed solutions. In fact, when issuing a proximity query, the issuer contacts only the SP, which stores the approximate location of all the participants and computes the distance with all the buddies. Furthermore, even if the buddies collude with the SP, it is not possible to locate the position of A inside the granule of G_{SP}. However, since the approximation given by the granules may degrade the service precision, especially when granules of G_{SP} are very large, user A may choose to directly contact B whenever the answer from the SP is uncertain, in order to obtain a more precise answer. This consideration inspired the two other protocols *Hide&Seek* and *Hide&Crypt*. The *Hide&Seek* protocol consists in the *SP-Filtering* protocol, eventually followed by a two-parties computation. The two-parties computation is similar to the *SP-Filtering* protocol, with the notable difference that A communicates his location obfuscated accordingly to her G_U requirement to B without involving the SP. If G_U granularity is finer than G_{SP}, which means that regions in G_U are smaller, then the answer given by *Hide&Seek* is more precise than *SP-Filtering*. However, although this technique guarantees the minimum privacy requirement, it is not able to further improve the privacy protection. The third proposed protocol, called *Hide&Crypt*, addresses this problem and significantly improves the privacy obtained. The idea of the algorithm is that, when a two-parties computation is triggered, user A computes the set of all the possible granules of G_U which can be considered in proximity, and then A runs a set-inclusion two-party secure-computation protocol with B to determine whether B is in proximity or not. Using this protocol, in the worst case (i.e.: when B is in proximity), the uncertainty region for B is composed by the set of all the granules which are in proximity of A. In addition, B does not learn anything about A's location. Hence, the location privacy achieved by *Hide&Crypt* with respect to the other buddies is significantly higher than the minimum required. Furthermore, this protocol achieves a better service precision than *Hide&Seek* using the same privacy requirements.

Table 9.5 shows a classification of the protocols presented above. As can be observed, the main common disadvantage of the three distributed protocols is that the communication costs grow linearly with the number of buddies of each user. The Louis and Leslie protocols are not able to guarantee privacy with respect to the other participating users. However, they achieve a very high service precision. The Pierre protocol is able to give a certain location privacy under the assumption that the user chooses the same proximity threshold for all the buddies. If this is not the case, colluding buddies may be able to

Protocol	Architecture	Privacy wrt SP	Privacy wrt buddies	Service precision	Comm. costs
Louis	Distributed	Total	None	High	High
Leslie	Distributed	Total	None	High	High
Pierre	Distributed	Total	Partial	Medium	High
SP-Filtering	Centralized	User defined	User defined (same as SP)	Low	Low
Hide &Crypt	Hybrid	User defined	User defined	Medium	Medium
FriendLocator	Centralized	Total	Partial	Medium	Low
Longitude	Centralized	Total	User defined	Medium	Low

Table 9.5: Classification of the proximity based privacy preserving techniques

triangulate the user position. Furthermore, the approximation introduced by the grid cells does impact on the service precision. The *SP-Filtering* and the *Hide&Crypt* solutions always guarantee that the requirements defined by the user are satisfied. In the comparison we assumed that a user is more concerned about her privacy with respect to the SP, rather than the other buddies. However, it is possible for the user to specify different requirements. It should be noted that also the extreme cases in which a user requires no privacy protection or total privacy protection can be modeled. For all the protocols, the service precision strictly depends on the privacy requirement of the user. This means that the less privacy a user requires, the higher service precision is obtained. Finally, communication costs are considerably lower than the ones we expect from the distributed protocols, thanks to the filtering done by the SP.

The last two protocols included in Table 9.5 represent preliminary efforts that take advantage of both of the approaches presented above [38, 28]; They propose three-party secure computation techniques involving the SP, taking advantage of its presence to reduce the communications between buddies without disclosing any location data; moreover, Longitude also allows the user to precisely tune the level of location privacy with respect to the buddies.

9.4   Conclusions and Open Issues

In this chapter we have first presented our view on the relationship between online defense techniques, mostly proposed for privacy protection in LBS, and offline techniques mostly investigated in privacy preserving data mining for the publication of location and trajectory data. Focusing on the first class of defenses, we have presented our view of the state of the art, and illustrated in more detail two emerging defense techniques. Considering that positioning technology on mobile devices is enabling the acquisition of huge amount of timestamped georeferenced data, we believe that we still underestimate the range of applications that this data can enable. Partly for this reason, we argue that the research on location and trajectory data management is still in its infancy, and even more so for the privacy protecting techniques that have to deal with the diffusion of this data.

Among the many interesting open issues, the following are the ones that we would like to highlight.

Protection from sequential publication

Current offline techniques do not satisfactorily address the privacy problem in the presence of multiple sequential releases of location data. When different subsets of the transactions dataset covering different and possibly overlapping time windows are published, or obtained by an adversary, offline techniques have to take into account the possible correlations among published data, which may include segments of overlapping trajectories published using different obfuscation methods, as well as disjoint segments of trajectories that can be associated to the same individual. This scenario still deserves attention by the research community.

Evaluation of privacy-preserving techniques

A great effort should be made in the formal specification of adversary models and more generally on the attacks being considered. This is a precondition for being able to give solid theoretical guarantees about a specific defense. In some cases, probabilistic analysis would also be desirable. Theoretical analysis must be complemented by extensive experimental results. Current experiments are often based on limited real data regarding specific types of moving objects and for relatively small time windows. Others use synthetic data obtained from moving object simulations that do not resemble the real deployment scenario of the considered applications.

The great majority of papers that use an experimental evaluation simulate the user movements through a moving-object generator. The main functionality of these applications is to simulate the movement, generally on a road network, between two points randomly chosen on a map. This operation, repeated several times, generate a dataset of many spatio-temporal locations that are then used as users' location. The main problem with this approach is that real users' movements are very different from the random ones generated by these simulators [19]. Hence, it is worth wondering if the experimental results obtained using mainly random movements are reliable, how it is possible to measure how realistic a simulation is and, finally, how it is possible to generate a realistic simulation. While Mascetti et al. made a first attempt to answer the first question ([33]), these issues are mainly unexplored. We believe that the development of a flexible, agent-based user movement simulator would be of great help to our research community.

Acknowledgments

This work was partially supported by National Science Foundation (NSF) under grant N. CNS-0716567, and by Italian MIUR under grants InterLink-II04C0EC1D and PRIN-2007F9437X.

References

[1] Osman Abul, Francesco Bonchi, and Mirco Nanni. Never walk alone: Uncertainty for anonymity in moving objects databases. In *Proc. of the 24th International Conference on Data Engineering*, pages 376–386. IEEE Computer Society, 2008.

[2] Claudio Agostino Ardagna, Marco Cremonini, Sabrina De Capitani di Vimercati, and Pierangela Samarati. Access control in location-based services. In Claudio Bettini, Sushil Jajodia, Pierangela Samarati, and Sean Wang, editors, *Privacy in Location Based Applications*. Springer, 2009.

[3] Bhuvan Bamba, Ling Liu, Péter Pesti, and Ting Wang. Supporting anonymous location queries in mobile environments with privacygrid. In *Proc. the 17th International Conference on World Wide Web*, pages 237–246. ACM, 2008.

[4] Alastair R. Beresford and Frank Stajano. Location privacy in pervasive computing. *IEEE Pervasive Computing*, 2(1):46–55, January–March 2003.

[5] Alastair R. Beresford and Frank Stajano. Mix zones: User privacy in location-aware services. In *Proc. of the 2nd Annual Conference on Pervasive Computing and Communications*, pages 127–131. IEEE Computer Society, 2004.

[6] Claudio Bettini, Sushil Jajodia, and Linda Pareschi. Anonymity and diversity in LBS: a preliminary investigation. In *Proc. of the 5th International Conference on Pervasive Computing and Communications*, pages 577–580. IEEE Computer Society, 2007.

[7] Claudio Bettini, Sergio Mascetti, X. Sean Wang, and Sushil Jajodia. Anonymity in location-based services: towards a general framework. In *Proc. of the 8th International Conference on Mobile Data Management*, pages 69–76. IEEE Computer Society, 2007.

[8] Claudio Bettini, X. Sean Wang, and Sushil Jajodia. Protecting privacy against location-based personal identification. In *Proc. of the 2nd VLDB workshop on Secure Data Management*, volume 3674 of *LNCS*, pages 185–199. Springer, 2005.

[9] Francesco Bonchi, Ycel Saygin, Vassilios S. Verykios, Maurizio Atzori, Aris Gkoulalas-Divanis, Selim Volkan Kaya, and Erkay Savas. Privacy in spatiotemporal data mining. In Fosca Giannotti and Dino Pedreschi, editors, *Mobility, Data Mining and Privacy. Geographic Knowledge Discovery*. Springer, 2008.

[10] Chi-Yin Chow and Mohamed Mokbel. Enabling private continuous queries for revealed user locations. In *Proc. of the 10th International Symposium on Spatial and Temporal Databases*, pages 258–275. Springer, 2007.

[11] Chi-Yin Chow, Mohamed F. Mokbel, and Xuan Liu. A peer-to-peer spatial cloaking algorithm for anonymous location-based service. In *Proc. of the 14th International Symposium on Geographic Information Systems*, pages 171–178. ACM, 2006.

[12] Landon P. Cox, Angela Dalton, and Varun Marupadi. Smokescreen: flexible privacy controls for presence-sharing. In *Proc. of the 5th International Conference on Mobile Systems, Applications, and Services*, pages 233–245. ACM, 2007.

[13] Matt Duckham and Lars Kulik. A formal model of obfuscation and negotiation for location privacy. In *Proc. of the 3rd International Conference, on Pervasive Computing*, pages 152–170. Springer, 2005.

[14] Bugra Gedik and Ling Liu. Protecting location privacy with personalized k-anonymity: Architecture and algorithms. *IEEE Transactions on Mobile Computing*, 7(1):1–18, 2008.

[15] Gabriel Ghinita. Private queries and trajectory anonymization: a dual perspective on location privacy. *Transactions on Data Privacy*, 2(1):3–19, 2009.

[16] Gabriel Ghinita, Panos Kalnis, Ali Khoshgozaran, Cyrus Shahabi, and Kian-Lee Tan. Private queries in location based services: Anonymizers are not necessary. In *Proc. of SIGMOD*, pages 121–132. ACM Press, 2008.

[17] Gabriel Ghinita, Panos Kalnis, and Spiros Skiadopoulos. Mobihide: A mobile peer-to-peer system for anonymous location-based queries. In

Proc. of the 10th International Symposium of Advances in Spatial and Temporal Databases, pages 221–238. Springer, 2007.

[18] Gabriel Ghinita, Panos Kalnis, and Spiros Skiadopoulos. Prive: anonymous location-based queries in distributed mobile systems. In *Proc. of the 16th international conference on World Wide Web*, pages 371–380. ACM Press, 2007.

[19] Marta C. Gonzalez, Cesar A. Hidalgo, and Albert-Laszlo Barabasi. Understanding individual human mobility patterns. *Nature*, 453:779–782, June 2008.

[20] Marco Gruteser and Dirk Grunwald. Anonymous usage of location-based services through spatial and temporal cloaking. In *Proc. of the 1st International Conference on Mobile Systems, Applications and Services*, pages 31–42. The USENIX Association, 2003.

[21] Marco Gruteser and Xuan Liu. Protecting privacy in continuous location-tracking applications. *IEEE Security & Privacy*, 2(2):28–34, 2004.

[22] Baik Hoh and Marco Gruteser. Protecting location privacy through path confusion. In *Proc. of the First International Conference on Security and Privacy for Emerging Areas in Communications Networks*, pages 194–205. IEEE Computer Society, 2005.

[23] Baik Hoh, Marco Gruteser, Hui Xiong, and Ansaf Alrabady. Preserving privacy in GPS traces via uncertainty-aware path cloaking. In *ACM Conference on Computer and Communications Security*, pages 161–171. ACM, 2007.

[24] Panos Kalnis, Gabriel Ghinita, Kyriakos Mouratidis, and Dimitris Papadias. Preventing location-based identity inference in anonymous spatial queries. *IEEE Transactions on Knowledge and Data Engineering*, 19(12):1719–1733, 2007.

[25] Ali Khoshgozaran, Houtan Shirani-Mehr, and Cyrus Shahabi. Spiral: a scalable private information retrieval approach to location privacy. In *Proc. of the 2th International Workshop on Privacy-Aware Location-based Mobile Services*. IEEE Computer Society, 2008.

[26] Hidetoshi Kido, Yutaka Yanagisawa, and Tetsuji Satoh. Protection of location privacy using dummies for location-based services. In *Proc. of the 21st International Conference on Data Engineering Workshops*, page 1248. IEEE Computer Society, 2005.

[27] Ashwin Machanavajjhala, Johannes Gehrke, Daniel Kifer, and Muthuramakrishnan Venkitasubramaniam. *l*-Diversity: Privacy Beyond *k*-Anonymity. In *Proceedings of the 22nd International Conference on Data Engineering*, page 24. IEEE Computer Society, 2006.

[28] Sergio Mascetti, Claudio Bettini, and Dario Freni. Longitude: Centralized privacy-preserving computation of users' proximity. In *Proc. of 6th VLDB workshop on Secure Data Management*, Lecture Notes in Computer Science. Springer, 2009.

[29] Sergio Mascetti, Claudio Bettini, Dario Freni, and X. Sean Wang. Spatial generalization algorithms for LBS privacy preservation. *Journal of Location Based Services*, 2(1):179–207, 2008.

[30] Sergio Mascetti, Claudio Bettini, Dario Freni, X. Sean Wang, and Sushil Jajodia. Privacy-aware proximity based services. In *Proc. of the 10th International Conference on Mobile Data Management*, pages 31–40. IEEE Computer Society, 2009.

[31] Sergio Mascetti, Claudio Bettini, X. Sean Wang, Dario Freni, and Sushil Jajodia. *ProvidentHider*: an algorithm to preserve historical k-anonymity in lbs. In *Proc. of the 10th International Conference on Mobile Data Management*, pages 172–181. IEEE Computer Society, 2009.

[32] Sergio Mascetti, Claudio Bettini, X. Sean Wang, and Sushil Jajodia. k-anonymity in databases with timestamped data. In *Proc. of 13th International Symposium on Temporal Representation and Reasoning*, pages 177–186. IEEE Computer Society, 2006.

[33] Sergio Mascetti, Dario Freni, Claudio Bettini, X. Sean Wang, and Sushil Jajodia. On the impact of user movement simulations in the evaluation of LBS privacy-preserving techniques. In *Proc. of the International Workshop on Privacy in Location-Based Applications*, volume CEUR-WS Vol-397, pages 61–80, Malaga, Spain, 2008.

[34] Mohamed F. Mokbel, Chi-Yin Chow, and Walid G. Aref. The new casper: query processing for location services without compromising privacy. In *Proc. of the 32nd International Conference on Very Large Data Bases*, pages 763–774. VLDB Endowment, 2006.

[35] Mehmet Ercan Nergiz, Maurizio Atzori, Yucel Saygin, and Baris Guc. Towards trajectory anonymization: a generalization-based approach. *Transactions on Data Privacy*, 2(1):47 – 75, 2009.

[36] Daniele Riboni, Linda Pareschi, Claudio Bettini, and Sushil Jajodia. Preserving anonymity of recurrent location-based queries. In *Proc. of 16th International Symposium on Temporal Representation and Reasoning*. IEEE Computer Society, 2009.

[37] Pierangela Samarati. Protecting respondents' identities in microdata release. *IEEE Transactions on Knowledge and Data Engineering*, 13(6):1010–1027, 2001.

[38] Laurynas Siksnys, Jeppe R. Thomsen, Simonas Saltenis, Man Lung Yiu, and Ove Andersen. A location privacy aware friend locator. In *Proc. of*

the 11th International Symposium on Spatial and Temporal Databases, volume 5644 of *Lecture Notes in Computer Science*, pages 405–410. Springer, 2009.

[39] Manolis Terrovitis and Nikos Mamoulis. Privacy preservation in the publication of trajectories. In *Proc. of the 9th International Conference on Mobile Data Management*. IEEE Computer Society, 2008.

[40] V. Verykios, M.L. Damiani, and A. Gkoulalas-Divanis. Privacy and security in spatio-temporal data and trajectories. In Fosca Giannotti and Dino Pedreschi, editors, *Mobility, Data Mining and Privacy. Geographic Knowledge Discovery*. Springer, 2008.

[41] Toby Xu and Ying Cai. Location anonymity in continuous location-based services. In *Proc. of ACM International Symposium on Advances in Geographic Information Systems*, page 39. ACM Press, 2007.

[42] Man Lung Yiu, Christian S. Jensen, Xuegang Huang, and Hua Lu. Spacetwist: Managing the trade-offs among location privacy, query performance, and query accuracy in mobile services. In *Proc. of the 24th International Conference on Data Engineering*, pages 366–375. IEEE Computer Society, 2008.

[43] Ge Zhong, Ian Goldberg, and Urs Hengartner. Louis, lester and pierre: Three protocols for location privacy. In *Privacy Enhancing Technologies*, volume LNCS 4776, pages 62–76. Springer, 2007.

Part IV

Time Series

Chapter 10

Privacy Preservation on Time Series

Spiros Papadimitriou

IBM T. J. Watson Research Center, Hawthorne, New York

Feifei Li

Computer Science Dept, Florida State University, Tallahassee, Florida

George Kollios

Computer Science Dept, Boston University, Boston, Massachusetts

Philip S. Yu

Computer Science Dept, University of Illinois at Chicago, Chicago, Illinois

10.1   Introduction

Time series data are sequence of values based on observations at periodic time instants and appear in a wide range of domains and applications, such as financial, retail, environmental and process monitoring, defense and health care. Additionally, massive volumes of data from various sources are continuously collected. However, when a data owner wants to publish this data he may not be willing to exactly reveal the true values due to various reasons, most notably privacy considerations. A widely employed and accepted approach for partial information hiding is based on random perturbation [4], which introduces uncertainty about individual values. Consider the following examples:

(E1)   A driver installing a vehicle monitoring system [5, 35] may not wish to reveal his exact speed. How can he, e.g., avoid revealing small violations of the speed limit (say, by 3–5 mph) but still allow mining of general driving patterns or detection of excessive speeding?

(E2) A financial services company may wish to provide a discounted, lower-quality price ticker with a specific level of uncertainty, which is not useful for individual buy/sell decisions but still allows mining of trends and patterns. How can they ensure that the level of uncertainty is indeed as desired?

(E3) Similarly, a financial institution [43] may not wish to reveal amounts of individual transactions over time, but still wants to allow mining of trends and patterns. How can it control the level of uncertainty (or, privacy) in the published data and ensure that nothing more can be inferred?

Prior work on numerical and categorical data has focused on the traditional relational model, where each record is a tuple with one or more attributes. Existing methods can be broadly classified into two groups and work (i) either by direct perturbation of individual attributes separately [4, 3, 18] or of entire records independently [24, 23, 31, 10], (ii) or by effectively swapping or concealing values among an appropriately chosen small group of "neighboring" records [37, 2, 6, 32].

Although some of the prior work on relational data has considered certain forms of privacy breaches that are possible by exploiting either the global or local structure of the data [32, 23, 24, 10], the additional aspect of time poses new challenges, some of which are related to fundamental properties of time series [17]. In particular: (i) sophisticated filtering techniques may potentially reduce uncertainty thereby breaching privacy; (ii) time series can be "described" in a large number of ways (in a sense, a univariate time series is a single point in a very high-dimensional space [1]—e.g., if the series has 1000 points, there are many 1000-dimensional bases to choose from); (iii) time series characteristics may change over time and, in a streaming setting, new patterns may start emerging in addition to old ones changing (for example, we cannot know about quarterly or annual trends while still collecting the first week of data), making both static, global as well as fixed-window analysis unsuitable.

In this chapter we focus on univariate time series, examine the trade-offs of methods for partial information hiding via data perturbation, and propose a practical approach that we evaluate against both filtering attacks and, also, true value leaks. Additionally, it is suited for time-evolving (i.e., non-stationary) series and can be adapted for on-the-fly data hiding in a streaming setting.

The main idea is exemplified by the two extreme cases, which are explained in more detail in Section 10.3.1. True value leaks reveal the perturbation at particular time instants. If we wish to ensure that such information does not help infer anything about the perturbation of other time instants, then necessarily each time instant must be perturbed independently of others. However,

Sym.	Description
x_t	True value at time t, $1 \leq t \leq N$.
$\{x_t\}$	Set of all values (i.e., series).
N	Number of points (total or so far).
n_t	Perturbation at time t.
y_t	Published value at time t, $y_t := x_t + n_t$.
$\tilde{y}_t$	Reconstruction via filtering.
$\hat{y}_t$	Reconstruction via linear regression.
$w_{\ell,t}$	Wavelet (aka. detail) coeff. at level ℓ and time t.
$v_{\ell,t}$	Scaling (aka. approximation) coeff. at level ℓ and time t.
$\{w_{\ell,t}\}$	Set of all wavelet coefficients.
L	Maximum wavelet level, $L \leq \log_2 N$.
χ_k	Fourier coefficient.
$\{\chi_k\}$	Set of all Fourier coefficients.
σ	Discord, $\sigma^2 := \mathrm{Var}[n_t] = \mathrm{E}[n_t^2]$.
$\tilde{\sigma}$	Uncertainty after filtering, $\tilde{\sigma}^2 := \mathrm{Var}[\tilde{y}_t - x_t]$.
$\hat{\sigma}$	Uncertainty after regression, $\hat{\sigma}^2 := \mathrm{Var}[\hat{y}_t - x_t]$.
K	Number of coefficients with magnitude greater than σ.

Table 10.1: Symbols and their descriptions.

if the series exhibit certain patterns, such independent perturbation of each value in the time domain can be distinguished from the original data and filtered out. On the other hand, to ensure complete protection against any filtering method by making the perturbation completely indistinguishable from the original series, then the only way to achieve this is to make the perturbation a rescaled, exact copy of the data. However, in this case, even a single true value reveals how all other values have been perturbed.

In the first case, *each* time instant is perturbed independently, while in the second case *all* time instants are perturbed in the same way. But what if we perturb groups (or, windows) of values in the same way within a group, but differently across groups? How should these groups be chosen? Based on this insight, we address these questions using both Fourier and wavelet transforms. We demonstrate the trade-offs between privacy and compressibility, as well as the efficiency and effectiveness of our approach on real-time series.

10.2 Background

In this section we summarize the necessary background on wavelets and filtering. The main notation is summarized in Table 10.1.

10.2.1   Discrete Wavelet Decomposition

Wavelets are best introduced with the Haar transform, because of its simplicity. A more rigorous introduction to wavelets along with an introduction to the Fourier transform can be found, e.g., in [34]. Given a series with N points, we define $v_{0,t} := x_t$ to start the Haar DWT construction. At each iteration, or level, $\ell = 1, 2, \ldots, \log_2 N$ we perform two operations on $v_{\ell-1,t}$ to compute the coefficients at the next level:

- Differencing, to extract the high frequencies of $v_{\ell-1,t}$, which gives the *wavelet coefficients* $w_{\ell,t} = 2^{-1/2}(v_{\ell-1,2t} - v_{\ell-1,2t-1})$ that form the *detail* component of level ℓ.

- Smoothing, which averages each consecutive pair of values and extracts the remaining low frequencies of $v_{\ell,t}$, obtaining the *scaling coefficients* $v_{\ell,t} = 2^{-1/2}(v_{\ell-1,2t} + v_{\ell-1,2t-1})$ that form the *smooth* component of level ℓ.

The scaling factor of $2^{-1/2}$ ensures that the total energy (i.e., sum of squares of all values) is preserved. The coefficients of level $\ell + 1$ are half as many as those of ℓ and correspond to a time window twice the size. We stop when $w_{\ell,t}$ consists of one coefficient, which happens at $\ell = \log_2 N + 1$. The total number of wavelet coefficients across levels is $N - 1$.

There are several families wavelet transforms that follow the above recursive *pyramid algorithm*, using a pair of filters, one high-pass and one low-pass. For example, in Haar wavelets, this pair consists of the simple first-order differencing and averaging filters, respectively. More generally, for each $L \geq 1$, Daubechies-L (or DB-L) wavelets use an L-th order difference filter for the high-pass operation and the corresponding low-pass filter (for more details, see [34]). These filters have $2L$ non-zero coefficients.

Time/frequency decomposition   Figure 10.1[a] illustrates how Haar wavelets decompose a series into time and scale. Each scale approximately corresponds to a frequency band and each wavelet coefficient within that band "summarizes" the corresponding frequency content within a localized time window. For comparison, Figure 10.1[b] shows a pure-frequency decomposition. Each coefficient contains information about a single frequency (sinusoid), but has no time information, since the basis (i.e., sinusoid) for each coefficient is not localized. In practice, series often exhibit jump discontinuities, frequency shifts or changes and other non-stationarities, therefore some localization is necessary [13]. Short-window Fourier analysis uses DFT on a fixed-size window. This poses limitations on the minimum frequencies that can be captured, as well as the localization in time of each coefficient. In a wide range of application domains, the jointly varying window size and bandwidth make wavelets ideally suited for analysis and representation [13, 28].

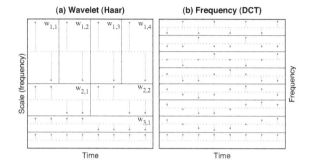

FIGURE 10.1: Illustration of time-frequency properties.

Streaming estimation In the above example, note that estimation of both $v_{\ell,t}$ and $w_{\ell,t}$ requires only the two last scaling coefficients from the previous level, $v_{\ell-1,2t}$ and $v_{\ell-1,2t+1}$. In general, Daubechies-L DWT requires the last $2L$ scaling coefficients from the previous level. Thus, it is possible to perform the DWT incrementally as new points arrive, by buffering only $2L$ numbers for each of the $\ell \leq \log_2 N$ levels. The total time required is still proportional to N, i.e., constant per new value.

10.2.2 Compressibility and Shrinkage

Because of their time/frequency decomposition properties, wavelets have been successfully used in signal estimation and de-noising [16, 14]. Our presentation in this section summarizes that of [13].

Assume that we are given the representation of a time series with N points in some basis. This representation consists of N numbers and can be obtained by applying an orthonormal transform (i.e., change of coordinates) to the original series $\{x_t\}_{t=1}^{N}$. Also assume that the noise is i.i.d. (i.e., white) and its variance σ is known. Given the above, the ideal de-noiser is simple: any coefficient whose magnitude is below σ is discarded as noise, otherwise it is retained. Then, the important questions are: (i) how to choose an appropriate basis, (ii) how to estimate σ when it is not known, and (iii) what to do with the retained coefficients.

For the first question, we ideally want the basis that compresses the signal into the smallest possible number of coefficients or, equivalently, has the largest possible number of zero coefficients. This implies that the remaining, non-zero coefficients will have a large magnitude, making them easy to distinguish from noise coefficients. Of course, it is not possible to know this optimal representation for a single series; differently put, the optimal basis for a specific realization of a series is always just the series itself, which is not very useful. Therefore, we want to choose a representation that is appropriate for a class of signals. As already mentioned, wavelets successfully compress many real-world series [13], because of their time/frequency decomposition

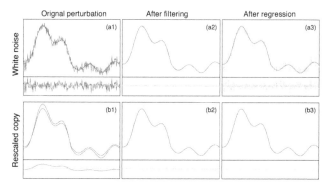

FIGURE 10.2: Illustration of intuition, via two simple, extreme examples: (a1–3) perturbation most resilient to any true value leaks, and (b1–3) most resilient to any linear filtering.

properties and are thus an appropriate choice.

Having chosen wavelets to represent the series, it can be shown that the risk-optimal estimate of the noise variance is the median over t of the absolute magnitude, $|w_{1,t}|$, of the first-level coefficients [16]. Additionally, the best way to perform thresholding is to shrink each retained coefficient towards zero, rather than keeping them intact. This is also known as *soft thresholding* and its application to the wavelet representation is known as *wavelet shrinkage*.

10.3 Privacy and Compression

We first explain the fundamental intuition in Section 10.3.1, which exposes the key issues and questions. Subsequently, we address each of those questions in the remainder of this section and in Section 10.4.

10.3.1 Intuition and Motivation

We illustrate the intuition with two extreme cases in Figure 10.2. The original series is shown in the smooth dark line, and consists of 200 points. The perturbation added and the published series are shown in the jitter line in Figure 10.2[a1]. The perturbation that remains after either a filtering attempt or after true value leaks are shown in the smooth or the jitter gray line in Figure 10.2[a2] or Figure 10.2[a3].

For both extremes we assume that, in the worst case, an attacker may have full knowledge of the true data, but in different ways. In the first, we allow an attacker direct access to an arbitrary number of true values (in the time domain). In the second extreme, we allow the attacker to know the shape of the series with arbitrary accuracy (i.e., the attacker may know the one-dimensional subspace spanned by the series itself). We always assume that an attacker uses linear functions/filters to obtain estimates of the true data [23, 27].

Figure 10.2[a1–3] illustrate the perturbation that is resilient to any number of true value leaks. In this case, each time instant must be perturbed independently of others, in order to prevent any inferences across values. This requirement is always satisfied by white noise, i.e., independent, identically distributed random values. A realization of a white noise process is shown in the bottom panel of Figure 10.2[a1]. We add this to the original series and obtain the published series, shown with a jitter line in the top panel of Figure 10.2[a1]. The linear regression estimate of the true values versus the perturbed values is shown in Figure 10.2[a3]. As expected, the true values cannot be accurately recovered. However, white noise is also uncorrelated with the original data (no matter what the data are), leading to the potential vulnerability illustrated in Figure 10.2[a2], which shows the output of a wavelet-based filter.

Figure 10.2[b1–3] illustrate the perturbation that is resilient to knowledge of the exact shape of the series. In this case, the perturbation must be completely indistinguishable from the original series. In other words, it should be perfectly correlated with the original series. Clearly, this is guaranteed if the perturbation is an exact copy of the original series, except for rescaling of all values by the same factor. The result is shown in Figure 10.2[b1], with the same perturbation magnitude as in the previous example. As expected, any kind of linear filtering is unable to separate the perturbation from the true series—Figure 10.2[b2]. However, if even a single true value is leaked, then evidently all true values can be inferred, as illustrated in Figure 10.2[b3], which shows the linear regression estimates.

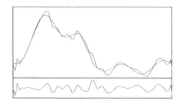

FIGURE 10.3: Our goal is to automatically find a perturbation with the same "smoothness" properties as the data, under a broad linear class of series (here, signals with compact wavelet representation), while simultaneously allowing for enough variation to also prevent linear reconstruction based on true value leaks.

Summarizing, the two extreme assumptions about background knowledge, and the corresponding best choices for perturbation, as illustrated in Figure 10.2, are as follows:

An adversary may have a combination of such knowledge, therefore we need to automatically find a balance between fully "deterministic" and fully independent perturbation—see Figure 10.3 for an example of our technique, in which case neither filtering nor linear estimation based on leaks can remove more than 1% of the perturbation. We propose practical techniques to address this challenge and evaluate them on a number of real datasets. We give the necessary definitions in Section 10.3.2 and describe our proposed techniques in Section 10.4.

10.3.2 Measuring Privacy

A common measure of uncertainty is standard deviation, i.e., root mean square value of a series. We will use standard deviation to measure two important aspects: (i) discord between perturbed and original data, and (ii) remaining uncertainty about the true values, after attempts to recover them. We want the discord to be as low as possible and, in particular, at most equal to a chosen threshold. The utility of the published data drops as the discord increases [20, 26]. On the other hand, given the discord, we want the remaining, "true" uncertainty to be as high as possible, ideally equal to the discord. Next, we formally define these notions.

DEFINITION 10.1 Additive perturbation   *Given a series x_t, for $t \geq 1$, we choose a corresponding perturbation series n_t with zero mean, $\mathrm{E}[n_t] = 0$, and publish the series $y_t := x_t + n_t$, for all $t \geq 1$.*

DEFINITION 10.2 Discord   *The discord σ is the standard deviation of the perturbation, i.e.,*

$$\sigma^2 := \mathrm{Var}[y_t - x_t] = \mathrm{Var}[n_t] = \mathrm{E}[n_t^2].$$

The discord threshold is given and determines both the maximal loss of information we are willing to tolerate, as well as the maximum uncertainty that can be introduced. In fact, these two quantities should be equal and this is precisely our goal. However, they may not be equal, because an adversary can apply techniques that reduce the uncertainty.

Given the discord threshold, we will always fully exploit all the available perturbation latitude, i.e., our goal will be to add a perturbation amount equal to the threshold. Thus, from now on, we will not distinguish between the discord and its threshold, using σ to denote both.

Given the published values y_t, for $t \geq 1$, an adversary may attempt to obtain an estimate of the true values, which may reduce the overall uncertainty. The discord (i.e., uncertainty originally introduced by the data publisher) is the standard deviation of the difference between true and published values. Similar to this, we will measure the remaining uncertainty with the standard deviation of the difference between true values and the adversary's estimates. This remaining uncertainty is a measure of privacy achieved under each attack setting.

We shall consider two attempts for estimating the true values, each with different, worst-case assumptions about the background knowledge available. In both cases, we assume that an adversary applies *linear* functions or filters to obtain an estimate of the true values.

Reconstruction via filtering The first one relies on linear filtering methods, which attempt to separate the perturbation from the true data. The filtering technique we shall employ is described in Section 10.2.1 and has been proven very successful in a wide range of domains and applications. [16, 14].

DEFINITION 10.3 Filtering uncertainty *Let $\tilde{y}_t$ be the result of a linear filtering operation on the published series y_t. The filtering uncertainty is the remaining uncertainty after this operation, i.e.,*

$$\tilde{\sigma}^2 := \mathrm{Var}[\tilde{y}_t - x_t].$$

In practice, we estimate the standard deviation $\tilde{\sigma}$ of the filter's output by applying the filtering operation on a finite time series consisting of N points and using the sample estimate of the standard deviation, $\tilde{s}^2 := \sum_{t=1}^{N}(\tilde{y}_t - x_t)^2/N$. With a slight abuse of notation, we will denote the sample estimate also with $\tilde{\sigma}$ instead of $\tilde{s}$.

In this case, an adversary has the background knowledge that the signal has a compact representation in some space, and more specifically, that the largest fraction of its energy is concentrated on a few transform coefficients. This is a very common assumption in signal estimation and recovery [15, 14], and amounts to a constraint on the "shapes" that the series is allowed to have. All practical applications of signal recovery need to make an assumption about the actual transform. Wavelet-based techniques have been shown most successful for a wide range of real-world signals [16], performing at least as well as Fourier-based techniques.

Reconstruction from true value leaks The second kind of attempt to partially remove the perturbation relies on true value leaks. By construction $y_t = x_t + n_t$ and, if n_t is Gaussian white noise, this is precisely the model for least-squares linear regression. This observation leads naturally to the next definition.

DEFINITION 10.4 Leak uncertainty   *Let $\hat{y}_t$ be the linear regression estimate obtained by fitting a line to the true vs. perturbed values, i.e., $\hat{y}_t = \alpha y_t + \beta$ where $\hat{y}_t$ are chosen so as to minimize the residual error $\sum_t (x_t - \hat{y}_t)^2$. This RMS error is our measure of* true value leak uncertainty, *i.e.,*

$$\hat{\sigma}^2 := \mathrm{Var}[\hat{y}_t - x_t].$$

In practice, we need to estimate $\hat{\sigma}$ from a finite sample. The least-squares estimators of α and β are

$$a := \frac{\sum_{t=1}^{N}(x_t - m_x)(y_t - m_y)}{\sum_{t=1}^{N}(x_t - m_x)^2}, \text{ and } b := m_y - am_n$$

where $m_x = \sum_{t=1}^{N} x_t/N$ and $m_y = \sum_{t=1}^{N} y_t/N$ are the sample means. The sample estimate of the residual variance is $\hat{s}^2 := \sum_{t=1}^{N}(x_t - ay_t - b)^2/N$. Since a and b are unbiased estimators, their expectation over all finite samples is $\mathrm{E}[a] = \alpha$ and $\mathrm{E}[b] = \beta$.

Leak uncertainty is the minimum error that can be achieved by any linear function for estimating the true values, *even if* we assume that an adversary knows almost all true values (except at least one). Therefore, our measure is a worst-case estimate of privacy loss, under the assumptions that an adversary uses linear estimation techniques and has access to any number of true values.

Furthermore, the distribution of $N\hat{s}^2/\tilde{\sigma}^2$ is χ^2 with $N-2$ degrees of freedom [11]. Therefore, even if a small subset of $M < N$ samples was used to estimate $\hat{s}$, its expectation over all leaks of size M would still be $\mathrm{E}[\hat{s}^2] = \hat{\sigma}^2(M-2)/M \approx \hat{\sigma}^2$. The standard deviation $\mathrm{Dev}[\hat{s}^2]$ drops quickly, in proportion to $\hat{\sigma}^2/M$. Finally, again with a slight abuse of notation, from now on we will use $\hat{\sigma}$ instead of $\hat{s}$.

Utility   For single time series, trends and patterns often refer to bursts [42] and dominant periods [39]. Such analysis is largely performed on the spectrum of the signal. Whether a perturbation preserves these key properties depends on (i) how much perturbation is added, which is the discord, and (ii) how the perturbation is added. In most perturbation methods, the first is a parameter determined by the end user. Additionally, both of our perturbation techniques, naturally preserve the spectral and "smoothness" properties of the original signal, by design. Hence, the proposed perturbation techniques will be useful in preserving both privacy and utility of time series.

Summary   We consider two potential breaches, with different assumptions about background knowledge. In the first case, we assume that an adversary knows that a series has a compact representation in some linear subspace (e.g., few non-zero wavelet or Fourier coefficients). In the second case we assume that an adversary knows any number of true values, in the time domain. In both cases we assume that linear estimation techniques are used. We propose practical techniques to address both challenges and we evaluate our techniques under the two different attack models on a number of real datasets.

10.4 Compressible Perturbation

As pointed out, the simple solution of perturbing the series with white noise does not work, because white noise is incompressible under any representation (or basis). As a result, the added perturbation is "diluted" over coefficients that are not important in representing the series. Consequently, a large portion of the white noise can be removed, leading to a significant decrease in remaining, true uncertainty over individual true values. Thus, our goal is to avoid this problem, by appropriately adapting the perturbation to the original series.

10.4.1 General Algorithm

The perturbation n_t for each value at time t will be chosen based on a given discord σ and, of course, the series $\{x_t\}$ itself. Since (i) it is impossible to design a method that is optimally resilient against *both* filtering and leak attacks, and (ii) filtering is possible at any and all time instants since it requires no prior knowledge about the true data, we consequently use resilience to filtering as the primary guide in designing our techniques, but also taking leak attacks into consideration, and we evaluate our methods with respect to both potential attacks. The general steps to construct the perturbation are:

(S0) Choose a "description" or basis.

(S1) Perturb only those coefficients that are "important" (to be made precise later) in the chosen description.

(S2) Determine by how much to perturb them.

The first step consists of applying an orthonormal transform which, given the N time domain values x_t, for $1 \leq t \leq N$, will produce another set of N coefficients, c_i for $1 \leq i \leq N$. Next, let us assume for the moment that we add Gaussian white noise with variance σ^2. This simply means that we perturb *each* coefficient by a random number c_i' drawn according to a Gaussian distribution with zero mean and standard deviation σ, $c_i \leftarrow \text{GAUSSRANDOM}(0, \sigma)$ for all $1 \leq i \leq N$. We may think of this as allocating N noise "units" (each corresponding to a per time instant perturbation of magnitude σ) equally into all N coefficients. Note that the resulting perturbation sequence n_t for $1 \leq t \leq N$ has the same statistical properties (i.e., Gaussian white noise with

---

Algorithm 1 COMPRESSIBLEPERTURBATION $(\{x_t\}_{t=1}^{N}, \sigma)$

---
[0] $\{c_i\} \leftarrow$ TRANSFORM$(\{x_t\})$ //*Transform coefficients*
[1] $\mathcal{I} \leftarrow \{i : |c_i| \geq \sigma\}$ //*Important w.r.t. σ*
[2] $\rho_i \leftarrow \begin{cases} \text{IMPORTANCE}(c_i) & \text{if } i \in \mathcal{I} \\ 0 & \text{if } i \notin \mathcal{I} \end{cases}$, for all $1 \leq i \leq N$

    such that $\sum_i \rho_i = N^2$
for each coefficient c_i **do**
    $c_i' \leftarrow$ GAUSSRANDOM$(0, \sqrt{\rho_i})$ //*Perturbation coeffs*
    $\{n_t\} \leftarrow$ INVERSETRANSFORM$(\{c_i'\})$ //*Perturbation*
    $y_t \leftarrow x_t + n_t$, **for all** $1 \leq t \leq N$ //*Published series*

---

the same variance) under any orthonormal basis. Therefore, for i.i.d. Gaussian n_t, the choice of representation is not important.

However, we have established that this approach is susceptible to filtering attacks. Therefore, we will choose a basis that successfully compresses a large class of time series, in the sense that it concentrates its energy into a few transform coefficients. Recall that the ideal de-noiser, given a basis, discards all coefficients below the (true or estimated) noise variance. Therefore, any noise embedded into such coefficients is "wasted," as it can be easily separated from the dominant coefficients. This observation leads to the conclusion that only those coefficients with magnitude greater than σ are "important" for perturbing the data in a way that is resilient to filtering attacks.

Therefore, instead of allocating the N available noise units into all N coefficients, we will allocate them to the set of coefficients whose magnitude exceeds σ. Let $\mathcal{I} := \{i : |c_i| \geq \sigma\}$ be the set of their indices. However, in order to ensure that $\text{Var}[n_t] = \sigma^2$, we need to also change the variance of the random number that will be added to each c_i, for $i \in \mathcal{I}$. For example, a simple choice would be a random number with variance $\rho_i := N/K$ to each of them, where $K := |\mathcal{I}|$ is the number of coefficients that exceed σ. This ensures that $\text{E}[\sum_i c_i'^2/N] = \text{E}[\sum_{i \in \mathcal{I}} c_i'^2]/N + \text{E}[\sum_{i \notin \mathcal{I}} c_i'^2]/N = K\sigma_i^2\sigma^2/N + (N-K)\cdot 0/N = K(N/K)\sigma^2/N + 0 = \sigma^2$, since each $c_i' \in C$ is perturbed independently. In other words, the expected sample variance of the perturbation series will be σ^2 as desired. More generally, we can choose any ρ_i such that $\sum_i \rho_i^2 = N$.

The general steps (S0–2) are shown in detail above (algorithm COMPRESSIBLEPERTURBATION). We will make them concrete next, in Sections 10.4.2 and 10.4.3.

10.4.2 Batch Perturbation

In this section, we propose two batch perturbation methods that rely on pure frequency or time/frequency representations of the series. In particular, the first is based on the well-established Fourier representation of the entire, length-N series. The second is based on the wavelet representation. First, we

Algorithm 2 FOURIERPERTURB $(\{x_t\}_{t=1}^N, \sigma)$

$M \leftarrow (N-1)/2$ //*Case N odd only, due to space*
$\{\chi_k\} \leftarrow \text{FFT}(\{x_t\})$ //*Fourier transform*
for $k = 1$ **to** M **do**
    [1] $p_k \leftarrow \sqrt{2}|\chi_{k+1}|$ //*All freqs, except DC (i.e., mean value)*
$\mathcal{I} \leftarrow \{k : p_k \geq \sigma\}$
$K \leftarrow 2|\mathcal{I}|$ //*No. of freqs exceeding σ*
[2] $P \leftarrow \sum_{k \in \mathcal{I}} p_k^2$
$\nu_1 \leftarrow 0$ //*Zero DC coeff for perturbation*
for $k = 1$ **to** M **do**
    if $p_k \geq \sigma$ **then**
        [3] $\rho_k \leftarrow (p_k/P) \cdot (M/K)$
        [4] $\nu_{k+1} \leftarrow \text{GAUSSRND}\left(0, \frac{\sigma}{2}\sqrt{\rho_k}\right) + i\,\text{GAUSSRND}\left(0, \frac{\sigma}{2}\sqrt{\rho_k}\right)$
        [5] $\nu_{n-k+1} \leftarrow \nu_{k+1}^*$ //*Complex conjugate*
    else
        ν_{k+1} and $\nu_{n-k+1} \leftarrow 0$
$\{n_t\} \leftarrow \text{INVFFT}(\{\nu_k\})$ //*Inverse FFT (zero DC)*
$y_t \leftarrow x_t + n_t$, **for all** t //*Published series*

---

study Fourier and wavelet perturbation in a batch setting and we revisit the wavelet-based scheme in Section 10.4.3, adapting it to a streaming setting.

Pure frequency perturbation COMPRESSIBLEPERTURBATION using the Fourier representation, which decomposes the series into pure sinusoids, is shown in algorithm FOURIERPERTURB. We denote with χ_k, $1 \leq k \leq N$ the Fourier transform of x_t, $1 \leq t \leq N$, and with ν_k the Fourier transform of the perturbation n_t that we want to construct. For simplicity, the pseudocode only shows the case for N odd. If N is even, then the Fourier coefficient $\chi_{N/2+1}$ at the Nyquist frequency must be treated as a special case.

Intuitively, each sinusoid is perturbed by randomly changing its magnitude and phase (lines 4–5 in FOURIERPERTURB). In more detail, since x_t is real-valued, its Fourier transform is symmetric, i.e.,

$$\chi_{k+1} = \chi_{N-k+1}^*, \text{ for } k = \begin{cases} 1, \ldots, (N-1)/2 & \text{if } N \text{ odd} \\ 1, \ldots, N/2 - 1 & \text{if } N \text{ even} \end{cases}, \qquad (10.1)$$

where χ_{N-k+1}^* denotes the complex conjugate of χ_{N-k+1}. The DC coefficient χ_1 is always real and equal to the series' mean. If N is odd, then $\chi_{N/2+1}$ is also real (case not shown in FOURIERPERTURB). We ensure that ν_k, $1 \leq k \leq N$, also satisfies the same property (line 5 in FOURIERPERTURB), so that the perturbation is also real-valued.

Because of Equation 10.1, essentially the first half of the Fourier transform carries all the necessary information. We compute the per-frequency energy (or, more accurately, its square root) in line 1 of FOURIERPERTURB. From Equation 10.1, $|\chi_{k+1}| = |\chi_{N-k+1}|$, so that $\sum_k p_k^2 = \sum_t x_t^2$ (assuming that x_t is zero mean). We then use this information to decide which frequencies to perturb.

For each frequency that exceeds σ, we choose a complex Gaussian random number, which perturbs the amplitude and phase independently, as shown in Figure 10.4.

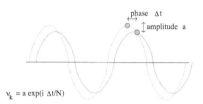

FIGURE 10.4: Illustration of lines 4–5 in FOURIERPERTURB.

The allocation of "noise units" into the important frequencies is done in proportion to N/K (as explained in Section 10.4.1) as well as in proportion to the energy content of each perturbed frequency (factor of p_k^2/P in line 3 of FOURIERPERTURB). This is the best choice for resilience to filtering attacks, as it tends to concentrate most of the perturbation into a few dominant frequencies. However, this may increase the "regularity" of the perturbation and make it somewhat more susceptible to true value leaks. We found that *per-band weighting* of the frequencies above the threshold σ (i.e., inclusion of the p_k/P factor in ρ_k, line 3 of FOURIERPERTURB) has small impact on true value leaks, while in certain cases significantly reduces resilience to filtering attacks. As we shall see later, the wavelet representation does not suffer from such problems, allowing a simpler decision on how to allocate "noise units."

Fourier-based perturbation generally performs well for series that are dominated by a few frequencies which do not change over time. If the series has discontinuities or frequency shifts, then Fourier may perform worse, because phenomena localized in time are spread across frequencies. This effect would allow a potential attacker to remove more uncertainty, roughly in proportion to the magnitude of such discontinuities (either in time or in frequency) and in inverse proportion to the number of frequencies.

Finally and more importantly, the Fourier transform of a growing series cannot be updated incrementally. One potential solution might be to use the short-time Fourier transform (STFT), but a fixed-size time window is undesirable, as we shall see. Next, we develop a wavelet-based perturbation method. Wavelets employ multiple window sizes to decompose the series and are also amenable to streaming estimation.

Algorithm 3 WAVELETPERTURB $(\{x_t\}_{t=1}^N, \sigma)$

$\{w_{\ell,t}\} \leftarrow \mathrm{DWT}(\{x_t\})$ //*Wavelet transform (detail coeffs)*
$\mathcal{I}_\ell \leftarrow \{t : |w_{\ell,t}| \geq \sigma\}$ for each level ℓ
[1] $K \leftarrow \sum_\ell |\mathcal{I}_\ell|$ //*No. of coeffs exceeding σ*
$\rho \leftarrow N/K$ //*Noise "density"*
for each detail $w_{\ell,t}$ do
   [2] if $t \in \mathcal{I}_\ell$ then //$|w_{\ell,t}| \geq \sigma$
      [3] $\omega'_{\ell,t} \leftarrow \mathrm{GAUSSRND}\left(0, \sigma\sqrt{\rho}\right)$
   else
      [4] $\omega'_{\ell,t} \leftarrow 0$
$\{n_t\} \leftarrow \mathrm{INVDWT}(\{\omega'_{\ell,t}\})$ //*Inverse DWT (zero smooths)*
$y_t \leftarrow x_t + n_t$, for all t //*Published series*

Time/frequency perturbation COMPRESSIBLEPERTURBATION using the wavelet transform, is shown in algorithm WAVELETPERTURB. We denote $w_{\ell,t}$ and $\omega'_{\ell,t}$ the wavelet coefficients of the data x_t and the perturbation n_t, respectively. WAVELETPERTURB follows the same general design of Section 10.4.1. In fact, wavelet coefficients are always real numbers and the procedure is simpler and more intuitive than FOURIERPERTURB. We allocate "noise units" only to those coefficients that exceed σ in absolute value. The perturbation is allocated equally among them, i.e., only in proportion to N/K (without weights in proportion to per-coefficient or per-level energy). This simple choice makes the perturbation more resilient to true value leaks, but without sacrificing resilience to filtering attacks in practice, unlike FOURIERPERTURB. The reason is that time-localized phenomena do not lead to smearing of energy across coefficients.

Wavelets have been successful in a wide range of settings [28] and are more resilient to changes in series' characteristics. They decompose the series into translated and dilated, localized waves at multiple scales, which correspond to a particular time and frequency window. Short windows are employed for high frequencies (i.e., short periods) and longer windows for lower frequencies (i.e., longer periods).

The localization of bases in time has the additional desirable characteristic that, intuitively, each period is perturbed independently of others. For example, assume that by following an automobile, we learn its true speed over a period of 15 minutes. However, if periodic trends shorter than 15 minutes are perturbed independently, our collected true values can tell us nothing about the future perturbation at scales of up to 15 minutes. For periodic trends in the next scale of 30 minutes, perhaps the information learned will be useful for another 15 minutes, but not longer, and so on for scales of 60 minutes, etc.

Finally, the DWT can be computed in $O(N)$ time, as opposed to $O(N \log N)$ time required by FFT [34]. Thus, even in a batch setting they are computationally more efficient. Furthermore, wavelets can be estimated incrementally, using just $O(\log N)$ total space and $O(1)$ amortized time per value (see Section 10.2.1). From now on we focus on wavelets, since they have several desirable benefits.

10.4.3 Streaming Perturbation

Our goal is to choose an effective perturbation that is hard to remove, but we want to perturb values as they arrive, before seeing the entire series, which grows indefinitely. Furthermore, we want to minimize or eliminate publishing delay. We explain this requirement next.

The Fourier transform needs, by definition, the entire series which is clearly not possible in this case. One solution is to partition the series into fixed-size windows and apply Fourier on each of them. However, if we use a small window, we cannot capture trends with period larger then the window length. For example, if we use a 5-minute window to perturb driving speed, it is still possible to leverage hourly or daily driving patterns to reduce uncertainty. If we use a large window, then we may have to delay publishing the data until the window is filled up, so we analyze it and perturb it. Alternatively, we could use the frequencies from the previous window to perturb the current one. However, if the window is large, it may not capture trends that have substantially changed in the new window. For example, a car might have been on the highway driving with a constant speed during the last hour, but has now entered a city and is in stop-and-go traffic. If we use a single one-hour window, the perturbation will follow the wrong trends.

Thus, the time/frequency decomposition of wavelets, which use multiple windows proportional to the period is desirable. In this case, we would use the information of the last, e.g., 5 minutes to decide if and how to perturb, during the next 5 minutes, patterns up to that long. However, we use the information of the last 10 minutes to make the same decision for smoother, longer patterns (up to 10 minutes) during the next 10 minutes, and so on. However, steps (S1–2) in the general algorithm (see Section 10.4.1) need to be re-examined in a streaming context.

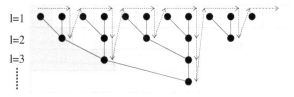

FIGURE 10.5: Order of incremental estimation: post-order traversal of wavelet coefficient tree.

Revisiting step (S1) If we want to make an exact decision whether to perturb a coefficient $w_{\ell,t}$ based on its actual magnitude (lines 2 and 3–4 in WAVELETPERTURB), then we have to wait time proportional to 2^ℓ for coefficients at level ℓ. In order to perform the inverse wavelet transform to publish a value, we need to wait for all coefficients across all levels that may affect its value. However, since the series size N grows indefinitely, so does the number of levels $L = O(\log N)$, which implies an indefinite publication delay.

We can impose a maximum delay (equivalently, a maximum level we are willing to wait for), but that is effectively the same as using a fixed-length window. Instead, we embed the noise into the *next* coefficient of the same level, i.e., we use $w'_{\ell,t+1}$ instead of $w'_{\ell,t}$ in lines 3 and 4. Said differently, the important coefficients in step (S1) are chosen based on the magnitude of *previous* coefficient at same band. For example, in Figure 10.5 the first coefficients of each level (darker shade) won't be perturbed, whereas the decision on whether to perturb the lightly shaded coefficients will be based upon the previous (darker) coefficient on the same level.

This simple one-step prediction is effective, since we are only interested whether a coefficient exceeds σ, rather than in its exact value. More specifically, periodic trends result in uniformly large coefficients at the corresponding wavelet level. Bursts also tend to affect more than one consecutive coefficient— if not, that is the only case we may "miss." However, such very short bursts generally occur at small scales and can safely be ignored.

Revisiting step (S2) The number K of coefficients exceeding σ (lines 1 of WAVELETPERTURB) is not available at the time we need to make a decision about how to perturb the data. This quantity is needed to determine $\rho := N/K$. Our approach is to substitute these with incremental estimates. Therefore, whenever a new wavelet coefficient $w_{\ell,t}$ for any ℓ and t is produced, we update our estimate of ρ as follows:

$$N \leftarrow N + 1$$
$$\textbf{if } |w_{\ell,t}| \geq \sigma \textbf{ then}$$
$$K \leftarrow K + 1$$
$$\rho \leftarrow \lambda\rho + (1 - \lambda)(N/K)$$

The order in which wavelet coefficients are incrementally computed is shown in Figure 10.5. This is the order in which the running counters N and K are updated. The decay factor $\lambda = 0.9$ is meant to prevent wild fluctuations, particularly in the beginning of the series when both N and K are relatively small. The inverse wavelet transform can be performed incrementally in a similar fashion.

LEMMA 10.1 Incremental inverse DWT
The inverse DWT can be computed incrementally in $O(1)$ time per value, using $O(\log N)$ space.

PROOF   (Sketch)The forward transform can be performed incrementally because it is a post-order traversal of the coefficient tree (see Figure 10.5). The inverse transform is a pre-order traversal of the same tree.   ☐

10.5   Related Work

Privacy preserving data mining was first proposed in [4] and, simultaneously, in [30]. Various privacy techniques have been proposed since, which apply to the traditional relational model can be broadly classified into methods based on secure multiparty computation (SMC) [30, 38] and into methods based on partial information hiding. The latter can be further subdivided into data perturbation [4, 3, 18, 24, 23, 31, 10, 27] and k-anonymity [37, 2, 32, 26, 41, 6] methods.

Wavelets have been successfully applied on a wide variety of data mining or data summarization applications [40, 22, 33, 8, 29, 21, 25]—see [28] for a comprehensive survey. Thus, the ability of wavelets to succinctly describe data in several application domains and their effectiveness in practice as a general analysis tool is beyond doubt.

The work of [24] and [23] also use a linear transformation to detect patterns in the data and, consequently, leverage them to add noise that is hard to remove. In particular, they use principal components analysis (PCA) on a static, relational table with n numerical attributes and obtain a rank-k, $k < n$, approximation of its covariance matrix. This covariance is used to perturb each tuple with noise that has the same correlation among attributes. The work [27] has extended the discussion into streaming data to deal with dynamic correlation and auto-correlation exhibited by multiple data streams. However, even though [27] mentions the techniques of using the auto-covariance from a stream data, neither propose a method suitable for time series data. Moreover, they do not consider connections between privacy and compressibility, nor address true value leaks. The streaming perturbation techniques in [27] concentrates on non-transformed streaming data and thus they are fundamentally different from the streaming algorithm presented in this chapter (in frequency domain).

Among other work on privacy, ℓ-diversity [32] and personalized privacy [41] are similar in spirit to our work, in the sense that they point out potential privacy breaches that exploit certain structure of the data. For example, among several aspects studied, both [32] and [41] point out that if all k tuples with the same generalized quasi-identifier are associated with the same sensitive value, the privacy of these tuples is compromised. This *homogeneity attack* [32] may be viewed as a very specific case of compressibility: the distribution of the sensitive values for this set of k tuples has zero variance. Both [32] and [41] make a number of important observations. However, none of them addresses the challenges posed by the aspect of time.

More generally, recent work has begun to realize that, when the entire collection of values is considered as a single data object, any regularity or structure that is present may lead to potential privacy breaches. In this chapter we address these challenges for time series data. We consider filtering attacks as well as true value leaks and we propose a practical, effective method that automatically strikes an appropriate balance between the two. When the number of attributes becomes very high, the well-known *dimensionality curse* [1] poses additional challenges for privacy. In our context, a univariate time series is a *single* point in a very high-dimensional space (and in a streaming setting, the dimension increases indefinitely) and the challenges faced are even harder.

A different model of *interactive privacy*, similar in spirit to that of [12], has been proposed in a series of works, including [7, 19]. In contrast to the non-interactive model, where the dataset itself is perturbed, the interactive model adds a perturbation to the outputs of arbitrary aggregate queries over the dataset. This thread of work provides an important theoretical analysis on privacy, under certain assumptions. First, the weak form of independence assumption made by [7] may be reasonable for datasets with millions or billions of tuples (e.g., a global census database, where we may assume that an adversary's belief about my age is largely independent of their belief about my parents' age). However, in ordered data, such as time series, this assumption may be problematic. More generally, our work focuses on practical aspects that may arise in real-world settings.

The work on watermarking numeric data streams [36] faced similar challenges as we do, i.e., how to inject digital watermarks into continuously arriving data tuples in a streaming fashion while maintaining high resilience under various attacks. However, the goal of watermarking is different, considering different types of attacks. In particular, it is generally assumed that the entire original data (or, at least, a large fraction thereof) are available, so the "noise" component of watermarked data can be exactly recovered and subsequently analyzed to verify the presence of a watermark.

Finally, in the field of statistical signal processing, notion of *compressed sensing* [15, 9] has recently emerged, building upon previous fundamental results in signal estimation and recovery [17, 16] and is partly related to our chapter. Traditional signal recovery assumes that a time series has a concise representation in some space and examines the relationship between reconstruction accuracy versus number of observed samples. Compressed sensing generalized these results from individual sample observations to arbitrary observed functionals on the signal (such as the total energy, or the averages of neighboring values, etc). However, this chapter does not address issues that arise in information hiding.

10.6   Conclusion

We consider two potential breaches, with different assumptions about background knowledge, each of which captures situations that may arise in practice. In particular, the first set of assumptions is most common in signal estimation and recovery applications, and essentially imposes either "global smoothness" constraints (via the background assumption of compact representation in the frequency domain) or "local smoothness" constraints (via the assumption of compact representation in the wavelet domain). The second set of assumptions deals with true value leaks and efforts for linear estimation of other true values, based on those that were leaked. In this case we take the worst-case view that an arbitrary number of true values may be leaked. Our leak uncertainty is a statistical measure of the maximum possible loss of privacy under these assumptions.

In this chapter, we focus on practical aspects and we have extensively evaluated our methods under both attack models, demonstrating that both are important in practice (results were not included in this chapter). Our evaluation demonstrates the practical robustness of our techniques on a number of datasets. In summary, we focus on two novel aspects of partial information hiding and privacy. We consider two real-world scenarios, design robust and practical techniques which are also suitable for a streaming setting. A challenging and interesting problem for future research is to come up with a unified attack model, which combines background knowledge of both types (i.e., knowledge about some true values and also about the shape of the series).

From the first seminal work on privacy preservation via partial data hiding [4, 37] until today, there is an increasing realization that subtle potential privacy breaches may arise when any regularity or structure is present in the entire collection of values considered as a single, complex data object [24, 23, 41, 32]. In this chapter we address these challenges for time series data. We consider true value leaks as well as filtering attempts, study the fundamental trade-offs involved in addressing both and propose a practical, effective method that is based on the wavelet transform, which has been widely successful in capturing the essential characteristics of data [28].

Acknowledgments

This work was supported in part by NSF Grants CNS-0831281 and CNS-0831278.

References

[1] Charu C. Aggarwal. On *k*-anonymity and the curse of dimensionality. In *VLDB*, 2005.

[2] Charu C. Aggarwal and Philip S. Yu. A condensation approach to privacy preserving data mining. In *EDBT*, 2004.

[3] Dakshi Agrawal and Charu C. Aggarwal. On the design and quantification of privacy preserving data mining algorithms. In *PODS*, 2001.

[4] Rakesh Agrawal and Ramakrishnan Srikant. Privacy preserving data mining. In *SIGMOD*, 2000.

[5] Davis Automotive. CarChip. http://www.carchip.com/.

[6] Elisa Bertino, Beng Chin Ooi, Yanjiang Yang, and Robert H. Deng. Privacy and ownership preserving of outsourced medical data. In *ICDE*, 2005.

[7] Avrim Blum, Cynthia Dwork, Frank McSherry, and Kobbi Nissim. Practical privacy: The SuLQ framework. In *PODS*, 2005.

[8] Ahmet Bulut and Ambuj Singh. SWAT: Hierarchical stream summarization in large networks. In *ICDE*, 2003.

[9] Emmanuel Candés, Justin Romberg, and Terence Tao. Robust uncertainty principles: Exact signal reconstruction from highly incomplete frequency information. *IEEE TOIT*, 52(2), 2006.

[10] Keke Chen and Ling Liu. Privacy preserving data classification with rotation perturbation. In *ICDM*, 2005.

[11] Morris H. DeGroot and Mark J. Schervish. *Probability and Statistics*. Addison Wesley, 3rd ed. edition, 2002.

[12] Dorothy E. Denning. Secure statistical databases with random sample queries. *TODS*, 5(3), 1980.

[13] David L. Donoho. Progress in wavelet analysis and WVD: A ten minute tour. In Y. Meyer and S. Rogues, editors, *Progress in Wavelet Analysis and Applications*. Frontiéres, 1993.

[14] David L. Donoho. De-noising via soft thresholding. *IEEE TOIT*, 41(3), 1995.

[15] David L. Donoho. Compressed sensing. *IEEE TOIT*, 52(4), 2006.

[16] David L. Donoho and Iain M. Johnstone. Adapting to unknown smoothness via wavelet shrinkage. *J. Am. Stat. Soc.*, 90, 1995.

[17] David L. Donoho and Philip B. Stark. Uncertainty principles and signal recovery. *SIAM SIAP*, 49(3), 1989.

[18] Wenliang Du and Zhijun Zhan. Using randomized response techniques for privacy-preserving data mining. In *KDD*, 2003.

[19] Cynthia Dwork, Frank McSherry, Kobbi Nissim, and Adam Smith. Calibrating noise to sensitivity in private data analysis. In *TCC*, 2006.

[20] Alexandre Evfimievski, Johannes Gehrke, and Ramakrishnan Srikant. Limiting privacy breaches in privacy preserving data mining. In *PODS*, 2003.

[21] Minos Garofalakis and Philip B. Gibbons. Wavelet synopses with error guarantees. In *SIGMOD*, 2002.

[22] Anna C. Gilbert, Yiannis Kotidis, S. Muthukrishnan, and Martin Strauss. Surfing wavelets on streams: One-pass summaries for approximate aggregate queries. In *VLDB*, 2001.

[23] Zengli Huang, Wenliang Du, and Biao Chen. Deriving private information from randomized data. In *SIGMOD*, 2005.

[24] Hillol Kargupta, Souptik Datta, Qi Wang, and Krishnamoorthy Sivakumar. On the privacy preserving properties of random data perturbation techniques. In *ICDM*, 2003.

[25] Panagiotis Karras and Nikos Mamoulis. One-pass wavelet synopses for maximum-error metrics. In *VLDB*, 2005.

[26] Daniel Kifer and Johannes Gehrke. Injecting utility into anonymized datasets. In *SIGMOD*, 2006.

[27] Feifei Li, Jimeng Sun, Spiros Papadimitriou, George Mihaila, and Ioana Stanoi. Hiding in the crowd: Privacy preservation on evovling streams through correlation tracking. In *ICDE*, 2007.

[28] Tao Li, Qi Li, Shenghuo Zhu, and Mitsunori Ogihara. A survey on wavelet applications in data mining. *SIGKDD Explorations*, 4(2), 2002.

[29] Jessica Lin, Michalis Vlachos, Eammon Keogh, and Dimitrios Gunopulos. Iterative incremental clustering of time series. In *EDBT*, 2004.

[30] Yehuda Lindell and Benny Pinkas. Privacy preserving data mining. In *CRYPTO*, 2000.

[31] Kun Liu, Jessica Ryan, and Hillol Kargupta. Random projection-based multiplicative data perturbation for privacy preserving distributed data mining. *IEEE TKDE*, 18(1), 2006.

[32] Ashwin Machanavajjhala, Johannes Gehrke, and Daniel Kifer. ℓ-diversity: Privacy beyond *k*-anonymity. In *ICDE*, 2006.

[33] Spiros Papadimitriou, Anthony Brockwell, and Christos Faloutsos. AW-SOM: Adaptive, hands-off stream mining. In *VLDB*, 2003.

[34] Donald B. Percival and Andrew T. Walden. *Wavelet Methods for Time Series Analysis*. Cambridge Univ. Press, 2000.

[35] Walter P. Schiefele and Philip K. Chan. SensorMiner: Tool kit for anomaly detection in physical time series. *Technical Report*, `http://www.interfacecontrol.com/`, 2006.

[36] Radu Sion, Mikhail Atallah, and Sunil Prabhakar. Rights protection for discrete numeric streams. *IEEE TKDE*, 18(5), 2006.

[37] Latanya Sweeney. *k*-anonymity: A model for protecting privacy. *IJUFKS*, 10(5), 2002.

[38] Jaideep Vaidya and Chris Clifton. Privacy preserving association rule mining in vertically partitioned data. In *KDD*, 2002.

[39] Michail Vlachos, Philip S. Yu, Vittorio Castelli, and Christopher Meek. Structural periodic measures for time-series data. *DMKD*, 12(1), 2006.

[40] Changzhou Wang and X. Sean Wang. Supporting content-based searches on time series via approximation. In *International Conference on Scientific and Statistical Database Management*, pages 69–81, 2000.

[41] Xiaokui Xiao and Yufei Tao. Personalized privacy preservation. In *SIGMOD*, 2006.

[42] Yunyue Zhu and Denis Shasha. Efficient elastic burst detection in data streams. In *KDD*, 2002.

[43] Yunyue Zhu and Dennis Shasha. StatStream: Statistical monitoring of thousands of data streams in real time. In *VLDB*, 2002.

Chapter 11

A Segment-Based Approach to Preserve Privacy in Time Series Data Mining

Yongjian Fu

Cleveland State University, 2121 Euclid Ave. Cleveland, Ohio

Ye Zhu

Cleveland State University, 2121 Euclid Ave. Cleveland, Ohio

11.1   Introduction

As more and more data become available electronically, data privacy has been a serious concern. The recent advance in data mining technology and its widespread adoption make privacy an even more critical issue. On the one hand, data producers must protect the privacy of their data due to business interests or government regulations. On the other hand, data producers want to publish their data for analysis and mining to find global patterns and trends which are not present in local data. To resolve the conflicting requirements, data mining researchers have proposed privacy preserving data mining [1, 14]. In privacy preserving data mining, data privacy is protected without seriously hurting data mining performance.

Many approaches have been proposed for privacy preserving data mining. They can be broadly grouped into two categories: data perturbation approaches and secure multiparty computing approaches. To preserve privacy, data perturbation approaches modify original data by adding noise, generalization, transformation, swapping, and so on. Secure multiparty computing approaches assume that data is distributed among multiple parties who securely compute global patterns without revealing data. Both categories of approaches assume that data is in the format of a relational table with rows representing objects and columns representing attributes.

A very popular kind of data in data mining is the time series. A time series consists of data points measured at constant time intervals that make up the time dimension. Time series data mining has attracted a lot of interest due to the abundance of time series in nature and society, and their special characteristics not found in relational data. Examples of time series include daily stock prices, monthly sales, and daily weather. However, the time dimension also makes privacy in time series more sophisticated than relational data.

With the high dimensionality of time series data, secure multiparty computing approaches are impractical due to overhead cost in computation and communications. Meanwhile, many existing data perturbation approaches developed for relational data is ineffective if directly applied on time series data. For example, one method in data perturbation approaches adds random noise to original data and publishes the noised data. For time series data, if the noise is independent of the original data, the noise can be filtered out to reveal the original time series.

In this chapter, we first discuss issues related to privacy protection in time series data mining. Existing methods for preserving privacy are summarized and their applicability to time series data is examined. We then propose a method to preserve privacy in time series data mining by adding segment-based noises. In our method, a time series is first divided into segments. In each segment, noise that is dependent on the segment data is added. Our method can prevent privacy breaching under attacks such as filtering and regression. We also study the effect of noise on classification accuracy. The method is implemented and tested using a real dataset. Its effectiveness in privacy protection and its impact on classification accuracy are reported.

The rest of the chapter is organized as follows. In Section 11.2, issues related to privacy protection in time series data mining are discussed, including protection and threat of time series privacy, methods for privacy preserving data mining, and measurements of privacy breach. Our method for privacy preservation using segment-based noise is given in Section 11.3 with an algorithm. Experimental results and performance evaluation are presented in Section 11.4. Section 11.5 concludes our study and points to some future work.

11.2   Preserving Privacy in Time Series Data Mining

In this section, we first describe properties of time series which may need to be protected as private data, followed by potential attacks to time series privacy. Privacy preserving methods are then summarised from related research work in privacy preserving data mining, with their applicability for time series privacy. Finally, measurements of privacy breach are discussed.

11.2.1 Properties of Time Series

A time series has extra properties other than data values. These properties may be considered private and need to be protected in data mining. Like relational data, a time series consists of values in the time domain. Unlike relational data, a time series has properties in the frequency domain.

A time series consists of a series of values which can be interpreted as measurement of a variable at constant time intervals. Besides its values, its statistics such as mean and variance may be sensitive just like relational data. Unlike relational data, it has other properties that may be sensitive, including peaks, troughs, trends, and seasonal effects. For example, a peak may represent a sales promotion event that is private.

A time series can also be represented by its counterpart in a frequency domain, for example, through Fourier transformation. Its values in the frequency domain represent the amplitudes at various frequencies. Obviously, the amplitudes should be kept private, as well as statistics such as mean and variance. Besides, the frequency spectrum also needs to be protected because its peaks imply periods.

In this chapter, we deal with privacy of time series in the time domain. The privacy of time series in the frequency domain will be an interesting topic for future research. Moreover, we consider only the privacy of time series data, not the privacy of its properties such as peaks and trends. Data is the basis of other properties. The privacy of data is the first step toward the privacy of other properties. Our focus is privacy preservation of time series data under the attacks that target specifically such data.

11.2.2 Attacks on Time Series Privacy

Time series are under the usual attacks on privacy just as relational data. Because of the nature of time series, there are some extra attacks that are specific to time series. Three of them are listed below.

- Filtering
  Filtering is an attack that uses statistical or mathematical filters to separate noise from data. When noises added to data are independent to data, and their characteristics are known, they can be removed using filters. For example, assume the noises are independent and identically distributed, and mostly in high frequencies. Adding such white noise is not enough to preserve data privacy. Given the published, noised data, an adversary can use a low pass filter to throw out noises and uncover true values.

- Regression
  In a regression attack, an adversary builds a regression model of a time series and uses the model to predict the time series. If an adversary can obtain some true values of the time series, either by other means or by guessing, he can use linear regression to separate noise from data. If noise is dependent on the true values, just a few true values are enough to reveal the whole time series.

- Blind Source Separation
  This attack uses the blind source separation techniques [3] from signal processing to separate aggregated time series. To preserve privacy, multiple time series are often aggregated and published instead of individual time series. When individual time series are independent of each other, an adversary can use the blind source separation techniques to unmix the aggregated time series and uncover the individual time series.

As pointed out in [16], adding independent noise is effective against regression, but ineffective against filtering. On the other hand, adding dependent noise is just the opposite, effective against filtering, but ineffective against regression. Therefore, we propose a segment-based approach to add noise where noises are dependent in each segment but independent among segments.

11.2.3   Methods for Preserving Privacy

Many approaches have been proposed for privacy preserving data mining. These approaches can be broadly classified into two categories. The first category of approaches can be labeled as data perturbation approaches, in which data is modified to preserve privacy and mining is performed in modified data. The second category of approaches does not modify data. Instead, data is split among multiple parties, who use secure multiparty computing to find global patterns without sharing local data, therefore preserving privacy. Most of them use encryption as well. We call the second category secure multiparty computing approaches.

The following is a list of some common data perturbation approaches. This is of course not an exclusive list.

- Adding random noise
  The added noise is independent from data, though its distribution is known. Data mining algorithms are extended to accommodate the uncertainly in noised data [1, 6]. Various randomization techniques have been studied[5, 8, 23].

- Generalization
  In generalization, a numerical value is replaced by a range to preserve privacy. For categorical attributes, a specific value such as "Doctor" is replaced by a more general term such as "Professionals." Generalization

has been used extensively to achieve k-anonymity where each tuple is identical to at least $k-1$ other records in the dataset [17, 2, 13, 9, 7, 15].

- Aggregation
  Data from multiple sources are aggregated and published[21]. The simplest form of aggregation is addition, where individual values are added up and the total is published.

- Suppression
  Original data is removed or replaced by a universal value such as a null value. It is usually used when generalization is not able to hide true values [7, 9]. For example, when there is only one woman in a group of people, to protect her information, the attribute gender may be dropped because it is impossible to further generalize.

Secure multiparty computing was introduced as a technique for privacy preserving decision tree construction in [14]. It had been used for association rule mining [18, 11], clustering with k-means [19, 10], and learning Bayesian network structures [20].

Some recent research specifically addresses privacy issues of time series data.

A privacy preserving algorithm for mining frequent patterns in time series data has been proposed by Silva and Klusch [4]. The time series is first segmented, then discretized and represented as a sequence of symbols. Secure multiparty computing is used to find frequent patterns which are sequences of symbols that occur frequently in the time series.

Time series data privacy has been studied by Papadimitriou et al. [16]. They argue that time series data has unique characteristics in terms of privacy. In order to preserve privacy, they propose two perturbation methods based on Fourier and wavelet transformations respectively. It is shown that white noise perturbation does not preserve privacy while the proposed methods are effective.

In [22], Zhu et. al. also point out that privacy of time series data is more than just the identity of data. They argue that existing privacy preserving techniques such as aggregation and white noise are ineffective for preserving privacy in time series data. The paper presents a privacy attack that can separate individual time series from aggregate data, without giving a solution to the problem.

Based on our analysis of previous work, we propose a segment-based approach for adding noise to preserve privacy in time series. Though adding dependent noise has been proposed by other researchers [8], it was for relational data. Adding noise for privacy preservation of time series was also proposed in [16]. However, our approach adds noise in time domain, whereas [16] adds noise in frequency domain. Besides, the effect of noise on data mining performance was not considered in [16]. Though [22] suggested adding dependent noise as an effective counter measure against blind source separation based privacy attacks, it did not give details.

11.3 A Segment-Based Approach for Preserving Privacy

As discussed in Section 11.2, the direct application of existing methods for privacy preserving in relational data is ineffective for preserving privacy in time series data mining. The inclusion of a time dimension in time series adds more complexities in privacy preservation.

In particular, adding noise to data has been a popular approach for privacy preserving in relational data. One approach is to add noise that is totally independent from data. This approach is very effective for protecting privacy against regression attacks. However, it is susceptible to filtering attacks. On the other hand, adding totally dependent noise is effective against filtering attacks, but weak against regression attacks. It is obvious that both approaches are extreme cases and neither is desirable in practice.

We propose a segment-based approach to preserve privacy in time series. A time series is divided into equal size segments. Noise is calculated and added in each segment independently. However, within a segment, the noise is dependent on the data. This avoids completely dependent or independent noise and thus is robust against both kinds of attacks.

Our approach is a generalization of the two extreme approaches mentioned above. When every segment consists of a single value, our approach is basically adding totally independent noises. When the whole time series is a single segment, our approach is the same as adding totally dependent noise.

To put it more formally, given a time series $x = \{x_1, x_2, \cdots, x_n\}$ and a segment size w, we divide the time series into m segments, where $m = n/w$. The i-th segment $s_i = \{x_{(i-1)*s+1}, \cdots, x_{i*s}\}$, $i = 1, \ldots, m$. We assume a time series can be separated into segments of equal size, i.e., n is divisible by w. It is straightforward to deal with the case when the last segment has a smaller size. In each segment, noise is calculated as a percentage of data and added to the data. The percentage is a random number between $-T$ and T, where T is the noise threshold.

It is obvious that noise will adversely affect data mining results. Since we select classification as our data mining task, to limit noise's effect on classification accuracy, a threshold is introduced for noise. The threshold, T, limits the maximum level of noise that may be added. The noise threshold is represented as a percentage of a data point in the time series. For example, a noise threshold of 10% allows noises between -1 and 1 for a point whose value is 10.

The algorithm for our method is given in Algorithm 4. It takes a time series, a segment size, and a noise threshold, and returns a noised time series as described.

It is obvious that Algorithm 4 has a linear time and space complexity.

Algorithm 4 An Algorithm for Adding Segment-Based Noise

Require: x: a time series

   T : a noise threshold //*Maximum level of noise allowed*

   W: a segment size

Ensure: A perturbed time series, $D' = D+$ random noise

1: break x into a set of segments of size W

2: $s_i \Leftarrow$ segment i of x

3: **for** each segment s_i **do**

4:    $r = random();$ //*a random number in [-1,1]*

5:    **for** each data point $p \in s_i$ **do**

6:       $D'(p) \Leftarrow D(p) * (1 + r * T)$ //*noise is a percentage of data*

11.4 Experimental Results and Performance Evaluation

The method proposed in Section 11.3 has been implemented in MATLAB. A set of experiments has been conducted using a dataset from the UCR Time Series Classification/Clustering data collection [12]. All experiments are done on a PC with Intel Core 2 CPU and 1GB of RAM. Every experiment is repeated 10 times and the average of the 10 runs is reported.

The dataset we used is the "Swedish Leaf" dataset. It contains a training set and a test set. Since the data mining task is classification, the training set is used for building classification models and the test set is used for evaluating these models. The dataset has 15 classes, 500 time series in training set, 625 time series in test set, with a time series length of 128. That is, there are 128 data points in each time series.

In all experiments, noises are added to the training set only. An original time series is denoted as x and its noised version is denoted as y. To evaluate the effect of noise on privacy preservation, noised time series are subject to privacy attacks described in Section 11.4.1. A time series obtained by a privacy attack on y is denoted as $\hat{y}$.

11.4.1 Privacy Attacks and Classification Algorithm

Two attacks are used in our experiments. The first is linear regression. We assume an adversary can obtain the true value of d data points of a time series. Based on these values and the noised time series y, a standard linear regression procedure is used to obtain $\hat{y}$. In our experiments, we randomly select d points in the original time series x, which are then used with corresponding points in y to build a linear regression model. We estimate $\hat{y}$ from y using the model. The second attack is linear filtering. We use a simple moving average filter of order $2p + 1$. That is, $\hat{y}_t = \frac{1}{2p+1} \sum_{i=-p}^{p} y_{t+i}$, for $t = p + 1, \ldots, n - p$. For the boundary points, we simply copy the available data, i.e., $\hat{y}_t = y_t$ for $t < p+1$

Table 11.1: Notations.

Symbol	Description
x	an original time series
y	a noised time series
$\hat{y}$	a time series uncovered from y by an attack
$MSE(a,b)$	mean square error between two time series a and b
acc	classification accuracy

and $t > n - p$.

The classification algorithm used in our experiments is kNN (k Nearest Neighbors). For every time series in test set, kNN finds k time series in the noised set y that are closest to it. The most popular class in this neighborhood is predicted as the class of the time series. In case two or more classes have the same number of votes in the neighborhood, we arbitrarily break the tie. If the predicted class and the actual class are the same for a time series in the test set, the time series is corrected classified. In our experiments, the Euclidean distance is used in determining neighbors.

11.4.2 Performance Metrics

We measure the performance of our method in terms of privacy preservation and classification. The metric for privacy preservation is mean square error(MSE). The metric for classification is classification accuracy (ACC).

Given two time series, $x = \{x_1, x_2, \cdots, x_n\}$ and $y = \{y_1, y_2, \cdots, y_n\}$, the MSE between x and y is defined as:

$$MSE(x,y) = \frac{\sum_{i=1}^{n}(x_i - y_i)^2}{n} . \tag{11.1}$$

The larger the MSE, the more privacy of x is preserved from y.

The MSE measures the difference in magnitude between two time series. In our experiments, we measure the MSE between the original time series and its noised version, i.e., $MSE(x,y)$. In addition, we measure the MSE between the original time series and the time series revealed by an attack, i.e., $MSE(x,\hat{y})$. The difference between these two MSEs shows the effectiveness of privacy preservation under the attack.

The classification accuracy measures the percentage of time series in the test set that are correctly classified by kNN using the noised set. It is defined as:

$$acc = cc/N \tag{11.2}$$

where cc is the number of time series in the test set that are correctly classified by kNN and N is the total number of time series in the test set.

The notations are summarized in Table 11.1.

Table 11.2: Parameters.

Parameter	Description	Values in Experiments
s	segment size	1, 2, 4, *8*, 16, 32, 64, 128
T	noise threshold	5%, 10%, *15%*, 20%, 25%
d	number of known data points	4, 8, *16*, 32, 62
p	$2p+1$-th order moving average	*1*, 2, 3, 4, 5
k	number of neighbors in kNN	*1*, 2, 3, 4, 5

Table 11.2 lists the the parameters used in our experiments. For each parameter, a brief description is given with its values used in experiments. The default value of each parameter is in *italics*. Unless specified otherwise, a parameter takes its default value.

11.4.3   Experimental Results in Privacy Preservation

In this section, we look at the effectiveness of proposed method in privacy preservation.

Figure 11.4.3 shows the MSE between the original time series and its noised counterpart, and the MSE between the original time series and the one uncovered by a privacy attack, for different segment sizes. Two attacks are considered as described above. The time series uncovered by linear regression and linear filtering are represented as y_r and y_f, respectively. In other words, Figure 11.4.3 shows $MSE(x, y)$, $MSE(x, y_r)$, and $MSE(x, y_f)$.

It can been seen from Figure 11.4.3 that when segment size is very small, $MSE(x, y_f)$ is much smaller than $MSE(x, y)$, i.e., linear filtering is able to uncover most of the original time series. On the other hand, when segment size is very large, $MSE(x, y_r)$ is much smaller than $MSE(x, y)$, i.e., linear regression is able to uncover most of the original time series. When the segment size is not at extreme, $MSE(x, y_r)$ and $MSE(x, y_f)$ are the same as or larger than $MSE(x, y)$, which means neither attack is able to get more private information than the published data (the noised time series y).

To examine how effective our method can be against regression attack, we look at the effect of d, the number of points known to an adversary. Figure 11.2 shows the $MSE(x, y_r)$ for various values of d and s, the segment size. As expected, $MSE(x, y_r)$ decreases when s increases for a fixed d, since larger s means less number of segments and therefore more precise regression. Also, $MSE(x, y_r)$ decreases when d increases for a fixed s, since more known points lead to better regressions.

It should be noted that Figure 11.2 shows that $MSE(x, y_r)$ declines noticeably only when s is greater than 32 and is relatively insensitive to s, except for $d = 4$. It shows that the proposed method is very effective against regression attack even though the adversary may obtain a number of original date points.

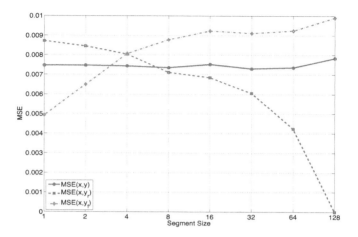

FIGURE 11.1: Privacy preservation with segment-based noise.

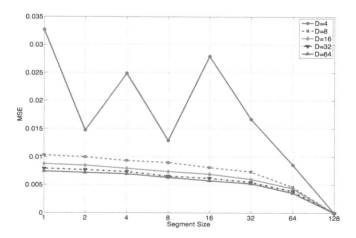

FIGURE 11.2: Performance of regression attack with various s and d.

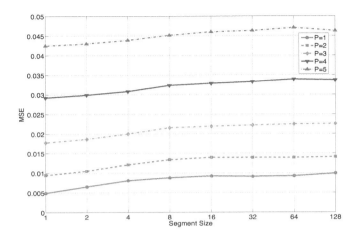

FIGURE 11.3: Performance of filtering attack with various s and p.

Figure 11.3 shows the $MSE(x, y_f)$ with various values of p and s. It is obvious from the figure that filtering attack is ineffective except when s is 1, i.e., noise is totally independent. Besides, larger p values cause larger $MSE(x, y_f)$ and are less effective because the moving average filter includes more points when p increases.

To sum up, our experiments demonstrate that our method to preserve privacy is effective against privacy attacks including regression and filtering.

11.4.4 Experimental Results on Classification

In this section, the effects of noise on classification accuracy are studied.

Figure 11.4 shows classification accuracy for various segment sizes. It is clear that segment size does not affect classification accuracy. Also, smaller k is slightly better for classification accuracy.

As shown in Figure 11.5, classification accuracy decreases when noise threshold increases, especially when the noise threshold is 20% or higher. This is understandable since more noises make classification harder. Again, smaller k is slightly better for classification accuracy.

In summary, classification accuracy is unaffected by segment size and holds well for reasonable noise thresholds. This shows our method does not degrade much in term of classification accuracy.

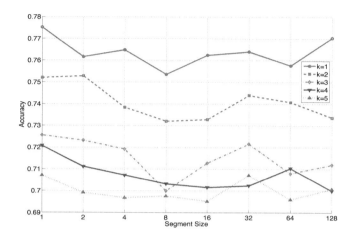

FIGURE 11.4: Classification accuracy for various segment sizes.

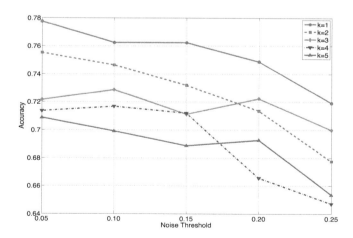

FIGURE 11.5: Classification accuracy for various noise thresholds.

11.5 Conclusion

In this chapter, we discuss issues related to privacy in time series data mining and propose a segment-based method for preserving privacy in time series data mining. Our experimental results show that the method is effective against privacy attacks and in the meantime does not seriously degrade classification performance.

More experiments are needed to evaluate the method in other datasets with different characteristics, such as mean, variance, length, number of classes, etc. Though our method does not depend on data, its effectiveness is certainly influenced by data.

Another interesting direction is to investigate privacy attacks using other regression and filtering techniques. Moreover, it will be interesting to see how our method works with other classification algorithms.

Acknowledgments

We thank Professor Keogh for the dataset used in our experiments.

References

[1] Rakesh Agrawal and Ramakrishnan Srikant. Privacy-preserving data mining. In *SIGMOD Conference*, pages 439–450, 2000.

[2] Roberto J. Bayardo and Rakesh Agrawal. Data privacy through optimal k-anonymization. In *ICDE '05: Proceedings of the 21st International Conference on Data Engineering*, pages 217–228, Washington, DC, USA, 2005. IEEE Computer Society.

[3] J. Cardoso. Blind signal separation: statistical principles. 9(10):2009–2025, 1998. Special issue on blind identification and estimation.

[4] Josenildo Costa da Silva and Matthias Klusch. Privacy-preserving discovery of frequent patterns in time series. In *Industrial Conference on Data Mining*, pages 318–328, 2007.

[5] Wenliang Du and Zhijun Zhan. Using randomized response techniques for privacy-preserving data mining. In *SIGKDD*, pages 505–510, 2003.

[6] Alexandre V. Evfimievski, Ramakrishnan Srikant, Rakesh Agrawal, and Johannes Gehrke. Privacy preserving mining of association rules. In *SIGKDD*, pages 217–228, 2002.

[7] Benjamin C. M. Fung and Ke Wang. Anonymizing classification data for privacy preservation. *IEEE Trans. on Knowl. and Data Eng.*, 19(5):711–725, 2007. Fellow-Philip S. Yu.

[8] Zhengli Huang, Wenliang Du, and Biao Chen. Deriving private information from randomized data. In *SIGMOD Conference*, pages 37–48, 2005.

[9] Vijay S. Iyengar. Transforming data to satisfy privacy constraints. In *KDD '02: Proceedings of the eighth ACM SIGKDD international conference on Knowledge Discovery and Data Mining*, pages 279–288, New York, NY, USA, 2002. ACM.

[10] Geetha Jagannathan and Rebecca N. Wright. Privacy-preserving distributed k-means clustering over arbitrarily partitioned data. In *SIGKDD*, pages 593–599, 2005.

[11] Murat Kantarcioglu and Chris Clifton. Privacy-preserving distributed mining of association rules on horizontally partitioned data. *IEEE Trans. Knowl. Data Eng.*, 16(9), 2004.

[12] E. Keogh, X. Xi, L. Wei, and C. A. Ratanamahatana. The UCR time series classification/clustering homepage. `http://www.cs.ucr.edu/~eamonn/time_series_data/`, 2006.

[13] Kristen LeFevre, David J. DeWitt, and Raghu Ramakrishnan. Workload-aware anonymization. In *KDD '06: Proceedings of the 12th ACM SIGKDD International Conference on Knowledge Discovery and Data Mining*, pages 277–286, New York, NY, USA, 2006. ACM.

[14] Yehuda Lindell and Benny Pinkas. Privacy preserving data mining. In *CRYPTO*, pages 36–54, 2000.

[15] Ashwin Machanavajjhala, Johannes Gehrke, Daniel Kifer, and Muthuramakrishnan Venkitasubramaniam. l-diversity: Privacy beyond k-anonymity. In *22nd IEEE International Conference on Data Engineering*, 2006.

[16] Spiros Papadimitriou, Feifei Li, George Kollios, and Philip S. Yu. Time series compressibility and privacy. In *VLDB '07: Proceedings of the 33rd International Conference on Very Large Data Bases*, pages 459–470. VLDB Endowment, 2007.

[17] Pierangela Samarati and Latanya Sweeney. Generalizing data to provide anonymity when disclosing information (abstract). In *PODS '98: Proceedings of the seventeenth ACM SIGACT-SIGMOD-SIGART Symposium on Principles of Database Systems*, page 188, New York, NY, USA, 1998. ACM.

[18] Jaideep Vaidya and Chris Clifton. Privacy preserving association rule mining in vertically partitioned data. In *SIGKDD*, pages 639–644, 2002.

[19] Jaideep Vaidya and Chris Clifton. Privacy-preserving k-means clustering over vertically partitioned data. In *SIGKDD*, pages 206–215, 2003.

[20] Rebecca N. Wright and Zhiqiang Yang. Privacy-preserving bayesian network structure computation on distributed heterogeneous data. In *SIGKDD*, pages 713–718, 2004.

[21] Nan Zhang and Wei Zhao. Privacy-preserving data mining systems. *Computer*, 40(4):52–58, 2007.

[22] Ye Zhu, Yongjian Fu, and Huirong Fu. On privacy in time series data mining. In *PAKDD'08: Proceedings of the 33rd International Conference on Very Large Data Bases*, pages 479–493, May 2008.

[23] Yu Zhu and Lei Liu. Optimal randomization for privacy preserving data mining. In *SIGKDD*, pages 761–766, 2004.

Part V

Biomedical Data

Chapter 12

A Survey of Challenges and Solutions for Privacy in Clinical Genomics Data Mining

Bradley Malin

Department of Biomedical Informatics, Vanderbilt University, Nashville, Tennessee

Christopher Cassa

Children's Hospital Informatics Program, Harvard-MIT Division of Health Sciences and Technology, Boston, Massachusetts

Murat Kantarcioglu

Computer Science Department, University of Texas at Dallas, Dallas, Texas

12.1   Introduction

Numerous government-sponsored ventures, such as the U.S. Department of Health and Human Services' Personalized Health Care Initiative [22], have fueled growth in personalized medicine research and its application. This, in combination with increasing ubiquity of clinical information systems and DNA sequencing technology, has stimulated an explosion in the quantity of patient-specific clinical and genomic data stockpiled in electronic medical records [1, 35] and biomedical research environments [40, 96]. Until recently, the collection, analysis, and application of clinical and genomic data were mainly localized to specific investigators or institutions. [81] Increasingly, however, scientists need to share data to strengthen the statistical power of complex association studies, allow the research community the opportunity to replicate and verify clinically-relevant findings, and comply with a host of laws and regulations. [29]

To assist in data sharing, agencies around the globe have invested considerable monetary and social capital to construct information technology infrastructure, such as the Database of Genotype and Phenotype (dbGaP) at the U.S. National Library of Medicine, National Institutes of Health (NIH) [61], which will facilitate the consolidation, standardization, and dissemination of person-specific records from disparate investigators. The availability of such databanks for widespread data mining activities is contingent on the protection of patient anonymity [70] and, while biomedical privacy policies and protection technologies exist, many studies (e.g., [64]) show they are vulnerable to various privacy-compromising attacks. This is particularly a concern because demographic and clinical data derived from patients' medical records are increasingly shared [56], thus heightening the probability that sensitive information can be "re-identified" to the originating patient [58]. As DNA sequences cannot be revoked or changed once they are released, any disclosure of such data poses a life-long privacy risk.

Beyond the clinical environment, there is an increasing push to circumvent anonymity issues and make personal genomic information available in a public setting in a fully identifiable format. A clear example of this grassroots movement is the Personal Genome Project [12], which is publishing the complete genome sequences and fully identified medical records of ten initial volunteers for its PGP-10 project with hopes of scaling up to 100,000 volunteers [23]. However, even as such projects march toward an "open" access environment, there is still a concern over privacy. Several years ago, for instance, James Watson, one of most preeminent scientists of the twentieth century, and a co-discoverer of the double-helix model of DNA, agreed to have his full genome sequenced and made available in an online searchable format. [103] That is, all of his genome, minus the sequence for his APOE gene, which is an indicator of an individual's potential to develop Alzheimer's disease. [84] Following suit, the same request for APOE suppression has been made by members of the PGP-10 program as well. [80] Despite such requests, the residual information in one's genome sequence may be sufficient to infer the status of a suppressed gene, and several scientists recently reported on a statistical model developed to infer Watson's APOE gene status with a high degree of certainty. [75]

The aforementioned violation is only one of many concerns looming for biomedical data sharing. In this chapter, we review various threats to privacy in the context of genomic data collection, sharing, and mining. In general, we believe that there are several aspects of genomic data that make it unique with respect to databases, data mining, and privacy. First, the inclusion of genomic data into the clinical realm creates a complex regulatory context (e.g., medical privacy laws and data sharing requirements) that is not found elsewhere. Second, the semantics of the data itself are unique in that it allows for the direct inference of genetic and clinical information of familial relations that have not consented to having their data collected or shared. Third, genomic data consists of a very high-dimensional space (each individual's genome is over 3 billion pieces of DNA), which allows for it to be tracked across locations and poses a challenge to standard database obfuscation techniques. To derive and apply real privacy protection solutions, it is necessary to understand the interplay of these facets of the problem.

The focus of this paper is not on the specific technical minutiae of the attacks, the database architecture in which such attacks are applicable, or the details of how to prototype the solutions to thwart the problems. Rather, due to the fact that many genomic database systems are currently in initial development or beta stage, we aim to provide the reader with a broader perspective of how such privacy violations come to be and the potential ways in which they can be addressed in the context of such data. In doing so, we hope to provide genomic database and system architects with general guidelines and reasoning tools they can apply when considering potential privacy concerns. We provide the reader with pointers to further reading and details beyond various attacks and protection mechanisms as necessary.

The remainder of this chapter is organized as follows. Section 12.2 surveys the social mechanisms that have led to biomedical data sharing as well as certain policies that govern and proscribe privacy protection requirements. Given this regulatory basis, Section 12.3 reviews various approaches that have been devised for re-identifying seemingly anonymous biomedical records, as well as inferring knowledge suppressed from such records. Section 12.4 follows with a review of emerging computational models and technologies for formally protecting biomedical records from privacy violations. We close this chapter in Sections 12.6 and 12.7, where we discuss the direction of this field and opportunities for genomic data privacy methods development, deployment, and integration.

12.2 Data Sharing, Policy, and Potential Misuse

The study of person-specific biomedical information raises serious privacy issues at a social level. [13, 82] Many people fear that information derived from their medical or genomic records will be used against them in employment decisions [52, 83], limit access to insurance [30, 46, 47, 104], or cause social stigma [48, 79]. Such fears are not unfounded. In 2002, for instance, the Burlington Northern Santa Fe Railroad Company tested employees for a DNA marker linked to carpal tunnel syndrome and at least one employee was threatened with disciplinary action for refusing to undergo examination. [27] In an out-of-court settlement, the company compensated 36 employees for $2.2 million and pledged to discontinue DNA testing for employment decisions. [53] As the relationships between genomic markers and disease are refined, the potential for discrimination will increase.

Various citizen rights advocates argue that banning genetic-based discrimination is the key to mitigating this concern. To this effect, the U.S. government recently passed the Genetic Information Nondiscrimination Act (GINA) of 2008. [21] GINA partially mitigates the threat of direct discriminatory action by employers or insurers [36], but there will continue to be other uses of genomic data that pose privacy risks, including the use of genetic testing in setting life, disability, and long-term care insurance premiums [38, 51, 89]. Furthermore, such regulation can only be enforced when it can be detected that genetic data has been used for discrimination. If de-identified genetic data is re-identifiable through public resources, or knowledge can be inferred from suppressed information, it could be used illicitly (e.g., discrimination, blackmail) without detection.

Regardless of the potential for misuse, many people want to contribute personal biospecimens or data for scientific research — provided protections are in place. When data is identifiable, for instance, patients want to specify the research topics for which data is applied (e.g., physical vs. mental health studies) [86, 90] and be consented prior to inclusion [39]. Yet, the consent process can bias the participant pool, be an administrative burden, and be prohibitively expensive for large research projects. [71, 105] The last issue is highlighted by a study that performed "re-consent" via residential mailings to 14,330 tumor registry subjects. [100] The cost was approximately $31,000, or $2 per subject. If such costs scale, consent management could exceed $1 million per modern databank.

12.2.1   Policies and Protections

To reduce complications, many countries have enacted regulations that permit data sharing without consent when the data lacks personal identifiers. For example, the European Union Data Protection Directive prohibits unconsented secondary uses of person-specific data, but makes an exception so that the "principles of protection shall not apply to data rendered anonymous in such a way that the data subject is no longer identifiable." [16] In the U.S. there is no centralized regulation; rather, biomedical information is controlled by a variety of federal and state policies, the appropriateness of which is context-dependent. Nonetheless, these policies also provide consent exemptions for data devoid of personal identifiers, as illustrated in the following summaries.

12.2.1.1   HIPAA Policy

In the United States, when a "covered entity," as defined by the Health Insurance Portability and Accountability Act of 1996 (HIPAA), wishes to share data collected in the context of clinical activities, it must adhere to the Privacy Rule. [97] The regulation outlines several routes by which personal health information is sharable for research: 1) safe harbor, 2) limited dataset, and 3) statistical certification.

The *Safe Harbor Standard* allows covered entities to publicly share data once it is stripped of a list of personal identifiers. These include explicit identifiers (e.g., names), "quasi-identifiers" (e.g., dates, geocodes), and traceable elements (e.g., medical record numbers). Neither clinical nor genomic data is explicitly labeled as a personal identifier and, arguably, can be released under this policy. For years, clinical data has been shared in public resources, such as hospital discharge databases. [72, 85] Similarly, person-specific DNA sequences have been disclosed to public repositories, such as the Entrez PopSet at the National Center for Biotechnology Information [7], which provides a population's aligned DNA sequences for a specified genomic region.

Various groups argue against disclosing data via Safe Harbor out of re-identification concerns. [55, 70] Rather, an alternative called the *Limited Dataset Standard* is advocated, which allows covered entities to share more detailed data, including dates and zip codes. The tradeoff is that investigators must enter into an acceptable use contract that prohibits re-identification. De-identified data in combination with a use contract satisfies this standard. This policy is appropriate for trusted investigators, but as the quantity of centralized data and investigators increases, such an approach may become infeasible to manage. Moreover, this policy does not actually prevent an individual from attempting re-identification nor does it measure the risk of re-identification.

The *Statistical Standard* allows sharing data in any format, provided an expert certifies "the risk is very small that the information could be used by the recipient, alone or in combination with other reasonably available information, to identify an individual." Methods to quantify risks have been researched [76, 95], but no standards have emerged and it is not clear how data should be protected or risk should be measured. For instance, one proposed method is to "perturb" DNA sequences; e.g., *aacctata* shared as *aatcaata*. [55] As perturbation increases, the likelihood that an investigator can determine the original sequence decreases, implying greater privacy protection. The tradeoff is perturbation can obscure, or lead to false, associations. A second criticism is that research has shown certain types of perturbation can be filtered to reveal or bound original data. [45] Despite such problems, data protection based on scientific models can be achieved, but care must be taken to design them with formal principles, as we illustrate below.

12.2.1.2   National Institutes of Health Policy

HIPAA does not necessarily apply to data collected for NIH-funded research. To address this issue, the NIH structured its "genome wide association," or GWA, data sharing policy such that providers must submit data without "identifiable information." [74] The NIH recognizes that residual information can lead to the re-identification of an individual. Thus, GWA dataset investigators must sign a use agreement with prohibitions akin to limited datasets. Again, however, such contracts do not technically address the re-identification risks.

12.2.1.3 Institutional Review Board Oversight

Institutional Review Board (IRB), also referred to as Research Ethics Board in certain countries, approval is required when research is federally funded. One of the exemptions to oversight, and patient consent, an IRB will issue is when data are believed to be anonymous. But if IRBs base their decisions on false beliefs about the identifiability of such data, then shared biomedical data may be vulnerable to re-identification and use agreements and IRB protections may be inappropriately designed. While data re-identification is often prohibited by an IRB's approval or use agreement, the policy itself is insufficient to prevent someone from performing the act.

Rather than argue the extent to which IRBs and use agreements delegate responsible research, we believe it is better to infuse policy with technology that has provable properties to control and enforce protection from curious insiders and malicious hackers.

12.2.2 Implications for Family Members

Beyond the privacy of an individual, there are substantial discrimination and privacy concerns that can arise from genomic data with respect to inferences about familial relatives. Consider, beyond the clinical setting, genetic sequencing is increasing in forensics [8]. A genetic fingerprinting provision in the renewal of the federal Violence Against Women Act [101], alone, may result in one million new sequenced individuals each year, markedly increasing the number of available links between identities and genotypes. Beyond concerns of civil liberties, there is a significant privacy concern in that the genotypes of family members can be used to assist in forensic or criminal investigations for indirect identification of genotype, increasing the number of people who may be identified [5, 6]. Similarly, Freedom of Information Act (FOIA) [19] requests related to federally-funded genome wide association studies could potentially be used to identify research participants and their family members. Clinically, choosing the detail and type of disease propensity information that must be disclosed to patients and their potentially affected family members is also under debate [17, 50, 77].

12.3 Technical Protections and Weaknesses

A database of DNA sequences appears anonymous because there is no public registry against which the DNA could be compared to reveal the associated persons' identity. Over the past decade, many data protection systems have relied on this premise and partition DNA from explicit identifiers through a variety of methods. Some systems, such as the Utah Resource for Genetic and Epidemiologic Research, apply a de-identification approach that removes explicitly, and potentially, identifiable values from shared datasets.[106] Beyond simple de-identification, an approach called denominalization was designed to code and disseminate genomic and familial information in Montreal, Canada. [20] The primary difference between simple de-identification and denominalization is that the latter uses structured coding to represent familial relationships. A random number is assigned to each family as well as each individual within the family. Then, a set of codes, consistent across families, is applied to represent relations, such as if two individuals are siblings, or the precedence of siblings (i.e., birth order). Other systems, such as that proposed by deCode Genetics, Inc. of Iceland, facilitates data sharing through a trusted third party, sometimes called an honest broker, who converts identified research participants' Social Security Numbers into encrypted codes. [28] Yet another approach, posed by the University of Gent, uses "semi-trusted" third parties that serve as a centralized repository for many providers, but each provider obscures participants' identities prior to supplying data to the third party. [15]

None of these systems obscure biomedical data, only identifiers. As a result, the aforementioned examples say nothing more than the data "looks anonymous." This is a dangerous practice because personal data is collected, shared, and studied with rapidly diminishing computational constraints that erode legal and policy safeguards. As mentioned earlier, and will be demonstrated in the following section, various research investigations have shown that de-identified biomedical data can be re-identified to named individuals through a number of mechanisms without "hacking" into computer systems. Nonetheless, such vulnerabilities are not tantamount to the realization of intrusions. In fairness, many of these systems are wrapped with acceptable use policies and utilize oversight boards that vet the trustworthiness of the individuals requesting access to such resources. However, many emerging repositories hope to make portions of their records publicly available at a person-specific or aggregated level. Regardless, it is our intention to point out where the technological protections can be improved so that assurances in data sharing policies can be strengthened.

12.3.1   A Model of Re-Identification

We will review some of the techniques designed for privacy invasion in a moment, but first it is important to recognize the basic model by which re-identification transpires. Specifically, the process requires several necessary conditions to be satisfied, as shown in Figure 12.1. First, it requires that the de-identified data is unique or "distinguishing." In other words, we must be able to pinpoint an individual in a group of size X or less. Second, we need a naming resource. Without such a naming resource, we have no way of linking the de-identified resource to an identity. Granted, we recognize that the lack of a readily available naming resource does not imply that data is sufficiently protected from re-identification, but it does indicate that it is much harder to identify an individual, or group of individuals, given the current resources at hand. Finally, we need a mechanism to relate the de-identified and identified resources.

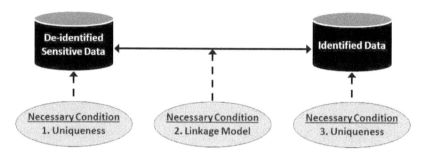

FIGURE 12.1: Conditions required to achieve a successful re-identification.

For instance, it is remarkably easy to positively identify a person with fewer than 100 independent, commonly varying single nucleotide polymorphisms (SNPs) (features that are common to genotype-phenotype investigations) using a physical sample or a copy of those values. [55] Now, imagine you were provided with a collection of DNA sequences and a randomly ordered list of names that corresponded to the same underlying population of individuals. Clearly, we have a de-identified resource and an identified resource, but there is no relation between the two types of resources. Thus, an attacker would have no way of relating the records beyond a random allocation. Yet, if we provided a feature set that was common between the resources, such as demographic information or the diagnosis codes associated with the individuals (e.g., see the attack laid out in the following section), then we have a route by which re-identification may be achieved. In many instances the information that is associated with genomic data, particularly genomic data derived from a clinical setting, permits relationships to be established between de-identified and identifiable resources.

12.3.2   From Genotype to Phenotype and Back Again

The first type of attack we review, summarized in Figure 12.2, takes into account the fact that there exists an inherent relationship between genomic data and physical manifestations in the form of phenotypic information. A phenotype is often structured through standardized biomedical coding ontologies, such as the International Classification of Diseases (ICD) and may be disclosed in various settings including semi-private data, such as administrative or insurance records, but also more public records, such as hospital discharge databases. This latter class of resource is important to note because it was applied in one of the most famous biomedical re-identification attacks to date. Specifically, in the mid-1990s, it was shown that de-identified, and publicly available, hospital discharge databases retained patient demographics, such as date of birth, gender, and disease. At the same time, it was found that the same demographics resided in identified voter registration lists. Thus, crossing the two types of resources facilitated the unique identification of many individual's medical records. [92] Statistically, it has been shown that this combination of features is somewhere between 63% to 87% unique for the U.S. population. [26, 92]

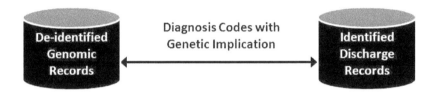

FIGURE 12.2: Re-identification through genotype-phenotype relationships.

Returning to the re-identification of genomic data, there exist a number of diseases, and subsequently ICD codes, that can be directly inferred from genomic sequences. In earlier work [68], ICD version 9 (ICD-9) codes* were cross-referenced with key words from two publicly available resources provided by the National Center for Biotechnology Information (NCBI): a) the Genes and Diseases online book [73] and b) the Online Mendelian Inheritance in Man (OMIM) database [31]. Most of the genetic disorders listed on these websites are the direct result of mutations in a single gene. The ICD-9 codes represent diseases that manifest as the result of mutations in single genes. The preliminary search was not exhaustive, since the names of some diseases are classified differently in the clinical information than its genetic counterpart. Examples of such well-defined diseases with different names in the database include diastrophic dysplasia, spinal muscular atrophy (SMA), and Angelman syndrome.

At least 40 ICD-9 codes were found to be related to over 35 DNA-mutation causing diseases. This information is represented in Table 12.1. Furthermore, the pharmacogenomics community continues to uncover relationships between genomic variation and the ability to process drugs and treatments. [4, 33, 99]

---

*Available for download from the National Center for Health Statistics at http://www.cdc. gov/nchs/about/otheract/icd9/abticd9.htm.

Thus, given such domain knowledge, in certain instances we can construct relationships between genotype and phenotype through treatments as well.

12.3.3   We Are Family

While the genotype-phenotype attack requires biomedical domain knowledge, a second type of attack is possible because genomic and clinical data is increasingly disseminated in the context of familial information. This is a practice that is common in gene hunting expeditions. In this context, the familial information is represented in the format of a de-identified pedigree, which reports the gender, disease state, and information regarding the mortality of the individuals in the pedigree. In other words, it is often reported if the individual in the pedigree is living or deceased. At the same time, there is a variety of publicly available identified information available. When asked, most people first think of online genealogy websites as a potential venue for collection of identifiable resources. And, while such venues do reveal the identities of certain people, they do not necessarily provide the best coverage on the population from which de-identified pedigrees are often derived. Rather, an alternative resource that has been exploited for identifying information is obituary and death records. These tend to have greater coverage on a population, especially when it is free to post such information in the local newspaper. Moreover, such resources tend to include information on the recently deceased individual as well as the family relations. Research has shown that such information tends to have robust population coverage and is relatively distinguishing of the corresponding population. In a study with records derived from a particular U.S. state capital, it was shown that approximately 70% of the population was identifiable using a two-generation pedigree. [66]

12.3.4   Following the Bread Crumbs

Beyond biomedical knowledge and family information, it was recognized that many patients are transient and visit multiple institutions providing care. In this setting, a patient's location-visit pattern becomes a distinguishing feature and facilitates what has been termed a "trails" attack. [69] In this scenario, a patient visits multiple hospitals, where his clinical and DNA data is collected. The facilities forward de-identified DNA records, tagged with the submitting institution, to a public centralized databank. [4, 15, 18] In addition, by state law, the hospitals send identifiable discharge records, including patient demographics and diagnoses to a public state-controlled database. [91] Even if there is no clear biomedical relationship between the diagnosis codes and DNA, we can construct more robust profiles on patients by tracking the hospitals they visited (i.e., the "trail") in the discharge data and tracking the hospitals where DNA records were collected in the repository (See Figure 12.3). Research has shown that substantial portions of patient populations diagnosed with DNA-based disorders are highly susceptible to re-identification

Table 12.1: Sample of diagnosis codes and DNA counterparts derived from crossing the ICD-9 registry with NCBI's OMIM and Genes and Disease database.

#	Disease Name	ICD-9 Code	Known Gene(s)
1	Adrenoleukodystrophy	3300	ALD
2	Amyotrophic Lateral Sclerosis (ALS)	33520	SOD1, ALS2, ALS4, ALS5
3	Burkitt's Lymphoma	2002	MYC
4	Chronic Myeloid Leukemia	2051, 20510, 20511	BCR, ABL
5	Cystic Fibrosis	27700, 27701, V181, V776	CFTR, CFM1
6	Duchenne's Muscular Dystrophy (paralysis)	33522	DMD
7	Ellis-van Creveld (chondroectodermal dysplasia)	75655	EVD
8	Essential Tremor (idiopathic) (autosomal dominant account for 1/2 of the cases)	3331	ETM1 (FET1), ETM2
9	Familial Mediterranean Fever (amyloidosis)	2773	FMF
10	Fragile X	75983	FMR1
11	Friedreich's Ataxia	3340	FRDA
12	Galactosemia	2711	GALT
13	Gaucher's disease (cerebroside lipidosis)	2727, 3302	GBA
14	Hemophilia Type A	2860	HEMA
15	Hereditary Hemorrhagic Telangiectasia	4480	HHT
16	Huntington's Chorea	3334	HD
17	Hyperphenylalaninemia (Phenylketonuria)	2701	PAH
18	Immunodeficiency with hyper-Igm (HIM)	27905	TNFSF5
19	Machado-Joseph Disease (Spinocerebellar Ataxia 3)	3348	MJD
20	Marfan Syndrome	75982	FBN1
21	Menkes Syndrome	75989	ATP7A
22	Methemoglobinemia	2897	HBB, HBA1, DIA1
23	Myotonic dystrophy	3592	DM
24	Pendred's syndrome	243	PDS
25	Prader-Willi Syndrome	75981	SNRPN
26	Refsum's Disease	3563	PAHX
27	Sickle Cell Anemia	28260	HBB
28	Spinocerebellar ataxias - or atrophy	3349	SCA1
29	Tangier disease	2725	ABC1
30	Tay-Sachs	3301	HEXA
31	Tuberous Sclerosis (Pringle's disease)	7595	TSC1, TSC2
32	Vitelliform Macular Dystrophy (Best Disease)	36276	VMD2
32	von Hippel-Lindau	7596	VHL
33	Werner's disease or syndrome	2598	WRN
34	Werdnig-Hoffmann disease	3350	SMA1
35	Kugelberg-Welander	33511	SMN/NAIP region
36	Wilson's Disease	2751	ATP7B

via trails. In studies with populations diagnosed with DNA-based disorders, extracted from the State of Illinois discharge databases, we found that data was trail re-identifiable in 33–100% of the populations' patients. [69] Moreover, this attack is more generalized in that it is not completely dependent on hospital discharge databases and that trails can manifest in a number of environments. [63]

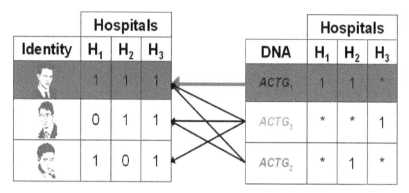

FIGURE 12.3: Re-identification of DNA samples to named individuals via location visit patterns, or "trails." In this representation "1," "0," and "*" correspond to presence, absence, and ambiguity with respect to such knowledge for a particular record.

12.3.5 Vulnerability Is a Matter of Context

In earlier work, a survey of real-world genomic data privacy technologies in the face of various re-identification attacks was performed. [64] The findings, summarized in Figure 12.4, revealed that all systems were vulnerable to multiple types of attack. Susceptibility varied with the type of protection adopted, as well as the environment in which the protection is deployed. For instance, the deCode model is protected from trail re-identification not because it explicitly addresses the attack, but because there is only one data provider. If the deCode approach were adopted in a distributed environment, such as emerging GWA repositories in the United States, then the system might be susceptible to this attack.

12.3.6 I Am My Sister's Keeper: Familial Inference of SNP Genotypes

Disclosure of genotypes can have an impact beyond those directly sequenced because genomic data contains implicit information regarding the genetics of family members. Consider that siblings, on average, share half of their

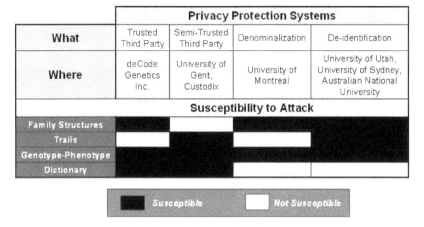

FIGURE 12.4: Summary of biomedical data privacy technology susceptibilities to various attacks. All technologies are susceptible to privacy compromise.

contiguous chromosomal segments, and well over half of a sibling's allelic values[†] can be inferred using only population-specific allele frequency data and the genotypes of another sibling.

A recently published attack [11] highlights the risks to the genetic privacy of family members when a relative shares genetic data with research investigators or clinicians. The following sections provide some additional context on how such associations can be exploited for SNP inference and sibling predictions.

Specifically, let us provide some general intuition into how inference of a sibling's SNPs can be achieved. Recognize that at each location (locus) in a child's genome, each parent transmits only one allele from his or her two chromosomes. Thus, if we have the genotype of one child, Sib_1 and would like to use that information to infer the genotype of a sibling, Sib_2, we consider both the known parental genotypes (based on the alleles that have already been transmitted to Sib_1) and also the alleles on the chromosomes that they have, but have not transmitted to Sib_1. We assume that the unknown parental alleles are drawn from a reference population, such as is available from the International HapMap Project[‡]. Now, with probability 0.25, Sib_2 will receive the same 2 chromosomes transmitted to Sib_1, in which case they will have the same genotype. With probability 0.25, the inferred sibling will receive both previously untransmitted chromosomes, in which case the sibling will have the same genotype distribution as the reference population. If only one of the same chromosomes is transmitted, then one chromosome will be the same and the other will be drawn from the population.

[†]An allele is the term used to represent one value of a set of possible values for a genomic region.

[‡]See http://www.hapmap.org/

We explored above that it is possible to use the underlying population frequency data to infer which alleles may not have been transmitted by parents when attempting to infer the alleles a second sibling has at a specific locus. When calculating the probability of a specific Sib_2 genotype given a known Sib_1 genotype, it is possible to apply Sib_1's genotype to improve the inference of Sib_2 genotype [11]. We can then use the population allele frequencies and the genotype (set of alleles at a specific locus) of the known sibling to quantify the quality of the inference of Sib_2's genotype at that same locus. This involves measuring the difference between the prior probability for the genotype, given only population frequencies, and the posterior probability using the genotype of Sib_1.

Additionally, sibling SNP data can be used to quantify an individual's disease propensity through genotypic inference, without that individual's actual sequence data. For example, a likelihood ratio test statistic may be used to describe relative risk. This can be applied to a single SNP and is easily extended to a multiplicative model for multiple independent SNPs that are important for diseases in which a set of common or rare variants dictates disease likelihood [34, 87]. As SNPs are both clinically informative and there is a wealth of supporting allele frequency data, they have been the focus of our analysis; however, there are other genomic data types which should be considered in a rigorous privacy and propensity analysis, including copy number variant and mutation data.

For instance, these inferences also extend to other types of familial genetic inference. It is straightforward to infer the probabilities of a child's genotype from the genotypes of his parents, but it is also possible to perform more complicated genotyping inferences, specifically where all of the allele information is not available. Moreover, it is possible to statistically infer the genotype of each parent given an observed child's genotype, and also to statistically infer the genotype of a child given only one parent's genotype using similar techniques outlined above.

12.4   Achieving Formal Protection

We can formally thwart re-identification by specifying guidelines for the relationships between features in shared data and the population from which the data was derived. To understand how to derive formal protection models, we need to return to how re-identification occurs. Recall, re-identification has several necessary conditions. The first and third conditions are satisfied when unique values exist in sensitive biomedical and identified records. The previous section illustrated the uniqueness of various features, such as patient-location visit patterns. Moreover, in the context of genomic data, the uniqueness of

DNA sequences, is relatively easy to satisfy. As mentioned earlier, less than 100 SNPs can uniquely represent an individual [55], but more recently it was shown that an individual can be identified in the pooled results of 5,000 SNPs [37]. This latter discovery prompted the NIH and Wellcome Trust to remove summary statistics of case and control populations from publicly accessible websites [110]. However, recall that, by itself, uniqueness is insufficient to claim re-identification is possible. To complete re-identification, we must satisfy a second condition, which is a method to link to a resource containing a subject's identity (e.g., name). Thus, as we depict in Figure 12.5 we can formally prevent re-identification by (1) making data non-unique or (2) limiting how de-identified data is linked to identity. Unfortunately, we can not work with data that is already in the public realm. Thus, we must concentrate on the sensitive data and ensure that it can not be linked with available resources.

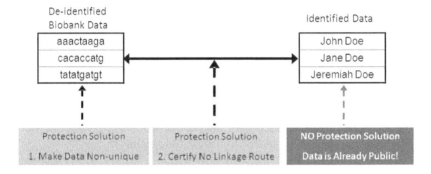

FIGURE 12.5: Points at which genomic data protection solutions can, and can not, be implemented.

12.4.1   Protecting Privacy by Thwarting Linkage

Some threats can be addressed without augmenting the underlying biomedical data. For example, it was shown that formal privacy models to thwart trail re-identification can be designed. A simple solution is to "suppress if in violation," such that providers withhold DNA records that can be linked to less than k names via their trails. This tactic guarantees the re-identification risk of each DNA record is within an acceptable range. As an improvement, we invented an algorithm called TRANON (TRail ANONymizer) that assists data providers to suppress only the portions of trails that cause re-identification. [67] Figure 12.6 recasts results (derived from [67]) with a cohort of 1149 patients diagnosed with cystic fibrosis distributed over 174 hospitals, as observed in public discharge databases from the state of Illinois. Notice that TRANON (denoted as "partial suppression") centralizes significantly more records than the basic suppress if in violation approach (denoted as "complete suppression") at every protection level k.

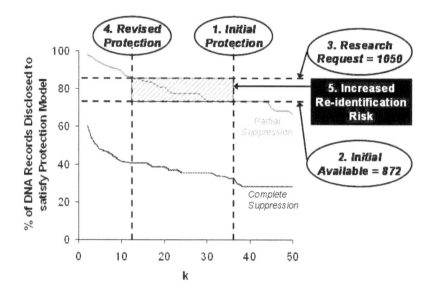

FIGURE 12.6: Flexible protection of a databank's cystic fibrosis person-specific DNA records (n = 1149) from trail re-identification.

Beyond a proof of privacy, such a formal protection approach illustrates that re-identification risks can be tied to policy. Let us walk through the steps necessary to achieve such an integration, while using 12.6 as an illustrative example. First, imagine that data providers agree on a policy with k set to 35 (Step 1). When providers run TRANON at this level, they will disclose 872 of the total 1149 genetic records available (Step 2 in Figure 12.6) and, in the process, have confirmation that each record links to at least 35 people. Next, a biomedical researcher performs a power calculation and determines he needs approximately 1000 records to conduct a hypothesis test with statistical significance (Step 3). The researcher can submit this request to the data providers, who, with the help of TRANON, will discover that to satisfy this request, they will need to push k back to a protection level of 12 (Step 4). Given the initial and final policies (i.e., k equal to 35 and 12, respectively), the data providers can determine the total increased risk to the population (Step 5). This risk can be addressed through a variety of mechanisms, both technically (e.g., increased auditing of the researcher's activities) or legally (e.g., a data use agreement that imparts a greater fine for misuse of the dataset with a k of 12 in comparison to a k of 35).

The primary benefit of thwarting linkage, such as through trails, is that it permits explicit protection against known attacks with quantifiable levels of protection. However, there are several drawbacks to such an approach that should be recognized. First, it assumes that data providers are able to be aware of, and are capable of computationally specifying, all linkage scenarios. In certain environments though, this may be an unrealistic assumption. Second, assuming that all linkage routes could be defined, the application of linkage prevention methods requires data providers to assume that the genomic data itself does not facilitate the privacy violation. When such assumptions do not hold true, then data providers must apply protections that augment the genomic data itself, as illustrated in the following subsections.

12.4.2   Protecting Privacy by Preventing Uniqueness

An example of a formal data protection model is "k-map," which states that each shared record must refer to no less than k subjects in a population. [94] Such models can be satisfied by measuring the number of identities to which a particular record can be linked. The TRANON solution mentioned in the previous section uses a variant of the k-map model for the basis of its protection. However, unlike in the trails scenario, we may not know the resources available to an investigator for performing linkage. In this case, we can use a restricted version of k-map, called k-anonymity, which is achieved when each disclosed record is equivalent to $k - 1$ other records. [94] This ensures each record links to no less than k entities in the population, thus satisfying k-map, regardless of additional knowledge known to the investigator.

Biomedical data can be made k-anonymous through generalization along a domain-specific hierarchy. For instance, geographic information, such as cities, can be generalized into counties and then into states. This approach, also known as binning, has been applied to field-structured medical information. [93, 102] Similarly, a solution based on generalization hierarchies was proposed to achieve k-anonymity for SNPs. [54] In this approach, SNPs were generalized in a two-step process. First, for each nucleotide position, the records are generalized until there are at least k records for each value. Second, records are further generalized so that the combination of values across nucleotides does not violate the k-anonymity requirement. Though it satisfies a formal protection model, there are several limitations to this approach. One limitation of the approach is that it does not scale gracefully to genomic regions with variation greater than two residues. For example, a C-G transversion value and a C-T transversion value will be generalized to an indeterminate value for the region, instead of utilizing the union of values, which would be C-G-T. A second limitation is that it does not attempt to minimize the distance between sequences before data is generalized. As such, this technique could overgeneralize released data.

To overcome the limitations of prior generalization models, we designed a software prototype called DNA Lattice Anonymization (DNALA). [65] In contrast to generalization hierarchies, DNALA uses a more robust space in the form of a generalization lattice of biochemical relations. DNALA was designed to minimize the generalization introduced into DNA sequences to achieve k-anonymity. Theoretically, discovering the minimal quantity of generalization is computationally challenging [3], so DNALA employs sampling to discover a stable solution. Computationally, DNALA first measures the similarity between each pair of sequences. The similarity between two sequences is the sum of similarities for each nucleotide position, based on an ontology of the biochemical relationships. Then DNALA applies a greedy heuristic to generalize groups of records that are the most similar.

The DNALA algorithm was evaluated with several publicly available datasets [32, 62, 109] of human DNA sequences from the NCBI PopSet. A variable region was defined as a point in an aligned set of sequences where at least two records had a different value. The increase in generalization was measured by summing the generalization hierarchy level score for each nucleotide (leaves have a generalization score of 0). The increase in generalization is dependent on the number of variable regions available for anonymization. All of the sample sets had an average increase in generalization of less than 1. In other words, on average, sequences required less than 1 region to be generalized to be made equivalent to another sequence. The analysis further suggested, however, that, intuitively, as the number of sequences and regions increase, the quantity of generalization needed to satisfy k-anonymity decreases.

Though a feasible model, k-anonymity is limited in its applicability to large-scale genomic records for several reasons. First, k-anonymity is known to have scalability problems, such that the curse of dimensionality is of concern [2]. In particular, when a dataset contains a large number of attributes, the resulting k-anonymized database is marred by a significant number of suppressed records. Second, k-anonymity was designed to address the issue of anonymity and not inference. Thus, we could k anonymize genomic records, and prevent "identity" disclosure, but the resulting records could have the same sensitive clinical information (e.g., HIV positive diagnoses). To counteract this problem of "attribute" disclosure, various solutions have been proposed, such as l-diversity [60], which force a mixture of sensitive attributes. Though this approach has not been explicitly applied to genomic or biomedical data, this model requires an even greater amount of data augmentation to reach the desired level of protection, and thus may not be acceptable for large scale genomic records.

12.5 Secure Multiparty Computation in the Biomedical Realm

As was alluded to in the previous section, perturbation or generalization of DNA sequence data is not necessarily a desirable solution. Alternatively, it would be ideal if we could leave sequence data in its most specific state while still sharing the data beyond the boundaries of the organization that collected the records. In this line of protection, secure multi-party computation (SMC) methods may provide a potential solution. SMC enables organizations to collaborate by revealing only encrypted versions of their records. [9, 24, 108] Informally, if a distributed protocol meets the SMC definitions, the participating parties learn only the final result and whatever can be inferred from the final result and their own inputs. A simple example is Yao's millionaire problem [107] in which two millionaires, Alice and Bob, want to learn who is richer without disclosing their actual wealth to each other.

In SMC protocols, the privacy protection guarantees are provided by employing cryptographic tools that involve expensive operations such as modular exponentiation [44]. In recent years, SMC techniques have been applied to support data mining endeavors, such as association rule learning and decision-tree induction. [10, 14, 41, 57, 98]

One caveat in using SMC is that no matter how secure the computation is, some privacy sensitive information may be revealed due to the computation results. For example, even if we can securely compute some statistics needed for genome wide association studies without revealing any individual's information, the statistics themselves in combination with other information could be used to violate individual privacy. Thus, there are two kinds of information leaks; the information leak from the function computed irrespective of the process used to compute the function and the information leak from the specific process of computing the function. Whatever is leaked from the function itself is unavoidable as long as the function has to be computed [43]. Therefore, SMC could be used to guarantee that there is *no* information leak whatsoever due to the process. In achieving this secure computation, the SMC literature defines two basic adversarial models:

Semi-Honest: Semi-honest (or Honest but Curious) adversaries follow the protocol faithfully, but can try to infer the secret information of the other parties from the data they see during the execution of the protocol.

Malicious: Malicious adversaries may do anything to infer secret information. They can abort the protocol at any time, send spurious messages, spoof messages, collude with other (malicious) parties, etc.

Most SMC protocols are mathematically correct, but, for various reasons, are inappropriate for real world application. They are often proof-of-concept models with unrealistic assumptions, such that they expect the majority of participating parties to be "semi-honest," i.e., participants follow the protocol's specifications, but can use observed values to compromise security. When parties are corrupt, however, they can exploit a number of tricks to gain an advantage, influence results, or simply wreak havoc. Moreover, though the SMC protocols developed for the malicious model provide more security guarantees, they are much more costly compared to the semi-honest model. [59].

Recently, we designed an SMC framework based on a "semantically secure" homomorphic public-key encryption system (HPE) for the storage and querying of genotype data stored on a third party's server. [42] A typical HPE could be defined as follows: Let $E_{pk}(.)$ denote the encryption function with public key pk and $D_{pr}(.)$ denote the decryption function with private key pr. A secure public key cryptosystem is called homomorphic if it satisfies the following requirements:

(1) Given the encryption of snp_1 and snp_2, $E_{pk}(snp_1)$ and $E_{pk}(snp_2)$, there exists an efficient algorithm to compute the public key encryption of $snp_1 + snp_2$, denoted $E_{pk}(snp_1 + snp_2) := E_{pk}(snp_1) +_h E_{pk}(snp_2)$. (2) Given a constant k and the encryption of snp_1, $E_{pk}(snp_1)$, there exists an efficient algorithm to compute the public key encryption of $k \cdot snp_1$, denoted $E_{pk}(k \cdot snp_1) := k \times_h E_{pk}(snp_1)$. We refer the reader to [78] for more details.

Using the properties of a HPE, the framework [42] incorporates four types of participants: 1) providers, 2) investigators, and multiple third parties: 3) a data storage site (DS), which is basically a consolidator and 3) a key holder site (KHS). Basically, DS stores and processes encrypted biomedical data. KHS manages the keys for encryption of the records and decryption of the results to biomedical researchers' queries. Distribution of the third party's role allows the majority of data management to be designated to DS, whereas KHS serves as a final point of control in the system. As a result, a data warehousing facility can assume the DS role without being liable for the maintenance of the keys. The use of multiple third parties also ensures that there is no single point of failure, so that if either of the third parties is compromised (e.g., a hacker breaks into the system), the contents of the stored records will not be revealed.

In the HPE system, the KHS keeps a private key secret and publishes the public key. When a provider wants to submit records to the repository, it encrypts the records using the public key. The encrypted records can only be decrypted by the corresponding private key, so the KHS is the only entity that can decipher the records. The semantic security property of the system ensures it is computationally infeasible to recover the original data when in possession of the encrypted data and the encryption key. [25] Informally, the repeated encryption of the same message will be indistinguishable to an eavesdropper. For example, when Alice and Bob encrypt the same genomic sequence, say *gtc*, the resulting encryptions will be different in binary format, e.g., "010111011100" is not equal to "110011100101."

From a data analysis perspective, the additively homomorphic property of

HPE allows for DS to use an encryption function $E_{pk}()$ to compute $E_{pk}(snp_1 + snp_2) := E_{pk}(snp_1) +_h E_{pk}(snp_2)$ given the encryptions of snp_1 and snp_2 (i.e., $E_{pk}(snp_1)$ and $E_{pk}(snp_2)$). As a result, a scientist can issue a query, such as "How many records have $SNP_1 = A$ and $SNP_2 = T$ and Alzheimer's Diagnosis $=$ Positive?" to the database and the consolidator can compute which records match using only the encrypted information. The encrypted results are sent to KHS, who decrypts and forwards the aggregated results (i.e., the total number) to the scientist. Another important aspect of our system is that during the query processing DS only learns the query (e.g., DS knows that the query is being evaluated) and the query result (e.g., say, ten records satisfy the given query), but DS does not learn which specific records satisfy the query. In addition, KHS does not learn the query or the records that satisfy the query. Instead, it just learns the query result. Thus, even if a hacker compromises the DS or KHS during the query evaluation, he cannot learn the records that satisfy any given query.

We prototyped the above described HPE system in the Java programming language and ran experiments on a computer with an Intel Pentium D 3.4GHz processor with 2GB of memory. We set the key size to 1024 bits and evaluated the efficiency of our computations using a range of simulated datasets of 20,000 records and 40 SNPs. For simulation purposes, we assumed that DS and KHS have a fast network connection, so that data transfer time is negligible. Our evaluations demonstrate that for a query consisting of 5 SNPs and a database of 5,000 records, we can complete the computations over the encrypted records and decryption of the results in approximately 20 minutes. Scaling up the system, our experiments indicate that a query for 40 SNPs over a database of 20,000 records requires 120 minutes. Of course, these results could be easily improved by one order of magnitude by more optimized implementations. We refer the reader to [42] for further details.

12.6   Discussion and the Future

Technologies for sequencing large numbers of SNPs, and genomic sequences in general, are rapidly dropping in cost, which will help realize the promise of personalized medicine, but pose substantial personal and familial privacy risks. While electronic storage and transmission of genetic tests is not yet a common component of medical record data, these tests will soon be stored in electronic medical records and personally controlled health records [88]. This mandates the need for improved informed consent models and access control mechanisms for genomic data. The increasingly common practice of electronically publishing research-related SNP data requires a delicate balance between the enormous potential benefits of shared genomic data through NCBI and other resources, and the privacy rights of both sequenced individuals and their family members.

This chapter provided an overview of various concerns and potential solutions for sharing genomic data captured in the clinical and research realm. The current status quo, however, is not sufficient to guarantee anonymity or confidentiality as may be required by existing regulatory requirements. The solutions we have posed are currently in a proof-of-concept and prototyping stage; however, we anticipate evaluating these approaches with emerging large-scale population genomics and clinical systems. In doing so, we hope to gain insight into which approaches will not only be the most accurate and efficient from a computational perspective, but also determine the feasibility of their implementation in real world environments with complex organizational and policy-based limitations.

The authors of this chapter strongly believe that quantifying the information content of disclosed genomic data will add clarity to the informed consent process when a patient shares genotypic data for research use. For research investigations, it is conceivable that a subject would want to limit the impact of her genomic disclosure on her family members, or be asked to have a discussion with specific family members before proceeding. Providing subjects with different levels of anonymity based on their genomic sequence data, along with an estimate of the probability of re-identification and familial impact for each of those anonymity levels, will allow patients to trade off altruistically motivated sharing [49] with privacy consideration, especially when they volunteer to share all the variants in their genome [12]. However, in doing so, this raises a crucial, and currently unaddressed, issue that must be clarified before such approaches are realized, regarding the notion of re-identification and/or disclosure "risk." Until recently, protection in data sharing was achieved through policies such as the Safe Harbor and Limited Dataset standards of the HIPAA Privacy Rule. Yet, such policies do not quantify protections or the amount of residual risk that resides in the system. Thus, as we move forward, it will be necessary to characterize how organizations (or individuals) sharing such genomic data will respond to approaches that quantify the risk associated with sharing genomics data.

12.7   Conclusions

The increasing prevalence of genomics in the clinical environment provides tremendous opportunities for novel clinical data mining projects and association studies on large populations. At the same time, various regulations are requiring such data to be shared beyond the initial point of collection in a manner that respects the anonymity of the corresponding research participants.

As we have demonstrated in this chapter, there are a number of potential concerns with sharing clinical and genomic data in an ad hoc privacy protecting manner. We have surveyed several approaches to protect such information with formal guarantees, with various tradeoffs in their scalability, accessibility, and potential impact on detailed data analysis. As we move toward the future, it is necessary to determine how best to integrate technical and policy-based data protections for clinical genomics data sharing and research environments. This will require collaboration between experts in databases and data mining, clinical and genomics domain knowledge, and policy and legal scholars, but will be necessary to ensure that data is widely-distributed in accordance with the privacy guarantees required by existing regulations.

Acknowledgments

This work was supported in part by grants 1R01LM009989 (Malin & Kantarcioglu) from the U.S. National Library of Medicine, 1U01HG00460301 (Malin) from the National Human Genome Research Institute, Career-0845803 (Kantarcioglu) and CNS-0716424 (Kantarcioglu) from the National Science Foundation.

References

[1] B. Adida, and I.S. Kohane. Geneping: secure, scalable management of personal genomic data. *BMC Genomics*, 7:93, 2006.

[2] C. C. Aggarwal. On k-anonymity and the curse of dimensionality. In *Proceedings of the 31st International Conference on Very Large Data Bases*, pages 901–909, 2005.

[3] G. Aggarwal, T. Feder, K. Kenthapadi, R. Motwani, R. Panigrahy, D. Thomas, and A. Zhu. Approximation algorithms for k-anonymity. *Journal of Privacy Technology*, page 20051120001, 2005.

[4] R. Altman and T. Klein. Challenges for biomedical informatics and pharmacogenomics. *Annual Review of Pharmacology and Toxicology*, 42:113–133, 2002.

[5] F. Bieber, C. Brenner, and D. Lazer. Human genetics. finding criminals through DNA of their relatives. *Science*, 312(5778):1315–1316, 2006.

[6] F. Bieber and D. Lazer. Guilt by association: should the law be able to use one person's DNA to carry out surveillance on their family? Not without a public debate. *New Sci*, 184(2470):20, 2004.

[7] S. Brawley. Submission and retrieval of an aligned set of nucleic acid sequences. *Journal of Phycology*, 35:433–437, 1999.

[8] C. Brenner and B. Weir. Issues and strategies in the dna identification of world trade center victims. *Theoretical Population Biology*, 63(3):173–178, 2003.

[9] R. Canetti, U. Feige, O. Goldreich, and M. Naor. Adaptively secure multi-party computation. In *Proceedings of the 28th ACM Symposium on Theory of Computing*, pages 639–648, 1996.

[10] J. Canny. Collaborative filtering with privacy. In *Proceedings of the 23rd IEEE Symposium on Security and Privacy*, pages 238–245, 2002.

[11] C. A. Cassa, B. W. Schmidt, I. S. Kohane, and K. D. Mandl. My sister's keeper?: genomic research and the identifiability of siblings. *BMC Medical Genomics*, 1(1):32, 2008.

[12] G. Church. The personal genome project. *Molecular Systems Biology*, 1:2005.0030, 2005.

[13] E. W. Clayton. Ethical, legal, and social implications of genomic medicine (review). *New England Journal of Medicine*, 349(6):562–569, 2003.

[14] C. Clifton, M. Kantarcioglu, J. Vaidya, X. Lin, and M. Zhu. Tools for privacy preserving data mining. *ACM SIGKDD Explorations*, 4(2):28–34, 2002.

[15] G. J. de Moor, B. Claerhout, and F. de Meyer. Privacy enhancing technologies: the key to secure communication and management of clinical and genomic data. *Methods of Information in Medicine*, 42:148–153, 2003.

[16] Directive 95/46/EC on the protection of individuals with regard to the processing of personal data and on the free movement of such data. *Official Journal of the European Union*, October 24, 1995.

[17] R. Dugan, G. Wiesner, E. Juengst, M. O'Riordan, A. Matthews, and N. Robin. Duty to warn at-risk relatives for genetic disease: genetic counselors' clinical experience. *American Journal of Medical Genetics: Part C, Seminars in Medical Genetics*, 119C(1):27–34, 2003.

[18] M. Dugas, C. Schoch, S. Schnittger, A. Kohlmann, W. Kern, T. Haferlach, and K. Uberla. Impact of integrating clinical and genetic information. *In Silico Biology*, 2:383–391, 2002.

[19] Freedom of Information Act. 5 U.S.C. 552, H.R. 3802, 1996.

[20] D. Gaudet, S. Arsenault, C. Belanger, T. Hudson, P. Perron, M. Bernard, and P. Hamet. Procedure to protect confidentiality of familial data in community genetics and genomic research. *Clinical Genetics*, 55:259–264, 2007.

[21] Genetic Information Nondiscrimination Act of 2008. Public Law No. 110-233, 122 Stat. 881, 2008.

[22] J. Glaser, D. Henley, G. Downing, K. Brinner, and Personalized Health Care Workgroup of the American Health Information Community. Advancing personalized health care through health information technology: an update from the American Health Information Community's Personalized Health Care Workgroup. *Journal of the American Medical Informatics Association*, 15(4):391–396, 2008.

[23] T. Goetz. How the Personal Genome Project could unlock the mysteries of life. *Wired Magazine*, 18(8), 2008.

[24] O. Goldreich, S. Micali, and A. Wigderson. How to play any mental game - or - a completeness theorem for protocols with honest majority. In *Proceedings of the 19th Symposium on Theory of Computing*, pages 218–229, 1987.

[25] S. Goldwasser and S. Micali. Probabilistic encryption. 28:270–299, 1984.

[26] P. Golle. Revisiting the uniqueness of simple demographics in the U.S. population. In *Proceedings of the 2006 ACM Workshop on Privacy in the Electronic Society*, pages 77–80, 2006.

[27] S. Gottlieb. U.S. employer agrees to stop genetic testing - Burlington Northern Santa Fe - News. *British Medical Journal*, Feb 24, 2001.

[28] J. Gulcher, Kristjansson, H. Gudbjartsson, and K. Stefansson. Protection of privacy by third-party encryption in genetic research in Iceland. *European Journal of Human Genetics*, pages 739–742, 2000.

[29] A. E. Guttmacher and F. S. Collins. Realizing the promise of genomics for biomedical research. *Journal of the American Medical Informatics Association*, 294:1399–1402, 2005.

[30] M. Hall and S. Rich. Patients' fear of genetic discrimination by health insurers: the impact of legal protections. *Genetics in Medicine*, 2:214–221, 2000.

[31] A. Hamosh, A. Scott, J. Amberger, C. Bocchini, and V. McKusick. Online mendelian inheritance in man (omim), a knowledgebase of human genes and genetic disorders. *Human Mutation*, 15:57–61, 2000.

[32] E. Harris and J. Hey. X chromosome evidence for ancient human histories. *PNAS USA*, 96:3320–3324, 1999.

[33] P. Hess and D. Cooper. Impact of pharmacogenomics on the clinical laboratory. *Molecular Diagnosis*, 4(4):289–298, 1999.

[34] J. Hirschhorn and M. Daly. Genome-wide association studies for common diseases and complex traits. *Nature Reviews Genetics*, 6(2):95–108, 2005.

[35] M. Hoffman. The genome-enabled electronic medical record. *Journal of Biomedical Informatics*, 40(1):44–46, 2007.

[36] C. Holden. Genetic discrimination: long-awaited genetic nondiscrimination bill headed for easy passage. *Science*, 316(5825):676, 2007.

[37] N. Homer, S. Szelinger, M. Redman, D. Duggan, W. Tembe, J. Muehling, J. Pearson, D. Stephan, S. Nelson, and D. Craig. Resolving individuals contributing trace amounts of dna to highly complex mixtures using high-density snp genotyping microarrays. *PLoS Genetics*, 4:e1000167, 2008.

[38] K. Hudson, M. Holohan, and F. Collins. Keeping pace with the times– the genetic information nondiscrimination act of 2008. *New England Journal of Medicine*, 358(25):2661–2663, 2008.

[39] S. Hull, R. Sharp, J. Botkin, M. Brown, M. Hughes, J. Sugarman, D. Schwinn, P. Sankar, D. Bolcic-Jankovic, B. Clarridge, and B. Wilfond. Patients' views on identifiability of samples and informed consent for genetic research. *American Journal of Bioethics*, 8(10):62–70, 2008.

[40] J. Kaiser. Biobanks: Population databases boom, from Iceland to the U.S. *Science*, 298(5596):1158–1161, 2002.

[41] M. Kantarcioglu and C. Clifton. Privacy-preserving data mining of association rules on horizontally partitioned data. *IEEE Transactions on Knowledge and Data Engineering*, 16(9):1026–1037, 2004.

[42] M. Kantarcioglu, W. Jiang, Y. Liu, and B. Malin. A cryptographic approach to securely share and query genomic sequences. *IEEE Transactions on Information Technology in Biomedicine*, 12(5):606–617, 2008.

[43] M. Kantarcioglu, J. Jin, and C. Clifton. When do data mining results violate privacy? In *Proceedings of the 10th ACM SIGKDD International Conference on Data Mining and Knowledge Discovery*, pages 599–604, 2004.

[44] M. Kantarciouglu and C. Clifton. Privacy-preserving distributed mining of association rules on horizontally partitioned data. *IEEE TKDE*, 16(9):1026–1037, Sept. 2004.

[45] H. Kargupta, S. Datta, Q. Wang, and K. Sivakumar. Random-data perturbation techniques and privacy-preserving data mining. *Knowledge and Information Systems*, 7:387–414, 2005.

[46] N. Kass. Insurance for the insurers: the use of genetic tests. *Hastings Center Report*, 22:6–11, 1992.

[47] N. Kass and A. Medley. Genetic screening and disability insurance: what can we learn from the health insurance experience. *Journal of Law, Medicine, and Ethics*, 35(2 Suppl):66–73, 2007.

[48] R. Kenen and R. Schmidt. Stigmatization of carrier status: social implications of heterozygote genetic screening programs. *American Journal of Public Health*, 68:116–120, 1978.

[49] I. Kohane and R. Altman. Health-information altruists—a potentially critical resource. *New England Journal of Medicine*, 353(19):2074–2077, 2005.

[50] K. Kohut, M. Manno, S. Gallinger, and M. Esplen. Should healthcare providers have a duty to warn family members of individuals with an hnpcc-causing mutation? A survey of patients from the Ontario familial colon cancer registry. *Journal of Medical Genetics*, 44(6):404–407, 2007.

[51] R. Korobkin and R. Rajkumar. The genetic information nondiscrimination act—a half-step toward risk sharing. *New England Journal of Medicine*, 359(4):335–337, 2008.

[52] J. Kupfer. The ethics of genetic screening in the workplace. *Business Ethics Quarterly*, 3:17–25, 1993.

[53] T. Lewin. National briefing: Washington: accord on genetic tests. *New York Times*, May 9, 2002.

[54] Z. Lin, M. Hewett, and R. Altman. Using binning to maintain confidentiality of medical data. In *Proceedings of the American Medical Informatics Association Annual Fall Symposium*, pages 454–458, 2002.

[55] Z. Lin, A. Owen, and R. Altman. Genetics: genomic research and human subject privacy. *Science*, 305:183, 2004.

[56] D. A. Lindberg and B. Humphreys. Rising expectations: access to biomedical information. *Yearbook of Medical Informatics*, 3(1):165–172, 2008.

[57] Y. Lindell and B. Pinkas. Privacy preserving data mining. *Journal of Cryptology*, 15(3):177–206, 2002.

[58] W. W. Lowrance. Learning from experience: privacy and the secondary use of data in health research. White paper, National Human Genome Research Institute, October 2006. Available online at http://www.nuffieldtrust.org.uk/ecomm/files/161202learning.pdf (85 pages).

[59] O. Kardes and M. Kantarcioglu. Privacy-preserving data mining in the malicious model. *International Journal of Information and Computer Security*, 2(4):353–375, 2008.

[60] A. Machanavajjhala, D. Kifer, J. Gehrke, and M. Venkitasubramaniam. *l*-diversity: Privacy beyond *k*-anonymity. *ACM Transactions on Knowledge Discovery from Data*, 1(1), 2007.

[61] M. D. Mailman, M. Feolo, Y. Jin, M. Kimura, K. Tryka, R. Bagoutdinov, L. Hao, A. Kiang, J. Paschall, L. Phan, N. Popova, S. Pretel, L. Ziyabari, M. Lee, Y. Shao, Z. Y. Wang, K.Sirotkin, M. Ward, M. Kholodov, K. Zbicz, J. Beck, M. Kimelman, S. Shevelev, D. Preuss, E. Yaschenko, A. Graeff, J. Ostell, and S. Sherry. The NCBI database of genotypes and phenotypes. *Nature Genetics*, 39(10):1181–1186, 2007.

[62] K. Makova, M. Ramsay, T. Jenkins, and W. H. Li. Human DNA sequence variation in a 6.6-kb region containing the melanocortin 1 receptor promoter. *Genetics*, 158:1253–1268, 2001.

[63] B. Malin. Betrayed by my shadow: learning data identity via trail matching. *Journal of Privacy Technology*, page 20050609001, 2005.

[64] B. Malin. An evaluation of the current state of genomic data privacy protection technology and a roadmap for the future. *Journal of the American Medical Informatics Association*, 12:28–34, 2005.

[65] B. Malin. Protecting genomic sequence anonymity with generalization lattices. In *Methods of Information in Medicine*, volume 44, pages 687–692, 2005.

[66] B. Malin. Re-identification of familial database records. In *Proceedings of the American Medical Informatics Association Annual Fall Symposium*, pages 524–528, 2006.

[67] B. Malin. A computational model to protect patient data from location-based re-identification. *Artificial Intelligence in Medicine*, 40(3), 2007.

[68] B. Malin and L. Sweeney. Determining the identifiability of DNA database entries. In *Proceedings of the American Medical Informatics Association Annual Fall Symposium*, pages 537–541, 2000.

[69] B. Malin and L. Sweeney. How (not) to protect genomic data privacy in a distributed network. *Journal of Biomedical Informatics*, 37(3):179–192, 2004.

[70] A.L. McGuire, R. Fisher, P. Cusenza, K. Hudson, M.A. Rothstein, D. McGraw, S. Matteson, J. Glaser, and D. E. Henley. Confidentiality, privacy, and security of genetic and genomic test information in electronic health records: points to consider. *Genetics in Medicine*, 10(7):495–499, 2008.

[71] A. Mitchell and J. Kline. Systematic bias introduced by the informed consent process in a diagnostic research study. *Academic Emergency Medicine*, 15(3):225–230, 2008.

[72] National Association of Health Data Organizations. *NAHDO Inventory of State-wide Hospital Discharge Data Activities*. National Association of Health Data Organizations, May 2008.

[73] National Center for Biotechnology Information. *Genes and Disease*. National Library of Medicine, Bethesda, MD, 2005.

[74] National Institutes of Health. Policy for sharing of data obtained in nih supported or conducted genome-wide association studies (gwas). Notice NOT-OD-07-088, August 28, 2007.

[75] D. Nyhold, C. E. Yu, and P. Visscher. On Jim Watson's APOE status: genetic information is hard to hide. *European Journal of Human Genetics*, 17:147–149, 2008.

[76] D. O'Brien and W. Yasnoff. Privacy, confidentiality, and security in information systems of state health agencies. *American Journal of Preventative Medicine*, 16(4):351–358, 1999.

[77] K. Offit, E. Groeger, S. Turner, E. Wadsworth, and M. Weiser. The "duty to warn" a patient's family members about hereditary disease risks. *Journal of the American Medical Association*, 292(12):1469–1473, 2004.

[78] P. Paillier. Public key cryptosystems based on composite degree residuosity classes. In *Advances in Cryptology - Proceedings Eurocrypt '99, Lecture Notes in Computer Science*, number 1592, pages 223–238. Springer-Verlag, 1999.

[79] J. Phelan. Geneticization of deviant behavior and consequences for stigma: the case of mental illness. *Journal of Health and Social Behavior*, 46(4):307–322, 2005.

[80] S. Pinker. My genome, my self. *New York Times*, January 7, 2009.

[81] H. A. Piwowar, M. J. Becich, H. Bilofsky, and R. S. Crowley. Towards a data sharing culture: recommendations for leadership from academic health centers. *PLoS Medicine*, 5(9):e183, 2008.

[82] M. A. Rothstein. Genetic screening in employment: some legal ethical and social issues. *International Journal of Bioethics*, 1:244, 1990.

[83] M. A. Rothstein. *Genetic secrets: promoting privacy and confidentiality in the genetic era*. Yale University Press, 1997.

[84] R. Rubin. Test can tell if you're destined for Alzheimers, but then what? *USA Today*, march 5, 2008.

[85] J. Schoenman, J. Sutton, S. Kintala, D. Love, and R. Maw. The value of hospital discharge databases: final report to the Agency for Healthcare Research and Quality under contract number 282-98-0024 (task order number 5). White paper, NORC at the University of Chicago, in cooperation with the National Association of Health data Organizations, May 2005. Available online at http://www.hcup-us.ahrq.gov/reports/final_report.pdf (102 pages).

[86] M. D. Schwartz, K. Rothenberg, L. Joseph, J. Benkendorf, and C. Lerman. Consent to the use of stored dna for genetics research: a survey of attitudes in the Jewish population. *American Journal of Medical Genetics*, 98:336–342, 2001.

[87] P. Sebastiani, M. Ramoni, V. Nolan, C. Baldwin, and M. Steinberg. Genetic dissection and prognostic modeling of overt stroke in sickle cell anemia. *Nature Genetics*, 37(4):435–440, 2005.

[88] W. Simons, J. Halamka, I. Kohane, D. Nigrin, N. Finstein, and K. Mandl. Integration of the personally controlled electronic medical record into regional inter-regional data exchanges: a national demonstration. *Proceedings of the American Medical Informatics Association Annual Fall Symposium*, page 1099, 2006.

[89] L. Slaughter. The genetic information nondiscrimination act: Why your personal genetics are still vulnerable to discrimination. *Surgical Clinics of North America*, 88(4):723–738, 2008.

[90] R. Sterling, G. Henderson, and G. Corbie-Smith. Public willingness to participate in and public opinions about genetic variation research: a review of the literature. *American Journal of Public Health*, 96(11):1971–1978, 2006.

[91] L. Sweeney. Guaranteeing anonymity when sharing medical data, the datafly system. In *Proceedings of the American Medical Informatics Association Annual Symposium*, pages 51–55, Nashville, TN, 1997.

[92] L. Sweeney. Uniqueness of simple demographics in the us population. *Technical Report* LIDAP-WP04, Data Privacy Laboratory, Carnegie Mellon University, Pittsburgh, PA, 2000.

[93] L. Sweeney. Achieving k-anonymity privacy protection using generalization and suppression. *International Journal of Uncertainty, Fuzziness, and Knowledge-Based Systems*, 10(5):571–588, 2002.

[94] L. Sweeney. *k*-anonymity: a model for protecting privacy. *International Journal of Uncertainty, Fuzziness and Knowledge-Based Systems*, 10:557–570, 2002.

[95] Testimony of Latanya Sweeney, Ph.D. before the privacy and integrity advisory committee of the U.S. Department

of Homeland Security, June 15, 2005. Available online: http://www.dhs.gov/xlibrary/assets/privacy/privacy_advcom_06-2005_testimony_sweeney.pdf (5 pages).

[96] D. Thomas. Are we ready for genome-wide association studies? *Cancer Epidemiology, Biomarkers, and Prevention*, 15(4):595–598, 2006.

[97] U.S. Department of Health and Human Services. Standards for privacy of individually identifiable health information, final rule, 45 cfr, parts 160-164. *Federal Register*, 67, 2002.

[98] J. Vaidya and C. Clifton. Secure set intersection cardinality with application to association rule mining. *Journal of Computer Security*, 13(4):593–622, 2005.

[99] L. T. Vaszar, M. K. Cho, and T. A. Raffin. Privacy issues in personalized medicine. *Pharmacogenomics*, 4(2):107–112, 2003.

[100] J. Vates, J. Hetrick, K. Lavin, G. Sharma, R. Wagner, and J. Johnson. Protecting medical record information: start your research registries today. *Laryngoscope*, 115:441–444, 2005.

[101] Violence Against Women and Department of Justice Reauthorization Act of 2005. H.R. 3402, Public Law 109-162, 2005.

[102] D. Wang, C. Liau, and T. Hsu. Medical privacy protection based on granular computing. *Artificial Intelligence in Medicine*, 32:137–149, 2004.

[103] D. A. Wheeler, M. Srinivasan, M. Egholm, Y. Shen, L. Chen, A. McGuire, W. He, Y. J. Chen, V. Makhijani, G. T. Roth, X. Gomes, K. Tartaro, F. Niazi, C. Turcotte, G. Irzyk, J. Lupski, C. Chinault, X. Z. Song, Y. Liu, Y. Yuan, L. Nazareth, X. Qin, D. Muzny, M. Margulies, G. Weinstock, R. Gibbs, and J. M. Rothberg. The complete genome of an individual by massively parallel DNA sequencing. *Nature*, 452(7189):872–876, 2008.

[104] S. M. Wolf and J. P. Kahn. Genetic testing and the future of disability insurance. *Journal of Law, Medicine, and Ethics*, 35(2 Suppl):6–32, 2007.

[105] S. Woolf, S. Rothemich, R. Johnson, and D. Marsland. Selection bias from requiring patients to give consent to examine data for health services research. *Archives of Family Medicine*, 9(10):1111–1118, 2000.

[106] J. Wylie and G. Mineau. Biomedical databases: protecting privacy and promoting research. *Trends in Biotechnology*, 21:113–116, 2003.

[107] A. Yao. Protocols for secure computations [extended abstract]. In *Proceedings of the 23rd Annual Symposium on Foundations of Computer Science*, pages 160–164, 1982.

[108] A. Yao. How to generate and exchange secrets. In *Proceedings of the 27th IEEE Symposium on Foundations of Computer Science*, pages 162–167, 1986.

[109] Y. G. Yao, L. Nie, H. Harpending, Y. X. Fu, Z. G. Yuan, and Y. P. Zhang YP. Genetic relationship of chinese ethnic populations revealed by mtdna sequence diversity. *American Journal of Physical Anthropology*, 118:63–76, 2002.

[110] E. Zerhouni and E. Nabel. Protecting aggregate genomic data. *Science*, 322:44, 2008.

Chapter 13

Privacy-Aware Health Information Sharing

Thomas Trojer

Research Group Quality Engineering, University of Innsbruck, Austria

Cheuk-kwong Lee

Hong Kong Red Cross Blood Transfusion Service, Hong Kong

Benjamin C. M. Fung

CIISE, Concordia University, Montreal, QC, Canada

Lalita Narupiyakul

University of Ontario, Institute of Technology, Oshawa, ON, Canada

Patrick C. K. Hung

University of Ontario, Institute of Technology, Oshawa, ON, Canada

13.1 Introduction

Gaining access to high-quality health data is a vital requirement for informed decision making by medical practitioners and pharmaceutical researchers. Driven by mutual benefits and by regulations, there is a demand and necessity for healthcare institutes to share patient data with various parties for research purposes. However, health data in its raw form often contains sensitive information about individuals, and publishing such data will violate individual privacy. The current practice in information sharing primarily relies on policies and guidelines on the types of data that can be published, and agreements on the use of shared data. This approach alone may lead to excessive data distortion or insufficient protection. A problem of utmost importance, known as *privacy-aware information sharing*, is to provide methods and tools for sharing person-specific, sensitive information for the purpose of performing data mining.

This chapter exploits a real-life information sharing scenario in the Hong Kong Red Cross Blood Transfusion Service (BTS) to bring out the challenges of preserving *both* individual privacy and data mining quality in the context of healthcare information systems. Using the Red Cross BTS scenario, we present a unified privacy-aware information sharing method for two specific data mining tasks, namely *classification analysis* and *cluster analysis*. Furthermore, we present a data schema taken from the Health Level 7 (HL7) framework, which is a standard for electronic data interchange (EDI) among healthcare organizations. The presented schema defines many elements including the data hierarchy of blood usage records that can be employed in the Red Cross BTS scenario.

A closely related research area is *privacy-preserving data mining* [3]. The term privacy-preserving data mining (PPDM) emerged in 2000 [2]. The initial idea of PPDM was to extend traditional data mining techniques to work with the data modified to mask sensitive information. The key issues were surrounding how to modify the data and how to recover the data mining results from the modified data. The solutions were often tightly coupled with the data mining algorithms under consideration. In contrast, privacy-aware information sharing may not necessarily tie to a specific data mining task, and the data mining task is sometimes unknown at the time of data publishing. Furthermore, some privacy-aware information sharing solutions emphasize preserving the data truthfulness at the record level, but PPDM solutions often do not preserve such property. In recent years, the term "PPDM" has evolved to cover many other privacy research problems, even though some of them may not directly relate to data mining [9].

This chapter is organized as follows. Section 13.2 presents an overview of the information sharing scenario, together with information and privacy requirements, in the Hong Kong Red Cross Blood Transfusion Service. Section 13.3 reviews the literature of privacy-aware information sharing. Section 13.4 describes the problem of privacy-aware information sharing for classification analysis and an anonymization algorithm to achieve the privacy requirement while preserving the usefulness of information for classification analysis. Section 13.5 describes the problem of privacy-aware information sharing for cluster analysis and extends the anonymization algorithm for classification analysis to tackle the anonymization problem for cluster analysis. Section 13.6 concludes the chapter with a summary and some possible extensions.

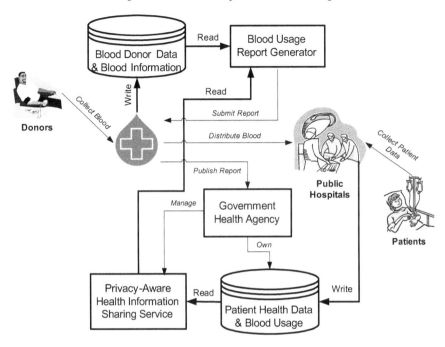

FIGURE 13.1: Data Flow in Hong Kong Red Cross Blood Transfusion Service

13.2 Reference Scenario

Figure 13.1 illustrates the data flow in the Hong Kong Red Cross BTS. After examining the blood collected from donors, the Red Cross BTS distributes the blood to different hospitals. The hospitals collect and maintain the health records of their patients, and transfuse the blood to them if necessary. All information used and maintained throughout the transfusion procedure, including the type of operation, participating medical practitioners, and reason for transfusion, is clearly documented and stored in the database of a hospital. The patient information as well as the blood usage listings have been made accessible to the Red Cross BTS so that this institution can perform certain data mining and auditing tasks. The objectives of the data mining and auditing procedures are to improve the estimated future blood consumption in different hospitals and to make recommendation on the blood usage in future medical cases. In the final step, the Red Cross BTS submits a report to the Government Health Agency. Referring to the privacy regulations, such reports have the property of keeping patients' privacy protected, although useful patterns and structures have to be preserved. The data published along with the Privacy-Aware Health Information Sharing Service gets refined in a way to meet certain privacy criteria. This Red Cross example brings out a typical dilemma in information sharing and privacy protection faced by many healthcare institutions in the world nowadays. In general, we can study this use case from different perspectives as follows.

Information needs: The Red Cross BTS wants to have access to the health and blood usage data, not statistics, from the public hospitals for several reasons. First, the practitioners in hospitals have no expertise in doing data mining. They simply want to share the patient data with a party, such as the Red Cross BTS in this example, who needs the health data for a legitimate reason. Second, having access to the data, the Red Cross BTS has much better flexibility to perform the required data mining. It is impossible to request the practitioners in a hospital to produce different types of statistical information and fine-tune the results for research purposes. In this chapter, the term "data mining" has a broad sense. The data mining conducted by the Red Cross BTS could be anything from a simple counting of men with diabetes using Type A blood to sophisticated classification and cluster analysis.

Privacy concerns: There are legitimate reasons to allow the Red Cross BTS to have access to the health and blood usage. However, it also raises some concerns on the patients' privacy. In the information collection phase, the public hospitals collect person-specific data from individual patients. In the information sharing phase, the hospitals release the collected information to the Red Cross BTS, who will then conduct data mining and auditing on the shared data. The patients are willing to submit their data to a hospital because the hospital is a trustworthy entity. Yet, the trust to the hospital may not necessarily be transitive to a third party. Nowadays, many agencies and institutions consider that the released data is privacy-preserving if the explicit identifying information, such as name, social security number, address, and telephone number, is removed. However, substantial research has shown that simply removing the explicit identifying information is often insufficient for privacy protection. Sweeney [30] even shows that many patients can be re-identified simply by matching their other attributes, called the *quasi-identifier*, such as gender, age, and postal code.

How can healthcare institutions share patient-specific information with a third party without compromising the privacy of individual patients? The study of privacy-aware information sharing is to address this problem by anonymizing the released data. Insufficient anonymization leads to privacy threats. Over-anonymization heavily leads to loss of information, which, in turn, lowers the quality of applied data mining. The key challenge is how to perform the anonymization so that both privacy and usefulness of information throughout a data mining process are preserved in the derived data advertising privacy-protection.

In the most basic form of privacy-aware information sharing, the data publisher (e.g., the hospitals and/or the Government Health Agency in this case) has a table of the form of a tuple

$$T(Explicit\_Identifier, Quasi\_Identifier,$$
$$Sensitive\_Attributes, Non-Sensitive\_Attributes)$$

where $Explicit\_Identifier$ is a set of attributes, such as name and social security number (SSN), containing information that explicitly identifies record owners; $Quasi\_Identifier$ (QID) is a set of attributes that could potentially identify record owners; $Sensitive\_Attributes$ consist of sensitive patient-specific information such as disease, medical history, and disability status; and $Non-Sensitive\_Attributes$ contain all attributes that do not fall into the previous three categories [5]. The four sets of attributes are disjoint. Most work assumes that each record in the table represents a distinct record owner.

In addition to the privacy and information requirements, one major challenge in the BTS scenario is the problem of high dimensionality in the shared data [21]. Many privacy models, such as k-anonymity [27, 30] and its extensions [22, 33], have been proposed to thwart privacy threats caused by identity and attribute linkages in the context of relational databases. The usual approach is to generalize the records into equivalence groups so that each group contains at least k records with respect to some QID attributes, and the sensitive values in each QID group are diversified enough to disorient confident inferences. However, Aggarwal [1] has shown that when the number of QID attributes is large, that is, when the dimensionality of data is high, most of the data have to be suppressed in order to achieve k-anonymity. Our experiments confirm the *curse of high dimensionality on k-anonymity* [1] in the BTS case, which has more than 60 attributes. Applying k-anonymity on the high-dimensional patient data would significantly degrade the data quality. In order to overcome this bottleneck, we exploit one of the limitations of the adversary: in real-life privacy attacks, it is very difficult for an attacker to acquire all the information of a target patient because it requires non-trivial effort to gather each piece of prior knowledge from so many possible values. Thus, it is reasonable to assume that the attacker knows only some subsets of QID attributes of a target victim. Based on this assumption, we define a new privacy model called *multi-QID k-anonymity* [13], which will be discussed in the rest of the chapter, for anonymizing high-dimensional data.

13.3 Literature Review

What is privacy protection? Dalenius [6] provided a very stringent definition:

Access to the published data should not enable the attacker to learn anything extra about any target victim compared to no access to the database, even with the presence of any attacker's background knowledge obtained from other sources.

Dwork [8] shows that such absolute privacy protection is impossible due to the presence of attacker's background knowledge. Let us consider the age of an individual as sensitive information. Assume an attacker knows that Alice's age is of 5 years younger than the average age of American women. If the attacker has access to a statistical database that discloses the average age of American women, then Alice's privacy is considered to be compromised according to Dalenius' definition, regardless whether or not Alice's record is in the database [8].

Most literature on Privacy-Aware Information Sharing, also known as *Privacy-Preserving Data Publishing* [9], considers a more relaxed, more practical notion of privacy protection by assuming the attacker has limited background knowledge. Below, the term "victim" refers to a patient in the Red Cross example targeted by an attacker. We can broadly classify privacy models to two categories based on their attack principles. In general, a privacy threat occurs when an attacker is able to link a record owner to a record in a published data table, or to a sensitive attribute in a published data table. We call them *record linkage* and *attribute linkage*, respectively. In both types of linkages, we assume that the attacker knows the QID of the victim.

13.3.1   Record Linkage

In a *record linkage attack*, some value qid on QID identifies a small number of records in the released table T, called a *group*. If the victim's QID matches the value qid, the victim is vulnerable to being linked to the small number of records in the group. In this case, the attacker faces only a small number of possibilities for the victim's record, and with the help of additional and supporting knowledge, there is a high chance that the attacker can uniquely distinguish the victim's record from the group.

Example 1. Suppose that a hospital wants to publish patients' records as listed in table 13.1 to a research center. Therefore, the hospital should have to protect the data table against privacy threats by simply removing all identifying attributes. Suppose that the research center has access to the external table, table 13.2, and knows that every person with a record in table 13.1 has a record in table 13.2. Joining the two tables on the common attributes Job, Gender and Year of Birth may link the identity of a person to his/her sensitive information Diagnosis. For example, Doug, a male lawyer born in 1968, is identified as an HIV patient by $qid = \langle Lawyer, Male, 1968 \rangle$ after the join. ∎

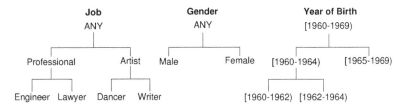

FIGURE 13.2: Taxonomy Trees.

k-**Anonymity**: To prevent record linkage through QID, Samarati and Sweeney [28, 29, 27, 30] proposed the notion of *k*-anonymity: if one record in the table has some value qid, at least $k - 1$ other records also have the value qid. In other words, the minimum group size on QID is at least k. A table satisfying this requirement is called *k*-anonymous. In a *k*-anonymous table, each record is indistinguishable from at least $k - 1$ other records with respect to QID. Consequently, the probability of linking a victim to a specific record through QID is at most $\frac{1}{k}$.

Example 2. Table 13.3 shows a 3-anonymous table by generalizing $QID = \{Job, Gender, Year\ of\ Birth\}$ from table 13.1 using the taxonomy trees in figure 13.2. It has two distinct groups on QID, namely $\langle Professional, Male, [1965-1969]\rangle$ and $\langle Artist, Female, [1960-1964]\rangle$. Since each group contains at least 3 records, the table is 3-anonymous. If we link the records in table 13.2 to the records in table 13.3 through QID, each record is linked to either no record or at least 3 records in table 13.3. ∎

We broadly classify record linkage anonymization algorithms into two families: *optimal anonymization* and *minimal anonymization*. Algorithms in both families primarily use generalization and suppression to achieve the *k*-anonymity privacy model.

The first family finds an optimal *k*-anonymization, for a given data metric, by limiting to full-domain generalization and record suppression. Since the search space for the full-domain generalization scheme is much smaller than other schemes, finding an optimal solution is feasible for small datasets. Due to the large number of data records in the scenario of Red Cross BTS, finding the optimal anonymization is not practical.

Sweeney's *MinGen* algorithm [30] exhaustively examines all potential full-domain generalizations to identify the optimal generalization, measured in minimal distortion. Sweeney acknowledged that this exhaustive search is impractical even for the modest sized datasets, motivating the second family of *k*-anonymization algorithms to be discussed later. Samarati [27] proposed a *bi-*

Table 13.1: Patient Table

Job	Gender	Year of Birth	Diagnosis
Engineer	Male	1965	Hepatitis
Engineer	Male	1968	Hepatitis
Lawyer	Male	1968	HIV
Writer	Female	1960	Flu
Writer	Female	1960	HIV
Dancer	Female	1960	HIV
Dancer	Female	1960	HIV

Table 13.2: External Table

Name	Job	Gender	Year of Birth
Alice	Writer	Female	1960
Bob	Engineer	Male	1965
Cathy	Writer	Female	1960
Doug	Lawyer	Male	1968
Emily	Dancer	Female	1960
Fred	Engineer	Male	1968
Gladys	Dancer	Female	1960
Henry	Lawyer	Male	1969
Irene	Dancer	Female	1962

Table 13.3: 3-Anonymous Patient Table

Job	Gender	Year of Birth	Diagnosis
Professional	Male	[1965-1969]	Hepatitis
Professional	Male	[1965-1969]	Hepatitis
Professional	Male	[1965-1969]	HIV
Artist	Female	[1960-1964]	Flu
Artist	Female	[1960-1964]	HIV
Artist	Female	[1960-1964]	HIV
Artist	Female	[1960-1964]	HIV

nary search algorithm that first identifies all minimal generalizations, and then finds the global optimal generalization. Enumerating all minimal generalizations is an expensive operation and, therefore, not scalable for large datasets, especially if a more flexible anonymization scheme is employed. LeFevre et al. [16] presented a suite of optimal bottom-up generalization algorithms, called *Incognito*, to generate all possible k-anonymous full-domain generalizations.

Another algorithm called *K-Optimize* [4] effectively prunes non-optimal anonymous tables by modeling the search space using a set enumeration tree. Each node represents a k-anonymous solution. The algorithm assumes a totally ordered set of attribute values, and examines the tree in a top-down manner starting from the most general table and prunes a node in the tree when none of its descendants could be a global optimal solution based on discernibility metric and classification metric. Unlike the above algorithms, K-Optimize employs the subtree generalization and record suppression schemes. It is the only efficient optimal algorithm that uses the flexible subtree generalization.

The second family of algorithms produces a minimal k-anonymous table by employing a greedy search guided by a search metric. Being heuristic in nature, these algorithms find a minimally anonymous solution, but are more scalable than the previous family. The anonymization algorithms in this family are usually more scalable than the anonymization algorithms in the aforementioned family.

μ-argus. The *μ-argus algorithm* [14] computes the frequency of all 3-value combinations of domain values, then greedily applies subtree generalizations and cell suppressions to achieve k-anonymity. Since the method limits the size of attribute combination, the resulting data may not be k-anonymous when more than 3 attributes are considered. Sweeney's *Datafly* system was the first k-anonymization algorithm scalable to handle real-life large datasets. It achieves k-anonymization by generating an array of qid group sizes and greedily generalizing those combinations with less than k occurrences based on a heuristic search metric that selects the attribute having the largest number of distinct values. Datafly employs full-domain generalization and record suppression schemes. These works aim at minimizing the data distortion, but minimally distorted data does not necessarily preserve the information usefulness for classification and cluster analysis, which are the information requirements of the Red Cross BTS case.

Iyengar [15] was among the first who aimed at preserving classification information in k-anonymous data by employing a genetic algorithm with an incomplete stochastic search based on classification metric and a subtree generalization scheme. The idea is to encode each state of generalization as a "chromosome" and encode data distortion by a fitness function. The search process is a genetic evolution that converges to the fittest chromosome. Iyengar's experiments suggested that, by considering the classification purpose, the classifier built from the anonymous data produces a lower classification error than the classifier built from the anonymous data using a general purpose metric. However, experiments also showed that this genetic algorithm is inefficient for large datasets [12, 13].

The *Top-Down Refinement* (TDR) method [12, 13] masks a table by refining it from the most general state in which all values are masked to the most general values of their taxonomy trees. At each step, TDR selects the refinement according to the search metric that maximizes the information gain and minimizes the privacy loss. The refinement process is terminated if no refinement can be performed without violating k-anonymity. TDR handles both categorical attributes and continuous attributes in a uniform way, except that the taxonomy tree for a continuous attribute is grown on the fly as specializations are searched at each step. Fung et al. [10, 11] further extended the k-anonymization algorithm to preserve the information for cluster analysis. The major challenge of anonymizing data for cluster analysis is the lack of class labels that could be used to guide the anonymization process. Their solution is to first partition the original data into clusters, convert the problem into the counterpart problem for classification analysis where class labels encode the cluster information in the data, and then apply TDR to preserve k-anonymity and the encoded cluster information. Since the framework of TDR fits well to the requirement of Red Cross case, the subsequent sections of this chapter study TDR extensively in the context of the Red Cross case.

Multidimensional k-anonymity. A variant of traditional k-anonymity is the multidimensional k-anonymity [17]. Let D_i be the domain of an attribute A_i. A single-dimensional generalization, such as full-domain generalization and subtree generalization, is defined by a function $f_i : D_{A_i} \leftarrow D'$ for each attribute A_i in QID. In contrast, a multidimensional generalization is defined by a single function $f : D_{A_i} \times \cdots \times D_{A_n} \rightarrow D'$, which is used to generalize $qid = \langle v_1, \ldots, v_n \rangle$ to $qid' = \langle u_1, \ldots, u_n \rangle$ where for every v_i, either $v_i = u_i$ or v_i is a child node of u_i in the taxonomy of A_i. This scheme flexibly allows two qid groups, even having the same value v, to be independently generalized into different parent groups. For example $\langle Engineer, Male \rangle$ can be generalized to $\langle Engineer, ANY\_Gender \rangle$ while $\langle Engineer, Female \rangle$ can be generalized to $\langle Professional, Female \rangle$. The generalized table contains both Engineer and Professional. Nergiz and Clifton [24] further evaluated a family of clustering-based algorithms that even attempts to improve data utility by ignoring the restrictions of the given taxonomies.

This scheme produces less distortion than the traditional full-domain and subtree generalization schemes because it needs to generalize only the qid groups that violate the specified threshold. The trade-off is that multidimensional generalization is less scalable than other schemes due to the increased search space. Nonetheless, it is important to note that the utility of data is adversely affected by this flexibility, which causes a data exploration problem; most standard data mining methods treat *Engineer* and *Professional* as two independent values, but, in fact, they are not. For example, building a decision tree from such a generalized table may result in two branches, *Professional* $\rightarrow$ *class2* and *Engineer* $\rightarrow$ *class1*. It is unclear which branch should be used to classify a new engineer. This data exploration problem prohibits applying multidimensional k-anonymity to the Red Cross BTS scenario.

LeFevre et al. [17] presented a greedy top-down specialization algorithm for finding a minimal k-anonymization in the case of the multidimensional generalization scheme. Both TDR and this algorithm perform a specialization on a value v one at a time. The major difference is that TDR specializes in all qid groups containing v. In other words, a specialization is performed only if each specialized qid group contains at least k records. In contrast, Mondrian performs a specialization on one qid group if each of its specialized qid groups contains at least k records. Due to such a relaxed constraint, the resulting anonymous data in multidimensional generalization usually has a better quality than in single generalization. Since Mondrian is a minimal anonymization algorithm, which uses heuristics to guide the search, it is quite scalable.

13.3.2 Attribute Linkage

In the attack of attribute linkage, the attacker may not precisely identify the record of the target victim, but could infer his/her sensitive values from the published data T, based on the set of sensitive values associated to the group that the victim belongs to. In case some sensitive values predominate in a group, a successful inference becomes relatively easy even if k-anonymity is satisfied. Several approaches have been proposed to address this type of threat. The general idea is to diminish the correlation between QID attributes and sensitive attributes.

Example 3. From table 13.1, an attacker can infer that all female dancers born in 1960 have HIV, i.e., $\langle Dancer, Female, 1960 \rangle \rightarrow HIV$ with 100% confidence. Applying this knowledge on table 13.2, the attacker can infer that Emily has HIV with 100% confidence provided that Emily comes from the same population of table 13.1. ∎

ℓ-**diversity**. Machanavajjhala et al. [22, 23] proposed the diversity principle, called ℓ-diversity, to prevent attribute linkage. The ℓ-diversity requires every *qid* group to contain at least ℓ "well-represented" sensitive values. There are several instantiations of this principle, which differ in the definition of being well-represented. The simplest understanding of "well-represented" is to ensure that there are at least ℓ distinct values for the sensitive attribute in each *qid* group.

Confidence Bounding. Wang et al. [32, 33] considered bounding the confidence of inferring a sensitive value from a *qid* group by specifying one or more *privacy templates* of the form, $\langle QID \rightarrow s, h \rangle$. s is a sensitive value, QID is a quasi-identifier, and h is a maximum confidence threshold. Let $Conf(QID \rightarrow s)$ be $max\{conf(qid \rightarrow s)\}$ over all *qid* groups on QID, where $conf(qid \rightarrow s)$ denotes the percentage of records containing s in the *qid* group. A table satisfies $\langle QID \rightarrow s, h \rangle$ if $Conf(QID \rightarrow s) \rightarrow h$. In other words, a privacy template bounds the attacker's confidence of inferring the sensitive value s in any group on QID to the maximum h. For example, with $QID = \{Job, Gender, Year of Birth\}$, $\langle QID \rightarrow HIV, 10\% \rangle$ states that the confidence of inferring HIV from any group on QID is no more than 10%. For the data in table 13.3, this privacy template is violated because the confidence of inferring HIV is 75% in the group $\{Artist, Female, [1960 - 1964]\}$.

t-closeness. Li et al. [19] observed that when the overall distribution of a sensitive attribute is skewed, ℓ-diversity does not prevent attribute linkage attacks. Consider a patient table where 95% of records have Flu and 5% of records have HIV. Suppose that a *qid* group has 50% of Flu and 50% of HIV and, therefore, satisfies 2-diversity. However, this group presents a serious privacy threat because any record owner in the group could be inferred as having HIV with 50% confidence, compared to 5% in the overall table. To prevent *skewness attack*, Li et al. [19] proposed a privacy model, called *t*-closeness, which requires the distribution of a sensitive attribute in any group on QID to be close to the distribution of the attribute in the overall table. *t*-closeness uses the Earth Mover Distance function to measure the closeness between two distributions of sensitive values, and requires the closeness to be within t.

Proximity attacks. Most works on k-anonymity and its extensions assume categorical sensitive attributes. Zhang et al. [35] proposed the notion of (k, e)-anonymity to address continuous sensitive attributes such as salary. The general idea is to partition the records into groups so that each group contains at least k different sensitive values with a range of at least e. However, (k, e)-anonymity ignores the distribution of sensitive values within the range λ. If some sensitive values occur frequently within a subrange of λ, then the attacker could still confidently infer the subrange in a group. This type of attribute linkage attack is called the *proximity attack* [20]. Consider a *qid* group of 10 data records with 7 different sensitive values, where 9 records have sensitive values in [30-35], and 1 record has value 80. The group is $(7, 50)$-anonymous because $80 - 30 = 50$. Still, the attacker can infer that a victim inside the group has a sensitive value falling into [30-35] with 90% confidence. Li et al. [20] proposed an alternative privacy model called (ϵ, m)-*anonymity*: given any continuous sensitive value s in T, this privacy model bounds the probability of inferring $[s - \epsilon, s + \epsilon]$ to be at most $1/m$. Wang et al. [34] introduced a privacy model called (ϵ, δ)-*dissimilarity*, which requires that for all qid_i group, every sensitive value to be dissimilar to at least $\delta \times (a(qid_i) - 1)$ other sensitive values, where $a(qid_i)$ denotes the number of records in qid_i and two sensitive values are considered dissimilar if their semantic distance is larger than ϵ.

Probabilistic inference. Du et al. [7] model the privacy threats caused by attribute linkages as probabilistic inferences, $P(sensitive\ value|qid)$: given a qid value of a target victim, compute the probability that the victim has the sensitive value. Due to the large number of combinations of QID values, computing all these conditional probabilities are very expensive and infeasible in real-life problem. Their proposed approach is based on the maximum entropy principle. They treat all the conditional probabilities $P(sensitive\ value|qid)$ as unknown variables, consider the background knowledge as the constraints of these variables, and formulate constraints from the published data. They basically transform the problem to an optimization problem for finding variable values that satisfy all these constraints.

Background knowledge. Many privacy models lie in how to model the attacker's background knowledge. Yet, in real-life information sharing, a data publisher may not able to specify such background knowledge. In some cases, for example publishing data on the Web, the data publisher may not even know who the data recipients are. Thus, it is unreasonable to require manual specification of the background knowledge. Li and Li [18] proposed to generate such knowledge by mining the data to be released. The method is developed based on the rationale that the knowledge should manifest itself in the published data; therefore, we should able to identify them using data mining. Then, their approach uses the extracted knowledge in the data anonymization process. As a result, the method improves both privacy and utility at the same time.

In this chapter, we show an anonymization method to achieve Multi-QID k-anonymity while preserving the information usefulness for data mining. The one may enforce any privacy models discussed above, but the impacts on the information usefulness for data mining should be further studied.

13.4   Privacy-Aware Information Sharing for Classification Analysis

Most work in section 13.3 focuses on achieving a privacy requirement. Yet, another requirement is making the released data useful to data mining, which is the primary purpose of sharing the information. For example, in the data flow of the Red Cross blood transfusion system depicted in figure 13.1, the Government Health Agency has to share patient-specific data with the Red Cross for classification analysis. Is it possible that both the privacy and data mining goals can be achieved at the same time? Our insight is that these two goals are indeed dealing with two types of information. The privacy goal requires masking sensitive information, usually specific descriptions that identify individuals, whereas the classification goal requires extracting general structures that capture trends and patterns. Both goals can be achieved by *carefully* performing generalization and suppression on some selected data. This insight is supported by extensive experimental results on real-life datasets [12, 13]. This section summarizes the essential property and presents a high-level anonymization algorithm for achieving both privacy and data mining goals.

Another major challenge to be addressed is the problem of high dimensionality. Most of the previously discussed k-anonymization methods consider only a single QID. As a result, every combination of qid values on QID has to be shared by at least k records in the anonymous table, resulting in high information loss when the number of QID attributes is high. Below, we define a variant of the k-anonymity privacy model to tackle the problem of high dimensionality as discussed in the Red Cross BTS scenario.

13.4.1   The Problem: Multi-QID k-Anonymity for Classification Analysis

To prevent record linkages, the Government Health Agency wants to k-anonymize the patient data before sharing the data with the Red Cross for data mining and report generation. Sharing the patient data in the Red Cross BTS case poses several challenges to the traditional anonymization algorithms [28, 29, 27, 30, 16].

- The Hong Kong Red Cross wants to utilize the patient data as training data for building a classification model, and then use the model to classify future cases. Most traditional anonymization methods aim at minimizing the distortion of the data. These methods may well-preserve some basic count statistics, but experiments have shown that achieving minimal distortion does not imply preserving the data quality for classification analysis [12, 13].

- The patient data contains both categorical attributes and continuous attributes. Some categorical attributes come with a taxonomy tree while many of them do not. Some anonymization methods suggest pre-discretizing continuous attributes into intervals; however, this approach does not take classification into account. We need an anonymization algorithm that can mask all three types of attributes, while preserving a certain classification quality.

- The number of patient data records can be huge. The anonymization algorithm must be efficient and scalable to perform well on large datasets.

The problem of k-anonymity for classification analysis in the Red Cross case can be formally described as follows: Given a raw data table

$$T(QID, Sensitive\_Attributes, Class\_Attribute),$$

a specified k-anonymity requirement, and an optional taxonomy tree for each categorical attribute in QID, the Government Health Agency wants to determine a masked version of T, denoted by T^*. In the modified and privacy-protected table T^* records are made k-anonymous while essential structures for classifications are preserved (that is, the masked table remains useful for classifying the $Class\_Attribute$). Therefore it is important to extract certain patterns, e.g., most dominant attributes (which are not necessarily sensitive ones), from T, which are then preserved in T^* in way to gain most information about the table for analysis. In parallel it has taken care that no privacy violation occurs when generating T^* from the raw table T. The $Sensitive\_Attributes$ should be important for the task of classification analysis, otherwise, they should be removed.

To tackle the problem of high dimensionality, Fung et el. [13] introduced a variant of k-anonymity requirement called multi-QID k-anonymity. The modified notion does not require every combination of qid values to be shared by at least k records. Instead, it relaxes the requirement by decomposing a single QID into smaller subsets based on the assumption that the attacker is unlikely to know all attributes of a victim. The modified notion is formally described below.

Definition 1. Multi-QID anonymity requirement: Consider p quasi-identifiers $QID_1, \ldots, QID_p$ on T. $a(qid_i)$ denotes the number of data records in T that share the value qid_i on QID_i. The *anonymity* of QID_i, denoted by $A(QID_i)$, is the smallest $a(qid_i)$ for any value qid_i on QID_i. A table T satisfies the *multi-QID anonymity requirement* $\{\langle QID_1, k_1 \rangle, \ldots, \langle QID_p, k_p \rangle\}$ if $A(QID_i) \geq k_i$ for $1 \leq i \leq p$, where k_i is the *anonymity threshold* on QID_i specified by the data provider. ■

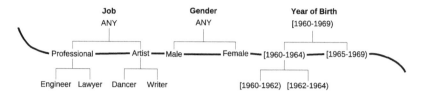

FIGURE 13.3: Taxonomy trees indicating a cut

Definition 1 generalizes the classic notion of k-anonymity by allowing multiple QIDs (with possibly different thresholds). Suppose that the data provider wants to release a table $T(A, B, C, D, S)$, where S is the sensitive attribute, and knows that the recipient has access to previously released tables $T1(A, B, X)$ and $T2(C, D, Y)$, where X and Y are attributes not in T. To prevent linking the records in T to X or Y, the data provider only has to specify the k-anonymity on $QID1 = \{A, B\}$ and $QID2 = \{C, D\}$. In this case, enforcing the k-anonymity on $QID = \{A, B, C, D\}$ will distort the data more than what is necessary. All previous works suffer from this problem because they handled multiple QIDs through the single QID made up of all attributes in the multiple QIDs.

We discuss a particular anonymization method, called *Top-Down Refinement* (TDR) [12, 13], because TDR does not only achieve multi-QID k-anonymity for classification analysis, but also provides extensibility to deal with the problem of k-anonymity for *cluster analysis*, which will be discussed in Section 13.5.

13.4.2   Masking Operations

To transform T to satisfy the multi-QID k-anonymity requirement, we consider three types of masking operations on the attributes D_j in QID.

1. Generalize D_j if D_j is a categorical attribute with a taxonomy tree. A leaf node represents a domain value and a parent node represents a less specific value. A generalized D_j can be viewed as a "cut" through its taxonomy tree. A cut of a tree is a subset of values in the tree, denoted by Cut_j, which contains exactly one value on each root-to-leaf path. For example in figure 13.3, the cut indicated by the dashed line represent generalized values of the 3-anonymous table from table 13.3.

2. Suppress D_j if D_j is a categorical attribute with no taxonomy tree. The suppression of a value on D_j means replacing all occurrences of the value with the special value $\perp_j$. All suppressed values on D_j are represented by the same $\perp_j$, which is treated as a new value in D_j by a classification algorithm. We use Sup_j to denote the set of values suppressed by $\perp_j$.

This type of suppression is at the value level in that Sup_j is, in general, a subset of the values in the attribute D_j.

3. Discretize D_j if D_j is a continuous attribute. The discretization of a value v on D_j means replacing all occurrences of v with an interval containing the value. Our algorithm dynamically grows a taxonomy tree for intervals at runtime, where each node represents an interval, and each non-leaf node has two child nodes representing some "optimal" binary split of the parent interval. A discretized D_j can be represented by the set of intervals, denoted by Int_j, corresponding to the leaf nodes in the dynamically grown taxonomy tree of D_j.

13.4.3 The Algorithm: Top-Down Refinement (TDR)

A table T can be masked by a sequence of refinements starting from the most masked state in which each attribute is either generalized to the topmost value, suppressed to the special value $\perp$, or represented by a single interval. TDR iteratively refines a masked value selected from the current set of cuts, suppressed values, and intervals, until violating the anonymity requirement. Each refinement increases the information and decreases the anonymity since records with specific values are more distinguishable. The key is selecting the "best" refinement at each step with both impacts considered. Below, we formally describe the notion of refinement on different types of attributes D_j in $\cup QID_i$ and define a selection criterion for a single refinement.

1. *Refinement for Generalization*: Consider a categorical attribute D_j with a user-specified taxonomy tree. Let $child(v)$ be the set of child values of v in a user-specified taxonomy tree. A refinement, written $v \rightarrow child(v)$, replaces the parent value v with the child value in $child(v)$ that generalizes the domain value in each (generalized) record that contains v.

2. *Refinement for Suppression*: For a categorical attribute D_j without taxonomy tree, a refinement $\perp_j \rightarrow \{v, \perp_j\}$ refers to disclosing one value v from the set of suppressed values Sup_j. Let $R_{\perp_j}$ denote the set of suppressed records that currently contain $\perp_j$. Disclosing v means replacing $\perp_j$ with v in all records in $R_{\perp_j}$ that originally contain v.

3. *Refinement for Discretization*: For a continuous attribute, refinement is similar to that for generalization except that no prior taxonomy tree is given and the taxonomy tree has to be grown dynamically in the process of refinement. Initially, the interval that covers the full range of the attribute forms the root. The refinement on an interval v, which is written as $v \rightarrow child(v)$, refers to the optimal split of v into two child intervals $child(v)$ that maximizes the information gain. The anonymity is not used for finding a split good for classification. This is similar to

defining a taxonomy tree where the main consideration is how the taxonomy best describes the application. Due to this extra step of identifying the optimal split of the parent interval, we treat continuous attributes separately from categorical attributes with taxonomy trees.

A refinement is *valid* (with respect to T) if T satisfies the anonymity requirement after the refinement. A refinement is *beneficial* (with respect to T) if more than one class is involved in the refined records. A refinement is performed only if it is both valid and beneficial. Therefore, a refinement guarantees that every newly generated qid has $a(qid) \geq k$.

We propose a selection criterion for guiding our TDR process to heuristically maximize the classification goal. Consider a refinement $v \rightarrow child(v)$, where $v \in D_j$, and D_j is a categorical attribute with a user-specified taxonomy tree or D_j is a continuous attribute with a dynamically grown taxonomy tree. The refinement has two effects: it increases the information of the refined records with respect to classification, and it decreases the anonymity of the refined records with respect to privacy. These effects are measured by "information gain," denoted by $InfoGain(v)$, and "anonymity loss," denoted by $AnonyLoss(v)$. v is a good candidate for refinement if $InfoGain(v)$ is large and $AnonyLoss(v)$ is small. Our selection criterion is choosing the candidate v, for the next refinement, that has the maximum information-gain/anonymity-loss trade-off, which is defined as

$$Score(v) = \frac{InfoGain(v)}{PrivLoss(v)}$$

.

For $InfoGain(v)$, we employ Shannon's information theory to measure information gain of a refinement on v with respect to the Class attribute. For $PrivLoss(v)$, it is the decrease of the anonymity of QID by the refinement on v.

We present a high-level description of the TDR algorithm. In a preprocessing step, we compress the given table T by removing all attributes not in $\cup QID_i$ and collapsing duplicates into a single row with the Class column storing the class frequency. The compressed table is typically much smaller than the original table. Below, the term "data records" refers to data records in this compressed form. Algorithm 1 summarizes the conceptual algorithm. Initially, Cut_j contains only the top-most value for a categorical attribute D_j with a taxonomy tree, Sup_j contains all domain values of a categorical attribute D_j without a taxonomy tree, and Int_j contains the full-range interval for a continuous attribute D_j. The valid beneficial refinements in

---

Algorithm 5 Top-Down Refinement (TDR)

Require: Raw data table T

1: Initialize every value of categorical attribute D_j with taxonomy tree to the topmost value, suppress every value of D_j without taxonomy tree to $\perp_j$, and include every value of continuous attribute D_j into a full-range interval, where $D_j \in \cup QID_i$.

2: Initialize Cut_j of D_j to include the topmost value if D_j is a categorical attribute with taxonomy tree, Sup_j of D_j to include all domain values of D_j if D_j is a categorical attribute without taxonomy tree, and Int_j of D_j to include the full-range interval if D_j is a continuous attribute, where $D_j \in \cup QID_i$.

3: **while** some refinement $x \in \langle Cut_j, Sup_j, Int_j \rangle$ is valid and beneficial **do**

4:     Find the refinement *Best* from $\langle Cut_j, Sup_j, Int_j \rangle$ that has the highest *Score*

5:     Perform *Best* on T and update $\langle Cut_j, Sup_j, Int_j \rangle$

6:     Update $Score(x)$ and validity for $x \in \langle Cut_j, Sup_j, Int_j \rangle$

7: **return** multi-QID k-anonymous T^* and solution set $\langle Cut_j, Sup_j, Int_j \rangle$

$\langle Cut_j, Sup_j, Int_j \rangle$ form contain the set of candidates fulfilling the definitions of being valid and beneficial. At each iteration, we find the candidate of the highest Score, denoted by *Best* (Line 4), apply *Best* to T, update $\langle Cut_j, Sup_j, Int_j \rangle$ (Line 5), and update *Score* and the validity of the candidates in $\langle Cut_j, Sup_j, Int_j \rangle$ (Line 6). The algorithm terminates when there is no more candidate in $\langle Cut_j, Sup_j, Int_j \rangle$, in which case it returns the masked table together with the solution set $\langle Cut_j, Sup_j, Int_j \rangle$.

13.4.4 The HL7-Compliant Data Structure for the Blood Usage Record

The HL7 data hierarchy of blood usage record is designed to support the HL7 schema version 3 which is a standard for the electronic data interchange (EDI) in the healthcare organization. The importance of HL7 lies within the unifying and well-defined structures on the maintaining of Electronic Health Records (EHR) within domain boundaries as well as concerning a wider perspective. Any electronic documents or records need to follow the HL7 standard and the HL7 current version (version 3) supports the XML platform representation. Therefore, the data fields of blood usage records are transformed to the HL7-compliant XML document structure in a matching way. To compare our data hierarchy of the blood usage record with the data fields in table 13.4, we match the elements of the data fields from table 13.4.

Algorithm 6 OT Reference Data Time

Require: OT records interfaced from CMS into Data Warehouse
 1: **if** OT Record has non-empty OT Start Date Time **then**
 2:    OT Start Date Time
 3: **else if** OT Record Creation Date Time = OT Date **then**
 4:    OT Record Creation Date Time
 5: **else**
 6:    OT Date (Time = 00 : 00)

In the Red Cross BTS scenario, the Government Health Agency first collects the patient data from the hospitals, integrates and anonymizes the data, transforms it to the HL7 XML standard format, and submits the data to Red Cross BTS.

The HL7 data hierarchy consists of two main sections: a head and a body section. The head section contains the information related to the patient identification, physicians, and hospital information while the body section contains the information about the patient medical history, laboratory results, and physical examination. For example, in HL7 Version 3, the elements named "title" and "patient" of the head section can be matched with the data field "product" and "patient name", respectively. For the body section, each element "entry" (content entries) has a particular laboratory result or a measurement value and can be matched with the data fields from table 13.4 and 13.5, e.g., like the element "entry" code = (Blood Group) with the "Blood Group" attribute contained in tables 13.4. The HL7-compliant XML document structure can provide the flexibility of simple interchanging, updating, and analyzing of data which improves the overall performance in the management of blood usage records. Referring to figure 13.1, the data in both databases "Blood Donor Data and Blood Information" and "Patient Health Data and Blood Usage" will be stored in this HL7-compliant format.

13.4.5   Experimental Results

Our goal in this section is to evaluate the proposed method, TDR, in terms of preserving the usefulness for classification analysis. We compare the classifier built from the masked data with the classifier built from the unmodified data. This comparison makes sense because the anonymization is due to the privacy consideration and the data will be released without modification in the absence of such consideration. In addition, the unmodified data has the lowest possible cost, therefore, serves the best possible candidate according to previous cost metrics [4, 15, 16]. Iyengar [15] has evaluated the impact of anonymity on classification with single dimensional generalization. Our evaluation uses the baseline of the unmodified data and the reported results in [15].

Table 13.4: Data Field Description

Field Name	Data Type*	Description
LIS Hospital (Identifiable)	Char(3)	From LIS
Issue Date Time	DateTime	From LIS
Issue Date ID	Int	Issue Date ID of blood product
No of Unit	Int	From LIS
Blood Group	Char(6)	From LIS
Product	Char(11)	From LIS
LIS Case No	Char(12)	From LIS
Patient Name	Char(48)	From LIS
Reference Key	Int	Non-HKID identifier for patient, from Data Warehouse
Sex	Char(1)	From LIS
Age	Int	From LIS
Age Unit	Char(6)	From LIS
DOB	DateTime	From LIS
Patient Blood Group	Char(6)	From LIS
IP Hospital (Identifiable)	Char(3)	Hospital code of the IP episode for the patient at "Issue Date Time" from Data Warehouse
IP Case No	Char(12)	HN number of the IP episode for the patient at "Issue Date Time" from Data Warehouse
Specialty (EIS)	Char(7)	EIS specialty code of the IP episode for the patient at "Issue Date Time" from Data Warehouse
Pre Issue Hb	Decimal(11, 4)	For study on a) red cells
Pre Issue Platelet Count	Decimal(11, 4)	For study on b) platelet concentrates
Pre Issue PT	Decimal(11, 4)	For study on c) fresh frozen plasma
Pre Issue INR	Decimal(11, 4)	For study on c) fresh frozen plasma
Pre Issue APTT	Decimal(11, 4)	For study on c) fresh frozen plasma
Pre Issue D-dimer	Decimal(11, 4)	For study on c) fresh frozen plasma
Pre Issue Fibrinogen	Decimal(11, 4)	For study on c) fresh frozen plasma Non standardized test, pending for entity ID(s) for searching

*Char(n): n is the number of characters. DateTime: date and time; format depends on system locale. Int: Integer. Decimal(p,s): p is the maximum total number of decimal digits and s is the maximum number of decimal digits to the right of the decimal point.

Table 13.5: Data Field Description

Field Name	Data Type[†]	Description
Dx1 ... Dx15	Char(7)	Diagnosis codes (in ICD9CM) of the IP episode for the patient at "Issue Date Time" from Data Warehouse
OT Reference	Char(12)	OT Reference number of the IP episode for the patient at "Issue Date Time" from OT records interfaced from CMS into Data Warehouse; Note that one HN may have multiple OT records.
OT Reference Date Time	DateTime	see Algorithm 6
OT Nature	Char(1)	C - Elective E - Emergency From OT records interfaced from CMS into Data Warehouse
OT Magnitude Description	Char(16)	OT magnitude input by surgeon, from OT records interfaced from CMS into Data Warehouse
Blood Loss (ml)	Int	Blood loss in ml, from OT records interfaced from CMS into Data Warehouse
OT Related Px1 ... Px15	Char(7)	OT Record Related procedure codes in ICD9CM, from OT records interfaced from CMS into Data Warehouse

[†]Char(n): n is the number of characters. DateTime: date and time; format depends on system locale. Int: Integer. Decimal(p,s): p is the maximum total number of decimal digits and s is the maximum number of decimal digits to the right of the decimal point.

Table 13.6: The *Adult* dataset

Attribute	Type	Numerical Range	
		# of Leaves	# of Levels
Age (Ag)	cont.	17 - 90	
Capital-gain (Cg)	cont.	0 - 99999	
Capital-loss (Cl)	cont.	0 - 4356	
Education-num (En)	cont.	1 - 16	
Final-weight (Fw)	cont.	13492 - 1490400	
Hours-per-week (H)	cont.	1 - 99	
Education (E)	cat.	16	5
Marital-status (M)	cat.	7	4
Native-country (N)	cat.	40	5
Occupation (O)	cat.	14	3
Race (Ra)	cat.	5	3
Relationship (Re)	cat.	6	3
Sex (S)	cat.	2	2
Work-class (W)	cat.	8	5

All experiments on TDR were conducted on an Intel Pentium IV 2.6GHz PC with 1GB RAM. We used the C4.5 classifier [26] as the classification model and adopted a widely used benchmark dataset, *Adult*, from the UCI repository [25]. Unless stated otherwise, all attributes were used for building classifiers.

13.4.5.1 Data Quality

In a typical real life situation, the data provider releases all data records in a single file, leaving the split of training and testing sets to the data miner. Following this practice, we combined the training set and testing set into one set for masking, and built a classifier using the masked training set and collected the error using the masked testing set. This error, called the *anonymity error*, denoted by AE, was compared with the *baseline error*, denoted by BE, for the unmodified training and testing sets. Note that AE depends on the anonymity requirement. $AE - BE$ measures the quality loss due to data masking.

The *Adult* dataset has 6 continuous attributes, 8 categorical attributes, and a binary *Class* column representing two income levels, ≤50K or >50K. Table 13.6 describes each attribute (*cont.* for continuous and *cat.* for categorical). After removing records with missing values from the pre-split training and testing sets, we have 30,162 records and 15,060 records for training and testing respectively. This is exactly the same dataset as used in [15].

For the same anonymity threshold k, a single QID is always more restric-

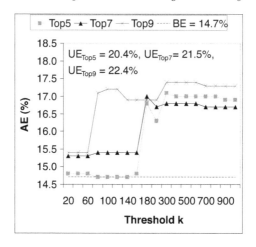

FIGURE 13.4: Suppress and discretize TopN in *Adult*

tive than breaking it into multiple QIDs. For this reason, we first consider the case of single QID. To ensure that masking is working on attributes that have impact on classification, the QID contains the top N attributes ranked by the C4.5 classifier. The top rank attribute is the attribute at the top of the C4.5 decision tree. Then we remove this attribute and repeat this process to determine the rank of other attributes. The top 9 attributes are Cg, Ag, M, En, Re, H, S, E, O in that order. We specified three anonymity requirements denoted Top5, Top7, and Top9, where the QID contains the top 5, 7, and 9 attributes respectively. The *upper error*, denoted UE, refers to the error on the data with all the attributes in the QID removed (equivalent to generalizing them to the top most ANY or suppressing them to $\perp$ or including them into a full range interval). $UE - BE$ measures the impact of the QID on classification.

Figure 13.4 displays AE with the anonymity threshold $20 \leq k \leq 1000$ by applying discretization on the 6 continuous attributes and suppression on the 8 categorical attributes without taxonomy trees. Note that k is not spaced linearly. We summarize the analysis for Top7 as follows. First, $AE - BE$, where $BE = 14.7\%$, is less than 2.5% over the entire range of tested anonymity threshold, and AE is much lower than $UE = 21.5\%$. This supports that accurate classification and privacy protection can coexist. Second, AE *generally* increases as the anonymity threshold k increases, but not monotonically. For example, the error slightly drops when k increases from 180 to 200. This is due to the variation between the training and testing sets, and the fact that a better structure may appear in a more masked state.

We further evaluate the effectiveness of generalization on categorical at-

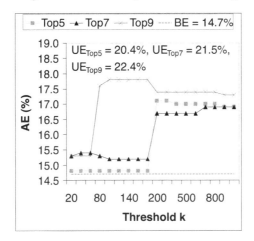

FIGURE 13.5: Generalize and discretize TopN in *Adult*: C4.5.

tributes with taxonomy trees. Although the author of [15] has specified taxonomy trees for categorical attributes, we do not agree with the author's groupings. For example, the author grouped *Native-country* according to continents, except Americas. We followed the grouping according to the World Factbook published by the CIA (http://www.cia.gov/cia/publications/factbook/).

Figure 13.5 displays AE with the anonymity threshold $20 \leq k \leq 1000$ by applying discretization on the 6 continuous attributes and generalization on the 8 categorical attributes according to our specified taxonomy trees. We summarize the analysis for Top7 as follows. $AE - BE$, where $BE = 14.7\%$, is less than 2% over the range of anonymity threshold $20 \leq k \leq 600$, and AE is much lower than $UE = 21.5\%$. These results are similar to the results in Figure 13.4 although the finally masked versions of data are very different. This suggests there exist redundant "good" classification structures in the data.

TDR took at most 10 seconds for all previous experiments. Out of the 10 seconds, approximately 8 seconds were spent on reading data records from disk and writing the masked data to disk. The actual processing time for generalizing the data is relatively short.

In an effort to study the effectiveness of multiple QIDs, we compared AE between a multiple QIDs requirement and the *corresponding* single united QID requirement. We randomly generated 30 multiple QID requirements as follows. For each requirement, we first determined the number of QIDs using the uniform distribution $U[3, 7]$ (i.e., randomly drawn a number between 3 and 7) and the length of QIDs using $U[2, 9]$. For simplicity, all QIDs in the same requirement have the same length and same threshold $k = 100$. For each QID,

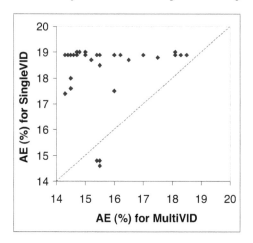

FIGURE 13.6: SingleQID vs MultiQID ($k = 100$).

we randomly selected some attributes according to the QID length from the 14 attributes. A repeating QID was discarded. For example, a requirement of 3 $QIDs$ and length 2 is $\{\langle\{Ag, En\}, k\rangle, \langle\{Ag, Ra\}, k\rangle, \langle\{S, H\}, k\rangle\}$, and the corresponding single QID requirement is $\{\langle\{Ag, En, Ra, S, H\}, k\rangle\}$.

In Figure 13.6, each data point represents the AE of a multiple QID requirement, denoted MultiQID, and the AE of the corresponding single QID requirement, denoted SingleQID. Most data points appear at the upper left corner of the diagonal, suggesting that MultiQID generally yields lower AE than its corresponding SingleQID. This verifies the effectiveness of multiple $QIDs$ to avoid unnecessary masking and improve data quality.

13.4.6   Comparing with Other Algorithms

Iyengar [15] presented a genetic algorithm solution. This experiment was customized to conduct a fair comparison with the results in [15]. We used the same *Adult* dataset, same attributes, and same anonymity requirement as specified in [15]:

$$GA = \langle\{Ag, W, E, M, O, Ra, S, N\}, k\rangle.$$

We obtained the taxonomy trees from the author for generalization, except for the continuous attribute Ag which we used discretization. Following the procedure in [15], all attributes not in GA were removed and were not used to produce BE, AE, and UE in this experiment, and all errors were based on the 10-fold cross validation and the C4.5 classifier. For each fold, we first masked the training data and then applied the masking to the testing data.

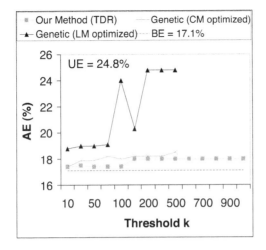

FIGURE 13.7: Comparing with genetic algorithm.

Figure 13.7 compares AE of TDR with the errors reported for two methods in [15], Loss Metric (LM) and Classification Metric (CM), for $10 \leq k \leq 500$. TDR outperformed LM, especially for $k \geq 100$, but performed only slightly better than CM. TDR continued to perform well from $k = 500$ to $k = 1000$, for which no result was reported for LM and CM in [15]. This analysis shows that TDR is at least comparable to genetic algorithm [15] in terms of accuracy. However, TDR took only 7 seconds to mask the data, including reading data records from disk and writing the masked data to disk. Iyengar [15] reported that his method requires 18 hours to transform this data, which has about only 30K data records. Clearly, the genetic algorithm is not scalable.

13.5 Privacy-Aware Information Sharing for Cluster Analysis

Performing classification analysis on anonymous data is a privacy preservation requirement for data mining. Another data mining task to perform is cluster analysis in order to obtain better insight on the common characteristics of blood transfusion cases. The major challenge of masking data for cluster analysis is the lack of class labels that could be used to guide the masking process. In this section we convert this problem into the counterpart problem of classification analysis, wherein class labels encode the cluster structure of the data, and present a framework to evaluate the cluster quality on the masked data.

13.5.1 The Problem: Multi-QID k-Anonymity for Cluster Analysis

The data holder wants to transform a raw patient data table T to a masked table T^* for the purpose of *cluster analysis*, with its goal to group similar objects closer (i.e., into the same cluster) and dissimilar objects away from each other (i.e., into different clusters).

What kind of information should be preserved for cluster analysis? Unlike classification analysis, wherein the information utility of attributes can be measured by their power of identifying class labels [4, 12, 13, 15, 17], no class labels are available for cluster analysis. One natural approach is to preserve the cluster structure in the raw data. Any loss of structure due to the anonymization is measured relative to such "raw cluster structure."

The problem of multi-QID k-anonymity for cluster analysis in the Red Cross case can be formally described as follows: given a raw data table $T(QID, Sensitive\_Attributes)$, a multi-QID k-anonymity requirement, an optional taxonomy tree for each categorical attribute in $\cup QID_i$, the Government Health Agency wants to determine a masked version of T, denoted by T^*, such that the masked table T^* satisfies the multi-QID k-anonymity requirement and has a cluster structure as similar as possible to the cluster structure in the raw table T. The *Sensitive_Attributes* should be important for the task of classification analysis; otherwise, removed from the set.

13.5.2 The Solution Framework

In this section, we present a framework to show the steps of the algorithm for generating a masked table T^*, represented by a solution set $\langle Cut_j, Sup_j, Int_j \rangle$ that satisfies a given k-anonymity requirement and preserves as much as possible of the raw cluster structure. Figure 13.8 provides an overview of our proposed framework. First, we generate the cluster structure in the raw table T and label each record in T by a class label. This labeled table, denoted by T_l, has a Class attribute that contains a class label for each record. Essentially, preserving the raw cluster structure is to preserve the power of identifying such class labels during masking. Masking operations that diminish the differences among records belonging to different clusters (classes) are penalized. As the requirement is similar to the anonymity problem for classification analysis, we can apply TDR, the anonymization algorithm for classification analysis, to achieve the requested degree of anonymity. We explain each step in figure 13.8 as follows.

1. Convert T to a labeled table T_l. Apply a clustering algorithm to T to identify the raw cluster structure, and label each record in T by its class label. The resulting labeled table T_l has a Class attribute containing the labels.

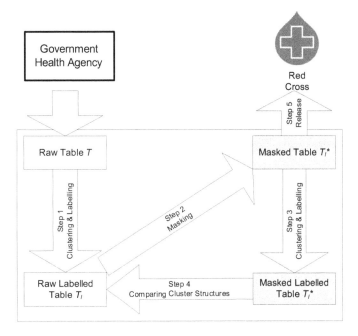

FIGURE 13.8: The Framework for Privacy-Aware Cluster Analysis

2. Mask the labeled table T_l. Employ an anonymization algorithm for classification analysis, such as TDR, to mask T_l. The masked T_l^* satisfies
the given k-anonymity requirement.

3. Clustering on the masked T_l^*. Remove the labels from the masked T_l^*
and then apply a clustering algorithm to the masked T_l^*, where the
number of clusters is the same as in Step 1. By default, the clustering
algorithm in this step is the same as the clustering algorithm in Step 1,
but can be replaced with any other choice requested by the Red Cross
BTS.

4. Evaluate the masked T_l^*. Compute the similarity between the cluster
structure found in Step 3 and the raw cluster structure found in Step
1. The similarity measures the loss of cluster quality due to masking.
If the evaluation is unsatisfactory, the Government Health Agency may
repeat Steps 1–4 with different specification of taxonomy trees, choice
of clustering algorithms, masking operations, number of clusters, and
anonymity thresholds if possible. We further explain this step in Section 13.5.3.

5. Release the masked T_l^*. If the evaluation in Step 4 is satisfactory, the
Government Health Agency can release the masked T_l^* together with
some optional supplementary information: all taxonomy trees (including

those generated at runtime for continuous attributes), the solution set, the similarity score computed in Step 4, and the class labels generated in Step 1.

13.5.3 Evaluation

Step 4 compares the raw cluster structure found in Step 1, denoted by $\mathcal{C}$, with the cluster structure found in the masked data in Step 3, denoted by $\mathcal{C}_g$. Both $\mathcal{C}$ and $\mathcal{C}_g$ are extracted from the same set of records, so we can evaluate their similarity by comparing their record groupings. We present two evaluation methods: *F-measure* [31] and *match point* [11].

13.5.3.1 F-measure

F-measure [31] is a well-known evaluation method for cluster analysis with known cluster labels. The idea is to treat each cluster in $\mathcal{C}$ as the relevant set of records for a query, and treat each cluster in $\mathcal{C}_g$ as the result of a query. The clusters in $\mathcal{C}$ are called "natural clusters," and those in $\mathcal{C}_g$ are called "query clusters."

For a natural cluster C_i in $\mathcal{C}$ and a query cluster K_j in $\mathcal{C}_g$, let $|C_i|$ and $|K_j|$ denote the number of records in C_i and K_j respectively, let n_{ij} denote the number of records contained in both C_i and K_j, let $|T|$ denote the total number of records in T^*. The *F-measure* for C_i and K_j is calculated as follows:

$$F(C_i, K_j) = \frac{2 * Recall(C_i, K_j) * Precision(C_i, K_j)}{Recall(C_i, K_j) + Precision(C_i, K_j)} \qquad (13.1)$$

where $F(C_i, K_j)$ measures the quality of query cluster K_j in describing the natural cluster C_i, by the harmonic mean of *Recall* and *Precision*. The *recall* for C_i and K_j

$$Recall(C_i, K_j) = \frac{n_{ij}}{|C_i|} \qquad (13.2)$$

read as the fraction of relevant records retrieved by the query. The *precision* for C_i and K_j

$$Precision(C_i, K_j) - \frac{n_{ij}}{|K_j|} \qquad (13.3)$$

read as the fraction of relevant records among the records retrieved by the query.

The success of preserving a natural cluster C_i is measured by the best matched cluster K_j for C_i, i.e., K_j maximizes $F(C_i, K_j)$. We measure the quality of $\mathcal{C}_g$ using the weighted sum of such maximum F-measures for all natural clusters. This measure is called the *overall F-measure* of $\mathcal{C}_g$, denoted

$F(\mathcal{C}_g)$:

$$F(\mathcal{C}_g) = \sum_{C_i \in \mathcal{C}} \frac{|C_i|}{|T|} max_{K_j \in \mathcal{C}_g}\{F(C_i, K_j)\} \qquad (13.4)$$

Note that $F(\mathcal{C}_g)$ is in the range [0,1]. A larger value indicates a higher similarity between the two cluster structures generated from the raw data and the masked data, i.e., better preserved cluster quality.

13.5.3.2 Match Point

F-measure is an efficient evaluation method, but it considers *only* the best query cluster K_j for each natural cluster C_i; therefore, it does not capture the quality of other query clusters and may not provide a full picture of the similarity between two cluster structures. Thus, we present an alternative evaluation method, called match point, to directly measure the preserved cluster structure.

Intuitively, two cluster structures $\mathcal{C}$ and $\mathcal{C}_g$ are similar if two objects that belong to the same cluster in $\mathcal{C}$ remain in the same cluster in $\mathcal{C}_g$, and if two objects that belong to different clusters in $\mathcal{C}$ remain in different clusters in $\mathcal{C}_g$. To reflect the intuition, we build two square matrices $Matrix(\mathcal{C})$ and $Matrix(\mathcal{C}_g)$ to represent the grouping of records in cluster structures $\mathcal{C}$ and $\mathcal{C}_g$, respectively. The square matrices are $|T|$-by-$|T|$, where $|T|$ is the total number of records in table T. The $(i, j)^{th}$ element in $Matrix(\mathcal{C})$ (or $Matrix(\mathcal{C}_g)$) has value 1 if the ith record and the jth record in the raw table T (or the masked table T^*) are in the same cluster; 0 otherwise. Then, we define *match point* to be the percentage of matched values between $Matrix(\mathcal{C})$ and $Matrix(\mathcal{C}_g)$:

$$Match\ Point(Matrix(\mathcal{C}), Matrix(\mathcal{C}_g)) = \frac{\sum_{1 \le i,j \le |T|} M_{ij}}{|T|^2}, \qquad (13.5)$$

where M_{ij} is 1 if the $(i, j)^{th}$ element in $Matrix(\mathcal{C})$ and $Matrix(\mathcal{C}_g)$ have the same value; 0 otherwise. Note that match point is in the range of [0,1]. A larger value indicates a higher similarity between the two cluster structures generated from the raw data and the masked data, i.e., better preserved cluster quality.

13.6 Conclusions and Extensions

This chapter presents the major privacy issues when sharing sensitive information in the context of healthcare applications and services. The strong need to protect individual privacy for data mining activities should be encountered by different healthcare stakeholders (e.g., the Hong Kong Red Cross Blood

Transfusion Services) on arbitrary kinds of client-related datasets, in our case of discussion Health Level 7 (HL7)-compliant ones. In general, this is done by extracting valuable structures and patterns to perform such an activity, e.g., classification analysis over given medical datasets. We describe some well-known methods suitable to secure person-specific data and use an iterative method called Top-Down Refinement (TDR) on how the medical datasets can be published in a way in which one's privacy is protected.

An approach in the area of privacy-aware information processing which comes along with the TDR method is called k-anonymity which gives a measure of privacy protection. This chapter deals with the problem of reaching k-anonymized data for classification analysis; additionally it describes a framework for solving the problem of cluster analysis on the records of the datasets. Future work will include further improvements of the discussed TDR method to cover other privacy models, like ℓ-diversity and t-closeness, discussed in the literature review. Ongoing effort will also be put to design methods to directly apply privacy-protection algorithms securing the data represented in healthcare documents in the illustrative case of the Hong Kong BTS which is compliant with HL7 version 3. During the past cooperation with the institution of the Hong Kong Red Cross BTS we were able to verify the applicability of our approach and future efforts will be put towards the full adoption of the needs of privacy-preservation in such a real-world scenario.

References

[1] C. C. Aggarwal. On k-anonymity and the curse of dimensionality. In *Proc. of VLDB*, 2005.

[2] R. Agrawal and R. Srikant. Privacy preserving data mining. In *Proc. of ACM SIGMOD*, pages 439–450, Dallas, Texas, May 2000.

[3] C. C. Aggarwal and P. S. Yu. *Privacy-Preserving Data Mining: Models and Algorithms*. Springer, March 2008.

[4] R. J. Bayardo and R. Agrawal. Data privacy through optimal k-anonymization. In *Proc. of the 21st IEEE International Conference on Data Engineering (ICDE)*, pages 217–228, Tokyo, Japan, 2005.

[5] L. Burnett, K. Barlow-Stewart, A. Pros, and H. Aizenberg. The gene trustee: A universal identification system that ensures privacy and confidentiality for human genetic databases. *Journal of Law and Medicine*, 10:506–513, 2003.

[6] T. Dalenius. Towards a methodology for statistical disclosure control. *Statistik Tidskrift*, 15:429–444, 1977.

[7] W. Du, Z. Teng, and Z. Zhu. Privacy-maxent: integrating background knowledge in privacy quantification. In *Proc. of the 2008 ACM SIGMOD International Conference on Management of Data*, pages 459–472. ACM, 2008.

[8] C. Dwork. Differential privacy. In *33rd International Colloquium on Automata, Languages and Programming (ICALP)*, pages 1–12, Venice, Italy, 2006.

[9] B. C. M. Fung, K. Wang, R. Chen, and P. S. Yu. Privacy-preserving data publishing: A survey on recent developments. *ACM Computing Surveys*, 42(4), December 2010.

[10] B. C. M. Fung, K. Wang, L. Wang, and M. Debbabi. A framework for privacy-preserving cluster analysis. In *Proc. of the 2008 IEEE International Conference on Intelligence and Security Informatics (ISI)*, pages 46–51, Taipei, Taiwan, 2008.

[11] B. C. M. Fung, K. Wang, L. Wang, and P. C. K. Hung. Privacy-preserving data publishing for cluster analysis. *Data & Knowledge Engineering (DKE)*, 68(6):552–575, June 2009.

[12] B. C. M. Fung, K. Wang, and P. S. Yu. Top-down specialization for information and privacy preservation. In *Proc. of the 21st IEEE International Conference on Data Engineering (ICDE)*, pages 205–216, Tokyo, Japan, 2005.

[13] B. C. M. Fung, K. Wang, and P. S. Yu. Anonymizing classification data for privacy preservation. *IEEE Transactions on Knowledge and Data Engineering (TKDE)*, 19:711–725, 2007.

[14] A. Hundepool and L. Willenborg. μ- and τ-argus: Software for statistical disclosure control. In *Proc. of the 3rd International Seminar on Statistical Confidentiality*, Bled, Slovenia, 1996.

[15] V. S. Iyengar. Transforming data to satisfy privacy constraints. In *8th ACM SIGKDD*, pages 279–288, Edmonton, AB, Canada, 2002.

[16] K. LeFevre, D. J. Dewitt, and R. Ramakrishnan. Incognito: Efficient full-domain k-anonymity. In *Proc. of the ACM SIGMOD*, pages 49–60, Baltimore, ML, USA, 2005.

[17] K. LeFevre, D. J. Dewitt, and R. Ramakrishnan. Workload-aware anonymization. In *Proc. of the 12th ACM SIGKDD*, Philadelphia, PA, USA, 2006.

[18] Tiancheng Li and Ninghui Li. Injector: Mining background knowledge for data anonymization. In *Proc. of the 2008 IEEE 24th International*

Conference on Data Engineering (ICDE), pages 446–455. IEEE Computer Society, 2008.

[19] N. Li, T. Li, and S. Venkatasubramanian. *t*-closeness: Privacy beyond *k*-anonymity and ℓ-diversity. In *Proc. of the 21st IEEE International Conference on Data Engineering (ICDE)*, Istanbul, Turkey, 2007.

[20] J. Li, Y. Tao, and X. Xiao. Preservation of proximity privacy in publishing numerical sensitive data. In *Proc. of the ACM Conference on Management of Data (SIGMOD)*, pages 437–486, Vancouver, Canada, June 2008.

[21] N. Mohammed, B. C. M. Fung, P. C. K. Hung, and C. K. Lee. Anonymizing healthcare data: A case study on the blood transfusion service. In *Proc. of the 15th ACM SIGKDD International Conference on Knowledge Discovery and Data Mining (SIGKDD)*, pages 1285–1294, Paris, France, June 2009. ACM Press.

[22] A. Machanavajjhala, J. Gehrke, D. Kifer, and M. Venkitasubramaniam. ℓ-diversity: Privacy beyond *k*-anonymity. In *Proc. of the 22nd IEEE International Conference on Data Engineering (ICDE)*, Atlanta, GA, USA, 2006.

[23] A. Machanavajjhala, D. Kifer, J. Gehrke, and M. Venkitasubramaniam. ℓ-diversity: Privacy beyond *k*-anonymity. *ACM TKDD*, 1, 2007.

[24] M. E. Nergiz and C. Clifton. Thoughts on *k*-anonymization. *Data and Knowledge Engineering*, 63:622–645, 2007.

[25] D. J. Newman, S. Hettich, C. L. Blake, and C. J. Merz. UCI repository of machine learning databases, 1998.

[26] J. R. Quinlan. *C4.5: Programs for Machine Learning*. Morgan Kaufmann, 1993.

[27] P. Samarati. Protecting respondents' identities in microdata release. *IEEE Transactions on Knowledge and Data Engineering (TKDE)*, 13(6):1010–1027, 2001.

[28] P. Samarati and L. Sweeney. Generalizing data to provide anonymity when disclosing information. In *Proc. of the 17th ACM SIGACT-SIGMOD-SIGART PODS*, page 188, Seattle, WA, USA, 1998.

[29] P. Samarati and L. Sweeney. Protecting privacy when disclosing information: *k*-anonymity and its enforcement through generalization and suppression. *Technical Report*, SRI International, 1998.

[30] L. Sweeney. *k*-anonymity: a model for protecting privacy. *International Journal on Uncertainty, Fuzziness and Knowledge-Based Systems*, 10(5):557–570, 2002.

[31] C. J. van Rijsbergen. *Information Retrieval, 2nd edition*. London, Butterworths, 1979.

[32] K. Wang, B. C. M. Fung, and P. S. Yu. Template-based privacy preservation in classification problems. In *Proc. of the 5th IEEE International Conference on Data Mining (ICDM)*, pages 466–473, 2005.

[33] K. Wang, B. C. M. Fung, and P. S. Yu. Handicapping attacker's confidence: An alternative to k-anonymization. *Knowledge and Information Systems (KAIS)*, 11(3):345–368, 2007.

[34] T. Wang, S. Meng, B. Bamba, L. Liu, and C. Pu. A general proximity privacy principle. In *Proc. of the 2009 IEEE International Conference on Data Engineering (ICDE)*, pages 1279–1282, Washington, DC, USA, 2009.

[35] Q. Zhang, N. Koudas, D. Srivastava, and T. Yu. Aggregate query answering on anonymized tables. In *Proc. of the 23rd IEEE International Conference on Data Engineering (ICDE)*, April 2007.

Part VI

Web Usage Data

Chapter 14

Issues with Privacy Preservation in Query Log Mining

Ricardo Baeza-Yates

Yahoo! Labs, Spain

Rosie Jones

Yahoo! Labs, USA

Barbara Poblete

Yahoo! Labs, Chile

Myra Spiliopoulou

University of Magdeburg, Germany

14.1 Introduction

The Web has profoundly changed the way we live and work in a very short period of time. One of the main drivers for that change is *trust*. Trust encompasses trusting information found in the Web, trusting e-commerce applications, trusting that personal data will not be shared, etc. The main trust discussed in this chapter, is that of trusting that search engines keep the queries issued by a person as private information.

In each of the cases mentioned above, guarding and enhancing that trust should be one of the main goals of Web service providers. In the case of search engine query logs, this is crucial for their business success. In particular, we show that even a sequence of queries can disclose private information, and that it is important to be aware of what type and how much information we are potentially exposing when using a search engine.

Query log mining is of great interest to industrial and academic researchers because of its tremendous capability to provide useful information. Applications of query log mining range from improving the performance, quality and functionality of search engines [7, 35, 30], to extracting knowledge from *the wisdom of the crowds* of users searching the Web. The world knowledge that can be derived from query logs comprehends knowledge about language, including semantic relationships [17, 8], spelling [16] and even sociology [31].

In August of 2006, the online services provider America Online (AOL) made a public release of 6 months of anonymized Web search logs [4]. The intention was to aid the academic research community, but the outcome was a public relations nightmare. One of the people whose queries were in the log was quickly identified by journalists from *The New York Times* [11]. This led to a great increase in public awareness of the potential privacy risks involved in Web search.

This confidentiality issue is not only important for people, but can also become a problem for businesses. For example, all of the queries issued from a company, may not disclose any private information for an individual, but may disclose information that is considered confidential by a company. As we will discuss later, this type of business privacy breach may not even be as explicit as it is in our example.

An important technique used for analysis of privacy preservation is k-anonymity [32, 34, 33, 36], which we describe in Section 14.3. In this work, we walk-through the possible applications of k-anonymity to independent query log issues, and discuss the existing problems for the success of this technique on real query logs.

This chapter is organized as follows. In Section 14.2 we define the notion of privacy in our context, we characterize query logs and the risks behind sharing them. In Section 14.3 we discuss the problem of query log privacy preservation from a k-anonymity perspective. Section 14.4 gives an overview of the main and newer privacy-enhancing techniques for query log privacy preservation. An excellent survey of query log privacy techniques from a policy perspective is provided by Cooper in [15]. We complement this paper by analyzing the state of the art with the k-Anonymity framework, and update it by covering the most recent work in the area. We close the chapter by discussing the main issues still unsolved with privacy preservation for query logs.

14.2   Private Information in Query Logs: Setting the Scene

In this section we define our "privacy protection" problem for query log analysis. The *context* of our study is the publication of a search engine access log for future analysis by third parties. This scenario is inspired by the precedence of the case of the AOL dataset which was made publicly available after an anonymization process that turned out to be insufficient. We first elaborate on the non-trivial question about which information should be considered private in this context. Second we characterize query logs and discuss the risks of sharing one. We then identify the information sources that can be combined with the published query log for the disclosure of private or confidential information.

14.2.1 Which Information Is Private?

There has been a debate about which information should be considered private, even before the issue of privacy in query logs arose. Experience has shown that some Web users are willing to share personal information that other users would consider private. For our purposes, it is appropriate to make explicit *who* accesses and analyzes the information in the query log, since a person may be willing to make their personal information available to the query log owner but not to another institution.

Under the title "Query log retention rationales," Cooper [15] identifies reasons why query logs are or should be retained. We distinguish categories where the query log is exploited by its owner from categories where the log is made available to another party. As Cooper points out, *improvement of ranking algorithms, improvement of language-based features, query refinement and personalization, combating fraud and abuse* are good reasons for retaining and analyzing a query log. These improvements refer to the quality of the services offered by the search engine, hence the analysis of the query log is done internally and the data is not shared. This situation is quite different from the other two retention rationales mentioned in the same article: *sharing data for academic research* and *sharing data for marketing and other commercial purposes*. As the names imply, the query log data is *shared* with a third party. This third party may be a company or other for-profit organization that is interested in gaining insight into interests, preferences and behavior patterns of users. It may also be an academic institution that is interested in understanding the behavior of individuals and in extracting implicit human knowledge for use in tasks like natural language processing, document translation, extraction of semantics from non-textual sources, etc. It can be argued that the willingness of users to make their data available depends on the purpose of the analysis *and* on the entity who analyzes the data.

From the privacy perspective it is important to differentiate the entity that *owns* the data from the entity that *obtains access* to the data. Therefore we define the following criteria to help us understand which data is private:

1. The owner of a data item may grant *access privileges* of this item to another entity. We consider this second entity as the *recipient* of the privilege.

2. Only the owner can grant access privileges to its data items. Therefore, access privileges are not transferable, unless the owner gives up explicitly its ownership in favor of the recipient.

3. We consider a data item as public if and only if the owner has explicitly given access privileges to everyone.

4. Data that is not public is private.

5. We consider privacy to be a *non-composable* property, i.e., a composite object consisting of public data items is private, unless made public by its owner.

6. Access privileges to data may be granted *implicitly* (given that it is allowed by national and international regulations).

We apply this criteria only in the context of the Web. Therefore, information that has been published on-line is considered public, since it can be accessed by anyone. On the other hand, a query submitted to a search engine is considered private, unless its owner (i.e., the user that generated it) decides to make it public. The non-decomposability property ensures that the query is private, even if it is made of public elements, such as the user ID, query string and clicked URLs.

The observation that *all* of the information which is not public is private is taken from the work on business confidentiality of Poblete et al. [28]. Poblete et al. define as *confidential all* of the information about a company which (a) is not published data and (b) cannot be concluded trivially by combining publicly available information. In a similar way, they say that data or information about a company becomes *public* when (i) it is published by the institution itself or (ii) it is published by some entity that is legally authorized (or obliged) to do so. This reasoning can be indistinctly applied to entities such as people (Web users) or businesses (Web sites).

The last entry of our privacy criteria deals with an issue that draws much debate: many national regulations state that a user must give their permission to access and use their data explicitly. In our work, we have decided to assume that if implicit granting of access privileges is not prohibited, then it is allowed. For example, in the case of search engines we assume that when submitting a query the user implicitly grants access privileges to their searching data to the search engine. This would allow the user to conduct their queries and obtain an improved service through query log analysis. Nevertheless, since the access privileges are not transferable, then *sharing query logs without proper anonymization* implies disclosing private data.

The criteria we have just defined concerns data owned by *one* entity. However, there is data that is owned by many entities; this includes public knowledge. Hence, we extend this criteria by stating that *a data item owned by more than k distinct and independent entities is public*. This definition contains k as a variable, allowing for k-anonymity methods to protect private data during data sharing.

14.2.2   Characteristics of a Query Log

Query logs store information sequentially and preserve the time order of the requests. This quality enables data mining algorithms to establish user sessions and follow the traces left by users who query and click on results. The applications of such techniques include recommendations on returned items and personalized ordering of the search results. For our work, we assume that query log records have at least the following fields: {*UserID, Query, ClickTime, ClickURL*} where *UserID* is the user ID and *Query* is the query string. If the user clicked on a result, this is recorded in the next two fields: *ClickTime* is the time in which the user clicked on a returned URL *ClickURL*.

Query logs grow at a fast pace. Growth implies not only additional recordings, but also new objects being recorded: new URLs appear in the results of a query that has been launched also in the past, new query terms emerge, some of them being new words (e.g., SARS*) or recently coined word combinations (e.g., "dwarf planet," a term much younger than the well-known "dwarf star"). Therefore, query log analysis requires efficient privacy-protection algorithms that can deal with a huge amount of concept drifting data.

Query log growth and evolution imply that query log analysis is not an once-in-a-lifetime event. Rather, one expects a regular analysis that includes (a) model discovery, (b) model adaptation to changes and (c) model monitoring to identify, quantify and interpret changes. Nonetheless, for the purpose of this study we concentrate on a single query log analysis event: this implies that our privacy-preservation approach, which is based on information hiding, is irreversible: once data is hidden it cannot become accessible later on. Intuitively, revealing information that has once been hidden would be counterproductive, because such information would be bound to draw an attacker's attention.

Another interesting characteristic of query logs concerns their statistical properties: the frequency distribution of queries, query terms and clicked URLs show a small number of very frequently recorded objects (queries, terms, URLs) followed by a vast number of objects that are recorded very rarely. Power laws with a heavy tail have been observed, presented in a similar way in different query logs (except of parameter values) [6]. For our analysis, skewed distributions are of interest because the information that is potentially private (and should be hidden) is more likely to be found in the heavy tail.

---

*SARS is a virus which appeared as an epidemic in late 2002 and early 2003 and was first named then.

14.2.3   Sharing a Query Log

There are two ways in which query log data can be shared with a third party. One possibility is that the search engine performs data analysis on behalf of a third party and provides only the results of this analysis. However, Atzori et al. [5] have shown that publishing association rules derived from data, even those with high support, might lead to anonymity leaks from single individuals. Thus even sharing derived data can have the potential to cause privacy leaks. Do not consider this case further. Another possibility is to share primary data directly. This can be implemented by (a) providing the query log to the third party, (b) publishing the query log for access and analysis by arbitrary, *a priori* unknown third parties or (c) providing an interface through which arbitrary third parties can extract data from the query log. The delivery of the query log to a specific recipient is a special case of (b) publishing the log for unknown recipients. On the other hand, (c) is a known approach for providing limited access to on-line information sources and is practiced for querying census or health data [18]. Since census data is privacy-sensitive, access to it is usually governed by restrictive protocols that e.g., reject queries that return less than k results. Algorithms that guarantee k-anonymity in querying are employed for this kind of data retrieval.

Query interfaces that guarantee k-anonymity might be used to extract data from a query log. However, this method is not adequate by itself. As Bar-Yossef and Hurevich [9] show, there are ways of mining aggregate query logs via the applications interfaces made available by the search engines themselves. They have estimated query frequencies, as well as the number of impressions on a website [10] using publicly available data sources, such as query suggestion tools and answer pages in search engines. These algorithms mean that we can infer information from a query log that has not even been released. Hence, we believe that data hiding before providing access to a query log is a necessary precaution.

14.2.4   The Risk of External Sources

As mentioned before, another key issue in query log privacy protection is the large amount of background knowledge and external databases that can be involved in the disclosure of anonymized data. This ranges from *public* data sources to *private* data sources:

- **public data sources** include previously published query logs, such as the AOL log. It also includes publicly available data, such as census or health data, white pages, and basically any data that has been previously published with or without anonymization. We also include in this category, data that can be obtained from the output of on-line data mining applications, such as search engine advertising keyword suggestion tools or search engine results themselves. In Section 14.4 we will also discuss recent work demonstrating how additional information can be derived from public data sources.

- **private data sources** include privately owned data and personal or corporate background knowledge about users and businesses. Also, we include private website logs in this category, which can be later matched to anonymized logs (see [28]).

14.3   *k*-Anonymity in Query Log Privacy Protection

In this section we analyze the query log privacy preservation problem from a *k*-anonymity perspective. We discuss the issues that make effective query log anonymization particularly difficult.

In seminal work by Samarati and Sweeney [32, 34, 33, 36] a formal protection model for anonymizing data releases, named *k*-anonymity is presented. This model seeks to guarantee that the individuals who are the subjects of released data cannot be re-identified by linking or matching the data to other data or by studying unique characteristics in the released information, all of this while retaining technical usefulness of the data. The main principle of this approach is that the released data provides *k*-anonymity protection if the information of each person cannot be distinguished from at least $k - 1$ individuals also included in the release. Nevertheless, Samarati and Sweeney acknowledge that the precise elimination of all the possible inferences with respect to the identifiers of the people portrayed in the data is *impossible* to secure. This would require the data holder to know beforehand all of the possible attacks that the released data could be subject to. Therefore *k*-anonymity protection attempts to protect only against known attacks.

Following Samarati and Sweeney's work, we look mostly into known issues in query log privacy protection. However, Kumar et. al. [25] have already said that there are two concerns with the application of *k*-anonymity to query logs: 1) That the data is not naturally structured (not like relational databases), so it is unclear how to extend *k*-anonymity. For example, it is not practical to make the entire session history of a user identical to that of $k - 1$ other users. In fact, they maintain that it is not clear which parts of a query session should even be treated as values in a relation. And 2) that even revealing that somebody in a set of one hundred users is querying about sensitive topics is already revealing too much information.

In Section 14.4 we show how most of the existing query log anonymization schemes end up targeting only a small subset of the privacy problem, which then can be accommodated to a *k*-anonymity protection solution. Nevertheless, these solutions stop being effective once the problem is combined with other possible attacks on the query log. Therefore we come back to the original issues stated by Kumar et. al.

First, we start by defining the *entities* that should be protected in a query log. At first sight the only apparent entity is the *user* that interacts with the search engine. It would be logical to assume that no user wants their *queries* or *visited URLs* to be associated with their identity in a data release. Due to the sensitive nature that these fields could have. In most query logs the user identity is not explicitly in the data, rather than it is represented by the search engine user-id (if there is one). On the other hand, a user can be identified by one or more queries that they issue, in particular if these queries, or their combination, is rather unique and discloses information about the user. For example, *vanity queries* as described by Jones et al. [21], which include the name of the person behind them. We will look into this issue further ahead.

Secondly, previous work by Poblete et. al. [29] presents businesses or websites, as an entity that should also be protected in query logs, mostly due to the business related confidential information that can be disclosed from the URLs visited by users. Therefore, we include also the entity *website* along with the entity *users* as properties in the query log that should be protected against disclosure. These entities are explicitly reflected in the fields *ClickURL* and *UserID* of the query log.

Therefore, according to the criteria for private data discussed in Section 14.2 there are two types of private data contained in query logs: *queries associated with a particular user* and *traffic bound to a particular website*. This is, data that the log owner has access to, but not ownership upon.

Next, we define the set of *attributes* that are contained within a query log. In Samarati and Sweeney's work [32, 34, 33, 36], they generally refer to data that is conceptually organized as a table of records and columns (i.e., attributes). Each row is referred to as a *tuple*, and tuples do not have an order within their containing table. In our query log analogy, we will consider as a tuple a single request (or record) to the search engine. Notice that each user generally has more than one tuple associated with them (i.e., a user session) and that the order of these tuples is of importance and cannot be omitted. So, in a sense, query log tuples have a temporal dimension, which the standard k-anonymity framework does not admit. Shuffling of query log records would destroy valuable session information, which is commonly used in query log data mining analysis. In particular, a specific user may click on zero or more URLs for a same query, and a user may issue one or more queries.

Hence, we can refer to two types of query log attributes:

1. **Explicit attributes:** These attributes that appear as a field in the query log record, such as, UserID, Query, ClickTime, ClickURL.

2. **Implicit attributes:** These attributes refer to distinguishing statistical properties of explicit attributes in the query log. Such as, query frequency, query term frequency, coocurrence of query terms frequency,

URL click frequency. They are important, because they can uniquely identify or approximate the explicit attribute that they are mapped to. Therefore, this must be considered for the purpose of anonymizing explicit attributes.

The last important concept for applying k-anonymity is that of *quasi-identifiers* [32, 34, 33, 36]. These are attributes that without including explicit identifiers, can be combined to uniquely identify any of the entities being protected, or be linked to external data. In the case of query log anonymization we have two explicit identifiers that should be anonymized, the UserID and the ClickURL. In the case of the UserID we find that a quasi-identifier is the Query, which on its own or in combination with other queries issued by the user, can identify uniquely the user. For example, this is the case of the previously mentioned *vanity queries*, such as full names, visa card numbers, social security numbers, or of combinations of queries that include zip code and an uncommon last name.

In the case of the ClickURL, we also find that the Query is a quasi-identifier, because it can be linked to the live search engine results to discover the ClickURL, or because it can be linked using its query-clicked document distribution to find the ClickURL as shown in [28].

At this point the logical next step is to find a k-anonymity solution to hide the explicit identifiers UserID, ClickURL and the quasi-identifier Query. But, there are several difficulties for doing this. First, the explicit identifiers UserID and ClickURL cannot be removed from the released data without destroying the utility of the query log. These two attributes need to be anonymized in a fashion which preserves their properties while protecting their values. This should be done while keeping in mind that the *frequencies* of each the anonymized versions of ClickURL, Query and (ClickURL, Query) pairs, can also be quasi-identifiers for the anonymized data. Second, unique combinations of queries from a particular user pose a possible privacy breach, as well as particular queries themselves. Also, the temporal property of query log records is fundamental for data mining purposes, so it cannot be suppressed from the release. So, even though we have presented a very basic mapping of k-anonymity properties to a simplified view of query log privacy, we come across many issues that increase the complexity of any general k-anonymity solution.

The most important observation is that *most* of the attributes in the query log require anonymization, and that each independently can be satisfied by a k anonymity solution. The problem resides in that a query log requires that all of the anonymizations to its fields are applied in conjunction, and, most importantly, the overall anonymization must be applied while preserving the independent statistical properties of the query log. As we will see in the following section, this is what is currently being addressed in recent research. In general, anonymization is attempted for one or two fields in the query log, having a k-anonymity solution. But later when the problem is expanded to the complete log it becomes impossible to find an overall solution, due to the increased complexity of the data relations.

One of the challenges of privacy protection in the k-Anonymity framework is that we must consider not only the dataset itself, but also external resources that can be joined to it, for example voter registration information [32, 34, 33, 36]. The increasing use of social network sites means that increasing amounts of information about users are publicly available, increasing their identifiability in private datasets [42].

14.4   Anonymization Techniques for Query Logs

The k-anonymity approach provides us with three tools for analyzing and implementing approaches to privacy in query logs. First, by *measuring* the ability to identify users — finding the size of the set k containing the user, we can understand how much the dataset identifies users. Second, by *aggregating* and *generalizing* the records in the dataset to increase the size of k, we can seek to reduce the identifiability of individuals. Third, by *suppressing* sensitive information we can reduce the impact of what is learned about a user. In this section we describe work in query log privacy analysis in terms of these three tasks and include techniques based on noise aggregation: this topic lies outside the k-anonymity framework but may offer the best prospects for anonymization of query logs.

14.4.1   Measurement

Reporters from *The New York* Times were able to identify one of AOL's users by investigating clues in a query log after the log was released [11]. This was an existence proof that the query log could provide enough information that the user was in a set of small enough size k that reporters could head to a small town and follow leads to track the user down.

Jones et al. quantify the number of users trackable to sets of size of k in a query log [20], by looking at how much information is revealed in query logs when no attempt is made to provide privacy protection. They show that automatic classifiers which can approximately guess a user's age, location and gender based on their query logs can be used to map the user to sets of relatively small size k. They show that simple attempts at scrubbing identifying information by removing names and addresses do not greatly reduce the identifiability of users. However, reducing the time-span over which queries are linked by identifiers does provide some protection.

As already mentioned, Kumar et al. found that queries about sensitive topics can be identity-disclosing even if k is as big as one hundred [25]. Jones et al. further show that *combinations of queries* can uniquely identify a user

Aggregation Type	Contains fields				
	user ID	query	timestamp	URL	clicks
No aggregation	user ID	query	timestamp	URL	whether-clicked
Partial bundling	grouped userID	query	timestamp	URL	whether-clicked
Complete bundling	-	query	timestamp	URL	whether-clicked
Query frequency	-	query	-	-	-
Query graph	-	query session pairs	-	-	-
Click graph	-	query	-	URL	clicked-frequency
Query click graph	-	query session pairs	-	URL	clicked-frequency

Table 14.1: Summary of kinds of Aggregation on Query Log Data.

[21]: even a few of a user's queries suffice for identity disclosure if the log connects them to each other with some system identifier.

14.4.2 Aggregation and Generalization

In conventional k-anonymity approaches, *aggregation* implies grouping records and reporting the number of individuals within a group that have some characteristics in common. Xiong and Agichtein [40] give an overview of some of the aggregations that can be performed on query logs; they are summarized on Table 14.1.

One aggregation proposed by a major commercial search engine involves IP masking: queries from multiple users are placed in a single bucket by deleting bits from their IP addresses and using the remaining bits for grouping. However, Jones et al. show that this aggregation does not prevent the disclosure of very frequent users: user search frequency follows a power-law distribution, with few users making a lot of searches and many others searching infrequently, so that it is still possible to identify a dominant user within the group [21].

An aggregation technique combined with *data suppression* has been proposed by Poblete et al. [28]: it involves building a graph of associations between the entities in the logs and removing the individual entities that led to those associations. The method has been used by Boldi et al. upon the associations between users and queries in a query log [12], while Poblete et al. have performed graph pruning upon a combination of query log data and web clickstream data [27].

Korolova et al [24] propose combining aggregation with suppression and the addition of noise: we give more detail on this in Section 14.4.4.

14.4.3 Suppression

Suppression in the conventional k-anonymity context involves eliminating sensitive values so that groups of larger size k can be built. In the case of query logs, the information to be suppressed may be personally-identifying or otherwise sensitive queries. Poblete et al. consider also the suppression potentially privacy disclosing query terms from the graph [28].

Xiong and Agichtein [40] give an overview of the kinds of identifying information that can be found in queries and relate them to the HIPAA standard: such personally-identifying information pieces include geographic subdivisions smaller than a state, dates directly related to the individual, phone numbers, email addresses, and names. However, Jones et al. show that simply scrubbing out such data is not adequate, because further personally-identifying information can be derived [20]; for example, age and gender may be derived from the topics searched for. Xiong and Agichtein [40] also stress that the sensitive information in query logs could include *financial information*, *health information*, and even *political viewpoints*. Such types of information may be very difficult to suppress, since there are many different ways of querying and referring to them.

Hence, simply suppressing queries or terms known to be sensitive or personally-identifying is not adequate. The graph-based techniques in [28, 12, 27] suppress information on the basis of statistics and graph properties.

14.4.4 Adding Noise to Query Log Data

The idea of privacy preservation by adding noise while preserving some statistical properties has been long exploited in statistics [39] and more recently in data mining literature [22]. Methods of this category add noise to the counts or reported data values. Adding noise to a query log could have different implementations, depending on where it takes place and at what level of aggregation.

The TrackMeNot system [19] follows the approach of adding noise to the individual user's query stream. The system, installed as a client-side web browser plug-in, issues queries automatically, and clicks on results. This masks the true queries from the user, amid a sequence of queries which were not issued by that user. A strength of this approach identified by the authors is that it places control in the hands of the users themselves.

A weakness of TrackMeNot is the need to generate queries for users from the client-side. As such, the generated queries could be detectable either by being nonsensical, if automatically generated by combining words from a dictionary, or by being detectable as coming from TrackMeNot, if generated from a list.

A search engine provider can provide some degree of statistical anonymity by mixing queries from different users. This has the advantage of providing plausible deniability for the *sensitive* information, while also obfuscating identifiability of the *identifying* information.

If a user frequently queries for sensitive information, then adding noise by mixing queries may not be adequate. In important recent work, Korolova et al. [24] show that by limiting the number of queries considered per user and setting a lower bound for the query frequency by adding noise to a threshold selection function, the main part of the query-click distribution can be released with provable privacy properties. One variation would be to combine the two restrictions mentioned above and consider a lower bound for the query frequency from different users.

14.5   Conclusions and Future Work

None of the attempts towards privacy preservation that we have surveyed can guarantee protection against all possible adversarial attacks. In fact, because we can cross query logs with a growing number of external data sources, preserving privacy is at the end unsolvable.

Even in a restricted setting, the research results are mostly negative, in the sense that it is very hard to protect privacy without making the query log unusable. Even in the successful cases like adding noise to the query log, the most diverse part of the data, the long tail, cannot be disclosed.

Finally, one of the main purposes of this chapter is to create awareness of how important this problem is and how it affects the different parties involved, from individuals to businesses.

References

[1] Eytan Adar. User 4xxxxx9: Anonymizing query logs. In *Query Log Analysis: Social and Technological Challenges, Workshop in WWW '07*, 2007.

[2] C. C. Aggarwal, J. Pei, and B. Zhang. On privacy preservation against adversarial data mining. *Proceedings of the 12th ACM SIGKDD International Conference on Knowledge Discovery and Data Mining*, pages 510–516, 2006.

[3] AOL. AOL research website, no longer online. http://research.aol.com.

[4] Michael Arrington. AOL proudly releases massive amounts of private

data.   http://www.techcrunch.com/2006/08/06/aol-proudly-releases-
massive-amounts-of-user-search-data/, 2006.

[5] Maurizio Atzori, Francesco Bonchi, Fosca Giannotti, and Dino Pedreschi. Anonymity preserving pattern discovery. *VLDB J.*, 17(4):703–
727, 2008.

[6] R. Baeza-Yates. Query usage mining in search engines. In A. Scime,
editor, *Web Mining: Applications and Techniques*, pages 307–321. Idea
Group, 2004.

[7] R. Baeza-Yates. Applications of web query mining. In D. Losada and
J. Fernández-Luna, editors, *European Conference on Information Retrieval (ECIR'05)*, number 3408 in LNCS, pages 7–22, Santiago de Com-
postela, Spain, March 2005. Springer.

[8] R. Baeza-Yates and A. Tiberi. Extracting semantic relations from query
logs. In *Proc. of the 13th ACM SIGKDD International Conference on
Knowledge Discovery and Data Mining*, pages 76–85. ACM, 2007.

[9] Ziv Bar-Yossef and Maxim Gurevich. Mining search engine query logs
via suggestion sampling. In *VLDB 2008*, 2008.

[10] Ziv Bar-Yossef and Maxim Gurevich. Estimating the impression rank
of web pages. In *WWW 2009*, 2009.

[11] M. Barbaro and T. Zeller. A face is exposed for AOL searcher no.
4417749. *New York Times*, 2006.

[12] Paolo Boldi, Francesco Bonchi, Carlos Castillo, Debora Donato, Aristides Gionis, and Sebastiano Vigna. The query-flow graph: model and
applications. In *CIKM*, pages 609–618, 2008.

[13] S. Chawla, C. Dwork, F. McSherry, A. Smith, and H. Wee. Toward
privacy in public databases. *Theory of Cryptography Conference*, pages
363–385, 2005.

[14] C. Clifton, M. Kantarcioglu, and J.Vaidya. Defining privacy for data
mining. In *Proceedings of the National Science Foundation Workshop
on Next Generation Data Mining*, Baltimore, 2002.

[15] Alissa Cooper. A survey of query log privacy-enhancing techniques from
a policy perspective. *ACM Transactions on the Web (TWeb)*, 2(4), 2008.

[16] Silviu Cucerzan and Eric Brill. Spelling correction as an iterative process
that exploits the collective knowledge of Web users. In *EMNLP*, 2004.

[17] Hang Cui, Ji-Rong Wen, Jian-Yun Nie, and Wei-Ying Ma. Probabilistic
query expansion using query logs. In *WWW*, pages 325–332, 2002.

[18] Cynthia Dwork and Kobbi Nissim. Privacy-preserving datamining on
vertically partitioned databases. In *CRYPTO*, pages 528–544, 2004.

[19] D. Howe and H. Nissenbaum. Trackmenot: Resisting surveillance in web search. In Ian Kerr, Carole Lucock, and Valerie Steeves, editors, *On the Identity Trail: Privacy, Anonymity and Identity in a Networked Society*. Oxford: Oxford University Press, Forthcoming.

[20] Rosie Jones, Ravi Kumar, Bo Pang, and Andrew Tomkins. I know what you did last summer: query logs and user privacy. In *CIKM '07: Proceedings of the sixteenth ACM Conference on Information and Knowledge Management*, pages 909–914, New York, NY, USA, 2007. ACM.

[21] Rosie Jones, Ravi Kumar, Bo Pang, and Andrew Tomkins. Vanity fair: privacy in query log bundles. In *CIKM '08: Proceeding of the 17th ACM Conference on Information and Knowledge Management*, pages 853–862, New York, NY, USA, 2008. ACM.

[22] H. Kargupta, S. Datta, Q. Wang, and Krishnamoorthy Sivakumar. On the privacy preserving properties of random data perturbation techniques. In *Proceedings of Third IEEE International Conference on Data Mining (ICDM 2003)*, 2003.

[23] D. Kifer and J. Gehrke. Injecting utility into anonymized datasets. *Proceedings of the 2006 ACM SIGMOD international Conference on Management of Data*, pages 217–228, 2006.

[24] Aleksandra Korolova, Krishnaram Kenthapadi, Nina Mishra, and Alexandros Ntoulas. Releasing search queries and clicks privately. In *WWW 2009*, pages 171–180, 2009.

[25] Ravi Kumar, Jasmine Novak, Bo Pang, and Andrew Tomkins. On anonymizing query logs via token-based hashing. In *WWW '07: Proceedings of the 16th International Conference on World Wide Web*, pages 629–638, New York, NY, USA, 2007. ACM Press.

[26] Ercan M. Nergiz, Chris Clifton, and Erhan A. Nergiz. MultiRelational k-anonymity. In *Proc. of IEEE Int. Conf. on Data Engineering (ICDE'07)*, pages 1417–1421. IEEE, 2007.

[27] Barbara Poblete, Carlos Castillo, and Aristides Gionis. Dr. Searcher and Mr. Browser: a unified hyperlink-click graph. In *CIKM*, pages 1123–1132, 2008.

[28] Barbara Poblete, Myra Spiliopoulou, and Ricardo Baeza-Yates. Business privacy protection in query log mining. Technical report, Center for Web Research (CWR), 2008.

[29] Barbara Poblete, Myra Spiliopoulou, and Ricardo Baeza-Yates. Website privacy preservation for query log publishing. In *Proceedings of the First SIGKDD International Workshop on Privacy, Security, and Trust in KDD (PinKDD'07), Lecture Notes in Computer Science*, volume 4890. Springer, 2008.

[30] Filip Radlinski and Thorsten Joachims. Query chains: Learning to rank from implicit feedback. *CoRR*, abs/cs/0605035, 2006.

[31] Matthew Richardson. Learning about the world through long-term query logs. *TWEB*, 2(4), 2008.

[32] P. Samarati and L. Sweeney. Protecting privacy when disclosing information: k-anonymity and its enforcement through generalization and suppression. *Technical report*, Computer Science Laboratory, SRI International, 1998.

[33] Pierangela Samarati. Protecting respondents' identities in microdata release. *IEEE Trans. Knowl. Data Eng.*, 13(6):1010–1027, 2001.

[34] Pierangela Samarati and Latanya Sweeney. Generalizing data to provide anonymity when disclosing information (abstract). In *Proceedings of the Seventeenth ACM SIGACT-SIGMOD-SIGART Symposium on Principles of Database Systems, June 1-3, 1998, Seattle, Washington*, page 188. ACM Press, 1998.

[35] F. Silvestri. Mining query logs: Turning search usage data into knowledge. *Foundations and Trends in Information Retrieval*, To appear.

[36] Latanya Sweeney. K-anonymity: a model for protecting privacy. In *Int. J. Uncertain. Fuzziness Knowl.-Based Syst.*, pages 557–570, 2002.

[37] Richard G. Vedder, Michael T. Vanecek, C. Stephen Guynes, and James J. Cappel. CEO and CIO perspectives on competitive intelligence. *Commun. ACM*, 42(8):108–116, 1999.

[38] V. S. Verykios, E. Bertino, I. N. Fovino, L. P. Provenza, Y. Saygin, and Y. Theodoridis. State-of-the-art in privacy preserving data mining. *SIGMOD Record*, 33(1):50–57, 2004.

[39] S. L. Warner. Randomized response: a survey technique for eliminating evasive answer bias. *Journal of the American Statistical Association*, 1965.

[40] Li Xiong and Eugene Agichtein. Towards privacy preserving query log publishing and analysis. In *Query Log Analysis Workshop, in Conjunction with International Conference on World Wide Web (WWW)*, 2007.

[41] Alessandro Zanasi. Competitive intelligence through data mining public sources. *Competitive Intelligence Review*, 9(1):44–54, 1998.

[42] Elena Zheleva and Lise Getoor. To join or not to join: The illusion of privacy in social networks with mixed public and private user profiles. In *WWW 2009*, 2009.

Chapter 15

Preserving Privacy in Web Recommender Systems

Ranieri Baraglia

HPC Lab, ISTI-CNR, Pisa, Italy

Claudio Lucchese

HPC Lab, ISTI-CNR, Pisa, Italy

Salvatore Orlando

Department of Computer Science, Ca' Foscari University, Venice, Italy

Raffaele Perego

HPC Lab, ISTI-CNR, Pisa, Italy

Fabrizio Silvestri

HPC Lab, ISTI-CNR, Pisa, Italy

15.1 Introduction

The goal of Web recommendation and personalization techniques is to *"provide users with the information they want or need, without expecting from them to ask for it explicitly"*[19].

Web Mining has shown to be a viable technique to discover information "hidden" in Web-related data [11]. In particular, Web Usage Mining (WUM) is the process of extracting knowledge from Web user's access data (or clickstream) by exploiting Data Mining (DM) technologies [14]. It can be used for different purposes such as *recommendation, personalization, system improvement* and *site optimization*.

A typical way to exploit WUM techniques for the recommendation task is the extraction of a model from usage data that permits to group users in different clusters, according to their interests, and to adaptively provide them useful recommendations. Obviously, the learning of a model from past usage data, or simply the collection of such data, can introduce privacy breaches, by either disclosing personal information or allowing malicious queries capable of reconstructing the knowledge collected by the system.

In this chapter, we first survey the techniques that have appeared in the literature and aim to automatically generate suggestions and recommendations to users, by also discussing their privacy preserving features.

In the second part of the chapter, we present our privacy-enhanced Web recommender system, called $\pi SUGGEST$, which is designed to dynamically generate personalized contents of potential interest for users of a Web Site, without providing privacy breaches to malicious users.

The architecture of $\pi SUGGEST$ is based on a two-tier architecture. The server-based tier monitors and collects Web usage information in order to build a global model, whereas the client-based tier, to be plugged-in into the user browser, exploits this model to provide personalized recommendations to the single user. In particular, the plug-in is able to to personalize *on-the-fly* a requested HTML page, by appending a list of page links (*suggestions*). The privacy-preserving strength of $\pi SUGGEST$ relies of its capability of building an accurate model of Web usage, even if users hide and protect their own *user sessions* with the aim of not disclosing their complete activity records or preferences. The only information which is collected and maintained by the server is the single navigation hops of users, i.e., from browsing a given Web page to visiting the next one. The current user session is obviously maintained on the client-tier, which exploits it to give suggestions to the user, by comparing the current session to the usage model built and provided by the server.

Eventually, we define a measure of privacy in order to evaluate with which confidence a malicious user can infer users' activities from the provided suggestions. In other words, we only discuss the case of malicious users who can make new HTTP requests to the server and analyze the supplied recommendations, and we do not deal with the case of malicious users who can access private information stored on the client-tier.

The quality of suggestions provided to users is evaluated by adopting the metric introduced in [3]. This metric tries to estimate the effectiveness of a recommendation system as the capacity of anticipating the requests that users will submit to the system in the future.

Summarizing, the main contributions of this chapter are:

- a comprehensive survey of the main recommender systems proposed in the literature, by also considering their possible privacy breaches;

- a new algorithm to incrementally generate users' profiles in a privacy preserving way;

- a general privacy measure for Web recommender systems, which is used to evaluate how $\pi SUGGEST$ is able to successfully preserve users privacy.

The rest of the chapter is organized as follows. In Section 15.2 we survey the main literature proposals concerning recommender systems, by also considering their possible privacy breaches. Section 15.3 presents the architecture and the algorithms used by $\pi SUGGEST$. Section 15.4 presents a framework for analyzing privacy in cluster-based recommender systems. This framework is then used for the analysis of $\pi SUGGEST$ from the point of view of privacy preservation. Section 15.5 discusses the quantitative evaluation of the accuracy of the suggestions made by $\pi SUGGEST$. Finally, Section 15.6 concludes the chapter.

15.2 Taxonomy of Web Personalization and Recommendation

In general, a recommendation system accomplishes two tasks. The first is to collect data about users in order to understand the frequent patterns of interests. The second is to provide interesting recommendations related to the current activity of the user.

Concerning the employed usage data, such data can be directly collected by logging the actions of users/customers who voluntarily registered in a collaborative service and accepted their preferences/interests/buying information to be recorded. This is the typical case of e-commerce and social networking websites.

Sometimes, the users are not willing to register, or they simply cannot. This is the most general case with Web-site recommender systems. However, similar data can be obtained from server logs. The quality of this data might be lower, mainly due to the uncertainty in distinguishing the identities of different users to build their profiles.

We do not address the problem of dealing with this type of raw data, but we need to introduce the useful concept of *user session*, which is the ordered set of actions performed by the user to accomplish a goal. Examples of sessions are the set of product description pages visited before actually buying an item, or the set of queries submitted to a Web search engine before landing on the desired page. Detecting user sessions is a complex task, since they are usually interleaved and hierarchically structured [10]. Nevertheless, several methodologies and techniques can be found in literature.

If, in addition to sessions it is possible to identify users, then sessions associated with a given user can be aggregated, thus yielding a *user profile*.

The collection of user data, the management of user profiles and the generation of personalized recommendations raise a number of privacy issues. This is quite a wide topic, since privacy aspects are manifold, including several laws in different countries. Here we will focus on two aspects only, called privacy risks:

- **Risk I:** How are sensitive data collected and maintained?

- **Risk II:** Is the recommendation process introducing any privacy breach?

Concerning the first aspect, it is clear that users must disclose information about their activity, that is, preferences/interests/buying information. This can be done with different level of detail, ranging from a very general profile, to fine-grained temporal monitoring, from anonymous interaction to a logging-in requirement.

Concerning the second aspect, that is the privacy risks of recommender systems, a preliminary paper [24] tried to formalize the problem and to measure the amount of privacy provided to users. In the paper, a recommender system is proposed that considers similar users that share a similar profile, e.g., if they share at least w identical ratings. Given this similarity relationship, a social network over users' data can be built by linking similar users. This network will be likely to be naturally clustered, so that it can allow to detect similar habits among groups of users. Once a user enters the system, recommendations based on the ratings previously expressed by other "similar" users can be provided for the items not been already visited (or purchased) by the user herself.

Dispensing recommendations in such a way turns out to constitute a strong privacy breach, where by privacy breach we mean the chance for a malicious user to track users activities or preferences. For example, suppose that a user rates items $\{a, b, c, d\}$ and receives as a recommendation item e. Then, we know that there is a bunch of users who actually rated items in $\{a, b, c, d, e\}$. This is a first kind of breach, since we have detected the actual behavior of a group of users.

Moreover, recommendations are usually given only when they are supported by a certain number $minfreq$ of users, i.e., by a statistically relevant group. We could think that if just a single user has rated items $\{a, b, c, d, e\}$, since this information will not be considered during the classifier training, his privacy will be preserved. However, a malicious user could perform consecutive interactions with the system and discover that after rating $\{a, b, c, d, e\}$ for $minfreq - 1$ times, this new pattern will appear in the recommendations, thus detecting the preferences of one single user. In other words, such a system can be exposed to queries and this is a second kind of privacy breach.

In the following section, we survey the techniques proposed in literature to automatically generate suggestions and recommendations, and, in some cases, personalization of a user service. Differently from other surveys [1, 18], we will also take privacy issues into account. For each technique, we illustrate and discuss the following characteristics:

- **Model Building**: how information to understand user interests are gathered and stored.

- **Recommendation Generation**: how recommendations are generated as a response to user interaction.

- **Sensitive Data**: the personal data collected by the system.

- **Privacy Preservation**: the privacy concerns and guarantees.

To the best of our knowledge, the only recommender system taking into account both the two risk types discussed above is $\pi SUGGEST$, which is illustrated in detail in Section 15.3.

15.2.1 Content-Based Filtering

15.2.1.1 Model Building

This method [20, 13] works by collecting the content descriptions of all the items that a user has previously expressed interest in. By aggregating and weighting the set of features extracted from all such contents, we can build a *user profile*.

For example, in Web site recommendation we can consider the content of pages visited by a user, and collect all the terms appearing in these pages. These textual features can be opportunely weighted to build a *weighted term vector* representing the user profile. Analogously, in electronic commerce, items have an associated textual description that can be exploited in a similar way. Finally, in the context of query suggestion, it is possible to describe a query with the text of the pages returned by a search engine and clicked by users.

15.2.1.2 Recommendation Generation

To generate a recommendation, the user profile is compared with all the objects not already seen by the user. This comparison produces a ranked list of items, and consequently the highest ranked items may be suggested. To this aim, methods like cosine similarity can be exploited.

This approach is mainly used as a filtering process. Given a set of candidates, those non relevant to the user profile are pruned and the others are returned to the user, possibly with an associated rank. An example is [12], where a browser plug-in highlights interesting links during the navigation.

A problem of this approach is the impossibility of providing serendipitous recommendations. Given the user profile, only very similar items are used to build suggestions, and therefore, such recommendations do not bring any new information to the user.

15.2.1.3   Sensitive Data

The system records every expression of interest, and therefore most of the activity of a user, e.g., items rated or pages visited, is monitored. However, if this method is used to implement a filtering process, such sensitive data can be kept on the client computer.

15.2.1.4   Privacy Preservation

If realized as a filtering based approach, it can be entirely implemented on the client side. The activity of the user is monitored in order to build the model, and a set of candidate items, resulting from the user activity, is filtered and possibly ranked. Since no information flows outside the user client, no privacy concern is raised. However, the applicability is limited since only passive filtering is applied.

An alternative approach [30] stores the user profile on a centralized server. This is applied to a Web search engine, where the profile is used to re-rank results of submitted queries. To achieve some privacy guarantee, the user is allowed to exclude from the profile the least frequent terms. The underlying assumption is that infrequent terms may identify a user, while frequent ones let him hide in the crowd. There is a trade-off, since the least frequent terms are obviously important in the recommendation process.

15.2.2   Collaborative Filtering

15.2.2.1   Model Building

The model consists of a global *Users* × *Items* matrix, where each element (i, j) stores the rating of item i given by user j [9]. Such a matrix describes all the preferences expressed by all the users.

Depending on the application, the rating can be explicit or implicit. In electronic commerce, the items correspond to products purchased along with their discrete ratings (e.g., one to five stars) assessing product quality or user satisfaction. In a Web scenario, items are the Web pages visited by a user. The implicit item rating may be measured by considering the number of page visits, or the cumulative time spent on the page.

One of main issues is related to the data sparsity. Since the number of user ratings is usually small with respect to the number of possible items, the model will contain mostly missing values, which makes it difficult to generate relevant recommendations [27].

15.2.2.2   Recommendation Generation

The profile of a user is defined as the set of ratings for the visited/purchased/seen items. By using a *kNN* search, it is possible to identify the k most similar user profiles in the model. Then, the most popular items in such profiles are used to build recommendations.

Scalability and churn are two important issues [7]. The scalability is related to the exploitation of a lazy *kNN* classifier on a large *Users* × *Items* matrix. The churn is related to the possibly large amount of items that can appear over time, e.g., in a news personalization system. Also, new items and new users are associated with a very small number of ratings, and therefore they can hardly play a role in the recommendation process.

Clustering and, more generally, model-based algorithms can be used to improve the efficiency and scalability of the real-time personalization tasks. By grouping together similar users and similar terms, it is possible to reduce the complexity of the recommendation process.

15.2.2.3 Sensitive Data

As for content-based filtering, the activity of a user is monitored. In this case, however, the recommendation is based on a search operation for similar user profiles, and therefore such information is stored, maintained and indexed in a centralized server.

15.2.2.4 Privacy Preservation

The method suffers from privacy breaches, since users have to grant to third parties personal information about their preferences, in order to speedup *kNN* search operation.

There exists a proposal [6] that uses a blend of secure multiparty computation and factor analysis. The model consists of a matrix *Users* × *Topics*, where the topics and the mapping between items and topics are automatically learned through factor analysis. However, user profiles are not shared to build the model. Rather, a secure multiparty computation technique is used to learn the model by exchanging encrypted messages. At the end of the process, every user has a copy of the model. A drawback of the method is that several customers must be on-line in order to participate simultaneously in the computation and subsequent model construction. While the approach is safe for what regards risk I, it does not deal with risk II.

There are some other proposals that try to reduce somewhat risk I. For example, by avoiding collecting all data in a single site, or by perturbing sensitive data regarding user activities. In [2] the authors propose to split customer data between the merchant and a semi-trusted third party. For example, this other party could be trusted to only maintain the customers' demographic information, while the merchant only manages item ratings. A proposal that still aims to split users' data among many parties appeared in [23]. In that paper these parties hold disjoint sets of item ratings collected by the same user, but the devised privacy-preserving protocol is able to supply a recommendation service using their joint data without disclosing them to each other.

An interesting proposal [22] is to provide the perturbation of users' ratings before submitting them to a central database on which the collaborative filtering algorithm is run. Of course the amount of privacy is directly proportional to the amount of perturbation, whose drawback is a reduction of the accuracy of recommendations achieved.

15.2.3 Item-Based Collaborative Filtering

15.2.3.1 Model Building

The method adopts the same user-based profiles of standard collaborative filtering [26], thus building the same *Users × Items* matrix.

15.2.3.2 Recommendation Generation

Rather than finding similarities among users, the objective is to find similarities among items. Two items are considered similar if they share similar ratings, that is, if the corresponding columns of the *Users × Items* matrix are similar. Differently from content-based collaborative filtering, the content/description of objects does not affect the similarity.

In order to make a suggestion, a target item is needed, e.g., the product the user has just purchased. The method suggests items not previously seen that are in the neighborhood of the target item.

15.2.3.3 Sensitive Data

For each visited/purchased/seen item, we need to collect its ratings by all the users, as in a classical collaborative filtering method.

15.2.3.4 Privacy Preservation

The basic units of information, on the basis of which the method makes its recommendations, exactly correspond to the ratings of an item by all the users. The need of collecting, for each item, the private ratings of all the users, constitutes a clear privacy breach.

15.2.4 Recommending by Clustering Unordered User Sessions

15.2.4.1 Model Building

In the previous approaches we have seen different models that do not account for the temporal aspect of each single user interaction. The sequence of all the ratings of each user is flattened in a single set, as if they occurred simultaneously.

It is possible to see the interactions of a user with the system as a set of sessions, where a session is an ordered sequence of items visited by a user within a given time interval. A session thus contains items that can be considered as related from the user-side.

Many techniques take into account sessions, but do not exploit the sequential ordering of items within each session [31, 15]. A session is simply considered an n-dimensional vector, where the i-th element is the weight or degree of interest.

In [16], the Association Rule Hypergraph Partitioning (ARHP) technique is proposed. The idea is to group together items that frequently occur together in a user's session. The frequent itemsets, i.e., sets of items that occur not less than a given threshold in user sessions, returned by an *Apriori*-like algorithm are considered as hyperedges of a hypergraph. A hypergraph is an extension of a graph in the sense that each hyperedge can connect more than two vertices. A set of clusters is finally obtained by recursively partitioning the hypergraph into components with high connectivity. Finally, a cluster of items can be characterized by its median, or any other aggregation of the profiles of the various items in the cluster.

The whole model building process can be performed off-line, before and independently of the on-line recommendation generation. Whereas this allows more expensive model generations to be exploited, aiming to provide more accurate suggestions, we have to deal with the aging of the model built.

15.2.4.2 Recommendation Generation

The active user session is used to generate recommendations. As the user continues its activity, the user profile is updated by aggregating information about the items being viewed. This profile is compared with the cluster representatives in the model. The items in the most similar cluster, which were not already visited, are used to create recommendations [31].

Depending on the application, different similarity measures can be exploited. In most cases, a good measure is simply counting the number of items the user has accessed in each cluster: a cluster matches the profile if the count is above a certain threshold.

15.2.4.3 Sensitive Data

We need to collect user sessions, that is, the groups of items visited by each user during a given time interval, in particular, the complete sessions to build the model, and the partial ones to make a recommendation.

15.2.4.4 Privacy Preservation

In this approach, neither risk I nor risk II are considered. The user is monitored during her activity, and the data contained in her sessions managed by the centralized recommender system.

15.2.5 Recommending through Association Analysis of Unordered User Sessions/Profiles

15.2.5.1 Model Building

Association rules are a powerful tool for the discovery of strong dependencies between sets of items in a database. A model consists of a set of rules, with given support (number of times the rule occurs in the database) and confidence (conditional probability of the consequent given the antecedent).

In the context of recommender systems, it would be possible to mine for association rules by considering sessions as transactions, thus discovering correlation between sets of items, pages, queries, etc. Such rules, in conjunction with the activity or profile of a target user, can be used for recommendation generation.

Also in this case, the model construction is performed off-line.

15.2.5.2 Recommendation Generation

We illustrate two scenarios: collaborative filtering and query recommendation. In the first scenario, the preferences of the target user are matched against the items in the antecedent of each rule, and the items in the consequent are used to create recommendations. The confidence of rules is used to rank recommendations [25].

In the second scenario, only rules with a single query both in the antecedent and in the consequent are considered. The query submitted by the user is searched among rules antecedents. The matching rules, and thus the queries in the rules' consequent are sorted according to confidence, and used to build the recommendations [8].

15.2.5.3 Sensitive Data

Also in this case, the data contained in the user session must be sent to a centralized server, where they are used to build the model. The same remarks made above and concerning the exploitation of unordered user sessions hold.

15.2.5.4 Privacy Preservation

The same remarks made above concerning the exploitation of unordered user sessions for building a model and recommending hold in this case.

15.2.6 Recommending by Clustering Ordered User Sessions

15.2.6.1 Model Building

In addition to considering users' sessions, it is also possible to take into account the order of the items in each session. We illustrate two algorithms for web page recommendation, *SUGGEST* [3, 5] and *PageGather* [21], that find clusters of pages based on this idea.

The model built by the two algorithms is an undirected graph whose vertices are the pages visited by the users so far, and the edges represent the jump through a link from one page to another. Note that the graph is undirected, meaning that a link is interpreted as a symmetric similarity between two pages.

PageGather needs the whole collection of the user sessions to build the graph. The arc (i, j), is labeled with $\min P(i|j), P(j|i)$, where $P(j|i)$ is the conditional probability that page j is visited during a session given that page i has been visited in the same session.

SUGGEST uses less information than *PageGather* from the various sessions to build the graph. Each undirected arc (i, j) is labeled with the number of times pages i and j have been accessed consecutively, in any order, by a user. Analogously, graph nodes are labeled with the number of times the associated page has been visited. Note that such graph labeling can be carried out even if the complete user session is not available. It is sufficient to know the referral of each requested page.

Both algorithms remove noise by dropping arcs with small weight. Finally, graph clustering algorithms are used, aimed at finding the connected components of the graph, i.e., corresponding to clusters of pages frequently occurring in users visiting paths.

15.2.6.2 Recommendation Generation

SUGGEST provides an on-line component that keeps track of the last recently visited pages, and suggests new pages belonging to the cluster with the largest intersection with these pages.

In *PageGather* there is no on-line component. It simply generates from the clusters a static index of correlated pages which is kept in a separate "Suggestion Section" of the web-site.

15.2.6.3 Sensitive Data

PageGather and *SUGGEST* exploit the information regarding the page visiting order in the user sessions to build the graph used to cluster the pages. Indeed, *SUGGEST* only needs to collect single page transitions from each session. A user session composed of n page visits is thus completely equivalent to *n-1* short sessions made by distinct users, and visiting the same pages.

15.2.6.4 Privacy Preservation

The method exploited by *PageGather* suffers from privacy breaches, since complete (ordered) user sessions need to be collected, although the identities of users can be preserved, so that global user profiles cannot be reconstructed by joining different sessions. On the other hand, *SUGGEST* only needs to collect user transitions from one page to another.

15.2.7   Recommending through Sequential Analysis of Ordered User Sessions/Profiles

15.2.7.1   Model Building

So far we have discussed the use of frequent itemsets, and the resulting association rules. These are the least restrictive type of navigational patterns, since they take into account the presence of items in a session, disregarding their order.

When considering a session as an ordered set of items, there are a number of data mining tools able to extract significant patterns that take into account that order. In particular, it is possible to use sequential patterns and contiguous sequential patterns to analyze users' navigational trails [29, 17]. A sequential pattern S is an ordered set of items, and it requires all of its items to appear in the same temporal order. In addition, a *contiguous* sequential pattern requires its items to be adjacent in the users' sessions.

The resulting set of patterns can be used as a model of frequent users' behavior. In order to perform efficient operation on the model, it can be stored with a trie data structure.

15.2.7.2   Recommendation Generation

As usual, recommendations stem from the current session of a given user. Given the ordered set of items recently visited (purchased, etc.), this can be used to traverse the trie of the frequent sequential patterns. If the current profile matches part of a profile stored in the model, then the remaining items are used to create recommendations.

In [17] contiguous sequential patterns were judged as too much restrictive in the general context of recommendation generation, even if very valuable in page prefetching applications.

15.2.7.3   Sensitive Data

Similarly to the other session-aware algorithms, the activity of the user must be continuously monitored in order to build/update the model and to generate recommendations.

15.2.7.4   Privacy Preservation

The same remarks made above concerning the exploitation of ordered user sessions for building a model and recommending hold in this case.

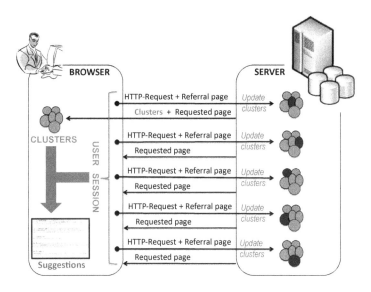

FIGURE 15.1: $\pi SUGGEST$ two-tier architecture.

15.3 The $\pi SUGGEST$ System

$\pi SUGGEST$, is an evolution of $SUGGEST$ [3, 5], the on-line recommender mentioned in Section 15.2.6. The main novelty of $\pi SUGGEST$ is that its two components, the one that updates the knowledge base, and the one that builds and provides recommendations, are well separated (see Figure 15.1). The former is placed on the Web server (it is indeed a module of the Apache Web server). The latter runs on the client-side as a browser plug-in.

In order to collect information about navigational patterns, $\pi SUGGEST$ does not need to maintain the complete user sessions. It only needs to manage an undirected graph $G = (V, E)$ with weighted edges. Each vertex $v_i = V$ corresponds to a page hosted by the Web site. Since in our model the interest in a page depends on its visiting order during the various sessions, each edge $e_{ij} = E$, which connects vertices v_i and v_j, is associated with a weight $W_{ij} = N_{ij}/max\{N_i, N_j\}$. N_{ij} is the number of times the two pages, corresponding to v_i and v_j, have been accessed consecutively (and in any order) by the user community, while N_i and N_j are, respectively, the number of times the same two pages have been visited. We divide by $max\{N_i, N_j\}$ since we want to reduce the relative importance of links involving *index pages*. Generally, even if such pages do not contain useful content, they are used as a starting point for a browsing session. Moreover, users often return to these pages several times, in order to start the visit of a new branch of the Web site. Therefore, though it is very likely that index pages are visited along with any other page, nevertheless they are of little interest as potential suggestions.

A triangular adjacency matrix N is indeed used to store the knowledge base corresponding to graph G: each entry $N[i, j]$, $i \neq j$, stores N_{ij}, while each entry $N[i, i]$ stores N_i. The adjacency matrix is incrementally maintained by the $\pi SUGGEST$ component on the server-side (see Figure 15.1), by only considering single HTTP requests coming from clients. Note that each HTTP request contains both the URL of the requested page and the referral one, i.e., the page from which the user is coming. The server-side component of $\pi SUGGEST$ exploits the adjacency matrix to find disjoint clusters of strongly related pages. In particular, it partitions G on the basis of its connected components, by using a modified version [3, 5] of the well known incremental connected components algorithm [28]. The algorithm is driven by two threshold parameters, aiming to limit the number of edges to visit, but also to avoid the generation of clusters that may be statistically irrelevant (because they might over-fit the knowledge base). In particular,

1. we filter out from G all the edges whose weight $W_{i,j}$ is below the constant *minfreq*. The pairs of pages connected by such edges are indeed poorly correlated, and thus are not considered by our clustering algorithm;

2. we only take into consideration those connected components whose size is greater than a fixed number of nodes, namely *minclustersize*. All the other components are indeed discarded because considered not significant enough.

The extracted information, i.e., the cluster identifiers together with the various vertices/pages of G, is maintained in another a vector L. Since in large Web sites the size of matrix N and vector L might exceed the maximum available main memory, the server-side component of $\pi SUGGEST$ adopts an LRU-based strategy to store in main memory only the portions of the data structures associated with those pages that have been recently accessed by users.

As illustrated by Figure 15.1, the client-side component of $\pi SUGGEST$ asks the server for the page clusters (stored in L) when a session starts. The same component is responsible for tracking the user and maintaining her/his session. It also builds suggestions by finding the cluster that has the largest intersection with the *PageWindow* (i.e., the last portion of the current session). The suggestions only include the most relevant pages in the cluster, according to an order determined during the clustering phase.

15.3.1   Privacy-Preserving Features of $\pi SUGGEST$

We have previously introduced two kinds of privacy risks. The first risk is due to the data collected by the recommender service, and the second risk is related with the recommendation generation process. The two-tier architecture of $\pi SUGGEST$ makes it possible to overcome both these two kinds of risks.

The information collected by $\pi SUGGEST$ is just a couple of web-page URLs for each user interaction: requested and referral pages. This allows the user to protect his privacy against the recommender system by adopting a number of technological solutions. Such techniques range from cookies-related stuff to methods aimed at masking or scrambling the client IP address*. In such a way, the user may achieve two goals: changing his identity at every request, and avoiding the recommender system to reconstruct the user session.

Regarding the second risk type, the system needs the current user session in order to provide recommendations. Thanks to the two-tier structure, the user session is only built and kept locally at the client-side, and never communicated to the recommender service. Therefore, the server component of $\pi SUGGEST$ is not aware of the user sensitive data, i.e., identity and sessions, but still it can build a model for the generation of good recommendations.

The model built by the centralized component is sent to every client, which uses the model to generate recommendations. The model is general enough to prevent any malicious user from deducing any sensitive information.

In the theoretical framework of $\pi SUGGEST$ we are not considering those forms of threats that may affect a specific user, his software or his hardware. For example, these issues may arise in context where the attacker is able to sniff the Internet traffic of a single client, or when the client browser is compromised so that an attacker can access to the complete user sessions. Finally, we are not considering the case where a significant number of clients perform artificial HTTP requests to sabotage the model building phase.

15.4 $\pi SUGGEST$ and Privacy

In order to evaluate the privacy features of $\pi SUGGEST$, we start quantifying the level of confidence associated with the capability of inferring information about users activities.

In general, a recommender system tries to classify a user on the basis of the visited pages. Each class of users is associated with a subset of pages, which are of interest for them. In $\pi SUGGEST$, these subsets of pages (i.e., the clusters of pages) are a public information, since L is returned to each client when a user session starts. In other systems, such class representatives are kept private, even if part of them are published in the form of user recommendations. We

---

*See, for example, `http://www.torproject.org/index.html.en`.

are interested in investigating which kind of information is revealed when information about the composition of a generic cluster is disclosed.

From the point of view of the plug-in on the client-side, a cluster is simply a set of pages $C = \{p_0, p_1, ..., p_n\}$, obtained by partitioning graph G on the server-side. Cluster C actually corresponds to a (partially or completely) connected component of G. However, the plug-in cannot be aware of which pairs of pages actually correspond to edges in the G graph. On the other hand, a *user activity* (or session) corresponds to a set of visited pages. Since the user moved from a page to another, there must exist a partially (or completely) connected graph behind such a set of pages.

Since we are interested in analyzing which kind of user activities may have generated a given cluster, it is useful to introduce the concept of *valid cluster generator*.

DEFINITION 15.1   *Let $C = \{p_0, p_1, ..., p_q\}$ be a cluster of pages, and $\mathcal{U} = \langle U_1, ..., U_n \rangle$ be a set of user activities. Each U_i is a subset of pages belonging to C that has been visited by some user. $\mathcal{U}$ is a* valid cluster generator *iff the following three conditions hold:*

1. **covering** $\bigcup_{i=1}^{n} U_i = C$.
2. **connectivity** $\forall\ U_i \in \mathcal{U},\ \exists\ U_j \in \mathcal{U},\ i \neq j,\ such\ that\ U_i \cap U_j \neq \emptyset$.
3. **minimality** $\forall i,\ (\mathcal{U} \setminus U_i)$ *is not a* valid cluster generator.

Since a connected graph exists behind each U_i, the *connectivity* condition ensures that the union of all the connected graphs associated with the various U_i surely generates one of the possible connected graphs that are able to *support/generate* C.

Therefore, a cluster generator is the *minimal* set of user activities (sessions), that are able to create the connected component C. We introduce *minimality* to avoid anomalous combinations that may be useless in this context. For example, we do not want the two sessions $\langle \{abcd\}, \{abc\} \rangle$ to be a valid generator for cluster $\{abcd\}$, since the cluster is also supported by the first session only.

DEFINITION 15.2   *Given a cluster $C = \{p_0, p_1, ..., p_q\}$, a valid cluster generator $\mathcal{U}$, and a recommender system Σ, the privacy level Π of Σ with respect to $\mathcal{U}$ is:*

$$\Pi_\Sigma(\mathcal{U}, C) = 1 - P(\mathcal{U} \mid C)$$

If we can estimate $\mathcal{U}$ with high probability on the basis of the knowledge of a cluster C, the system has a very low level of privacy. On the other hand, if there is no $\mathcal{U}$ which is likely to be a generator of C, then the system has a high level of privacy.

For example, suppose that the client-side plug-in of $\pi SUGGEST$ receives a cluster of pages, namely $C = \{a, b, c, d, e\}$. Many different events may have generated C. For example, a single user who visited all the pages $\{a, b, c, d, e\}$, or two users who visited respectively the pages $\{a, b, c\}$ and $\{c, d, e\}$, or three users who visited the pages $\{a, b, c\}$, $\{a, c, d\}$ and $\{d, e\}$, and so on. Note that different users' activities may have generated not only the same cluster, but also the same knowledge base.

Although this example is very small, we were able to find a lot of valid cluster generators. Before considering this example more formally, let us consider clusters of smaller sizes. If $|C| = 2$, since $\pi SUGGEST$ creates an edge between two pages if and only if they were visited consecutively, we can conclude that some user visited the two pages with probability 1, and therefore our privacy level is $1 - 1 = 0$. Clearly, we only have one acceptable user activity and thus no privacy. For the case $|C| = 3$, we have only four valid cluster generators (the three subsets of two elements of C, and the set C itself) leading to a privacy level of $1 - 1/4 = 0.75$. However, the recommendations provided by using these "*small*" clusters are of little significance. Moreover, they would lead to the generation of an over-fitted model with respect to the training data. For this reason, our system builds clusters whose cardinality is greater than or equal to 4.

THEOREM 15.1

Given a cluster $C = \{p_1, ..., p_q\}$, where $q \geq 4$, and a valid cluster generator $\mathcal{U}$, the privacy level Π provided by πSUGGEST can be bounded, and its lower bound is:

$$\Pi_{\pi SUGGEST}(\mathcal{U}, C) = 1 - P(\mathcal{U} \mid C) \geq 1 - \frac{1}{2^{|C|}}$$

The previous theorem, whose proof can be found in [4], states that the amount of possible valid cluster generators is very high. Therefore this makes it impossible to understand which set of user activities have actually lead to cluster C. But we are pretty much interested not only in giving a confidence level for a set of users' activities as above, but also a confidence level for the activity of a single user.

DEFINITION 15.3
Given a cluster $C = \{p_0, p_1, ..., p_{n_1}\}$, let $U = \{q_0, q_1, ..., q_{n_2}\}$, $U \subseteq C$, be the set of pages visited by a single user. The privacy level Π^* provided by a recommender system Σ with respect to U is:

$$\Pi^*_{\Sigma}(U, C) = 1 - P(U \mid C)$$

Given that the system created and suggested cluster C, we want to weigh the chance that some users have actually visited a set of pages U, where $U \subseteq C$.

THEOREM 15.2

Given a cluster $C = \{p_0, p_1, ..., p_q\}$, and a set of pages $U = \{q_1, ..., q_h\}$ visited by a user, where $U \subseteq C$, the privacy level Π^* provided by πSUGGEST with respect to U can be lower bounded, and the bound is:

$$\Pi^*_{\pi SUGGEST}(U, C) = 1 - P(U \mid C) \geq 1 - \frac{1}{3^{\frac{|C|}{2}}}$$

Interested readers can refer to [4] for the proof of the previous theorem.

Theorem 15.1 and Theorem 15.2 state that if the $\pi SUGGEST$ system is plugged into a privacy safe system, it will not provide any privacy breach. We say that a system is *privacy safe* if two conditions hold: (i) the user activity cannot be tracked, (ii) the user activity cannot be inferred. Condition (i) holds by definition in a safe system. Moreover, neither publishing the clustered structure can be considered a privacy breach, even if it could be inferred with consecutive queries to the system. Theorem 15.1 assures that the privacy provided by $\pi SUGGEST$ increases exponentially with the size of the published cluster. Given one recommendation, there are exponential many aggregate behaviors that might have generated it, and therefore it is not possible to detect the actual behavior among them, i.e., condition (ii) holds.

15.4.1   Discussion

The classification-based approach, which is used by many popular recommender systems, could be a privacy breach by itself. It may disclose to a malicious person which pages a group of users have actually visited.

In $\pi SUGGEST$ we have defined a new privacy measure that models the chance for a malicious user to recover the real behavior of a group or a single user, on the basis of the information disclosed (under the form of recommendation) by the system. Finally, we have introduced a two-tier system for privacy-enhanced recommendation. On the server-side, a knowledge base is updated on-line. On the client-side, a plug-in creates a list of links to pages of interest.

$\pi SUGGEST$ has been shown to be privacy safe. From its knowledge base, a cluster C of web pages is extracted and used to build recommendations. The probability to guess whether a user has visited a set of pages U, $U \subseteq C$, on the basis of the extracted cluster only, decrease exponentially with the cardinality of $|U|$. This probability is the same, both for any third party user and for the server providing this service as well. In other words, the server that also collects information to build the knowledge base cannot breach users' privacy.

15.5 $\pi SUGGEST$ Evaluation

Measuring the quality of a recommendation system is considered a very difficult task. We have to characterize the quality of the suggestions obtained, by quantifying how useful the suggestions are for the users.

The $\pi SUGGEST$ effectiveness can be evaluated by using the performance measure introduced in [3], which is based on the intersection of real user sessions with the corresponding set of suggestions. For every session S_i, and a set of suggestions R_i provided by the system, we could derive the quality of suggestion by using:

$$\omega_i = \frac{\mid S_i \cap R_i \mid}{\mid S_i \mid} \qquad (15.1)$$

Unfortunately, this simple measure cannot capture the potential impact of the suggestions on the user's navigational session. For example, suppose that a page that the user would visit at the end of the session is instead suggested at the beginning of the session: in this case the suggestion should be very valuable for the user, who can find a shorter way to what he is looking for. Therefore we can extend expression 15.1 by taking into account the distance between the suggestions and the actual pages visited during the session. To this end, we need to split S_i into two halves. Only the first half S_i^1 is used to generate the set of suggestions R_i. The second half is instead used to measure the intersection with the suggestions. For every page $p_k \in S_i^2 \cap R_i$, where p_k appears in position k within S_i^2, we add a weight $f(k)$. We choose f so that more importance is given to pages actually visited at the end of the session. In conclusion, for the whole session log, we can measure the quality of the suggestions by:

$$\Omega = \frac{1}{F} \sum_{i=1}^{N_S} \sum_{k=1}^{\mid S_i^2 \mid} [\![p_k \in (S_i^2 \cap R_i)]\!] \ f(k) \qquad (15.2)$$

where N_S is the number of sessions, $[\![expr]\!]$ is the truth function (which is equal to 1 if $expr$ evaluates to True, 0 otherwise), while F is a normalization factor on the weights.

For a quantitative evaluation of $\pi SUGGEST$, refer to [3], where we used three real-life access logs[†]: Berkeley, NASA, USASK, produced by the Web servers of the Computer Science Department of Berkeley University, Saskatchewan University and Kennedy Space Center, respectively. In these experiments, we chose $f(k) = k$, so that the page weights increase linearly with the corresponding positions in the session. For each test, we generated

---

[†]`www.web-caching.com`

requests to an Apache server running $\pi SUGGEST$, and recorded the suggestions generated for every navigation session contained within the access log file considered.

For each log file, we measured Ω as a function of the *minfreq* parameter, which is used to filter out from the graph G all the "infrequent edges." Suggestions generated by $\pi SUGGEST$ show a higher quality than a random generator of suggestions, and this quality reaches the maximum for *minfreq*=0.2 for almost all the log files.

15.6   Conclusion

In this chapter we have described the distinguishing features of privacy preserving recommender systems, and have discussed the main features and evaluation methodologies of a privacy-preserving Web recommender system.

The chapter is divided into two main parts. In the first part we introduce the problem, survey the approaches existing in literature, and highlight the implications from a privacy point of view. For each technique we illustrate how models are built, how recommendations are generated, what data are retained and stored, and, finally, privacy concerns and guarantees it offers. In particular, we point out two different kinds of risks for privacy that are related to what kind of data is retained, and what kind of breach of privacy the recommendation models are subjected to.

Regarding the two risks just mentioned, in the second part of the chapter we present $\pi SUGGEST$, a recommender system that has been specifically designed to address and overcome those risks. $\pi SUGGEST$ builds upon a previous work on online web recommender systems [3, 5] and addresses the problem of privacy preservation using a two-tier architecture. The major difference from previous versions of the system is that information about users' sessions and visited pages is stored only on the client-side. This limits considerably the amount of knowledge that can be inferred by querying the knowledge base (stored at server-side), and this makes it practically impossible to disclose navigational information about single users.

There are some open questions that will become important in the future as recommender systems will be used more and more. It is very important to think of how to construct data repositories able to manage large numbers of subjects and objects along with actions performed by those subjects on the objects stored. As an example, consider the effort to cope with the large amount of new object ratings. Privacy concerns, in this case, are very important. Furthermore, related topics like: advertising, reputation based discovery, and other processes will have to be able to model and identify, in a privacy preserving manner, dynamic trends, such as emerging "topics," and to take these dynamic behaviors over time into account in making recommendations. Privacy (as well as trust enforcement) mechanisms are an important requirement for making recommender system usable. Users, not feeling protected enough from privacy breaches, will stop using them.

References

[1] G. Adomavicius and A. Tuzhilin. Toward the next generation of recommender systems: A survey of the state-of-the-art and possible extensions. *IEEE TKDE*, 17(6):734–749, 2005.

[2] E. Aimeur, G. Brassard, J. M. Fernandez, and F. O. Onana. Alambic: a privacy-preserving recommender system for electronic commerce. *International Journal of Information Security*, 7(5):307–334, 2008.

[3] R. Baraglia and F. Silvestri. An online recommender system for large web sites. In *Proceedings of WI 2004*, September 2004.

[4] R. Baraglia, C. Lucchese, S. Orlando, M. Serranó, and F. Silvestri. A privacy preserving web recommender system. In *SAC*, pages 559–563. ACM, 2006.

[5] R. Baraglia and F. Silvestri. Dynamic personalization of web sites without user intervention. *CACM*, 50(2):63–67, 2007.

[6] J. Canny. Collaborative Filtering with Privacy via Factor Analysys. In *Proc. of ACM SIGIR'02*. ACM Press, 2002.

[7] A. S. Das, M. Datar, A. Garg, and S. Rajaram. Google news personalization: scalable online collaborative filtering. In *WWW '07: Proceedings of the 16th International Conference on World Wide Web*, pages 271–280. ACM, 2007.

[8] B. M. Fonseca, P. B. Golgher, E. S. de Moura, and N. Ziviani. Using association rules to discover search engines related queries. In *LA-WEB '03: Proceedings of the First Conference on Latin American Web Congress*, page 66. IEEE Computer Society, 2003.

[9] J. L. Herlocker, J. A. Konstan, L. G. Terveen, and J. Riedl. Evaluating collaborative filtering recommender systems. *Transactions on Information Systems*, 22(1):5–53, 2004.

[10] R. Jones and K. L. Klinkner. Beyond the session timeout: automatic hierarchical segmentation of search topics in query logs. In *CIKM '08:*

Proceeding of the 17th ACM Conference on Information and Knowledge Management, pages 699–708. ACM, 2008.

[11] R. Kosala and H. Blockeel. Web mining research: A survey. *ACM SIGKDD*, 2(1):1–15, July 2000.

[12] H. Lieberman. Letizia: An agent that assists web browsing. In Chris S. Mellish, editor, *Proceedings of the Fourteenth International Joint Conference on Artificial Intelligence*, pages 924–929. Morgan Kaufmann publishers Inc.: San Mateo, CA, USA, 1995.

[13] D. Mladenic. Text-learning and related intelligent agents: A survey. *Intelligent Systems*, 14(4):44–54, July/August 1999.

[14] B. Mobasher, R. Cooley, and J. Srivastava. Automatic personalization based on web usage mining. *CACM*, 43(8):142–151, August 2000.

[15] B. Mobasher, H. Dai, T. Luo, and M. Nakagawa. Discovery and evaluation of aggregate usage profiles for web personalization. *Data Mining and Knowledge Discovery*, (6):61–82, 2002.

[16] B. Mobasher, H. Dai, T. Luo, and M. Nakagawa. Discovery and evaluation of aggregate usage profiles for web personalization. *Data Mining and Knowledge Discovery*, 6(1):61–82, January 2002.

[17] B. Mobasher, H. Dai, T. Luo, and M. Nakagawa. Using sequential and non-sequential patterns for predictive web usage mining tasks. In *IEEE Int.l Conf. on Data Mining (ICDM)*, pages 669–672, 2002.

[18] B. Mobasher. Data mining for web personalization. In *The Adaptive Web, Methods and Strategies of Web Personalization*, pages 90–135. LNCS 4321, Springer, 2007.

[19] M. D. Mulvenna, S. S. Anand, and A. G. Buchener. Personalization on the net using web mining. *CACM*, 43(8), 2000.

[20] M.J. Pazzani and D. Billsus. Content-based recommendation systems. In In P. Brusilovsky et al., eds.: The Adaptive Web: Methods and Strategies of Web Personalization, volume LNCS 4321. Springer, 2007.

[21] M. Perkowitz and O. Etzioni. Adaptive web sites: Automatically synthesizing web pages. In *15th National Conference on Artificial Intelligence*, pages 727–732, 1998.

[22] H. Polat and W. Du. Privacy-preserving collaborative filtering using randomized perturbation techniques. In *IEEE Int.l Conf. on Data Mining, ICDM*, page 625. IEEE Computer Society, 2003.

[23] H. Polat and W. Du. Privacy-preserving collaborative filtering on vertically partitioned data. In *9th European Conf. on Principles and Practice of Knowledge Discovery in Databases - PKDD*, number LNCS 3721, pages 651–658. Springer, 2005.

[24] N. Ramakrishnan, B. J. Keller, B. J. Mirza, A. Y. Grama, and G. Karypis. Privacy risks in recommender systems. *IEEE Internet Computing*, pages 54–62, 2001.

[25] B. Sarwar, G. Karypis, J. Konstan, and J. Riedl. Analysis of recommender algorithms for e-commerce. In *Proc. of the 2nd ACM E-Commerce Conference (EC00)*, pages 158–167, 2000.

[26] B. Sarwar, G. Karypis, J. Konstan, and J. Riedl. Item-based collaborative filtering recommendation algorithms. In *Proc. of the 10th Int.l WWW Conference*, pages 285–295, 2001.

[27] B. M. Sarwar, G. Karypis, J. A. Konstan, and J. T. Riedl. Application of dimensionality reduction in recommender systems a case study. In *In ACM WebKDD Workshop*, 2000.

[28] J. G. Siek, L. Lee, and A. Lumsdaine. *Boost Graph Library, The: User Guide and Reference Manual.* Addison Wesley Professional, 2001.

[29] M. Spiliopoulou and L. C. Faulstich. Wum: A web utilization miner. In *Workshop on the Web and Data Bases (WebDB98)*, pages 109–115, 1998. http://citeseer.nj.nec.com/spiliopoulou98wum.html.

[30] Y. Xu, Ke Wang, B. Zhang, and Z. Chen. Privacy-enhancing personalized web search. In *WWW '07: Proceedings of the 16th International Conference on World Wide Web*, pages 591–600. ACM, 2007.

[31] T. W. Yan, M. Jacobsen, H. Garcia-Molina, and D. Umeshwar. From user access patterns to dynamic hypertext linking. *Fifth International World Wide Web Conference*, May 1996.

Part VII

Social Networks

Chapter 16

The Social Web and Privacy: Practices, Reciprocity and Conflict Detection in Social Networks

Seda Gürses

K.U.Leuven, Leuven, Belgium

Bettina Berendt

K.U.Leuven, Leuven, Belgium

16.1 Introduction

In the Social Web, the Internet and Web are coming into their own, offering an infrastructure for self-expression, information and communication to everyone regardless of their technical expertise. The Social Web comprises many facets: wikis, blogs, photographs/video/etc., portals, tagging systems, etc. Most of these have functionalities that allow "social networks" of people with shared interests or other forms of interdependency to grow and become manifest by links such as blogrolls, comments, etc. One group of applications and portals has made this network building into its core purpose: social network sites (SNS). SNS are web-based services that allow individuals to (1) construct a public or semi-public profile within a bounded system, (2) articulate a list of users with whom they share a connection, and (3) view and traverse their list of connections and those made by others within the system [11]. SNS are not only popular, but also highly effective at turning otherwise often passive users into active contributors: In 2008, more than 30% of Internet users were members of at least one SNS, and more than 80% of SNS users became active network members [18]. The publishing of personal information in a network and the ease with which such information travels through different sites and beyond, allows providers and users to profile each other based on personally and relationally revealed data. Thus, on the one hand SNS *exemplify* functionality that permeates the whole Social Web, on the other hand they are *prime examples* of profiling functionality.

More recently, privacy has shifted into the focus of social-network researchers and practitioners. A common view is that SNS play an active role in the (general) "privacy nightmare" of the Internet. Empirical analyses of SNS support this view, showing that vast amounts of data are collected, often without a clearly defined purpose, that privacy settings are cumbersome and their use poorly communicated, and that privacy setting defaults reveal a lot of information and (see [8] for a detailed analysis of 45 major SNS). Interestingly, millions of users appear to think otherwise, delighting in the new possibilities for self-expression, finding new friends online and sharing resources. Nevertheless, a number of those users also complain about unexpected revelations of their personal information and related privacy concerns. How can these views, which at first sight appear to be opposed, be considered together in order to help users, companies, and society at large to reach common understandings and working implementations of privacy protection in a world in which information sharing is a desirable daily practice?

We argue that a solution to this problem lies in studying different approaches to privacy. The dominant approach to privacy in computer science is to define privacy as data confidentiality — hiding data in an environment in which SNS act as drivers of the privacy-nightmare seducing users to disclose personal information. In this view, solutions consist of formal approaches to ensuring confidentiality through access control methods, data perturbation and other modifications of data to counter unwanted information inferences and leakages. We show later that this approach is not sufficient to address users' privacy concerns in social networks, is often inappropriate in collaborative sharing environments, and is solely preemptive — most confidentiality and anonymity models do not engage with the information that has already been revealed or leaked. Hence, in this chapter we categorize complementary approaches to privacy and show how the approaches can be used to address the different types of concerns.

Once we have sketched out the different approaches, we explore in depth one of these in the context of social networks, an approach we call privacy as practice. In order to be able to do that we step out of the privacy nightmare discourse, assume that SNS are an interesting space on the Internet for engaging in privacy [2] and that therefore a detailed study of user behavior and concerns in them will yield a more accurate description of the privacy concepts that are relevant. Further, we presume that privacy is not something concrete, in consensus and in constant danger. Rather, we conceive privacy as a set of practices to negotiate what should remain public or private in social contexts. Legal and other regulatory frameworks and various social mechanisms exist to ensure that individuals can practice their privacy. We hence argue that we also need approaches to defining and developing technology that target the same.

Further, SNS provide a prime example for studying the the privacy and related concerns manifest on the (Social) Web: by virtue of being public and popular, SNS make evident privacy problems elsewhere on the Internet such as emails, discussion forums, chats, or e-Commerce. At the same time, in no other web applications are the user communities so actively involved in privacy debates although similar concerns apply.

The chapter is organized as follows. In Section 16.2, we review some dominant approaches to privacy and emphasize the importance of methods other than confidentiality and anonymity for privacy practices. There we also show how the present chapter and Chapters 15 and 18 of this book, which give detailed overviews of mechanisms for protecting profile privacy and methods for private analysis of networks, complement one another. We also shortly contextualize the three approaches by analyzing privacy concerns articulated by users and other stakeholders of social networks. Based on those concerns, in Section 16.3 we categorize the types conflicts that arise among users as a result of two characteristic features of SNS: relational information and transitive access control. We then introduce the initial concepts for a method to detect these conflicts. In Section 16.4, we construct a formal model of the conflicts and describe our conflict discovery method. We then apply our method to four cases which are typical in SNS and discuss their differences. In Section 16.5, we suggest that in order to negotiate the conflicts identified using our method, data-mining and feedback techniques as well as access control alternatives can be used. The method hence not only serves to assemble *requirements* and study interactions between those requirements; further, by showing outcomes and possible conflicts, it suggests how data-mining can be the core of *awareness tools* that help users better oversee consequences of their actions. An outlook is given in Section 16.6.

In the work presented here, the role of data mining changes. Today data mining is often seen as a a technology that is at the core of privacy concerns and at the same time is the starting point of a group of methods ("privacy-preserving data mining") that help avoid these. In this chapter, we show how data mining methods and technologies may also inform individuals and groups about the (possible) consequences of various privacy-related behaviors.

Finally, it is not the objective of this chapter to propose new access control models that limit how information can travel according to some specification. Rather, we develop a method to investigate the consequences and conflict potential of information travel resulting from common SNS designs. These detected conflicts can be used to elicit requirements for solutions — these requirements may in turn be useful in designing access control models.

16.2   Approaching Privacy in Social Networks

In this section we motivate and define different approaches to privacy. In order to do that, we start from the way the privacy problem is currently framed in privacy debates and in data protection legislation. We then proceed to describe the three relevant privacy approaches and the privacy definitions they rely on. For each approach we also state their advantages and disadvantages. Later, we return to the data question by identifying the privacy-relevant data most characteristic of social networks.

16.2.1   Data I: Personal Data

Since computers are about data and data processing, any concept of privacy in computational environments will concern (centrally or also) data, in particular "personal data." *Personal data* is "any information relating to an identified or identifiable natural person [...]; an identifiable person is one who can be identified, directly or indirectly, in particular by reference to an identification number or to one or more factors specific to his physical, physiological, mental, economic, cultural or social identity" (EU Directive 95/46/EC [15], Art. 2 (a); this is defined in a similar way in other legal contexts). Notice the emphasis on identity, which is assumed to be unique and identifiable for one natural person; in line with this emphasis, US terminology talks about *personally identifiable* data. The standard types of personal data are profile data describing individuals, including name, address, health status, etc.

16.2.2   Privacy as Hiding: Confidentiality

In one of its historical moments, privacy has been defined as "the right to be let alone" [50]. Although originally formulated as a right that protects individuals against gossip and slander, this construct has since then acquired a wider meaning. Namely, it refers to an individualistic liberal tradition in which an intrinsic pre-existing self is granted a sphere of autonomy free from intrusions from both an overbearing state and the pressure of social norms [39]. This definition has also been popularly used by computer scientists and has been interpreted as an autonomous (digital) sphere in which the data about persons is protected, outside of which the data remains confidential.

Data confidentiality — the protection of data from unauthorized access — is a strong and useful translation of such privacy concerns into digital space. After all, once data about a person exists in a digital form, it is very difficult to provide individuals with any guarantees on the control of that data. Data collected using current technologies represent activities of individuals in social life that for many are assumed to be private. To preserve privacy, in that sense, is then to keep this data private, in other words confidential from a greater public. Not exchanging any data would preserve privacy but is inconvenient and probably also not desirable. Therefore, a lot of the privacy research in computer science is concerned with other forms of partial confidentiality, like anonymity.

Anonymity is achieved by unlinking the identity of the person from the traces that her activities leave in information systems. Anonymity keeps the identity of the persons in information systems confidential but is not necessarily concerned with how public the traces subsequently become. This is also reflected in data protection legislation which by definition cannot and does not protect anonymous data [21].

In technical terms, anonymity can be based on different models. In communications, anonymity is achieved when an individual is not identifiable within a limited set of users, called the anonymity set [38]. An individual carries out a transaction anonymously if she cannot be distinguished by an observer from others in that set. The observer, often also called the adversary, may obtain some additional information [12]. Depending on the observer's capabilities, different models can be constructed with varying degrees of anonymity for the given anonymity set. Exactly what degree of anonymity is sufficient in a given context is dependent on legal and social consequences of a data breach and is an open question [12].

In databases and SNS, the conditions for establishing anonymity sets and the targeted objectives are different. Anonymity is a popular requirement when (SNS) data are to be analyzed (e.g., data-mined), especially when this is done by third parties. One difference to communications anonymity is that methods to anonymize databases aspire to protect the utility of the anonymized data for analysts. More specifically, it is an objective of these methods to provide the analyst with data that allow the inference of certain information, while forestalling the inference of certain other information (information that could lead to privacy breaches). This type of research is called privacy preserving data mining (PPDM). PPDM research on relational databases as well as network data has shown that simple anonymization approaches do not work, because ill-meaning or even unsuspecting analysts ("adversaries") may, through additional information based on the network structure, recover the supposedly-unlinked identities and/or find more information about these data subjects [46, 28, 30, 42, 13]. In Chapter 18 of this book, Hay, Miklau and Jensen give a detailed account of opportunities and challenges for network anonymization, again with the additional goal of preserving the utility of the network data.

These results demand that the scope of what is defined as "personal data" be expanded. The expansion of the definition of personal data raises important research questions about the usability, efficiency, utility and practicability of privacy-as-confidentiality methods in social networks and in general. Further, where it is difficult to make confidentiality or anonymity guarantees, other approaches that address the privacy concerns raised may be considered. In the following two sections we motivate and describe two such approaches.

16.2.3   Privacy as Control: Informational Self-Determination

A wider notion of privacy, appearing in many legal codifications, defines the term not only as a matter of concealment of personal information, but also as the ability to control what happens with it. One reason for this notion, which does not call for strict data parsimony, is that the revelation of data is necessary and beneficial under many circumstances — and that control may help to prevent abuses of data thus collected.

This idea is expressed in Westin's [51] definition of *(data) privacy*: "the right of the individual to decide what information about himself should be communicated to others and under what circumstances" and in the term *informational self-determination* [9]. Informational self-determination is also expressed in international guidelines for data protection such as the OECD's Guidelines on the Protection of Privacy and Transborder Flows of Personal Data [35], the Fair Information Practices (FIP) *notice, choice, access, and security* [49, 19], or the principles of the EU Data Protection Directives [15, 16]. As an example, consider the principles set up in the OECD Guidelines: collection limitation, data quality, purpose specification, use limitation, security safeguards, openness, individual participation, and accountability.

An important class of tools to exercise (more) control over personal data is called *Identity Management Systems* (IDMS). There are different types of identity management systems, but here we refer to mechanisms that support separation of context-dependent virtual identities represented by pseudonyms of varying strength. IDMS allow individuals to establish and secure identities, describe those identities using attributes, follow the activities of their identities, and delete identities. They are often based on credentials, policies and access control methods.

In SNS an essential part of the configuration of one's profile is who gets to access what; and these "whos" are specified not on the basis of identity (only Mr. Ali gets to see my health data) or individual attributes (only people who are doctors get to see my health data), but on relationships, or in other words, the topology of the network (only my friends get to see my health data or only my friends and their friends get to see my health data). Thus, social network sites are in that sense identity management tools, which in turn are tools that implement the idea of privacy as control through topological vicinity.

A simple form of such access control defines access based on the path distance from the node that owns the data. Popular access models in current SNS comprise "friends" (only nodes one hop away from the data owner may see that profile) and "friends-of-friends" (only nodes at most two hops away may see the profile), or in some cases, friends at a longer path length [8]. An overview of current work related to identity management in social networks and a detailed description of different access-control models that protect a user's profile or relationships is given by Carminati, Ferrari, Kantarcioglu and Thuraisingham in Chapter 15 of this book.

Although informational self-determination principles are desirable, suggesting that individual control is always possible, desirable and effective can be misleading. This is the case for a number of reasons. First of all, collection limitation in one system does not protect against the aggregation of that data in many systems. Monitoring all revealed information in SNS may be overwhelming where the number of data controllers increase exponentially. A user may be overwhelmed by the difficulties of individual participation and unable to judge the risk of revealing information or using automated agents for such decision-making. Further, even if all these principles were implemented, it would be very difficult to identify violations. In the case of trusted parties, system security violations (i.e., hacked systems) or design failures (i.e., information leakages) or linking of different sources of safely released data may cause unwanted release of information. Last, data protection and most IDMS, by focusing on individual and identifiable data provides little protection with respect to aggregation of anonymized data, profiling based on correlations and patterns found in this aggregated data, and the consequent desirable or undesirable discriminations. In addition, privacy as control is an abstract concept that does not consider how people actually do and want to construct their identities. Hence, further approaches are needed, which assist in establishing an identity management practice. This is the topic of privacy as practice, to which we turn next.

16.2.4   Privacy as Practice: Identity Construction

Despite interesting research results in the area of privacy preserving methods and tools, individuals are daily confronted with the collection of massive amounts of data about them. This could be due to the market interests in collecting information; the lack of popular and usable privacy enhancing technologies; surveillance technologies that collect information on a mass level without consent; contexts in which identification is central to the services provided (i.e., in hospitals or in employment situations); or, simply due to the desire of individuals to reveal information about themselves with their names etc. By *privacy as practice*, we refer to the definition of the right to privacy as the freedom from unreasonable constraints on the construction of one's own identity, be it by strategically being able to reveal or conceal data. This approach requires domain specific and sociological analysis of users' and communities' information revelation and concealment needs as in the recent examples given in [23, 6, 7]. Such diversity of user concerns resulting in or in tension with privacy are often not emphasized in the privacy-as-confidentiality and privacy-as-control approaches.

Privacy as practiced demands the possibility to intervene in the flows of existing data and the re-negotiation of boundaries with respect to collected data. These two activities rest on, but extend the idea of privacy as informational self-determination in that they demand transparency with respect to aggregated datasets and the analysis methods and decisions applied to them. In this sense, these approaches define privacy not only as a right, but also as a public good [25].

Sociologists have investigated the idea that privacy is (social) practiced from various viewpoints. Linking these discussions to the discussions on privacy on the Internet and concrete PETs, Phillips [39] distinguishes between four *kinds of privacy* (which are not mutually exclusive). These comprise the above-mentioned right to be let alone and the possibility of separating identities. The third type is the *construction of the public/private divide*. This distinction concerns the social negotiation of what remains private (i.e., silent and out of the public discourse) and what becomes public. For example, in the case of voting, individuals may want to keep their choice private, and in the case of domestic violence, interest groups and individuals may have an interest in defining the "domestic" as a public issue. The fourth type of privacy is the *protection from surveillance*. In this context, surveillance refers to the creation and managing of social knowledge about population groups. This kind of privacy can easily be violated if individual observations are collated and used for statistical classification, which applied to individuals makes statements about their (non)compliance with norms, their belonging to groups with given properties and valuations, etc. Market segmentation is an example of the classification of population groups which may constitute a breach of this kind of privacy.

In a similar fashion, Palen and Dourish argue that "privacy management in everyday life involves combinations of social and technical arrangements that reflect, reproduce and engender social expectations, guide the interpretability of action, and evolve as both technologies and social practices change" [37]. Boyd and Ellison state that privacy in social networks sites is also implicated in users' ability to control impressions and manage social contexts [11].

These definitions emphasize that confidentiality and individual control are part of privacy, but not all. Privacy includes strategic concealment, but also revelation of information in different contexts, and these decisions are based on — and part of — a process of collective negotiation. Tools should therefore support data concealment and revelation to help individuals practice privacy individually and collectively.

For example, Lederer et al. [29] suggest improving privacy sensitivity in systems through feedback that enhances users' understanding of the privacy implications of their system use. This can be coupled with control mechanisms that allow users to conduct socially meaningful actions through them. These ideas have led to suggestions like the identityMirror [31] which learn and visualize a dynamic model of user's identity and tastes. A similar approach is suggested in the concept of privacy mirrors [33]. The authors criticize purely technical privacy preservation solutions that do not take the social and physical environments in which the technical systems are embedded into consideration. Making the collected data visible would make the underlying systems more understandable, enabling users to better shape those socio-technical systems, not only technically, but also socially and physically. A first implementation of privacy mirrors exists in Facebook through which users can set controls on their profile information and then check how their profile is seen by their friends, but not by non-friends.

Hansen's [24] proposal for linkage control in IDMS is a further example of these ideas. In her proposal to extend and improve the user experience of IDMS she suggests mechanisms that provide information about collected data to individuals and the general public. These mechanisms include informing users on possible and actual linkages, as well as de-linking options; communicating privacy breaches to individuals concerned; documenting the sources of data and algorithms used by data controllers as well as the recipients of analyzed data; making accessible personal data and also other data suitable to affect individuals; and providing effective tools to intervene in data linkages in order to execute corrections or deletions.

Social Networks as a Locus of Privacy as Control and Practice We frame existing Web-based social networks services as one of the first massively adopted IDMS (privacy as control) with the potential of providing insight into how improved practices can be developed (privacy as practice). SNS provide numerous and rich examples of user-provider-negotiation with respect to privacy. This can be anywhere from the privacy settings which have evolved immensely in the last two years, via the introduction of usable and integrated privacy policies, to the introduction of some simple forms of "privacy mirrors" as a standard feature etc. The latter are exemplary of tools designed to raise awareness, on which we from now on we will focus.

Summing up, all three approaches to privacy: privacy as confidentiality, privacy as control and privacy as practice can and should be used in developing systems. Each type of privacy requires different kinds of research, the compositionality of which also demands further study.

In this chapter, we emphasize the view of privacy as practice, investigate social networks as a locus of such practices, and describe methods to better support the identified processes and requirements.

16.2.5 Privacy in Social Network Sites: Deriving Requirements from Privacy Concerns

Before we review the definition of personal data and suggest ways in which privacy as practice may be developed, we shortly summarize the results of a media study on privacy concerns that may or have lead to privacy breaches in SNS. Our objective is to understand what the privacy concerns are, how the underlying principles and design of SNS lead to these concerns, and how a practice around these problems can be developed. To understand privacy concerns in today's SNS, we combined a literature study of a wide range of computer science, sociological and legal approaches, a study of large SNS' design and privacy-strategy communications, and a manual content analysis of news and blogs during a time of intensive discussion of Facebook's and Myspace's privacy practices. The result was a categorization of privacy breaches in SNS into the following [22]:

Indeterminate visibility denotes the problem of a user's profile information being visible to others without the user's explicit knowledge or approval. *Separation of digital identities and aggregation Separation of digital identities* refers to the construction of social identities by individuals that selectively reveal and conceal information in specific contexts and roles [39, 34]; *aggregation* is the de-separation of these identities. *Contested ownership:* are explicit and implicit definitions of data ownership on SNS that may lead to privacy breaches.* *Misappropriation* is the use of SNS data out of context or for previously undefined purposes.

16.2.6 Data II: Relational Information and Transitive Access Control

In the reports on privacy breaches in SNS that we analyzed in [22], a common theme arose throughout the different types of breaches: many concerns were raised about the practices in SNS with respect to what we term relational information and transitive access control.

In short, relational information (RI) is data that, unlike profile information, is regarded as "belonging" or "related" to more than one user; for example, the information representing the "friends relationship" between A and B may be said to belong to both A and B. With relational information, both A and B have some control rights on that information. Which rights these are depends on if both have equal permissions on the relational information — as is the case with a friends relationship — or, if there are differences in the permissions distributed to the various related parties. The latter can, for example, depend on whose profile the information is placed: the owner of the profile usually has more rights than those who post information on that profile.

Transitive access control (TAC) refers to the fact that by defining topology based access control based on path lengths greater than or equal to two, a profile A allows her friends to co-define who can access her information; for example, if A specifies that "friends of friends" may see his profile, then a friend B — by her choice of friends — co-defines who may access A's profile. Hence, effectively A's friends are assigned the right to give and revoke to their friends access permissions to A's selected objects. There again is a hierarchy in the permissions; a friend B can grant and revoke permissions to their friends

---

*While we called the third breach category "contested ownership," we would like to point out that this term was chosen to reflect the wording used in the materials, and that we do not claim to make any statements about the associated legal concepts. To motivate our choice of terminology and put it into context, we will discuss the more general question of how a resource pertains to a person (such that the person has or should have "something to say" about its use). In this chapter, we cannot solve the legal issues, and we therefore avoid the term "ownership" and its derivatives wherever possible, preferring the (intentionally) underspecified "belonging to" or "related to".

that are not already assigned permissions by A. Further, if the access path length defined by A is $p > 2$, then friends at path length $p - 2$ are able to delegate the permission to co-define the access list of A to their friends.

There are various reasons why RI and TAC are useful for the different stakeholders of SNS. First, TAC makes it easier to share resources by allowing friends of a certain path length to grant further profiles in the network access to that resource. The TAC model hence overlaps with the SNS providers inter-est in achieving maximum sharing.[†] Second, many of the information objects in SNS, even at the time of creation, are related to many. The combination of TAC and RI addresses this problem by giving all users related to an in-formation object access and some control permissions. It enables information objects to be collectively managed by multiple profiles who are granted a lim-ited set of control permissions throughout the information objects' lifetime. Third, TAC provides a collaborative solution to deal with the expansion and contraction of the network and maybe even a solution to deal with issues of privacy collectively.

Yet, while RI and TAC are cornerstones of the attractiveness of social net-works for users, they also give rise to numerous privacy breaches [22]. Own-ership of RI may be contested in various ways (what can be decided by A, what by B, and what happens when they grant and revoke different access rights with respect to a relational information object?), and TAC may lead to a wide and indeterminate visibility of (profile or relational) information. This usually has a consequence for any functionality to keep identities or audiences separated.

In addition, different profiles may have different preferences on how the consequences should be handled. The misappropriation of RI is a distinct and commercially attractive possibility in SNS whose business model rests on the "network value of customers." Misappropriation may for example occur if, in order to reveal relational information to third parties, it is sufficient for one of the related profiles to agree to the third party's terms. Finally, misappropriation may also occur because deletion of relational information is complicated as long as one or more of the related profiles want to keep their relational information and hence the integrity of their profiles.

Analyzing privacy concerns in SNS only with respect to "personal data" belonging to individual users falls short of analyzing many of the problems arising from relational information and TAC. This is also a problem for ex-isting data protection legislation which is focused on classical definitions of personal data and has no terms dealing with relationality of data or with the transparency of data collections and data mining methods.

As a step forward, in the next section we will model both of these concepts in detail. We will then use that model to develop a method with which we

---

[†]A recent user study of Facebook users show that 87% of the users have default or permissive privacy settings [45] which reinforces privacy salience practices by the providers of SNS [8]

can identify types of conflicts that lead to privacy concerns. Later, we will discuss possible solutions to these conflicts using privacy awareness raising data mining techniques.

16.3   Relational Information, Transitive Access Control and Conflicts

Relational information objects raise a number of requirements and design questions: Which of the data subjects or controllers can access, distribute or delete such information? What conflicts may arise when relational information and Transitive Access Control are applied in an SNS, and how can these conflicts be systematically detected prior to implementation? How can these conflicts be addressed? In addition to keeping attributes of profiles confidential, as discussed in Chapter 15, what alternative solutions may data mining techniques offer for users of SNS? To answer these questions, we first define the notions in more detail.

16.3.1   Transitive Access Control and Relational Information

Access control in information systems defines which principals (persons, processes, machines, ...) have access to which resources in the system — which files they can read, which programs they can execute, how they share data with other principals, and so on [3]. Often a distinction is made between mandatory and discretionary access control. Mandatory access control occurs when there is a central instance defining access rules, where resources have trust levels that they require and principals have trust levels that they can prove — also called label-based access control. Mandatory access control is limited in responding to the needs of systems with dynamic principals and resources.

Under certain conditions, SNS make use of discretionary access control models. The specifics of these conditions are described below. *Discretionary access control* is a mode in which the creators or "owners" of files assign access rights, and a subject with a discretionary access to information can pass that information on to another subject [17].[‡] In [27] the authors make a distinction between access permission and control permission. *Access permission* is the permission of a principal to access a resource in some manner. *Control per-*

[‡]TCSEC (1985) defines discretionary access control without mention of "ownership," but rather as "a means of restricting access to objects based on the identity of subjects or groups, or both, to which they belong. The controls are discretionary in the sense that a subject with a certain access permission is capable of passing that permission (perhaps indirectly) on to any other subject [...]."

mission allows principals to grant or revoke access permissions. Sometimes, this includes the ability to pass a subset of the available control permission to other users [27].

Transitive access control is the type of discretionary access control that is activated in SNS when users grant and revoke both access permissions and a subset of their control permissions to others. Transitive access control is used when users manage relational information or allow friends-of-friends, or friends at longer path lengths to access their information objects.

Each information resource of a profile in SNS we call an *information object*. If an information object has two or more profiles with some control permissions at some point in its lifetime, it is called a *relational information object*. Some resources have multiple controllers during initialization. In an SNS in which friendship is bidirectional, each relationship between two profiles, by virtue of both profiles having control permissions on the relationship, is relational information. A photograph of a profile A, once commented by another profile B, becomes relational information, since by commenting B henceforth receives permission to grant her friends of a desired path length access to both her comment and the photograph [§].

In our definition of relational information, we focus on explicit relatedness. We disregard the less clear-cut cases where the establishment of relatedness is technically difficult although legally relevant, such as the data subjects of a photograph made public by somebody who do not inform all the data subjects.

16.3.2 Inconsistency and Reciprocity Conflicts with TAC and RI

Privacy concerns with respect to relational information and transitive access control, and resulting privacy breaches, have been expressed by users and experts in the media and the blogosphere as we discussed briefly in Section 16.2. With respect to the underlying design and configuration of TAC, two types of conflicts can occur among profiles that may lead to the articulated privacy concerns: inconsistencies among users' TAC settings and reciprocity conflicts. These are defined as follows:

Inconsistency among users' TAC settings. TAC settings can easily lead to unexpected visibilities. As an example, consider that user A's friends are $\{C, D, E\}$, and B's friends are $\{C, F, G\}$. If both A and B have set their access permissions to "friends" and then enter a relationship, for both A and B, the

---

[§]Recently Facebook has changed their privacy settings. As a result, now there is a hierarchy between the owner's privacy settings and the privacy settings of those users who post information objects on the owner's profiles: the profile owner's settings may override the settings of the posting user, although not always. There are many varieties of how these conflicts are resolved on Facebook. The conflict detection model that we develop can be adopted to also address conflicts arising from the way privacy settings are negotiated with respect to such information objects.

new relationship becomes visible to the union $\{C, D, E, F, G\}$, a set greater than their respective set of friends. This leads to an inconsistency between the permissions granted by each profile and the actual accessibility of their relationship information. This type of access inconsistency is pervasive in today's social networks: For example, in a German social network with 120,000 users investigated in [41], more than two thirds of the users' hidden relationships were disclosed to the public due to unilateral friendship disclosure by their immediate friends.

Reciprocity among users' access to information objects. Differing privacy preferences with varying sets of friends may be desirable in SNS. Hence, inconsistency among users' TAC settings may be acceptable. But then, the profiles should be provided with information about the collective effect of the privacy settings of their sub-networks. In order to inform the user of the extent to which her relational information is accessible, reciprocity of some degree in the flow of information is a required condition. This idea of reciprocity is derived from the theory of social translucence. Social translucence is an approach to designing digital systems that emphasizes making social information visible to the participants of a system. It is mapped to digital systems through the use of "social proxies," minimalist graphical representations of the online presence and activities of people. Specifically, these systems work with the concepts of visibility, awareness and accountability [14]. For social networks, social translucence can be applied through different degrees of reciprocity in information flow and access. In its stronger form it is possible to stipulate that if a profile A can access profile B's information, then that accessibility should also hold in the opposite direction. This is called strong reciprocity and usually holds when a relationship is established between two profiles. Strong reciprocity may not always hold with immediate friends and/or with friends of a greater path length. In some cases, a weaker reciprocity may suffice, consisting of B knowing that A can access her profile. A feedback system that informs profile B of the set S of users who have access to her relational information can be implemented only if "weak" reciprocity is permitted. Not all members of the feedback set S may agree with being listed in a feedback mechanism. This may lead to weak reciprocity conflicts. Depending on the degree of reciprocity required, different types of conflicts may occur ¶.

Depending on the preferences of different profiles and the way TAC is implemented, inconsistencies and reciprocity conflicts may occur. We argue that if the design options with respect to relational information and transitive access control can be handled during requirements engineering, such that the different inconsistencies and reciprocity conflicts are discussed with the different system stakeholders, then some of the privacy breaches mentioned in Section

---

¶It is always possible to expect reciprocity of higher orders recursively: if B knows that A can access her profile, then A should know that B knows that A can access her profile. This is a typical problem of auditing the audits or awareness of awareness. For now we are only concerned with "first order" reciprocity.

16.2 can be avoided. Depending on the different stakeholders' requirements, alternative TAC and relational information models can be designed.

Where the mitigation of inconsistencies is not possible, data mining tools can be used to improve users' awareness of information distribution in order to support their privacy practices and negotiations. These tools can usually be implemented if weak reciprocity conflicts do not occur. After all, if users do not want to be mentioned in feedback systems (do not agree to weak reciprocity), then tools that mention their profile and access information to others would lead to a violation of their privacy needs.

In the following, we develop a method with which inconsistencies and reciprocity conflicts based on relational information and transitive access control can be discovered and can be handled during requirements engineering to address users' privacy concerns. As an example, we analyze four alternative TAC models with respect to one of the articulated privacy concerns: indeterminate visibility. We show how the possible solutions interact with the functional requirements of sharing information and enabling social networking.

16.3.3 Formal Definitions

In this section, we formalize SNS, permissions, inconsistencies and reciprocity conflicts.

SNS are typically modeled as a graph. In a common form of such graph models, each node stands for the user's profile and all the information objects contained therein, while the set of edges stands for the relationships between the profiles.[||] In such models, it is assumed that every information object is related to and controlled by a single profile.

Since the conflicts we study are about relational information objects and the conflictual permissions granted to those, we model each social network profile as a set of information objects. Each information object, be it the relationship between two profiles, a photo or a comment, is represented explicitly by a node in the graph. Each edge models the relatedness of that information object to other profiles or other information objects. A profile node in our graph therefore does not represent all the information that a user has put online, but rather is a root node that functions as a quasi "object id" for all the related information objects.

The notation We introduce the notation for the graph to represent the SNS profiles and their information objects. We assume that the social network only

---

[||]From now on we refer to a "profile" in an SNS rather than to a "user." This is for a number of reasons: firstly, a user may have multiple profiles; secondly, the profile of a user is not the user herself, but a set of information objects she collects, creates and distributes; and last, profiles may have no user behind them i.e., attacks on social networks may consist of injecting spam profiles into the network that may have serious implications for the functionality as well as the security of a social network.

contains relationships that are confirmed by both related parties i.e., there are no unidirectional relationships. The information objects in the graph are defined as follows:

- $P = p_1, p_2, ..., p_n$ is the set of profiles in the SNS.

- R stands for the set of relationships, r_{ij} denotes a relationship between two profiles $p_i, p_j \in P$. Each tuple (i,j) is in the set $R^{<>} \subset 1, ..., n \times 1, ..., n$ as follows: if $(i, j) \in R^{<>}$ then $(j, i) \in R^{<>}$, and $(i, i) \notin R^{<} >$.

- M stands for any other informational object, which can be multimedia or comments or links.

- O is the set of informational objects o where $O = R \cup M \cup P$.

Next, we introduce the permissions. In order to enable transitive access control, profiles should be able to delegate control permissions. Hence, we define two types of permissions:

- access permissions: If a profile grants access permission to another profile for an information object, then that profile may read that information object. For the sake of simplicity, we define access permissions only as the right to read an information object, and not the right to edit, execute or delete an information object.

- control permissions: A principal with control permissions with respect to an information object has access permissions, can grant and revoke additional access permissions, and, in some cases, can delegate the right to grant access permission to others for that information object.

We assume that all profiles may create new information objects. The creators of an information object have control permissions for that object. If permitted, profiles may add textual or media comments to existing information objects.

Deletion and disconnection from information objects is an important functionality and a complicated matter in social networks. With relational information, deletion becomes a locus for conflicts. For now, we do not consider commenting, disconnection or deletion in our models. Hence, we assume that once permissions are distributed, these can no longer be changed. Thus:

- $C(o)$ and $A(o)$ respectively denote the set of profiles that have control and access permissions on an information object $o \in O$.

- $F(p)$ returns the set of profiles that establish a relationship with p. For a subset of the profiles $Q \subseteq P$, $F(Q)$ returns the union of $F(p)$ for each $p \in Q$. p is not included in $F(p)$ so that we can distinguish between the different sets "friends" and "friends-of-friends." The union of those two sets is denoted with $FoF(p)$.

- If $p \in C(o)$ for some information object o, then it can assign some permissions to that information object. The union of all the access permissions assigned to an object by profiles in $C(o)$ define who can access o.

  $S(p, o)$ returns the permissions a profile assigns to an information object o. The permissions return the tuple $(controlPermission, accessPermission)$. The value of each permission set may vary between $C(o)$ and P. An information object o is private if $S(p, o).controlPermission = S(p, o).accessPermission = p$. We also add a convention in order to keep profiles with no access permissions from being able to grant or revoke control permissions:

$$S(p, o).controlPermission \subseteq S(p, o).accessPermission \subseteq P$$

- $T(p)$ refers to all the permissions set by a profile p, such that $\{S(p, o) : p \in C(o)\}$.

- $s, t \in \mathbb{N}$ are variables that state the length of a path in a graph.

Rules describing who can belong to $C(o)$, and what kind of control rights will be assigned, need to be defined for each information object o. These definitions may contain conflicts and may sometimes not be desirable. Further, the permissions themselves may reveal information that was not meant for a greater public.

In this chapter we concentrate on one type of relational information, namely, relationships themselves. Relationships are information objects that become relational as soon as they are established i.e., $C(r_{ij}) = \{p_i, p_j\}$. The set $C(o)$ of a relationship is static and never gets extended. Both profiles in $C(r_{i,j})$ have the right to grant access rights to and/or delete $r_{i,j}$. We plan to study further types of relational information and address conflicts with respect to the assignment of control permissions in future work.

The graph   We can now construct our SNS graph $G = (V, E)$ that includes relationships and profiles:

- V: there are two different types of vertices in G:

  - there are vertices labeled with an element of P.
  - there are vertices labeled with an element of R.

- E: edges connect vertices labeled with an element of P and vertices labeled with an element of R. When two profiles p_i and p_j establish a relationship, a vertex r_{ij} and edges (p_i, r_{ij}) and (p_j, r_{ij}) are inserted to the graph. The edges are undirected. If two profiles establish a relationship, then a path of length two exists between them.

Example: Figure 16.1 is a depiction of a graph H which only includes profiles and relationships as information objects. The profiles in H are $P = \{p_1, p_2, p_3, p_4\}$, and the relationships are $R = \{r_{12}, r_{13}, r_{23}, r_{14}\}$. The $C(r_{ij})$ for each of the relationships are the relationship partners. So far, we have not defined any permissions for information objects in H.

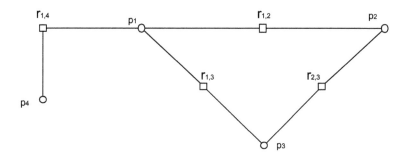

FIGURE 16.1: SNS graph H. Each user is represented by a profile and her relationships.

The conflicts:

- **Inconsistency Conflicts:**

    - **Control Permission Inconsistency**: There is a control permission inconsistency if:

        $$\exists p_i, p_j \in P: S(p_i, o).controlPermission \neq S(p_j, o).$$
        $$controlPermission \text{ where } p_i, p_j \in C(o)$$

        Thus, a network is free of control-permission inconsistency if for all o:

        $$\bigcup_{\forall p_i \in P} S(p_i, o).controlPermission = \bigcap_{\forall p_i \in P} S(p_i, o).$$

    - **Access Permission Inconsistency**: There is an access permission inconsistency if:

        $$\exists p_i, p_j \in P: S(p_i, o).accessPermission \neq S(p_j, o).$$
        $$accessPermission \text{ where } p_i, p_j \in C(o)$$

        The global rule for freedom from access-control-permission inconsistency is analogous to that for control permissions.

If permission inconsistencies exist and are acceptable, and awareness mechanisms are desirable, then it is also necessary to determine existing reciprocity conflicts.

- **Reciprocity Conflicts**: The type of reciprocity may vary for different kinds of information objects. This may result from the definition of the set $C(o)$ for that information object: profiles contain information that belong to one, relationships are information that belong to two, whereas other information objects may belong to different sets of profiles over time. The types of reciprocity may also vary. In the case of relationships and profiles, we distinguish between two kinds of reciprocity:

  - strong reciprocity: if p_i has access or control permissions to p_j's information object o, then p_j has the same access or control permissions with respect to an equivalent information object m of profile p_i. Strong reciprocity can be a pre-condition for socially translucent systems by virtue of making all participants aware and accountable of their sharing and privacy practices.

  - weak reciprocity: if p_i has access or control permissions to p_j's information object o, then p_j knows that p_i has these permissions with respect to information object o. "Knowing" here does not necessarily include monitoring whether and how often information object o has been accessed by p_i. Weak reciprocity is a pre-condition for most awareness mechanisms.

  - no expectation of reciprocity: This means that p_i makes information object o public and has no expectations of reciprocity.

  If strong or weak reciprocity is required and not fulfilled, then we say that there is respectively a strong or weak reciprocity conflict between two users.

Ultimately, we would like to check on a given graph how given permissions on information objects, some of which are relational information, behave on a social network represented by a graph G. We would like to verify if and when inconsistencies appear that are not evident from the individual definitions of access permissions. In particular, we would like to see how the graph structure of social networks affects the behavior of the permissions. If inconsistencies exist and are acceptable, then we would like to know which reciprocity conflicts have to be addressed to implement awareness mechanisms in SNS.

In order to analyze reciprocity conflicts, we define some helping sets. For each source profile p_i, we need the sets of profiles and the relationship boxes that p_i can access. We also need the sets of profiles that p_i knows about, by virtue of either accessing their relationships or permissions, although she cannot access their profile. We call these the *outbound sets* of a profile. What p_i can access depends on the permissions of the other profiles on their information objects. The *inbound sets* of a profile are those profiles that can access p_i's profile and relationships, as well as those profiles that know p_i but cannot access its profile. These sets depend on the permissions set by p_i's subnetwork. By comparing the outbound and inbound sets, we can determine if reciprocity conflicts occur between profiles in an SNS.

16.4 Social Network Construction and Conflict Analysis

In the following, we show our method for detecting conflicts based on RI and TAC using the outbound and inbound sets. In order to do that, we define tokens that model permissions. Then we describe the behavior of the permission tokens, given the permitted activities in the SNS. We summarize four alternative TAC cases, for which we analyze the conflicts using our conflict detection method. Finally, we evaluate the advantages and disadvantages of each case with respect to the privacy concerns raised in Section 16.2 and the functionality of social networks.

In general, the way permissions behave in a graph are dynamic and are based on the activities of profiles. By *activities*, we mean any profile action that updates the graph. These include establishing new relationships, introducing new media objects, commenting on existing information objects, etc. Here, we solely study the establishment of relationships and study its effects on discovering information objects. The information discovery activity also returns the outbound and inbound sets necessary for conflict detection.

16.4.1 Constructing the Graph with Tokens for Permissions

In order to check the permission inconsistencies, as well as reciprocity conflicts, we use tokens, and we rename relationship nodes r_{ij} as *relationship boxes*. Each relationship box r_{ij} is labeled and the permission tokens are inserted to related boxes as relationships are established. These tokens enable the enforcement of the permissions set by the various profiles.

We focus on a basic SNS model. In this basic model, we fix control permissions to always be limited to the creators of information objects, where $o \subset P \cup R$. Therefore, control permissions are static and are not further discussed in our model.

Token distribution Each access permission token is a tuple (p, s), where $p \in P$ and s is a path length. In our model, each profile initially has a permission preference for all its information objects that is fixed (since we do not study deletion, it is also not possible to consider changes in permissions). Thus, all her information objects are accessible to a previously selected set based on path length, which can be defined as friends (s=2), friends-of-friends (s=4), etc. The size of the set changes as the profiles in the SNS establish relationships.

The existence of a token enables the traversal of certain paths. The information objects that can be traversed to starting from a given profile are the information objects accessible to that profile. The p in a token (p, s) can be used as both: permission for some other profile to access a profile p, and for p to access the information objects of another profile.

When a relationship is established between two profiles p_i and p_j, two edges and a node are inserted into the graph between the two profiles. We stipulate that when a relationship is established then at a minimum the profile information and the relationship box are accessible to the newly befriended profile. Therefore, two tokens (pi, s) and (p_j, t) are inserted for each of the newly befriended profiles to enable access to the new relationship box and the corresponding profile.

Further, depending on the path lengths defined by tokens in the existing relationship boxes and the path lengths of the new tokens inserted into the newly created relationship box, propagation of tokens takes place. The path length of each token is reduced by two when propagated. The *Propagation Algorithm* consists of three steps given in the following algorithm:

[**Propagate** Step 1:] p_i and p_j propagate tokens from existing relationship boxes with $s > 0$ to the newly established relationship box r_{ij}.

[**Propagate** Step 2:] p_i and p_j propagate tokens in the established relationship box r_{ij} with $s > 0$ to all their existing relationship boxes.

[**Propagate** Step 3:] depending on the maximum path length $s > 0$ of all the tokens propagated in Steps 1 and 2, profiles at a maximum path length $s - 2$ from p_i and p_j propagate the new tokens to further relationship boxes.

The tokens only contain information with respect to propagation path length. Further constraints with respect to distribution can be defined. For example, if "common friends only" is the preference in the network, then in Step 3 tokens are only propagated to the relationship boxes of common friends.

Further, paths to friends beyond friends-of-friends results in tokens traveling in cycles. This has an effect on if and how duplicate tokens are treated in relationship boxes. Since these cycles occur in none of the four cases we study, we erase all duplicate tokens (tokens referring to the same profile), keeping only those with maximum path length.

Graph Traversal based on tokens The traversal rules based on the permission tokens are as follows:

1. traversal to a relationship box: a profile p_i can traverse to a relationship box, if p_i can traverse to a profile neighboring the relationship box, and if the relationship box contains a token (p_i, s) where $s \geq 0$.

2. traversal to a profile: a profile p_i can traverse to another profile p_k, $k \neq i$ if:

  - there is a token (p_k, t) where $t > 0$ in every relationship box which p_i has access to on a path between p_i and p_k, and
  - in each token (p_k, t) that p_i collects on its path, t is increasing.

Example   Figure 16.2 shows a graph that resulted from three profiles interacting with each other. p_1 and p_2 wish to give their friends access permissions to their information objects – these being $p_1, p_2, r_{12}, r_{23}-$, while p_3 wishes to give her friends and friends-of-friends access permissions, written $FoF(p_3)) = F(p_3) \cup F(F(p3))$. Their permissions result in the token settings shown in the figure.

  - p_1 and p_2 can traverse to each other's profiles and access all relationship boxes

  - p_2 and p_3 can traverse to each other's profiles and access all relationship boxes

  - p_1 can traverse to p_3's profile, while the opposite is not the case. This is a result of the traversal to profiles defined above: there are tokens (p_3, s) with increasing path lengths in the relationship boxes on the path to p_3, and both relationships boxes are accessible to p_1. In the other direction, there is no token (p_1, s) where $s > 0$ in r_{23}. p_3 can see the relationship box r_{12} because p_2 has allowed p_3 to do so according to the traversal rule to relationship boxes.

FIGURE 16.2: Example: tokens define traversals to profiles and relationships boxes.

   In order to perform conflict analysis, we use the *Information-Objects Discovery Algorithm*. This algorithm traverses the graph once the permissions are distributed with an exhaustive traversal procedure such as breadth-first. For each profile node encountered during this traversal, a tuple $(profile, inboundsets, outboundsets)$ is added to an initially empty set $Traversable_{I}nformation_{O}bjects$. The set $Traversable_{I}nformation_{O}bjects$ is the output of the algorithm. The inbound and outbound sets are then used to identify inconsistencies and reciprocity conflicts among profiles.

16.4.2 Relationship Building and Information Discovery in Different Types of Social Networks

We now summarize conflict detection for four cases. The four cases involve making profiles and relationships accessible to others, i.e., beyond the profiles in $C(o), o \in P \cup R$. As argued above, this type of access is necessary for a functioning social network – on the one hand, profiles should be accessible enough to make interesting discoveries, on the other hand, the profiles' privacy preferences should be observed and undesired access should be minimized. We have selected four cases that are (a) as simple as possible and show the basic features of this problem, that (b) build on one another, that (c) reflect existing default and other possible settings in existing SNS [8].

In particular, in most existing SNS, establishing a relationship between two profiles p_i and p_j means that by default, it becomes visible to all friends, i.e., $F(p_i) \cup F(p_j)$ (Case 1). An alternative, which is currentlt not available on SNS, is to make the relationships only visible to common friends, denoted $F(p_i) \cap F(p_j)$ (Case 2). In some existing SNS, profiles can be made accessible to friends and friends-of-friends, shortly stated as $FoF(p)$. This means relationships are accessible to $FoF(p_i) \cup FoF(p_j)$ (Case 3). Case 4 investigates what happens when preferences differ, with some users preferring a Case-1 setting and others a Case-3 setting. More complex and differentiated settings can be constructed on this basis, also including information objects shareable by many; they are the subject of future work.

Here, we will describe in detail our model for Case 1, shortly summarize the other three cases, and move on to an evaluation of all four models with respect to inconsistencies, reciprocity conflicts and of the privacy concerns raised earlier — indeterminate visibility.

16.4.2.1 Case 1: Information objects accessible only to friends $(F(p_i) \cup F(p_j))$

Constructing the Model: This is the most open model possible that is limited to friends of first degree. If a relationship is established, then both relationship partners can see each others' profiles and list of all friends. $F(p_i)$ can see p_i's relationship with p_j but cannot access p_j's profile, unless they are also in the set $F(p_j)$. The opposite is also the case. We call this the SimpleFriendsOnlySNS.

The algorithms The algorithm consists of a straightforward application of the relationship box insertion and the *Propagation Algorithm* sketched above. Since tokens are propagatcd at most once (maximum s value is 2, and hence any token with $s = 2$ can only be propagated once) by the newly related profiles, no cycles occur that affect the propagation of tokens. Hence, it is enough if two profiles that establish a relationship complete the first two propagation steps described above.

In order to complete the conflict analysis, we run the *Information-Objects Discovery Algorithm*. For the model SimpleFriendsOnlySNS, the relevant outbound sets and the inbound sets for each p_i returned by the algorithm is as follows:

- *AccessibleProfiles$_{p_i}$*: only p_i's friends are accessible to p_i.

- *AccessibleRelations$_{p_i}$*: various subsets of the relationship boxes of $F(p_i)$ are accessible to p_i.

- *KnowsProfiles$_{p_i}$*: through being able to access friends' relationship boxes, p_i knows the friends of $F(p_i)$, that is $p_x \in F(F(p_i))$ such that $p_x \notin AccessibleProfiles_{p_i}$.

- *ProfilesAccessibleTo$_{p_i}$*: p_i's profile is only accessible to her friends $F(p_i)$.

- *RelationsAccessibleTo$_{p_i}$*: p_i's relationship boxes are accessible to $F(p_i)$, and since friends of $F(p_i)$ can access their relationship boxes, a subset of her relationship boxes are also accessible to friends of $F(p_i)$. In total, different subsets of p_i's relationship boxes are accessible to $FoF(p_i)$.

- *ProfileKnownTo$_{p_i}$*: although they are not mentioned in the permissions, by virtue of being able to access subsets of p_i's relationship boxes, $p_x \in F(F(p_i))$ knows p_i, and belongs to the set *ProfileKnownTo$_{p_i}$* unless $p_x \notin AccessibleProfiles_{p_i}$.

Conflict analysis:

We will now check for access permission inconsistencies and reciprocity conflicts in the SimpleFriendsOnlySNS model. Control permission inconsistencies are not an issue, since we decided to keep the control permissions fixed.

- access permission inconsistency: If $F(p_i) \neq F(p_j)$, then we have an access permission inconsistency. If $F(p_i) \neq F(p_j)$, then some $p_k \in F(p_j)$ and not in $F(p_i)$ can access the relationship box r_{ij}, although p_i had limited the access permission for r_{ij} to $F(p_i)$. According to p_j's settings, the access to r_{ij} for p_k is allowed.

- reciprocity conflict: Strong reciprocity exists for profiles and relationship boxes, since for every p_i the following holds:

$$AccessibleProfiles_{p_i} = ProfilesAccessiblcTo_{p_i},$$

$$AccessibleRelations_{p_i} = RelationsAccessibleTo_{p_i}$$

$$KnowsProfiles_{p_i} = ProfilesKnownTo_{p_i}.$$

Strong reciprocity also implies weak reciprocity. Thus, there are no reciprocity conflicts in SimpleFriendsOnlySNS.

Model evaluation: We conclude that with the SimpleFriendsOnlySNS, the only conflict is the access permission inconsistency. We have also verified that there are no reciprocity conflicts. The access permission inconsistency can be eased by inserting feedback systems that show the difference between permissions and their behavior (see Section 16.5.1 below). The SimpleFriendsOnlySNS model is open to socially translucent design, as it produces no reciprocity conflicts. As a design, SimpleFriendsOnlySNS is static and offers the users little flexibility with respect to preferences with alternative path lengths. The access to relational information is co-determined by friends, and can only be extended to friends-of-friends of a given profile. Hence, although the model is not optimal for sharing beyond immediate friends, it is a model which provides a good overview of how and how far information can travel in the network.

16.4.2.2 Case 2: Information objects accessible only to common friends $(F(p_i) \cap F(p_j))$

Constructing the model: The SimpleCommonFriendsOnlySNS model is constrained in that only common friends are able to see that a relationship exists. This also means that access to a profile only reveals the list of common friends. If there is no central instance of the SNS, the SimpleCommonFriendsOnlySNS causes the problem of verifying p_i and p_j's common friends without revealing information about the friends they do not have in common. This could be solved using zero-knowledge proofs or through a trusted third party that would do comparisons of encrypted lists of friends. This is not the focus of this chapter, so we simply assume that there is a function that returns the list of common friends.

Model evaluation: The SimpleCommonFriendsOnlySNS model avoids inconsistencies and reciprocity conflicts. At the same time, it is a very conservative model in which the network visibility of profiles is very small. As a design, SimpleCommonFriendsOnlySNS is static with respect to preference alternatives. Further, the model makes it difficult to discover and establish new communities where common friends are sparse.

16.4.2.3 Case 3: Relationship accessible to $FoF(p_i) \cup FoF(p_j)$

Constructing the Model:
The SimpleFoFOnlySNS allows relationships to be visible to friends of friends. If a relationship r_{ij} is established, both $FoF(p_i) \cup FoF(p_j)$ can see that this relationship exists. The model is similar to the SimpleFriendsOnlySNS.

The relationship establishment algorithm is the same as that of the model SimpleFriendsOnlySNS up until the last propagation step (see Propagate Algorithm Step 3) in which friends of p_i also update their relationship boxes, so that the access permissions also hold for friends-of-friends.

Model evaluation: Case 3 is a straightforward generalization of Case 1, and therefore the analysis of Case 1 carries over directly. The resulting inconsistent permissions and reciprocity conflict analysis are shown in Table 16.1. Case 3 is problematic from a usability perspective: it is probably more difficult for users to imagine access permission inconsistencies across longer path lengths, although this is more interesting from a sharing perspective. Again, there are no alternative preferences available to the profiles.

16.4.2.4   Case 4: Relationship accessible to friends or to friends-of-friends

Constructing the Model: Next, we construct a model that allows users some flexibility in their choice of permission path length. Users can choose between making their information objects available only to friends or to friends-of-friends. The model becomes complicated as soon as a profile p_i wants to make her information objects accessible only to her friends, but a $p_j \in F(p_i)$ wants to make her information objects accessible to friends-of-friends.

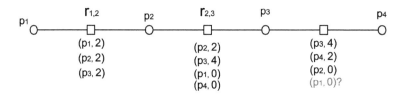

FIGURE 16.3: Graph with profiles setting access to either $F(p)$ of $FoF(p)$.

Consider the example graph in Figure 16.3. There are two options:

1. $FoF(p_i)$ overrides $F(p_j)$: p_3 sets access permissions for her information objects to $FoF(p_3)$. This means that p_1 can access p_3's profile and her relationship boxes, although the opposite is not the case. Further, p_4 has set her access permission for her information objects to $F(p_4)$. However, according to p_3's permissions, p_1 can access relationship box r_{34}. Hence, in this model we prioritize p_3's permissions and suggest that they override p_4's access permission that limits access to its relationship boxes to $F(p_4)$. We call it the FoFDominantSNS model.

2. $F(p_j)$ overrides $FoF(p_i)$: Alternatively, p_4's access permissions can be prioritized, meaning that relationship box r_{34} is not accessible to p_1. This we call the FDominantSNS model.

Model evaluation: The model FoFDominantSNS offers greater flexibility to users, since they can now choose between making their information objects accessible to friends or to friends-of-friends. Although this produces access permission inconsistencies, with appropriate feedback systems these can be seen as a feature of the model (see Section 16.5.1 below). The dominance of one permission over another does cause problems. Namely, in the worst case, when a profile p_i with access permissions set to friends is surrounded by neighbors p_j with access permissions set to friends-of-friends, then her permissions have no effect on the accessibility of her relationship boxes. Therefore, if users like the profile p_i are not aware of the effects of the FoFDominantSNS model, they may harbor false perceptions of control. If they are aware of the effect, it may cause frustration or simply confusion.

An alternative model like the FDominantSNS may solve these problems for profiles p_i, but then cause problems for profiles p_j who have the feeling that their ability to share their resources with a greater community can be dampened by their very own friends. Therefore, although the two models in Case 4 provide the users with more flexibility, they also come along with their problems, especially with respect to reciprocity. As a result, a socially translucent design may be more difficult to implement with such models.

16.4.3 Comparing Models

In Table 16.1, we give an overview of the conflict analyses in the four cases (each case is listed in Column 1). In the second column, we have abbreviated $S(p_i, p_i).accessPermission$ to $S(p_i)$ since control permissions are fixed and are hence not used in the table. In columns two and three, we indicate whether permission inconsistencies or strong reciprocity conflicts occur. In the remaining columns, we list the outbound and inbound sets necessary to identify whether conflicts occur. In column $KnowsProfile_{p_i}$, after the first row we abbreviated $AccessibleProfiles_{p_i}$ to AP_{p_i} to save space. In column $RelationsAccessibleTo_{p_i}$, we listed the profiles that have access, but did not specify which relationship boxes each profile can access. These are usually subsets of the profile p_i's relationship boxes: relationships of p_i known to another profile p_x by virtue of accessing the profiles of another profile $p_j \in F(p_i)$. We also did not add a column for weak reciprocity conflicts. If no strong reciprocity conflicts occur, then weak reciprocity conflicts do not occur either. On the other hand, in Case 4, not only is strong reciprocity not guaranteed, but depending on the permutations of the neighbors preferences, different types of weak reciprocity conflicts occur. For the sake of readability and giving an overview, we chose not to list the different permutations of preferences that lead to weak reciprocity conflicts.

The most important conclusion to be drawn from the table is that the many privacy preferences offered by SNS providers produce inconsistent access permissions which are as a rule not communicated to the users of SNS. Further, it becomes evident from the table that the only case in which conflicts are avoided and information visibility is controlled is the model SimpleCommonFriendsOnlySNS (Case 2). This model is also the most conservative: for cliques in a graph, access to information objects remains very open; for profiles that are not grouped in such close communities, access to information objects is very limited. Next, the problems that occur in Case 1, the model SimpleFriendsOnlySNS are simply amplified in Case 3, the model SimpleFo-

FOnlySNS.

We numbered the two sub-models of Case 4. Case 4.1 represents the mixed model with the FoFDominantSNS, whereas Case 4.2 is the FDominantSNS that privileges profiles p_i with access permissions set to friends. In Case 4.2, regardless of the access permissions of $p_j \in F(p_i)$, p_i is guaranteed protection of its information objects equivalent to those of SimpleFriendsOnlySNS. If privacy can be seen as the ability to keep information close to a profile, then Case 4.2 can be favorable. However, Case 4.1 is the common model in existing SNS. This could be because it privileges sharing over privacy. Given the evaluation of the model of Case 4.1, it is no surprise that many users complain about indeterminate visibility of their information objects.

We conclude that already in a comparatively simple model in which profiles can choose between two permission settings, challenging complexities occur. In current SNS, there are also relational information objects for which the $C(o)$ can be extended after the creation of the object. It is nevertheless clear in the four cases that combinations of permissions from networked profiles can produce unexpected visibility of information objects depending on the relationships and access permissions. Depending on the model, a profile's permissions can be completely overridden by the permission of their friends at different path lengths. Access permission inconsistencies may be easier to determine, but determining reciprocity conflicts exhaustively can be a challenge.

Through relational information and transitive access control settings, it becomes evident that privacy in social networks is not only about individual decisions but also about collective ones. As simple as they may seem, the models for access control used in existing SNS are full of inconsistencies that are often brushed away. These become evident as users state indeterminate visibility and breaches of separation of identities as privacy concerns. Making the underlying relationality of access control evident and opening its design to users, or developing it to fit the users' requirements, is a step forward in improving systems according to users' differing privacy needs. The Information-Objects Discovery Algorithm hence can be used to detect conflicts, discuss requirements and design solutions with users and other stakeholders. In the next section, we make proposals on how the conflicts made explicit through our models and analyses can be resolved using requirements engineering and data mining methods.

16.5 Data Mining and Feedback for Awareness Tools

Many privacy proponents observe that abstract warnings of the kind "If you disclose data, others may see and abuse them" are too abstract to have much effect on people's behavior. Various authors have therefore proposed

Model	S(pi)	Access Perm Conflict	Strong Recip. Conflict	Outbound Sets			Inbound Sets		
				Accessible Profiles pi	Accessible Relations pi	Knows Profile pi	Profile Accessible To pi	Relations Accessible To pi	Profile Known To pi
C.1	$F(pi)$	yes	no	$F(pi)$	$\{rxy: F(pi) ! C(rxy)\}$	$\{px: px ! F(F(pi)) ! px\ {}^{*}\#ccessibleProfilepx\}$	$F(pi)$	$FoF(pi)$	$\{px: px ! F(F(pi)) ! px\ {}^{*}\ ProfileAccessibleTopx\}$
C.2	$F(pi)$	no	no	$F(pi)$	$\{rxi: pxi\ F(pi)\} {}^{*} \{rxy: px,py ! (F(pi)! F(px))\}$	\$	$F(pi)$	$F(pi)$	\$
C.3	$FoF(pi)$	yes	no	$FoF(pi)$	$\{rxy: FoF(pi) ! C(rxy)\}$	$\{px:px ! FoF(F(F(pi))) ! px\ {}^{*}\#ccessible\ Profilepx\}$	$FoF(pi)$	$FoF(pi) {}^{*} F(FoF(pi))$	$\{px: px ! FoF(F(F(pi))) ! px\ {}^{*}\ ProfileAccessibleTopx\}$
C.4.1	$F(pi)$	yes	yes	$F(pi) {}^{*} \{px: px ! F(F(pi)) ! S(px) = FoF(px)\}$	$\{rxy: pxi\ F(pi)\} {}^{*} \{rxy: px ! F(F(pi)) ! S(px) = FoF(px)\}$	$(FoF(pi) {}^{*} \{FoF(px):pxi\ F(pi) ! S(px)=FoF(px)\} {}^{*} \{py: py! F(F(px)) ! S(py)=FoF(py)\}\} \setminus AP_{pi}$	$F(pi)$	$FoF(pi) {}^{*} \{FoF(px):pxi\ F(pi) ! S(px)=FoF(px)\}$	$(\{FoF(px);pxi\ F(pi) ! S(px)=FoF(px)\} {}^{*} \{py:pyi\ F(F(pi)) ! S(py)=FoF(py)\}\} \setminus ProfileAccessibleTopi$
C.4.2	$F(pi)$	yes	yes	$F(pi) {}^{*} \{px: px ! F(F(pi)) ! S(px) = FoF(px)\}$	$\{rxy: pxi\ F(pi)\} {}^{*} \{rxy: px ! F(F(pi)) ! S(px) = FoF(px)\}$	$FoF(pi) {}^{*} \{py:pyi\ FoF(px) ! S(py)=FoF(py)\} {}^{*} \{py:pxi\ FoF(px) ! S(py)=FoF(px) ! pyi\ F(px) ! S(py)=FoF(py)\} {}^{*} \{pz:pzi\ FoF(px)\} \setminus AP_{pi}$	$F(pi)$	$FoF(pi)$	$\{px:px ! F(F(pi)) ! px\ {}^{*}\ ProfileAccessibleTopx\}$
	$FoF(pi)$	yes	yes	$F(pi) {}^{*} \{px: px ! F(F(pi)) ! S(px) = FoF(px)\}$	$\{rxy: pxi\ F(pi)\} {}^{*} \{rxy: px ! F(F(pi)) ! S(px) = FoF(px)\}$	$FoF(pi) {}^{*} \{py:pyi\ FoF(px) ! S(py)=FoF(py)\} {}^{*} \{py:pxi\ FoF(pi) ! S(py)=FoF(px) ! pyi\ F(px) ! S(py)=FoF(py)\} {}^{*} \{pz:pzi\ FoF(pz)\} \setminus AP_{pi}$	$FoF(pi)$	$FoF(pi) {}^{*} \{FoF(px):pxi\ F(pi) ! S(px)=FoF(px)\}$	$(\{F(px): pxi\ FoF(pi) ! S(px)=F(pi) ! \{FoF(px) ! pxi\ FoF(pi) ! S(px)=FoF(px)\}\} \setminus ProfileAccessibleTopi$

Table 16.1: An overview of the conflicts, outbound and inbound sets for the different cases.

more concrete demonstrations of what is already known about the user, or about other people, in an attempt to be more effective by raising awareness.

Many of these techniques are based on *retrieval*. Tools allow a user to search for her name on various search engines and Social Web sites, and compile the results in one page (see www.123people.com as one example). A variant of this technique, which relies on *pull* activities and is thus more likely to reach users who are privacy-conscious anyway, is the "Identity Angel" [48] that employs a *push* technique. This is a specialized search engine that visits online job boards and other sources to look for either of three types of personally identifying information: a person's name, address, and Social Security Number. Although the first two are often easy to find on the Web, finding all three is the gold standard for anyone who wants to commit fraud or steal someone's identity. If the Identity Angel program finds all three, and can locate the person's e-mail address, it will send an automated message to that person, warning that his/her identity may potentially be in danger.** Push techniques may work even without reference to specific information: [32] found that sending teenagers on MySpace an email from "Dr. Meg," mentioning that "you seem to be quite open about sexual issues or other behaviors such as drinking or smoking," caused many of them to clean up their profiles and boost privacy settings.

Other techniques emphasize *inference*: that the presence of such different explicit pieces of information on a person means that there is even more — implicit — information about them. With the help of a mashup that visualizes the homes (including addresses) of people interested in "subversive" books, [36] demonstrated the simplicity of combining existing information to infer people's identity. The technique is attribute matching, which was shown by Sweeney [47] to be an easy way of circumventing simple anonymization schemes. In social networks, recent studies have shown that attributes revealed by friends in a profile's vicinity may be used to infer confidential attributes [53, 4]. These methods are powerful and at the same time controversial. For example, although inferencing attributes through social networks may return mathematically accurate results, the assumptions such inferences are based on are socially questionable. In [52], for example, the authors problematize some of the heuristics used to probabilistically infer information from the attributes of a profile's network vicinity. They argue that the heuristics are comparable to notions like "birds of a feather flock together," "judge a man by the company he keeps," or "guilty by association."

Hence, such inference techniques should be made visible to users to raise awareness of both, the (in)appropriateness of their underlying heuristics, as well as the potential risks accruing if they are applied. Along these lines, in [5],

---

** Related business models are becoming common practice. For example, an entrepreneur in the UK has launched Lucid Intelligence, a database of personal data available on phishing and hacking sites. Concerned individuals can pay to check whether their data security has been breached [1].

we have presented a P3P extension and a Web-based service for helping businesses to avoid computing analytics that would indirectly violate their own P3P policies and therefore data-protection agreements with their customers. This service was based on computing inferences implicit in data configurations. We have proposed an analogous extension to P3P for different groups of "friends" in social network services in [40].

Data mining can extend the scope of these applications and simulations for information inference by employing more sophisticated forms of induction and deduction for demonstrating the possible consequences of a user's actions. In Section 16.4, we have shown how the spread of visibility/accessibility of a user's profile and relational data may be computed. The same could be done for the spread of control permissions over such data. In the remainder of this section, we first outline how inferencing could be employed in the SNS models we studied and then sketch more sophisticated approaches.

16.5.1 Toward Conflict Avoidance and Resolution: Feedback and Trust Mechanisms

The analyses of the cases in Section 16.4 have shown, among other things, access permission inconsistencies: some information becomes visible beyond the group of people originally intended. A "feedback mechanism" could be implemented to make users aware of this. It would signal, upon the intention of p_i and p_j to establish a relation to them, that the actual group of people who will be able to see the relationship will be larger than what they (probably) expect based on their individual permissions. A simple feedback mechanism could rest on showing $AccessReachFeedback(r_{ij}) = \bigcup_{\forall p \in C(r_{ij})} S(p, r_{ij})$.

If such access permission inconsistencies are judged to be acceptable, there is no problem. However, if users disagree, other models will have to be considered that either avoid access permission conflicts or allow users to articulate conflicting requirements and find designs that allow users to negotiate these prior to design or during run time. It is important to underline the fact that users cannot and do not decide on their preferences alone as long as RI and TAC is implemented.

In Cases 1–3, these problems occur in a symmetric fashion. However, in Case 4, model 4.1, the access to information objects can become asymmetric. Assume again that p_i is the more restrictive side of a relationship to be established. If p_i is surrounded by profiles such that for all $p_x \in F(p_i)$ the permissions for profiles are $S(p_x, p_x).accessPermission = FoF(p_x)$, then p_i's choice of limiting her access permissions to its information objects to $F(p_i)$ is close to meaningless. It only serves to protect her profile, which may be important, but nevertheless, may not be sufficient. The reverse, that p_j is surrounded by profiles p_y that all set their access permissions to friends might not be problematic, unless p_j feels that her intentions to share her resources have been limited by her friends.

In order to avoid such cases, one could introduce trust models. In these trust models, p_j may be allowed to make r_{ij} accessible only to those friends-of-friends who can prove a threshold trust level that the two profiles p_i and p_j determine together (see Chapter 15 of this book for further uses of trust in social-network access modeling). In any case, p_i should be provided with feedback similar to the feedback proposed in Case 1, informing her about how far her relationship information travels through the graph. This feedback can be coupled with collective privacy setting negotiation mechanisms, building on policy visualization techniques like the Expandable Grids [43].

16.5.2 Design Choices in Feedback Mechanisms Based on Data Mining

Going beyond straightforward what-if simulations, we believe that feedback for awareness-raising simulations should not only be limited to the application of data-mining models such as classifiers or graph inference results. Rather, it is vital to consider also the dynamics with which users' data-related activities contribute to the learning of these models. Thus, we propose to integrate data mining more fully — by considering also statistical information, by considering also the learning stages of a model — into creating privacy awareness tools.

As one example in social networks, consider the problem of inserting structure into the set of "friends." In current SNS, these sets have no internal structure, or friends can be assigned to predefined classes [8]. These sets grow too fast for many users and easily become unmanageable. This is reminiscent of the email structuring problem (which has been addressed by several machine-learning approaches such as [10]). In addition, it is however an increasing privacy problem, because profile and relational information is distributed either to all friends or to none. To improve on this situation, the user's set of "friends" could be clustered by connectivity, a classifier could be learned from the user's own past communication behavior with these different clusters, and a recommender could be derived from it to suggest that in the future, it might be advisable to withhold certain information from this group. Exactly such a mechanism was implemented in [20] based on tie strength characterized by multiple dimensions representing trust and closeness among friends. This type of clustering / classification / recommendation mining could be incremental, such that the effects of decisions such as accepting an invitation to become friends attain visibility.

This basic idea gives rise to a number of choices and questions: (a) The implications could be shown to users in pull or push fashion. Push has the advantage of potentially reaching more people, but the disadvantage of potentially becoming tiresome and ignored if too many warnings are issued. Machine learning could in turn be used to learn how and when to make proposals to a user to maximize effectiveness (cf. earlier work on desktop agents). (b) Inferences can be based on already-stored data or on what-if simulations. The latter have the advantage of warning people "before it's too late," but may therefore also create a false sense of security. This tradeoff remains an open issue for interaction design. (c) The target groups to whom inferences are shown can range from end users (natural persons in SNS applications, businesses in applications like [5]) to SNS providers.

Simulations issued to end users are particularly interesting when conflicts between end users are possible: Simulation runs in simultaneous interaction with several users may show a conflict about to evolve. This could pave the way for a *negotiation* between the users as a way of solving the conflict. Such solutions will often require a *preference aggregation* function. For example, a minimum strategy may be applicable in situations like that of Fig. 16.3, where it would imply that the conflict between p_1 and p_3 will be resolved in favor of the more restrictive preference of p_1, such that neither of them can see the other's profile. This also involves the challenge of (d) how to best address groups (rather than individuals). Some of the issues involved (such as preference aggregation) will be similar to those in issuing recommendations to groups [26], but further ones will surface due to the as-yet little-explored nature of privacy seen as a collective good.

On the other hand, simulations can also be helpful for service providers to help them make well-informed choices when introducing new features into their applications. Choices made in response to public outrage at previous choices (such as Facebook's alterations of the Beacon functionality from opt-out to opt-in after the widespread anger expressed in the blogosphere, cf. http://news.bbc.co.uk/2/hi/technology/7120916.stm) may show a certain responsiveness to user interests, but participatory design would preview and integrate concerns in a much earlier phase of software development and maintenance.

16.6 Conclusions and Outlook

In this chapter, we have analyzed challenges for privacy on today's Social Web. We have focused on social network services as Social Web applications that are both highly popular at the moment and regarded by many as prime players in the "privacy nightmare" of the Web. We have argued that this seeming contradiction shows that a re-investigation of the notion of privacy itself is necessary. This investigation has shown that privacy is not only about hiding or controlling information, but also about the practices with which collectives — such as the users of a social network service — constantly explore and (re-)negotiate what information to disclose and what to hide, and the construction of identities therein. We described empirically identified types of concerns and breaches in detail and derived *relational information* and *transitive access control* as central to both sharing and privacy concerns. The latter is the case because the individual profile privacy settings in SNS, when aggregated in a network with the privacy settings of other profiles, often lead to unexpected visibility of information objects and to privacy concerns. This shows that access to information objects is not determined solely through individual privacy settings but depends on the permissions of friends of different path lengths — depending on the SNS design. Hence, tools are necessary that make transparent collective data practices and access to information objects, as are tools for negotiating differences. All of these developments affect how personal data is constructed legally and question the viability of using existing data protection frameworks in social networks.

We therefore proposed formal definitions of conflicts resulting from relational information and transitive access control, and a method for detecting the occurrence of these conflicts in various types of social networks. As an example, we provided an analysis of different design settings typical of SNS and studied the conflicts that may emerge in them. We also briefly described proposals for avoiding or resolving those conflicts. Concluding, we proposed to use this analysis to infer which conflicts can emerge, along with other inference methods from data mining, to create both techniques for requirements engineering and privacy awareness tools.

Many open issues remain for future work. Models should be considered in which control permissions may also be granted and deletion of both permissions and information objects is possible. We expect that the inbound and outbound sets will become impermeable as these parameters are included in the model, emphasizing the importance of data mining and visualization of collective permissions for privacy as practice. We plan to develop and implement simulation models and awareness tools which we will use to gather and analyze requirements, support negotiations between users and other stakeholders – that include service providers and privacy commissioners– prior to wide-spread privacy breaches and during run-time. In general, modeling relational information and transitive access control explicitly will enable different analyses on social network groups, affect the possible inferences made from networks, and change understandings of information, sharing and social ties in SNS.

In this chapter, our main objective was to treat data mining not only as a technology that can cause privacy breaches or that can help build new privacy-preserving algorithms, but also as a technology for privacy and information literacy. Data mining techniques can be used to build "privacy mirrors" that inform individuals and groups about the possible consequences of various privacy-related behaviors at the requirements phase, design phase and run time. Further collaboration between research on data mining, access control, interaction design, and other fields mentioned in this chapter may make data practices transparent and hence actively support the establishment of privacy-conscious behaviors on the Social Web.

References

[1] M. B. Ahmed. Four million british identities are up for sale on the internet. Times Online, 18. July 2009.

[2] A. Albrechtslund. Online social networking as participatory surveillance. *First Monday*, 13(3), 2008.

[3] Ross J. Anderson. *Security Engineering: A Guide to Building Dependable Distributed Systems*. Wiley Computer Publishing, 2001.

[4] Justin Becker and Hao Chen. Measuring privacy risk in online social networks,. In *Web 2.0 Security Symposium*, 2009.

[5] B. Berendt, S. Preibusch, and M. Teltzrow. A privacy-protecting business analytics service for online transactions. *International Journal of Electronic Commerce*, 12:115–150, 2008.

[6] Andrew Besmer and Heather Lipford. Tagged photos: concerns, perceptions, and protections. In *CHI '09*, pages 4585 – 4590, 2009.

[7] Jens Binder, Andrew Howes, and Alistair Sutcliffe. The problem of conflicting social spheres: effects of network structure on experienced tension in social network sites. In *CHI '09*, pages 965–974, 2009.

[8] Joseph Bonneau and Sören Preibusch. The privacy jungle: On the market for data protection in social networks. In *WEIS 2009*, 2009.

[9] Bundesverfassungsgericht. BVerfGE 65, 1 – Volkszählung. Urteil des Ersten Senats vom 15. Dezember 1983 auf die mündliche Verhandlung vom 18. und 19. Oktober 1983 – 1 BvR 209, 269, 362, 420, 440, 484/83 in den Verfahren über die Verfassungsbeschwerden, 1983.

[10] R. Cole and G. Stumme. Cem – a conceptual email manager. In B. Ganter and G. W. Mineau, editors, *Proc. ICCS 2000*, volume 1867 of *LNAI*, pages 438–452. Springer, 2000.

[11] Danah Boyd and Nicole Ellison. Social network sites: Definition, history and scholarship. *Journal of Computer-Mediated Communication*, 2007.

[12] Claudia Diaz. *Anonymity and Privacy in Electronic Services*. Katholieke Universiteit Leuven, 2005.

[13] J. Domingo-Ferrer and V. Torra. A critique of k-anonymity and some of its enhancements. In *Third International Conference on Availability, Reliability and Security, 2008. ARES 08.*, 2008.

[14] Thomas Erickson and Wendy A. Kellogg. Social translucence: An approach to designing systems that support social processes. *ACM Transactions on Human Computer Interaction*, 7(1):59–83, 2000.

[15] EU. Directive 95/46/ec of the European parliament and of the council of 24 October 1995 on the protection of individuals with regard to the processing of personal data and on the free movement of such data. *Official Journal of the European Communities*, (L. 281), November 1995.

[16] EU. Directive 2002/58/ec of the European parliament and of the council concerning the processing of personal data and the protection of privacy in the electronic communications sector, 2002.

[17] David F. Ferraiolo, D. Richard Kuhn, and Ramaswamy Chandramouli. *Role-Based Access Control*. Artech House Publishers, 2003.

[18] M. Fisch and C. Gescheidle. Mitmachnetz web 2.0: Rege beteiligung nur in communitys. *Media Perspektiven*, 7:356–364, 2008.

[19] Federal Trade Commission (FTC). Privacy online: Fair information practices in the electronic marketplace: A federal trade commission report to congress, May 2000. `http://www.ftc.gov/reports/privacy2000/privacy2000.pdf`.

[20] Eric Gilbert and Karrie Karahalios. Predicting tie strength with social media. In *CHI '09*, 2009.

[21] Paolo Guarda and Nicola Zannone. Towards the development of privacy-aware systems. *Information and Software Technology*, 51(2):337 – 350, 2009.

[22] Seda Gürses, Ramzi Rizk, and Oliver Günther. Privacy design in online social networks: Learning from privacy breaches and community feedback. In *Twenty Ninth International Conference on Information Systems*, 2008.

[23] Jeff Hancock, Heremy Birnholtz, Natalya Bazarova, Jamie Guillory and Josh Perlin, and Barrett Amos. Butler lies: awareness, deception and design. In *CHI '09*, 2009.

[24] Marit Hansen. Linkage control - integrating the essence of privacy protection into identity management. In *eChallenges*, 2008.

[25] Mireille Hildebrandt. *Profiling the European Citizen: Cross Disciplinary Perspectives*, chapter Profiling and the Identity of the European Citizen. Springer Science and Business Media B. V., 2008.

[26] Anthony Jameson. Adaptive interfaces and agents. In Julie A. Jacko and Andrew Sears, editors, *Human-Computer Interaction Handbook*, pages 305–330. Erlbaum, Mahwah, NJ, 2003.

[27] Carole Jordan. *A Guide to Understanding Discretionary Access Control in Trusted Systems.* DIANE Publishing, 1987.

[28] Daniel Kifer and Johannes Gehrke. l-diversity: Privacy beyond k-anonymity. In *ICDE'06*, 2006.

[29] Scott Lederer, Jason I. Hong, Anind K. Dey, and James A. Landay. Personal privacy through understanding and personal privacy through understanding and action: Five pitfalls for designers. *Personal Ubiquitous Computing*, 8(6):440–454, 2004.

[30] Ninghui Li and Tiancheng Li. t-closeness: Privacy beyond k-anonymity and -diversity. In *ICDE'07*, 2007.

[31] Hugo Liu, Pattie Maes, and Glorianna Davenport. Unraveling the taste fabric of social networks. *International Journal on Semantic Web and Information Systems*, 2(1):42–71, 2006.

[32] Megan A. Moreno, Ann VanderStoep, Malcolm R. Parks, Frederick J. Zimmerman, Ann Kurth, and Dimitri A. Christakis. Reducing at-risk adolescents' display of risk behavior on a social networking web site. a randomized controlled pilot intervention trial. *Arch Pediatr Adolesc Med.*, 163(1):35–41, 2009.

[33] David H. Nguyen. Privacy mirrors: Understanding and shaping sociotechnical ubiquitous computing. *Technical Report*, 2002.

[34] Helen Nissenbaum. Privacy as contextual integrity. *Washington Law Review*, 79(1), 2004.

[35] OECD. Guidelines on the protection of privacy and transborder flows of personal data.

[36] T. Owad. *Data Mining 101: Funding subversives with Amazon wishlists*, 2006.

[37] Leysia Palen and Paul Dourish. Unpacking "privacy" for a networked world. In *CHI '03*, pages 129 – 136, 2003.

[38] Andreas Pfitzmann and Marit Hansen. Anonymity, unobservability, and pseudonymity: A consolidated proposal for terminology. Technical Report, Technical University, Dresden, 2008.

[39] D. J. Phillips. Privacy policy and pets: The influence of policy regimes on the development and social implications of privacy enhancing technologies. *New Media Society*, 6(6):691–706, 2004.

[40] S. Preibusch, B. Hoser, S. Gürses, and B. Berendt. Ubiquitous social networks – opportunities and challenges for privacy-aware user modelling. In Ryan Baker, Joseph Beck, Bettina Berendt, Ernestina Menasalvas, Alexander Kröner, and Stephan Weibelzahl, editors, *Proceedings of the Workshop on Data Mining for User Modelling at UM 2007*, 2007.

References

[41] Sören Preibusch and Alastair R. Beresford. Establishing distributed hidden friendship relations. In *Seventeenth International Workshop on Security Protocols (SPW 2009), 1-3 April 2009, Cambridge / United Kingdom*, 2009.

[42] David Rebollo-Monedero, Jordi Forné, and Josep Domingo-Ferrer. From t-closeness to pram and noise addition via information theory. In *PSD '08: Proceedings of the UNESCO Chair in Data Privacy International Conference on Privacy in Statistical Databases*, 2008.

[43] Robert W. Reeder. *Expandable Grids: A User Interface Visualization Technique and a Policy Semantics to Support Fast, Accurate Security and Privacy Policy Authoring*. PhD thesis, Carnegie Mellon University, 2008.

[44] William Robinson, Suzanne Pawlowski, and Vecheslav Volkov. Requirements interaction management. *ACM Computing Surveys*, 35(2), 2003.

[45] Katherine Strater and Heather Richter. Examining privacy and disclosure in a social networking community. *Proceedings of the 3rd Symposium on Usable Privacy and Security*, pages 157–158, 2007.

[46] Latanya Sweeney. k-anonymity: a model for protecting privacy. *International Journal on Uncertainty, Fuzziness and Knowledge-Based Systems*, 10(5):557–570, 2002.

[47] Latanya Sweeney. Achieving k-anonymity privacy protection using generalization and suppression. *International Journal of Uncertainty*, 10(5):571–588, 2003.

[48] Latanya Sweeney. Protecting job seekers from identity theft. *IEEE Internet Computing*, 10(2), 2006.

[49] Education U.S. Department of Health and Welfare (HEW). Secretary's advisory committee on automated personal data systems, records, computers, and the rights of citizens viii, 1973.

[50] S. Warren and L. Brandeis. The right to privacy. *Harvard Law Review*, 4:193–220, 1890.

[51] A. F. Westin. *Privacy and Freedom*. Atheneum, New York, 1970.

[52] David Wills and Stuart Reeves. Facebook as a political weapon: Information in social networks. *British Politics*, 4(2):265 – 281, 2009.

[53] E. Zheleva and L. Getoor. To join or not to join: the illusion of privacy in social networks with mixed public and private user profiles. In *WWW '09*, 2009.

Chapter 17

Privacy Protection of Personal Data in Social Networks

Barbara Carminati, Elena Ferrari

DICOM - University of Insubria, Varese - Italy

Murat Kantarcioglu, Bhavani Thuraisingham

University of Texas at Dallas, Dallas, Texas

17.1   Introduction

The Web has evolved from a simple tool for publishing text data, into a complex collaborative knowledge management system. This evolution is mainly due to the rapid spread of social computing services, such as blogs, wikis, social networks, social bookmarking, collaborative filtering, and recommendation and reputation systems. Social computing services are now starting to be used also at the enterprise level to communicate, share information, make decisions, and do business. This is in line with the emerging trend known as Enterprise 2.0, that is, the use of Web 2.0 technologies within the intranet, to allow for more spontaneous, knowledge-based collaborations. One of the main witnesses of this new trend is represented by online social networks, platforms that allow people to publish details about themselves and to connect to other members of the network through friendship or other kind of links. Recently, the popularity of online social networks is increasing significantly. For example, Facebook now claims to have more than two hundred and fifty million active users.* The existence of online social networks that include person-specific information creates both interesting opportunities and challenges. For example, social network data could be used for marketing products to the right

---

*http://www.facebook.com/press/info.php?statistics. Retrieved on August 10, 2009.

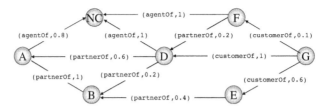

FIGURE 17.1: A portion of *SellNet*

customers. At the same time, security and privacy concerns can prevent such efforts in practice [3].

In this chapter we first introduce the main privacy issues in online social network (Section 17.2). Then, we go into more details of the most interesting research proposals appeared so far to deal with these issues. Finally, we conclude with the discussion of other related research challenges in Section 17.6.

17.2 Privacy Issues in Online Social Networks

Online social networks are collecting data from more than 250 million users. A great part of these data consists of personal information. If we further consider the data users publish in their virtual spaces (e.g., photos, or group membership), it is easy to conclude that social networks represent the hugest source of personal data available on the Web. They become a precious source for user profiles generation, with the obvious drawbacks for user privacy. Proofs of this risk are the recent complaints of some privacy activists against Facebook for the use of News Feed and Beacon [3]. These complaints resulted in several online petitions with several thousand signatures. Despite petitions, Facebook continues to see user personal data as a possible source of income, as it is recently demonstrated by its announcement to allow companies to send users questionnaires based on user profile information. Having in mind these recent complaints as well as privacy breaches introduced in Chapter 16 by Gürses et al. of this book, in this section we overview the main privacy issues that in our opinion it is required to address in order to obtain privacy-aware social networks. Before doing that we introduce the reference example we will use throughout the chapter.

Example 17.1

In the chapter, we use the standard way to model a social network, that is, as a directed graph, where each node corresponds to a network user and edges denote relationships between two different users. In particular, the initial node of an edge denotes the user who established the relationship, whereas the terminal node denotes the user who accepted to establish the relationship.

Each edge is labeled by the *type* of the established relationship and the corresponding *trust* level. The scenario we refer to in the remainder of the chapter is that of an online social network in the Enterprise 2.0 domain. The network (that we refer to as *SellNet*) has been established by a company (*New-Comp*) to support its sales agents in their day to day activities. Figure 17.1 illustrates a portion of *SellNet*, where node *NC* denotes *NewComp*. *SellNet* aims at providing a space where sales agents can find updated information on the company products, obtain support from company experts, exchange their experiences with other agents, ask for suggestions and so on. Additionally, *SellNet* provides the possibility for the nodes of the community to share a variety of information (e.g., opinions on new products, marketing strategies, data about the sales). The social network may also involve agents from different companies (i.e., partners of *NewComp*) that should have a selective access to the network services, or customers, that may access selected portions of the offered services, and can exploit *SellNet* to communicate with sales agents and to share experiences with other customers. Nodes can also form smaller networks or groups (for instance related to products of a particular type, or denoting a partnership among some of the agents).

☐

Privacy issues in data mining. Companies holding social networks may be interested in releasing collected data to other companies for data mining purposes. In this case, the company receiving the data could use it for violating users' privacy. The challenge in this scenario is how release *useful* social network dataset without violating individual privacy. This challenge is addressed in another chapter in this book (please see the Chapter by Miklau et al.), therefore we will not deal with it here.

Privacy protection of personal data. Another privacy issue that arises in the context of social networking is how to protect users' personal data from other network participants and, in some cases, from the social network hosting company. Indeed, since users could post privacy and sensitive information online, restricting unauthorized access to online profiles/resources will be the first step in limiting potential privacy violations. For example, a user may need to be able to specify that a picture posted online by her could be seen by her friends but not by her boss, or that a report distributed in an intranet social network should be accessible only to selected colleagues. There is thus the need of tools allowing a selected sharing of information among social networks users. If we consider today social networks, a user can basically decide which personal information, relationships, and/or resources are accessible to other members by marking a given item as public, private, or accessible to their direct contacts. Some online social networks provide variants of these settings, in order to give more flexibility, but the principle is the same [9]. For instance, besides the basic settings, Bebo (`http://bebo.com`), FaceBook (`http://facebook.com`), and Multiply (`http://multiply.com`) support the option "selected friends"; Last.fm (`http://last.fm`) the option "neighbors" (i.e., the set of users having musical preferences and tastes similar to mine); Facebook, Friendster (`http://friendster.com`), and Orkut (`http://www.orkut.com`) support the option "friends of friends"; Xing (`http://xing.com`) supports the options "contacts of my contacts" (2nd degree contacts), and "3rd" and "4th degree contacts." All these approaches have the advantage of being easy to implement, but they lack flexibility. In fact, the available protection settings do not allow users to easily specify their access control requirements, in that they are either too restrictive or too loose (e.g., the options "my connections" and "my network" in LinkedIn). In general, social networks create some unique access control challenges that are not easily addressable by existing access control solutions. In Section 17.3, we will discuss more deeply these challenges, and we will introduce some of the ongoing researches trying to address some of the limitations of current approaches.

Privacy issues in relationship-based access control enforcement. As briefly introduced in previous paragraph, there is a general consensus in considering relationships established by social networks participants as the key parameter to perform access control. Indeed, access control policies are mainly specified by considering the relationships that should exist between the resource provider and the resource requester in order to obtain access to the requested resource. However, relationships are in general sensitive resources whose privacy should be properly guaranteed during access control enforcement. In Section 17.4 we will discuss in more detail the privacy threats that may arise during relationship-based access control enforcement, by then illustrating some solutions to achieve a *privacy-aware access control enforcement*, that is, an access control enforcement where users' privacy preference on relationships' disclosure are taken in account.

Preventing private information inference. Another privacy problem is individual private information leakage due to being part of an online social network. To understand the private information leakage, we must first distinguish between *revealed* and *unrevealed* data. We consider unrevealed data to be any data which a user is not privy to. For a general user, this means any information which they are explicitly denied from seeing. For the social network site, this means data which is not entered into their site. An individual with access to a portion of the entire social network and the link structure can then develop a learning model upon which they classify "unknown" nodes to obtain the unrevealed traits. Trivially, an example of this is someone who hides their political affiliation because of privacy concerns, but displays that he has joined a group called "College Democrats." This naturally poses the question of whether merely hiding these traits (e.g., hiding the political affiliation) is enough to secure that knowledge. More specifically, in Section 17.5 we discuss how online social network data could be used to predict some individual private trait that a user is not willing to disclose (e.g., sexual orientation) and discuss the effect of possible data sanitization alternatives on preventing such private information leakage.

17.3   Access Control for Online Social Networks

In what follows, we start by introducing some requirements of an access control systems for a social network. We then analyze the state of the art w.r.t. these requirements. Finally, we show how semantic Web technologies can be used to specify and enforce access control policies for online social networks.

17.3.1   Challenges in Access Control for Online Social Networks

An access control model and mechanism for online social networks needs to consider various issues specific to social networks. First of all, some of the security/privacy requirements may be quite different than the ones seen in a traditional access control system. Let consider a generic social network, supposing, for instance, that a user, say Alice, is the owner of a set of resources, and that she wishes to share them with some of her friends. In this simple scenario, standard access control policies provided by Database Management Systems (DBMSs) fit well. Indeed, since an access control policy basically states who can access what and under which modes, and since Alice knows who her friends are, she is able to set up a set of authorizations to properly grant the access only to (a subset of) her friends. However, if we consider a more general scenario, the traditional way of specifying access control policies is not enough. For instance, let us consider the discretionary access control model and suppose that Alice decides to make her resources available not only to her friends, but also to their friends, the friends of their friends, and so on. The problem is that Alice is not able to specify the authorizations for all her possible indirect friends, since she does not know them *a priori*. Nonetheless, even if she knows them, she should specify a huge number of authorizations. Moreover, if we consider that relationships among users of an online social network could change dynamically over time, this solution implies a complex policy management. An access control model for online social networks should therefore take into account relationship information during policy specification. Therefore, a first requirement is supporting access control based on users' relationships and their types. Unfortunately, this is not enough for generic online social networks. For example, let us assume that Alice wishes to share her data with some of her direct and indirect friends. In particular, she wants to grant the access to her direct friends. Moreover, since Alice knows them very well, she wants to grant the access also to their direct friends. However, Alice may not want to propagate the access rights also to contacts of the friends of her direct friends, in that, she does not know how they choose their friends. Therefore, when considering an online social network, the length of the path connecting two nodes (i.e., the depth of a relationship) is relevant information for access control purposes. Thus, an access control model for online social networks should make a user able to state in a policy not only the type but also the maximum depth of a relationship. Another key parameter to be used for policy specification is represented by trust. Although the notions of depth and trust may be related, they are not equivalent. For instance, let us consider the *SellNet* social network in Figure 17.1. Node D, say user David, has two relationships of *partnerOf* with A, say Alice, and B, say Bob. However, David considers Alice more trustworthy than Bob. In this case, the depth of the relationship is the same for both Bob and Alice (i.e., depth=1, since they are both direct partners of David), but the trust level is different. Therefore, access policies for online social networks should also support constraints on the minimum trust level of a relationship. Besides policy specification issues, we see other important challenges in how access control is enforced. For example, assume that a picture taken by a user is uploaded to a social network, and suppose that the owner of the photo tagged some other users on the photo. Because of this tagging process, tagged users may have some rights on the photo (e.g., removing the tags about them or controlling the release of the photo to other users) even if they are not the owner of the photo. Thus, there is the need of a collaborative tools for access control management that traditional access control solutions may not offer. Moreover, existing solutions, such as the one adopted in DBMSs and OSs, imply that the entity in charge of data management also plays the role of enforcing access control policies. However, applying this kind of access control solution to social networking implies that users have to completely delegate the control of their data to social network management systems of companies holding social networks, by simply stating how data must be released to other network nodes. Since access control is enforced by a social network management system, users actually do not know whether access control is correctly enforced. They do not have any assurance about the behavior of these systems with respect to their data (for instance, they could maliciously release them to unauthorized users). They have to totally trust social networking management systems. The increasing privacy concerns about how these systems manage personal information lead us to believe that a centralized access control solution is not the most appropriate in the online social network scenario. Indeed, we believe that in the near future social network participants would like to have more and more control over their data. In view of this, we believe it is necessary to investigate alternative ways of enforcing access control, which make users not totally dependent on social networking management systems. A possible solution is to make the network participants themselves able to evaluate their access control policies. In this scenario, which we refer to as decentralized access control enforcement, each user should be in charge of specifying and enforcing his/her access control policies.

17.3.2 Overview of the Literature

Research work focusing on online social network privacy is quite recent. As far as privacy is concerned, current work is mainly focused on protecting information related to the network, i.e., relationships/nodes, while performing social network analysis (please see the Chapter by Miklau et al. for more details on these aspects). By contrast, issues concerning the protection of user profiles and relationships when users browse a social network have been up to now poorly addressed. Moreover, if we examine what is provided by current social networking services, we see that most of them provide very simple privacy protection mechanisms for user profiles, and almost none for user relationships protection. In contrast, user privacy concerns are increasing. Recently some research proposals are trying to overcome the restrictions of the privacy protection mechanisms provided by current online social networks.

For example, Ali et al. [1] propose a multi-level security approach, according to which with each user and resources is associated with a security level, and resource access is granted only if the security level of the user requiring access is equal or greater than the level of the required resource. In [1] the security levels are determined based on trust. More precisely, to each user u a reputation value $r(u)$ is assigned, computed as the average of the trust ratings specified for u by other users in the system.

After having logged in, user u chooses an operating level T, T $<$ $r(u)$. A resource o created by user u will then be assigned a level equal to T, whereas user u can read only resources having a level equal to or less than T. Moreover, access control is enforced according to a challenge-response based protocol. This proposal has the drawback of considering only direct relationships, which in a dynamic and complex scenario like an online social network limits the privacy preferences a user may specify.

Authors of this chapter have also investigated the problem of privacy protection. In particular, [7] addresses access control issues arising in online social networks, and proposes a model according to which access control requirements are expressed in terms of access rules specified by the resource owners. Such access rules denote authorized members in terms of the type and trust level of the relationships they must have with other network nodes. The system implementing this model exploits a client-based approach to enforce access control, according to which the requester must provide the resource owner with a proof of being authorized to access the requested resource. By contrast, [9] highlights privacy issues related to the disclosure of relationship information during access control. In addition, [9] proposes a method to specify privacy requirements on existing relationships, based on the notion of distribution rules, which denote which online social network nodes can be aware of a given relationship, and use it in order to gain access to a resource. Enforcement of privacy preferences and distribution rules has been proposed both for semi-decentralized and fully-decentralized architectures [5, 8]. More details about this proposal will be given in Section 17.4.2. The above models have been extended in [10] and [11]. In particular, in [10] authors improve protocols proposed in [9] by using public-key cryptography to reduce the overhead caused by distribution rule enforcement. By exploiting homomorphic encryption, in [11] authors propose a solution to enforce privacy preferences on relationship disclosure in a fully-decentralized architecture. Another project is represented by the D-FOAF system [17], which is primarily a FOAF-based [4] distributed identity management system for online social networks, where access rights and trust delegation management are provided as additional services. As described in [17], D-FOAF also denotes authorized users based on the relationships existing in the network. A weak point in this approach is that it does not prevent the forging of fake relationships, which implies possible authorized accesses. To overcome this point the solution proposed in [9] implies to associate with each relationship a certificate ensuring its correctness (please see discussion in Section 17.4.2). Moreover, this approach does not protect relationship privacy during access control enforcement. Another effort to protect users' privacy inside social networks is the one in [2]. Here, authors propose an approach aiming to create a P2P (Peer-to-Peer) network based on the relationships of a given social network, such that two peers are connected only if there exists a relationship between them. In such a way, since each node communicates directly with the target node, access control can be performed directly by the owner of the resource, in that, s/he can decide on his/her own whether or not to release the requested resource. However, the main focus of this work is the generation of a P2P network reflecting the social network. In contrast, the access control aspect has been roughly addressed by simply delegating this task to the owner, which obviously is not an efficient solution for real social networks, in that it implies a decision from the user for each request, without the possibility to set up some rules to automatically enforce access control. Moreover, since the P2P network created in [2] models only generic relationship without trust level, in the access control decision the owner is not able to consider the trust level and the relationship type together. Furthermore, this simple access control mechanism does not ensure a relationship's privacy. Note that other strategies for generating a P2P network reflecting a social network have been proposed (see for example the Social Virtual Private Network project [13]); however, these solutions also do not cope with privacy protection of user profiles and relationships. It is interesting to note that the emerging trend in semantic Web technologies is to provide much richer social network data (e.g., representing relationships

Access control enforcement	Decision based on relationship types	Decision based on relationship trust	Decision based on relationship depth	Relationship protection
Centralized	[2, 6, 12]	[1, 6]	[6]	
Semi-decentralized	[7, 8, 9, 10, 17]	[7, 8, 9, 10, 17]	[7, 8, 9, 10, 17]	[7, 8, 10]
Fully-decentralized	[5, 11]	[5, 11]	[5, 11]	[5]

Table 17.1: Summary of the Related Work

among users and resources in detail) [19]. On these semantically enriched social networks, more flexible and expressive privacy protection mechanisms can be devised, as shown by recent work [6, 12]. For example, in [12] authors focus on online communities, by proposing a semantic framework based on OWL — Web Ontology Language — for defining different access rights exploiting the relationships between the individuals and the community. In contrast, in [6] an extensible fine grained access control model based on semantic Web rules has been proposed. However, except for the work in [5, 8, 7], which will be discussed in Section 17.4.2, and [10, 11] not all the above discussed proposals cope with relationship privacy concerns that might arise during access control enforcement.

Table 17.1 summarizes the discussion on related work presented in this section. Proposals are organized according to the their supported access control and privacy preferences (i.e., defined based on type, trust and depth of relationships) and their proposed architectures (i.e., centralized, semi-centralized and fully decentralized access control and privacy enforcement).

17.3.3 Semantic-Based Access Control in Online Social Networks

In this section, we show how by using semantic Web technologies it is possible to design an access control solution addressing requirements pointed out in Section 17.3.1. In doing that, we will focus on the framework presented in [6], which proposes an extensible, fine-grained online social network access control model based on semantic Web technologies. During our discussion, we assume that a centralized reference monitor hosted by the social network management system will enforce the required access control policies.[†] In presenting the framework proposed in [6], we first introduce the access control policy specification and then the corresponding access control enforcement.

Semantic-based Access Control Policy Specification in Online Social Networks

A typical policy language defines access control policies according to three main components: a *subject specification*, aiming to specify the entity to which an access control policy applies (e.g., users, processes), an *object specification*,

---

[†]In Section 17.4.2, we will discuss an alternative solution adopting decentralized architectures.

to identify the resource to which the policy refers to (e.g., files, HW resources, relational tables), and an *action specification*, specifying the action (e.g., read, write, execute) that subjects can exercise on objects. Moreover, to make the task of policy evaluation easier, policies are usually enforced through a set of *authorizations*, stating for each subject the rights she has on the protected resources, according to the specified policies. In [6], access control policies and entailed authorizations are encoded by means of rules. In general, a rule consists of two formulae and an implication operator, with the obvious meaning that if the first formula, called the antecedent, holds, then the second formula, called the consequent, must also hold. In [6] each access control policy is encoded as a *access control rule*, that is, a rule whose antecedent represents the conditions stated in the policy subject and object specifications, and the consequent represents the entailed authorizations.

For example, an access control policy authorizing sales agent Bob's customer to access his phone number can be represented by the following high level access control rule:

(targetSubject is a customer of Bob) $\wedge$ (targetObject is Bobs Phone-No) $\implies$ Access control authorization for targetSubject to read targetObject

This means that the system should contain the following access control authorization: (targetSubject, targetObject, Read).

In [6], semantic Web technologies are used to encode social network-related information, such as: (1) user's profiles, (2) relationships among users (e.g., Bob is Alice's close friend), (3) resources (e.g., reports), (4) relationships between users and resources (e.g., Bob is the owner of a report, Alice is tagged to a photo), (5) actions (e.g., post a message on someone's wall). The main advantage for using ontology for modeling online social network data is that relationships among many different social network concepts can be naturally represented using OWL.

As such, all social network-related information is contained in a knowledge base, hereafter called social network knowledge base. This implies that access control rules have to be encoded by means of semantic Web rule language, thus to pose subject and object specifications conditions directly on knowledge base. In [6] authors exploit SWRL [16] to encode such access control rules. SWRL has been introduced to extend the axioms supported by OWL to also support rules. This enables users to write rules to reason about OWL individuals and to infer new knowledge about those individuals. In SWRL, the antecedent, called the body, and the consequent, called the head, are defined in terms of OWL classes, properties, and individuals. More precisely, they are modeled as positive conjunctions of atoms. Atoms can be of the form: (1) $C(x)$, where C is an OWL description or data range; (2) $P(x,y)$, where P is an OWL property and x and y could be variables, OWL individuals or OWL data values; (3) sameAs(x,y); (4) differentFrom(x,y); (5) builtIn$(r,x,...)$, where r is a built-in predicate that takes one or more arguments and evaluates to true if the arguments satisfy the predicate. More precisely, an atom $C(x)$ holds if x is an instance of the class description or data range C, an atom $P(x,y)$

holds if x is related to y by property P, an atom sameAs(x,y) holds if x is interpreted as the same object as y, an atom differentFrom(x,y) holds if x and y are interpreted as different objects, and builtIn(r,x,...) holds if the built-in relation r holds on the interpretations of the arguments.

Exploiting SWRL to specify access control rules implies that authorizations must be represented in some ontology, thus to be encoded as a SWRL head. For this reason, in [6], a Security Authorization Knowledge Base (SAKB) ontology to model authorizations is introduced. The proposed framework translates each access control policy as a SWRL rule where the antecedent encodes the conditions specified in the policy (e.g., conditions denoting the subject and object specifications), whereas the consequent encodes the implied authorizations. In particular, since access control rules are modeled as SWRL rules, the SWRL body states policy conditions over the social network knowledge base, whereas the SWRL head entails new instances of the SAKB. Such SWRL rules could be used to enforce various access control policies, according to the requirements of the considered domain.

Using such SWRL rules, it is possible to easily specify access control rules encoding policies with conditions on ontologies modeling user relationships and user profiles. For example, a SWRL rule that encodes an access control policy specifying that company documents where Alice is mentioned can be accessed by her direct contacts (e.g., customers) could be specified as follows:

```
Document(?targetObject) ∧ Mentioned(Alice,?targetObject)
∧ Contact(Alice,?targetSubject) ⟹ Read(?targetSubject,
?targetObject)
```

One down side of using SWRL to specify access control rules is that the specification of SWRL rules is strictly bound to the ontologies supported by the online social network to model the required knowledge bases. This implies that it is not possible to provide a formalization of generic SWRL rules, since these can vary based on the considered ontologies.

Semantic-based Access Control Enforcement in Online Social Networks

The framework presented in [6] acts like a traditional access control mechanism, where a *reference monitor* evaluates a request by looking for an authorization granting the request (please see Figure 17.2 for details). In particular, access control policies are evaluated when an *access request* is submitted. Authorizations necessary to evaluate the access request are retrieved by querying the policy store that contains the ontologies encoding authorizations (i.e., SAKB). Thus, for example, to verify whether a user u is authorized to read object o, it is necessary to verify if the instance Read(u,o) of SAKB could be inferred by some SWRL rule (e.g., access control policy). This implies that in order to evaluate access control requests, the reference monitor will retrieve the required part of the social network knowledge base needed to evaluate the SWRL rule (i.e., for a given request all the parts of knowledge base may not be needed), and send it to the reasoning engine. After this point, once authorizations are inferred, access control policy enforcement can be carried out.

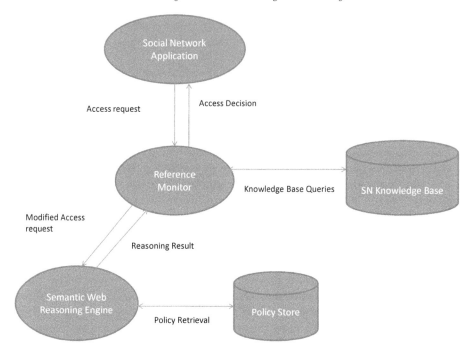

FIGURE 17.2: Framework layout

17.4 Privacy Issues in Relationship-Based Access Control Enforcement

In this section, we first discuss the main issues arising when protecting relationship privacy during relationship-based access control enforcement. We then present a proposal for enforcing a privacy-aware access control [5, 8] in online social networks.

17.4.1 Challenges in Privacy-Aware Access Control in On-line Social Networks

As we have seen in Section 17.3.2, there is a general consensus in considering relationships established by social network participants as the key parameter to perform access control. However, relationships are in general sensitive resources whose privacy should be properly guaranteed. Additionally, relationships may have associated a trust value that must be carefully protected. Therefore there are two main privacy threats in relationship-based access control: relationship disclosure and the disclosure of the associated trust value.

Relationship disclosure. Establishing a relationship in a community implies, in some sense, an exposure of personal information of the users involved in the relationship, which may give rise to some relevant privacy concerns (see also discussion provided by Chapter 16 by Gürses et al.). For instance, referring to our example, a customer that have bought some products from two different sales agents, may not want one of the two to be aware of the *clientOf* relationship existing between him/her and the other agent. One fundamental requirement is therefore that each participant in the social network is able to specify his/her privacy preferences with respect to the disclosure of the established relationships. Then, it must be ensured that such preferences are enforced when access control is performed. As it will become clear in Section 17.4.2, how to achieve this is highly influenced by the way access control is performed (e.g., centralized vs. decentralized architecture).

Trust disclosure. The other key factor to decide the result of an access request is the trust associated with network nodes and/or relationships. For instance, referring to *SellNet*, a customer may have different *clientOf* relationships with different sales agents belonging to the network, but he may not consider all of them equally trustworthy. For instance, he trusts some agents more than others, because of previous experiences and the reputation they have among other customers. The user may want to share some comments about the products he bought only with those agents whose trust level is above a given threshold. Modeling such requirements implies an answer to a variety of fundamental issues. The first is that of defining suitable trust models. Even if this issue is out of the scope of this chapter, it is important to note that in the literature there does not exist a unique definition of trust, since the semantics of trust usually varies depending on the domain and the considered purposes. For instance, in P2P systems, trust is mainly a measure of the reliability of a peer in providing a given service [20], whereas in online social networks supporting collaborative rating (e.g., movies, books) trust is mainly a measure of how much a user is an expert in a particular topic. If trust is used as a parameter to enforce access control, we believe that its semantics should also be related to the compliance with the specified access control policies and privacy preferences. Another important issue is trust computation, in that assigning a wrong trust value to a potentially malicious user could imply unauthorized releasing of information. Therefore, some mechanisms should be devised to help a user to precisely estimate the other network participants' trust level. Such mechanisms should also preserve user privacy when performing trust computation.[‡] Finally, similar to relationships, there is also the need of protecting trust when performing access control. Indeed, a user may not want to disclose to everybody the trust he assigns to other users in the community. For instance, referring to *SellNet*, a customer may accept to reveal his or her *customerOf* relationship with a given sales agent, but wants to keep

---

[‡]We will elaborate more on this in Section 17.4.2.

secret how much he trusts the agent. Similar to relationship disclosure, there is thus the need of supporting user preferences w.r.t. trust disclosure and such preferences should be enforced when performing access control.

In Section 17.4.2 we will describe a privacy-aware access control mechanism able to cope with the first class of requirements discussed above. Discussion on private trust computation is postponed to Section 17.6.

17.4.2 Privacy-Aware Access Control in Online Social Networks

To avoid the problem of relationship disclosure during access control, in [5, 8, 9] we have proposed a privacy-aware access control mechanism for online social networks, which is able to enforce relationship-based and trust-based access control, and at the same time, satisfy user preferences with respect to the release of relationship information. To the best of our knowledge, together with proposals in [10, 11], these are the only ones we are aware of in this direction, whereas the other access control solutions presented in Section 17.3.2 assume that relationships are public. Moreover, since works [10, 11] are based on models introduced in [7, 8, 9], in the following we will focus on them. In the model presented in [7, 8, 9], resources to be shared are protected by one or more *access rules*, which specify the access control requirements in terms of relationships, their depth and trust level. Each access rule has the form (rsc, AC), where AC is a set of access conditions that all need to be satisfied in order to get access to resource rsc. An access condition is a tuple $ac = (v, rt, d\_max, t\_min)$, where v is the member with whom the requester of a given resource must have a direct or indirect relationship to obtain access, whereas rt, d_max, and $t_{m}in$ are, respectively, the type, maximum depth, and minimum trust level that the relationship must have.

Example 17.2

Consider Figure 17.1 and suppose that a client G, say Greg, would like to share his opinions about a product (contained in the document $greg\_opinions$) with his suppliers but only if the trust he has assigned to them is greater than 0.5. He can specify this requirement through the following access rule: $(greg\_opinions, (G, customerOf, 1, 0.5))$. Referring to Figure 17.1, the nodes that can access $greg\_opinions$ are D, say David, and E, say Eric, whereas F, say Fred, is not allowed to access the document. Indeed, even if he satisfies the requirement on the relationship type, his trust level is less than 0.5. Suppose now that Fred, a sales agent, would like to share the document my_doc with $NewComp$ and with his direct and indirect partners, whose trust level is greater than 0.7. He can specify the following access rules: $(my\_doc, \{(F, agentOf, 1, *)\})$ and $(my\_doc, \{(F, partnerOf, 2, 0.7)\})$, where symbol '*' is a metacharacter to indicate any trust level. □

In a similar way, relationships can also be protected through a set of *distribution rules* [5, 8], which identify online social network members authorized to be aware of the relationship in terms of relationship type and depth. By properly customizing the distribution rules associated with a relationship, a user can express a variety of privacy preferences with respect to its disclosure. For example, with reference to our example, Greg can specify that the *customerOf* relationship linking him with Fred should be kept private, whereas David and A, say Alice, can decide to disclose their partnership relationships only to *NewComp*.

The way distribution rules are enforced strictly depends on the architecture on support of access control enforcement. The simplest solution is to let the Social Network Management System (SNMS) be in charge of access control and therefore of enforcing also distribution rules. This centralized architecture is the standard solution usually adopted by Data Management Systems. However, even if this solution has the advantage of being very easy to be implemented, we think that in an environment like social networks relying on an entity that has the right to know all the relationships existing in the community as well as the data to be shared and the access rules regulating their release is not appropriate. The main reason is that this implies that network users totally delegate to the SNMS the administration of their resources and relationships and therefore that they have to fully trust it with respect to the enforcement of their privacy and access control requirements. However, some recent events (see for instance [3]) have increased the privacy concerns of online social network users w.r.t. how SNMSs manage personal information. This leads us to believe that a centralized architecture for access control enforcement is not the most appropriate for the online social network scenario.

The alternative solution is to make the network participants themselves able to evaluate their access control policies. In this scenario, which we refer to as *decentralized architecture*, each participant is in charge of specifying and enforcing his/her access control policies. This solution can be further classified into *provider-side* and *requestor-side* access control. According to the provider-side paradigm, the resource provider is in charge of checking whether the access can be granted or not, on the basis of the specified access control policies. In contrast, according to the requester-side approach, the burden of answering an access request is mainly on the requester node. More precisely, according to this paradigm, which is the one we proposed in [9], the provider sends to the requester node the access rules he has to satisfy in order to gain access to the requested resource. The requester node should then provide the owner with a *proof*, certifying that he satisfies the requirements specified by the received rules. The proof consists of a set of *relationship paths*, as well as their trust levels. Moreover, the resource provider should receive some additional information that makes him able to check the correctness of the received proof. We refer the interested readers to [9] for all the details of the access control protocol.

Let us see now how both requester-side and provider-side access control can be extended to also ensure the satisfaction of the privacy preferences w.r.t. relationships disclosure. Let us start by explaining the two most important privacy breaches that should be prevented.

Example 17.3

Consider again the online social network in Figure 17.1 and suppose that, according to the specified distribution rules, David should not be aware of the *partnerOf* relationship between Bob and Alice. Suppose now that David requests a resource to NC and that in order to get access to this resource he should prove to be a partner of Alice. Suppose that relationships are public and available at the SNMS. Therefore, in order to gain access to the resource, David retrieves from the SNMS the *relationship path* of type *partnerOf* connecting it him to Alice. Since this path contains information about relationships of type *partnerOf* between Bob and Alice, and between David and Bob, by means of this path, David is also informed that Bob is a partner of Alice, and this violates the distribution rule specified by Bob. Suppose moreover that NC has established a *non_competition* relationship with another company and that it would like to share with this company a classified report *rep*. Moreover, suppose that for the moment, it does not want to disclose this relationship to its sales agents. Now assume that Fred asks NC to access *rep*. If requester-side access control is applied, NC would reply with an access rule containing conditions on *non_competition* relationship, in that, according to NC protection requirement, in order to gain access to *req* the requester has to have a direct *non_competition* relationship with NC. Therefore, by reading the received access rule, Fred will be informed that NC has established such a relationship with another company, since NC posed it as rule conditions. This violates the distribution rule specified by NC.

$\square$

Let us first consider the requester-based approach. First of all, since the generated proof, i.e., *relationship paths*, is based on the existing relationships, they should be certified in order to avoid having a node make use of fake relationships in order to get access to a resource. To avoid some of the problems discussed in Example 17.3, in [8], such certificates are encrypted with secret keys. When two nodes establish a new relationship, they generate an encrypted relationship certificate. Then, once they agree on the distribution rule, they distribute the corresponding secret key to all and only those members satisfying the distribution rule. Key distribution is performed according to a protocol involving all the members authorized to access the corresponding relationship certificate. More precisely, whenever an encrypted relationship certificate is generated, the members establishing the corresponding relationship send the secret key together with the distribution rule, regulating the certificate distribution, to those of their direct neighbors that satisfy that distribution rule. In turn, the neighbors propagate the secret key and the distribution rule only to those of their neighbors that satisfy the distribution rule. This process is iterated until all members authorized to access the certificate have been provided with the corresponding secret key. Moreover, encrypted certificates are available in a public repository, which is then acquired by online social network members to generate proofs. A member will then be able to decrypt only those certificates in the encrypted relationship path for which he has been provided with the corresponding key, that is, only those certificates whose distribution rules are satisfied by him. Moreover, the repository can not infer any information on online social network relationships since it does not receive any decryption key. To avoid the privacy breach arising by distributing access control rules (see Example 17.3), in [8] access rules are also encrypted with a secret key, called the *relationship key*. This key is managed and distributed in such a way that each member m holds a different relationship key K_rt for each different type rt of relationship he is involved in. The proposed key management scheme ensures that each relationship key K_rt is shared by all and only those users connected to m by a direct or indirect relationship of type rt. This ensures that a requester will be able to read an access condition only if there exists a direct or indirect relationship of the type required by the access rule between him and the resource owner, which limits the inferences he can perform. We refer the interested readers to [8] for more details about the protocols.

Clearly, the main drawback of this approach, as of any cryptographic based solution, is related to the cost of key management and key distribution. For instance, each time an access or distribution rule is updated, this may require the generation and distribution of new keys. To overcome this drawback, in [5] we have proposed a different approach which works when the provider-side paradigm is used. The protocol is based on a collaboration among selected nodes in the network to build a certificate path that satisfies an access control rule. More precisely, when a node receives an access control request, it first verifies which are the relationship paths required by the access rules associated with the requested resource. Then, he starts a collaborative process, by contacting his neighbors and asking them whether they have a relationship of the required type with the requester. If this is not the case, the neighbors contact their direct neighbors by propagating the request of collaboration. This process is iterated until the request cannot be further propagated (i.e., the process reaches a member that does not have any relationship of the required type) or a path satisfying one of the access rules associated with the resource is found. The collaborative protocol is defined in such a way that during the process, information on the traversed path (i.e., traversed relationships and corresponding trust levels) is gathered and forwarded to the new nodes taking part to the collaborative process. When the path is found, all this information is sent back to the resource owner, which is then able to locally verify if the found path satisfies the depth and trust level requirements specified in the access rule. A first benefit of this collaborative process is that it avoids the

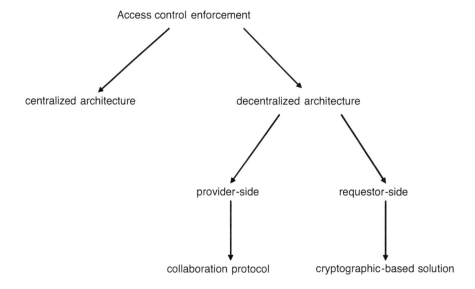

FIGURE 17.3: A taxonomy of architectural options on support of privacy aware access control

privacy inferences due to the revealing of access rules. However, the collaborative process also could lead to privacy breaches, in that, information on relationships a member inserts in the path (i.e., relationship type and trust level) is available to all the members that subsequently take part to the collaborative process. To overcome this drawback, the collaboration process is driven by the distribution rules specified by the members taking part to the collaboration. More precisely, before propagating the request of collaboration to one of his neighbors, a member verifies whether the neighbor satisfies the distribution rules associated with the relationships in the path built so far. If this is not the case, the request of collaboration is not propagated. Additionally, the use of cryptographic techniques and of a particular digital signature data structure (called an *onion signature*) makes it possible to detect if a malicious member propagates the request of collaboration to a neighbor even if he does not satisfy the distribution rules associated with the relationships in the path. We refer the interested reader to [5], for more information on the onion signature data structure and the collaborative protocol.

All the architectural options that support access control described so far are summarized in Figure 17.3.

Finally, as we have discussed in Section 17.4.1, there are relevant privacy issues related to trust disclosure and computation. As far as trust disclosure is concerned, the problem is similar to that of relationship protection. Both of the methods described above, that is, the collaborative protocol and the cryptographic-based solution, can be easily extended to also enforce privacy preferences related to trust distribution. For instance, if a cryptographic-based solution is used, the trust level contained into each relationship certificate can be encrypted with a key, which is then distributed only to the nodes which satisfy the privacy preference w.r.t. its disclosure.

17.5   Preventing Private Information Inference

In this section, we focus on the problem of individual private information leakage due to being part of an online social network. More specifically, we discuss how online social network data could be used to predict some individual private trait that a user is not willing to disclose (e.g., political or religious affiliation) and explore the effect of possible data sanitization alternatives on preventing such private information leakage. We would like to stress that the privacy issues discussed here are different from the social network anonymization techniques discussed in Chapter 18 by Miklau et al. The goal of the social network anonymization is how social network data that needs to be released could be sanitized so that identifying a given individual will be hard. For example, to preserve individual privacy, Facebook can apply such techniques to sanitize its data before selling it to other companies. Instead, here, we focus on private information leakage to anyone who can access a given user's profile. For example, assume that Alice wants to keep her political affiliation private (i.e., she does not release this information online). In this case, Facebook may build very accurate models to predict such private information. The goal of the research described in this section is to come up with techniques so that users like Alice can protect the privacy of their sensitive personal traits while enjoying the benefits provided by an online social network platform. In the rest of this section, first, we give an overview of the current work. Then, we discuss an example of how such an inference attack could be launched and discuss possible sanitization techniques to prevent it.

17.5.1   Overview of the Literature

The area of privacy inside a social network encompasses a large breadth, based on how privacy is defined. Many papers have tried to deal with private information inference using data mining inside social networks. In [15], authors consider ways to infer private information via friendship links by creating a Bayesian Network from the links inside a social network. While they crawl a real social network, Livejournal, they use hypothetical attributes to analyze their learning algorithm.

In [21], the authors propose a method of *link reidentification*. That is, they assume that the social network has various link types embedded, and that some of these link types are sensitive. Based on these assumptions, authors propose several methods by which these sensitive link types can be hidden. The general method by which they hide links is either by random elimination or by link aggregation.

In [22], Zheleva and Getoor attempt to predict the private attributes of users in four real-world datasets: Facebook, Flickr, Dogster, and BibSonomy. In addition to using general relational classification, they introduce a group-based classification by taking advantage of specific types of attributes in each of the social networks. However, their work does not attempt to sanitize the data; it only reveals the problems we also describe herein.

In [14], Gross and Acquisti examine specific usage instances at Carnegie Mellon. They also note potential attacks, such as node re-identification or stalking, that easily accessible data on Facebook could assist with. They further note that while privacy controls may exist on the user's end of the social networking site, many individuals do not take advantage such privacy controls. However, their paper focuses mostly on faults inside the Facebook platform. They do not discuss attempting to learn unrevealed traits of Facebook users, and do no analysis of the details of Facebook users.

Similarly, in [18], authors provide techniques to infer private information on social networks and how to selectively delete attributes and links to prevent such inference attacks. Basically, authors attempt to identify sensitive traits of individuals by using a graph that initially has a full listing of friendship links. Also, compared to [21, 22] and [15], instead of random elimination of links between nodes and profile attributes, they propose information sanitization strategies that will reduce the accuracy of the inference attack the most. In the following section, we discuss the work reported in [18] to illustrate such an inference attack.

In summary, current research just scratches the surface of this important problem. More research needs to be done on how to prevent such inference attacks without losing the utility provided by online social networks. For example, we need new sanitization techniques for social network data that can prevent the disclosure of individuals' sexual orientation and still outputs useful information that could be used for marketing various products.

17.5.2   Overview of a Typical Inference Attack on Social Networks

Usually inference attacks on social networks start with building some sort of a classifier. For example, in [18], authors present a modification of Naïve Bayes classification that is suitable for classifying large amount of social network data. The modified Naïve Bayes algorithm tries predict whether a person is conservative or liberal using both node traits and link structure. In this scenario, node traits capture the user's profile information such as the fa-

Classifier	0t, 0l	0t, 10l	10t, 0l	10t, 10l
Naïve Bayes	0.7533	0.7157	0.6838	0.6790

Table 17.2: Effect of link and details removal for Naïve Bayes classification method [18]

vorite hobbies, and link structure captures the information related to a user's friends. Later on, they compare the accuracy of their learning method based on link structure against the accuracy of their learning method based on node traits. After the inference attack scenario is developed, usually some sort of sanitization of the social network data is suggested. For example, in [18], to protect privacy, they sanitize both trait (e.g., deleting some information from a user's online profile) and link details (e.g., deleting links between friends) and explore the effect they have on combating possible inference attacks. The results reported in [18] indicate that just sanitizing trait information or link information may not be enough to prevent inference attacks and comprehensive sanitization techniques that involve both aspects are needed in practice. Usually these techniques are tested on real-life online social network data such as Facebook. For example, in [18], authors wrote a program to crawl the Facebook Dallas/Forth Worth (DFW) network to gather data for their research. Due to the data gathering process, if two people share a common friend that is outside the DFW network, this is not reflected inside their dataset. For their experiments, authors consider only the subset of the social network data for which a user specifically expressed political affiliation as either "Conservative" or "Liberal." This reduces the overall set size from approximately 160,000 to approximately 35,000 profiles. One interesting finding of current work is that we may not need too much sanitization to protect against some types of inference attacks. For example, in [18], authors examine the specific effects of removing traits and links. Authors provide heuristics to create a list of the most representative traits in the social network data, which they use to remove the 10 most predictive traits from the social network data. That is, when they remove K traits, they calculate which K traits are globally the most likely to reveal true political affiliation and then remove those traits from every node that originally had them. Similarly, they remove the 10 most telling links from every node in the graph. Unlike removing traits, which is done globally, removal of links is done locally. Finally, they combine the two methods and generate test sets with both 10 traits and 10 links removed from the graph. In the above table, those tests are referred as 0t, 0l; 10t, 0l; 0t, 10l; 10t, 10l removed, respectively. Following this, they randomly divide the nodes in the social network to form sets of 50% of the nodes in the training and 50% in the test sets. The previous process is repeated five times, and each experiment is run independently. Then the average of each of these five runs as the overall accuracy is reported.

The results, as shown in Table 17.2, indicate that a performance of Naïve

Bayes based inference attacks could be significantly reduced by deleting both links and traits. In summary, current research has explored the effect of removing traits and links in preventing sensitive information leakage. Initial results indicate that removing trait details and friendship links together is the best way to reduce classifier accuracy, but this is probably infeasible in maintaining the use of social networks. However, it looks like by removing only traits, we can greatly reduce the accuracy of the classifiers that predict private information.

17.6   Conclusion and Research Challenges

This chapter has provided an overview of some of the developments in protecting the privacy of online social network users. In particular, we have focused on three main issues, that is, (*a*) protecting the privacy of user profiles by exploiting access control solutions, (*b*) protecting the privacy of user relationships when performing access control, and (*c*) protecting the users' privacy avoiding private information inference. The field addressed by this chapter is new and leaves room for a lot of research. In the following, we discuss some of the most challenging research issues.

- **Trust computation and protection**. As we have seen in Section 17.4.1, one key issue to be addressed is the privacy threats that may arise during trust computation. When trust is used for access control purposes, the trust level assigned to a node must keep into account the compliance of the node to the specified access control rules and privacy preferences. In order to properly assess a node trust level, there is thus the need of monitoring the behavior of the online social network users w.r.t. the release of relationships or resources. There is thus the need of defining suitable methods to assess the behaviors of online social network users w.r.t. relations/resources disclosure. One intuitive method to do this is logging all the access control decisions into an audit file that can be inspected by the other users in the network, in order to assess a user trust level. However, this solution raises serious privacy concerns, because a participant might have privacy concerns in releasing information about the decisions he has made. For instance, a user might not want to reveal to another user the releasing of a given resource, even if this release does not violate the specified access control policies. Therefore, there is the need of devising privacy-preserving techniques to perform trust computation. If a log file is used, an option is to exploit anonymization strategies of the audit file, such that details about the performed access control decisions are kept private but, at the same time, it is possible to determine whether the decisions are a correct or not, with respect to the specified policies.

- **Policy specification**. In Section 17.3 we have discussed some of the requirements of a policy language to support access control in online social networks. However, in this section, we focused only on access control policies. We think that a comprehensive framework for online social network access control must support other kinds of security policies w.r.t. access control ones. First, of all, the model should also support administration policies, stating who can specify access control policies, on which data and under which conditions. In an online social network, besides the traditional, ownership-based administration policy, used by most of the current DBSMS, there is the need to support other more articulated policies. For instance the online social network administrator may want to specify an administration policy stating that users tagged to a given resource are authorized to specify access control policies for that resource. The policy language should therefore be able to cope with these requirements.

  Another class of policies that the model must support is the one preventing the fruition of inappropriate or unwanted content through the online social networks. These policies differ from traditional access control policies because they are not specified by the resource owner/administrator. Rather, they can be specified by every user in the online social network to state which data has to be filtered out when a given user browses the online social network pages. By means of a filtering policy, it is, for example, possible to state that from online social network pages fetched by user Alice, all resources that have not been published by Alice's colleagues have to be removed. As such, these policies can be used for spam prevention. Another option is to use them to prevent some particular categories of users (e.g., children) from accessing harmful content. In this case, the policies should not be specified by the users themselves, but by one or more of their supervisors (e.g., teachers, parents). The access control model should therefore be able to also support this kind of policy. Additionally, the system should be equipped with proper integration strategies to cope with possible conflicts arising among the various kinds of policies.

- **Privacy issues due to social network applications**. Online social networks such as Facebook allow external developers to develop applications using their infrastructure. For example, the SuperWall application on Facebook allows users to find and share videos, pictures, graffiti, etc. with their friends. Currently, a user needs to allow the application to access his entire profile information if they want to use the application. We believe that such an approach is too restrictive. Instead, we believe that users should be able specify fine grained access control policies on what kind of applications could access which part of the profile information. One important research challenge that is different from the current work on social network access control is that some kind of trust negotiation between users and application providers is needed to agree on reasonable service level for accessing particular profile information.

References

[1] B. Ali, W. Villegas, and M. Maheswaran. A trust based approach for protecting user data in social networks. In *Proceedings of the Conference of the Center for Advanced Studies on Collaborative Research (CASCON'07)*, pages 288–293, 2007.

[2] K. Ando, A. Fukagai, K. Ohshima and M. Terada. DHT network with link access control using a social network, In *Proceedings of the International Symposium on Applications and the Internet (SAINT 2008)*, 2008.

[3] S. Berteau. Facebook's misrepresentation of Beacon's threat to privacy: Tracking users who opt out or are not logged in. CA Security Advisor Research Blog, Mar. 2007.

[4] D. Brickley and L. Miller. FOAF vocabulary specification 0.91. RDF Vocabulary Specification, Nov. 2007. Available at http://xmlns.com/foaf/0.1.

[5] B. Carminati, and E. Ferrari. Privacy-aware collaborative access control in web-based social networks.. In *Proc. of the 22nd IFIP WG 11.3 Working Conference on Data and Applications Security* (DBSEC2008), London, UK, 2008.

[6] B. Carminati, E. Ferrari, R. Heatherly, M. Kantarcioglu, B. Thuraisingham. A semantic web based framework for social networks. In *Proc. of the 14th ACM Symposium on Access Control Technologies (SACMAT'09)*, Stresa, Italy, June 2009.

[7] B. Carminati, E. Ferrari, and A. Perego. Rule-based access control for social networks. In *Proceedings of OTM 2006 Workshops*, volume 2 of *LNCS 4278*, Springer Verlag, 2006.

[8] B. Carminati, E. Ferrari, and A. Perego. A decentralized security framework for web-based social networks. *International Journal of Information Security and Privacy, 2(4),22-53, 2010.*

[9] B. Carminati, E. Ferrari, and A. Perego. Enforcing access control in web-based social networks. *ACM Transactions on Information & System Security, 13(1), 2009.*

[10] J. Domingo-Ferrer. A public-key protocol for social networks with private relationships In *Proceedings of Modeling Decisions for Artificial Intelligence*, LNCS 4617, Springer Verlag, 2007.

[11] J. Domingo-Ferrer, A. Viejo, F. Sebe, and U. Gonzalez-Nicolas, Privacy homomorphisms for social networks with private relationships, *Computer Networks Journal*, 52(15), Elsevier, 2008.

[12] N. Elahi, M. M. R. Chowdhury, and J. Noll. Semantic access control in web based communities. In *Proceedings of the 2008 The Third International Multi-Conference on Computing in the Global Information Technology* (ICCGI 2008), Washington, DC, USA, 2008.

[13] R. Figueiredo, P. O. Boykin, P. St. Juste, D. Wolinsky Social VPNs: Integrating Overlay and Social Networks for Seamless P2P Networking In *Proceedings of the 17th IEEE International Workshop on Enabling Technologies*: *Infrastructures for Collaborative Enterprises*, Rome, Italy, 2008.

[14] R. Gross, A. Acquisti, and J. H. Heinz. Information revelation and privacy in online social networks. In *Proceedings of ACM Workshop on Privacy in the Electronic Society*, New York, NY, USA, ACM Press, 2005.

[15] J. He, W. Chu, and V. Liu. Inferring privacy information from social networks. In *Proceedings of Intelligence and Security Informatics*, volume LNCS 3975, Springer Verlag, 2006.

[16] I. Horrocks, P. F. Patel-Schneider, H. Boley, S. Tabet, B. Grosof, and M. Dean. SWRL: A Semantic web rule language combining OWL and RuleML. W3C Member Submission, World Wide Web Consortium, May 2004. Available at: `http://www.w3.org/Submission/SWRL`.

[17] S. R. Kruk, S. Grzonkowski, H.-C. Choi, T. Woroniecki, and A. Gzella. D-FOAF: Distributed identity management with access rights delegation. In *Proceedings of the 1st Asian Semantic Web Conference (ASWC 2006)*, LNCS 4185, pages 140–154. Springer Verlag, 2006.

[18] J. Lindamood, R. Heatherly, M. Kantarcioglu, and B. Thuraisingham. Inferring private information using social network data. *In Proceedings of the 18th International Conference on World Wide Web* (WWW 2009), Poster, Madrid, Spain 2009.

[19] P. Mika. Social Networks and the Semantic Web, volume 5 of *Semantic Web and Beyond Computing for Human Experience*. Springer, 2007.

[20] Xiong, L. and Liu, L. PeerTrust: Supporting reputation-based trust for peer-to-peer electronic communities. *IEEE Transactions on Knowledge and Data Engineering*, 16(7), 843-857, 2004.

[21] E. Zheleva and L. Getoor. Preserving the privacy of sensitive relationships in graph data. In *Proceedings of the First ACM SIGKDD Workshop on Privacy, Security, and Trust in KDD*, San Jose, USA, 2007.

[22] E. Zheleva and L. Getoor. To join or not to join: the illusion of privacy in social networks with mixed public and private user profiles. In *Proceedings of the 18th International Conference on World Wide Web (WWW 2009)*, Poster, Madrid, Spain 2009.

Chapter 18

Analyzing Private Network Data

Michael Hay, Gerome Miklau, and David Jensen

University of Massachusetts, Amherst, Massachusetts

18.1 Introduction

Many phenomena can be modeled as networks in which entities (represented by nodes) participate in binary relationships (represented by edges). In a social network, nodes are individuals and edges are personal contacts or relationships. In a communication network, nodes are individuals and edges are flows of information such as phone calls or email messages. In a technological network, nodes are machines, such as computers or power stations, and edges are some means of transmission.

Research into the structure and function of networks has wide-ranging applications. Network analysis is being used by businesses to market products [31], by epidemiologists to combat the spread of diseases [32], and by financial regulatory agencies to detect fraud among securities dealers [20]. Network analysis has also been applied to national security, industrial engineering, and computer network design.

The collection, dissemination, and analysis of networks has become much easier in recent years. In the early days of social network analysis, data was often collected manually through interviews or surveys. As a result of the cost of data collection, few networks were available to researchers, and those available were small—sometimes consisting of fewer than 100 nodes. Figure 18.1 reproduces a widely studied 34-node social network of karate club members, taken from Zachary [66]. Now, because so many of our interactions leave electronic traces, networks can be systematically recorded, sometimes on a nearly global scale. For example, Leskovec and Horvitz's [39] study of Microsoft Messenger users examined a network of 180 million nodes and 1.3 billion edges.

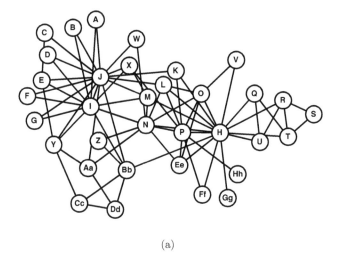

(a)

Id	Gender	Age	Belt	Injury
16	F	18	yellow	ankle
6	M	21	white	ankle
31	F	42	white	elbow
11	M	16	white	none
9	M	19	white	clavicle
21	M	21	white	knee
13	F	21	white	none
26	M	36	black	none
8	F	22	brown	none
2	M	45	black	ribs
...				

Edge	YearsKnown
{ 16, 8 }	2
{ 16, 2 }	3
{ 6, 8 }	10
{ 6, 2 }	11
{ 31, 2 }	20
{ 31, 9 }	1
...	

(b)   (c)

FIGURE 18.1: (a) A social network representing friendships among karate club members, from Zachary [66]. (b) An example vertex table V. The rows correspond to vertices (nodes) in the graph shown in (a). (c) An example edge table E. The rows correspond to edges in the graph shown in (a).

Some speculate that data at this scale can revolutionize the social sciences—much the way data has transformed biology and physics—leading to a data-driven "computational social science" [35]. However, scientific progress has been impeded because much of the data is not yet available to the scientific community at large. The institutions and service providers that collect the data are often unwilling to release it. Their reluctance is due, in part, to concerns about privacy, since network data can reveal sensitive facts about participating entities and their connections. As a result, computational social science is happening, but only at the institutions that own the data or by a limited set of researchers who have negotiated access to the data (e.g., [22, 34, 39, 50, 53]). If the data is not accessible to the larger scientific community, then results cannot be replicated and findings cannot be challenged. For the field of computational social science to flourish, we must remove the obstacles to data sharing caused by privacy concerns.

This chapter describes techniques for the private and accurate analysis of network data. We assume the data owner possesses a graph representing a network of interest to analysts, and we consider two strategies for the safe release of the data. In *private data publication*, a transformed network is released for analysis by the data owner. In *private query answering*, an analyst submits queries to the data owner and receives answers, often transformed or perturbed by the data owner to protect privacy. In order to be useful to the analysts, the transformed data must accurately reflect the original graph, and the techniques that transform this data must be efficient enough to scale to large datasets.

Both strategies have an important role in enabling safe dissemination of network data. In data publication, the analyst receives a transformed graph and performs analysis using local resources. This means the data owner does not have to devote resources on behalf of the analyst. It also allows the analyst to carry out tasks that are difficult to do through a query interface, such as data cleaning, exploration, and transformations. Lastly, the analyst's processing of the graph is not revealed to the data owner. In query answering, the analysts receive only the answers to specific queries. The main advantage of this strategy is that it can typically offer more accurate results since the distortion introduced to protect privacy is targeted to specific queries.

Both of these approaches have been explored in the literature, but most existing work assumes that the private data can be represented using a single table. Typically each record in the table corresponds to a separate entity and, in contrast to network data, and there are no relationships between the entities. Data publishing techniques for tabular data are not well-suited for network data because they fail to account for the interconnectedness of the entities. Naively applied, they tend to destroy the network structure, which can be a crucial part of the analysis of such data. At the same time, threats considered for tabular data do not account for the vulnerabilities posed by the connections in a network.

Existing query answering techniques can be applied to network data; however, the kinds of queries posed on network data differ from the typical queries posed on tabular data. We review recent work that adapts existing query answering techniques to accurately carry out important network analyses.

While the algorithms designed for tabular data do not always apply to network data, some of the definitions of privacy, such as k-anonymity [57, 58, 61] and differential privacy [13, 15], can be adapted to network data.

Much research has explored related privacy problems in network data, particularly on problems that surface with online social networks [1, 7, 18, 21, 23, 29, 33, 41, 67, 68]. While all of this work shares a common goal of keeping sensitive information private, the privacy issues that arise with data analysis are distinct from those that arise with, say, access control. Typically, the analyst is interested in facts about the network's overall topology and not with the particular connections between individuals. Thus, the overarching goal is to reveal properties of the network (in the aggregate) but hide sensitive properties of particular entities and their relations.

18.1.1   How Are Networks Analyzed?

If the techniques for protecting privacy are to have practical application, they must allow an analyst to measure important network properties and carry out common analyses. After introducing a network that will serve as a running example, we briefly review some ways that networks are studied.

We represent a network as a graph consisting of vertices, described by vertex table V, and edges, described by edge table E. Figure 18.1 shows the vertex and edge table for the karate club network. Each node has a unique identifier (e.g., $A, B, C \ldots$), and edges are unordered pairs of node identifiers (e.g., $\{A, I\}$). In some networks, nodes and edges may have attributes, which are represented as auxiliary columns in tables V and E. A directed graph can include a direction attribute in E. In the figure, the node attributes are *Name, Gender, Age, Belt*, and *Injury*, and the edge attribute is *YearsKnown*. (The attributes on the nodes and edges have been created for the purpose of illustration and were not present in the original network from Zachary [66].)

Many analyses focus solely on measuring the topology of the network as defined by the edge table. Such analyses include the distribution of node degrees, the distribution of path lengths (including the diameter—the longest minimum length path between two nodes), and measures of transitivity (defined as the likelihood that a node's neighbors are directly connected). Significant research effort has been devoted to models of network formation that generate graphs possessing the structural properties seen in the real world [3, 8, 6, 24, 36, 38, 37, 63].

Some analyses pinpoint specific structural features of the network. Analysis of network centrality [19] seeks to identify influential nodes. For example, in Figure 18.1, node H may be considered influential because a large number of shortest paths include H. In addition, community discovery [51] divides the network into meaningful clusters. Motif analysis [46] identifies interesting structures that occur repeatedly in a network.

Another category of research focuses on understanding the function of the network by modeling processes that occur within the network. Such processes include search or navigation within networks [59, 62] and diffusion across networks (e.g., rumors or epidemics spreading in a group) [31].

While the above analyses focus on the structure of the graph, the presence of attributes on edges or nodes allows for some new analyses and variants of those above. For example, homophily, the tendency for associations to form among similar individuals, can be measured in a network with attributes on nodes [44, 54]. Network models have been developed that model the correlation between structural features and attributes [24]. Finally, network data can include temporal information, allowing the study of network dynamics. This study includes the development of models of network formation and evolution [37] and models to accurately predict future links [34, 40].

The above summary is incomplete, but shows the diversity of analyses that are performed on network data. More complete surveys of network analysis appear in the literature [49, 12].

18.1.2 Why Should Network Data Be Kept Private?

Many networks contain sensitive information, which may be disclosed through network analysis. In cases where entities represent individuals, network data often contains personal information. Even if the entities in a network are not individuals, network data may still be sensitive. For example, detailed topological information about the power grid may reveal vulnerabilities to potential terrorists, or records of information flow between host machines in a computer network may reveal applications running on those hosts or facts about host operators.

The vertex table of a network raises the common privacy problems of tabular data: descriptive attributes associated with an entity may be sensitive, and even the inclusion of an entity in the data can itself be sensitive. For example, the first tuple in Figure 18.1(b) reveals that Alice is in the karate club, that she is 18 years old, and that she has injured her ankle.

Of course, the distinctive feature of graph data is the presence of relationships between entities represented by the edge table. The existence of an edge may be sensitive. For example, Alice may want to hide the fact that she and Ingrid are friends. Alternatively, Dave may be willing to disclose that Ingrid and John are his friends, but he may wish to hide the fact that he has only two friends. Other aspects of connections may also be sensitive. For example, Ingrid may prefer to hide the fact that she is friends with a 45 year-old man, or that she associates primarily with white belts. Or the degree of a vertex may be sensitive: academics in a scholarly collaboration network may wish to hide their low degree, while participants in a network of romantic contacts may wish to hide their high degree.

In summary, both the attributes of a node and the structure of connections around a node can be sensitive. The diversity of sensitive information in network data poses challenges for privacy mechanisms.

18.1.3   Are Privacy and Utility Compatible?

Given the range of sensitive information to be protected in networks, maintaining privacy and enabling accurate analysis may be impossible. As our review will show, existing work has encountered some limits on what analyses can be accurately studied. With each of the data publishing approaches, the transformations that are applied to protect privacy systematically distort some important network properties, and it is not clear how to lessen the distortion without weakening the privacy protection. With the query answering approaches, it has been shown that there are some network analyses that are impossible to answer accurately under existing privacy definitions.

At the same time, some positive results have emerged. Many network properties are preserved in the transformed networks, and the transformations provide practical privacy protection. In the query answering setting, it is possible to answer some queries very accurately while also ensuring strong privacy guarantees.

These results are encouraging, but leave many open questions about the nature of the relationship between privacy and utility. Understanding what properties of networks can be safely released remains one of the main open questions in this area of research.

18.1.4   Organization

In the remainder of this chapter, we first discuss attacks on network data and then discuss strategies for protecting privacy, reviewing both data publishing techniques and query answering techniques. In Section 18.2, we discuss attacks on networks that are anonymized simply by removing identifiers from nodes, showing that this common approach is insecure. We review three specific attack strategies, show how they can lead to the disclosure of sensitive information, and evaluate their effectiveness through simulated attacks on real networks. In Section 18.3, we review approaches that protect privacy by transforming the graph either through directed alteration, generalization, or random alteration. In Section 18.4, we review private query answering approaches, in which perturbed query answers are returned to the analyst. We conclude in Section 18.5 by addressing future challenges in the private analysis of networks.

18.2   Attacks on Anonymized Networks

A common strategy for protecting sensitive networks is *naive anonymization*. Naive anonymization is a simple transformation of a graph in which names of nodes (or other unique identifiers) are removed and replaced by

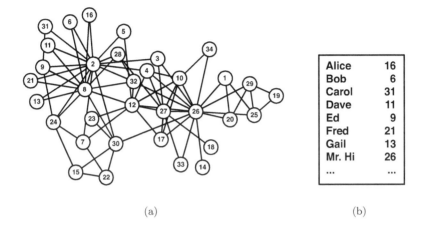

(a)

Alice	16
Bob	6
Carol	31
Dave	11
Ed	9
Fred	21
Gail	13
Mr. Hi	26
...	...

(b)

Id	Gender	Age	Belt	Injury
16	F	18	yellow	ankle
6	M	21	white	ankle
31	F	42	white	elbow
11	M	16	white	none
9	M	19	white	clavicle
21	M	21	white	knee
13	F	21	white	none
26	M	36	black	none
8	F	22	brown	none
2	M	45	black	ribs
		...		

(c)

Edge	YearsKnown
{ 16, 8 }	2
{ 16, 2 }	3
{ 6, 8 }	10
{ 6, 2 }	11
{ 31, 2 }	20
{ 31, 9 }	1
...	

(d)

FIGURE 18.2: (a) Naive anonymization of the network from Figure 18.1; (b) Secret mapping between names and synthetic identifiers; (c) Anonymized vertex table and (d) Anonymized edge table.

synthetic identifiers. For example, Figure 18.2 shows the naively anonymized version of the karate club network in Figure 18.1. Also shown (Figure 18.2(b)) is the random mapping between names and synthetic identifiers. This is secret and known only by the data owner.

A naively anonymized network can support many analyses accurately since the topology of the graph and non-identifying attributes are unmodified. Unfortunately, this also makes it vulnerable to attack by an adversary with some prior knowledge about entities in the network. Using knowledge of attribute values, graph structure, or both, the adversary may be able to re-identify targeted individuals in the naively anonymized network.

In this section, we categorize attacks on naively anonymized networks, and review empirical results on the effectiveness of these attacks. The results demonstrate that naive anonymization has considerable privacy risk. Equally important, the vulnerabilities of naive anonymization exposed by the attacks provide insight into strategies for improved anonymization techniques, such as those discussed in Section 18.3.

18.2.1   Threats: Re-Identification and Edge Disclosure

Most researchers have focused on one of two threats to naively anonymized data: *node re-identification* and *edge disclosure*. Node re-identification occurs when an adversary accurately identifies the named individual corresponding to a node in the naively anonymized graph. Once node re-identification occurs, further disclosures are likely. If the published network includes attributes, those attributes are now associated with the identified individual. In addition, the position of the individual in the network is now revealed, which can lead to disclosure of various structural properties, as discussed in Section 18.1.2.

Re-identification can either be *complete* or *partial*. Given a target individual, we say that the adversary has completely re-identified the target if the adversary knows which node in the anonymized graph corresponds to the target. For example, the adversary knows that Ed is node 9. With partial re-identification, the adversary may be uncertain about which node corresponds to the target, but the adversary has succeeded in winnowing the possibilities down to a small set of *candidates*. For example, the adversary may know that Ed is one of $\{7, 9, 17, 25, 28, 29\}$. The size of the candidate set is a natural measure of re-identification risk.

Edge disclosure occurs when an adversary is able to accurately infer the existence of an edge between two named individuals. Disclosing the *absence* of an edge may also be considered a violation of privacy. However, since most real networks are sparse—meaning most edges are absent—the adversary's ability to infer the presence of an edge tends to be a greater concern.

Node re-identification and edge disclosure are distinct threats, and researchers have often considered them separately. Of course, in a naively anonymized graph, re-identification of multiple nodes leads to edge disclosure: if both Alice and John are re-identified, then the presence of an edge between them can be determined by inspection. However, when we move beyond naive anonymization to more complex transformations in Section 18.3, we will see that re-identification does not necessarily imply edge disclosure since some of the edges in the anonymized network may be artificial. Edge disclosure can also occur without complete node re-identification. For example, suppose the adversary has identified a set of candidate matches for Alice—$\{6, 9, 11, 16, 28\}$—and a set of candidate matches for John—$\{2, 8\}$. The adversary can conclude that Alice and John must be connected because each candidate for Alice is connected to each of the candidates for John.

Node re-identification and edge disclosure are simple instances of disclosure and the two most commonly considered in the literature. In some settings, more complex disclosures may be of interest to an adversary, such as the disclosure of specific attributes or structural patterns. For example, in a network of sexual interactions, revealing a person's degree (i.e., the number of sexual partners) constitutes a sensitive disclosure.

18.2.2 Adversary Knowledge

The adversary's ability to attack a naively anonymized network depends critically on the adversary's background knowledge. Here we discuss adversary knowledge and its implications for attacks on naively anonymized networks. Section 18.2.3 reviews some specific attacks.

The adversary may use knowledge of node attributes to attack an anonymized graph. Such attacks have been widely studied in the context of tabular data (e.g., the widely reported attack of Sweeney [60] which re-identified anonymized medical records using voter registration data). Because attribute-based attacks are relatively well-understood, research on network attacks has focused on the novel threat of an adversary obtaining knowledge about the structure of the graph.

A common assumption is that the adversary has structural knowledge of a small subgraph surrounding the target(s) [2, 43, 27, 26, 67, 69]. For example, the adversary may know that Alice has degree 2, or that Alice has two neighbors who are themselves connected. The adversary may know about multiple targets—e.g., the adversary may know that Alice and Bob share two neighbors.

The above structural patterns describe *what* the adversary knows, but not how the knowledge was acquired. The adversary's knowledge could be derived from many possible sources (specific sources are discussed in Section 18.2.3). The source of the knowledge, particularly its credibility, is important because it affects the strategy that the adversary uses to find matches in the naively anonymized network.

We can distinguish sources in terms of whether they provide *precise* or *approximate* information. If the adversary's source is precise, then any facts learned about a target are also true of the corresponding node in the anonymized graph. In contrast, if the adversary's source is approximate, then it may assert properties about a target that are inaccurate or only roughly describe the corresponding node in the anonymized graph. Typically, it is assumed that the adversary knows whether the information source is precise or approximate.

Example 18.1

An example of an adversary with *precise* knowledge is one that learns that Alice has degree exactly 2. Therefore, the node in the anonymized network that corresponds to Alice also has degree 2.

An example of an adversary with *approximate* knowledge is one that learns that the network is dynamic and, at some point in recent time, Alice's degree was 3. Therefore, the node in the anonymized network that corresponds to Alice is likely to have degree 3 but may also have a smaller or larger degree. □

In practice, we might expect the adversary's knowledge will be approximate rather than precise. As Example 18.1 suggests, one reason is that networks change over time and the adversary's knowledge may be derived from a different snapshot than the published network. Approximate knowledge also arises when the adversary lacks direct access to the true network data but instead derives knowledge from a related auxiliary source, as is the case with the auxiliary-network attack discussed in Section 18.2.3.

While approximate knowledge may be more realistic, precise knowledge is nevertheless very useful to study. First, when assessing privacy risk, it makes sense to evaluate the worst-case scenario, and an adversary is most powerful when the knowledge is precise. Second, in some cases, the adversary can, in fact, acquire precise knowledge (see the injection attack discussed in Section 18.2.3). Finally, approximate knowledge is difficult to model: it is not always clear what kinds of uncertainty will arise in practice.

When knowledge is precise, the adversary can execute an attack on the anonymized network by simply looking for matching subgraphs. The anonymized network will contain at least one match, and if it contains only one match, then the adversary has re-identified the target. However, with approximate knowledge, the adversary must somehow account for the uncertainty of the knowledge about the target. Thus, the adversary may consider subgraphs that only partially match, and perhaps rank them based on the quality of the match. An appropriate measure of match quality will depend on the information source and what kinds of errors are likely.

18.2.3   Attacks

We highlight three attacks that have been proposed in the literature. First, we describe a family of attacks, proposed by Hay et al. [27, 26], that cover a range of adversaries and can be a useful tool for assessing re-identification risk. Second, we describe the injection attack of Backstrom et al. [2], in which an adversary injects a distinctive subgraph into the network *prior* to anonymization. Finally, we describe a recent attack of Narayanan and Shmatikov [48] which exploits the availability of noisy, approximate knowledge to conduct a large-scale attack.

18.2.3.1   Degree Signature Attacks

Hay et al. [27, 26] describe a sequence of attacks, of increasing power, that use knowledge of local graph structure to re-identify a single target node.

The attacks model an adversary who is capable of learning about node degrees. Specifically, given a target x, the adversary learns the *degree signature* of x, which is denoted $\mathcal{H}_i(x)$ for $i = 1, \ldots$. At $i = 1$, the signature $\mathcal{H}_1(x)$ simply reveals the degree of target x to the adversary. Each signature in the sequence reveals an increasingly detailed description of the neighborhood around the target: $\mathcal{H}_2(x)$ reveals the degrees of the target's neighbors, $\mathcal{H}_3(x)$ reveals the degrees of the neighbors' neighbors, etc. The signatures can be defined iteratively, where $\mathcal{H}_i(x)$ is a multi-set of the $\mathcal{H}_{i-1}$ signatures of x's neighbors:

$$\mathcal{H}_i(x) = \{\mathcal{H}_{i-1}(z_1), \mathcal{H}_{i-1}(z_2) \ldots, \mathcal{H}_{i-1}(z_m)\}$$

where $z_1 \ldots z_m$ are the neighbors of x. Degree signatures, which are called vertex refinement queries by Hay et al. [27, 26], are inspired by a process called iterative vertex refinement that was originally developed to efficiently test for the existence of graph isomorphisms [11].

Example 18.2
If Ed is the adversary's target, then $\mathcal{H}_1(Ed) = \{4\}$ since Ed has 4 neighbors. $\mathcal{H}_2(Ed) = \{2, 12, 16, 5\}$ because these are the degrees of Ed's neighbors $\{C, I, J, Y\}$.

Suppose the adversary attacks the naively anonymized network (Figure 18.2) using knowledge of Ed's $\mathcal{H}_1$ signature. Any node who has degree 4 is considered a match, so the candidates for Ed are $\{7, 9, 17, 25, 28, 29\}$. However, if the adversary attacks using knowledge of Ed's $\mathcal{H}_2$ signature, the adversary can re-identify Ed as node 9 because Ed's $\mathcal{H}_2$ signature is unique. □

Although degree signatures $\mathcal{H}_i$ for $i \geq 2$ might be considered unrealistically powerful knowledge, they are appealing as a tool for assessing re-identification risk. First, since they are parameterized, the data owner can assess risk across a range of adversaries. Second, it can be shown that for almost all graphs, the sequence of degree signatures converges to complete knowledge of graph structure, representing a worst-case adversary [26, 27]. Finally, degree signatures can be computed efficiently; in contrast, to measure risk using models based on subgraph patterns requires solving instances of the subgraph isomorphism problem, which is NP-Hard.

Degree signatures have also been used to understand what properties of a graph make it more or less vulnerable to adversary attacks. For example, density appears to play a key role, with re-identification risk increasing as graphs become more dense [26].

18.2.3.2 Injection Attack

Backstrom et al. [2] introduce the idea of an *injection attack*. It is a special case of a subgraph matching attack where the adversary is a participant in the network and capable of altering the network structure prior to its publication. Specifically, the adversary can create new nodes and, from these nodes, add edges to any other node in the network. For example, in a network of email communication, the adversary could add a node by creating a new user account and add an edge by sending an email from this account to another account.

The idea behind the attack is to insert a group of nodes with a distinctive pattern of edges among them. The adversary then links this distinctive structure to some set of targeted individuals. When the naively anonymized network is published, the adversary uses precise knowledge of the injected subgraph to perform a matching attack. If successful, the targets, who are connected to the subgraph, are re-identified and the edges between them are disclosed.

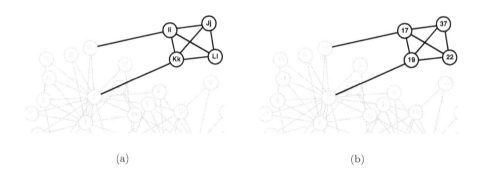

(a)   (b)

FIGURE 18.3: Example of injection attack: (a) injected subgraph $\{Ii, Jj, Kk, Ll\}$ connects to targets A and J; (b) Naive anonymization of the graph shown in (a). The injected subgraph is unique and can be re-identified.

Example 18.3

To illustrate the injection attack, we imagine that the karate club network of of Figure 18.1 is, in fact, a *virtual* karate club. A person can join the virtual karate club by creating an account on the club website; one can also create friendship links to other accounts. Thus, the graph represents user accounts connected by friendships.

The adversary performs an injection attack to determine whether there is an edge between Alice and John. First, the adversary creates four new accounts— $\{Ii, Jj, Kk, Ll\}$—and links them together in a distinctive pattern. Then the injected subgraph is connected to the targets, Alice and John. Figure 18.3(a) shows the injected subgraph.

When the anonymized network is published (Figure 18.3(b)), the adversary can re-identify the injected subgraph as the subgraph of nodes $\{17, 19, 22, 37\}$ because it is the only 4-clique in the graph. In turn, this allows the adversary to re-identify Alice and John as nodes $\{2, 16\}$, disclosing the edge between them. ▯

Designing a successful injection attack is challenging. The injected subgraph must be distinctive so it can be re-identified, but the adversary must inject the subgraph *before* seeing the rest of the graph. So the adversary must somehow create a subgraph that is likely to be distinctive regardless of the structure of the graph. In addition, the adversary must create a structure that can be re-identified efficiently, as solving the subgraph isomorphism problem is intractable in general. Finally, while the inserted structure should be distinctive to the adversary, it should not be so distinctive that the data owner can see that the network has been compromised. At the very least, this suggests that the inserted subgraph should be small relative to the size of the network.

Backstrom et al. [2] describe an injection attack that relies on randomness to ensure that the injected subgraph is distinct. They show theoretically that for a graph with n nodes and an injected subgraph with $k = \Theta(\log n)$ nodes, it is possible to construct a subgraph H that is unique with high probability regardless of both the structure of G and how H is connected to G. The argument relies on the fact that the number of subgraphs of size k in G is small relative to the the number of possible subgraphs of size k; thus, by choosing a subgraph uniformly at random, the adversary is unlikely to choose a subgraph that already exists in G. Furthermore, the subgraph is efficiently re-identifiable. This identifiable subgraph can be linked to as many as $\Theta(\log^2 n)$ targets.

Injection attacks are particularly effective for online networks, where it is possible to create new accounts and connections among them. However, executing an injection attack in a network of human contacts can be very difficult as it requires forming a coalition of adversaries who then physically interact with the targets.

18.2.3.3   Auxiliary-Network Attack

Most proposed attacks (including the ones described above) assume that (a) the adversary only has information about a small number of targets and (b) the information is precise. An exception is the attack recently proposed by Narayanan and Shmatikov [48]. It is a large-scale attack in which potentially all of the nodes in the graph are re-identified. Further, it relies on information that may be noisy and imprecise, thus the adversary must attempt to re-identify the targets using approximate knowledge.

The basis of the attack is that the adversary has access to an auxiliary network whose membership overlaps with the anonymized network. For example, suppose an online social network site decides to publish an anonymized version of its network. Often a single person has accounts on multiple sites.

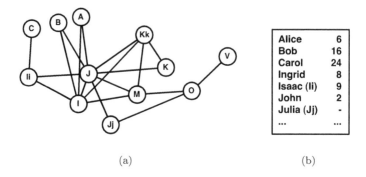

Alice	6
Bob	16
Carol	24
Ingrid	8
Isaac (Ii)	9
John	2
Julia (Jj)	-
...	...

(a)   (b)

FIGURE 18.4: Example of an auxiliary-network attack: (a) Auxiliary network of the bridge club, which overlaps partially with the karate club of Figure 18.1; (b) Adversary's proposed mapping between the bridge club and the nodes in the anonymized karate club of Figure 18.2.

Furthermore, some sites are public and it is possible for the adversary to obtain a copy of a public network through crawling [47]. The adversary could use knowledge of this auxiliary network to re-identify nodes in the anonymized network. An auxiliary-network attack can lead to breaches of privacy if, for instance, the anonymized network includes sensitive attributes and/or additional edges that are not present in the auxiliary network.

Example 18.4

Suppose an adversary wants to re-identify nodes in the anonymized karate club network (Figure 18.2). While the adversary lacks access to the private karate club network (Figure 18.1), the adversary does have knowledge of the social network of the bridge club, shown in Figure 18.4(a). Some individuals, specifically $\{A, B, C, I, J, M, V\}$, appear in both networks. Further, the friendships among these nodes in the bridge club are similar to those of the karate club. However, they are not identical: e.g., Carol is connected to John in the karate club but not the bridge club. Figure 18.4(b) shows a possible mapping between the auxiliary bridge network and the anonymized network, where "-" indicates that Julia is not mapped to any node in the anonymized karate club.   ⬚

An attack based on using an auxiliary network raises interesting challenges for the adversary. One such challenge is addressing the approximate nature of the information source. As Example 18.4 suggests, the networks are likely to have different sets of entities, plus, even where the entities overlap, the relationships in the anonymized network may differ from the relationships in the auxiliary network. This requires a more flexible matching strategy than when the knowledge is assumed to be precise. It also requires some way of scoring or ranking an inexact match.

A related challenge is the complexity of the attack. As discussed previously, a subgraph matching attack is in general NP-Hard. Earlier attacks circumvent the problem complexity by either using efficiently computable structural signatures (the degree signatures) or by considering small subgraphs with a highly constrained structure (the injection attack). With an auxiliary network attack, the subgraph can be arbitrarily large. Further, the matching is not restricted to exact matches.

Narayanan and Shmatikov [48] propose a heuristic, two-stage algorithm for auxiliary-network attacks. First, a small set of "seed" nodes are re-identified in the anonymized network. The assumption is that seeds can be re-identified using, for example, the injection attack of Backstrom et al. [2]. Importantly, the seeds must also appear in the auxiliary network, thereby giving the adversary a partial mapping between the auxiliary network and the anonymized network. In the second stage, called *propagation*, the partial mapping is iteratively extended. At each step, an arbitrarily chosen unmapped node u is mapped to a node v in the anonymized network, based on how many neighbors of u have been mapped to neighbors of v.

To help mitigate the uncertainty in the adversary's knowledge, Narayanan and Shmatikov [48] propose various heuristic strategies, such as early termination, revisiting mapped nodes and reverse mapping. However, the final output is a single mapping and does not reflect the adversary's uncertainty about its accuracy.

18.2.4   Attack Effectiveness

The effectiveness of these proposed attacks has been demonstrated on real networks. Below, we highlight some of the results.

18.2.4.1   Effectiveness of Degree Signature Attacks

Hay et al. [27, 26] simulate degree signature attacks on three real-world datasets: HepTh, a dataset of co-authorship relations among high-energy physicists; Enron, a network derived from email communication among Enron employees; and NetTrace, a bipartite graph derived from an IP packet trace. For each graph, a separate attack is simulated for each node and each degree signature $\mathcal{H}_i$ for $i = 1, \ldots, 4$.

Figure 18.5 summarizes the results, showing for what percentage of nodes the attack succeeds. For each degree signature $\mathcal{H}_i$ along the horizontal axis, the nodes are categorized based on the size of their candidate set under that $\mathcal{H}_i$. For example, the black region shows the percentage of nodes that have a candidate set of size 1 (i.e., are re-identified) under the specified $\mathcal{H}_i$. For those nodes not uniquely re-identified, the other shades of gray give an indication of their re-identification risk. For example, the lightest gray region corresponds

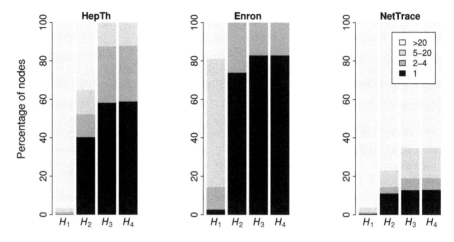

FIGURE 18.5: Effectiveness of degree signature attacks across three network datasets. For each node in a given network, we simulate an attack and measure the size of the resulting candidate set. The attack is simulated for increasingly refined degree signatures $\mathcal{H}_i$ from $i = 1, \ldots, 4$ (horizontal axis). Nodes are partitioned based on the size of their candidate set (vertical axis). The size of the candidate set is indicated by color: 1 (black), $2 \ldots 4$ (dark gray), $5 \ldots 20$ (gray), $21 \ldots$ (light gray).

to nodes that have a candidate set of size 21 or larger, and are therefore at relatively low risk of re-identification.

Overall, we observe that the vulnerability to attack varies significantly across different datasets. However, across all datasets, the most significant change in re-identification is from $\mathcal{H}_1$ to $\mathcal{H}_2$, illustrating the increased power of adversaries that can explore beyond the target's immediate neighborhood. Re-identification tends to stabilize after $\mathcal{H}_3$—more information in the form of $\mathcal{H}_4$ does not lead to an observable increase in re-identification in any dataset. Finally, even though many nodes are re-identified, a substantial number of nodes are *not* uniquely identified even with $\mathcal{H}_4$ knowledge.

In addition to simulating attacks on real networks, Hay et al. [26] also study random graphs to gain insight into what properties of a graph make it more or less vulnerable to re-identification attacks.

18.2.4.2   Effectiveness of Injection Attacks

Backstrom et al. [2] evaluate their injection attack on a real network, finding that in practice the attack can be successful even when the injected subgraph is smaller than required by their worst-case theoretical analysis. On a 4.4 million-node graph derived from LiveJournal, an online blogging and social network site, attacks succeed over 90% of the time with as few as $k = 7$

injected nodes. A successful attack re-identifies the injected subgraph along with roughly 70 targets, disclosing the presence or absence of the $\binom{70}{2}$ possible edges among the targets.

18.2.4.3 Effectiveness of Auxiliary-Network Attacks

Narayanan and Shmatikov [48] demonstrate their auxiliary-network attack using graphs derived from two online social networks, Twitter (224K nodes) and Flickr (3.3M nodes). Since both of these networks are in the public domain, the authors simulate an attack by naively anonymizing the Twitter graph, using the Flickr graph as the auxiliary network. A total of 150 nodes (less than 0.1% of the anonymized graph) were randomly selected as seeds.

To evaluate the attack, the authors must establish ground truth—the true mapping between nodes in Twitter and nodes in Flickr. This is done by matching the identifying attributes, such as username and geographic location. These attributes are available in both networks, but are not used in the attack, only to establish ground truth. Matching on identifying attributes produces a mapping of roughly 27K nodes, about 12% of Twitter users.

To measure the success of the attack, the authors argue that simply reporting the fraction of re-identified nodes is a "meaningless" metric since many nodes cannot be re-identified by graph structure. Instead, they propose a measure that gives more weight to correctly re-identifying nodes that are "central" in the graph. The *success rate* of an attack is defined as:

$$\frac{\sum_{v \in \mathcal{V}} \mathbf{I}\left[\mu(v) = \mu_{\mathcal{A}}(v)\right] \lambda(v)}{\sum_{v \in \mathcal{V}} \lambda(v)}$$

where $\mathcal{V}$ is the set of nodes that appear in both the auxiliary network and the anonymized network, μ is the ground-truth mapping, $\mu_{\mathcal{A}}$ is the adversary's mapping, and λ is the measure of centrality (the authors use degree).

Using this weighted measure of re-identification success, the attack has a success rate of over 30%. Furthermore, they report that many of the incorrectly mapped entities were mapped to a node that was close, either graphically or geographically, to the true node.

18.3 Algorithms for Private Data Publication

In this section, we review data publishing techniques for graphs. The goal of data publishing is to construct a graph or graph-like object that resists attacks and can be studied accurately by analysts. As discussed above, simply removing identifiers fails to provide privacy protection since an adversary can use background knowledge to re-identify target individuals. All techniques begin by removing identifiers, and then apply further transformations prior to publication so that the adversary's ability to re-identify nodes or infer edges is greatly diminished. The transformed graph should protect privacy and be useful, and the transformation process should be efficient to execute.

The graph transformations proposed in the literature to date can be categorized as *directed alteration, generalization*, and *random alteration*. With directed alteration, the graph structure is altered, using operations such as edge insertions, to create common structural patterns. Nodes in the output graph are more likely to look more similar to one another, but the graph may be missing data or contain spurious information. With generalization, the structure of the graph is generalized at a granularity that is coarse enough to provide some privacy but fine enough to reveal the essential features of the network's topology. Most approaches to generalization are based on clustering nodes into groups and then describing the graph at the group level. Finally, with random alteration, the graph is altered stochastically, through random edge additions and deletions. Structural patterns in the original graph are disguised by the random alteration.

The transformations are applied to produce an output graph satisfying some privacy or anonymity criterion. Many techniques measure privacy in terms of the transformed graph's resistance to subgraph matching attacks and are variants of k-anonymity [58, 57, 61]. Essentially, they ensure that, for given assumptions about an adversary's external information, any target node will have at least k matches in the transformed graph. This uncertainty hinders an adversary's ability to infer sensitive information.

Of course, the transformed graph should be useful to analysts. Each approach defines (sometimes implicitly) a measure of utility which is typically used to guide the transformation process. Utility is an important concern in existing work, but is typically secondary to privacy. While privacy is often guaranteed—for any input, an algorithm's output will satisfy the privacy condition—utility is typically only evaluated empirically and worst-case analysis is not considered.

Finally, the techniques presented below differ on the kind of network data considered. Some allow attributes on nodes or focus on limited graph structures, such as bipartite graphs. As a default case, we assume a graph without attributes and therefore an adversary with only structural knowledge. Differences are noted below.

18.3.1 Directed Alteration of Networks

One of the findings from Section 18.2 was that nodes can be distinguished by the local structure around them, making them vulnerable to re-identification in an naively anonymized graph. To counter the threat of re-identification, directed alteration techniques insert edges to make the nodes more structurally uniform. Uniformity ensures that when an adversary attacks the anonymized network, many nodes will match the target's structural pattern, hence preventing the adversary from uniquely identifying the target.

18.3.1.1 Degree Anonymity

The algorithm developed by Liu and Terzi [43] alters the graph to resist matching attacks by an adversary with knowledge of node degree. Edges are inserted into the graph until every node has the same degree as at least $k-1$ other nodes—thus, the graph can be considered k-anonymous with respect to degree. This privacy condition can be satisfied trivially by inserting edges until the graph is complete, but this destroys the utility of the data. To preserve utility, the objective of the algorithm is to find the minimal set of edge insertions to render the graph k-anonymous with respect to degree.

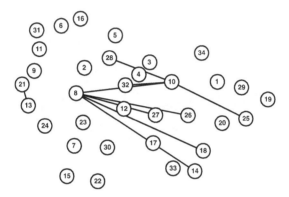

FIGURE 18.6: Examples of directed alteration applied to the anonymized karate club network of Figure 18.2. The original edges are shown in light gray. With directed alteration, edges are inserted until each degree occurs at least $k = 3$ times (inserted edges in solid black).

Example 18.5
Figure 18.6 gives an example of a graph that has been altered to ensure the graph is 3-anonymous with respect to degree. ⬜

While this privacy condition may not protect against more powerful adversaries (whose knowledge extends beyond node degree), this problem formulation satisfies another important criterion: scalability. A key insight is that the privacy condition can be assessed using only the graph's *degree sequence*, motivating a two-stage approach: first find the minimum change to the degree sequence to satisfy the privacy condition; then alter the graph to match the new degree sequence. This decoupling leads to a simple, efficient, and scalable solution. The first stage can be computed using an $O(kn)$ dynamic program over the degree sequence. In addition to being efficient, the output sequence has "optimal" utility in the sense that it corresponds to the minimum change necessary to meet the privacy condition.

However, some challenges remain in completing the second stage of altering the graph to match the k-anonymous sequence. First, it may be impossible to realize a graph whose degree sequence matches the k-anonymous sequence. Degree sequences must obey certain constraints (e.g., the sum of the degrees must be even) and the first stage may produce a sequence that is not realizable. Second, even if the sequence is realizable, the second stage requires that it is possible to realize the degree sequence by inserting edges to the original graph. This may not be possible (unless one allows self-loops or multiple edges between a pair of nodes). To address these challenges, Liu and Terzi draw on existing graph theoretic results and devise some heuristic strategies that are efficient and appear to work well on realistic graphs. The algorithm has a worst-case running time that is quadratic in the size of graph, but in practice, run-time is closer to linear. Finally, they also present an extension that alters the graph using edge deletions as well as insertions.

18.3.1.2 Neighborhood Anonymity

Zhou and Pei [69], in some of the earliest work in this area, propose a similar problem formulation as Liu and Terzi [43] but with a stronger privacy condition. The condition requires that for each node in the graph, its *neighborhood*—the subgraph induced by the node and its neighbors—is isomorphic with at least $k - 1$ other neighborhoods. Any graph satisfying this condition will also satisfy the condition of Liu and Terzi [43] because if two nodes have isomorphic neighborhoods, then they must have equal degrees. Another difference is that the data model includes labels on the nodes, which must also be anonymized.

Zhou and Pei seek to create isomorphic neighborhoods by inserting edges into a graph. Their utility objective, similar to Liu and Terzi [43], is to minimize the number of edge insertions. They show that the problem of determining the minimal set of edge insertions that satisfy the privacy condition is NP-Hard.

Since computing the optimal solution is intractable, Zhou and Pei give a greedy algorithm that iteratively anonymizes the nodes in batches of size k. In each round, a seed node is chosen from the remaining un-anonymized nodes, then $k - 1$ nodes are chosen greedily based on their structural similarity to the seed node. Edges are inserted until the batch of neighborhoods becomes isomorphic. To facilitate comparisons between neighborhoods, existing graph coding techniques, called minimum depth-first-search (DFS) codes, are employed. Minimum DFS-codes have the property that graphs are isomorphic if and only if they have matching minimum DFS-codes [64]. While computing the minimum code can require time that is super-polynomial in the size of the neighborhood, the average-case complexity appears to be much lower: the algorithm can anonymize graphs with 25K nodes in under 10 minutes.

With this iterative approach, a subtle issue can arise when an edge is inserted that connects to a node that has already been marked as anonymized. This causes the marked node to no longer be isomorphic with the other nodes in its batch. The algorithm addresses this by unmarking these nodes and returning them to the list of un-anonymized nodes. In the worst case, the algorithm returns a complete graph. This highlights a challenge with anonymizing graph data: the alterations that modify the local structure around a node can have unintended consequences on the global structure of the network.

The problem formulations of Zhou and Pei [69] and Liu and Terzi [43] are quite similar, and it is not clear which approach provides better utility. Since Zhou and Pei impose a more stringent privacy condition, one would expect more edge insertions, and thus perhaps lower utility. In general, the literature contains few direct comparisons of graph anonymization techniques. A thorough evaluation of their privacy-utility tradeoffs would be valuable to data owners who must choose among these competing techniques.

The empirical results of Liu and Terzi [43] provide some insight into how these techniques affect graph structure. First, edge insertion introduces bias into some common measures: degrees increase and average path length becomes shorter. The magnitude of the bias depends on the topology of the graph. For instance, Liu and Terzi evaluate their approach on power-law graphs—random graphs with power-law degree distributions—and on small-world graphs—random graphs with binomial degree distributions. For the same level of privacy, more edges must be inserted into power-law graphs than small-world graphs because the degree distribution of a power-law graph contains some large, outlying degrees. For example, at $k = 15$, the average degree increases by about 1 for a power-law graph but by less than 0.2 for a small-world graph [43].

Finally, the utility objective of both algorithms is to minimize the number of edge insertions. This assumes that the utility cost of an edge insertion is uniform across all edges. In fact, given that many graphs exhibit "community" structure—relatively dense subgraphs that are sparsely interconnected—the insertion of some edges (say, within community edges) would distort the graph topology "less" than others (say, between community edges). The generalization-based approaches (described next) present alternative utility objectives that explicitly attempt to minimize some measure of information loss.

18.3.2 Network Generalization

The goal of generalization techniques is to obscure the details of local structure while preserving global properties of the graph. Rather than create structural uniformity through alteration, node identity is hidden and local structure is summarized.

18.3.2.1   Anonymity through Clustering

Hay et al. [26] introduce a network anonymization algorithm that is based on *generalizing* the network to resist re-identification attacks. The algorithm outputs a generalized graph, which represents a coarse summary of the original input graph. Since a similar idea of graph generalization is also considered elsewhere [10, 5, 67], we now describe it in some detail.

The generalized graph, denoted $\mathcal{G}$, is based on a partition of the nodes into disjoint sets. Each subset can be thought of as a *super-node* since it contains nodes from G but is itself a node in $\mathcal{G}$. The edges of $\mathcal{G}$ are called *super-edges*, and there is a super-edge between two super-nodes if there is at least one edge in the original graph between their corresponding sets of nodes. If two nodes in the same super-node share an edge in the original graph, then their super-node has a self-loop in $\mathcal{G}$. Finally, the super-edges are assigned non-negative weights which report the number of edges in the original graph that exist within and between the partitions.

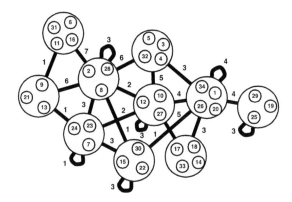

FIGURE 18.7: Examples of generalization applied to the anonymized karate club network of Figure 18.2. With generalization, nodes are grouped into super-nodes until each group contains at least $k = 3$ nodes (super-nodes in gray; super-edges in black).

Example 18.6
A generalized graph is shown Figure 18.7. The gray enclosing circles denote super-nodes and the thick black edges denote super-edges. The super-edge between super-node $\{1, 20, 26, 34\}$ and super-node $\{19, 25, 29\}$ has a weight of 4 because there are 4 edges between these two sets of nodes in the original graph. □

A generalized graph summarizes the structure of the original graph, but the accuracy of the summary depends on the choice of super-nodes. At one extreme, if the generalized graph contains a single super-node, then the only facts revealed about the input graph are its size (number of nodes) and density (number of edges). This provides considerable privacy but very low utility. At the other extreme, if there is a one-to-one correspondence between nodes and super-nodes, then the generalized graph encodes the original graph, providing perfect utility but no additional privacy. A generalized graph defines a set of graphs that are consistent with its summary description. The graphs in this set are called *possible worlds*.

Hay et al. [26] specify a privacy condition that each partition (super-node) must contain at least k nodes. Since nothing in the published output allows an adversary to distinguish between two nodes in the same partition, the output is k-anonymous with respect to *any* knowledge of graph structure. Therefore, this privacy condition is stronger than the conditions of the directed-alteration approaches, which assume bounds on adversary knowledge.

Example 18.7

In Figure 18.7, the generalized graph has a minimum group size of $k = 3$, thus ensuring that an adversary cannot re-identify a node beyond 3 possible candidates. □

To balance the competing goals of privacy and utility, Hay et al. [26] introduce an algorithm that outputs a generalized graph $\mathcal{G}$ such that each super-node contains at least k nodes and the number of possible worlds is minimized. The number of possible worlds is a measure of the utility of the output: more possible worlds implies greater uncertainty about the input graph. The algorithm uses local search over the exponential space of generalized graphs, applying operations such as merging/splitting super-nodes and moving a node between super-nodes. The output is a local optimum in the search space. The algorithm appears to scale roughly quadratically with the size of the graph.

In terms of utility, an analyst can study the generalized graph by sampling a graph from the set of possible worlds. This graph is a standard graph (not a summarized graph) and can be analyzed using standard techniques. The experiments of Hay et al. [26] suggest that graph generalization appears to preserve some important global properties such as network resiliency and the distribution of path-lengths. However, some local properties, such as clustering coefficient can be substantially diminished. This is because within a super-node, the sampled graph structure is a random graph, and random graphs tend to have low clustering coefficients.

Campan and Truta [5] Concurrently with the above work, Campan and Truta [5] devise a similar approach. In terms of graph structure, their *masked social network* appears to be equivalent to the generalized graph described above. Campan and Truta also include identifying attributes on the nodes. These attributes are generalized using conventional techniques from tabular data anonymization with the result that each super-node is assigned a vector of generalized attribute values. Aside from the additional condition on attribute values, the privacy condition is the same as above. Thus, the k-anonymous masked social network is k-anonymous with respect to knowledge of attributes and structure.

Campan and Truta formulate a slightly different utility objective than Hay et al. [26], with the main differences having to do with the inclusion of attributes. Subject to the privacy condition, the objective is to minimize a measure of *information loss* that combines both attribute and structural information loss. Campan and Truta adopt a measure of attribute information loss from existing work in tabular data anonymization. For structural information loss, they use a measure that is approximately equivalent to minimizing the number of possible worlds. These two loss functions are combined linearly, with weights that can be chosen by the user. So if the attribute information loss is given zero weight, this formulation appears to be roughly equivalent to the formulation of Hay et al. [26].

To generalize the graph, Campan and Truta apply an iterative, greedy algorithm that anonymizes nodes in batches of k, similar to the algorithm of Zhou and Pei [69]. At each iteration, a new super-node is created by choosing a seed node. Then $k - 1$ other nodes are added to the super-node based on their similarity (in terms of attributes and neighborhood) to the super-node.

18.3.2.2   Safe Groupings

Cormode et al. [10] also present a generalization algorithm for anonymizing graph data; however, the graphs considered have different semantics than the graphs discussed above. The data model is a bipartite graph (V, W, E) where V and W correspond to two distinct types of entities and E corresponds to the associations between them. (In addition, there is an attribute table associated with each of V and W.) For example, V could be customers at a pharmacy and W could be medications, and the edges in E connect each customer with the medications they have have purchased. In this setting, the private information is the association between customer and product. Their generalization algorithm prevents the disclosure of edges (e.g., who bought what medication). This is a departure from the above approaches which focus on preventing node re-identification.

The approach taken by Cormode et al. assumes that the adversary will use knowledge of attributes rather than graph structure in a matching attack. As a result, it is not considered a privacy risk to publish the exact graph structure. This is also a departure from the adversary models considered above. To prevent matching attacks based on attributes, their technique masks the mapping between nodes in the graph and real-world entities (with their associated attribute vectors). This is done by partitioning the nodes, and the corresponding entities, into groups. Within a group, the mapping between node and entity is secret. The most basic privacy definition used is a (k, ℓ)-grouping, essentially requiring that the minimum group size is k and ℓ for V and W, respectively. For a graph with a (k, ℓ)-grouping, the set of possible worlds corresponds to every possible bijective mapping of nodes and entities in each group.

Of course, a (k, ℓ)-grouping may not necessarily prevent edge disclosure. For example, if every customer in a group purchased the same group of medications, then the subgraph between this customer group and the medication group would be complete. Cormode et al. propose a notion of a *safe* grouping, which requires that no two nodes in the same group share a neighbor—in other words, the edges in the subgraph between any pair of groups must form a matching (i.e., edge-independent set). This definition necessarily imposes some constraints on the graph—it must be sparse for such a grouping to exist. Cormode et al. demonstrate the advantage of a safe grouping and prove that with a safe grouping, associations cannot be inferred using the published data alone. Further, they present a greedy algorithm for anonymizing the graph using groupings. While the algorithm is not guaranteed to find a safe-grouping (even if one exists), in practice it appears to work well for small values of k, ℓ.

18.3.3 Randomly Altering Networks

In contrast with the above approaches—which thwart the adversary by systematically transforming the graph to make it more general or structurally uniform—random-alteration approaches alter the graph structure randomly, thereby making the adversary uncertain about the true structure of the graph. It is an appealing approach that has been successfully applied to protect privacy in tabular data [4, 17, 56]. The algorithms developed for tabular data are quite simple, yet provide strong privacy guarantees and good utility. However, extending these techniques to network data appears challenging. We review one technique for tabular data and then discuss the challenges that arise with network data.

For tabular data anonymization, Rastogi et al. [56] give a simple randomized algorithm in which each record from the table is added to the output table with probability less than one. In addition, synthetic records are randomly sampled from the table's domain and added to the output. This ensures privacy because the adversary cannot determine whether a particular record in the output is genuine or synthetic. It also provides utility: one can estimate answers to any counting query—the number of records satisfying a predicate—with reasonably high accuracy (error scales with the square-root of the domain size). Note that computing query answers requires some post-processing: simply evaluating the query on the randomized output will give an inaccurate answer because the output contains many synthetic records. Instead, one must use statistical inference techniques to derive an estimate.

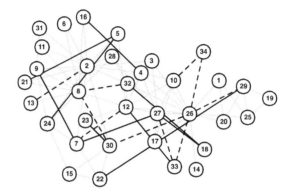

FIGURE 18.8: Examples of random alteration applied to the anonymized karate club network of Figure 18.2. The original edges are shown in light gray. With random alteration, edges are randomly chosen and rewired until $m = 10$ edges have been altered (deleted edges in dashed black; inserted edges in solid black).

While such random alteration preserves utility for tabular data, a number of challenges arise in devising random-alteration techniques for network data. The first problem is choosing a natural randomization operation. A direct application of the techniques of Rastogi et al. [56] would randomly remove some edges and insert others, resulting in an output graph that is a mixture of the input graph and a random graph. This limits the disclosure of individual edges, but the utility of the output is also limited. With network data, the queries of interest are not typically counting queries over the set of edges but instead often involve computing paths (self-joins on the edge table). Since the insertion or removal of a single edge can make or break many paths, accurate estimates are difficult to achieve. In fact, for a query such as the number of triangles (cycles of length 3), one can construct worst-case input graphs where the expected error is linear in the size of graph [55].

18.3.3.1   Uniform Randomization

There have been some initial efforts to apply random alterations to network data. Hay et al. [26] considered randomly permuting some fraction of the network's edges.

Example 18.8
An example of random alteration is shown in Figure 18.8. The network is altered by deleting $m = 10$ edges uniformly at random and then inserting m edges uniformly at random.   ⬚

Hay et al. show that this was effective at limiting an adversary's ability to re-identify a target based on node degree (see Ying and Wu [65] for a theoretical analysis of privacy). However, the graph structure was changed considerably: a 10% change in the edge structure resulted in a roughly 33% change in the value of some important graph metrics. Although the analyst may be able to reduce the error through statistical post-processing, the results suggest that the gain in privacy is offset by a substantial loss in utility.

18.3.3.2 Spectrum-Preserving Randomization

To address the loss of utility, Ying and Wu [65] considered a more complex randomization strategy that was guided by the graph structure, choosing a random alteration that preserves key properties of the network. The technique is based on the observation that many important network properties are related to the graph's spectrum—i.e., the set of eigenvalues of the graph's adjacency matrix or other matrices derived from it. Thus, they develop a random-alteration algorithm where edges are randomly added and deleted, but the random choice is guided based on how the change affects the graph's spectrum. They show that the utility of the randomly altered network—measured both in terms of common metrics and spectral properties—is much improved. However, they do not assess what impact spectrum-based randomization has on privacy. The protection must necessarily be weaker than pure randomization: the noise is influenced by the structure of the graph which means the adversary may be able to use his knowledge of graph structure to infer likely edge swaps. It is unclear how much this improves the adversary's ability to breach privacy.

18.4 Algorithms for Private Query Answering

The above approaches protect privacy by transforming the data prior to publication. The published output is an altered or a generalized graph. In this section, we review an alternative approach, in which a graph is never published. Instead, the only published information consists of the answers to specific queries. To ensure privacy, often the exact answer is not revealed; instead, the data owner publishes an approximate answer, perhaps by adding random noise to the true answer.

The distinction between these two approaches can be blurred, since a "query" could, in principle, be any request for data. Typically, however, the query is a summary statistic, such as the clustering coefficient of the graph, rather than a request for raw data. An advantage with the query answering approach is that the distortion can be tailored to the specific query, allowing for better utility. Intuitively, statistics that summarize the data at a coarse granularity can be answered more accurately than a query that asks about specific records.

Much of the recent work in query answering techniques has used a notion of privacy called *differential privacy* [13, 15]. It is an extremely robust notion of privacy that guarantees protection even against extremely powerful adversaries. Despite this strong guarantee, it is possible to satisfy differential privacy and yet provide accurate answers in a variety of practical applications.

While most work in differential privacy focuses on the query-answering setting, the privacy definition can also be applied to the data publishing setting as well. In fact, some differentially private data publishing algorithms have been proposed recently [4, 16, 56], but they are designed for tabular data. Developing differentially private algorithms for publishing network data is an interesting direction for future work.

While differential privacy has been the basis of an active area of data privacy research, most work assumes the data is tabular. For a survey of the tabular data results, see Dwork [13]. In this section, we highlight some of the results oriented specifically to network analysis. After formally defining differential privacy, we discuss how the definition can be adapted to network data. Then, we review the differentially private algorithm of Dwork et al. [15] that can be used to answer arbitrary queries. Finally, we describe some positive results for network analyses as well as some of the remaining challenges.

18.4.1 Differential Privacy

The formal definition of differential privacy assumes that the database consists of a single table of records where each record describes an individual's private information. We review the formal definition and then discuss how it can be adapted to network data.

Differential privacy is a property of an algorithm. Informally, it requires that an algorithm be insensitive to small changes in the input, such as the addition or removal a single record. The formal definition uses the concept of neighboring databases: two databases I and I' are *neighbors* if they differ in at most one record, i.e., $|(I - I') \cup (I' - I)| = 1$. Let $nbrs(I)$ denote the neighbors of I. Differential privacy is defined as follows:

DEFINITION 18.1 ϵ-**differential privacy** *An algorithm A is ϵ-differentially private if for all instances I, any $I' \in nbrs(I)$, and any subset of outputs $S \subseteq Range(A)$, the following holds:*

$$Pr[A(I) \in S] \leq \exp(\epsilon) \times Pr[A(I') \in S]$$

where probability Pr is over the randomness of A.

An example illustrates why a differentially private algorithm protects privacy. Suppose a trusted party is conducting a poll. Once responses have been collected, the pollster plans to analyze the responses using a differentially private algorithm and publish the output. The individual's concern is that if they respond, the output will reveal something about them personally and thus violate their privacy. The above definition assuages this concern because whether the individual opts-in or opts-out of the survey, the probability of a particular output is almost the same (differing by a factor of at most $\exp(\epsilon)$). Clearly, any observed output cannot reveal much about their particular record if that output could occur (with a similar probability) even when their record is excluded from the database.

This is a different notion of privacy than the ones considered in Section 18.3, which define privacy in terms of protection against an adversary with specific knowledge. The differential privacy guarantee is a condition on the algorithm, and thus it is independent of adversary knowledge. In fact, it can be shown that even if an attacker knows every record in the database except one, the adversary cannot use the output of a differentially private algorithm to infer much about the remaining record (more formally, the difference between the adversary's prior and posterior beliefs is bounded [15, 55]). Thus, it affords extremely strong privacy protection.

Differential privacy has been defined inconsistently in the literature, where neighboring databases are sometimes defined in terms of Hamming distance [14, 15] and sometimes defined, as it is above, in terms of symmetric difference [13, 45]. The technical implications are outside the scope of the present discussion, but suffice it to say that the definition based on symmetric difference is more general.

18.4.2 Differential Privacy for Networks

The above definition is predicated on a data model where an individual's private information is encapsulated within a single record. Thus, neighboring databases differ by the addition or removal of a person's private information. With network data, which is primarily about relationships among individuals, the correspondence between private data and database records is less clear. To adapt the definition to graphs, one must appropriately define the concept of neighboring graphs.

In the literature, neighboring graphs are assumed to differ by a single edge. Under this approach, a differentially private algorithm essentially protects against edge disclosure. This is a similar privacy objective as some of the data publishing techniques described in Section 18.3. However, differential privacy places no limiting assumptions on the input or on adversary knowledge. An adversary with knowledge of all of the edges in the graph except one, cannot use the differentially private algorithm to infer the presence or absence of the unknown target edge [55].

While individual edges are protected, this adaptation of differential privacy for graphs does not capture the same "opt-in/opt-out" notion of privacy that was described in the polling example (Section 18.4.1). It may still be possible to learn specific facts about a node. For example, this adaptation admits the disclosure of aggregate properties of sets of edges—e.g., a node's *degree* can be approximately revealed. Further, some networks, such as the example in Figure 18.1, also have attributes on the nodes. There may be alternative ways to adapt the definition to protect both edges and node attributes. Understanding the privacy-utility tradeoffs of these alternatives is an important area for future work.

18.4.3   Algorithm for Differentially Private Query Answering

Dwork et al. [15] present a differentially private algorithm for answering any query or sequence of queries. We illustrate the approach using the following example. Consider an analyst who wants to learn about the degrees of nodes. Let $\mathbf{D}[u]$ denote the query that returns the degree of node u if $u \in V$, and otherwise returns -1. Let $U = u_1, \ldots, u_n$ be a sequence of node identifiers. The query sequence $\mathbf{D}[U]$ returns a vector corresponding to the degrees of the nodes in U—i.e., $\mathbf{D}[U] = \langle \mathbf{D}[u_1], \ldots, \mathbf{D}[u_n] \rangle$.

Example 18.9
Given the network from Figure 18.1, the query $\mathbf{D}[Alice]$ returns 2. The query sequence $\mathbf{D}[Alice, Ed, Frances]$ returns $\langle 2, 4, -1 \rangle$ since 2 and 4 correspond to the the the degrees of Alice and Ed respectively and -1 reveals that Frances is not in the network.   ⬜

The algorithm of Dwork et al. [15] works by adding random noise to the answer, where the amount of noise depends on the query's *sensitivity*. Sensitivity is a worst-case notion that measures the maximum change in the query answer between any two neighboring databases.

DEFINITION 18.2 Sensitivity   *Let* $\mathbf{Q}$ *be a sequence of queries where each query returns a number in* $\mathbb{R}$*. The sensitivity of* $\mathbf{Q}$*, denoted* $S_\mathbf{Q}$*, is defined as*

$$S_\mathbf{Q} = \max_{I, I' \in nbrs(I)} \| \mathbf{Q}(I) - \mathbf{Q}(I') \|_1 .$$

We illustrate this concept by computing the sensitivity of some degree queries.

Example 18.10
The sensitivity of query $\mathbf{D}[Alice]$ is 1: Neighboring graphs differ by exactly one edge and there exist pairs of neighboring graphs where that edge is incident to Alice. So for those pairs of neighboring graphs, the query answer differs by 1.

The sensitivity of the query sequence $\langle \mathbf{D}[Alice], \mathbf{D}[Ed], \mathbf{D}[Frances] \rangle$ is 2 because neighboring graphs can differ by an edge that connects two of these individuals, causing each of their degrees to differ by one. ▯

Dwork et al. [15] have shown that the following algorithm is ϵ-differentially private. Given a query sequence $\mathbf{Q}$, the algorithm first computes the answer to the query on input I and then adds independent random noise to each answer in the sequence. The noise is sampled independently from a Laplace distribution with mean zero and scale $\sigma = S_\mathbf{Q}/\epsilon$. The magnitude of the scale controls the amount of noise: as σ increases, the answers become noisier. Thus, the noise in the answer increases with increasing query sensitivity, $S_\mathbf{Q}$, or with decreasing ϵ (corresponding to greater privacy).

Example 18.11
Let the query $\mathbf{Q}$ be $\mathbf{D}[Alice]$. To compute the answer to the query under differential privacy, the algorithm first computes the true answer, which is 2. Then it adds Laplace random noise with scale $\sigma = S_\mathbf{Q}/\epsilon$. Recall that for this query, $S_\mathbf{Q} = 1$.
When $\epsilon = 1.0$, the scale is $\sigma = S_\mathbf{Q}/\epsilon = 1.0$. With a 95% probability, the noisy answer will lie in the interval 2 ± 2.995. However, when $\epsilon = 0.1$, the scale becomes $\sigma = 1/0.1 = 10.0$ and the 95% probability interval is 2 ± 29.957. ▯

For a fixed query, or query sequence, the above algorithm is simple to implement and it is guaranteed to satisfy a strong privacy guarantee. For the output to be useful, however, the amount of random noise must be small relative to the query answer. Since the noise is determined by the sensitivity of the query, a key question is whether common network analyses have low sensitivity. The next section looks at some specific analyses and the extent to which they can be accurately estimated under differential privacy.

18.4.4 Network Analysis under Differential Privacy

Enabling accurate analysis of social networks is an often mentioned goal in the differential privacy literature, but relatively few concrete results exist that demonstrate the feasibility of differential privacy for network data. Below we highlight a few results and discuss some of the challenges.

18.4.4.1 Low Sensitivity Analyses

The previous section showed that the accuracy of Dwork et al.'s [15] algorithm depends on the query's *sensitivity*, with lower sensitivity yielding greater accuracy. Some analyses of networks can be computed with queries that are low sensitivity. For example, network resiliency can be approximated with a low sensitivity query. The query asks how many edges must be removed until the network becomes, say, disconnected, and it has a sensitivity of one [15]. In addition, for weighted graphs with edge weights in $[0,1]$, the weight of a minimum edge-cut or a minimum spanning tree are both low-sensitivity queries [15].

However, the fact that an analysis can be computed using a query, or sequence of queries, with low sensitivity does not necessarily imply that the analysis will be accurate under differential privacy. We present a more detailed look at one particular analysis: measuring the degree distribution of a network.

As discussed above, the query that asks for an individual degree, or a sequence of degrees, is a low sensitivity query. However, typically, an analyst is not concerned with individual degrees but with the distribution of degrees. While there are some natural strategies for obtaining the entire degree distribution—such as asking for each node's degree or asking for the number of nodes with a given degree—these approaches require asking many queries, and the total amount of noise grows linearly with the size of the graph. The consequence of asking so many queries is that the error introduced can substantially distort the degree distribution.

Hay et al. [25] give an accurate and efficient algorithm for estimating the degree distribution of a graph. It capitalizes on a recent innovation in differentially private algorithms that has been shown to boost accuracy without sacrificing privacy [28]. The technique performs a post-processing step on the differentially private output, using a set of known constraints to infer a more accurate result. Hay et al. [25] demonstrate that the post-processing step can reduce the error by orders of magnitude and the resulting degree distributions are extremely accurate. Also they show the post-processing requires only linear time and thus it scales to the large social networks commonly analyzed today.

18.4.4.2 High Sensitivity Analyses

While these are promising results, open questions remain about the accuracy obtainable for many common network analyses. For some important analyses, the prospects seem poor. Computations such as transitivity, clustering coefficient, centrality, and path-lengths involve joins on the edge table. It is not hard to construct examples showing that the sensitivity of such statistics is extremely high. We cannot hope to guarantee accurate answers for high sensitivity queries under differential privacy. (For a formal statement, see Rastogi et al. [55].)

To address these limitations, some alternative approaches have been proposed. We discuss two approaches for a particular high sensitivity query: counting the number of triangles in a graph.

The query that reports the number of triangles (i.e., cycles of length 3) is an important query in social network analysis and is related to properties such as clustering coefficient. It has a sensitivity of $n-2$ because, in the worst case, a single edge participates in a triangle with each of the remaining $n - 2$ nodes. Removing that edge changes the number of triangles by $n - 2$.

Nissim et al. [52] give an algorithm for approximating the number of triangles in a graph. It is based on a general technique called *smooth sensitivity*. The motivation is that a query can have high sensitivity because some worst-case inputs yield substantially different answers from their neighboring databases, but typical inputs yield only small changes. A tempting solution is to use the *local sensitivity* of I—i.e., the maximum change between $\mathbf{Q}(I)$ and $\mathbf{Q}(I')$ for any $I' \in nbrs(I)$. However, this can leak information because the local sensitivity itself can change substantially between neighboring instances and thus an approach that uses it directly would fail to satisfy differential privacy. Smooth sensitivity is a upper bound on local sensitivity that varies smoothly over the space of possible databases. Nissim et al. [52] show that adding noise according to the smooth sensitivity satisfies a slightly relaxed definition of differential privacy.

Nissim et al. [52] apply the smooth sensitivity idea to the problem of computing the number of triangles. They show how to efficiently compute the smooth sensitivity for a given graph and also show that random graphs are likely to have low smooth sensitivity.

Rastogi et al. [55] present an alternative approach for estimating the number of triangles. While the algorithm is not differentially private, it does guarantee a natural definition of privacy called *adversarial privacy*. Interestingly, they also characterize the relationship between differential privacy and adversarial privacy by defining the class of adversaries for which a differentially private algorithm is adversarially private. This class includes adversaries that are extremely powerful and arguably unrealistic. By restricting the protection to a weaker (and more realistic) class of adversaries, they are able to accurately estimate the frequency of triangles, as well as other subgraph patterns.

Finally, another potential solution for high sensitivity queries is to avoid them. High sensitivity means that for some networks, the change of a single edge can profoundly alter the query answer. Given that network data is often incomplete and noisy, analysts need measures that are robust to minor perturbations of network structure. In fact, robustness to small perturbations has been proposed as a way of evaluating the significance of the communities found by a community discovery algorithm [30]. The connection between robust statistics and differentially private algorithms has been explored, but existing results are limited to high sensitive queries of tabular data [14].

18.5   Conclusion and Future Issues

The investigation of the private and accurate analysis of network data is still in its early stages and many challenges remain. New attacks are being discovered and new protection mechanisms are actively being developed. Some of the outstanding challenges include: establishing formal guarantees of utility, devising methods to handle richer data representations, and scaling techniques to large networks.

In general, existing data publication techniques do not provide guarantees of accuracy for specific analyses, only empirical evidence that certain properties are maintained in the output. An analyst forced to study a surrogate dataset may be reluctant to trust conclusions drawn without guarantees of utility. In addition, a precise notion of network utility has yet to be defined, and the evaluation of utility has been somewhat ad hoc in existing work.

Further, few of the current privacy mechanisms support the release of attributes on nodes. Privacy protection for attributed networks deserves more study since attributes are crucial to many analyses. In addition, many networks encountered in the real world are derived from time-stamped streams of connections or contacts (e.g., email graphs, network traces, online social networks). Techniques proposed thus far do not support dynamic networks.

As mentioned in the introduction, network data is now collected on very large scales. Networks with over 100 million nodes are being collected and studied. Analysis of such networks can be challenging even in the absence of privacy concerns, as some analyses do not scale well. However, scalability of privacy mechanisms is a significant challenge. Most of the data publication schemes described above were tested on networks with fewer than 100 *thousand* nodes, and do not appear to scale to larger graphs. Unfortunately, the proposed attacks on networks scale better than some of the publication mechanisms. The query answering techniques based on differential privacy have an advantage here, as in most cases they do not add much overhead above the cost of computing the released query.

This review highlights some of the main challenges of protecting privacy while enabling accurate network analysis, but our coverage of this active area of research is admittedly incomplete. Two recent surveys [42, 70] provide additional perspective on this topic. In addition, more work on this topic is forthcoming, including new data publishing techniques by Cormode et al. [9] and Zou [71].

Acknowledgments

We thank the reviewers for insightful comments, Cindy Loiselle for editorial assistance, and Don Towsley, Dan Suciu, and Vibhor Rastogi for helpful discussions.

This material is based on research sponsored by the National Science Foundation (NSF CNS 0627642, NSF ITS 0643681, AND NSF DUE 0830876), and by the Air Force Research Laboratory and the Intelligence Advanced Research Projects Activity (IARPA), under agreement number FA8750-07-2-0158. The U.S. Government is authorized to reproduce and distribute reprints for Governmental purposes notwithstanding any copyright notation thereon. The views and conclusion contained herein are those of the authors and should not be interpreted as necessarily representing the official policies or endorsements, either expressed or implied, of the Air Force Research Laboratory and the Intelligence Advanced Research Projects Activity (IARPA), or the U.S. Government.

References

[1] Alessandro Acquisti and Ralph Gross. Imagined communities: Awareness, information sharing, and privacy on the Facebook. In *Privacy Enhancing Technologies Workshop*, 2006.

[2] Lars Backstrom, Cynthia Dwork, and Jon Kleinberg. Wherefore art thou R3579X? Anonymized social networks, hidden patterns, and structural steganography. In *WWW*, 2007.

[3] Albert-Laszlo Barabasi and Reka Albert. Emergence of scaling in random networks. *Science*, 1999.

[4] Avrim Blum, Katrina Ligett, and Aaron Roth. A learning theory approach to non-interactive database privacy. In *STOC*, 2008.

[5] Alina Campan and Traian Marius Truta. A clustering approach for data and structural anonymity in social networks. In *PinKDD*, 2008.

[6] Ramon Ferrer Cancho and Ricard V. Sole. Optimization in complex networks. In *ArXiv cond-mat/0111222*, 2001.

[7] Barbara Carminati, Elena Ferrari, and Andrea Perego. Rule-based access control for social networks. In *Workshop on Reliability in Decentralized Distributed Systems*, 2006.

[8] Aaron Clauset, Cristopher Moore, and Mark Newman. Hierarchical structure and the prediction of missing links in networks. *Nature*, 2008.

[9] Graham Cormode, Divesh Srivastava, Smriti Bhagat, and Balachander Krishnamurthy. Class-based graph anonymization for social network data. In *VLDB*, 2009.

[10] Graham Cormode, Divesh Srivastava, Ting Yu, and Qing Zhang. Anonymizing bipartite graph data using safe groupings. In *VLDB*, 2008.

[11] Derek Corneil and Calvin Gotlieb. An efficient algorithm for graph isomorphism. *Journal of the ACM*, 1970.

[12] Luciano da F. Costa, Francisco A. Rodrigues, Gonzalo Travieso, and P. R. Villas Boas. Characterization of complex networks: A survey of measurements. *Advances In Physics*, 2007.

[13] Cynthia Dwork. Differential privacy: A survey of results. In *Conference on Theory and Applications of Models of Computation*, 2008.

[14] Cynthia Dwork and Jing Lei. Differential privacy and robust statistics. In *STOC*, 2009.

[15] Cynthia Dwork, Frank McSherry, Kobbi Nissim, and Adam Smith. Calibrating noise to sensitivity in private data analysis. In *TCC*, 2006.

[16] Cynthia Dwork, Moni Naor, Omer Reingold, Guy N. Rothblum, and Salil P. Vadhan. On the complexity of differentially private data release: efficient algorithms and hardness results. In *STOC*, 2009.

[17] Alexandre Evfimievski, Johannes Gehrke, and Ramakrishnan Srikant. Limiting privacy breaches in privacy preserving data mining. In *PODS*, 2003.

[18] Adrienne Felt and David Evans. Privacy protection for social networking APIs. In *In Web 2.0 Security and Privacy Workshop*, 2008.

[19] Linton C. Freeman. A set of measures of centrality based on betweenness. *Sociometry*, 1977.

[20] Lisa Friedland and David Jensen. Finding tribes: Identifying close-knit individuals from employment patterns. In *KDD*, 2007.

[21] Keith Frikken and Philippe Golle. Private social network analysis: How to assemble pieces of a graph privately. In *WPES*, 2006.

[22] Marta C. Gonzalez, Cesar A. Hidalgo, and Albert-Laszlo Barabasi. Understanding individual human mobility patterns. *Nature*, 2008.

[23] Ralph Gross and Alessandro Acquisti. Information revelation and privacy in online social networks (the facebook case). In *WPES*, 2005.

[24] Mark Handcock, Garry Robins, Tom Snijders, Peng Wang, and Philippa Pattison. Recent developments in exponential random graph (p*) models for social networks. *Social Networks*, 2006.

[25] Michael Hay, Chao Li, David Jensen, and Gerome Miklau. Accurate estimation of the degree distribution of private networks. *Technical Report*, University of Massachusetts Amherst, 2009.

[26] Michael Hay, Gerome Miklau, David Jensen, Don Towsley, and Philipp Weis. Resisting structural re-identification in anonymized social networks. In *VLDB*, 2008.

[27] Michael Hay, Gerome Miklau, David Jensen, Philipp Weis, and Siddharth Srivastava. Anonymizing social networks. *Technical Report*, University of Massachusetts Amherst, 2007.

[28] Michael Hay, Vibhor Rastogi, Gerome Miklau, and Dan Suciu. Boosting the accuracy of differentially private queries through consistency. *Technical Report*, University of Massachusetts Amherst, 2009.

[29] Jianming He, Wesley W. Chu, and Zhenyu Liu. Inferring privacy information from social networks. In *ISI*, 2006.

[30] Brian Karrer, Elizaveta Levina, and M. E. J. Newman. Robustness of community structure in networks. *Physical Review E*, 2008.

[31] J. Kleinberg. Cascading behavior in networks: Algorithmic and economic issues. *Algorithmic Game Theory*, 2007.

[32] Alden Klovdahl, J. Potterat, D. Woodhouse, J. Muth, S. Muth, and W. Darrow. Social networks and infectious disease: the Colorado Springs study. *Social Science & Medicine*, 1994.

[33] Aleksandra Korolova, Rajeev Motwani, Shubha Nabar, and Ying Xu. Link privacy in social networks. In *CIKM*, 2008.

[34] Gueorgi Kossinets and Duncan Watts. Empirical analysis of an evolving social network. *Science*, 2006.

[35] David Lazer, Alex Pentland, Lada Adamic, Sinan Aral, Albert-Laszlo Barabasi, Devon Brewer, Nicholas Christakis, Noshir Contractor, James Fowler, Myron Gutmann, Tony Jebara, Gary King, Michael Macy, Deb Roy, and Marshall Van Alstyne. Computational social science. *Science*, 2009.

[36] J. Leskovec, J. Kleinberg, and C. Faloutsos. Graphs over time: Densification laws, shrinking diameters and possible explanations. In *KDD*, 2005.

[37] Jure Leskovec, Lars Backstrom, Ravi Kumar, and Andrew Tomkins. Microscopic evolution of social networks. In *KDD*, 2008.

[38] Jure Leskovec and Christos Faloutsos. Scalable modeling of real graphs using Kronecker multiplication. In *ICML*, 2007.

[39] Jure Leskovec and Eric Horvitz. Planetary-scale views on a large instant-messaging network. In *WWW*, 2008.

[40] D. Liben-Nowell and J. Kleinberg. The link prediction problem for social networks. In *CIKM*, 2003.

[41] Jack Lindamood, Raymond Heatherly, Murat Kantarcioglu, and Bhavani Thuraisingham. Inferring private information using social network data. In *WWW*, 2009.

[42] Kun Liu, Kamalika Das, Tyrone Grandison, and Hillol Kargupta. *Privacy-Preserving Data Analysis on Graphs and Social Networks*. 2008.

[43] Kun Liu and Evimaria Terzi. Towards identity anonymization on graphs. In *SIGMOD*, 2008.

[44] Miller McPherson, Lynn Smith-Lovin, and James M Cook. Birds of a feather: Homophily in social networks. *Annual Review of Sociology*, 2001.

[45] Frank McSherry. Privacy integrated queries: An extensible platform for privacy-preserving data analysis. In *SIGMOD*, 2009.

[46] R. Milo, S. Shen-Orr, S. Itzkovitz, N. Kashtan, D. Chklovskii, and U. Alon. Network motifs: Simple building blocks of complex networks. *Science*, 2002.

[47] Alan Mislove, Massimiliano Marcon, Krishna P. Gummadi, Peter Druschel, and Bobby Bhattacharjee. Measurement and analysis of online social networks. In *IMC*, 2007.

[48] Arvind Narayanan and Vitaly Shmatikov. De-anonymizing social networks. In *IEEE Symposium on Security and Privacy*, 2009.

[49] M. E. J. Newman. The structure and function of complex networks. *SIAM Review*, 45(2):167–256, 2003.

[50] Mark Newman, Stephanie Forrest, and Justin Balthrop. Email networks and the spread of computer viruses. *Physical Review E*, 2002.

[51] Mark Newman and Michelle Girvan. Finding and evaluating community structure in networks. *Physical Review E*, 2004.

[52] Kobbi Nissim, Sofya Raskhodnikova, and Adam Smith. Smooth sensitivity and sampling in private data analysis. In *STOC*, 2007.

[53] J.-P. Onnela, J. Saramaki, J. Hyvonen, G. Szabo, D. Lazer, K. Kaski, J. Kertesz, and A.-L. Barabasi. Structure and tie strengths in mobile communication networks. *PNAS*, 2007.

[54] Juyong Park and Albert-Laszlo Barabasi. Distribution of node characteristics in complex networks. *Proceedings of the National Academy of Sciences*, 2007.

[55] Vibhor Rastogi, Michael Hay, Gerome Miklau, and Dan Suciu. Relationship privacy: Output perturbation for queries with joins. In *PODS*, 2009.

[56] Vibhor Rastogi, Sungho Hong, and Dan Suciu. The boundary between privacy and utility in data publishing. In *VLDB*, 2007.

[57] Pierangela Samarati. Protecting respondent's privacy in microdata release. *IEEE Transactions on Knowledge and Data Engineering*, 2001.

[58] Pierangela Samarati and Latanya Sweeney. Protecting privacy when disclosing information: k-anonymity and its enforcement through generalization and suppression. *Technical Report*, SRI International, 1998.

[59] Ozgur Simsek and David Jensen. Navigating networks by using homophily and degree. *PNAS*, 2008.

[60] Latanya Sweeney. Uniqueness of simple demographics in the U.S. population. Technical Report LIDAP-WP4, Carnegie Mellon University, Laboratory for International Data Privacy, 2000.

[61] Latanya Sweeney. k-anonymity: a model for protecting privacy. *Journal of Uncertainty, Fuzziness, and Knowledge-Based Systems*, 2002.

[62] Duncan Watts, Peter Dodds, and Mark Newman. Identity and search in social networks. *Science*, 2002.

[63] Duncan Watts and Steve Strogatz. Collective dynamics of 'small-world' networks. *Nature*, 1998.

[64] Xifeng Yan and Jiawei Han. gSpan: Graph-based substructure pattern mining. In *ICDM*, 2002.

[65] Xiaowei Ying and Xintao Wu. Randomizing social networks: a spectrum preserving approach. In *SIAM Conference on Data Mining*, 2007.

[66] Wayne Zachary. An information flow model for conflict and fission in small groups. *Journal of Anthropological Research*, 1977.

[67] Elena Zheleva and Lise Getoor. Preserving the privacy of sensitive relationships in graph data. In *PinKDD Workshop*, 2007.

[68] Elena Zheleva and Lise Getoor. To join or not to join: The illusion of privacy in social networks with mixed public and private user profiles. In *WWW*, 2009.

[69] Bin Zhou and Jian Pei. Preserving privacy in social networks against neighborhood attacks. In *ICDE*, 2008.

[70] Bin Zhou, Jian Pei, and Wo-Shun Luk. A brief survey on anonymization techniques for privacy preserving publishing of social network data. *SIGKDD Explorations*, 2008.

[71] Lei Zou, Lei Chen, and Tamer Ozsu. K-Automorphism: A general framework for privacy preserving network publication. In *VLDB*, 2009.

Index

Milton Keynes UK
Ingram Content Group UK Ltd.
UKHW030902141024
449569UK00025B/1269